Praise for the First Edition

The following comments made by the Chinese critics are ordered by the number of strokes in their surnames.

MANAGEMENT PROFESSIONALS IN INTERNET COMPANIES

Online advertising is a complex system that plays multiple roles in the Internet ecological chain. In this book, Dr. Peng Liu introduces online advertising from a business perspective, analyzes the technologies and algorithms of advertising, and expounds the rationales and optimization opportunities for designing a large auction-based advertising market. This book is a pathway for learning about the online advertising market, a window for seeing through the design of Internet business patterns and profit models, and a valuable reference for the designers of Internet products.

– Wang Hua (@Super Derek), GVP of Alibaba and Director of Alimama

This book introduces computational advertising in a systematic and comprehensive manner. It is not only a must-read for online advertising professionals, but worth of being recommended to the business owners and decision makers that intend to harness the power of the Internet, as well as to the researchers and engineers that are keen on mining the value of big data. Although I have witnessed the revolution of advertising industry since the 1990s and devoted myself into the cause of online advertising, I dare not say that I have thoroughly understood the whole picture and subtleties of computational advertising until I have read this book.

– Mao Jianchang, Distinguished Engineer of Microsoft and Director of Bing Ads, former GVP of advertising science at Yahoo Labs

More than a decade of practice has proved that online advertising – which is capable of monetizing the Internet traffic directly – is the most effective Internet-based business model. From the pervasive banner ads at the outset to the search ads and recommendation engines with precise audience targeting, and finally to the native ads that blend into the browsing environment, the ever-changing needs and tastes of users have been promoting advertising products and technologies to be upgraded continuously. In this book, Dr. Peng Liu – a witness to the evolution of Internet advertising in China since it burgeoned – describes the design thinking and know-why of computational advertising systematically, and analyzes every aspect about direct monetization of the Internet traffic (e.g., ad presentation, pricing strategy and algorithms). No matter it is for advertising product managers or engineers, this book is an essential tool for them to exploit the biggest "gold mine" in the realm of Internet.

– Liu Zizheng (@Liu Zizheng), Deputy General Manager of Sina Weibo

In the field of computational advertising, this book is spoken highly for its wide-ranging content (involving all aspects of online advertising market) and elaboration on core technologies in simple language, as well as some topics that are seldom discussed in other books, such as advertising creative optimization, anti-fraud and privacy protection. The content is also up-to-date, covering new advertising forms and technologies that have emerged in recent years, e.g., RTB and native ads. With fluent description and clear topic, thorough introduction to core technologies and algorithms, and interpretation of theories, this book is a practical reference book for the practitioners in computational advertising.

– Liu Tieyan (@Liu Tieyan), lead researcher at Microsoft Research Asia

Dr. Peng Liu is a former colleague of mine at Microsoft. This learned and well-informed man has left a deep impression on me. I feel pleased to recommend Dr. Liu's book, it is the first monograph on computational advertising in China, and a crystallization of his years' working experiences and research achievements. By combining real business problems about computational advertising and corresponding technical solutions, this book is able to help readers fully understand the theories, technologies, application practice, systems and methodologies of computational advertising. For practitioners, technicians, teachers and students who have learned machine learning and data mining, this book will guide them to transfer to computational advertising and other related domains.

– Li Hang (@Dr. Li hang), Director of Huawei Noah's Ark Lab

Our team has spent a great deal of energy searching the materials and literatures about programmatic marketing, and even conducted surveys for this purpose at home and abroad, however, both business personnel and technicians have made detours for lacking of sophisticated theoretical guidance. That's why I have been expecting a helpful guide-book for a couple of years. This book written by Dr. Peng Liu, which materializes his expertise and insight in online advertising, will enlighten the practitioners in the field of digital marketing – a burgeoning industry that develops at a fast pace. Both programmatic marketing and big data application have been developing robustly and involving a large number of products, engineering science, algorithms and business logic. In this context, this book, with interpretation of the internal logic of online advertising that is applicable to programmatic marketing, will inspire readers to comprehend the profound changes and influences brought by big data to each industry.

– Yang Jiongwei (@Yang Jiongwei), GVP of
360 Group and CEO of Juxiao Advertising

Thanks to Andrei Broder, chief advertising scientist of Yahoo!, Stanford for the first time set up a course on computational advertising a couple of years ago. Thanks to Peng Liu, the Chinese readers for the first time a have a textbook on this emerging discipline. This book is the first one of this type in China that elaborates on computational advertising comprehensively and systematically. It introduces general knowledge about computational advertising before explaining complicated issues, it firstly outlines the macro background for the development of computational advertising and then goes deep into the technical details, business logic, product structure, engineering practices and application examples; both the traditional search ads and the latest RTB ads are discussed. It is not only a reference book for the operation specialists in online advertising, but a practical guide for the front-line technicians.

– Yu Kai (@Yu Kai, Migrant Worker at Xierqi), Deputy Director of Baidu Research and Director of Baidu Institute of Deep Learning

The traffic to the Internet is as important as the blood to human body – a common knowledge of the Internet industry insiders, the difference is that the Internet traffic is profit-driven, the direction and value of the traffic are determined by the ability of monetization, while computational advertising is one of the most essential ways to monetize the traffic. Only by understanding the essence of the Internet advertising can we truly understand the mystery of both the Internet traffic and the Internet itself. With a comprehensive and profound analysis of the Internet advertising market, products and technologies, this book will be a shortcut for the readers, either insiders or outsides, to probe into the Internet advertising industry. Being a veteran in the Internet advertising R&D for years, I can still get my knowledge refreshed by this book.

– Shen Dou (@Shen Dou), GVP of Baidu

Computational advertising has been a hot topic in recent years. Quite a number of algorithm engineers, system engineers and data scientists, who are working in the global Internet companies either large or small, are engaged in computational advertising. Just like Dr. Peng Liu has noted in this book, lots of the Internet companies have defined traffic and data monetization as their core business. Both academic and industrial circles have contributed research articles on computational advertising, but they focus on algorithms, systems or business logic separately, rather than stringing these dimensions together in a coherent, broad and in-depth manner like this book. In the past few years, Dr. Liu held lectures on computational advertising in Tsinghua University, Peking University and online education platforms, attracting quite a number of followers, some of them are currently or used to be my teammates. It's a good news that Dr. Liu now shares his insights into this topic in an official publication, which is sure to enlighten more readers. Let's give him a thumb-up!

– Zhang Xiaopei (@Joyce on the road), CTO of CreditEase and former GVP of Hulu

In the process where the Internet is vigorously transforming the traditional industry, the backward-monetization business strategy of "wool growing on pigs" has become especially important. Though there have been praises and discussions about this strategy in the market, it is Dr. Peng Liu's book that comprehensively sorts out the key business logic and product structure of this strategy from the perspective of actual combat, which is crucial for implementation of this strategy. That's why I recommend this book to all practitioners in the industries that are being revolutionized by the Internet. If you can integrate with your industry knowledge while reading, I'm sure you will find more instructive information from this book.

– Chen Tong (@Laochen), GVP of content operation and investment at Xiaomi

Computational advertising is quite a complicated discipline. Dr. Peng Liu, a scientific practitioner dedicated to this discipline, elaborates on the technical architecture and product forms of computational advertising in this book, which on the one hand popularizes the knowledge about computational advertising for beginners, and on the other hand broadens the horizon of professionals.

– Luo Zheng, GM of Tencent DMP

I'm so glad to see Dr. Peng Liu has written a book on computational advertising to share his wisdom and years' experience in the Internet advertising, understanding of commercial products, and summary of algorithms and engineering implementation. This book, for the first time, teases out the forms of the Internet advertising products, interprets the core algorithms and system implementation for each product, depicts an "ecosystem" with media and advertisers playing a central role, explains how technology promotes the evolution of this ecosystem and increases commercial value. For the Internet advertising practitioners, this book is sure to benefit them a lot.

– Jia Zhifeng (@Jia Zhifeng, Michael), Technical GVP of Auto Home

In the past decade or so, the Internet advertising has maintained an explosive growth, supporting the Internet giants like Google, Facebook, Alibaba and Baidu. Perhaps it has grown too quickly, or perhaps its design is so extensive that no single book is capable of expounding the Internet advertising in an all-round manner. Dr. Peng Liu has done a wonderful job that should have been done a long time ago. From business models to technical architecture, from algorithms to engineering implementation, from theoretical basis to implementation details, from historical background to the latest trends, Dr. Liu's book covers a detailed and systematic introduction of the Internet advertising. It is worth of reading by everyone that is involved in this complex trade, regardless of their roles.

– Gu Dawei (@Xiaomi Dawei), Director of Xiaomi advertising

All the technical procedures described in this book are not exclusively used for the Internet advertising, but applicable to the domains of search and recommendation. The author has sorted out the information and data about the key technologies and included them in this book, which is of great guidance to the newcomers in the Internet industry, and the frontier technologies mentioned in this book will also enlighten the practitioners.

– Huang Rongsheng, Chief Architect of Baidu

If you are engaged in or ready to enter the Internet advertising industry, this book is sure to be a must-read to develop your career. From a deeper and broader perspective, the author depicts the markets and technologies of the contemporary Internet industry in China and the world at large. In addition to the rich knowledge about the Internet big data, this book also lists the specific examples of the Chinese and western advertising markets to inspire the innovative thinking of the Chinese Internet practitioners (including product technicians). This book has made due contribution to the development of China's Internet industry.

– Yan Zhao (@Yan Zhao, AdMaster), founder and CEO of AdMaster

Today, the wave of big data is sweeping the world. Digital technology is changing our lifestyles, and in the meantime driving the development of business, marketing and advertising. Marketing is no longer simply associated with strategy, creative and ideas, but closely tied to the development of technology. After 2015, all industries are being transformed by big data: from sedimentary analysis and management of data to data onboarding, which seems like a revolution of the times. In this book, Dr. Peng Liu records the changes upon marketing techniques in this swiftly changing time, and introduces the latest digital advertising technologies in every detail; there are not only real-time updating of the advertising knowledge system, but a helpful exploration of a new digital marketing architecture in the future. I hope that what we are now exploring and exploiting will be one day written into history.

– Wu Minghui, founder, Chairman and CEO of Miaozhen Systems

Along with the rapid growth of the Internet, advertising has demonstrated a trend of refined development. How to maximize the overall yield of advertising with limited resources is a complicated, important and interesting topic, and also the research direction of computational advertising. Being an expert in this field, Dr. Peng Liu firstly outlines the computational advertising problems in this book, and then elaborates on the relevant products and key technologies. Through reading this book, the Internet advertising practitioners will have a systematic understanding of computational advertising.

– Zhou Lin (@Zhou Lin-KCN), co-founder of Souyidai.com and former SVP of Sohu

The content of this book, which is fairly close to the actual combat, is organized in a clear and logical manner. The Internet advertising practitioners shall carefully read this book and reflect on the problems therein. Whether the party concerned is medium, advertising agency or advertiser, it is the one that is good at capturing, understanding and applying data will win out in the increasingly fierce market competition.

– Zhao Shilu (@Zhao Shilu), founder and CEO of WiseMedia

The advertising ecosystem, in the Internet and mobile Internet, has been undergoing earth-shaking changes. The display forms, product types, market structure and industrial chain are constantly innovating, making people overwhelmed. Moreover, the computational advertising technology based on big data marketing has become increasingly mature. Dr. Peng Liu skillfully combines the two in this book, which not only helps practitioners understand the whole picture of the Internet advertising and the current situation of traffic monetization, but guide technicians to master the core technologies of computational advertising. It is a rare excellent work that involves both business logic and technical practice.

– Tang Jian, founder and CEO of OptAim

The Internet advertising is a 100-billion-yuan market. If we compare the Internet to a car, then the Internet advertising is "gasoline," because most websites rely on advertising to make money. This book covers a lot of basic knowledge, concepts and business models about online advertising, and is so far a comprehensive work in this field. It explains profound theories in simple language, introduces search ads, ad trading platforms, basic algorithms and key concepts such as open source system, as well as some ad-tech companies and their typical products in the Internet advertising. It is a suitable reference book for both the practitioners and students interested in this sunshine industry.

– Tang Zhaohui (@Tang Zhaohui, adSage), founder and CEO of adSage

In the last five years when the mobile Internet was growing at the fastest pace, developers have created so many applications and contents, user behavior and data accumulation has changed dramatically. In this process, the online advertising – the most important form of monetization – has gradually become a must-learn knowledge and technology for practitioners. However, because of a high learning threshold in this field, it remains a mystery to many practitioners. Most of the relevant articles just list or introduce some terms related to ads, they are unable to let everybody "know it and understand it." The publication of this book will fill this void by systematically introducing the history and logic of online advertising, as well as the key techniques and algorithms for the popular programmatic buying. What's more valuable is that Dr. Peng Liu integrates his years' knowledge and experience in computational advertising in this book, which makes the whole idea and arrangement of this book fairly smooth. This book is suitable for beginners or business people who want to know more about this field. It will become a required reading for the Internet practitioners. I hereby recommend it to all of you.

– Cui Xiaobo (@Cui Xiaobo, TalkingData), founder and CEO of TalkingData

MEDIA AND INDUSTRY EXPERTS

In essence, both the Internet economy and advertising economy belong to the specific technical or industrial form of information economy. The core element is data, and the economic feature is that "all commodities that can spread information will sell at their marginal cost." Therefore, it is very important to determine the logic, method and path of the transformation between data commercialization and advertising productization.

Dr. Peng Liu' book is an excellent description, combing and overview of the technology, innovation and business involved.

– Ma Qiji (@Ma Qiji), former SVP of Nielsen

I am both an advertiser and a college teacher since the 20th century, but I am facing the same problems and confusion. The marketing methods, especially the advertising forms, have kept bringing forth the fresh, and numerous technologies are emerging in an endless stream. Limited by my own knowledge background, I cannot fully understand every aspect. That's why I am happy to have an opportunity to read this book. A book written by an adverting expert has finally come, which is highly technical and practical. Advertisers can learn different ways of advertising display and the online marketing decision-making process of advertisers to make good choices. The media can also rely on similar advertising monetization decisions to reveal the future development direction. Professionals can further understand the technology behind to find the most targeted advertising and enhance the promotion effect. Therefore, I speak highly of the practical value and reference value of this book.

– Yang Shiming (@Yang Shiming), Associate Director of Institute for China Business, HKU SPACE, Director of Marketing and Media Management Center

The backward monetization brought by advertising is one of the core monetization models in the Internet economy, and also an important foundation of the Internet business model. This book provides a comprehensive summary of this field. We hope that the Internet enterprises, advertising services and technical firms, as well as the services companies like iResearch, to take this book as an opportunity to seriously discuss the division of labor and cooperation on the Internet business model, so as to promote the change and development of the industry.

– Yang Weiqing (@Yang Weiqing), President of iResearch Consulting

A kind of paid communication in the world – nature of advertising. In recent years, however, the Internet has changed the landscape of the entire advertising ecosystem, the world most powerful Internet companies rely almost entirely on advertising. Dr. Peng Liu's book systematically introduces these profound changes, and the technological tools and knowledge that have sprung up throughout the industrial chain. This book introduces the ecological position and the operational mechanism of almost every Internet advertisement from the simple to the profound. It is the most systematic work on computational advertising in China that I have ever seen. This book is a precious gift for the Internet, media, advertising companies, marketing professionals and even common consumers.

– Zhang Di (@adexchanger), founder of adexchanger. cn

No Internet, there will be no computational advertising: computational advertising has made ads targetable and measurable, which is a mission impossible for traditional advertising. In his spare time, Dr. Peng Liu summarized the systematic knowledge of computational advertising and years' practical experience into a book, which is very helpful to the engineers engaged in computational advertising and those who are eager to understand this discipline.

– Zhang Dong (@Zhang Dong, machine learning), former researcher at Google Research Institute

This book opens a window for me to see the mathematical models and algorithms behind the huge Internet advertising industry. Various methods involved in computational advertising remind me of a famous saying in management methodology: "If you can't measure it, you can't manage it!" Quantitative methods make computational advertising a new and important direction in computer science and engineering. Thank the author for sharing his expertise.

– Chen Huailin (@Tektalk), founder of Tektalk

The demand for computational advertising technology and talents has been rising rapidly in recent years. But computational advertising is a new interdisciplinary subject without a comprehensive and systematic monograph. This book provides a comprehensive overview of the business background, business requirements, and detailed technical implementation ideas in this field. An important feature of this book is the systematic introduction of the business challenges and the selection, application and implementation of technologies in this field, which integrates Chinese and western knowledge and enables readers with different knowledge backgrounds to gain a better understanding. In addition, this book has built a comprehensive and accurate knowledge system for the entire computational advertising technology, including the main knowledge points that practitioners and researchers need to understand; the readers with certain basis and practical experience can gain new insights through reviewing old material. The publication of this book will greatly promote the expansion of the talent pool in related industries in China.

– Fan Qiuhua (@RTBChina), founder of RTBChina

Interconnection is leading the trend, netizens distinguish themselves in eyeball economy. More yield comes from advertising, books on monetization are hard to find. Computational advertising is becoming popular through 20 years' development. Incorporating both theory and practice, Liu's book comes right in time. An overview comes first, showing how big the advertising market is. Product and technology are knives that cut the cake of market. Ad sales are guaranteed by search, promotion, auction and agreement. Programmatic trade increases efficiency, mobile platforms come up with new moves. Feed ad, social ad and native ad make people dazzled. Balanced exploration and utilization, click modelling for test and correction. Background and logic to lay a solid basis, core technologies reveal mysteries. Follow suit through encoding. Ten years of hard working and thinking, Dr. Liu makes a big move. I myself a veteran in advertising cannot give him thumbs up!

– Hong Tao (@zhazhaba), amateur poet and former senior scientist at Baidu

Computational Advertising

Computational Advertising

Market and Technologies for Internet Commercial Monetization

Second Edition

Peng Liu
Wang Chao

CRC Press
Taylor & Francis Group
Boca Raton London New York

CRC Press is an imprint of the
Taylor & Francis Group, an **informa** business

人民邮电出版社
POSTS & TELECOM PRESS

Second edition published 2020
by CRC Press
6000 Broken Sound Parkway NW, Suite 300, Boca Raton, FL 33487-2742,
Published with arrangement with the original publisher, Posts and Telecommunications Press

and by CRC Press
4 Park Square, Milton Park, Abingdon, Oxon OX14 4RN

First edition published by Posts and Telecommunications Press 2015

International Standard Book Number-13: 978-0-367-20638-3 (hbk)
International Standard Book Number-13: 978-0-429-26265-4 (ebk)

Contents

Figures, xxi

Tables, xxvii

Foreword, xxix

Preface (1), xxxvii

Preface (2), xxxix

Preface (3), xli

Authors, xliii

PART 1 **Market and Background of Online Advertising** 1

CHAPTER 1 ▪ Overview of Online Advertising 3

1.1 FREE MODE AND CORE ASSETS OF THE INTERNET 4

1.2 RELATIONSHIP BETWEEN BIG DATA AND ADVERTISING 5

1.3 DEFINITION AND PURPOSE OF ADVERTISING 8

1.4 PRESENTATION FORMS OF ONLINE ADVERTISING 10

1.5 BRIEF HISTORY OF ONLINE ADVERTISING 18

CHAPTER 2 ▪ Basis for Computational Advertising 25

2.1 ADVERTISING EFFECTIVENESS THEORY 26

2.2 TECHNICAL FEATURES OF THE INTERNET ADVERTISING 29

2.3 CORE ISSUE OF COMPUTATIONAL ADVERTISING 30

2.3.1 Breakdown of Advertising Return 32

2.3.2 Relationship between Billing Models and eCPM Estimation 33

2.4 BUSINESS ORGANIZATIONS IN THE ONLINE ADVERTISING INDUSTRY 36
2.4.1 Interactive Advertising Bureau 37
2.4.2 American Association of Advertising Agencies 38
2.4.3 Association of National Advertisers 38

PART 2 **Product Logic of Online Advertising** 39

CHAPTER 3 ▪ Overview of Online Advertising Products 41
3.1 DESIGN PHILOSOPHY FOR COMMERCIAL PRODUCTS 43
3.2 PRODUCT INTERFACE OF ADVERTISING SYSTEM 44
3.2.1 Demand-Side Management Interface 44
3.2.2 Supply-Side Management Interface 47
3.2.3 Multiple Forms of Interface between Supply and Demand Sides 48

CHAPTER 4 ▪ Agreement-Based Advertising 51
4.1 AD SPACE AGREEMENT 52
4.2 AUDIENCE TARGETING 53
4.2.1 Overview of Audience Targeting Technologies 54
4.2.2 Audience Targeting Tag System 57
4.2.3 Design Principles for Tag System 59
4.3 DISPLAY QUANTITY AGREEMENT 60
4.3.1 Traffic Forecasting 61
4.3.2 Traffic Shaping 61
4.3.3 Online Allocation 62
4.3.4 Product Cases 63
4.3.4.1 Yahoo! GD 63

CHAPTER 5 ▪ Search Ad and Auction-Based Advertising 65
5.1 SEARCH AD 67
5.1.1 Products of Search Advertising 67
5.1.2 New Forms of Search Ads 70
5.1.3 Product Strategy of Search Advertising 73
5.1.4 Product Cases 76
5.2 POSITION AUCTION AND MECHANISM DESIGN 79
5.2.1 Market Reserve Price 80
5.2.2 Pricing Problem 81

5.2.3 Squashing 83
5.2.4 Myerson Optimal Auction 84
5.2.5 Examples of Pricing Results 85
5.3 AUCTION-BASED ADN 85
5.3.1 Forms of ADN Products 86
5.3.2 Product Strategy for ADN 88
5.3.3 Product Cases 89
5.4 DEMAND-SIDE PRODUCTS IN AUCTION-BASED ADVERTISING 90
5.4.1 Search Engine Marketing 90
5.4.2 Trading Desk 91
5.4.3 Product Cases 91
5.5 COMPARISON BETWEEN AUCTION-BASED AND AGREEMENT-BASED ADVERTISING 93

CHAPTER 6 ▪ Programmatic Trade Advertising 95
6.1 RTB 97
6.1.1 RTB Process 98
6.2 OTHER MODES OF PROGRAMMED TRADE 100
6.2.1 Preferred Deal 100
6.2.2 Private Marketplace 101
6.2.3 Programmatic Direct Buy 102
6.2.4 Spectrum of Advertising Transactions 103
6.3 AD EXCHANGE 104
6.3.1 Product Samples 104
6.4 DEMAND-SIDE PLATFORM 105
6.4.1 DSP Product Strategy 106
6.4.2 Bidding Strategy 106
6.4.3 Bidding and Pricing Processes 108
6.4.4 Retargeting 108
6.4.5 Look-Alike 111
6.4.6 Product Cases 112
6.5 SUPPLY-SIDE PLATFORM 113
6.5.1 SSP Product Strategy 114
6.5.2 Header Bidding 115
6.5.3 Product Cases 117

CHAPTER 7 ▪ Data Processing and Exchange 119

7.1 VALUABLE DATA SOURCES 120

7.2 DATA MANAGEMENT PLATFORM 123

7.2.1 Tripartite Data Partitioning 123
7.2.2 First-Party DMP 123
7.2.3 Third-Party DMP 124
7.2.4 Product Cases 125

7.3 BASIC PROCESS OF DATA TRADING 129

7.4 PRIVACY PROTECTION AND DATA SECURITY 131

7.4.1 Privacy Protection 131
7.4.2 Data Security in Programmatic Trade 134
7.4.3 General Data Protection Regulations 136

CHAPTER 8 ▪ News Feed Ad and Native Ad 139

8.1 STATUS QUO AND CHALLENGES IN MOBILE ADVERTISING 140

8.1.1 Characteristics of Mobile Advertising 141
8.1.2 Traditional Creative of Mobile Advertising 142
8.1.3 Challenges in Front of Mobile Advertising 144

8.2 NEWS FEED AD 146

8.2.1 Definition of News Feed Ad 146
8.2.2 Key Points about News Feed Ad 149

8.3 OTHER NATIVE AD-RELATED PRODUCTS 150

8.3.1 Search Ad 150
8.3.2 Advertorial 151
8.3.3 Affiliate network 151

8.4 NATIVE ADVERTISING PLATFORM 151

8.4.1 Native Display and Native Scenario 152
8.4.2 Scenario Perception and Application 153
8.4.3 Product Placement Native Ad 154
8.4.4 Product Cases 157

8.5 NATIVE AD AND PROGRAMMATIC TRADE 161

PART 3 **Key Technologies for Computational Advertising** 163

CHAPTER 9 ▪ Technological Overview 165

9.1 PERSONALIZED SYSTEM FRAMEWORK 166

9.2 OPTIMIZATION GOALS OF VARIOUS ADVERTISING SYSTEMS 167

9.3 COMPUTATIONAL ADVERTISING SYSTEM ARCHITECTURE 169

9.3.1 Ad Serving Engine 169
9.3.2 Data Highway 172
9.3.3 Offline Data Processing 172
9.3.4 Online Data Processing 173

9.4 MAIN TECHNOLOGIES FOR COMPUTATIONAL ADVERTISING SYSTEM 174

9.5 BUILD A COMPUTATIONAL ADVERTISING SYSTEM WITH OPEN SOURCE TOOLS 175

9.5.1 Web Server Nginx 176
9.5.2 ZooKeeper: Distributed Configuration and Cluster Management Tool 178
9.5.3 Lucene: Full-Text Retrieval Engine 179
9.5.4 Thrift: Cross-Language Communication Interface 179
9.5.5 Data Highway 180
9.5.6 Hadoop: Distributed Data-Processing Platform 181
9.5.7 Redis: Online Cache of Features 182
9.5.8 Strom: Stream Computing Platform Storm 182
9.5.9 Spark: Efficient Iterative Computing Framework 183

CHAPTER 10 ▪ Fundamental Knowledge 185

10.1 INFORMATION RETRIEVAL 186

10.1.1 Inverted Index 186
10.1.2 Vector Space Model 189

10.2 OPTIMIZATION 190

10.2.1 Lagrange Multiplier and Convex Optimization 191
10.2.2 Downhill Simplex Method 192
10.2.3 Gradient Descent 193
10.2.4 Quasi-Newton Methods 195
10.2.5 Trust Region Method 199

10.3 STATISTICAL MACHINE LEARNING 201

10.3.1 Maximum Entropy and Exponential Family Distribution 202
10.3.2 Mixture Model and EM Algorithm 204
10.3.3 Bayesian Learning 206

10.4 DISTRIBUTED OPTIMIZATION FRAMEWORK FOR STATISTICAL MODEL 210

10.5 DEEP LEARNING 211
10.5.1 DNN Optimization Methods 212
10.5.2 Convolutional Neural Network 214
10.5.3 Recursive Neural Network 215
10.5.4 Generative Adversarial Nets 217

CHAPTER 11 ▪ Agreement-Based Advertising Technologies 219

11.1 ADVERTISING SCHEDULING SYSTEM 220
11.1.1 Scheduling and Mixed Ad Serving 220
11.2 GD SYSTEM 221
11.2.1 Traffic Forecasting 222
11.2.2 Frequency Capping 224
11.3 ONLINE ALLOCATION 227
11.3.1 Online Allocation Problem 228
11.3.2 Examples of Online Allocation Problems 230
11.3.3 Limit Performance Analysis 232
11.3.4 Practical Optimization Algorithms 233
11.4 HEURISTIC ALLOCATION PLAN HWM 240

CHAPTER 12 ▪ Audience-Targeting Technologies 245

12.1 CLASSIFICATION OF AUDIENCE TARGETING TECHNOLOGIES 246
12.2 CONTEXTUAL TARGETING 248
12.2.1 Near-Line Crawling System 249
12.3 TEXT TOPIC MINING 250
12.3.1 LSA Model 250
12.3.2 PLSI Model 251
12.3.3 LDA Model 252
12.3.4 Word Embedding (Word2vec) 253
12.4 BEHAVIORAL TARGETING 255
12.4.1 Modeling Problem for Behavioral Targeting 255
12.4.2 Feature Generation for Behavioral Targeting 257
12.4.2.1 Tagging Methods for Various Behaviors 260
12.4.3 Decision-making Process for Behavioral Targeting 261
12.4.4 Evaluation of Behavioral Targeting 262
12.5 PREDICTION OF DEMOGRAPHICAL ATTRIBUTES 264
12.6 DATA MANAGEMENT PLATFORM 266

Chapter 13 ▪ Auction-Based Advertising Technologies 267

13.1 PRICING ALGORITHMS IN AUCTION-BASED ADVERTISING 268

13.2 SEARCH AD SYSTEM 270

13.2.1 Query Expansion 272

13.2.2 Ad Placement 274

13.3 ADN 275

13.3.1 Short-Term Behavior Feedback and Stream Computing 275

13.4 AD RETRIEVAL 278

13.4.1 Boolean Expression 279

13.4.2 Relevance Retrieval 283

13.4.3 DNN-Based Semantic Modeling 288

13.4.4 ANN Semantic Retrieval 292

Chapter 14 ▪ CTR Prediction Model 301

14.1 CTR PREDICTION 302

14.1.1 CTR Basic Model 302

14.1.2 LR Model-Based Optimization Algorithm 303

14.1.3 Correction of CTR Model 312

14.1.4 Features of CTR Model 313

14.1.5 Evaluation of CTR Model 319

14.1.6 Intelligent Frequency Capping 321

14.2 OTHER CTR MODELS 322

14.2.1 Factorization Machines 322

14.2.2 GBDT 323

14.2.3 Deep Learning-Based CTR Model 324

14.3 EXPLORATION AND UTILIZATION 326

14.3.1 Reinforcement Learning and E&E 327

14.3.2 UCB 329

14.3.3 Contextual Bandit 329

Chapter 15 ▪ Programmatic Trade Technologies 331

15.1 ADX 332

15.1.1 Cookie Mapping 334

15.1.2 Call-out Optimization 336

15.2 DSP 338

15.2.1 Customized User Segmentation 340

15.2.1.1 Look-Alike Modeling 341

15.2.2 CTR Prediction in DSP 342
15.2.3 Estimation of Click Value 343
15.2.4 Bidding Strategy 344

15.3 SSP 345
15.3.1 Network Optimization 346

CHAPTER 16 ▪ Other Advertising Technologies 347

16.1 CREATIVE OPTIMIZATION 348
16.1.1 Programmatic Creative 349
16.1.2 Click Heat Map 350
16.1.3 Trend of Creative 351

16.2 EXPERIMENTAL FRAMEWORK 353

16.3 ADVERTISING MONITORING AND ATTRIBUTION 354
16.3.1 Ad Monitoring 355
16.3.2 Ad Safety 356
16.3.3 Attribution of Advertising Performance 357

16.4 SPAM AND ANTI-SPAM 359
16.4.1 Classification of Spam Methods 359
16.4.2 Common Ad Spam Methods 360

16.5 PRODUCT AND TECHNOLOGY SELECTION 366
16.5.1 Best Practices for Media 367
16.5.2 Best Practices for Advertisers 370
16.5.3 Best Practices for Data Providers 372

PART 4 **Terminology and Index** 375

REFERENCES, 381

INDEX, 387

Figures

Figure 1.1	Characteristics of big data problems	6
Figure 1.2	Example of banner ad	11
Figure 1.3	Example of textual ad	11
Figure 1.4	Example of pop-up ad	12
Figure 1.5	Examples of insert ad: front patch ad (L), pause ad (R)	12
Figure 1.6	Examples of playable ad	13
Figure 1.7	Example of social ad	14
Figure 1.8	Examples of mobile ad	15
Figure 1.9	Examples of EDM	15
Figure 1.10	Examples of integral wall	15
Figure 1.11	Examples of group-buying products	16
Figure 1.12	Exemplar game joint operation	17
Figure 1.13	Exemplar directindustry web guide	17
Figure 1.14	Monetization of network traffic and data	19
Figure 1.15	The atlas showing the structure of display advertising market and representative companies produced by LUMA	23
Figure 2.1	Generation process of the advertising effect	26
Figure 2.2	Examples of advertising positions (L: NY Times Square; R: Jingxin Mansion)	27
Figure 2.3	The process where online advertising produces effect	32
Figure 3.1	Evolution of online advertising products	42
Figure 3.2	Grading management of advertising products	44
Figure 3.3	Settings of an advertising campaign	45

Figure 3.4	Settings of an ad group	46
Figure 3.5	Settings of creative	47
Figure 3.6	Management of advertising positions in the media	48
Figure 3.7	Forms of interface between supply and demand sides	48
Figure 4.1	Agreement-based advertising products	52
Figure 4.2	Common audience targeting technologies	54
Figure 4.3	An exemplar bipartite graph for online allocation	62
Figure 5.1	Auction-based advertising	66
Figure 5.2	Exemplar positions for auction-based search ads	68
Figure 5.3	Examples of mobile search ads	69
Figure 5.4	Exemplar new products of search advertising	71
Figure 5.5	Examples of commodity-oriented advertising	73
Figure 5.6	Schematic decision-making process of search ad	73
Figure 5.7	Example of Taobao Express advertising	78
Figure 5.8	Example of position auction	79
Figure 5.9	Example of ADN	86
Figure 5.10	Examples of ADN products	87
Figure 5.11	Decision-making process in auction-based ADN	88
Figure 5.12	Example of "efficient frontier" in SEM	92
Figure 6.1	Programmatic trade advertising	96
Figure 6.2	Process of RTB	98
Figure 6.3	Process of preferred deal	101
Figure 6.4	Main transaction modes in online advertising	103
Figure 6.5	DSP decision-making process	106
Figure 6.6	Different bidding strategies in DSP	107
Figure 6.7	Bidding and pricing processes at DSP	108
Figure 6.8	Example of ad based on personalized retargeting	110
Figure 6.9	Example of Criteo personalized retargeting ad	112
Figure 6.10	Decision-making process for dynamic allocation	114

Figure 6.11	Decision-making process with Header Bidding	116
Figure 7.1	Data-driven computational advertising vs oil processing	120
Figure 7.2	Tripartite data sources	123
Figure 7.3	First-party DMP business model	124
Figure 7.4	Third-party DMP business model	125
Figure 7.5	Data trading process	129
Figure 7.6	Example of Ad Choices	132
Figure 7.7	Example of demand-side data security	135
Figure 8.1	Native advertising products	140
Figure 8.2	Examples of mobile ads	142
Figure 8.3	Landing page of the same ad on PC terminal (L) and mobile terminal (R)	145
Figure 8.4	Example of news feed ad: "Promoted Tweets."	146
Figure 8.5	Examples of news feed ad	147
Figure 8.6	Key features of news feed ad	148
Figure 8.7	Placement of news feed ad	150
Figure 8.8	Example of native interstitial ads	152
Figure 8.9	Product placement process in native ad	155
Figure 8.10	Examples of InMobi native ads	158
Figure 8.11	Elements of FAN native ad	159
Figure 8.12	Examples of rewarded video ad	160
Figure 9.1	General framework for personalized system	167
Figure 9.2	General architecture of online advertising system	170
Figure 9.3	Open source tools for computational advertising systems	177
Figure 10.1	Optimization process of gradient descent	194
Figure 10.2	Probabilistic graph model of a mixture distribution	204
Figure 10.3	MapReduce learning framework for exponential family of distribution	210
Figure 10.4	Multilayer perceptron (MLP)	211

Figure 10.5 Image transformational process with convolution kernel 214

Figure 10.6 Example of CNN structure 215

Figure 10.7 Example of RNN structure 216

Figure 10.8 Example of LSTM model structure 216

Figure 10.9 Schematic diagram of the GAN model 218

Figure 11.1 Decision logic for scheduling and mixed ad serving 221

Figure 11.2 Architecture of the GD system 223

Figure 11.3 Exemplar traffic forecasting based on inverted index 225

Figure 11.4 Relationship between frequency and advertising performance 226

Figure 11.5 An exemplar bipartite graph for online allocation 228

Figure 11.6 Schematic diagram of HWM-based online allocation plan 242

Figure 12.1 Common audience targeting technologies 246

Figure 12.2 Common audience targeting technologies 247

Figure 12.3 Schematic near-line crawling system for contextual targeting 249

Figure 12.4 PLSI probabilistic graphical model 252

Figure 12.5 LDA probabilistic graphical model 253

Figure 12.6 Word2vec model structure 254

Figure 12.7 Feature generation process for behavioral targeting 257

Figure 12.8 Methods for controlling behavior accumulation: sliding window (above); time decay (below) 258

Figure 12.9 Tagging methods for diverse behaviors 261

Figure 12.10 Reach/CTR curve 262

Figure 12.11 System structure of DMP 265

Figure 13.1 System architecture of search ad 271

Figure 13.2 System architecture of ADN 276

Figure 13.3 Stream computing process in advertising system 278

Figure 13.4 WAND relevance retrieval process 285

Figure 13.5 DSSM model structure 290

Figure 13.6 User vectorization process for semantic retrieval 291

Figure 13.7 Extreme case of random projection 293

Figure 14.1 Reasons for the bias of the CTR model in case of unbalanced samples 313

Figure 14.2 The CTR model training process with the CoEC feature 317

Figure 14.3 Statistics about evaluation of CTR model 320

Figure 14.4 PR curve (L) and ROC curve (R) 320

Figure 14.5 Deep learning-based CTR model 325

Figure 14.6 Structure of parameter server 326

Figure 15.1 System architecture of ADX 333

Figure 15.2 Cookie mapping between media and DMP 335

Figure 15.3 Cookie mapping between DSP and ADX 336

Figure 15.4 DSP system architecture 339

Figure 15.5 Different effect between look-alike tag and general audience targeting tag 342

Figure 16.1 Brand ad creative (L) and response ad creative (R) 348

Figure 16.2 Geo-creative of the same car ad in Beijing (L) and Shanghai (R) 349

Figure 16.3 Search retargeting creative 350

Figure 16.4 Influence of eye contact in ad creative on click heat map 351

Figure 16.5 Interactive creative of CrossInstall 352

Figure 16.6 Layered experimental framework 354

Figure 16.7 User ID matching attribution 359

Figure 16.8 Natural click (L) vs machine-based cheat click (R) on heat map 362

Figure 16.9 Example of a traffic hijacking for a TV ad 363

Figure 16.10 Example of traffic hijacking on mobile phone 364

Figure 16.11 The decision process by which a medium USES advertising to monetize its traffic 368

Figure 16.12 The decision-making process of advertisers in online marketing 371

Figure 16.13 The decision-making process of data monetization 373

Tables

Table 1.1	Size of main advertising markets in China and the United States	9
Table 2.1	Comparison of the billing models for online advertising	36
Table 4.1	Yahoo! GD audience targeting tag system	58
Table 5.1	Market size of search ads in China and the United States	67
Table 5.2	Ad bidding and pricing process based on the GSP pricing	85
Table 6.1	Developments in the US RTB market	98
Table 6.2	Summary of IAB on programmatic trade	100
Table 7.1	Main categories in BlueKai's tag system	127
Table 8.1	Market size of mobile advertising	141
Table 8.2	Status and sensor information of mobile devices	154
Table 9.1	Technical comparison by Web scale	168
Table 9.2	Decomposition of optimization goals of major advertising products	168
Table 10.1	Important forms of exponential family distribution	203
Table 10.2	Comparison of common model estimation methods	207
Table 11.1	Comparison of online allocation plans	234
Table 15.1	Systematic bias in offline testing of DSP CTR prediction model.	344
Table 16.1	Mobile-end advertising monitoring code parameters	355

Tables

Foreword

The rapid development of the Internet has changed the whole world. From portals to search engines, from social networks to e-commerce, from free Wi-Fi to app markets, the proliferation of online services has made life easier, and even disrupted the original business. Even more amazing, most of these services are free. Today, the term "Internet thinking" is being sought after and feared by more and more people inside and outside the Internet industry, and many of them are puzzled by the question: How do so many free services generate revenue, or even make a fortune? In fact, if we regard various Internet products or services as the front side of various coins, we will find that many of them have the same pattern on the back side, which is the backward monetization system with the core of advertising position. The front end of the free service is to get traffic and data, and the back end of the advertising business is to turn that traffic and data into money. This is one of the most critical thinking patterns of the Internet.

Having access to sufficient traffic or high-value data, we believe that all goods that can disseminate information will sell at a price close to their marginal cost. This view has a profound impact on the business models of many traditional industries, that's why we believe that people should have a deep understanding of advertising and the monetization of products in the Internet era. Therefore, although this book has the Internet advertising products and technology as its core, it does not mean everyone shall learn to build an advertising system. The prime purpose of this book is to enable readers to respond with reasonable logic and background knowledge when encountering product problems related to backward monetization on the basis of clear understanding of the whole picture of Internet advertising. In fact, in the Internet age, no matter what industry you are in, if you pay attention, you will find that such problems may be more common and more important than you think. For the most important of these, let's look at a few specific examples.

(1) Business model exploration. For example, movies are a typical commodity with a low marginal cost and a large amount of information dissemination. Then why are movie tickets so costly now? Can we explore a model of discovery in the film industry that sells for a very low price and makes full use of its ability to disseminate information to achieve higher economic and social benefits?

(2) Traffic monetization. Internet TV makers, for example, get a share of user traffic in addition to the return on hardware sales. What is the nature and value of this traffic and how is it monetized?

(3) Data monetization. For example, indoor navigation technology is an emerging Internet application that has developed rapidly in recent years. If indoor navigation products are operated free of charge by users, what valuable data assets will be obtained to support the corresponding backward monetization? What specific commercial products should be adopted to support it?

(4) Commercial product construction and operation. For example, what is the internal connection between the promotion modes of group buying, game co-op, rebate purchase and integral wall, and the general display ad or search ad? Can certain products and technology platforms be shared?

The typicality and value of these four types of problems are self-evident. But to answer these questions, it's not enough to think independently; we must have a good understanding of the business logic and product status of the current Internet traffic and data monetization market, and have corresponding schemes for reference and selection when concrete products are needed for implementation. This is what the book hopes to do.

From the perspective of traditional advertising, one would think that advertising in Internet services destroys user experience. This is actually a misunderstanding. First, the Internet advertising is no longer like offline advertising, which is dominated by propaganda banners. Instead, it exists in the form of paid information for various automatic decisions, which includes not only the traditional creative forms, but also the new forms of communication, such as game co-op, group buying, rebate and native ad, which are more consistent with user intention. In addition, although from a micro perspective, some advertising products that disregard the value of media and blindly turn into cash do have the problem of damaging users; however, from a macro perspective, it is precisely because of the existence of the backward monetization mode of advertising that the overall user experience of Internet products has reached an unprecedented height. In traditional enterprises, a number of business divisions are usually made according to the product line. While developing their own products, each business division is also responsible for the revenue and profit. However, in Internet enterprises or enterprises operating in line with the Internet mode, there is another organizational mode, i.e., the user-oriented free product department that is only responsible for optimizing product experience and not responsible for revenue, while the customer-oriented commercial product department creates revenue for enterprises through backward realization such as advertising. Practice has proved that in this way of organization, the user product department can often concentrate on improving the user experience. Therefore, we can see that compared with traditional software enterprises, the products of Internet enterprises are often able to do better in grasping user needs and optimizing user experience.

Therefore, in the Internet world, advertising is no longer just a matter of advertising companies, but every Internet company should care about it. As a result, online advertising is actually the most important engine of the Internet. In terms of revenue, it supports more than half of the Internet business. Of course, the concept of advertising itself has changed radically in the Internet business. First, in the Internet advertising, the ad serving small- and medium-sized businesses and aiming at direct sales, has replaced the brand advertising to become the mainstream, which also creates a new huge market. Second, its key is no longer the idea, strategy and other manual services, but data-backed traffic scale trading as a typical feature. In other words, machines and algorithms have replaced people and services as the defining features of online advertising. It can be said that the soul of the Internet advertising lies in data and computing. Therefore, the term "computational advertising" was born, with the complex products and technologies behind it.

The field of computational advertising gradually took shape after the generation of AdWords represented by Google AdWords and became increasingly mature after display advertising entered the stage of programmatic trade. But we should thank Andrei Broder, the then chief advertising scientist at Yahoo!, who has firstly summed up this discipline as a new research direction. Broder opened a course "Computational Advertising" at Stanford, and it was the first time that challenges in online advertising and practical algorithms were introduced comprehensively and systematically. Given the course on computational advertising, why there is still necessity for a monograph in this field? The first reason, of course, is that the field is changing so fast that in the years since the term "computational advertising" was coined, it has undergone significant changes in both meaning and denotation, and the changes of the last few years have gradually improved the field. Therefore, it is necessary to make a periodic summary of the current computational advertising field. Another important reason is that we have found in several teaching practices of computational advertising that the main barrier to understanding for students or those just coming into this field is not the algorithm and technology themselves, but the commercial logic and product objectives of advertising. With this as a starting point, this book is organized around advertising products. On the basis of a clear understanding of the product logic and commercial value of computational advertising, we will discuss the algorithm and architecture problems. Therefore, the upgrading of online advertising products and technologies driven by business logic is the most important main line of this book.

The book is also woven around the thread of processing, use and trading of data. Readers familiar with computational advertising and products will recognize that advertising revenue can only come from three aspects, i.e., data, traffic or brand attributes. The latter two are exclusive to media, while a large number of advertising platforms are mainly engaged in data processing and utilization. It is no exaggeration to say that the breadth and depth of data use for computational advertising is unprecedented, and all aspects of the industry are relatively complete. Given the emphasis on big data thinking and methods in all walks of life today, the in-depth understanding of computing advertising products and technology has a particularly strong model significance. Therefore, we have put special emphasis on data as a clue in the content organization, trying to explain how the evolution of advertising products makes more effective use of data step by step.

The current popularity of artificial intelligence also makes us re-examine the nature of computational advertising business from this perspective. In fact, the rapid development of artificial intelligence today is precisely due to the greatly improved computing efficiency of deep learning, and the greatly enhanced mining and using ability of big data in the future. The most important characteristic of the advertising field is the huge scale of data processing, and the potential of machines to interpret the data of user behavior is far greater than the rules set by human beings. At the first stage of the development of computational advertising, although we had dealt with a large number of data, it was often a relatively shallow model, but today, the methodology and technology represented by deep learning are getting more and more in-depth application in the field of computational advertising. In this edition, we also introduce the fundamental methodology of deep learning and its current key applications in computational advertising.

READERS OF THIS BOOK

Now that online advertising is no longer just a business for ad agencies, there is a wide range of people who need to understand the business and the technology behind it. We hope that readers of the following categories will find something valuable in this book.

(1) Product, technical and operations personnel in the commercialization division of an Internet company. For Internet companies, the most important commercial product is advertising product. However, we found that it is not easy to understand the overall picture of advertising product technology only from one's own business due to the specific product form of each company. Therefore, this book mainly aims at the readers who are related to these advertising products. We hope that by reading this book, they can have an overall understanding of the whole picture of Internet advertising and complex technical product series and avoid "seeing the forest for the trees."

(2) Persons interested in personalized system, big data realization or trading. Computational advertising is typical in all kinds of personalized systems and is relatively complex due to its business logic. In addition, calculated advertising has created a direct market for large-scale data use and monetization. Therefore, it is necessary for product technicians who recommend personalized system and product technicians related to big data to have a certain understanding of effect optimization, big data monetization and transaction, and many other problems under the constraints of personalized system architecture in industry by understanding the products and technologies of computational advertising.

(3) Internet process decision-makers in traditional enterprises. In the process of Internet transformation, traditional enterprises need to not only learn from the technologies and products of the Internet, but also transform traditional businesses according to the efficient operation and monetization mode formed by Internet enterprises. In this sense, the backward monetization system of Internet enterprises based on advertising is a crucial link in the whole process of Internet. Therefore, in such a traditional enterprise, the decision-makers of the Internet process must have a certain degree of understanding of the principles of advertising and the market.

(4) People in traditional advertising business. Traditional advertisement business and Internet advertisement business that are closely connected already have a huge difference again. Technology-oriented advertising strategies that precisely target audiences are profoundly affecting the entire advertising market. And with the rapid expansion of Internet advertising scale, such a strategy is more and more accepted and favored by advertisers. Therefore, practitioners of traditional advertising business must conform to the trend, understand and apply computational advertising methods and strategies, and integrate offline resources with online resources, so as to better serve advertisers and media.

(5) Internet entrepreneurs. Internet entrepreneurs for whom to find the user product pain point and beautiful solution is often not very difficult. However, what an enterprise ultimately needs is profit, and many entrepreneurs who are not familiar with the logic of monetization and thinking methods are often overwhelmed by the flow and data of products, and the slow process of commercialization will greatly bog down the operation schedule of user products, or even miss the golden development opportunity of enterprises. In this sense, understanding some ideas of flow and data realization will undoubtedly be of great help to the choice of entrepreneurial direction, the acceleration of entrepreneurial process, and the harvest of entrepreneurial fruits.

(6) Graduate student in computer science. Computational advertising talents are scarce in the Internet industry, and schools today are somewhat out of touch with the practical issues that are so closely tied to industry. An important purpose of this book is to provide some guidance for students who have a certain foundation in computer science and are interested in practical problems in industry, so that they can form a correct way of thinking about and designing commercial products and using technology to solve product problems.

CONTENT ORGANIZATION OF THIS BOOK

As we have mentioned earlier, the book is organized not simply to introduce computational advertising products and technology, but the more important purpose is to provide a new perspective, let everybody have a knowledge of how to achieve perfect product experience and how to maximize the monetization efficiency in Internet era through understanding the inner logic of advertisements. In our opinion, if you don't understand the products and markets of advertising monetization, you will never thoroughly understand the Internet, and you are sure to be held back in the design and operation of user products. For this purpose, the book is organized into three parts.

Part 1 outlines the online advertising market and background. This part introduces some basic issues in online advertising and background knowledge. Although the content is relatively simple, this part is the foundation of the whole book, especially the concentrated introduction of many related concepts and terms. Please do not skip it.

Part 2 introduces the logic of online advertising products, which is mainly aimed at product, operation, and sales personnel, as well as macro decision-makers of Internet products. The focus is on introducing the market structure, transaction mode, and main products of computational advertising. This part follows the development of online advertising products in order to help readers understand the inherent laws of various complex advertising products and trading mechanisms.

Part 3 introduces the key technology of computational advertising, which is mainly aimed at system engineers, algorithm engineers, and architects. Corresponding to the previous part of the advertising products, this part is also unfolded in the order of online advertising product development, focusing on the key technical challenges of realizing various advertising products and providing basic solutions.

Generally speaking, for the readers who want to operate online advertising business, or know how to use online advertising to monetize user products, they can focus on the first two parts and have an in-depth understanding of the products and business logic. For those who care about engineering implementation and revenue optimization, after the first two parts, take some time to dig into the third part, especially the technical sections related to the advertising products. The complexity of computational advertising lies in the fact that for any product or technology, it is necessary to judge its rationality in the corresponding business background, and to understand the goals that can be achieved in commercial products, it is necessary to have a fairly clear understanding of the current situation and difficulties of technology. Therefore, it is recommended that you read the whole book as much as possible, and simply skip over the parts that are really irrelevant or cannot be understood in the knowledge background.

There is a lot of jargon and terminology involved in discussing product technology in the online advertising market. For readers who are not familiar with the liquidity business, these terms will bring some obstacles to reading. In order to help readers search and find the relevant content of terms, the main terms, i.e., abbreviations, are indexed in the appendix for easy reading.

Due to space constraints, some of the details or background knowledge in this book cannot be fully developed. In this case, the corresponding references are given. However, as this book is not an academic work, the completeness of references is not guaranteed. Therefore, when the text is sufficient to explain the viewpoints and methods, the original literature may not be listed. In addition, in the third part of the book, to help readers understand, some key algorithms are given corresponding code snippets. But the code in this book is all exemplary code, intended only to more clearly describe the logic rather than to compile and execute programs directly, and some of the subfunction calls that are particularly easy to understand and implement may be omitted.

The content of this book is mainly composed of Dr. Peng Liu's open lectures at Tsinghua University and his postgraduate courses at Peking University and Beihang University. The content itself and its order have been adjusted for a wider audience. Among the two authors, Peng Liu is the main author, and Wang Chao is responsible for assistance in organizing the complex main body and the overall organization of the content, and Wang takes charge of the product cases and algorithm example codes. Due to the limited level of the authors, and coupled with the rush of time, the book inevitably has some mistakes, thus we will be grateful for all readers' comments and corrections. In addition, in the process of writing this book, we invited some experts and practitioners in the industry to help check the content, and got many useful suggestions from them, which made this book more complete and practical.

Preface (1)

In March 2009, I was attending CIKM'09 in Hong Kong and listened to a tutorial "Introduction to Computational Advertising" given by several scholars including Andrei Broder. I found everything fresh and new. I thought such course should be open in our university. After coming back, I got to know the situation of the young teachers around me and found no one was capable enough. Later, I learned Dr. Peng Liu is an expert in this field firstly from Weibo. I connected with him and felt happy to know that he is the one who I've been looking for. I invited him to give a similar lecture at Peking University, and he agreed. The lecture was scheduled one day in the summer of 2013. I designated Mr. Peng Bo, a young teacher in the laboratory, to be Liu's assistant. One of the purposes of doing so is that I hope Peng could learn the knowledge of computational advertising while being an assistant, and one day open classes by himself in Peking University. Liu's lectures went very well, Peng was present every time. In the fall of 2014, Peng succeeded in giving a lecture by himself. After the class, I asked him how he felt. He admitted that the content was too much and he could not grasp it well. As there was no textbook, it was difficult for both teacher and students.

In fact, when I first asked Dr. Liu to give lectures, I talked about the textbook with him. He promised to consider it, but as he has been busy with his work in the company, it would take a long time. But he did not forget it! After two years have passed, one day he sent me an email saying that the manuscript was finished and he expected me to write a preface for his book, which pleased me a lot.

It is not a big book, but it comprehensively covers the Internet-based advertising market background, product logic, and key technologies, and provides readers with a broad vision. Based on his years' experience, the author interprets the demand for products and technologies from the perspective of market behavior, rather than focusing on technology, thus having improved the idea of this book and is therefore suitable for a wider readership, including graduate students majored in computer science. It should be said that the style of this book is different from the usual teaching materials, if directly used for teaching, there will be higher requirements for teachers, but it is an excellent teaching reference book. In particular, the main thinking line of data processing, utilization, and transaction in this book can enable computer students to learn about the concrete technical demand. The emphasis on data in the context of the Internet advertising enables readers to have a more concrete experience of the significance of big data.

There are lots of difficulties and problems in computer professional education in Chinese universities (especially for senior and graduate students). One obvious point is that the teaching content is not modern enough. This is reflected in both breadth and depth. In line with the development of industry, some important courses cannot be opened timely and effectively. Computational advertising is one of them. This situation is incompatible with the booming information technology and industry. Therefore, we welcome experts who have a thorough understanding of technology and industry and are passionate about education to participate in college teaching activities, so that our students can learn more practical skills and meet the needs of industrial development. Dr. Liu opened the course on Computational Advertising at Peking University in 2013, which sets an example in this regard. The publication of his book is also a kind of dedication in this sense.

Li Xiaoming
Professor with Department of
Computer Science & Technology, Peking University

Preface (2)

All Internet companies are no strangers to the status and value of advertising monetization. At every stage of the growth of each user product, in addition to seriously solving the pain points of demand and optimizing user experience, we shall constantly evaluate the value of traffic and data, and actively discuss the strategy and product of commercial monetization. Among all kinds of commercial products, computational advertising is undoubtedly the most important.

At the early stages of product selection, development, and operation, it is very important to judge the growth space and commercial value of the product, if we can correctly evaluate the data and traffic value of the product in the future and know how to monetize these assets by utilizing advertising products. In addition, the early product promotion will use many advertising products, and the in-depth understanding of the principles of computational advertising will also be conducive to efficient marketing.

When a product is recognized by the market and has absorbed a certain number of users, it is a key step for each Internet company to actively formulate a systematic commercialization strategy and obtain cash flow in a reasonable way so to support the rapid development of product, which is a crucial stage in their growth process. If we can have a thorough understanding of the product technology of the Internet advertising market, it will be greatly helpful for the decision-making at this stage.

Although advertising technology is fairly important in the Internet industry, for a long time, there have been only a few monograph articles, and the introduction of the industry system architecture and algorithm from a global perspective lacked systematic collation and summarization. On the one hand, this is due to the rapid development of advertising market, from search bidding to programmatic trade and then to the native ad in the era of mobile Internet, and rapid product evolution has left no time for the entire industry to do a summary; on the other hand, the internal logic of advertising products is not as intuitive as that of user products. To conduct a comprehensive and thorough sorting and analysis, it requires both rich practical experience and considerable theoretical abstraction ability. Due to the lack of systematic information and incomplete talent cultivation in the Internet industry, there has been a lack of talents in advertising product technology.

Dr. Peng Liu had been working with me in Sohu for some time. Through our brief contact, I know that he has rich practical experience in monetization of media traffic and demand-side advertising products. Liu had once worked in Yahoo! Labs to do systematic research in the field of computational advertising. So Liu is the right person to do a comprehensive summary of the field. He could devote his time and energy to incorporate the product technology and business logic of computational advertising into a book that will greatly benefit the whole Internet industry.

My first impression of reading this book is that it is comprehensive and methodical: this book is an all-round introduction to computational advertising, a thorough dissection of its business logic and principles, and an in-depth discussion of its technical architecture and key algorithms. Moreover, in addition to audience targeting, CTR estimation, RTB, and other hot topics, there are detailed introductions to peripheral products and technology. I believe that readers who have carefully read this book will have an overall understanding of the whole advertising ecology, they will not only see the trees but see the forest, and readers can follow the picture and find specific ideas and even solutions in this book when they encounter various practical problems.

Another important aspect of this book, of course, is that it is the first systematic, formal publication in the field of computational advertising. I really hope that from the perspective of rational allocation of resources, the entire Internet field can gradually move toward standardization and division of labor in traffic and data monetization. This may promote Chinese Internet enterprises to get rid of vicious competition and march on the road of win-win cooperation.

In the end, I congratulate Dr. Liu for publishing this book and may it give you some enlightenment.

Wang Xiaochuan
CEO of Sogou

Preface (3)

Advertising marketing is at a turning point in its history, as the motivation and technical integration of the media has made the development of digital marketing an interesting and disturbing topic. The reason is simple: on the one hand, technology-driven digital ecology is flourishing, and programmatic marketing is getting better; on the other hand, the various concepts of advertising technology in the digital world have made marketizers confused.

It cannot be denied that the marketing industry, with its skilled professionals and data scientists helping us practice and innovate these technologies, seems to have everything it needs. Imagine sitting with one of our clients one afternoon, he might ask: What can you do for us in the future?

If technology represents the future of marketing, what is this technology? Why does technology exist? What can technology help people do? I often think that in order to break through the mists of technology, marketizers shall have a background that cuts through the blind spots of technical understanding, provides insight into the really crucial and clear attribution, and delivers the answers to these questions clearly and simply to our customers. So I'm looking for someone in the industry to explain the reality and role of advertising technology, whether it's commercial product concepts like DSP, DMP or RTB, or technical terms like "prediction models," "machine learning," and "demographical targeting."

With this expectation, I read through Dr. Liu's book. I would like to say that I have found the answers or clues while reading this book.

Dr. Liu has rich experience in the Internet field, especially in the field of advertising monetization. From Yahoo! global research and development center to Microsoft research, and now as the chief business architect of 360, he has not only presided over the design and development of demand-side marketing products and supply-side monetization products, but capable of grasping products, systems, and algorithms, and these experiences have become the foundation of the rich content in this book.

A good advertising book doesn't talk about trends, instead it examines the business logic in detail. A good technical book doesn't talk about common sense, but dissects the practical issues and come up with penetrating judgments. Dr. Liu's book is the one that crosses disciplines and has both at the same time.

I'd like to share two points of view about my reading experience. The first is the complicated digital ecology and technical rhetoric, which Dr. Liu has systematically sorted out and introduced. Even with highly professional product concepts, logic, and algorithm applications, readers from non-technical backgrounds can also establish a unified understanding of these concepts. The second is beyond the concept. The book lists classic international and domestic advertising platform products, analyzes their forms, technologies, and strategies, and depicts the interconnection and promotion between business and products. These are from the author's years of practice and accumulation of marketing and "Internet +" thinking perspective which are more valuable. The book is full of detailed data and illustrations, reflecting Dr. Liu's seriousness about technology and scholarship.

If you need to learn about the products and technologies of online advertising, you should do it now, open this book, and try to learn and explore.

May this book be accessible to every marketizer in digital advertising.

Li Guifen

CEO of Aegis Media Greater China

Authors

Dr. Peng Liu is senior director and chief architect of business products at Qihoo 360. He is also responsible for product and engineering for monetization of 360. After receiving his PhD from Tsinghua University in 2005, he joined Microsoft Research Asia and studied cutting-edge artificial intelligence technologies. In 2009, he participated in the founding of Yahoo! Labs Beijing as a senior scientist. He was also chief scientist of MediaV. Dr. Peng Liu is devoted to products and technologies related to big data and computational advertising. His public online course "computational advertising" has attracted more than 30,000 students on Netease.com, and has been adopted as a basic training material in many related companies. Moreover, this course has been selected by Peking University, Tsinghua University and Beihang University for their graduates.

Wang Chao received his master's degree from Peking University, and then worked at Weibo and Autohome's advertising department for some years. He is now a tech leader in the query recommendation group at Baidu's portal search department. His work focuses on machine learning algorithms in computational advertising, and he has won 7th place among 718 participants in "predict click-through rates on display ads" organized by Kaggle and Criteo. He is also interested in contributing code for open source machine learning tools such as xgboost.

Authors

1

Market and Background of Online Advertising

CHAPTER 1

Overview of Online Advertising

Online advertising, which is also known as network advertising or Internet advertising, refers to the ad serving via online media just as its name implies. Unlike the traditional advertising, online advertising has given birth to a technology-based and product-oriented ad serving model that targets specific user **segmentation**, though it was born just over a decade ago. It brings not only a new marketing channel for advertisers to accurately reach target audiences, but a means for large-scale monetization of the Internet-based free products and media. The fact is that no matter you are dealing with user products or commercial products you cannot fully understand the Internet business without a profound knowledge of online advertising. Given this, it is necessary for the Internet practitioners to spend some time figuring out the rationales and products of modern online advertising.

In addition, with regard to data application, online advertising takes the lead in large-scale and automated use of data to improve products and increase revenue. To say the least, for quite a long time in the past, online advertising was the only trade that fulfilled large-scale revenue-making with big data application. Even today, computational advertising remains the most mature and largest trade that relies on big data application. Therefore, the readers interested in big data are advised to carefully study the technical challenges and product problems concerning online advertising, which will guide them to apply big data in other domains.

The product forms and business logic of online advertising are fairly complex. In order to help readers have a macro-grasp of online advertising, this chapter firstly explains the connotations of online advertising (including its definition and purpose), and then analyzes its extensions, i.e., the key products of online advertising through years of development. Readers may at first feel confused at various concepts and ideas, but they will understand them one by one as the content unfolds progressively. Moreover, this chapter also introduces the products and technical terms of online advertising as much as possible, so as to lay the groundwork for the rest of the book.

Compared with offline advertising the products and creative forms of online advertising are represented in various forms, which is attributed to different forms and interactive modes of Internet media. We will briefly introduce some common forms of creative to help readers intuitively understand how online advertising works.

The content of this chapter is less to do with computing, because we intend to let readers get familiar with some important notions before accessing to computational advertising: first, advertising is not completely equal to search or recommendation, it is primarily a commercial activity and then a technology. Second, in this commercial activity, the interests of advertisers, media, and users shall be taken into account and satisfied, so as to achieve balanced and sustainable development of the entire advertising market. The evolution of all products and business forms in online advertising market shall keep with the theme of "interests." In order to understand the products, architectures, and algorithms mentioned in this book, the critical step is to think and explore the computational advertising technologies with a business logic.

1.1 FREE MODE AND CORE ASSETS OF THE INTERNET

It is known that the Internet-based products (websites and applications) are usually available for free. Some Internet companies also sell mobile phones, televisions, and other hardware products despite of meager direct profit or even economic loss. No matter it is free software or low-priced hardware, it is regarded as the "free mode." Well, what is the essence of the free mode? Our viewpoint is as follows:

> *The essence of free mode is to sell goods that can disseminate information in a large-scale and personalized manner at marginal cost.*

As for the websites and other software products, it takes a small marginal cost for them to serve one user, so these products could be provided for free, which is the "free mode" in a narrow sense. In contrast, if mobile phones and other hardware products are sold at marginal cost (the same with their mass production cost), their gross profit is almost zero, which is the "free pattern" in a broad sense. The two kinds of products share a common feature: disseminating information to different users in a personalized manner. But for the commodities that are unable to disseminate information, e.g., mineral water and charger, the Internet-based free pattern becomes inapplicable.

Now that these products themselves do not generate any profit, how can their developers make profit? The truth is that in the process of disseminating information, these free products will acquire three core assets that can be monetized, i.e., traffic, data and influence.

(1) Traffic. The value of traffic is that if someone uses your products, you can add some sponsored content (i.e., ads) to the proper functions of these products, thus turning traffic into revenue.

(2) Data. While using your products, users will leave some traces about their behaviors and attributes, e.g., the terms in their searches, browsing history of a certain product, or gender information. All of these traces are useful data based on which

you will learn about the attributes and interests of these users, and then adjust the policies for delivering sponsored content to raise the ad serving effectiveness.

(3) Influence. It means that your products or content have received the attention and trust above the average level. Of course, the sponsored content that you have delivered also gets better attention in the meantime, which is critical for increasing conversion rate (see Section 2.1). Therefore, the influential products or content can obtain brand premium during ad serving.

It is worth noting that a large number of Internet celebrities and We Media, which have been rising rapidly in recent years, actually rely on influence monetization rather than traffic and data monetization to gain profit. Compare the bid price of advertorials of official accounts (influence monetization) with the yield of end-of-text (ETX) ads (traffic and data monetization), we will find that the price of the former is usually dozens of times more than the latter. Such media monetization with influence as its prime asset, which is not the strength of the existing online advertising system, may become a new exploration direction in the future.

The process where the three assets are turned into revenue in the form of commercial products is called "monetization" or "backward monetization" since it is separate from the process where users are enjoying free products. The preceding paragraphs reveal a system in which traffic monetization lays the foundation for data and influence monetization, and it happens to be the modern commercial product system supported by computational advertising technology.

1.2 RELATIONSHIP BETWEEN BIG DATA AND ADVERTISING

In recent years, big data thinking and technology have developed into a noted school of thought, although the connotations of big data problems are not yet precisely defined. In reference [1] the author uses the "4Vs" (Volume, Variety, Velocity, and Value) to describe the characteristics of big data problems, but fails to give any definition standards for these problems. It may be easier to examine the big data problems from a practical perspective than from a theoretical perspective because big data have been put into practice since the Internet companies started mining the value from the numerous user behavioral data. In the industrial community, the prominent features of big data are its low cost and distributed computing architecture, which differs from the previous data processing system. The big data problems have distinct characteristics in the aspects of data source, processing mode, and application direction.

(1) Behavioral data. The traditional data processing usually deals with the transaction data which are generated from commercial activities and must be recorded, such as prepaid refills and call logs of telecom operators, deposit/withdrawal slips, and interest bills of banks. The processing of transaction data, though not in a large scale, is very strict with consistency and timeliness of data. The computing architecture of IOE (IBM, Oracle, and EMC) has become a mature solution for the

transaction data processing. In contrast, the behavioral data are also generated from commercial activities but they not necessarily recorded, such as location of telecom users, queuing at banks, and website visit logs. Compared with the transaction data, the processing of behavioral data is in a large scale and indifferent to consistency, e.g., a loss of 1/1000 of web logs is not a big deal for a website. Given this, the traditional IOE architecture is no longer applicable, which gives rise to construction of a big data computing architecture.

(2) Full processing. In case of a huge volume of data and impossibility of reducing the processing complexity by sampling, we have to utilize some computing and storage technologies (e.g., MapReduce and NoSQL) which are specifically designed for mass data processing. As shown in Figure 1.1, when examining the objective function of a data processing process, we may notice two typical problems:

- Type-A problems: Data sampling is no doubt preferred if it can significantly reduce the complexity of data processing, and not seriously weaken the problem-solving effect (i.e., the objective function). This type of problems, which usually includes statistical statements and general reports, is illustrated by Curve A in Figure 1.1.
- Type-B problems: As for other data problems, it is unlikely to achieve the effect of full data processing with only a small volume of data; in other words, due to lowering data sampling rate, the earnings from solving problems will drop rapidly. These problems are typical big data problems (illustrated by Curve B in Figure 1.1), personalized recommendation and computational advertising have the same characteristic, since they need to use each user's behavioral data for customized push, the data processing based on a fraction of users as data sample is far from enough.

(3) Automation application. There are two types of data application: (i) Insight application: make statistical analysis of data, produce a report on the analytical result, and then deliver the report to decision-makers for their instruction.

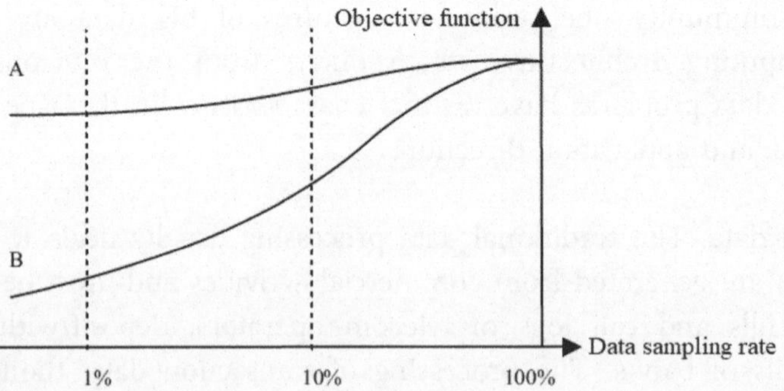

FIGURE 1.1 Characteristics of big data problems.

A typical example of insight application is the financial statement of enterprises. Business intelligence (BI) is also a kind of insight application. (ii) Automation application: deliver the data-processing result directly to the engine that decides the business affairs automatically. Computational advertising is a typical automation application, since its entire process – from collection of user behavioral data to audience targeting and finally to online automatic decision-making based on user tags – is automatically operated, while humans are only responsible for creating a work flow and adjusting strategies. The automatic replenishment system of e-commerce is also an automation application of big data.

In case of insight application, the data volume for producing statements could not be too large, since there are human beings involved in decision-making, which may result in loss of some information. Moreover, the interpretation and decision-making of statements need a strong professional background, just imagine how hard for a layman to understand a financial statement. In contrast, automation application enables machine-based decision-making, which processes data one by one to make better use of them. Therefore, if comparing with the traditional insight application, we believe automation application is a right option that exploits the advantages of big data to the full.

In view of the above three characteristics, the traditional IOE architecture for storing and computing medium-scale volume of transaction data is no longer applicable, and new solutions become a realistic need. Such demand has given rise to GFS, MapReduce, and BigTable – "troika" big data applications of Google, and such open source solutions as Hadoop and Spark.

Considering the key points of behavioral data, full processing, and automation application, the computational problems in online advertising are a typical big data application. In fact, for a long time in the past, computational advertising has been the only trade that is fully capable of commercialized and large-scale big data application, which sets an important example for the industry-wide big data application. The following three points shall be especially emphasized:

(1) Computational advertising has brought forth complete products and solutions for large-scale traffic and data monetization, and generated most of the profit for the Internet business.

(2) Online advertising has incubated a mature industrial chain for data processing and trading, which should be recommended to all big data practitioners for them to take reference.

(3) Because of the commercial constraints, computational advertising products and technologies are more complicated than the recommendation system. Given this, understanding the products and market of computational advertising is of great help for designing efficient commercial products.

In short, for the product managers, engineers, or administrators who deal with big data, business monetization or user growth, learning about advertising products and technologies is sure to benefit them a lot and help them quickly find the real challenges in this field. For this purpose, the content of this book will be unfolded along with an open line (evolution of advertising products and technologies) and a hidden line (data use degree).

1.3 DEFINITION AND PURPOSE OF ADVERTISING

Before learning computational advertising, we shall firstly know the general purpose of advertising. What is advertising? William F. Arens answered this question in his *Contemporary Advertising* [2]:

> *Advertising is the structured and composed nonpersonal communication of information, usually paid for and usually persuasive in nature, about products (goods, services, and ideas) by identified sponsors through various media.*

This definition contains two key points: (1) It points out the two active participants in advertising campaigns, i.e., sponsors and media. Considering the complex market structure of digital advertising, they can be described in general terms as "the demand" and "the supply." The former includes advertisers, agencies (representing the interests of advertisers), or buyers in other technical forms; the latter includes media and monetization platforms in other technical forms. (2) There is also a passive participant in advertising, i.e., audiences. Please do remember that the interest game relationship among sponsors, media, and audiences is the cardinal line of advertising campaigns, and this line runs through the entire evolutionary process of advertising business and product forms. In addition, the above definition makes clear that advertising is a "paid" and "nonpersonal" information dissemination activity: "paid" is the target of advertising, while "nonpersonal" means that the target could be optimized through computation; these two constraints are basis for generation of computational advertising.

What is the essential purpose of advertising? In different ages there are different answers to this question. In the era of traditional media, there has been a considerable gap between the supply and the demand in the advertising market. No matter it is TV, airport, or magazine, they are far from being able to generate the conversion behaviors as expected by most advertisers. The purpose of traditional advertising is to reach a large number of users promptly via media, so as to promote the brand image and increase the medium- and long-term conversion rate and profit margin; this kind of advertising is called "brand awareness advertising." Of course, some advertisers expect advertising to generate a great deal of purchases or other conversion behaviors as soon as possible, such kind of advertising is called "direct-response advertising."

The traditional media are apparently not good at delivering and optimizing the direct response advertising, since it lacks effective technical means to precisely deliver ads to target users so as to achieve the short-term effect. The most common response advertising via the traditional media may be the fast food leaflets distributed outside office buildings, which is a kind of "direct marketing" (DM). It is the digital media that have led to unprecedentedly vigorous development of direct response advertising, which is attributed to two aspects of reasons: (1) The distinctive digital media enables low-cost delivery of personalized ads, which is traffic monetization in essence. (2) It is easier for some online services like search and e-commerce – with better understanding of user intention – to optimize the advertising effect, which is data monetization in essence.

Online advertising has dual functions of brand awareness and direct response. But the robust development of online advertising is mainly for generating rich benefits to the direct response advertising market. As shown in Table 1.1, the online advertising market had been expanding rapidly from 2007 to 2015, and so far has surpassed TV advertising to occupy more than half of the Chinese advertising market; in the meantime, the traditional advertising market had shown faltering growth or fast decline. But the rapidly developing online advertising has not led to a significant contraction of TV advertising, because the major scenarios of online advertising (search engine marketing, mobile app downloading and e-commerce marketing) are oriented to direct response advertising, which is more like an increment rather than a substitute to TV advertising. In contrast, newspaper advertising has been declining rapidly, because users are spending more time on the Internet, and some classified ads in newspapers overlap with the response ads on the Internet. Presently, digital media are taking up more time of people; the strongly appealing media (e.g., online video) are becoming increasingly popular, so online advertising is bound to have more potential to perform the brand awareness function.

Now that an advertising campaign has two goals of brand awareness and direct response, how about its fundamental purpose? The answer is also in Arens's *Contemporary Advertising*:

> *The fundamental purpose of advertising is to connect advertisers with users through media at a low cost.*

It means that the fundamental purpose of advertising is to reach the corresponding groups of users based on a certain market intention, and then exert influence upon the

TABLE 1.1 Size of main advertising markets in China and the United States

State	Ad type	2007	2008	2009	2010	2011	2012	2013	2014	2015	2016
China	Online	1.7	2.7	3.3	5.2	8.3	12.2	17.9	23.3	31.7	42
	Radio & TV	9.7	11.4	12.7	15.3	18.2	20.7	21.2	21.9	22.6	22.3
US	Online	21.2	23.4	22.6	26	31.7	36.6	42.8	49.5	59.6	72.5
	TV	71.9	39.4	35.9	40.1	68.5	72.1	74.5	65.7	66.3	71.3
	Newspaper	48.6	34.4	24.6	22.8	20.7	19.4	18	16.7	15.1	-

Unit: US$ bln

Source: Market survey reports produced by IAB, iResearch, and other institutions potential users, so that they are more likely to choose certain products or less critical about the products' cost performance. The short-term conversion effects are not directly comparable due to different market intention or media nature. In other words, if we only stress the purpose of conversion effect, we may deviate from the correct methodology for ad serving. For example, if a cold medicine advertiser pursues a short-term effect, then the best strategy is to deliver ads to the people already have a cold, yet it is obviously an absurd decision. Take an automobile advertiser for example, he increases the product publicity among the users of competing brands to promote his own cars, but the direct response of the ad may be even worse than random ad serving. When comparing the effects of multiple advertising channels, a clear understanding of the advertising purpose will prevent us from drawing biased conclusions.

The "low cost" of advertising is relative to the cost of persuasion campaigns performed by marketing or sales personnel. Advertising is actually getting a free ride on media traffic and influence. In order to confirm whether the advertising cost is low or not, we need an evaluation index of return on investment (ROI), which is the ratio between total output and total input of an advertising campaign. In practice, it is easy to make sure of the total input into an advertising campaign, but the total output is not always definite and measurable, especially when delivering the brand ads that aim at medium- and long-term revenue. As a result, an absolute ROI is sometimes difficult to calculate, but we can assess whether the advertising cost is satisfactory by comparing different advertising channels.

In the Internet environment, the nature of advertising remains unchanged, but it has diverse and flexible forms of presentation to meet the keen demand for direct response. As for online banner ads (similar to offline banner ads), search ad and advertorials, or even game joint-operation which seems irrelevant to advertising, they are essentially paid information promotion and available to be categorized as advertising from the product perspective. Therefore, we can come to the following conclusion about online advertising:

> *All the channels through which paid information, products or services are disseminated fall into the category of advertising.*

The main presentation forms of online advertising are introduced below in Section 1.4.

1.4 PRESENTATION FORMS OF ONLINE ADVERTISING

Online advertising has multiple forms of presentation to contact users, and they have become increasingly diversified along with development of the mobile Internet (MI). Some common presentation forms are briefly introduced in the following paragraphs. Please note that these forms of advertising are somewhat overlapped in their concepts, rather than juxtaposed.

(1) Banner ad. It is the most traditional form of display advertising: embedding a picture – which usually takes up a fixed size of space – into a webpage. Nowadays, most banner ads are no longer static pictures, but become dynamic enabled by Flash or HTML5. See an example of a banner ad in Figure 1.2.

(2) Textual ad. This kind of advertising, which links the text to the landing page of an advertiser, is the mainstream form of search advertising and also widely used in display advertising. Textual ad sometimes takes up a fixed space like banner ad or is sometimes inserted into a large number of link entries (see Figure 1.3).

(3) Rich media ad. This kind of ad is presented in the forms with strong visual impact, in an aim to deliver the advertising materials to users in an intrusive manner. Pop-up ad, couplet ad, and full-screen ad are common forms of rich media ad. It is more appropriate for delivering the ads with strong brand attributes in high-quality media and influencing user experience. Some web portals sometimes place certain rich media ads – customized for brand advertisers and presented in complicated interactive mode – on their homepage. Such ad does not follow the logic of delivery to target audience, but highlights the impact force of creative and the features of interactive mode. Figure 1.4 shows a pop-up ad, which is a kind of rich media ad

(4) Video ad. Unlike static materials, the videolized advertising creative not only increases the quantity of disseminated information, but enhances its impact force. Video ad has become one of the most important trends in online advertising. In addition to click through rate (CTR), user duration and other indicators that better reflect the user impression are used to measure the effect of video ad.

Video ad mainly includes the following forms:

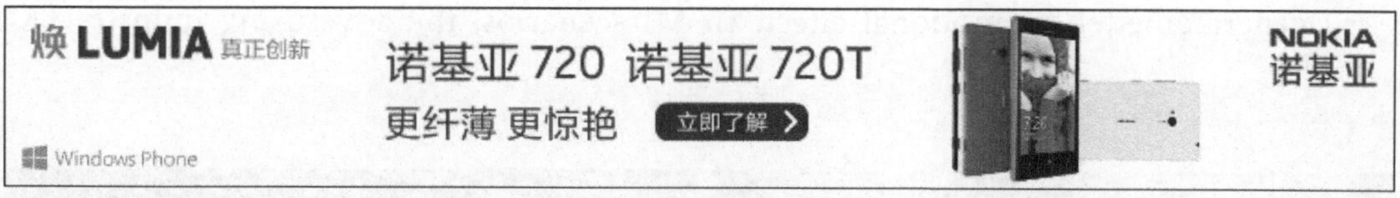

FIGURE 1.2 Example of banner ad.

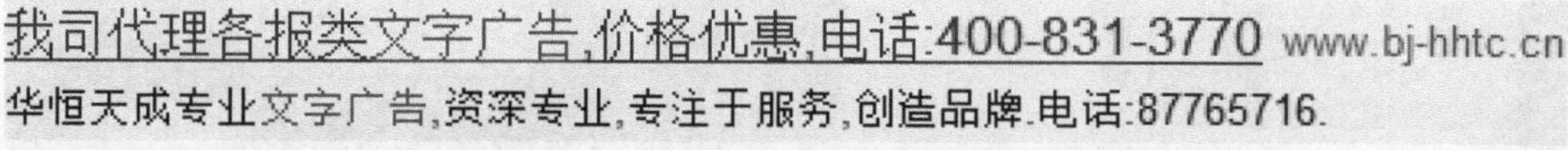

FIGURE 1.3 Example of textual ad.

FIGURE 1.4 Example of pop-up ad.

- Insert ad. There are front patch ad, end patch ad, and pause ad according to different insert positions (see the video ad examples in Figure 1.5). With a unique carrier, video ad has the similar effect and creative to offline TV ad. This kind of ad is usually in the form of short video, manifesting an expressive force much stronger than ordinary display ad, so the price is often higher.
- News feed video ad. It is played automatically in the scenes with Wi-Fi access, generating a much better effect than ordinary news feed display ad.
- Rewarded video ad in mobile games. Gamers will receive reward points by watching video ads. These ads usually have a higher watch rate and better advertising effect.

(5) Playable ad: By carrying more creative information, this kind of video ad is able to generate better promotional effect. In MI scenarios, the advertising industry has

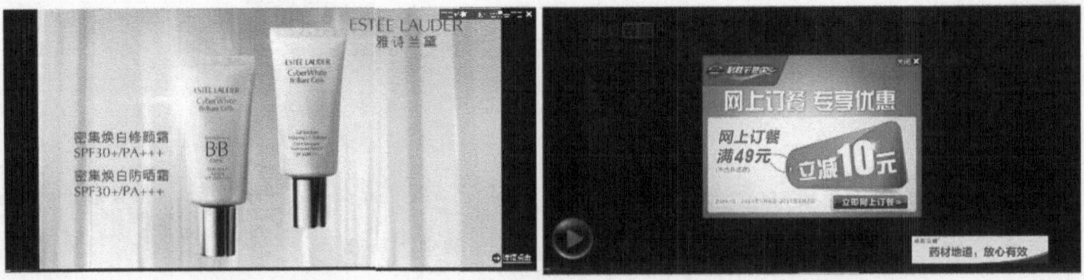

FIGURE 1.5 Examples of insert ad: front patch ad (L), pause ad (R).

started exploring interactive solutions that enable users to complete interaction directly in the creative process and experience the promoted products.

In mobile applications and game promotions, playable ad enables users to experience the advertising content without downloading the apps, which raises the conversion rate sometimes, but diverts users' attention from the media at the same time. The creative of playable ad is realized by two technical solutions: server-side interaction and HTML5-based simulation (the two solutions are to be introduced in Subsection 16.1.3). Figure 1.6 shows some examples of playable ad.

(6) Social ad: The rise of Social Networking Services (SNS) has broadened advertising channels and built up their capability. The ads embedded in SNS are collectively called "social ads." The most typical form of social ads is news feed ad, which was firstly seen in the "Promoted Tweets" introduced by Twitter. News feed ad falls into the category of native ad, since it strives to be inserted as naturally as possible during the interaction with users. The concepts of "social ad" and "ad in SNS" are not the same: for example, there is no substantial difference between the textual or banner ads auctioned on SNS pages and the display ads on regular websites, but the purpose of social ad is to exert greater influence through diffusion and communication among users; in this sense, there is a bright prospect in mining the value from news feed interaction (see an exemplar news feed ad in Figure 1.7).

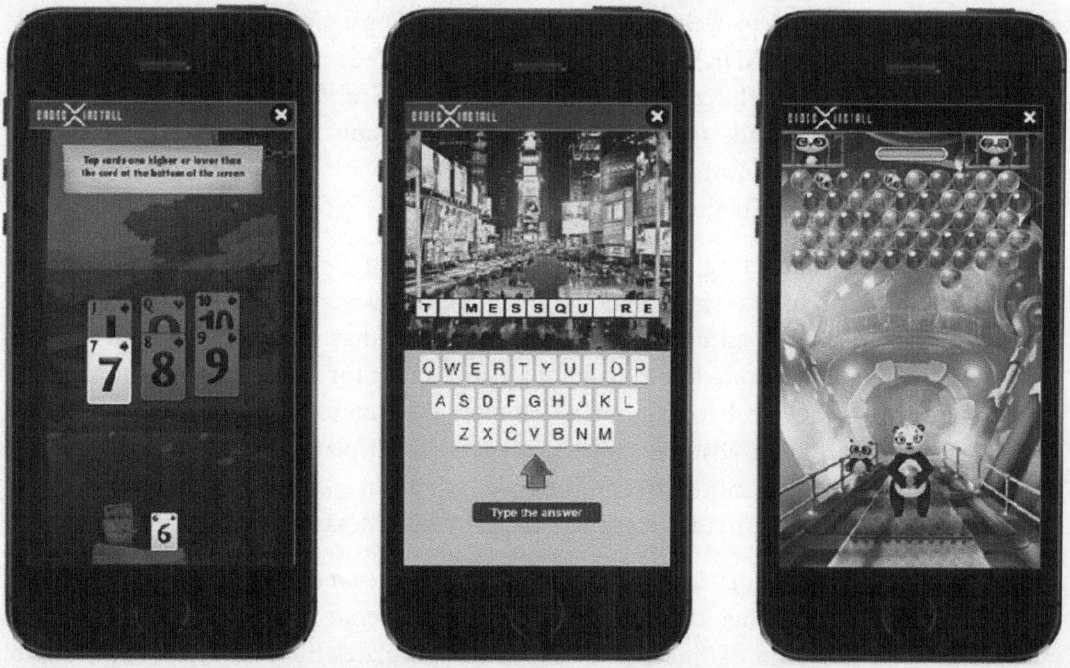

FIGURE 1.6 Examples of playable ad.

FIGURE 1.7 Example of social ad.

(7) Mobile ad: In recent years, the mobile Internet has experienced an explosive growth and tends to replace the desktop Internet. Strictly speaking, there is no essential difference between mobile advertising and desktop advertising. The only thing worth noting is that as result of popularization of mobile native apps, ads are no longer confined to webpages, but added into apps. Consequently, the Software Development Kit (SDK) is developed to insert ads into apps, and matching advertising products have come into being. The typical forms of mobile ad include banner ad, launch ad, screen ad, offer wall, and app wall (see the examples of mobile ad in Figure 1.8). The problems associated with mobile and native ads are to be explained in Chapter 8.

(8) E-mail direct marketing (EDM). It is a marketing tool that sends promotional information to users via e-mail. Unlike the abovementioned various forms of advertising, EDM is an active marketing approach that sends ads to right users at any time, but it is prone to be treated like junk mails for the same reason. For EDM operators, it is critical to accurately capture user interest and provide them with targeted information abstemiously. In contrast to display advertising, the audience targeting in EDM is more direct and more important (see the examples of EDM in Figure 1.9). In addition, the ad serving via SMS and iMessage is quite similar to EDM.

(9) Incentive ad. There is an important difference between digital advertising and traditional advertising: the former is able to generate conversion directly, thus giving rise to a kind of "incentive ad" which stimulates the conversion behavior of users directly and receives better advertising effect. One of the typical forms of incentive ad is the integral wall in mobile apps (see Figure 1.10).

FIGURE 1.8 Examples of mobile ad.

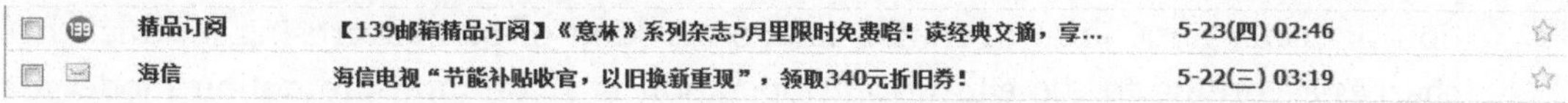

FIGURE 1.9 Examples of EDM.

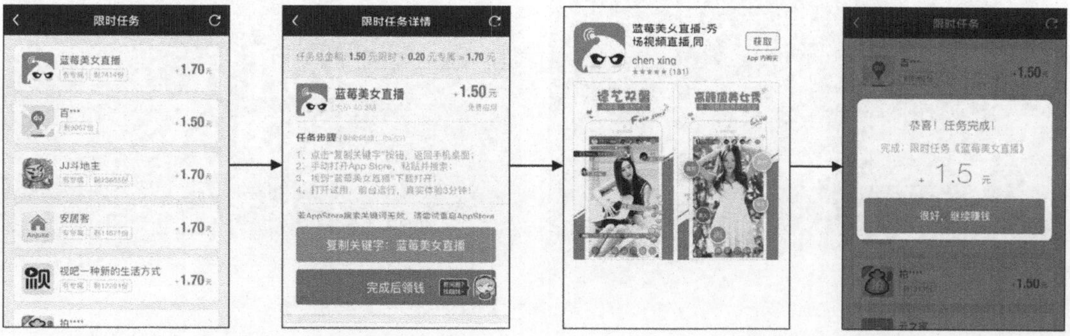

FIGURE 1.10 Examples of integral wall.

Rebate purchase is a common promotion model in e-commerce. It is also a kind of incentive ad since it uses discounts or shopping points to stimulate users to buy commodities. Apparently, this approach is able to yield arbitrarily high ROI, but it may also cause some old users to switch to rebate shopping guide websites.

In addition to integral wall and rebate, incentive ad is also presented in content lock and lock screen, etc. As the old saying goes, "There's no such thing as a free lunch." Although incentive ad can significantly raise the conversion rate, the users' real demand for products is not strong, meaning that the follow-up effect will be notably reduced, and its ability in extracting the value of new users is especially poor. Therefore, the price of incentive ad is usually much lower than that of non-incentive ad.

(10) Group buying. It is a kind of pan-advertising product that charges according to the effect, which is in essence a form of incentive ad. Most advertisers of the group-buying promotion are local stores that are eager to attract new customers. On the group-buying platforms, the ranking of products is the same with the ranking of ads (see Figure 1.11). Unlike the traditional group buying that adopts agreed pricing, the current group-buying websites have introduced auction-based direct sales. Moreover, the ad bank of group purchase only contains paid information rather than creative, which is conducive to developing the promotional models for native ad. Please refer to the detailed explanation in Chapter 8.

(11) Game joint operation. Being a commercial product with profits shared between promotion channels and game developers according to the final in-game consumption of users, game joint operation is another kind of pan-advertising product that charges according to the effect. Joint operation is a common promotion model for

FIGURE 1.11 Examples of group-buying products.

web games and mobile games. The game download centers (like the one shown in Figure 1.12) are usually subject to joint operation. In China's Android applications market, the revenue from game joint operation far exceeds that of other types of advertising. But the profit-sharing proportion varies greatly among different promotion channels. For some major foreign promotion channels like Apple Store, their profit-sharing proportion is generally 30%, while such proportion is above 90% for major promotion channels in China. The ideas for designing and operating advertising products are fully applicable to game joint operation.

(12) Navigation website. It mainly includes the location entrances of the directindustry web guide (see Figure 1.13), the recommended locations of the application distribution platforms and other paid promotion locations. In general, this kind of ad product charges by the hour rather than dynamic bidding, because advertisers,

FIGURE 1.12 Exemplar game joint operation.

FIGURE 1.13 Exemplar directindustry web guide.

though care about traffic attraction, are more interested in the window effect of these entrance locations. This type of advertising has similar sales and operation models with the contract advertising that charges on a daily basis.

The abovementioned advertising products and pan-advertising products are often operated by one advertising company at the same time, so it is not surprising that the company has to deal with the dilemma where its advertising products or even consumer products compete against each other for advertising space or other entrance resources. Under such circumstance, auction is the most reasonable approach for allocating advertising space or entrance resources, which is a very important operation principle for traffic monetization.

1.5 BRIEF HISTORY OF ONLINE ADVERTISING

Before talking about advertising technology, we shall firstly review the development history of online advertising to acquire a general knowledge of the multitudinous concepts, technologies, and terms about advertising, or else it will be hard to understand the specific ad products.

In the late 20th century, the online media like AOL and Yahoo! were still newborns. Enticed by their large-scale network traffic, the investors expected these media to bring them real money. The foremost direct way to monetize or commercialize the online traffic was to insert advertising space into webpages like magazines. So the offline advertising agencies treated the websites as new magazines, buying advertising space based on established ways of thinking. The banner ads placed on the Internet are categorized as "display advertising." From the aspect of sales model, display advertising is also described as "agreement-based advertising," i.e., there is a contract providing for a certain advertising space to be exclusively occupied by a specific advertiser for a prescribed period of time; creative ideas and ad delivery strategy shall be developed to meet the requirements of both sides. The ad space (left image) shown in Figure 1.14 was sold 10,000 yuan per day. Obviously, this type of advertising lacked personalized features since it was unable to deliver varied ad content to different users like the digital media capable of doing so.

Through explorations, it didn't take long for the Internet advertising operators to discover that digital media are essentially different from traditional media, i.e., the former are capable of presenting advertising originality in diverse forms to different audiences. Such knowledge, which seems commonplace nowadays, was actually the core driving force for the effect and scale of online advertising to keep growing. Being aware of this, the online media have developed a new train of thought to further raise the price for advertising space. Just like the pictures in Figure 1.14, the shaver ad only appeals to male audiences, so the online media allocate the male user traffic to this advertising space and set a price of 6,000 yuan; similarly, an advertising space for cosmetics, which targets at female audiences, is also priced at 6,000 yuan. Such kind of ad delivery is called "targeted advertising." For advertisers, they can win over the valid audiences like

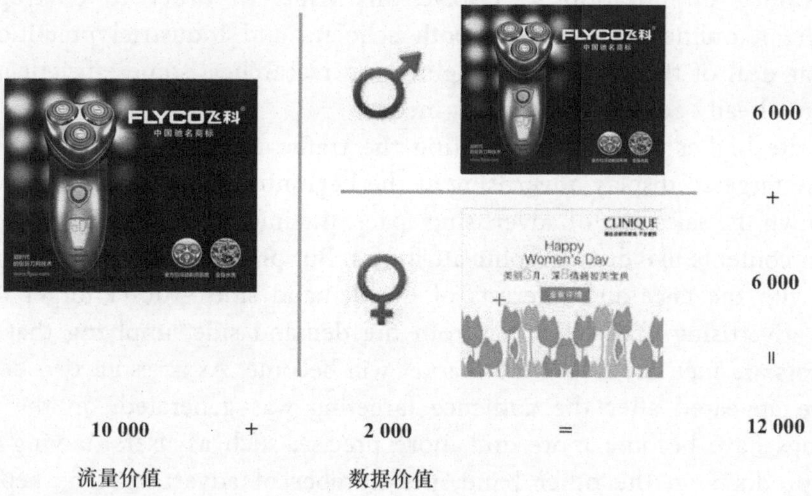

FIGURE 1.14 Monetization of network traffic and data.

the originally indiscriminate advertising space, but at a lower cost. For online media, they can earn a higher revenue of 12,000 yuan (used to be 10,000 yuan); the extra 2,000 yuan marks the monetized value of data (the data herein refer to the gender data of users). Readers shall keep the following point in mind:

In advertising business, data monetization is based on traffic monetization.

Targeted advertising system is supported by two computing technologies: (1) audience targeting: it identifies gender, age, or other characteristics of a certain user. (2) Ad serving: it turns ad serving from direct embedding into webpage to real-time response to front-end request, makes dynamic decisions, and reconsiders appropriate advertising originality. Since it is an extension of traditional advertising, targeted advertising is still carried out upon signing the contract: the media and the advertiser firstly agree on the advertising space, time frame, and serving quantity, and then determine the total amount of the contract and the compensation scheme if the quantity is not up to the standard. Such transaction model – guaranteed delivery (GD) – has gradually become the main model of Internet contract advertising. Generally speaking, most of these contracts are concluded with brand advertisers and billed by cost per mille (CPM).

GD involves an important computational problem, i.e., allocating better traffic to advertisers as much as possible while fulfilling the contract-specified quantity. This problem has two aspects of difficulties: (1) How to effectively allocate the traffic to the advertisers whose contract contents are crossed? (2) How to make each presentation decision in real time in an online environment? Given this, the issue of online allocation comes into being. If we take the quantity of each contract as a constraint and the advertising effect as an objective function, then we can use a mathematical framework with constrained optimization to resolve this issue. In order to develop practical solutions in an online environment, both scholars and industrial practitioners have done a great deal of theoretical and engineering researches, some efficient and simple solutions are already adopted by various media.

To generate higher revenue by splitting the traffic was the reason why the online media chose targeted display advertising at the beginning. Since fairly precise targeting may pull down the sales rate of advertising space, the initial targeting labels only showed some rough contents like demographic attributes. But precise audience targeting is more consistent with the taste and interests of the demand side – don't forget that all the money on advertising market comes from the demand side, implying that the better their interests are met, the larger the market will become. As a result, two development trends have appeared after the audience targeting was generated: on the one hand, targeting tags have become more and more precise, such as users' buying interest in a specific product; on the other hand, the number of advertisers has kept swelling. Because of these trends, the contract-based ad sales have fallen into increasing troubles: first, it is difficult to accurately estimate the traffic of these fine-grained tag combinations. Second, when multiple contracts are fulfilled in one impression, some traffic – though ought to be sold at a higher price – may be wasted by simply following the online allocation strategy. Now that constraint of quantity is culprit for these troubles, is it possible to get rid of it? This train of thought has fostered "auction-based advertising," which is a revolutionary product in the history of computational advertising. With this auction model, suppliers are only obliged to assure advertisers of "quality" (cost per unit of traffic) rather than "quantity"; and the decision for each impression is made according to the simple principle of highest return.

By reviewing the development history of display advertising, we can find the reasons for the emergence of auction-based advertising. But in fact, auction-based advertising was born in search ad – the foremost gold mine of Internet advertising. With mature technology, the search engines led by Google quickly became a new entry point of the Internet. Unlike portal websites, search engines were not regarded as media initially, so the monetization of search traffic also relied on paid search (sponsored search). But from the perspective of advertising, paid search is obviously a targeted advertising, i.e., targeted ad delivery based on instant interest of users, and the tags of instant interest thus becoming the keywords. It can be seen that as search ad boasts a high degree of accuracy since the very beginning, it is natural for it to adopt auction-based sales.

In addition to monetizing the search traffic itself, the keyword auction applicable to search engines has been promoted to other media: when users' search terms become the keywords on the webpage, then the product ads will transfer from the search engine results page (SERP) to the media page, here comes contextual advertising.

Viewing the advertising market at a macro level, in case of auction-based advertising, which is notably different from contract-based advertising, a large number of advertisers will be exposed to a multi-player game without contractual guarantee. In terms of charging the advertisers for each auction, implementing the optimal scheme at a micro level cannot always achieve the maximal benefit of the entire market. An in-depth study of the pricing mechanism has incubated an important theory about auction: generalized second price (GSP).

Based on such essential functions as auction and precise audience targeting, a new form of product – ad network (ADN) – has come into being. It operates the advertising spaces of online media in batch, sells them to demanders based on user groups or contextual tags, and allocates traffic through auction. ADN usually adopts the clearing form of cost per click (CPC), because of data, business, and reasons (see the details in Section 2.3.2). Generally speaking, the revenue per mille (RPM) of ADN is lower than that of contract-based advertising, but it can help a large number of media monetize their remnant inventory (the traffic unable to be sold via contract-based advertising): entrust their inventory to ADN directly and have their inventory monetized by ADN's sales and agent teams.

Search ad and ADN only have an offer interface, does it mean that advertisers no longer need the assurance for traffic quantity? In practice, the demand-side products are often used to guarantee the traffic quantity. After the generation of auction-based advertising, the forms for purchasing traffic have undergone the following changes: first, the purchase cares more about targeted audience than advertising space. Second, technological means are badly needed to satisfy advertisers' requirement for quantity, and advertising effect shall be optimized on this basis. It seems like another issue with constrained optimization similar to online allocation. But in fact, it is a fairly different issue, because the demand has no other choice but offer a price for the label combinations defined by the supplier, instead of controlling the offer price for each impression; the market is more like a "black box," the demand can only select appropriate label combinations, and make adjustments in different stages to control the advertising effect in an indirect manner. Here comes a new term "trading desk" (TD), which refers to one-stop purchase of advertising space from diverse ADNs or media based on user groups, and optimization of the products from the demand side in both quantity and quality.

ADN auction is an internal process, which cannot meet advertisers' requirementdemand for customized group selection and optimization. Consider the following two scenarios: (1) An e-commerce website is preparing to recall its lost users through advertising. (2) A bank intends to find similar potential customers based on existing credit card holders and reach them through advertising. Apparently, the advertising platforms are unable to sort out the appropriate user groups with their proprietary data. This requirementdemand has given rise to an open logic for auction: let the demand select traffic based on its own definition of user groups, which is known as "real-time bidding" (RTB), i.e., replacing the pre-bidding launched by advertisers with a real-time bidding for each display. By sending the contextual URL of the displayed ads and user ID to the demander, RTB will complete customized group selection and bidding. As a result, a new form of product named "ad exchange" (ADX) – which aggregates various media traffic and monetizes it through real-time bidding – has appeared on the market. "ADX" sounds like a stock exchange, and they do have some similarities if we regard ADN as an over-the-counter market.

The product that is available for RTB and ad purchase according to customized crowd tags is called "demand-side platform" (DSP). RTB usually charges by cost per visit (CPV) (see the explanations in Section 6.3), which means that DSP shall estimate the expected value of each impression as accurately as possible. In this regard, DSP is much more convenient than TD, because sufficient environmental information makes deep computation and estimation possible. The DSP-based ad purchase, which resembles the program trading on stock market, is also called "programmatic trade." In addition to RTB, there are other ways for program trading (the details are given in Section 6.2). In general, the position of programmatic trade in online advertising will continue to be strengthened, which is determined by the trend of maximizing the interests of advertisers.

For the readers who are unfamiliar with online advertising may be confused by the numerous concepts and business logic mentioned above. But they don't need to worry about it, as all the key concepts shown in bold font will be carefully explained in subsequent chapters. This section only provides readers with an overall knowledge of the topics in this book, so that they will see both trees and forest when they come across the specific problems in subsequent chapters.

Considering the sophisticated market structure of online advertising, LUMA Partners has comprehensively summarized the globally representative companies and shows them in the picture "DISPLAY LUMAscape"[1] (See Figure 1.15). The "skeleton" of this picture accords with the history of online advertising (see the preceding paragraphs), but it also outlines the advertising products covered in this book. In short, this "pedigree" develops gradually from both ends to the middle: firstly, in the phase of contract advertising, advertisers buy ads from the media via agencies, and then the publisher tools of the media side complete and optimize the contracts with multiple advertisers. Secondly, after the auction-based ad sales are practiced, such products (e.g., ADN) that tilt toward the supply side are launched; in order to adapt to this market change, the agencies on behalf of the demand side have put into operation of the **media buying platform**. Finally, after the programmatic trade becomes active, the supply side starts adopting ADX, so the demand side uses DSP to dock with it for ad delivery. The bottom half of Figure 1.15 depicts the products that prop up the market structure or specified products in subdivided fields. We will make detailed introduction to these products when they show up in the following sections.

Some terms in Figure 1.15 differ from those in this book, e.g., the "media buying platform" is replaced by a similar term "TD" in this book. Please don't get confused.

To sum up, the evolution of targeting technologies and transaction forms is a cardinal line in the history of online advertising. From the initial fixed-position contract to audience-targeting and CPM contract, and then to auction-based transaction, and finally to the open real-time bidding, the core driving force of this cardinal line is to enable more and more data sources to support advertising decisions, so as to enhance the effect of advertising. In addition, there is a second cardinal line of development path for Internet advertising, i.e., the development of ad display logic: at the initial stage of display advertising, the advertising space was decided and operated as a unit separated

1 Source: https://lumapartners.com/content/lumascapes/display-ad-tech-lumascape/

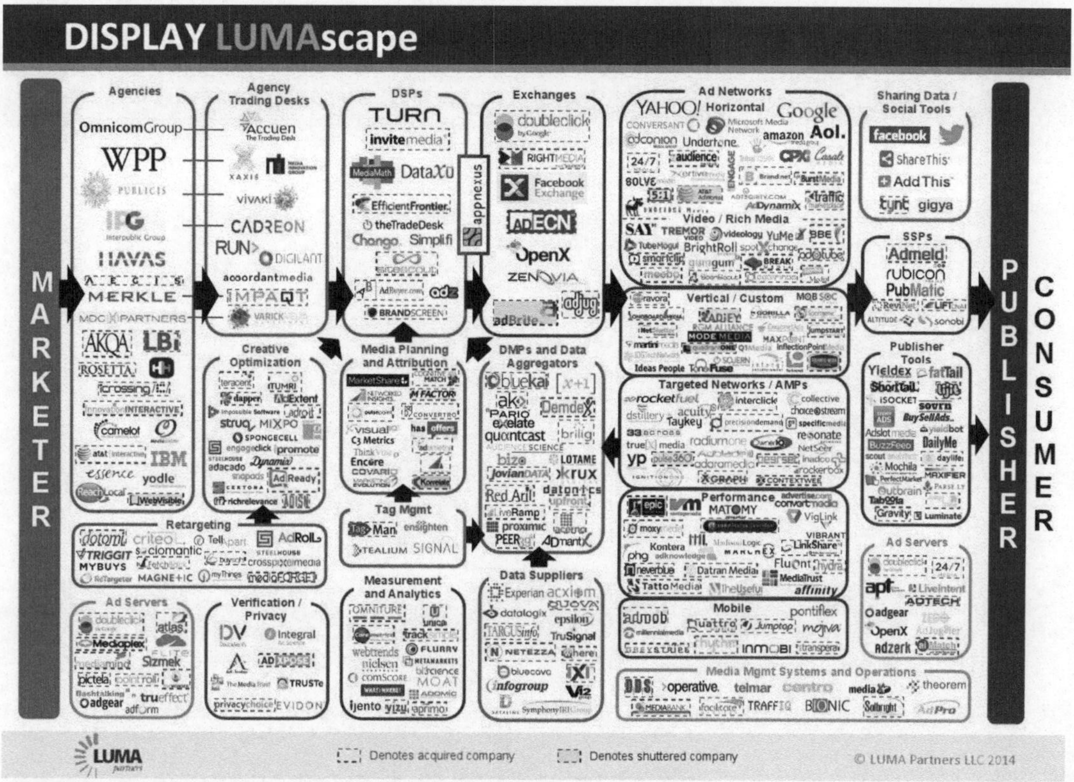

FIGURE 1.15 The atlas showing the structure of display advertising market and representative companies produced by LUMA.

from the ad content and only aimed to optimize revenue, but people are inspired by search ads and news feed ads that it is not always a good choice to set ad content against advertising (the reason why both search ads and news feed ads have prominent effects is for their high-level consistency between content display and trigger logic). Along this line of thinking, native ad – a form of product that unifies ad content and advertising in some way – has drawn increasing attention in recent years. How to combine the original decision-making habit with the mature advertising transaction forms is currently a hot topic in mobile Internet advertising. The relevant topics will be discussed in detail in Chapter 8.

CHAPTER 2

Basis for Computational Advertising

From this chapter we will start examining the computational problems in online advertising. What problems are solved by the computation in advertising? What kind of business description framework is needed to solve these problems? These questions are the focus of this chapter.

We will at first briefly review the advertising effectiveness theory born in the traditional advertising. By dividing the process where the advertising effect is generated into several stages and by analyzing the key influencing factors at each stage, we can have a perceptual knowledge of the know-why of such core technologies as audience targeting and creative optimization in online advertising. This part of content, though irrelevant to concrete computing technologies, profoundly reveals some rationales for computational advertising.

The reason why computation plays a significant role in the Internet advertising is for some of its fundamental technical features, which are the starting point of this chapter. In general, measurable results and computational optimization are the main features that distinguish online advertising from offline advertising. Based on these features, we have moderately broadened the core challenges upon computational advertising which are presented by Andrei Broder, and then identified the core problem about computational advertising – a conceptual framework for profit optimization – that runs through this book.

With regard to the most advertising products, it is their revenue that can be optimized through computation, while the expected cost per time (eCPM) is one of the foremost quantitative indicators in computational advertising. Being associated with the process where ad information is conveyed, eCPM can be resolved into a product of click-through rate (CTR) and click value; these two indicators, which often appear in the computational process of various advertising products, require thorough understanding and close attention of those responsible for product operation.

The breakdown of eCPM is helpful for understanding the market structure and billing methods of online advertising. Readers will find the multiple billing methods are able to reflect the different calculation division of online advertising market. To be specific, the billing methods are related to the ways through which the supply and the demand divide their labor to estimate CTR and click value, and finally optimize the resource allocation of the entire market. A thorough understanding of the common billing methods will enable readers to grasp the core problems about computational advertising and evaluate the difficulty of each problem under certain circumstances.

This chapter concludes with an introduction to several important industry associations in the field of advertising, of course, including online advertising. For the readers interested in advertising technologies and business affairs, it is necessary to identify the stakeholders (represented by industry associations) in advertising business and their role in promoting the development of online advertising products and technologies.

2.1 ADVERTISING EFFECTIVENESS THEORY

Before discussing the technologies for optimizing the advertising effect, we shall firstly learn about how an ad reaches users and ultimately generates effect. Such issue has all along been an important topic in advertising. In this section we directly borrow the previous study results, and use a three-segment information transmission model to dissect the entire process from materialization of an ad to conversion of user behavior (see Figure 2.1).

This process is made up of three phases as Selection, Interpretation, and Attitude, which are further split into six sub-phases as Exposure, Attention, Comprehension, Acceptance, Retention, and Decision. The significance and key points of each sub-phase are discussed below.

(1) Exposure. In this phase the ads are physically displayed, and the advertising effect is affected by the physical property of advertising position which has little room for technical optimization. In practice, in contrast to technical factors, effective exposure is far more important for the ultimate advertising effect, that's why the industry insiders like to say "position is everything." For example, the LED advertising displays at New York Times Square (Figure 2.2, L) and on the external façade of Beijing Jingxin Mansion at the north end of East Third Ring Road – one of Beijing's trunk roads (Figure 2.2, R) – are known for their stunning exposure effect. In the

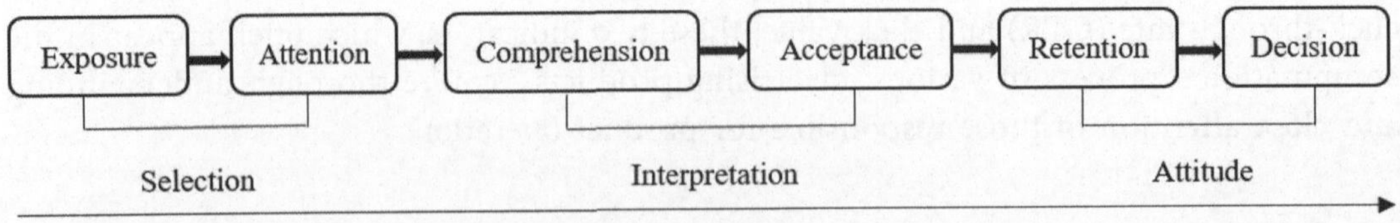

FIGURE 2.1 Generation process of the advertising effect.

FIGURE 2.2 Examples of advertising positions (L: NY Times Square; R: Jingxin Mansion).

Internet advertising, an advertising position sometimes plays a more significant role. As such, how to erase the CTR deviation caused by advertising positions algorithmically has become an important practical problem.

(2) Attention. In this phase the audiences are physically exposed to the ads and then gradually drawn to them. But in the domain of advertising, exposure may fail to draw user attention. For example, when a friend of mine was browsing a social networking site, his younger son shouted excitedly, "dad, look at the dinosaur on the page!" My friend looked for the dinosaur for a minute but found nothing. In fact, the dinosaur was in the most striking advertising position at the top of the page. This example shows that strong exposure cannot make sure of user attention.

How to raise user attention? Firstly, try not to interrupt what they are doing. This is the rationale for contextual targeting and one of the starting points of native ads. This rationale explains why the father failed to find the dinosaur, because when users have identified a fixed advertising position, if they don't think it is related to the page that they are browsing, they will subconsciously block its content. Secondly, clarify the reasons for delivering the ad to users, which is an important direction for optimizing the creative of target advertising. Finally, the ad content shall fit user interest or need, which is the basis for audience behavioral targeting.

(3) Comprehension. Though users may have noticed an ad, it does not mean they could comprehend its content. Take my experience for example, I once played a web game, and was later targeted by a web game "4D City War," so I was shown an ad promoting the new model of this game for several times. Such audience targeting is

of course accurate, and I even watched the ad carefully, but I could not understand it intuitively, let alone successful conversion.

How to improve the efficiency of comprehension? On the one hand, the advertising content shall be catering to user interest and understandable, which reveals the necessity to have accurate audience targeting. On the other hand, make sure that the target audience comprehends the content of varied forms of advertising. As such, TV ads can be presented in short stories, either touching or inspiring, to promote the brands; billboard ads shall express several major market requirements; in case of the Internet advertising, it is better to highlight a dominant requirement to attract user attention, since users are drawn to the webpage content most of the time.

(4) Acceptance. Even though the audience understands the ad content, it does not mean they accept it. The industry insiders always sigh that "half of my budget is wasted." Yet the actual situation may be even worse. If an ad contains inappropriate information, then one third of the advertising display may exert a negative effect. Therefore, special attention shall be paid when using some unconventional advertising approaches like humor and sex appeal.

The context of ads has a great impact on their degree of acceptance. For example, when users find the same ad in a game community and on the homepage of a web portal, they tend to think that the latter is more convincing, which is owing to the brand value of high-quality media. As target advertising becomes increasingly popular nowadays, the issue of ad safety – ensuring appropriate ads to show in right media – is a growing concern.

(5) Retention. The brand advertisers that aim at the long-term advertising effect certainly hope their ad content could leave a lingering impression on users so as to affect their choices in the long run. As a result, brand advertisers are especially serious about the creative design to enhance the effect of retention. If you just think of the TV ads invested with artistic glamour and romance, you can have an intuitive understanding of retention.

(6) Decision. The ultimate function of a successful ad is user conversion. The phase of decision is in fact beyond the scope of advertising, but a good ad is ought to lay the groundwork for raising the conversion rate. Especially for e-commerce and group-buying business, it is a very demanding job to determine which kind of information should be underlined in advertising creative so as to impress price-sensitive consumers.

Qualitatively speaking, the prior phases have greater impact on CTR, while the latter phases are more closely associated with the conversion rate. But these phases are by no means isolated or absolutely unconnected, because a concrete advertising strategy or technology may influence the effects of several phases concurrently. Although the advertising effectiveness model is often discussed in the studies on traditional advertising, its rules are still applicable for guiding the product direction of online advertising (esp. targeting).

2.2 TECHNICAL FEATURES OF THE INTERNET ADVERTISING

Through reading the preceding paragraphs, readers must have noticed the unique features of online advertising that distinguish it from traditional advertising. Some of these features will guide us to correctly understand the online advertising market and explore the appropriate plans for optimizing the advertising effect.

(1) Technology and computation oriented. The unique features of digital media have enabled online advertising to implement sophisticated audience targeting while the computing technology has made advertising decisions and transaction computationally driven. In fact, audience targeting was once attempted in offline advertising, e.g., some banks tried to customize the ads on the back of the paper bills of credit cards according to the age and gender of card holders, but they failed to vigorously promote such kind of advertising, because of the extremely high cost of doing so in non-digital media. In contrast, the cost of audience targeting in digital media is very low, which has directly unveiled a computational revolution of online advertising. In addition to audience targeting, online advertising also implements auction-based transaction, meaning that accurate estimation and optimization of advertising effect is particularly important.

(2) Measurability of effect. When online advertising was in its infancy, it was mostly praised for recording and optimizing the advertising effect directly during display and clicking. However, whether CTR is able to reflect the advertising effect in an absolute sense is a contentious issue. From 1998 to date, the average CTR of online banner ads kept dropping from 10% to 0.1%, does it mean their effect has decreased by two orders of magnitude? Of course not, the fast-growing online advertising market is the most powerful refutation. In our opinion, no matter it is in different times or for different products, the comparison of the absolute CTR value is not that important, it is the difference among various ads and algorithms in a given period that is truly meaningful. From this point of view, measurability of effect remains an important feature of online advertising.

(3) Standardization of creative and delivery approaches. Standardization is driven by audience targeting and programmatic trade. Since the demand side cares about user group rather than advertising position, it is critical to unify creative size and standardize some key interfaces. There are typical interface standards like the VAST [3] for video ads and the OpenRTB [4] for RTB ads. In the PC advertising market, more and more advertising platforms like to design products based on these standards, so that all parties can make full use of the mobility of the entire market and create value more quickly. However, in the mobile age, the demand for native ad – which features consistency between advertising form and content – is more urgent than the demand for standardization of creative. Therefore, the standards for advertising creative in the mobile age may have completely different ways of thinking.

(4) Diverse forms of online media. As Web 2.0 and the mobile Internet have become popularized, the online media with more interactive functions are substantially different from offline media. With varied functions, different online media have different distances from behavioral conversion of users. For example, in the conversion chain of portals, vertical sites, search engines, e-commerce sites, and rebate sites, the latter ones are closer to purchase behavior than the prior ones. We can intuitively tell that if delivering ads to the media is closer to behavioral conversion, their traffic will generate a higher ROI, but farther from the advertising goal of "guiding potential users." Therefore, when looking at online advertising from the demand side, we shall stress the coordination among different media, examine and optimize the overall effect through integrated marketing. Suppose that an online store only delivers ads on rebate sites, it will definitely harvest a high ROI, but how could it be sure of drawing a large number of potential users?[1]

(5) Data-driven delivery decisions. During the Industrial Revolution, the fundamental driving force of machine was electric power; in the contemporary era, the fundamental driving force of the Internet is deep processing and utilization of data. Now this knowledge sounds like a twice-told story, since the concept of big data is extensively recognized. The aforementioned computing technology for online advertising also relies heavily on large-scale use of data. In the domain of online advertising, there is a basic logic for ad delivery: widely collect user behavior data and ad feedback data, place proper tags on users in a cloud computing infrastructure, make decisions when multiple advertisers compete for the same ad display opportunity based on data, and then send the delivery result data to ad operators to adjust the delivery strategy. It can be said that the modern online advertising system is a big-data processing platform, and its data processing scale and velocity meet a high standard. Moreover, the biggest strength of online advertising is large-scale data collection and utilization, which has brought about exponential growth of users, no traditional advertising in any form is capable of doing so.

2.3 CORE ISSUE OF COMPUTATIONAL ADVERTISING

In addition to the subject of computational advertising, Andrei Broder also presented the core challenge to the corresponding studies: "find the best match between a given user in a given context and a suitable advertisement" [5] (do remember it is "core challenge" rather than "definition"). After reviewing the development of the advertising market in recent years and drawing the experiences from the practical business

1 At the end of 2012, Taobao announced to suspend the cooperation with Taobao Spreader (a platform that assists online vendors to promote their commodities and receive a cash rebate from them), proving that the attitudes of online media toward rebate are becoming consistent and rational.

operation, we slightly modified Broder's viewpoint and summed up the core problem of computational advertising as follows:

> *Find the most appropriate ad delivery strategy for a series of user-context combinations to optimize the profit of the overall advertising campaigns.*

We modified Broder's viewpoint in two aspects: (1) It is the effect of a group of ad displays that shall be optimized, rather than a single display, because of the quantitative constraint in advertising campaigns; while considering this constraint, the best decision for optimizing the profit usually differs from the decision for a single display. (2) The word "given" is deleted, because when delivering ads, the identified user or contextual tags are sometimes unavailable, but it does not mean computational optimization is infeasible. Moreover, it is the "delivery strategy" that shall be optimized, not necessarily the specific ads, because some delivery strategies are not the direct decisions for the final display. After reading the following chapters of this book, readers will fully understand the reasons for our modifications.

The above core challenge in computational advertising can be expressed by an optimization problem:

$$\begin{aligned} &\max \sum_{i=1}^{T} (r_i - q_i) \\ s.t. &\sum_{i=1}^{T} d_{ik} \leq D_k, \forall k \end{aligned} \tag{2.1}$$

In Formula (2.1), i represents an advertising display between the *1st* and the *T-th* display. Our goal of optimization is the gross profit in the *T-th* display, i.e., the balance between total revenue r and total cost q. For a specific advertiser k, he/she sometimes meets a budget constraint or has to guarantee the ad delivery quantity, which is one of the essential characteristics of advertising as a commercial activity, and also the constraint in the above formula, i.e., the demand-side constraint. Because of such constraint, the optimization of the advertising system greatly differs from search and recommendation, though the three of them have similar underlying technologies.

When the overall budget is definite, i.e., $\sum_{i=1}^{T} qi$ is a constant, it will be easy to verify that Formula (2.1) is consistent with $ROI = \sum_r ri / \sum_i qi$ – another goal which is more commonly seen. Further think about the specific dependence between revenue and cost, the above optimization problem can be rewritten as follows:

$$\begin{aligned} &\max_{a_1, \ldots, T} \sum_{i=1}^{T} \{r(a_i, u_i, c_i) - q(a_i, u_i, c_i)\} \\ s.t. &\sum_{i-1}^{T} d(a_i, u_i, c_i, k) \leq D_k, \forall k \end{aligned} \tag{2.2}$$

The variables a, u and c in Formula 2.2 respectively denote the ad, user, and context, which are major components of advertising campaigns. The revenue or cost of advertising display is related to the three factors. In fact, most advertising products (excluding DSP) either have self-running/monopoly resources or share revenue with the media based on the "revenue deciding expenditure" model, their cost is a constant or directly proportional to revenue. In this case, the cost can be removed from the above optimization formula. With the existence of constraint, the cost d is related not only to a, u and c, but to the specific advertiser k.

Please note an implicit assumption herein, i.e., suppose the overall revenue or cost could be broken down into each impression. Such assumption is of course unreasonable, but from a practical point of view, we still need it to promptly finish the computation for each impression, which is the basis for online decision-making. In practice, such methods as frequency capping and click feedback will address the problem of effect correlation of multiple impressions.

In terms of a specific advertising product, some contents or parameters may be omitted in Formula 2.2, and the constraint may have different forms or do not exist, which constitutes the unique optimization problem of this advertising product. Such optimization problem will be explained in detail in later chapters that discuss the key technologies for advertising products.

2.3.1 Breakdown of Advertising Return

Let's further break down the revenue r to draw forth the analysis of online advertising billing. For a specific advertising product, what can be initiatively optimized is its revenue rather than its cost, so we will mainly pay attention to the revenue optimization. After the end of an advertising display, are there any follow-up behaviors of users? As shown in Figure 2.3, when a user notices an ad in the media and shows some interest in it, what he/she will do next is to "click" the ad (the ratio between the number of clicks and the number of displays is "CTR"); then the user will open the landing page of the advertiser website (the ratio between the number of successful page openings and the number of clicks is "landing rate"); starting from the landing page, there may be

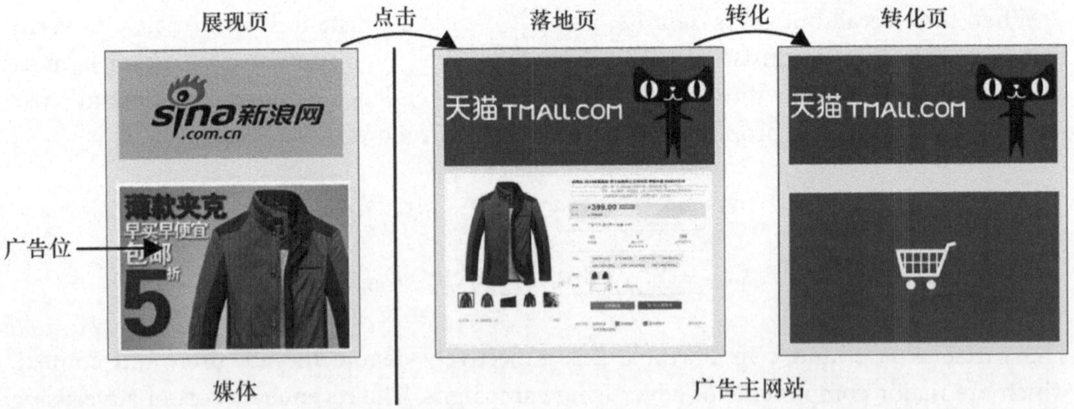

FIGURE 2.3 The process where online advertising produces effect.

behavioral conversion of the user (i.e., placing an order), the ratio between the number of conversion and the number of landing is "conversion rate" (CVR), which takes place on or off the advertiser website. In short, the breakdown of revenue r, which is based on the user behavior on the media and advertiser websites, is both reasonable and easily operable in practice:

$$\text{eCPM} = r(a, u, u) = \mu(a, u, c) \cdot \nu(a, u, c) \tag{2.3}$$

In the following text, we will continue using μ to denote click rate and ν to denote click value (the yield generated by a single click for advertisers): the former relates to the behavior on the media website, while the latter describes the behavior on the advertiser website. The product of μ and ν quantitatively represents the eCPM[2] of a display. We advise readers to pay special attention to eCPM, because it is the most frequently mentioned indicator in computational advertising, and the most critical indicator for quantitative revenue evaluation, it can be said that most of the computational problems in this book are revolving around eCPM. When ranking multiple candidate ads, the ranking by eCPM or CTR is an important strategic feature that distinguishes advertising products from user products. Furthermore, if all click values are equivalent, then the ranking by eCPM and CTR will yield the same result. Therefore, it is believed that the ranking by CTR is a special case of the ranking by eCPM, which makes it possible to produce the native ads that unify content and form.

eCPM has two similar concepts: revenue per mille (RPM) and CPM. The three terms are not always strictly distinguished in practice.

The conversion process shown in Figure 2.3 tells that click value can be further broken down into the product of reach rate, conversion rate and per customer transaction (PCT). Since this problem is more associated with website operation rather than advertising itself, it will be briefly discussed in Subsection 15.2.3.

2.3.2 Relationship between Billing Models and eCPM Estimation

For most advertising products, the eCPM for the given triad (a, u, c) needs to be computed for decision-making. But considering the complex cooperative relationship in the advertising market, it is not possible to reasonably estimate the two variables (μ and ν) of decomposed eCPM for each product. Which party is identified to estimate the variable(s)? It is the primary cause for the diverse billing models to come into being, and also the crucial link between the business logic and the product architecture in the advertising market. We will analyze the main billing models in the advertising market one by one.

(1) Cost per Time (CPT). This is the way by which an advertiser pays fees for monopolizing an ad space for a given period. Strictly speaking, CPT is a sales

2 eCPM cannot be compared with CPM before multiplied by a fixed coefficient of 1,000. But for simplicity, we have deliberately omitted this coefficient in this book.

model rather than a billing model, since the price is agreed by both parties in advance, no quantifying is needed. CPT mainly applies to the advertising positions of strong exposure attribute and somewhat customized. In the European and American markets, CPT is mostly used in the general display advertising, but in China, CPT prevails in portal advertising. Although CPT – an exclusive sales model – may generate additional brand effect and window effect, it goes against the development of audience targeting and programmatic trade, so its use ratio tends to decline in the long run.

(2) Cost per Mille (CPM). "Mille" is a Latin word meaning "a thousand times," so CPM refers to the settlement for a thousand times of impression. It is a billing model agreed by the supply side and the demand side. There may be risks that these impression fail to bring forth the expected revenue, so the demand side shall estimate and control the risks. For the brand ads that pursue a long-term ROI, it is difficult to directly calculate their click value based on short-term feedback data, and CTR is no longer the only key factor because of the core requirement for user contact. In this case, a reasonable trading mode is to let the demand side control the unit price for traffic in line with its market strategy and budget plan and settles by CPM. In fact, CPM is the dominant billing model for most online brand ads, especially video ads.

(3) Cost per Click (CPC). Though originating from search advertising, CPC soon became a common billing model for most response advertising. In the case where CPC applies, the supply side or intermediary market estimates CTR, the demand side estimates click value and inform the ad platform through bidding.[3] Such kind of calculation division is fairly reasonable for the online advertising that aims at direct response: the supply side is able to estimate CTR more accurately with its collection of massive user behavioral data; the demand side is able to estimate click value more accurately with its own data analysis system, since the conversion behavior occurs on the advertiser website. Therefore, CPC seems to monopolize the direct response market.

(4) Cost per Sale (CPS)/Return on Investment (ROI). They are variations of Cost per Action (CPA) which is an extreme billing model, i.e., the demand side settles accounts based on the final conversion earnings, thus avoiding risks to the greatest extent. Where CPA applies, the supply side or intermediary market has to estimate both CTR and click value, so as to properly decide traffic allocation. But there is an evident problem: conversion occurs on the advertiser website, so the supply side cannot directly detect or control it, let alone

3 Of course, the demand side will not offer a price fully based on the click value, but keep down its offer price to obtain arbitrage. Given this, the key for bidding system design is to prevent advertisers from frequently adjusting their offer price and promote market competition. This topic will be discussed in Chapter 5.

accurately estimate and optimize it. As such, CPA is only suitable for the advertising platforms constituted by the advertisers with the conversion process compatible with user experience, e.g., Taobao Spreader (the conversion occurs on Taobao site) and mobile app download center (the conversion occurs in Apple Store or Google Play). In addition, since DSP needs to fully represent the interests of advertisers, it is likely to charge advertisers by CPS. In general, for the demand-side products directly linking to the revenue of advertisers, CPS is feasible under certain conditions; but for the common intermediate advertising market, CPS is not the most reasonable billing model.

There are two special billing models deriving from CPA: one is Cost per Lead (CPL) – settlement based on the quantity of collected leads, which is applicable to the response advertising that gathers sales leads; the other one is Cost per Install (CPI) – settlement based on the number of app installation, which is applicable to the response advertising bound to mobile apps.

(5) Optimized CPM (oCPM). It is a new billing model vigorously promoted by Facebook, meaning that the advertising platform still settles by CPM, but optimizes it according to the conversion rate. In other words, though the settlement is still made on CPM, the supply side will estimate both CTR and click value. In practice, oCPM is usually a transitional billing model before implementing CPA. When dealing with new advertisers whose conversion rate is uncertain, the advertising platform dare not adopt the high-risk CPA, but prefers oCPM which facilitates advertisers to transfer their conversion data to the advertising platform; after the conversion data are accumulated to some extent and the advertising platform believes the time is ripe, then it will start implementing CPA. By carrying out this marketing strategy, Facebook has greatly reduced the workload of advertisers and quickly attracted a large number of app download advertisers, which is attributed to oCPM – the most critical product link in this process. In addition, this model is applicable to all scenarios where billing models are inconsistent with the goals of optimization: the advertising platform plans to implement CPC, but firstly attempts oCPC which is optimized on the basis of CPA.

The comparison of the above billing models is given in Table 2.1. To sum up, we believe that for response advertising, CPC is the most appropriate settlement to give play to the strengths of both the supply side and the demand side, that's why it is widely adopted in the advertising market. For brand advertising with effect and purpose sometimes not easy to measure directly, CPM is recommended. CPS/CPA/ROI are only suitable under certain circumstances. For the advertising platform highly capable of handling data, oCPM is better implemented before transitioning to CPA.

The billing demand of advertising has given rise to the demand for third-party monitoring. In CPM brand advertising where the ads are exposed on the media website,

TABLE 2.1 Comparison of the billing models for online advertising

Billing model	CTR estimation	Click value estimation	Merit and demerit	Applicable scenario
CPT	Demand side		Give full play to window effect Unable to use audience targeting technology	High-exposure brand advertising
CPM	Demand side		Choose target population with audience targeting technology Audience division based on contract sales may not be too elaborate	Brand advertising in need of audience selection RTB advertising trade
CPC	Supply side	Demand side	Fine division of audience Reasonable division of labor between supply and demand sides	Auction-based ADN
CPS/CPA/ROI	Supply side		Demand side free from any risk Supply side facing great difficulty in operation	Response advertising alliance Response DSP
oCPM	Supply side		Steady transition to CPA	Advertising platform highly capable of handling data

advertisers usually entrust a third-party monitoring firm to verify the ad impressions and clicks, which will be the basis for settlement. In CPC or CPS advertising where the billing indicators (clicks or conversions) appear on the advertiser website, no special monitoring service is required. It can be seen that the monitoring service is mainly provided to brand advertisers. As CPM advertising targeting becomes increasingly sophisticated, the content of advertising monitoring includes not only verification and measurement of ad impressions and clicks, but click frequency and demographical attributes. But in CPA advertising, advertisers may deliberately deduct conversions during the actual operation with an aim to increase brand exposure at a lower cost; in this case, a third-party attribution tool is needed to guarantee impartial monitoring of conversions and billing. The problems and techniques in this regard are introduced in Chapter 16.

2.4 BUSINESS ORGANIZATIONS IN THE ONLINE ADVERTISING INDUSTRY

Due to the game relationship between the supply side and the demand side on the online advertising market, some business organizations are needed to constrain and regulate the market. Through learning about the stance and mission of these organizations, readers will have a clearer understanding of the advertising business logic. In North America – the world foremost online advertising market – there are three online advertising organizations worthy of our attention.

2.4.1 Interactive Advertising Bureau

The Interactive Advertising Bureau (IAB), founded in the late 20th century, is the leading advertising business organization in the online advertising industry. The IAB studies and influences the online advertising market for safeguarding the long-term interests of the supply side. In other words, it cares more about the benefits of online advertising suppliers. "Dedicated to the growth of interactive advertising market" is the mission of the IAB. The major beneficiaries of this mission are online media and ad-tech companies, so the principal members of the IAB are ad suppliers (e.g., Google, Facebook, Yahoo!, and Microsoft) and technology suppliers (e.g., AudienceScience and MediaMath). The development of ad-tech companies and products will bring better service to advertisers and improve the online advertising effect, which will help divert more budgets into the online advertising industry. In terms of its specific work, the IAB has, by working with lots of online media and advertising platforms, developed several significant specifications which have greatly promoted the healthy development of the online advertising industry. Three important specifications are introduced as follows:

(1) The specification for display ad size. According to the advertising specifications released by the IAB in 2001, only seven of the commonly used ad sizes are standardized: 120*600 (skyscraper), 160*600 (wide skyscraper), 180*150 (rectangle), 300*250 (intermediate rectangle), 336*280 (large rectangle), 240*400 (vertical rectangle), and 250*250 (square pop-up). A uniform ad size is important for diluting the influence of advertising position and promoting audience targeting on the online advertising market. In contrast to the developed nations China has complicated ad sizes, so different advertising platforms may have their own requirements for ad sizes, and such a situation is of no good for developing target advertising and programmatic trade.

(2) The Digital Video Ad Serving Template (VAST) specification. Considering complex video ad creative and display forms, as well as large resource consumption, the IAB has developed a unified XML schema (i.e., VAST) for delivering video streaming ads on the online video media and completing normalized user description. VAST has reduced the technical obstacles to enter the domain of video ads, making it possible to rapidly develop the video ad market.

(3) The OpenRTB specification for RTB interface. The RTB technology is introduced in Chapter 6. To put it simply, RTB facilitates the demand side to purchase traffic more accurately based on its audience segmentation. Assuming that different advertising platforms have their own RTB interface, then the demand side has to pay several times more than the technical cost to realize extensive market docking. In view of this, the IAB has developed the OpenRTB to unify the RTB interfaces for delivering banner ads, video ads, and mobile ads on different platforms.

2.4.2 American Association of Advertising Agencies

The American Association of Advertising Agencies (4As) is an industry association representing the interests of both online and offline advertising (especially brand advertising) agencies in the United States. The 4As members charge a percentage of service fee from advertisers, partly for avoiding vicious internal competition and partly for motivating themselves to defend the interests of advertisers (the latter point is fairly important for the healthy development of advertising market in the long run). Ogilvy & Mather, JWT, and McCann are renowned 4As members in the United States. Theoretically speaking, the 4As members are domestic companies, but some foreign companies – with strong international influence and similar business models and norms to their American counterparts – are also eligible to join the 4As, the Japanese advertising giant Dentsu Group is one prominent example.

2.4.3 Association of National Advertisers

The Association of National Advertisers (ANA) is an organization of advertisers, defending the interests of the demand side the most steadfastly. Most of its members are the advertisers with abundant advertising budgets, such as AT&T, P&G, and NBA. There is an example showing how conscientiously the ANA safeguards the interests of advertisers: Microsoft was once considering to support a "do not track" (DNT) protocol in IE10 to restrict the third-party cookie abuse, but the ANA explicitly opposed the plan for fear of hurting the ability of accurate ad delivery on the online advertising market and harming the interests of advertisers.

2

Product Logic of Online Advertising

CHAPTER 3

Overview of Online Advertising Products

Unlike the traditional offline advertising, online advertising features rich forms of products (not the forms of creative). The development history of online advertising is briefly reviewed in Section 1.5. See Figure 3.1 for the same process illustrated from the perspective of advertising products.

This evolutionary process of advertising products and market is in fact driven by the need for data use and monetization. For the convenience of discussion, we hereby split this process into four stages.

(1) **Agreement-based ad.** It derives from the offline advertising trade and can be divided into CPT ad sold by time frame and CPM ad sold by agreed display quantity. This kind of ad is preferred by the brand advertisers whose follow-up advertising effect is unavailable for direct measurement, and often shown on portals and video websites. In case of quantity-guaranteed CPM ad – its prime power is the demand for data monetization – it can only monetize the large-scale data like demographical attribute owing to the quantity constraint in the agreement.

(2) **Auction-based ad.** Its most important form is search ad which is subject to bidding for search terms. When this ad extends to the offsite display ad, it will evolve into the product form of ADN which is subject to bidding for page terms or user tags. The auction-based ad has a business logic totally different from the agreement-based ad, and it is the key product to meet the demand for response advertising. The root cause for the emergence of auction-based ad is to monetize terms, fine user tags, and other high-value but small-quantity data, and to guarantee the subsequent effect despite the display quantity.

(3) **Programmatic trade ad.** The continuous development of auction-based ad has given rise to RTB. It is a trading mode that enables the demand side to segment

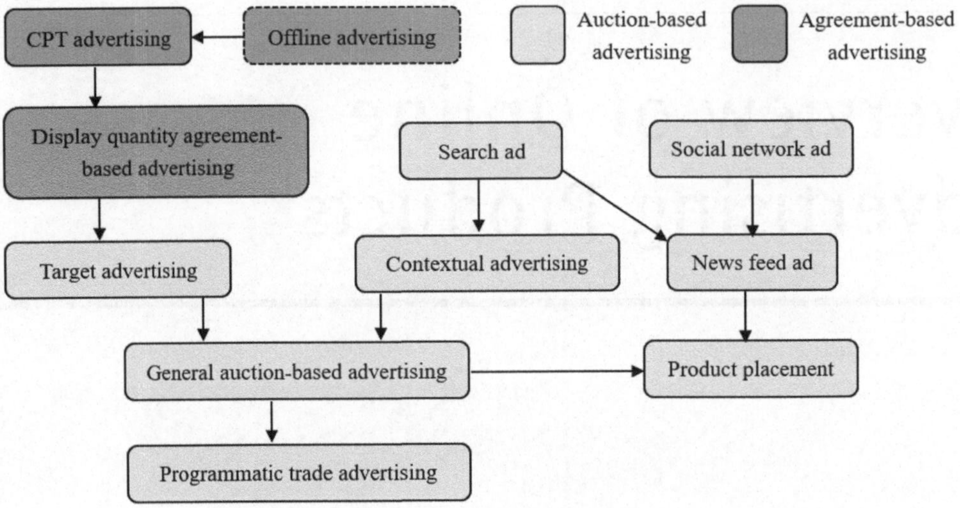

FIGURE 3.1 Evolution of online advertising products.

and choose its target audience more flexibly, and realizes extensive data use and rapid development of data trade. A series of trading mode, with RTB as the core, gradually evolved into an inter-machine and programmatic decision-making mode for advertising trade, the advertising product generated therefrom is known as "programmatic trade ad." Mainly driven by the use and monetization of advertiser data and third-party data, the programmatic trade has fueled the emergence of a corresponding data trading market.

(4) **Native ad.** In addition to the evolution of the advertising product system, another important topic is how to deal with the relationship between ad and its non-commercial content, so as to let them coexist in a "native" way as much as possible. Search ad and news feed ad are valuable explorations in this regard, but these forms of native ad have encountered lots of problems in large-scale development and monetization. In recent years, being stimulated by the robust demand from mobile devices, the development of native ad – mainly in the forms of news feed ad, rewarded video ad, and those containing flexibly assembled materials – has maintained a fast pace. From the perspective of data, native ad stresses the processing and use of scenario data, which represent the new problems and new thoughts in the mobile era.

Each advertising product basically has three components, i.e., the demand-oriented interface, the supply-oriented interface, and the intermediate ad serving system and matching strategy. In different products, the interface may be oriented for manual operation or inter-machine communication. The product link in advertising belongs to the category of commercial products.

3.1 DESIGN PHILOSOPHY FOR COMMERCIAL PRODUCTS

Commercial products refer to the products oriented to merchant customers rather than ordinary users; the most typical product is online advertising. Some other customer-oriented Internet products, e.g., customer relation management (CRM), Web analytics (WA), and data management platform (DMP), also fall into the category of commercial products. Both the design and operation of commercial products follow certain generality principle, which is to be introduced below.

The Internet is a product-driven industry. The readers familiar with product design may know that the fundamental driving force of user product evolution is people's natural instinct for convenience. Therefore, the design philosophy for user products has all along been "simpler, more intuitive and faster." And the corresponding product design shall highlight key functions and smooth operation.

However, if you have the opportunity to join in the design and operation of commercial products, you will find that there is a considerable gap between the focus and actual operation. Sometimes a commercial product that boasts a wonderful user experience cannot generate public praise or market success. Why is that? Commercial products usually have a clear business goal, and the motive of their users is to optimize this goal. Take advertising for example, it is used for optimizing the profit of users, no matter the user is medium, agent, or advertiser. Given this, there are objective and measurable criteria for choosing this kind of product. The reason why the Facebook ads are popular among the small- and medium-sized advertisers is for their conspicuous promotion effect, not because they are far more convenient than other similar ads. In a word, any functional improvement of a commercial product will be accepted as long as it fulfills the business goal, regardless of any inconvenience to use. Under the influence of such product philosophy (see Figure 1.15), the transaction links in the entire advertising market will become increasingly complex and the use threshold will get higher and higher, which differs from the situation of user products where the general trend is simplification.

While insisting on the general principle of optimizing the established business goal, some key points during operation of the commercial products are worth of our attention:

(1) Pay special attention to product strategy relative to product function. Strategy is a crucial part of commercial products. Take advertising for example, the formulation of a product strategy shall take account of bidding mechanism design, data exploration during cold start, and the tag system for audience targeting. Even some moderate adjustments in strategy can bring dramatic changes to advertising revenue. Unlike general products, the formulation of advertising strategy requires not only a profound understanding of advertising market, but solid basic knowledge in related fields. For the newcomers in advertising, it's better for them to carefully examine those "invisible product features."

(2) Pay special attention to data, let product operation and optimization form a closed loop. Since the goal of commercial products is definite and optimizable, all product features and success of strategy are strictly evaluated in reference to feedback data. Moreover, the planning for new product functions is also based on the insight into historical data and other user product data. The closed-loop iteration, which starts from data analysis and ends with data, is the most suitable development model for commercial products.

(3) In all product interfaces that deal with users, the design principle of ensuring convenience of user products remains important. But for commercial products, any overly novel or fascinating product appearance or any interactive model that is beyond the proper product functions shall be avoided.

Since the theme of this book is computational advertising – a typical commercial product, our focus will be placed on the product links of ad serving and trade, strategy, data use, and exchange. The interface between the advertising system and the demand/supply side will be briefly introduced below.

3.2 PRODUCT INTERFACE OF ADVERTISING SYSTEM

3.2.1 Demand-Side Management Interface

Considering the complexity of advertising market, the demand side of an advertising system may be an advertiser, agency, TD, or DSP. No matter which party becomes the demand side, it needs an operational interface to create a budget, ad serving conditions, and other strategies.

In general, the ad provided by the demand side is subject to grading management. For most advertising products, their management is delegated to the grades of "advertiser," "campaign," "ad group," and "creative" (see Figure 3.2). Among them, the "advertiser" grade manages the general information of an advertiser, while the other three grades deal with concrete ad serving matters.

(1) An advertising campaign – this concept corresponds to an advertiser's one-time ad serving contract – involves such basic information as budget and time frame

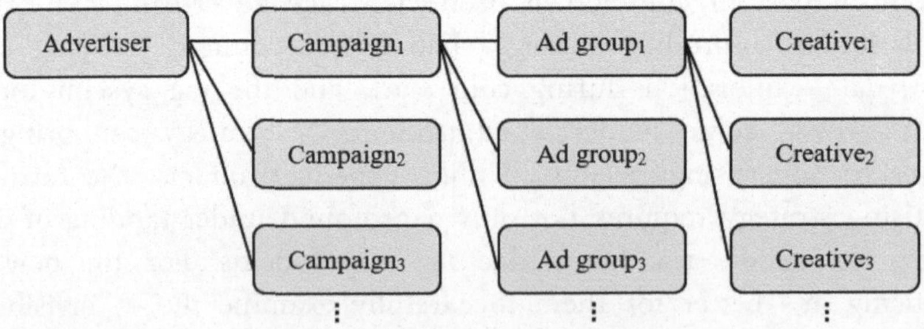

FIGURE 3.2 Grading management of advertising products.

FIGURE 3.3 Settings of an advertising campaign.

(see Figure 3.3). In addition, there are other settings in a campaign: (a) When there are several available advertising products, it is necessary to choose the one for ad serving (see "Ad serving choosing" in Figure 3.3). (b) Budget pacing (see "Budget allocation control" in Figure 3.3). For most advertising campaigns, it is reasonable to allocate their budget evenly, but for game development, mobile app rankings, and other types of promotion, the intensive spending of budget is more important.

(2) An ad group, which corresponds to a specific ad serving strategy, mainly sets conditions for audience targeting and offers a price (see Figure 3.4). The most important function of an ad group is to set various targeting conditions, so it is the key grade for the optimization of advertising effect. In addition, the media selection may also be regarded as a targeting condition. It should be noted that the bid – which is introduced later along with auction-based ads – is set by the advertiser rather than predetermined. It is difficult for the advertiser to have an intuitive knowledge of bidding and its relationship with traffic scale and quality. Given this, from a product perspective, an ad group shall offer some helpful hints, such as traffic prediction based on the current bid or the more direct "suggested bid" as shown in Figure 3.4.

FIGURE 3.4 Settings of an ad group.

(3) Advertising creative is the material displayed finally. There may be different sizes of creative despite of the same ad group (see Figure 3.5). For textual ad creative, the basic material includes title and description. For image ad creative, the picture materials are uploaded directly. In addition, the necessary settings for creative should also include the monitoring address of ad display and click. In order to facilitate the ad delivery staff to observe the display effect of the creative, the function of creative preview is often added (see the "Preview area" in Figure 3.5).

Though the detailed functions of demand-side management (DSM) may vary notably in different advertising products, this four-grade management approach is still applicable. In addition to raising efficiency of business management, this approach has provided a natural and reasonable stratified structure for making statistics and modeling, and for easier cold start of new creative. In the following chapters about various advertising products, we will focus on their commercial logic and product strategy, and no longer elaborate on the ad serving management on the interface.

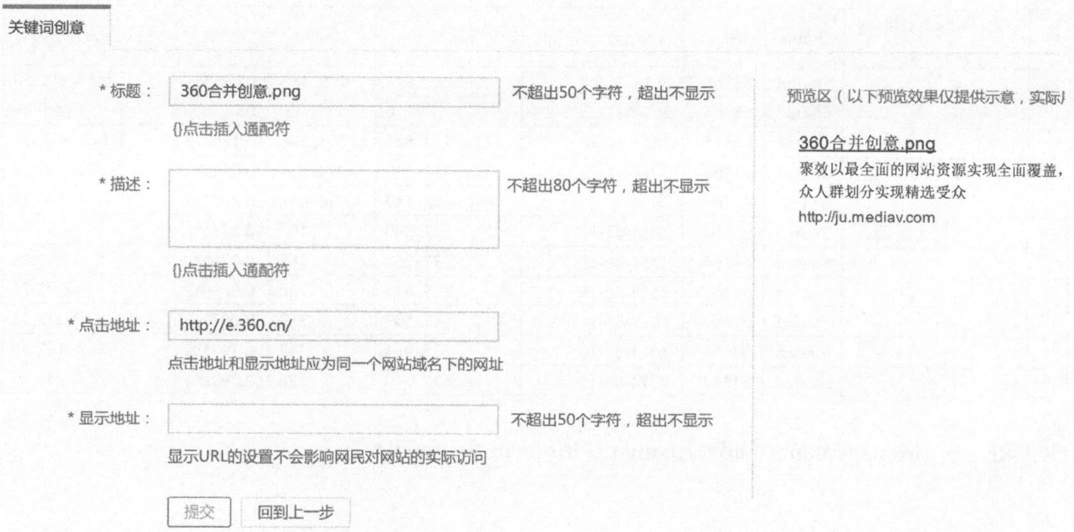

FIGURE 3.5 Settings of creative.

3.2.2 Supply-Side Management Interface

As for the currently mainstream advertising products, the supply side (i.e., the media) has much less business control than the demand side. The resource organization at the supply side consists of two levels: the media and the advertising position; the former may be websites or mobile app developers.

The operation of the media is simpler than that of advertisers. Generally speaking, the main functional requirements include adding and deleting advertising positions, as well as examining the operation data of each advertising position. The functionality of the interface is shown in Figure 3.6 (the names of advertising positions are hidden).

Based on varied functions of products, the specific advertising positions require different operating functions. But generally speaking, there are common requirements for the size of advertising position, ad serving code or SDK, and types of ads for each advertising position. In case of the supply-side products like advertising housekeeper or supply-side platform (SSP), there is often a function of fine traffic allocation. It should be noted that the advertising platform will protect the domain name or application name that corresponds to each advertising position, so as to prevent the traffic of other domains from embezzling the advertising position code.

The abovementioned supply-side management interface is relatively simple, usually applicable to general ADN or ADX, but not suitable for the native ads where the media are deeply involved, the relevant content is included in Chapter 8.

□	Name of advertising position	Status	Size	Date of creation	Displays	Clicks	CTR	Revenue (RMB)
□		Started	65*65	2014-11-28	238,602,848	199, 153	0.0835%	¥68, 692.58
□		Started	65*65	2014-11-28	0	0	0.0000%	¥0.00
□		Started	65*65	2014-11-28	376, 409, 825	704, 798	0.1872%	¥242, 941. 18
□		Started	63*63	2014-11-28	1,331, 921, 299	944, 687	0.0709%	¥321, 429.39
□		Started	64*64	2014-09-25	960, 408, 949	4,094, 441	0.4263%	¥1,261, 196.91
□		Started	64*64	2014-07-18	127, 600	104	0.0815%	¥34.76
□		Started	64*64	2014-06-10	237, 264	185	0.0780%	¥61.19
□		Started	64*64	2014-06-10	295, 444	266	0.0900%	¥91.78
□		Started	64*64	2014-06-10	362, 509	352	0.0971%	¥111.33
□		Started	64*64	2014-06-10	435, 934	447	0.1025%	¥147.65
□		Started	64*64	2014-06-10	530, 349	526	0.0992%	¥169.06

FIGURE 3.6 Management of advertising positions in the media.

3.2.3 Multiple Forms of Interface between Supply and Demand Sides

Both product managers and technicians shall have a basic knowledge of the ways in which online advertising supply and demand sides are connected. Figure 3.7 illustrates the major forms of interfaces among the media, supply-side products, demand-side products, advertisers, and other links.

There are three ways for the supply-side products, which are ought to be monetized, to dock with the media traffic.

(1) For Web/WAP media, JavaScript code can be embedded into the webpage to initiate an advertising request to the supply-side server and complete page rendering. This approach is also applicable to the mobile apps embedded with HTML5 sites.

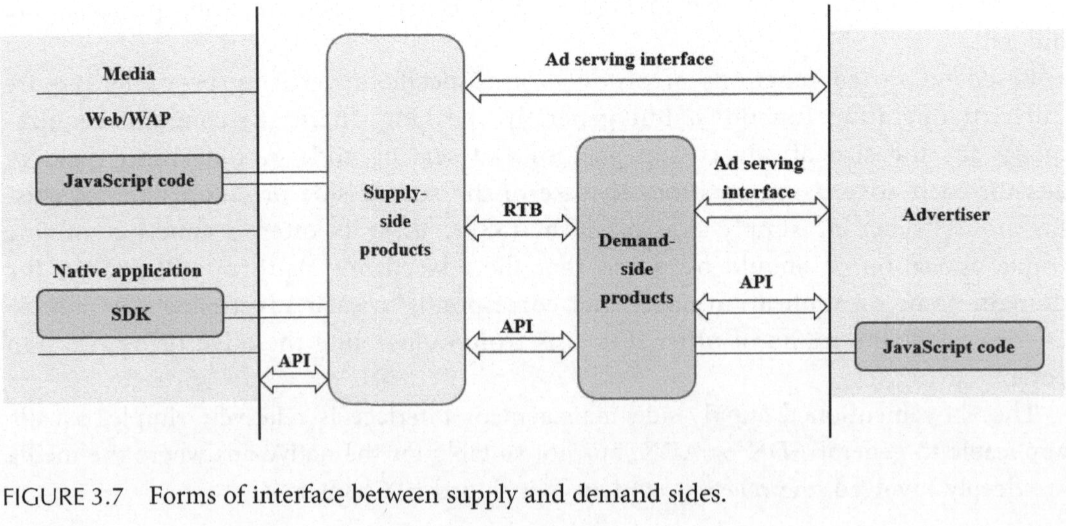

FIGURE 3.7 Forms of interface between supply and demand sides.

(2) For the iOS/Android applications implemented by native codes, it is necessary to integrate the SDK of the supply side in the applications, and its function is basically the same with the JavaScript code on the webpage. However, due to the large size of SDK and the possibility of application collapse, much work is ought to be done in integration and testing.

(3) Some media that lack faith in SDK or JavaScript code may use Application Programming Interface (API) for docking. To put it simply, the media server initiates an ad request to the supply-side server, and then makes decisions and renders on its own, but the media shall have enough technical strength to do so. This is a kind of Server-to-Server (S2S) docking. There are offline API and online API: in offline scenario, the supply side requests and caches ads in advance, and then ranks the ads and makes decisions by itself for each display; in online scenario, the supply side shall initiate an ad request for each display.

There are also three ways for the advertising products of the supply/demand side to dock with the ad serving demand of advertisers:

(1) The most common approach adopted by advertisers is to manage ad serving and optimize the effect manually via a user interface (the management interface for manual ad serving is already introduced in Subsection 3.2.1). When using a user interface for ad serving, the advertisers sometimes deliver ads on the demand-side products (e.g., DSP) or directly on the advertising platform of the supply side, but they have no essential difference to advertisers.

(2) When advertisers have a very complex ad serving (e.g., lots of terms shall be set) or need automatic adjustment and optimization, the advertising platform will provide an API corresponding to the interface functions of the demand side, so that the demand side can implement batch ad serving and optimization like programming. But it is possible for the demand side to abuse the API to make combined or trial ad serving, which will increase the pressure on the ad serving system. Therefore, in actual operation, the API is mainly open to large advertisers or agencies, and there is certain restriction of the bandwidth or the number of operations. Note that the API can play utterly different roles in different scenarios: the API herein transmits the setting conditions for ad serving, while the abovementioned API between the supply side and the media transmits the result of ad request.

(3) Some special ad serving calls for automatic docking with the advertisers' products and user behavior, a typical example in this regard is the personalized retargeting of e-commerce customers. In this case, the demand-side products also require to embed JavaScript code in advertiser webpage and make decisions based on the user behavior data collected by the JavaScript code.

The docking demand between the supply-side and demand-side products is usually satisfied via the following approaches:

(1) The same API docking between the supply side and the media as described above.

(2) The RTB for programmatic trade or other similar docking approaches. In case the RTB approach is adopted, there will be an offer from the demand side in addition to feedback of ad information, which is the essential difference from the API approach.

The abovementioned supply side and demand side are relative concepts. No matter which docking approach is adopted at each link, from media side to advertiser side, the S2S in each decision-making process for ad request may not be more than once, otherwise it will cause obvious delay at the user side and then affect the advertising effect. But in mobile native apps, such restriction is not that conspicuous because the client side is available for caching.

CHAPTER 4

Agreement-Based Advertising

Starting from this chapter, we will discuss the major products and business logic of online advertising. We will firstly introduce the agreement-based advertising products; their position in the evolutionary process of online advertising is shown in Figure 4.1.

At the initial stage of online advertising business, the media and the agents of advertisers had been the major participants in the market. The online advertising at that time was imitating the business logic of offline advertising: advertising agencies and media companies sign agreements to ensure that certain ad spaces would be occupied by designated advertisers for a prescribed period of time, and advertisers shall pay the advertising fees for the intact agreement. Such CPT-based sales features are less dependent on technology, as a simple ad scheduling system is enough.

An important form of advertising agreement is the CPM-based display quantity agreement, which keeps defining the total ad serving quantity and the unit display price of one advertising campaign via agreement, but the sales object has been upgraded from "ad space" to "ad space + audience." Such agreement is a milestone in the history of online advertising, since it enabled data to be directly used in ad sales. In terms of the complexity of the supply-side products and technologies, the agreement-based CPM advertising is even more complex than the auction-based advertising, because it has to fulfill the ad serving quantity provided in multiple agreements, which unveils the important allocation problem in online advertising.

The CPM-based display quantity agreement is a direct stimulus to the birth of audience targeting technologies. Yet the meaning and importance of audience targeting itself far exceeds the scope of agreement-based advertising. In this chapter we will comprehensively introduce the main product problems about audience targeting, including targeting technologies and tag system. This part of content is instructive to the later discussion about auction-based advertising.

When the agreement-based advertising prevails, the demand-side product technology fails to make notable progress, because the ad serving is carried out by the supply side through performing the agreement, leaving limited space for optimization by the

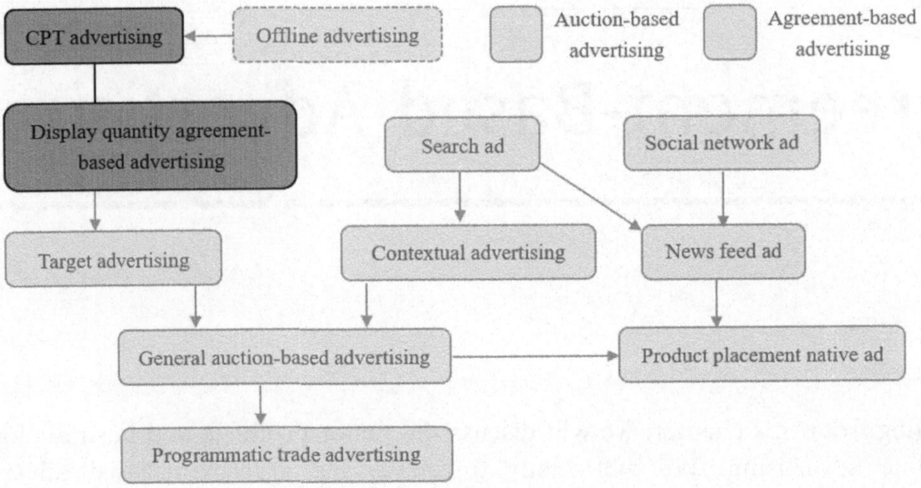

FIGURE 4.1 Agreement-based advertising products.

demand side. However, as time goes by, the demand side desires further optimization of advertising effect, which triggers the auction-based advertising to come into being. We hope the introduction of the agreement-based advertising in this chapter may help readers comprehend the internal driving force for the evolution of advertising trade.

4.1 AD SPACE AGREEMENT

Ad space agreement is the earliest sales model of online advertising: the media and advertisers agree to deliver the ads of the advertisers on fixed ad spaces within a prescribed time frame, and settled by CPT. This is a typical offline advertising model and was prevailing in the Internet advertising in the early days. But this model has an obvious defect, i.e., unable to deliver ads to target audience, let alone in-depth optimization of advertising effect, hence ad space agreement is not the mainstream advertising model at present.

But this model has some advantages in certain scenarios: (1) such exclusive ad serving in the ad spaces with strong exposure[1] will deeply impress users with the brand; and the long-term exclusive banner ad will exert a Windows Dress Effect to increase brand value and conversion rate. (2) This sales model enables monetization of the high-premium traffic by providing additional services to advertisers, e.g. exclusion of competitive products on the same page.

Along with the development of audience targeting technologies, the way of performing the ad space agreement has changed notably. Even if an ad space is monopolized by

1 Such as the splash ads in mobile apps and the special advertising positions on portal homepage.

an advertiser, it does not mean to deliver the same creative repeatedly, which requires audience targeting to play an important role. For example, if the advertiser is an automobile manufacturer who has multiple series of cars, e.g., small cars, compact cars, limousines and SUVs, his potential car buyers will be diversified. As such, delivering separate creatives to different audiences will generate a better advertising effect. Even if the audiences are hard to be segmented, a series of creative could be delivered to the same user progressively by means of frequency capping, so as to ensure a better advertising effect. In terms of system implementation, there is no substantial difference between the ad space agreement in combination with audience targeting and the non-exclusive advertising sales. The Programmatic Direct Buying (PDB), which is to be introduced in Chapter 6, has a lot to do with the above product scenarios.

There is a variant of ad space agreement, i.e., carousel of ad spaces, which means that a user visits the same ad spaces for multiple times, his/her accesses are marked with a set of cyclic sequence number (SN) like {1,2,3}, the impressions with the same SN are sold to advertisers as a virtual ad space. It should be noted that the first impression to a user may not be set as 1, but a random SN selected with equal probability, then the accumulation and cycling of SN will start from here, so that the traffic allocation for each carousel remains consistent. When the ad space are not enough for exclusive sales and advertisers ask for guaranteed displays, this carousel model will be widely adopted, especially for the brand advertising on Chinese portals.

In case of CPT advertising, both the supply and demand sides do not need sophisticated computation and technology. The demand of advertisers is usually summed up as "4As" (Ahead, Appreciation, Appropriate, and Arouse); sometimes they entrust an agency to purchase media advertising. Their demand for advertising quality and quantity is manually satisfied, i.e., based on the experiences of the agents in buying ad space and their knowledge of advertisers' business. With regard to the supply side (i.e., the media), they often use an ad management tool (also known as the ad scheduling system) to execute the agreements automatically after they are finalized.

The typical products of ad scheduling system include DoubleClick for Publishers (DFP), Allyes,[2] and Baidu Ad Manager, which is free for small- and medium-sized websites. The early products only had such basic functions as scheduling; however, as the audience targeting, RTB, and other ad serving approaches have become increasingly popular, their functions tend to be more complicated and applicable to other sales models, which seem like an SSP if combined with the functions of dynamic allocation and RTB.

4.2 AUDIENCE TARGETING

Including the display quantity agreement, the sales of most advertising products is audience-based, which is a core sales model for them. In view of this, audience targeting

2 Translator's note: Allyes is an all-in-one digital integrated marketing solution provider in China.

has become an important supporting technology. Yet the importance and application scope of audience targeting is far beyond the domain of agreement-based advertising, since it is also important for the auction-based advertising. Thus, we will comprehensively introduce audience targeting – the kernel of advertising product strategy.

With the development of online advertising business and technologies a great variety of audience targeting technologies has come into being. The comprehensive application of these technologies has made ad serving more and more accurate. When examining a targeting technology, two key points are worthy of our attention: one is the effect of targeting, i.e., the targeted traffic has better effect than the average traffic; the other one is the coverage of targeting, i.e., the proportion of targeted traffic to the overall inventory traffic. Of course, what we pursue is a targeting technology that is highly effective and widely covered, but it is difficult to make the best of both worlds. Therefore, it is a necessity for an advertising system to provide several targeting technologies at the same time, so as to qualitatively optimize the overall traffic.

The concept of "user portrait" has a similar connotation with audience targeting. But this term may cause an illusion that the focus is placed on the age, gender, and affordability and other state attributes of users. In fact, the focus of user portrait is usually their instant shopping interest and other tags that could be driven directly.

4.2.1 Overview of Audience Targeting Technologies

Let's firstly talk about some common audience targeting technologies. According to their effectiveness and the stages where they affect the acceptance of ad information, and in reference to the advertising effectiveness model in Section 2.1, we have drawn a diagram to show the qualitative evaluation of these technologies (see Figure 4.2).

In Figure 4.2, the horizontal direction denotes the stages where the targeting technology affects the acceptance of ad information, while the vertical direction shows

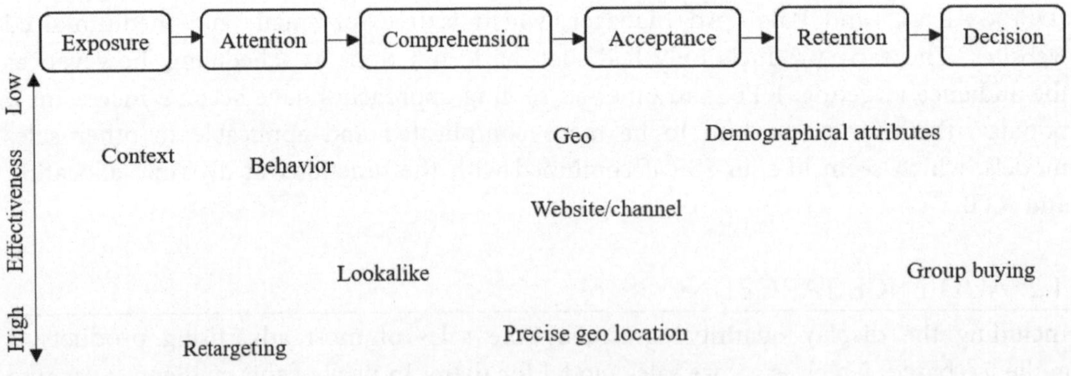

FIGURE 4.2 Common audience targeting technologies.

the effect of qualitative evaluation. Some typical audience targeting technologies are briefed as follows:

(1) **Geo-targeting.** This is an intuitive targeting technology that has been widely used since long. The business of many advertisers has regional characteristics, meaning that all online advertising systems shall be capable of geo-targeting (it is also regarded as contextual targeting). The computation of geo-targeting is fairly simple; some table look-up is already enough. Although the effect of geo-targeting is limited on the whole, it is still an indispensable means for selecting traffic. For example, if an e-commerce website operates and delivers goods only in Beijing, then its response advertising shall be targeted to local audiences; otherwise, the customers in other areas will find it unable to settle accounts after they click the ads and add the products to shopping cart, which will leave a bad impression on them.

(2) **Demographical targeting.** Although demographical targeting does not have any prominent effect, it is especially familiar to brand advertisers, because demographical tags have been extensively used to label the audience in the discourse system of traditional advertising. In online advertising, sometimes the brand ad agreements also contain some demographical requirements. The main demographical tags include age, gender, education level, and income level. The demographical tags are a little bit different from interest tags, since the former can be monitored – sampling and survey are concurrently implemented to estimate the correct proportion of demographical targeting in an advertising campaign. Therefore, in CPM advertising, the advertisers prefer demographical tags to other tags.

Unless there are special data sources, e.g., the registration information in Real Name System (SNS) or the online shopping records, it is generally not easy to make accurate demographical targeting. When the demographical attribute data are yet sufficient, we can make the users with known demographical attributes as the training set and develop a classifier to complete automatic tagging of unknown demographical attributes. But the accuracy of such classifier in defining demographical attributes is limited. In direct response campaigns, it is not necessary to predict demographical attributes, because the predicted data are based on users' other behavioral data and unable to provide additional information.

(3) **Contextual targeting.** It delivers ads with the content matching with the webpage being browsed or application being used. The contextual targeting is based on terms, themes, or other items decided by advertisers. A contextual tag may be a rough description of users' current task, and task matching is critical for increasing their attention to the ads. Although contextual targeting has notably different effect among the ads with varied content, it boasts a prominent advantage of a high coverage rate. For most advertising displays, no matter how much is known about the active users, their instant interest can be inferred from the webpages they are browsing, then the ads containing relevant information will be

pushed to them. Thanks to its high coverage rate, contextual targeting is also preferred in ADN.

(4) **Behavioral targeting.** It is an important targeting technology for display advertising; it deduces user interests based on their historical behaviors, which will be the basis for delivering the ads with relevant content. The reason why behavioral targeting is so important is that it provides a general way of thinking for monetizing user behavioral data that are collected on the Internet. Therefore, behavioral targeting framework, algorithms, and evaluation metrics determine that "data-driven" is the essential characteristics of online advertising, and incubate such derivative businesses as data processing and exchange. Contextual targeting is based on the single access behavior of users, while behavioral targeting is a fused result of several times of contextual targeting. In short, contextual targeting is the basis of behavioral targeting, and all kinds of contextual targeting have their corresponding behavioral targeting. For example, geo-targeting can be made on the basis of the currently active IP of users or the IPs that are most frequently located for some time in the past; the latter means is able to reveal the users' habitual residence, which is referred to as "where-on-earth" targeting by industry insiders.

(5) **Hyper-local targeting.** When delivering ads on mobile devices, we may get a precise geographical location of users. For example, when a user uses cellular network or GPS, he/she will be positioned to the block; when a user uses some indoor positioning technologies like Wi-Fi or blue-tooth, his/her location indicator will be as precise as several meters, which makes it possible for hyper-local targeting, and enables a large number of small advertisers (e.g., restaurants or beauty salons) with a strong regional feature to deliver hyper-local targeting ads. With a qualitative difference from the traditional geo-targeting, hyper-local targeting has become one of the most important opportunities for mobile advertising.

(6) **Retargeting.** It is the simplest customized tag; its rationale is to deliver ads to the visitors of the advertiser website for some time in the past to enhance the advertising effect. Of course, the visitor information is exclusive to the advertiser, meaning that it is a customized tag. Retargeting is acknowledged as the most accurate and effective targeting, but its population coverage is often small, because the ad delivery quantity via retargeting is co-decided by the number of advertiser's inherent users and its overlapping ratio to the media users. The retargeting rationale is to be explained in Chapter 6.

(7) **Look-alike targeting.** Retargeting cannot be solely relied for ad delivery since the delivery quantity is too small to meet the need of advertisers to reach potential customers. In contrast, the idea of look-alike targeting is to find potential customers with similar behaviors for advertisers based on the seed visitor information from advertisers and rich data from advertising platforms. The purpose of look-alike targeting is to achieve better result than common interest tags with the

same user coverage ratio, which essentially reflects the core value of advertiser data. Look-alike targeting is only a general idea rather than a concrete approach, and its rationale is to be introduced in Chapter 6.

(8) **Dynamic pricing.** It is not a targeting technology for advertising, but somewhat associated with it. According to our point of view, group buying is a disguised form of advertising which has two prominent characteristics: (i) Group buying is generally oriented to regional advertisers, so it has necessary functions of geo-targeting or taxonomic organization by region. (ii) Group buying mainly uses price tools to directly lower the threshold for decision-making by users, so as to significantly increase the conversion rate of those price-sensitive users. Of course, it takes some cost to use such means. The similar means – including discounts or price-off information in creative directly – are also widely used in other e-commerce advertising.

(9) **Scenario targeting.** Scenario targeting is a new problem born in the mobile environment. Richness of scenarios makes mobile devices different from PCs. During working out, eating, watching TV, or having a meeting, mobile phone is always by your side. All the background states are the scenarios where you are using mobile phone. The scenarios are of great importance in making decisions for advertising. Moreover, the abundant sensor and status information of mobile devices make it possible to judge the scenarios. The details about scenario targeting are discussed in Subsection 8.4.2.

4.2.2 Audience Targeting Tag System

To apply the audience targeting technologies that reflect user interest (e.g., behavioral targeting and contextual targeting), we need a tag system that maps each user to one or more tags. How to plan a reasonable tag system has a great impact on the operation of advertising products. Therefore, this is a particularly critical part of product strategy. Generally speaking, there are two ways for organizing the tag system: one is to develop a hierarchical tag system according to taxonomy, where the upper-layer tag is the parent node of the lower-layer tag and there is an inclusion relation in crowd coverage. Some audience targeting technologies for brand advertising often use this highly structured tag system. It should be pointed out that the tags in this system are developed according to the demand-side logic, and some classified tags with great significance in the media side, such as military, should not be included in the tag system for lacking of definite demand correspondence.

Another way to organize interest tags is to set corresponding tags according to the concrete requirements of advertisers. All tags cannot be described in the same classification system, and there is no definite set membership. This semi-structured or unstructured tag system usually contains a number of fairly accurate tag sets, so it is mainly applicable to the traffic requirements for multiple objectives, especially the requirement for coexistence of response and objective.

Whether to choose a structured or unstructured interest tag system is more of a business decision; the following two scenarios shall be taken into account:

(1) When tags are made as the direct target of ad serving (including the crowds that are directly selected by advertisers in CPM and auction-based advertising), these tags should not only be understood by advertisers, but convenient for their selection. Therefore, in this case, a structured hierarchical tag system is often a more reasonable product solution, especially in CPM advertising, where tag segmentation cannot be too detailed (see the explanation in Subsection 4.3.1). A typical example of this structured tag system is the Yahoo! GD audience targeting tag system given in Table 4.1. Such a tag system is easy to understand and operate, and is suitable for brand advertisers.

(2) When tags are only an intermediate variable required by the serving system and used as the input variable of CTR prediction or other modules, the structured tag system is actually unnecessary and should be fully planned and mined in an effect-driven way, and there is no need for the constraint of hierarchical relationship between tags. A typical representative of such a tag system is the BlueKai tag system; its purpose is to pursue the effect or special group targeting, thus making its organizational regularity give way to the result precision. See Subsection 7.2.4 for more information about the BlueKai tag system.

There is a special form of tag, i.e., terms. Users are often accurately divided into groups based on their search terms or browsed content. The term "tags" are not hierarchical and completely unstructured; although they are easy to understand, they are not easy to manipulate. However, due to the importance of search ad in the overall online advertising, the selection and optimization of ad serving terms, which is a specialized technology, has been developed quite fully, so this kind of tag is commonly seen in practice.

TABLE 4.1 Yahoo! GD audience targeting tag system

Tier-1 tag	Tier-2 tag
Finance	Bank Accounts, Credit Cards, Investment, Insurance, Loans, Real Estate …
Service	Local, Wireless, Gas & Electric …
Travel	Europe, Americas, Air, Lodging, Rail …
Tech	Hardware, Software, Consumer, Mobile …
Entertainment	Games, Movies, Television, Gambling …
Autos	Econ/Mid/Luxury, Salon/Coupe/SUV …
FMCG	Personal care …
Retail	Apparel, Gifts, Home …
Other	Health, Parenting, Moving …

4.2.3 Design Principles for Tag System

The most critical link of audience-targeted products is how to describe users, i.e., how to design a tag system, which is even more important than the audience targeting technology. We focus on the users who drive the direct response; for this purpose, a structured tag system is not necessary. Generally speaking, the design of tag system shall by be carried out by industry, and the key idea is to deeply study the decision-making process of users in the concerned industry. To put it simply, it is about understanding the reasons and logic behind what users decide to buy and not buy in this industry. We hereby cite a few common advertiser industries to interpret this principle.

(1) Auto industry. The user decision logic in the auto industry is fairly clear. The first consideration for a prospective car buyer must be price: if you have a budget of 200,000 yuan, but actually buys a car of 500,000 yuan, you are less likely to think about a car for less than 100,000 yuan. The second consideration is car models: if you have two children, you may prefer a seven-seater; if you're single, you may be interested in sports cars. Both of these considerations are reasonable or even rigid constraints. The consideration of brand only ranks the third place.

Therefore, the tag system for the auto industry is generally the price, model, and brand, and the ranking of importance is fixed.

(2) Game industry. The games have an artistic quality similar to movies and music, and their user decision-making process is generally difficult to grasp, because people's love for art is not rational, so it is difficult to summarize the law. Can we directly use RPG, ACT, SLG, RTS, and STG as the tag system? In fact, these categories are only for the purpose of organizing and indexing the game, and not to accurately reflect the decision-making logic of users. Would an "RPG lover" see an RPG as a must-play and dismiss all other games? Apparently not.

In order to do a good job in the user tag of game players, it is necessary to study the game scenarios in depth. For example, slot machine players often switch to new games with different materials, which means that "slot machine fans" as a user tag is consistent with the users' decision-making process. The users who are interested in the mobile game "Boom Beach" tend to admire SuperCell's new games, then the brand "SuperCell" becomes a valid user tag.

(3) E-commerce industry. From the perspective of consumers' decision-making, it is inappropriate to refer to e-commerce as an industry, but a collection of multiple industries. However, for the typical types of goods in e-commerce, such as clothing, the users' decision-making process is quite marvelous: assuming a girl notices an H&M dress, yet it is difficult to infer that she wants to buy a dress or fancy H&M, or maybe she is only interested in the style of the dress. For this kind of commodities, neither "H&M" or "dress" is a valid user tag. Therefore, the actual

practice of e-commerce is basically not to rely on classification, but mainly adopt the method of "single product + personalized recommendation" to build and use the tag system. See Subsection 6.4.4 for a detailed discussion.

4.3 DISPLAY QUANTITY AGREEMENT

Nowadays, even for the purpose of brand promotion, the ad space agreement is not the mainstream. In fact, the mainstream Internet brand advertising is the CPM-based display quantity agreement. This agreement provides for the display quantity under certain audience conditions and settles by the pre-agreed price for unit display quantity. This agreement is also known as Guaranteed Delivery (GD), in which "guaranteed" denotes the agreement on quantity. During the actual implementation, the media may be asked to bear certain compensation for the failure to fulfill the agreed quantity.

In many cases, we refer to display quantity agreement colloquially as "CPM advertising." In fact, CPM advertising also includes another way of selling which is settled by CPM but no agreement on display quantity, such as the sales in ad exchange. But such non-guaranteed advertising is categorized as auction-based advertising rather than agreement-based advertising, as their commercial logic differs greatly. Therefore, we still use the notion of display quantity agreement.

Let's talk about the rationality of this sales mode from both the supply and demand sides. From the sales of fixed ad space, the media have started the advertising sales settled by CPM, the original intention was to bring in data monetization in addition to traffic monetization, and still provide service to original brand advertisers. When buying ad space, it is easy for advertisers to predict their traffic allocation; when buying ads based on audience targeting, there will be lots of uncertainties in traffic allocation. Therefore, the demand side expects to prescribe the quantity guarantee in the agreement before buying.

Please note that although the display quantity agreement is sold with the crowd as an overt object, it has never broken away from the object of ad space.

Under the CPM settlement, it is impossible to package multiple and notably different ad space into one sales object, because the exposure effect of different ad space varies greatly, and the CPM will change significantly accordingly. In practice, the display quantity agreement is often based on some ad space with strong exposure, and then sold for separate audience segment. The most typical example is the post position of video websites or the advertising positions on the homepage of portals. The readers acquainted with RTB may wonder why is it possible to settle by CPM when there are so many different advertising positions in the market. We will discuss this topic later when we come to the product logic of RTB.

The display quantity agreement is still a relatively traditional trading mode, but from the perspective of technology, it actually reflects the essence of the computation-driven Internet advertising: obtain the user and contextual attributes through analysis, and then let the server side dynamically decide candidate ads based on these attributes and ad inventory. The emergence of this trading model is supported by several technical means, including audience targeting, traffic forecasting, and GD. Audience targeting is introduced in the preceding section, here we will discuss traffic forecasting and the product strategy for online allocation.

4.3.1 Traffic Forecasting

The display quantity agreement sells the number of ad impressions to a particular audience segment, which is different from the specified ad space, so the ad serving quantity shall be prescribed in the agreement. Thus, the problem of traffic forecasting comes into being. The traffic forecasting in advertising products mainly satisfies three purposes:

(1) **Pre-sales guidance.** In the agreement-based advertising, it is important to predict the traffic volume to each group of people as accurately as possible in advance, because the total number of impressions needs to be agreed upon. If the traffic is seriously underestimated, there will be insufficient sales of resources; if the traffic is seriously overvalued, then some agreements may fail to be fulfilled. These situations will directly affect the revenue of the advertising system.

(2) **Online traffic allocation.** In the agreement-based advertising, there will be lots of intersection in audience selection among different agreements. When an impression meets the requirements of more than two agreements at the same time, how to allocate the traffic so as to satisfy all agreements on the whole is a problem; this online allocation problem is to be discussed later. Various online allocation algorithms rely on the results of traffic forecasting to ensure of high efficiency and accuracy.

(3) **Bidding guidance.** In auction-based advertising, there is no guarantee of quantity. Advertisers need to know how much traffic they are likely to get based on their planned bidding, in order to evaluate whether their bidding is reasonable. Different from the agreement-based advertising, the traffic forecast herein also takes account of bidding.

To sum up, the general traffic forecasting problem in advertising can be described as the estimation of the traffic function $t(u, b)$. The parameter $\boldsymbol{u}$ denotes the given user tag or a combination of user tags, while the parameter $\boldsymbol{b}$ is bid. In the agreement-based advertising, there is no bid; it can be seen as an extreme case of $b \to \infty$. The technologies for traffic forecasting are introduced in Chapter 11.

4.3.2 Traffic Shaping

Traffic shaping is very important for display quantity agreement, but it is essentially a passive measurement of traffic. In some cases, we can actively influence the traffic to facilitate the conclusion of agreement. This product strategy problem is known as "traffic shaping."

The typical scenarios of traffic shaping can be referred to the agreement-based ad display on portals. The traffic of each sub-channel of portals relies heavily on the diversion of the key position links on the homepage. Take an auto show for example, there is a strong demand for ad displays on the car channel, where the links on the homepage shall divert more traffic to the car channel to increase revenue. This thought is fairly straightforward and widely practiced. However, with regard to the demand for commercial products, in order to achieve the goal of traffic shaping systematically and efficiently, it is necessary to link the demand for user products with advertising products, and then by following certain criteria, improve the efficiency of commercial monetization as much as possible without harming the user experience. The specific product technology is omitted here.

It is worth noting that the traffic shaping problem has involved the internal connection between user products and commercial products. This problem is inextricably connected with the native ads to be discussed in Chapter 8.

4.3.3 Online Allocation

The display quantity agreement will encounter the following problem: it is possible that the audiences of agreement-based advertising are largely overlapped, then how to develop an allocation plan to ensure each agreement is satisfied as much as possible. To interpret this problem, we will simplify it to a matching problem in a bipartite graph: one part of the graph represents the supply nodes of ad inventory, and each node represents the traffic set with the same user tags; the other part of the graph represents the demand nodes, and each node represents the user tag condition in the agreement.

An example of a bipartite graph of supply node, demand node, and online allocation is shown in Figure 4.3. In this graph, the six nodes below are supply nodes and the three nodes above are demand nodes. If the audience tag of a supply node can meet the requirement of a demand node, we will create a connecting edge between these two corresponding nodes. Each condition in the supply node is in an "and" relationship (if a "or" relationship is set in ad serving, it can be converted into multiple demand nodes). Apparently, the demand nodes may compete with each other for the traffic of the same supply node.

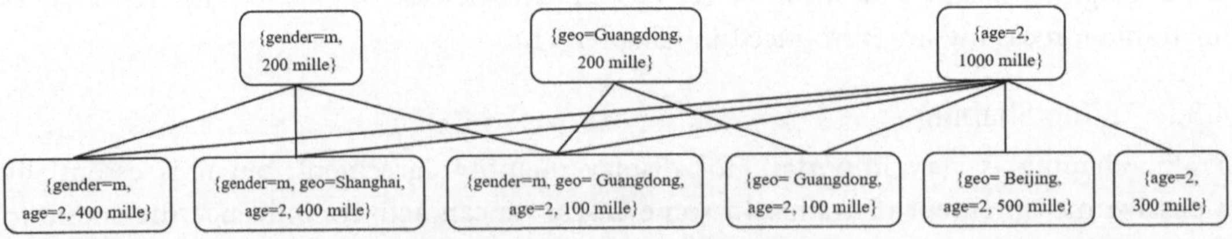

FIGURE 4.3 An exemplar bipartite graph for online allocation.

If the traffic allocation is allowed at the end of the day, it will be easy for us to develop an allocation plan: according to the traffic of each supply node and the constraints of each demand node, we can solve the above allocation problem and figure out the proportion of the traffic of each supply node to be allocated to a demand node. But in actual practice, we cannot wait until all the traffic data are known before making a decision, but make a real-time allocation decision at each exposure, so this problem is referred to as the online allocation problem. Online allocation requires an offline allocation plan based on historical data and a certain strategy, so that the online allocation plan is able to be executed.

If there are only a few optional tags, such as age and gender, then the number of supply nodes will be small; if the number of agreements is small, then the number of demand nodes could not be large either. In this case, we can still use the above offline method for online allocation: make traffic forecasting, replace the real traffic with the forecast result, solve the above allocation problem, and then calculate the proportion of the traffic per supply node to be allocated to a demand node, while the allocation in the online system is based on the solved proportion. The actual online allocation technologies are much more complex, which we will discuss in detail in Chapter 11.

As the number of tags increases, the number of supply nodes will increase exponentially, and the traffic per supply node will shrink rapidly. When the traffic per node is too small, it will be quite difficult to make relatively accurate prediction, and then the above plan will become completely unfeasible. Therefore, in case of rich and accurate user tags, such advertising products as display quantity agreement cannot operate effectively, which is one of the driving forces of auction-based advertising.

4.3.4 Product Cases

The advertising products based on ad space agreement are often seen on the home pages of Chinese portals and other exposure resources; considering their relatively simple logic, we will not illustrate them with examples. The display quantity agreement has two typical product scenarios: one is for video ad resources, and the other is for the brand advertising position on the global main portals. We hereby introduce Yahoo! GD for readers to take reference.

4.3.4.1 Yahoo! GD

YAHOO!
ADVERTISING

The display advertising of Yahoo! consists of two product systems: GD and non-guaranteed delivery (NGD). The former is for the brand advertising, while the latter is for ADN and programmatic trade. It seems like a relatively old perspective to divide advertising products by their satisfaction of high-value brand ads, which has held back the development of Yahoo! in programmatic trade, and its core business even exited from the advertising market. But Yahoo! GD advertising, from the perspective of historical development, is of great significance in the agreement-based advertising.

The Yahoo! GD market provides brand advertisers with agreement-based purchasing interfaces (orders are placed through API) and basic targeting functions to divide users. The user tags of Yahoo! GD include geo, demographical attributes (mainly age and gender), and behavioral targeting tags. The behavioral targeting tags are divided into several layers; some tags of the first two layers are given in Table 1.1.

In this behavioral targeting tag system, there are thousands of tags, but no more than 100 of them are incorporated into the sales agreement. This is a typical example of the awkwardness of agreement-based advertising: quite a number of precise tags are almost impossible to sell due to the constraints of agreed quantity. Therefore, it should be noted that even if an advertising product claims a sophisticated tag system and a rich variety of tags, it makes little sense since it is the size of tag holders that is truly convincing.

It should be said that Yahoo! GD is one of the earliest and relatively complete product systems for the advertising based on display quantity agreement. Before the RTB came into being, Yahoo! GD was able to offer simple tags to meet most demand. Some key product strategies and technical solutions for display quantity agreement are derived from this product, so it is worth of in-depth study. In addition, its methodologies and solutions can be directly employed in the present market where video ad has been developing at a fast pace.

CHAPTER 5

Search Ad and Auction-Based Advertising

Owing to the demand for monetization of the search business and development of the precise audience targeting technology, the auction-based trade has come into being in both search advertising and display advertising. In contrast to the agreement-based advertising, the essence of the auction-based trade is to remove the quantity constraint from the transaction process and only use the simple decision scheme ("the highest price obtained") to deliver ads. The bidding conforms to the development trend of refined targeted advertising, and provides monetization channels the remnant traffic not sold by agreement, which has greatly motivated a large number of small and medium advertisers to take part in online advertising, and substantially changed both the online and traditional advertising environment.

This chapter mainly introduces the auction-based advertising products (especially search ad and auction-based ADN) and the key product strategies. The position of these products in the overall ad evolution process is illustrated in Figure 5.1. The RTB-related products, which are greatly different from the ADN in terms of data utilization and business logic, will be introduced in Chapter 6.

Search ad is a flagship product in the auction-based advertising and even the entire online advertising. In addition to its advantages in monetization and market occupation, some core product strategies and technical solutions in computational advertising are derived from search ad. As such, an in-depth knowledge of search ad is critical for understanding the entire auction-based advertising market. The discussion of search ad in this chapter will focus on its leading points in the entire advertising market, and the most critical one is the generation of auction-based advertising products and the creation of corresponding mechanism design theory. How to develop reasonable market rules and pricing policies to make the competition in the bidding market more reasonable and sufficient has a considerable impact on the overall earnings. This

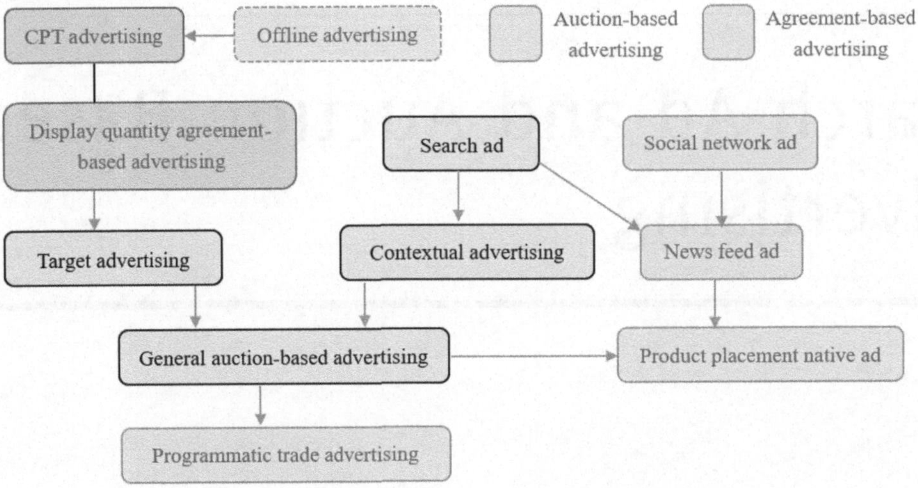

FIGURE 5.1 Auction-based advertising.

macro-market discussion has also become a well-studied topic in online advertising, and this chapter will focus on its problematic framework and practical approaches.

Influenced by auction trade, the domain of display advertising has seen the emergence of such forms of product as the ADN – which purchases the remnant traffic from various media in bulk and then sells the traffic to advertisers based on CPC. The ADN has played an important role in improving the liquidity of display advertising market. There are two types of bidding objects in ADN: one is the terms in the contextual page, which are directly derived from search ads; and the other is the user interest tags based on user behavioral data, which originates from the targeting logic of display advertising. The bidding environment in ADN differs from that of search ads: the effectiveness of contextual or user tags varies greatly, as does the ad space. Therefore, in addition to ranking ads according to eCPM estimation, the cold start problem and the normalization of CTR in various complex environments are fairly important, which makes the effect optimization of ADN a unique challenge.

Upon the emergence of auction-based advertising, the changes have taken place in the demand-side products and technologies. There are two key points in these changes: (i) The purchase of ad space is changed into the cross-network and audience-oriented purchase. (ii) Help advertisers fulfill the display quantity in a bidding environment, which is no longer guaranteed by the bidding market itself. The products that meet the purposes of the demand side are called the media-buying platform. In this platform, the problem of completing ROI optimization with the quantity constraint still exists and even becomes more difficult than the online allocation problem. The ROI optimization has become one of the services provided by the high-end purchasing platforms. Of course, the media acquisition and ROI optimization of search advertising are equally important, and this specialized service is referred to as "search engine marketing" (SEM).

5.1 SEARCH AD

When speaking of the auction-based advertising, we have to start with search ad. In the whole online advertising market, search ad has been holding the largest market share. More importantly, the overall architecture of bidding and ad serving is developed from search ad. Therefore, we shall comprehend the search ad profoundly at the first place and then learn about the entire auction-based advertising market.

As for search ad, it has different names in different search engines, e.g., paid search, search ad, and sponsored search. These names are conceptually similar but also slightly different; we prefer to use "sponsored search," since "paid search" may sometimes lead readers to misunderstand who is paying. As for "search ad," it should include other forms of ads in search engines. For more background and concepts about search ad, please consult with reference [6].

With a view to its market share, search ad occupies more than half of the entire online advertising market. The revenue data of China's integrated search engine advertising and vertical search engine advertising (e.g., Taobao through train – a marketing platform of Taobao) are listed in Table 5.1.[1]

Search ad is a typical auction-based advertising product, which is characterized by advertisers competing for advertising display opportunities through an auction for a certain bidding object (it means the term in this case), and occupy a number of positions of the advertising display according to the results of the auction. This is quite different from the quantity agreement detailed in Chapter 4: the quantity guarantee no longer exists, and advertisers have to adjust the balance between effect and quantity on their own; the price agreement is ruled out, and each advertiser can adjust his/her bidding for a term at any time. Now let's look at the specific product form of search advertising.

5.1.1 Products of Search Advertising

The audience targeting of search ad is based on query words as the granularity, and the search advertising products are sold via bidding and settled by CPC. Generally, search ads are displayed on the search results page (see Figure 5.2). The creative display area of the PC search advertising is generally divided into three parts: north, east, and south. All the ad spaces in the north and east parts constitute a set of positions for the auction of

TABLE 5.1 Market size of search ads in China and the United States

State	2012	2013	2014	2015	2016
China	3.75	5.08	7.59	10.04	13.66
US	17.03	18.85	20.19	21.53	29.20

Unit: bln US$

1 Data source: The market survey reports produced by IAB, IResearch, and other research institutions

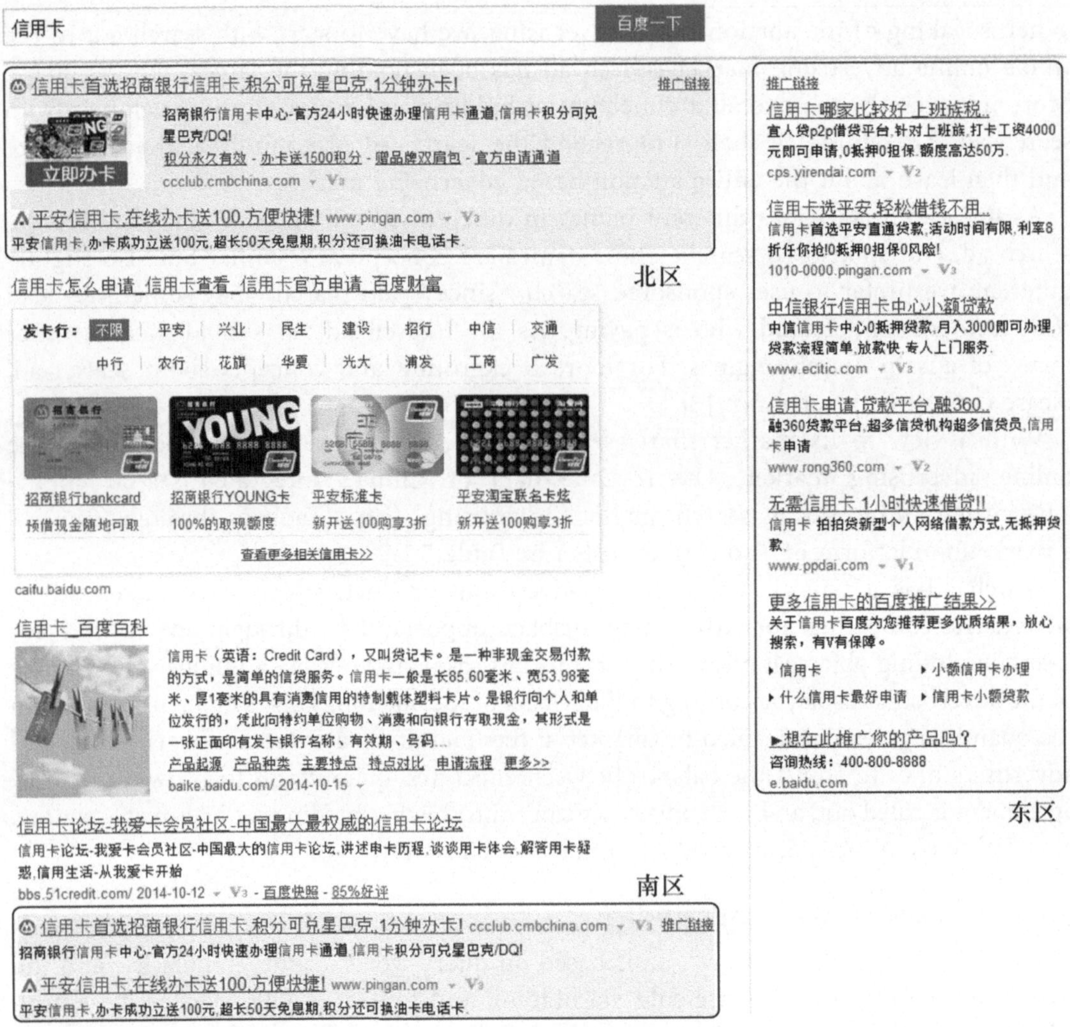

FIGURE 5.2 Exemplar positions for auction-based search ads.

the same term, the ranking during bidding is {north$_1$, north$_2$,···, east$_1$, east$_2$··}, which is basically ranked according to the CTR of each position. Meanwhile, there is no need for the ad display to occupy all of these positions, which is significantly different from the banner ad. For the ads in the south part, different search engines have different processing methods, some directly copy the ad displays in the north, and some directly copy the first a few ads display in the east.

The most basic form of search ad is the textual link that is consistent with the natural retrieval results, there will be bottom color and the words like "promotion," "sponsored links," and "Ad" at the corner to distinguish it from organic results, the purpose is to prevent the users not interested in the ads from false clicks, reduce invalid consumption of advertisers, and improve user experience.

Since mobile search results are generally organized in the form of a simple information flow, the form of mobile search ad is simpler than that of PC search ad: in general search, ads tend to appear at the top or bottom, the east part does not exist; in some vertical searches, ads may be inserted into the content. Figure 5.3 shows an exemplar product for mobile search ad.

The bidding object of search ad is the "bid term." Advertisers provide their queries to match with the terms so as to determine whether this ad is available to be triggered. There are simple and precise matching methods and more extended methods, which are known as "query extension" – a key product strategy in search advertising.

The search ad discussed in this chapter is based on general search engines. In fact, many vertical searches (especially e-commerce searches) also have strong ability of monetization, but the product forms may be somewhat different. Readers can select some of them to compare with the following problems.

In the entire product spectrum of the Internet advertising, search ad has a particularly important position with the following distinctive product and technical features.

(1) Monetization of search ad. Its eCPM is much higher than the general display advertising, and its market attention is thus highlighted. Therefore, the research on some unique problems and algorithms related to search ad has been highly valued. The most critical reason for the monetization ability of search ad is that the query entered by users directly reflects their intention.

(2) The audience targeting tag of search ad is the contextual search query. Since the search terms are fairly strong representations of user intention, search ads can be precisely targeted. In contrast to search terms, the importance of interest tags based on users' historical behaviors is greatly reduced, partly because the signals

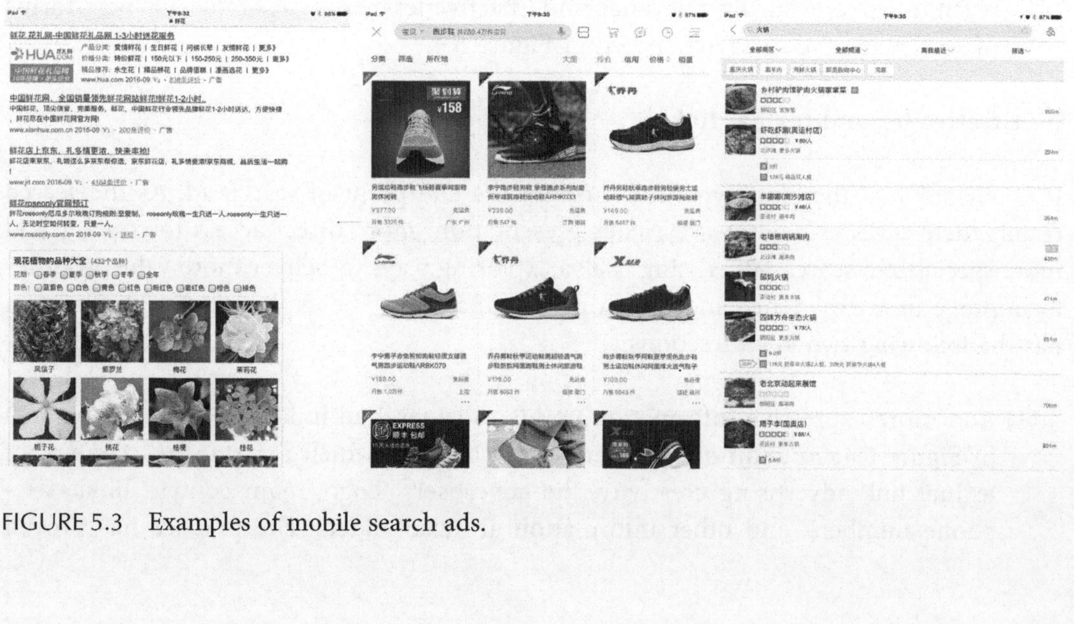

FIGURE 5.3 Examples of mobile search ads.

are much less strong than search terms, and partly because the users' tasks with a clear intention cannot be interrupted (see the principle of advertising effectiveness in Chapter 2). Therefore, the eCPM in search ads degenerates from $r(a, u, c)$ in general situations to $r(a, c)$.

(3) The display forms of search ad are quite close to those of natural results, but they have less dramatic hints in the background and textual links. Such product design endows it an implication of native ad, and further improves the advertising effect. However, such advertising result requires far more relevance than display ads, and therefore requires sophisticated policies and techniques to match ads based on queries.

(4) The auction-based transaction developed from search ad has gradually developed into the predominant transaction mode of the Internet advertising. This mode has fundamentally changed the operation mode of advertising and unleashed enormous productivity for rapidly improving its effectiveness.

5.1.2 New Forms of Search Ads

The technological focus of search advertising differs greatly from that of the agreement-based advertising, and also somewhat differs from that of the auction-based advertising. From the perspective of product development, search advertising has three aspects worthy of exploration:

(1) Enrich the forms of display for the textual link creative, and make it more expressive so as to increase CTR.

(2) Take advantage of the higher relevance tolerance of the east part to design some extended advertising products. Of course, this exploration is not applicable to mobile search advertising.

(3) Optimize the relationship between advertising and natural results, and increase revenue while ensuring relevance and effectiveness. Some examples of new forms of search ads products are shown in Figure 5.4.

I. **Creative beyond textual link**

It is obvious that the blue hyperlinks are not the end point of search ad. As the search results themselves evolve toward richer presentation, more direct access to content and more specialized, search advertising is also exploring ways to deliver more value in order to improve user experience and monetization efficiency. The exploration in this respect has the following two key directions:

(1) Add more expressive information points to general ad links. As shown in part ② in Figure 5.4, in addition to the title and abstract which are standard content of textual link advertising creativity, the advertisers' Logo, main content links, telephone numbers, and other information are also added. The practice has proved

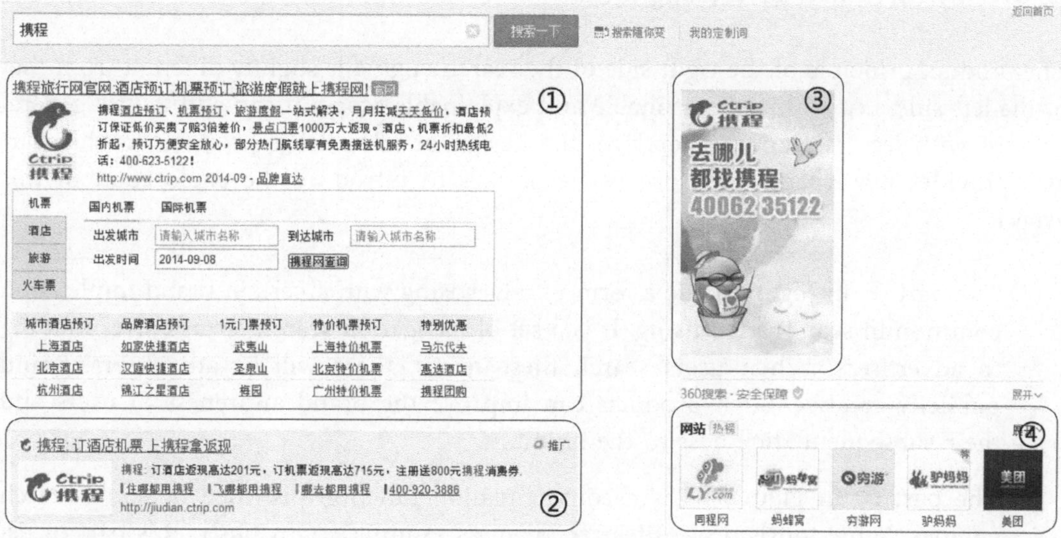

FIGURE 5.4 Exemplar new products of search advertising.

that it will improve the direct effect and brand value of the ads. What's more, such a development direction has little to do with the advertising industry and can be replicated on a large scale, so it has been widely adopted in search advertising.

(2) Directly display the abstract of the structured advertising content, and even provide some functions of direct access, which can reduce the cost of user jump and improve promotion efficiency. In part ① in Figure 5.4, the ad directly shows some main content links of the tourism website, and directly provides quick access to book air tickets and hotels in the results. Such commercialized results are often directly derived from the direct arrival products, such as Baidu's Aladdin and 360's OneBox. However, since the results are paid, they should also be classified as advertising or commercialized content. It should be pointed out that in order to ensure consistent user experience, this kind of content is often unable to be completely operated by the bidding mode of search advertising, and the general operation mode is to conduct periodic offline bidding for a certain industry.

The above development trend has provided a new space for improving the effect of search advertising, but has not yet become the mainstream of search advertising. The reason is that this mode requires product design and operation plan by industry, and the development scale is limited. In addition, if it is a single product that is involved directly, it will produce the same complex engineering problems as the personalized retargeting, such as docking of the goods warehouse, which will be discussed later along with the introduction of DSP.

II. **Weakly correlated advertising forms**

The product principle of the right side of the search engine is slightly different from that of the left side, i.e., within a reasonable and explainable scope, it can add a little general content with less relevance. Therefore, the design of advertising products in this part also provides new space. Let's use two examples to introduce the exploration in this aspect:

(1) The part ③ in Figure 5.4 is a form of advertising with a certain brand implication common in search advertising. It is a set of navigation search terms corresponding to advertisers. When users search these terms, there will be advertisers' brand publicity creative. Such products can improve the brand awareness of users and their subsequent stickiness to the brand.

(2) The part ④ in Figure 5.4 is a commendation function provided by some search engines. Some tourism websites are taken as examples. Obviously, this part of list and ranking can be operated according to the logic of auction-based advertising. Through this advertising product, search engines can provide some ads far away from the decision-making and aiming to contact with potential users. In this figure, it is possible that the users of Ctrip have not used LY.COM, but after seeing the ad here, they may want to have a try and grow interest in it. Of course, such product should never be displayed in the results on the left side of a search, because that would lead its users to question the relevance of the results.

III. **Exploration of native ad**

Search ad has the characteristics of native ad from the beginning: its commercialization results are the same as the organic results, triggered by the active intention of users, and the display form not greatly different from the organic results. In fact, a significant percentage of users are completely unable to distinguish between organic and advertising results. Therefore, exploring the natural combination of search ad and content, and deliver ads in an increasingly "native" manner is also an important direction of products.

Unlike Google, Chinese search ads have mixed competitive ranking among natural search results, the standard form similar to Figure 5.2 is only a late comer, but this mixed ranking has all along been existing in advertising products, and still plays an important role in generating revenue. Although this mixed ranking has received different judgments, and somewhat reduced the quality of query results, it could be seen as an exploration of native ad. There is another trend of native ad: when delivering structured content results as shown in Figure 5.5, the commercial results are mixed into some information searches directly oriented to commodities and ranked uniformly. It builds up monetization ability in contrast to only providing natural results, and avoids the degradation of results due to scant demand in contrast to just providing ad results. This kind of advertising is also known as "commodity-oriented advertising."

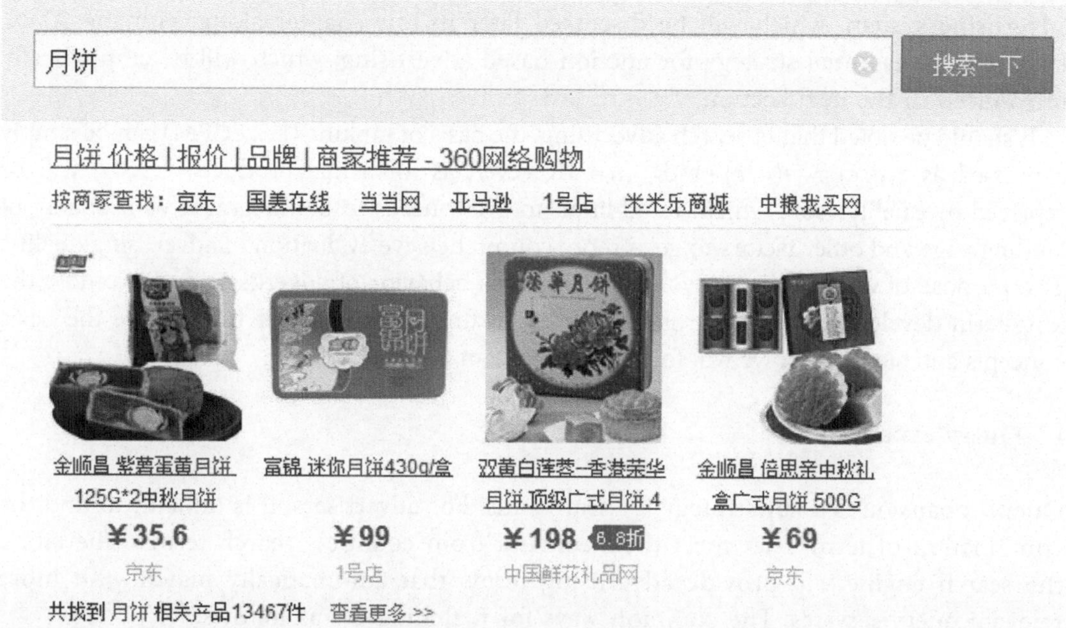

FIGURE 5.5 Examples of commodity-oriented advertising.

We believe that search ad is an origin of native ad far more important than news feed ad, and some features of search ad can inspire the native advertising products; see the relevant discussion in Chapter 8.

5.1.3 Product Strategy of Search Advertising

In addition to innovation of product forms, the strategy for ad serving and optimization is an important part of search advertising products. In order to understand such product strategy, we shall firstly acquaint with the decision-making process of search advertising.

As shown in Figure 5.6, the decision-making process of search advertising can be divided into several stages: query expansion, retrieval, ranking, placement, and pricing. Query expansion is a unique strategy of search advertising, aiming to automatically expand relevant query terms for advertisers and expand matching traffic. Advertising

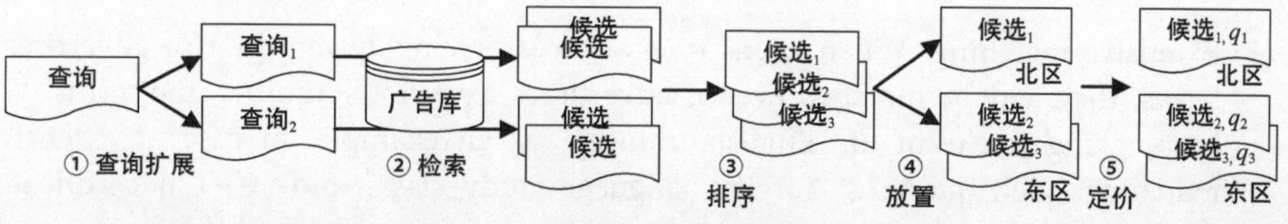

FIGURE 5.6 Schematic decision-making process of search ad.

retrieval and ranking of candidate ads according to eCPM are the core processes of advertising system, which will be discussed later in this chapter along with the ADN. Pricing is an essential strategy for auction-based advertising, which will be emphatically introduced in the next section.

It should be noted that in search advertising, the basis of ranking (i.e., eCPM) can be simply expressed as $r(a, c) = \mu(a, c) \cdot \text{bid}_{cpc}(a)$. However, as for actual products, CTR μ will be replaced by quality score which, in addition to CTR, needs to be integrated with quality of landing page and other factors to get a more comprehensive evaluation of advertising quality. The purpose of doing so is to avoid the malicious behavior of advertisers and promote the long-term development of advertising market. In this book, in order to illustrate the basic concepts and algorithms, we will focus on the role of CTR.

I. **Query expansion**

Query expansion is a key strategy for search ads. For advertisers, it is difficult to find the combination of terms that meet their demand from countless search terms. Therefore, the search engine will provide advertising terms that automatically match with more relevant query services. The common ways for matching are as follows:

(1) Precise matching. Does not make any expansion of the terms provided by advertisers, and ensures accurate implementation that is faithful to the intention of advertisers. The way to perform precise matching is to firstly segment the query terms input by users, such as "English training," and then divide into a word set of {English, training}. When the word set is completely consistent with the terms set by advertisers, the accurate matching will be triggered. Take the term "English training" as an example, by employing the accurate matching approach, the queries "English training" and "training English" will trigger the advertisement.

(2) Phrase matching. When a user query contains a complete set of advertisers' terms or term set (including synonyms of terms), the match is successful and able to trigger the corresponding ad candidates. Take the term "English training" as an example, with the phrase matching approach, the searches that may trigger the ads include the terms "English training," "English training summer class," "which English training institution is good," "training of English," "English-related training," and "English language learning." The terms like "English songs" or "computer training" are unable to trigger the ads. Generally speaking, since this approach is to match a broad range of concepts with refined concepts, it is precise on the whole.

(3) Extensive matching. When users' query words are highly matched to advertisers' terms, they may be matched even if advertisers have not submitted the terms. We keep taking the term of "English training" as an example, in case of extensive matching, such query as "foreign language study class" and "CET 4 certificate" may trigger the ads. The extensive matching logic is not clearly defined and is usually obtained automatically by the data mining algorithm. Therefore, although

extensive matching can get more traffic, the accuracy of the traffic may be discounted.

(4) Negative matching. Since phrase matching and extensive matching are automatically completed by the system, it is inevitable to incur some inaccurate matching results. Therefore, it is necessary to provide advertisers with the function of negative matching, i.e., to clarify which words cannot be matched, so that some inefficient traffic can be shut down flexibly.

Both phrase matching and extensive matching are typical query extension methods. By combining them with negative matching, advertisers will find a balance between traffic and quality. However, due to the inconsistency between the interests of media and advertisers, the extension of words provided by search engines may not be the best for advertisers, which will be discussed later when we introduce SEM products.

II. **Ad placement**

After the candidate ads are ranked, the number of ads in the north foot and east foot needs to be determined; this process is referred to as "ad placement." Since these two areas form a unified bidding queue, the conditions for entering the north foot and east foot shall be set respectively. The most critical condition is the one to enter the north foot.

The north foot is a prime location for advertising display. Generally speaking, the vast majority of the advertising revenue of general search engines comes from the north foot. Thus, the average number of ads in the north foot is directly related to revenue. But at the same time, the north foot advertising directly lowers the position of natural search results, so we shall pay special attention to the ad quantity and quality in north foot while focusing on revenue indicators. The average number of ads in north foot of the whole search engine is known as "north foot print" (NFP) or "average show number" (ASN). We should pay attention to NFP when we examine the effect of a new algorithm on RPM. However, when the NFP changes significantly, it is often of little significance to compare the corresponding RPM changes.

To determine whether an ad is able to enter the north foot, two key factors should be considered: whether the ad is relevant enough and whether the RPM of the ad is sufficient, the former is to ensure of user experience, while the latter is to make use of the display position more efficiently. Generally speaking, the north foot sets an upper limit for the number of ads. Based on the overall NFP constraints and revenue goals, we can easily determine the correlation and optimal threshold value of RPM by means of data simulation, which will be discussed in Chapter 13.

As mentioned earlier, the decisions for search advertising usually do not take account of the influence of user $\boldsymbol{u}$, but the NFP is an exception to this problem, which is personalized ad placement. Due to the differences in personal preference and comprehension of advertising, the advertising tolerance and CTR among users vary greatly: some users always skip ads and start browsing directly from organic results, while some users who are not good at distinguishing ads or more tolerable to ads will treat ads like natural search results, thus resulting in a large number of clicks. Obviously, for the former type of users, the NFP should be reduced to provide them with better experience without significantly reducing the revenue; for the latter type of users, try to make full use of the ad spaces in north foot when there are eligible ads.

5.1.4 Product Cases

I. Google AdWords

AdWords, which is a term bidding advertising product launched by Google, generates billions of dollars of revenue for Google every year. At its initial stage, AdWords was based on search terms as targeting condition and sold by CPM which was the most popular at that time. Unfortunately, the sales result was not satisfactory. Later, the CPC sales model developed by Overture was adopted, and the concept of CTR was creatively introduced. The expression of the advertising relevance by CTR has expedited the increase in advertising revenue.

When Overture invented the CPC sales model, the ad serving was only ranked by advertisers' bidding, that is, those offered the highest price would win the exposure opportunity. Google detected the defect in this model: the highest-bid ad wins a lot of exposure, but if no one clicks it, the advertising platform still has no revenue. Therefore, Google changed the strategy to estimate the CTR of each ad during the ad serving process, and then rank the ads according to the product of CTR and bidding price, thus forming the logic of eCPM-based strategy that prevails in the current auction-based advertising.

After the introduction of CTR to express the relevance, an ecosystem beneficial to advertisers, users, and platforms was formed under the CPC model. In this ecosystem, advertisers can target audiences by selecting keywords, and lower their bids by improving ad creatives and increasing CTRs. Google increases revenue by placing ads with high CTRs and high bids. Because of "personalized" advertising, search engine users see more relevant paid information, and a high click rate reduces the interference of advertising on the user.

With higher relevance, advertisers will be able to win more clicks at a lower price, so they have an incentive to increase CTR with more precise terms and better creatives. In 2013, the revenue of Google websites in Google financial report reached US$37.4 billion,[2] which mainly came from Google AdWords.

2 Note that this is based on the Google global market, which is even close to the US total online advertising revenue in Table 1.1.

For simplicity, the AdWords herein is a past product category of Google. Currently, Google has unified the demand-side entrance of its display advertising network and mobile advertising network into AdWords, in an aim to create a universal marketplace for advertisers and facilitate the optimization of unified effect tracking, which is actually an important trend of advertising products oriented to the demand-side interface.

II. **Taobao express**

In contrast to AdWords – an advertising product available for general search engines, Taobao Express, which is developed by a C2C e-commerce company Taobao, is a special advertising product oriented to sellers. As shown in Figure 5.7, Taobao Express mainly appears on the search results page of Taobao website. Since there is a notable difference between the search result display and general search engine, their corresponding advertising display also differs greatly. In Figure 5.7, the ads only appear on the east foot and south foot of the page.

Taobao Express was used to be known as Yahoo! Express; at that time sellers were able to place ads on both Yahoo! search engine and website. It was renamed as Taobao Express in 2008. At the beginning, the ad ranking rules were very simple, high-bid advertisers won ad placement opportunities. Later, Taobao improved its advertising strategy and began to adopt the eCPM ranking similar to AdWords. Compared with the previous ad ranking, the CTR of the ads was relatively higher, which increased the conversion rate of sellers. And the increase in CTR had generated more revenue for Taobao, thus forming a win-win landscape.

Unlike general search engines – their advertisers are distributed in different industries – the advertisers of Taobao Express are constituted by the sellers on the Taobao platform. There is a symbiotic relationship between Taobao and its advertisers, which enables Taobao to exert a greater influence on its advertisers and boasts obvious advantages in the following aspects:

(1) Advertisers can promote single products and directly reuse the pictures, descriptions, and other information of the products, without producing creative for advertising channel, therefore it only takes a small additional cost for small- and medium-sized sellers to use Taobao Express.

(2) Since the site search is closely related to user purchase intention, the advertising effect is very satisfying.

(3) Taobao understands the entire conversion process of its advertisers; as a result, Taobao Express is highly skilled in optimizing the advertising system (e.g., conversion estimation and synchronization of goods on/off shelves) with follow-up data, much better than the ordinary search ads.

FIGURE 5.7 Example of Taobao Express advertising.

Therefore, although Taobao Express is only a vertical search engine advertising system, its ecosystem supports most of the revenue and profit of Alibaba – China's largest Internet company – and serves as one of the main monetization channels of Taobao. This example tells that in some high commercial value vertical search engines (e.g., e-commerce, real estate, automobile, and app download), the search advertising system shall be given top priority in monetization of traffic.

5.2 POSITION AUCTION AND MECHANISM DESIGN

The auction-based advertising, with search advertising as its representative, sells ad display opportunities by means of auction. In other words, the advertising system determines who will get the position for a particular ad display according to advertisers' bidding and estimated eCPM. In the closed auction-based advertising market, the bidding is adjusted periodically by advertisers, but in the phase of RTB, advertisers can adjust their bidding in real time for each impression.[3] But with a view to the auction mechanism, there is no essential difference between these two kinds of bidding.

Let's describe the problem of auction-based advertising and introduce some important conclusions from a macro market perspective. As shown in Figure 5.8, suppose there is a group of advertising positions to be occupied, rank these positions according to their empirical value and mark them as $s = 1, 2, \cdots, S$ (S is usually 1 for display ad). In an advertising request, a set of ads $a = 1, 2, \cdots, A$ is available for bidding and the bidding of each ad is marked as $\boldsymbol{b_a}$, and the system places the former S ads with a higher price on the S-th advertising position; this kind of problem is called "position auction." According to the above discussion, when an ad a is placed in position $\boldsymbol{s}$, its expected revenue is expressed as eCPM $r_{as} = \mu_s v_a$. Here we make some assumptions, such as CTR μ is only related to position $\boldsymbol{S}$, and click value $\boldsymbol{v}$ only related to ad a, which does not affect the discussion on the macro auction-based advertising market.

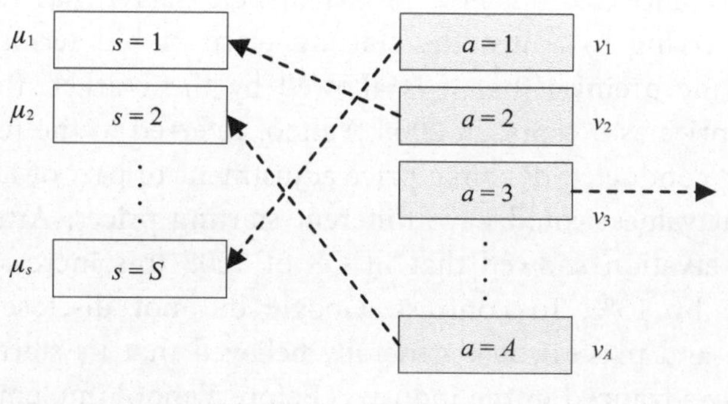

FIGURE 5.8 Example of position auction.

3 RTB is to be introduced in Chapter 6.

The design of major mechanisms for the position auction problem has a huge impact on the revenue, stability, and fairness of the whole auction market. This problem is referred to as the mechanism design problem. The common mechanism design problems in advertising include pricing, market reserve price, and price squeeze.

5.2.1 Market Reserve Price

In order to control the quality of ads and maintain a certain unit price for sale, the auction-based advertising market often sets a minimum price to win the auction position, and this price is called "market reserve price" (MRP) or commonly known as "starting price" or "reserve price." Advertisers cannot win the auction unless their bidding is above the MRP; besides, after winning an auction position, if their planned price is lower than the MRP (such situation is likely to take place with a view to the general "second price"), they shall adjust it up to level with the MRP.

Determining the MRP is an important product strategy for the auction-based advertising. If the MRP is set too low or too high, it will be no good for maximizing the profit the whole market. Generally speaking, when the competition is sufficient and the advertisers are fairly reasonable, the MRP can be set relatively high; otherwise, it should be appropriately adjusted down. There are two ways to set the MRP: one is to implement the same reserve price to the whole auction-based advertising; the other one is to set different reserve prices according to the characteristics of diverse objects (e.g., the terms in search ads). When adopting the second approach, we have to set a higher MRP for the more competitive terms.

There is another key point in the practice of search advertising: although the ads in north foot and east foot share the same bidding queue, in order to guarantee better monetization of the prime position at the north foot, we usually set a higher MRP for the north foot ads.

There are some theoretical studies and practical methods on how to calculate the optimal MRP. To put it simply, the optimal starting price of a particular term is only related to the distribution of bidding price and quality degree. By fitting the distribution that is truncated by the MRP, the optimal starting price can be solved with a theoretical calculation formula. Since the business model of paid search has taken shape, search engines have been trying to adjust the starting price of bid terms to improve their profitability under the premise that it is allowed by the market. In 2001, Yahoo! set a uniform starting price as 5 cents. In 2008, Yahoo! referred to the results of theoretical derivation and then conducted dynamic price adjustment to part of its search terms: the terms with different values would have different starting prices. After this adjustment, the continuous observation showed that in Q3 of 2008 this increase in starting price raised the revenue by 13%. In contrast, Google did not disclose its starting price calculation method and process; it is generally believed that its starting price formulation strategy is fairly advanced in the industry. Before Yahoo! implemented the dynamic pricing, researchers had found that Google's starting price was also dynamic.

Whether it is to adjust the overall MRP of the market or dynamically set MRP for different traffic allocation, the basic principle is to find a CPM reserve price with no significant decrease in filling rate according to the eCPM distribution of bidding advertisers, and then invert the CPC reserve price based on the quality degree. In fact, considering the quality degree, the dynamic reserve price can be related to all of the three parameters (*a*, *u*, *c*) at the same time to achieve complete dynamic performance. Readers may consult with reference [7] to find more literatures about the dynamic MRP theories and algorithms [7].

5.2.2 Pricing Problem

Pricing mechanism is of the foremost importance in position auction. It discusses how to charge a right price for an ad that wins an advertising position through auction, based on given bidding price of advertisers and their expected revenue.

The discussion about pricing sounds unnecessary at first, isn't it okay to charge based on an advertiser's bidding? To explain the motivation for this discussion, let's firstly look at some examples: suppose there is an advertising position ($S = 1$) for sale, Advertiser A offers 1 yuan and Advertiser *B* offers 2 yuan, then *A* wins this bidding and he/she shall pay 2 yuan for this position in case the MRP prevails. In the advertising market, this auction opportunity will appear repeatedly (corresponding to the demand for constant display), so advertisers have the opportunity to adjust their bid. Assuming that B wins the position with an offer price at 2 yuan, he/she may think that is it possible to lower the bid and obtain the traffic with a lower cost? *B* will keep lowering the bid until it drops to 1.01 yuan and finds that he would miss the position if he/she keeps doing so. So the pricing is finally stabilized at 1 yuan from A and 1.01 yuan from *B*. Now suppose that another advertiser *C* enters the competition and hopes to win the position, and then by that analogy, *C* will offer a price at 1.02 yuan through multiple adjustment, then the market revenue is also 1.02 yuan. Is it possible to adjust the pricing strategy in an aim to affect the total revenue of the system? The answer is yes. For example, if *A* bids 2 yuan and B bids 1 yuan, we do not charge *B* for the bidding of 2 yuan, but charge the bidding of 1 yuan to the next bidder (i.e., *C*), and then *A* has no incentive to lower his/her bid. When Advertiser *D* joins in the auction, he/she has to bid more than 2 yuan to win the auction, and then the market revenue will also become 2 yuan, no matter how much *C* offers, we will charge Advertiser *A* (the one next to *C*). This simple example shows that in an auction environment where participants such as advertisers can keep adjusting their bids for the same object, it is fully possible to create higher revenue and better market stability for the whole market through smart pricing strategies.

When concerning the pricing problem, the micro-level intuition may not be translated to the macro-level market. With a view to the entire market, we need to study the benefits and other characteristics that maintain market stability. The so-called stability refers to that the whole bidding system is in the Nash Equilibrium, which means that each advertiser gets the most advantageous position through bidding. The Symmetric Nash Equilibrium [8] of a position auction can be expressed by the following formula:

$$\begin{aligned} \mu_s(v_s - q_s) &\geq \mu(v_s - q_t), \forall t > s \\ \mu_s(v_s - q_s) &\geq \mu_t(v_s - q_{t-1}), \forall t < s \end{aligned} \tag{5.1}$$

Where the subscript is somewhat adjusted: v_s denotes the click value of the ad placed in the position s, rather than the click value brought by the position s; q_s denotes the price that the market charges for the ad placed in the position s, i.e., the pricing or the advertiser's single investment. The implications of this equilibrium are easy to understand: for each ad in the bid ranking for position auction, its revenue is higher than that for any other ad. Obviously, in such a state, each ad has reached its optimal state, and the whole system will be stabilized accordingly.

In Formula (5.1) only q_s or the pricing strategy that is subject to adjustment. With the different pricing strategies, the macro-revenue and degree of stability will be different when the market reaches a stable state. Therefore, the main purpose of the research on the macro-nature of the auction market is to find a better pricing strategy to optimize the overall returns. The mathematical analysis of the Nash Equilibrium state of position auction is not introduced in this book. Readers may consult with reference [8] to find relevant materials.

With regard to the auction-based online advertising, the Generalized Second Price (GSP) is most common pricing strategy; while the Vickrey-Clarke-Groves (VCG) pricing strategy is sometimes used.

I. GSP

What is the "second price" [9]? When there is only one position for auction, charge the advertiser that wins this auction at the price of the second advertiser's bid, such kind of auction is also known as "Vickery auction." In the search ads where there are multiple positions for auction, it is easy to intuitively generalize the second price strategy into a strategy like this: no matter which advertiser wins a position, he/she will be charged by the next advertiser's bid, i.e., Generalized Second Price (GSP) [10]. The GSP is the optimal mechanism of social value. In other words, under this mechanism, advertising platforms will allocate advertising opportunities to the advertisers with the highest subsequent return value, rather than the optimal revenue of the platforms. It is understandable that the key to optimal social value is a mechanism that allows advertisers to bid truthfully based on their return value, then the advertisers will be ranked by their bid.

The intuitive plausibility of the second price and the GSP is explained above. But in fact the GSP is not the optimal mechanism for social value during multi-position auction (the optimal strategy is the VCG described below). However, the GSP has the advantages of simple implementation and easy explanation to advertisers, so it has become the most mainstream pricing strategy in the auction-based advertising system.

In case of CPM-based settlement, the GSP can be applied directly. But in the auction-based advertising settled by CPC, the advertisers bid for clicks, while the auction is for eCPM. Therefore, a conversion between the two is needed to achieve the GSP under CPC [10]. The pricing formula is as follows:

$$q_s = \mu_{s+1} b_{s+1} / \mu_s + \Delta \tag{5.2}$$

Multiply both sides of this equation by μ_s, we can find that the GSP remains the second price based on eCPM.

Readers can verify by themselves that, whether it is based on CPM or CPC, in the scenario of the GSP, the pricing will not be higher than the bid of the concerned advertiser. In fact, this pricing strategy is also applicable to the CPS-based auction market, where we only need to replace μ in Formula (5.2) with ν. In this formula, Δ denotes the smallest unit of currency for settlement in the advertising system, such as 1 cent, which is a historical practice and makes advertisers feel more reasonable psychologically.

II. **VCG**

The VCG [9, 11, 12] is an optimal pricing strategy for social value developed by Vickrey, Clarke and Groves when they were studying the equilibrium state of the bidding system. The basic principle is that the cost of an advertiser in winning a position shall be equal to the lost value of other market players. The VCG strategy can be expressed as follows:

$$q_s = \sum_{t>s} (\mu_{t-1} - \mu_t) v_t \tag{5.3}$$

The intuitive logic of this pricing strategy is easy to understand. Through a theoretical analysis, we can find the advantages of the VCG pricing strategy in two aspects: (i) When this strategy is steadily implemented, the rational advertisers will offer a truthful price, i.e., if everyone offers a price based on their own return value, then they will be in their optimal state. (ii) The VCG charges the least in comparison with other pricing strategies. In the case of a single position auction, the VCG will degenerates into the second price.

It can be proved that the VCG is the optimal pricing strategy for social value, i.e., the overall interests of advertising platforms and advertisers reach the maximum. However, when the VCG pricing strategy is implemented, the revenue of advertising platforms is no better than the case of GSP.

The VCG is not a mainstream pricing strategy in auction-based advertising, mainly because the logic of this pricing strategy is too complex to explain to advertisers. In addition, it is difficult to verify whether the media have correctly calculated the "value loss to other market players" when there is a game relationship between advertisers and media. But this pricing strategy has its own market space. Some advertisers, such as Facebook, apply this pricing mechanism to their products.

5.2.3 Squashing

In CPC-based advertising, eCPM can be expressed as the product of CTR and bid, that is, $r = \mu \cdot v = \mu \cdot \text{bid}_{\text{CPC}}$ However, in the mechanism design of bidding, we sometimes make some slight adjustments to this formula, which will turn into the following form:

$$r = \mu^k \text{bid}_{\text{cpc}} \tag{5.4}$$

where k is a real number bigger than 0. We can consider two extreme cases to understand the role of k: when $k \to \infty$, the ranking is only based on CTR regardless of bid; when $k \to \mathbf{0}$, the ranking is only based on bid. Consequently, as $\boldsymbol{k}$ increases, it seems like we are squashing the role of bid in the entire auction system, this factor is called "squashing factor."

The role of the squashing factor is to influence the bidding system to develop toward the demand side more actively in reference to the market situation. For example, if a large number of advertisers offer a higher bid but lower quality, the k value should be raised to highlight the effect of quality and user feedback; if the auction market lacks fierce competition, the k value should be lowered to encourage competition, and such a practice will increase the short-term revenue to deal with the temporary financial pressure. In order to encourage advertisers to improve the quality and relevance of their ads, the $\boldsymbol{k}$ value should be lowered to alleviate the impact of bid.

5.2.4 Myerson Optimal Auction

The second price and VCG are the optimal pricing mechanisms for social value. But in practice, advertising platforms care more about optimization of revenue, that is, the methods for optimizing the value of platforms. This problem is known as the "optimal auction problem." When the auction object is a single and indivisible item, Roger Myerson gives the theoretical optimal mechanism, which is called "Myerson auction" [13].

In Myerson auction, assume that the expected click value v_a of an advertiser is a random variable with probability density function f_a and cumulative distribution function F_a; the advertiser bid is b_a. To simplify this problem, let's assume all candidates ads has the same CTR, in this case, the optimal auction mechanism is described as follows.

(1) Map the advertiser bid to a virtual bid: $b'_a = b_a - [1 - F_a(b_a)]/f_a(b_a)$

(2) Make 0 as the MRP on the virtual bid to filter the bidders.

(3) The virtual bid is priced at the second price and converted back to the real bid for fee deduction.

To sum up, this mechanism does not guarantee that the ranking is based on bid, and sometimes it even rejects all bidders. When f_a is uniformly distributed within [0, 1], this mechanism is equivalent to the second price plus a base price of 0.5. Its function is also intuitively easy to explain. For those large players who are likely to have high expected returns, we will impose some penalty upon them through virtual bidding transformation, so as to stimulate them to offer higher prices.

The Myerson auction affects not only the pricing result, but the ranking result, it is hard to explain to advertisers its fairness; therefore, the major advertising platforms, although more or less adopt the idea of the Myerson auction (e.g., impose somewhat price discrimination upon the buyers with strong bidding ability), rarely employ the form of the Myerson auction as the market rules. Of course, even if some platforms do use a similar mechanism, they won't admit it in public.

5.2.5 Examples of Pricing Results

We hereby use a specific example to intuitively illustrate the above integrated bidding and pricing process: assume that a group of ads competing for several search advertising positions, their bid and estimated CTR[4] are shown in the second and third columns in Table 5.2, the calculated eCPM and the prices based on the GSP pricing strategy with different ***k*** values are also shown in the table.[5] The figures in Table 5.2 tell that the CPC pricing based on the GSP is not in descending order and may be lower than the MRP (such as the ad ranking the third place), in this case, it is necessary to set the price at the MRP compulsively; the ***k*** value has obvious influence on both ranking and pricing.

Those who want to learn more about the implementation of the ad bidding/pricing process may refer to the sample code in Section 13.1. As for the price charged to each advertiser according to the VCG pricing strategy, readers can explore by themselves.

5.3 AUCTION-BASED ADN

While the bidding mechanism in search advertising becomes gradually mature, it has been widely used in the domain of display advertising. As for display ads, the agreement-based sales cannot consume all of the traffic inventory. In order to control the sales proportion and obtain a higher brand premium, there is rich advertising traffic not sold by the agreement, this part of the traffic is known as the "remnant inventory." The emergence of auction-based trade provides an opportunity for monetization of this part of traffic, and triggers the emergence of ADN. The function of ADN is to aggregate the remnant inventory of various media in batch and sell it to advertisers by means of traffic segmentation based on user or contextual tags.

TABLE 5.2 Ad bidding and pricing process based on the GSP pricing

Bid	**CTR (%)**	**Ranking/pricing (k = 1.0)**	**Ranking/pricing (k = 2.5)**	**Ranking/pricing (k = 0.5)**
0.80	1.6	1/0.50	1/0.25	2/0.25
2.00	0.4	2/0.75	3/0.70	1/1.60
0.30	1.0	3/0.25	2/0.25	3/0.28
0.40	0.5	4/0.25	4/0.25	4/0.25

Unit: yuan, MRP=0.25

4 The CTR here is only suggestive since it only takes account of the influence of position and other factors.
5 The Δ in Formula (5.2) in pricing is omitted in the calculation.

For some small- and medium-sized media, they don't have any traffic for agreement-based advertising; instead, the monetization of their ad spaces is subject to the ADN (see an example of the ADN in Figure 5.9, the parts marked by wireframe are monetized by the ADN).

As for the ADN in mobile apps, the most common forms include banner ad and interstitial ad. But in recent years, the mobile ADN has shown a native development trend (see Chapter 8). The following subsection mainly introduces the product logic of ADN in decision-making.

5.3.1 Forms of ADN Products

Generally speaking, the decision-making process in ADN is similar to a black box for media: we only need to call the ADN's ad serving code or SDK on the remnant traffic, and do not care about the results of each impression. In the actual operation, the ADN is available for both auction-based and agreement-based sales, but the former will be our focus.

The product logic of the auction-based ADN is shown in Figure 5.10. The key to the products here is that the target of sales are the audience segments, while the ad spaces are diluted. The content in Chapter 4 tells that it is difficult for agreement-based advertising to dilute the ad space. In addition, when the traffic meets the requirements of multiple advertising campaigns simply adopt the bidding model and do not think about the quantity constraints.

The ADN products come from two sources based on different models of audience segmentation: (i) Some of them are the contextual advertising products developed by search engines, i.e., the ad serving according to the terms extracted from the page. (ii) Some of them are based on the refined interest tags derived from display ads. Both the contextual tags and interest tags are for the purpose of audience targeting, so they are classified as the ADN products.

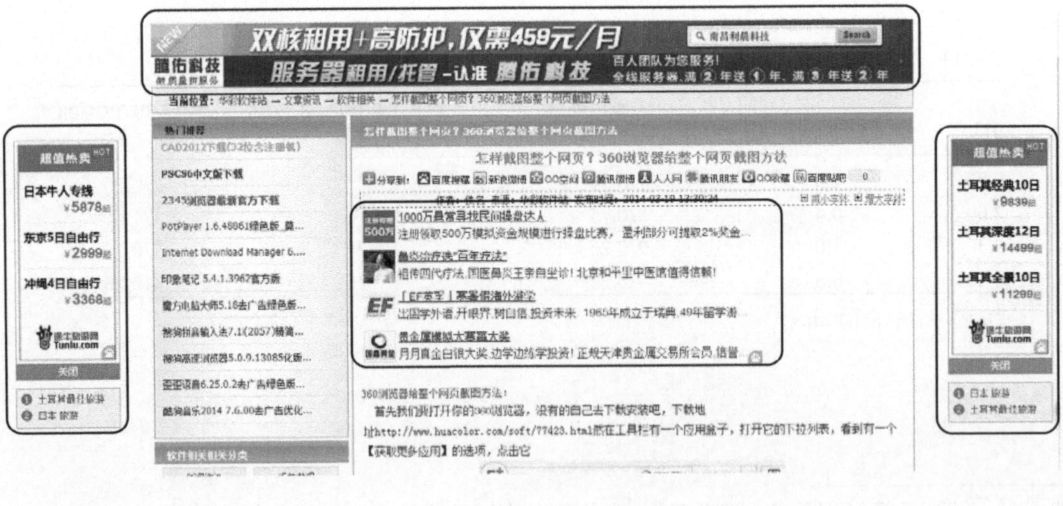

FIGURE 5.9 Example of ADN.

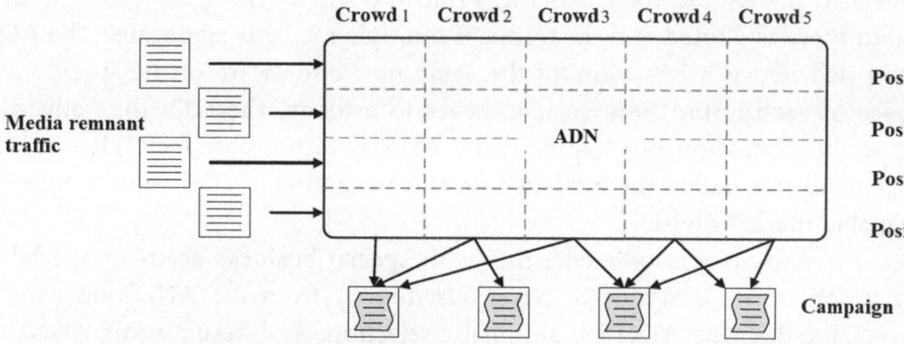

FIGURE 5.10 Examples of ADN products.

The auction-based ADN has the following key features:

(1) The bidding is based on the monetization ability of advertisers, i.e., each display opportunity is allocated to an advertiser based on eCPM, instead of based on the quantity constraint. Unlike the agreement-based advertising, in the auction-based ADN, there is little necessity to design sophisticated online allocation algorithms to guarantee execution of agreement, the computing techniques will concentrate on the estimation of eCPM.

(2) Based on audience segmentation, the ADN downplays the significance of media and ad space. As such, it is difficult for the ADN to get the ad spaces with high brand premium, making it generally not suitable for brand advertisers.

(3) From a business perspective, compared with the agreement-based sales, the ADN does not need to meet the requirement for exclusivity of brand advertisers, but let Gome and Suning – Chinese appliance sales giants – bid for the advertising displays oriented to the same audience segment concurrently, thus making it possible to improve market liquidity, which is difficult to do in agreement-based advertising.

(4) The settlement in the ADN is based on actual consumption, so advertisers usually pay for the ad serving in advance, which is different from the agreement-based advertising where the settlement is done after the ad serving, such practice has greatly improved the cash flow situation of the ADN operators.

There are different settlement methods in the ADN, such as CPM, CPC and CPS, but the most mainstream one is CPC. It is necessary to analyze the rationality of CPC from the perspective of computation: (i) From the demand-side perspective, since different advertising positions of various media are sold together, advertisers cannot know the specific ad space on each media. Position is of great significance in ad exposure, so it's virtually impossible for advertisers to evaluate the bid per display, and this awkwardness will be alleviated if they bid for clicks. (ii) From the supply-side perspective, since the concept of ad space is diluted and the traffic of multiple media is aggregated, the ADN is accessible to rich network behaviors of the same user and aware of the specific media and ad space of each impression, so it is easier to estimate the CTR than advertisers. According to the discussion in Chapter 1, the ADN is responsible for CTR estimation, while the demand side makes the bid based on the estimation of click value, which is the most reasonable market division.

However, for some media or media mix with special business needs or special data sources, it is sometimes desirable to select ads directly from the AND's ad bank and create more value than the ADN-led automatic selection. As a result, some ADNs open their ad bank to their partner suppliers for their selection such operational model of ADN is known as "affiliate."

5.3.2 Product Strategy for ADN

Compared with search advertising, the advertising decision-making process in the ADN is simpler, as shown in Figure 5.11. It is divided into several stages, such as retrieval, ranking and pricing. Although the process is relatively simple, the ad retrieval and ad ranking in the ADN are different from that of search advertising, and there are also some challenges in its product strategy.

I. **Ad retrieval**

Advertising and search actually deal with different documents, the former often employs a Boolean Expression to describe the ad serving conditions, rather than a simple word set. The word set-based retrieval in search is not the most efficient for Boolean expressions. In the case of search advertising, this problem is not prominent, but in the display ADN, such a difference is worth of attention.

Search advertising retrieval is basically consistent with search; the conventional inverted index is enough to solve this problem. Unlike search advertising, the display advertising does not have clear user intention, we usually need more terms and interest tags for the retrieval at the same time, and the practice has proved more tags can directly improve the advertising effect. Using lots of tags for a single search is also very

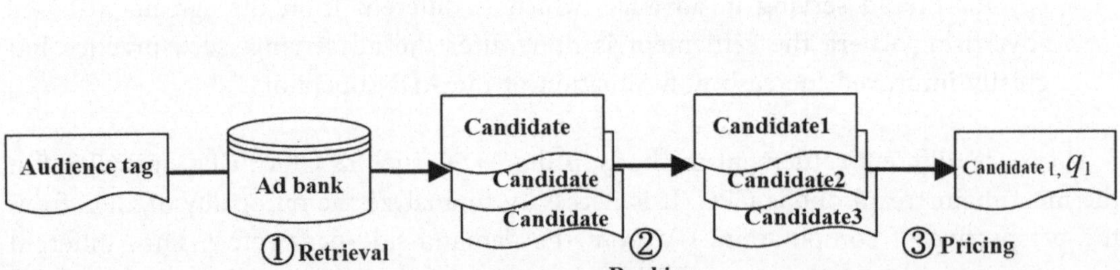

FIGURE 5.11 Decision-making process in auction-based ADN.

different from the short query in search, which can be described as a relevance search problem requiring exploration of specialized methods.

The above two problems are mainly related to specific algorithms, which will be discussed in detail in Chapter 13.

II. **Ad ranking**

It is known that the ranking criterion in auction-based advertising is eCPM, and in the case of CPC settlement, the estimation of eCPM turns into the estimation of CTR. It should be said that in search advertising and display advertising – both auction-based advertising products, the problem of CTR prediction encounters a real challenge.

Compared with the search advertising with more regular ad spaces and higher CTR, the CTR prediction in the ADN has two aspects of difficulties: (i) The click data are more sparse and the context and user information need to be considered at the same time, which makes the cold start of various new ads and new policies a prominent problem. How to design a reasonable and feasible cold start strategy is very important for the display network. (ii) There are great differences in ad spaces in the ADN, and the change range of CTR is very large, which makes it relatively difficult to estimate the CTR robustly. When we discuss CTR estimation techniques later, we will focus on the complex scenarios of display advertising and compare them with the specific cases of search advertising.

5.3.3 Product Cases

The actual ADN has two different lines of business: (i) To undertake a wide range of advertising inventory, and provide service to the advertisers with all categories of products, we call it a "horizontal ADN." (ii) Dedicated to serving a certain type of advertisers (such as e-commerce and games), and looking for relevant media resources to build a network, we call it "vertical ADN." Some examples are listed below to illustrate these two types of ADN.

I. **Google Display Network**

Google Display Network

The AdSense is the first advertising product that marks Google accessed to the display advertising. Unlike the AdWords that only uses terms to target audiences, the AdSense boasts diverse targeting approaches: it is able to identify the webpages through a series of terms or topics, and target audiences with such attributes as interest, gender and historical access information or with a combination of these targeting conditions; therefore, advertisers are able to choose the webpages or audience more accurately as they like. Compared with the AdWords, the AdSense enables advertisers to access to more webpages and traffic.

Despite of the differences in targeted audience, the AdSense and AdWords are basically the same in their bidding process and both of their ads are ranked by eCPM. In its targeting and bidding processes, the AdSense has an additional participant of websites (i.e., the media), in contrast to the AdWords which only has Google, advertisers, and users. In the AdSense ecosystem, the media will adjust the ad spaces and formats or add appropriate terms to pages to attract more similar varieties of ads so as to increase CTR. Advertisers can choose the right targeting conditions and bid to raise CTR. Under this mechanism, users will see more relevant ads and the platforms will have better benefits.

After the AdSense, in 2008 Google bought DoubleClick – a giant in display advertising. Through integration of some advertising resources including Utunbe, Google Finance and AdSense, Google Display Network (GDN) was launched, becoming one of the most important products in the field of display advertising. From the AdSense – a derivative product of search advertising – to the independent GDN, Google attaches great importance to display advertising and is determined to develop this business independently. The downstream business of GDN includes DoubleClick ADX and some TDs. The advertising platform will transfer the low-bid traffic to DoubleClick ADX for RTB, making some long-tail traffic likely to be sold at a higher price, while TD will buy traffic from multiple ADX and optimize ROI. Currently, the GDN is the largest display advertising network in the world, reaching 90% of the Internet users and over 2 million websites.

In its 2013 financial report, Google pointed out that the revenue of Google network members' websites reached US$13.1 billion.

5.4 DEMAND-SIDE PRODUCTS IN AUCTION-BASED ADVERTISING

Although search advertising and auction-based ADN are greatly different in their effect, their products are similar in essence. The emergence of auction-based ADN presents new requirements for the demand-side technologies: the original purchase based on display quantity agreement directly signed with the media will turn into the purchase based on auction to satisfy the quantity and quality demand of advertisers. Specifically, such a new purchase model shall have a basic function: cross-media and one-stop purchase based on the advertiser budget. In addition, there may be an advanced function as the ROI optimization enabled by machine-based decision-making.

Such requirement gives rise to two basic problems: one is how to select the right target group, and the other one is how to offer a right price to each target group. Since the decision-making process in the auction-based advertising platform is a "black box" for the demand side, it is not easy to solve these two problems.

5.4.1 Search Engine Marketing

The demand-side product corresponding to search advertising is Search Engine Marketing (SEM), i.e., to launch promotions by purchasing the search engine terms through bidding. The above-said two basic problems respectively correspond to the term selection and bidding in SEM. With regard to SEM, the traffic of each tag (i.e., term) does not overlap with each other, which is different from the complex Boolean operation that can be done between the audience targeting tags in display advertising, and seems more direct than user tag optimization.

Neither term selection nor bidding is an easy job. Let's firstly look at term selection. If advertisers provide some seed words, then this problem looks like the query expansion problem detailed in Subsection 5.1.3, but there is also a significant difference: search engine query expansion is to improve their own revenue; the demand side chooses terms for increasing the ROI of advertisers' traffic purchase. These two goals are obviously greatly different; advertisers prefer to trust SEM which represents the interests of the demand side. However, considering the data sources, SEM needs long-term data accumulation to achieve better results. At the same time, for a large number of long-term small advertisers, it is often difficult to accumulate enough data for optimization, so this kind of SEM companies mainly provide service medium and above advertisers.

As for the problem of bidding, the traditional knowledge is that advertisers estimate the click value based on the reach rate and conversion rate on their own webpages and per customer transaction, and then offer a bid in reference to this click value. However, one problem is ignored: the conversion rate per customer transaction and market competition of each term is notably different; given this, only by making different bids for different terms can the ROI of the overall acquisition be further optimized. Because the targeting granularity of search advertising is very fine, it can be seen that term selection and bidding are large-scale optimization problems, and because of the semi-closed bidding mechanism of ADN, the data feedback and adjustment are not timely enough, so the technical challenge of this optimization problem is relatively big.

5.4.2 Trading Desk

The one-stop shopping platform facing the ADN and DSP is known as "trading desk" (TD), which may be classified with the media-buying platform into the same type of product.

From the perspective of market development, many TDs are subsidiaries acquired or incubated by 4A or agency companies to adapt to the changes on market landscape and technologies, which can be seen from the connection line between the two products in Figure 1.15. In the auction-based advertising market, the display quantity demand of advertisers still exists. Therefore, the display quantity agreement does not disappear, it no longer exists between agents and media, but between advertisers and media-buying platform.

5.4.3 Product Cases

For non-RTB advertising products, it is difficult to optimize the demand side, so they are mainly developing in SEM with a high ROI. We hereby take an example of SEM product for your reference.

EfficientFrontier™

Efficient Frontier (EF) was used to be an ad-tech company specialized in SEM optimization and later extends to the field of optimization of display ADN. In 2011, EF was bought by Adobe's Omniture at a price of US$400 million as part of the "Adobe digital market suite," known as "Adobe adlens." At the time of acquisition, EF was managing a search engine advertising budget of over US$600 million a year and more than 40 million search terms, with an average of more than 40,000 bids per customer per day.

Looking at the name of EF, we can get a general idea of the technical direction of this company. Their business is to optimize ROI for search advertisers based on a large number of terms through term selection and bidding. EF solves these two problems with the "portfolio selection" approach [14] which is popular in finance. And the phrase "efficient frontier" itself is a financial term. This problem is to identify the investment proportion of each variety in a portfolio through calculation, so as to minimize the risks under the circumstance of an optimal ROI. At each level of expected ROI, the curve that corresponds to the portfolio with minimum risk is called the "efficient frontier."

If the object in search ads (i.e., terms) is analogous to stocks, then the investment allocated to each term with certain budget limit shall try to fulfill an optimal overall ROI, its problematic framework is quite similar to the above portfolio problem. Thus, EF creatively developed a large-scale term bid optimization technology by combining the portfolio theory of quantitative finance with computational advertising technology. There is an example of efficient frontier in Figure 5.12, where each dot represents an ad placement setting, i.e., the term combination and its bid, and each combination corresponds to a revenue and cost. Connect the ad serving setting with the maximum revenue corresponding to each cost, then there will be an efficient frontier curve. With this efficient frontier curve and a given advertiser budget, we can determine an optimal ad serving strategy. When the number of optional terms is very large, the term combinations for ad serving setting are considerably large, and coupled with the non-real-time data feedback of search engines, there is great difficulty in solving this optimization problem.

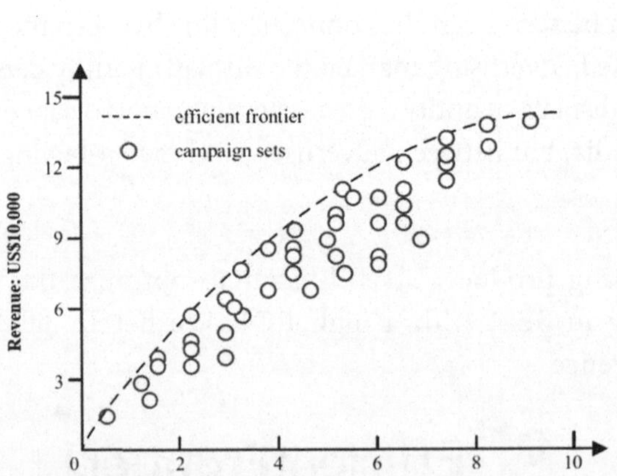

FIGURE 5.12 Example of "efficient frontier" in SEM.

The problem of optimizing advertising revenue is actually more complex than optimizing stock returns because advertising revenue is ROI and both the CTR and click value estimation are heavily dependent on data. As such, the accumulation of data is actually the core competitiveness of EF. So it becomes justifiable that EF was bought by Adobe's Omniture to gain more data to enhance its competitiveness, because Omniture is specialized in supplying web analytics tools, and it has accumulated a large amount of site behavior data, which is very valuable for optimizing ROI.

In addition to SEM, Adobe Adlens has also started the business of optimizing display ads in Facebook, because its technology is universal for display and search ads – the two are essentially the same from an ADN product perspective.

5.5 COMPARISON BETWEEN AUCTION-BASED AND AGREEMENT-BASED ADVERTISING

After learning about the two main types of advertising transactions – auction-based and agreement-based advertising, let's compare their advantages and disadvantages.

From the perspective of supply side or advertising market, the comparison between auction-based and agreement-based advertising is in analogy with the comparison between planned economy and market economy. In the case of agreement-based advertising, the display quantity and quality optimization are subject to the ad servers of media; in the case of auction-based advertising, the market is only responsible for developing the bidding and charging rules, the fulfillment of display quantity is subject to market competition. In this case, the market side shall carefully develop a macro-competition mechanism, but there is no need for any transaction-level scheduling as in the agreement-based advertising.

From the perspective of demand side, the purchase of agreement-based advertising is lack of transparency for advertisers. The only thing to do is to agree on some of the most concerned interest terms in the agreement in advance, but it is difficult to make in-depth optimization. However, such kind of purchase has certain benefits, in particular the quantity can be guaranteed in advance, which is more meaningful for the brand advertising campaigns.

In the auction-based advertising, the agreement between the supply side and the advertiser is relatively loose: the supply side no longer promises the ad serving quantity to the advertiser; accordingly, the unit click price is at discretion of the advertiser. Owing to such transaction logic, the advertising agreement no longer prioritizes the display quantity but firstly makes sure of the cost. This is actually a very revolutionary change, which makes the advertising market present a development trend that is conducive to greatly improving the advertising effect.

(1) A very sophisticated audience targeting can be used in transactions without hindrance, which is hard to do with in agreement-based advertising. Because of this, the efficiency of the advertising market has been greatly improved.

(2) A large number of small- and medium-sized advertisers gradually become the main body of bidding, which makes the market scale expand rapidly.

(3) Compared with agreement-based advertising, the data value in auction-based advertising is highlighted, and the whole market starts to organize and operate advertising products with data as the core.

CHAPTER 6

Programmatic Trade Advertising

By the time when the auction-based online advertising has come out, a computing landscape has taken shape in the main, and most important products and technologies have emerged and been studied. However, the demand is increasingly stricter with the optimization effect of advertising and the product forms of ADN can no longer fully satisfy the demand, while the development tendency of the market is to completely open to the demand. To be specific, advertisers are ought to buy ads based on the defined user segment, choose traffic on their own and offer a price independently for each impression. To perform such a function, ad request, offering, and bidding shall be implemented during the impression, thus giving rise to a programmatic trade market with real-time bidding (RTB) as its core. The position of programmatic trade products in the entire evolutionary process of advertising is shown in Figure 6.1.

Upon the emergence of RTB, the advertising market has incubated an open bidding platform, which is called the ad exchange (ADX). Its main feature is to use RTB to get the candidate ads in real time and make the ad serving decision by following the bidding procedure. The buyer platform corresponding to ADX is the demand-side platform (DSP). In the programmatic trade market, the ability of the demand side to select and control the traffic has reached perfection, which is quite a challenge to the relevant technologies and algorithms.

With regard to the demand side, the function of customized user segmentation enables advertisers to optimize ad purchase like they optimize their own recommendation systems, with the only difference being that it is an off-site recommendation system. The product demand at dynamic bid and the arbitrage within the budget of advertisers require the DSP to have the computational ability of CTR prediction, click value estimation, traffic forecasting, and off-site recommendation. In addition to off-site recommendation, the new technological development trend is to find potential users with similar behaviors based on the seed users of advertisers and the media data. Such

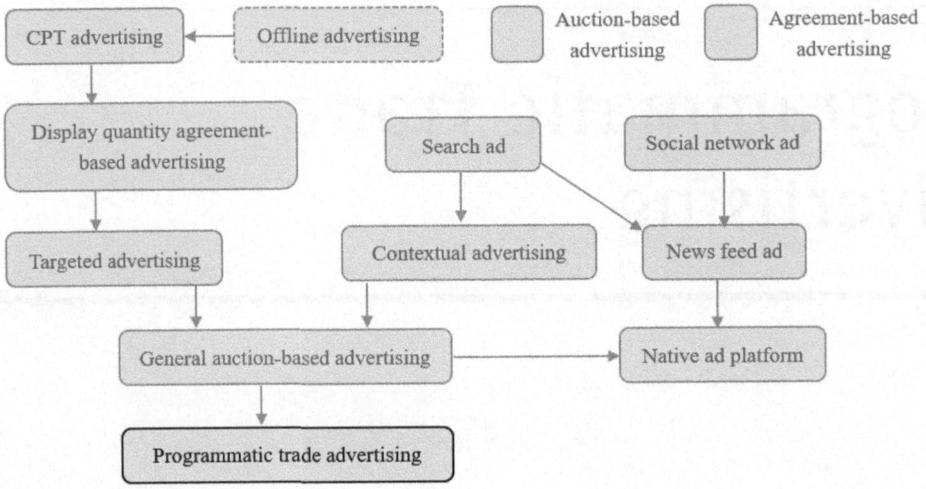

FIGURE 6.1 Programmatic trade advertising.

targeting methods are all customized user segmentation for the combination of (a, u), which makes the audience targeting accuracy reach a new level.

After the demand-side interests are fully guaranteed, the monetization means for the media have also changed accordingly. At present, there are at least four advertising monetization models for the media: agreement-based sales, self-run auction-based ADN, integrated ADN, and RTB. The demand pain point of the supply side is to choose the model that is the best in monetization and interest maximization. Driven by such a demand, such product as the SSP that optimizes the benefits of media has come into being.

In addition to the changes on trading patterns, the programmatic trade has spawned another important market: data processing and trading market. The open trading model allows advertisers to freely use a variety of data to guide their advertising campaigns, and the RTB provides a natural infrastructure for the derivative data transactions. Therefore, in the era of programmatic trade, data processing and trading has been experiencing scale development. The two key products of data processing and trading – ADX and DMP – provide valuable data sources or data processing services for the market based on the third-party and first-party data, respectively. A knowledge of the data transaction logic in advertising is of great guiding significance for the big data monetization in various industries.

Along with the continuous development of online advertising, the programmatic trade has become a decisive force that makes the whole online advertising market move more and more toward a data-driven and computing-oriented direction. In this chapter, we will summarize several main modes of programmatic trade and their corresponding supply-/demand-side products, and compare them with the agreement-based sales.

6.1 RTB

Let's firstly have an intuitive idea of why advertising trade is moving toward RTB. Although the audience targeting in the auction-based ADN is fairly accurate, it seems useless in certain scenarios: an advertiser wants to organize an advertising campaign to its lost users; an advertiser expects an advertising platform to find potential users with similar behaviors to their existing users. Obviously, it is impossible to complete these kinds of tasks no matter how to choose the existing audience tags in the ADN. In fact, the two tasks have a common feature: we need to use advertisers' own data in audience selection. Such an audience tag is referred to as "customized audience segmentation."

The ad serving with customized audience segmentation is not completely infeasible in the traditional ADN: when there is the need for retargeting – the most common scenario – ADN may lay out codes or uses SDK in the advertiser website, collect crowd data, or deliver ads; for the general customized segmentation, the advertiser may upload the user ID set (cookie or mobile device ID), and then the ADN will make decisions for ad serving, just like the advertising products of Facebook. Yet there are still some problems with this approach.

(1) The number of customized tags is directly proportional to the magnitude of the advertiser; given this, the centralized processing and use of these tags by an advertising platform is obviously an inefficient solution.

(2) In addition to the customized audience database, the demand side often has comprehensive decision-making requirements for many factors such as frequency, time, and region, where the simple uploading of the user ID set cannot achieve such a purpose.

(3) Simple crowd library interactions are not enough for sophisticated bidding and budget control.

Therefore, the use of ADN, which is a closed bidding solution, is unable to implement the ad serving based on customized tags on a large scale and refined manner. What kind of solution makes more sense? In fact, it is very simple; as long as the bidding process is open, let the demand side decide the bidding during the ad display, then this problem will be solved. Such a train of thought has generated RTB. So we have drawn up the following conclusion:

The crucial purpose of RTB is to implement ad serving under guidance of customized audience segmentation.

The RTB not only frees up the demand for relevant response advertising, but creates new opportunities for brand advertising. As we know, the core of brand advertising lies in its audience targeting strategy, but irrespective of agreement-based or auction-based advertising, the audiences segments are defined by the advertising platform, and the demand side has little freedom to process it. However, in case of RTB, the DSP can process the data about a specific audience segment for an advertiser according to various data bought from the market, so as to reach the crowd that is more consistent with its market strategy. As a result, we find that the budget for brand advertising is largely absent in the ADN, but shifting toward programmatic trade. In Table 6.1, we list the size and growth of the US RTB market.[1] The data show that RTB has become a very important part of the display advertising market and is still growing at a high speed. The data about Chinese advertising market is omitted due to the confused understanding about RTB.

6.1.1 RTB Process

The product interface of RTB is divided into two processes (see Figure 6.2): (i) the cookie mapping process for corresponding the user ID of ADX and DSP; (ii) the bidding and ad serving process for ad call.

(1) User ID mapping (cookie mapping): When both the supply and demand sides can get the same user ID, such as the IDFA or Android ID in mobile devices, this mapping process is not required. However, in case of ad serving based on cookies in the Web environment, this mapping process is inevitable. Cookie mapping is generally initiated by DSP on the advertiser website, and the reason for this is that DSP is responsible for processing advertisers' customized audience tags, so there is no need to map all users. The mapping process is further divided into the following two steps:

TABLE 6.1 Developments in the US RTB market

Year	2010	2011	2012	2013	2014	2015	2016
Trading volume (bln US$)	0.4	0.99	1.95	3.36	4.55	5.78	7.06
YoY growth (%)	-	149	98	72	36	27	22
Share in display ads (%)	4	8	13	19	22	25	28

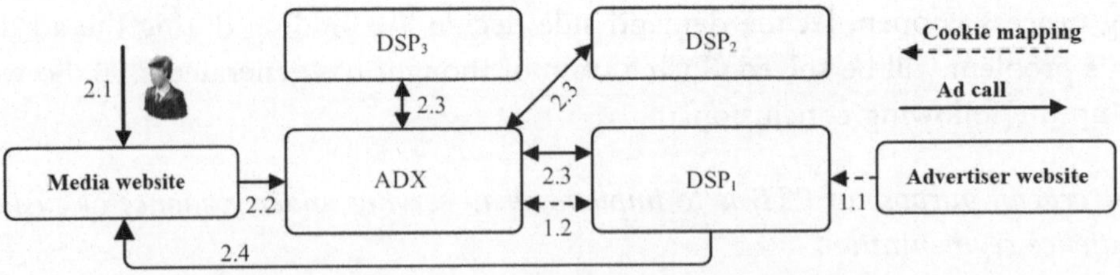

FIGURE 6.2 Process of RTB.

1 Data source: www.eMarketer.com.

Step 1.1: initiate a cookie mapping request from the advertiser website to the DSP server.

Step 1.2: the communication between DSP and ADX servers completes cookie mapping. Since the application of cookie mapping technology is not limited to RTB, we will discuss it in detail in Chapter 15 when we introduce RTB.

(2) Ad call: the ad call in RTB is further divided into the following three steps:

Step 2.1: when a user contacts the advertising position of the media website, the front-end will initiate an ad call to ADX.

Step 2.2: ADX transfers the URL (or application ID) and user ID to each DSP and initiates an ad request. In the case of a Web environment, the DSP will also look up the corresponding user ID based on cookie mapping, then the DSP will decide whether to bid based on the data, and if so, calculate and return to its own bid. After waiting for a fixed time slot, ADX will pick out the DSP with the highest bid and return it to the media site.

Step 2.3: the media site gets the ad creative from the winning DSP and displays it.

Steps 2.2 and 2.3 can be combined into one step, i.e., DSP returns both the ex-works price and the creative advertising address, which is returned to the media by ADX. This has the advantage of reducing a round trip to the server and reducing the delay of seeing ads. The disadvantage is that ADX can obtain the relevant audience data of an advertiser in DSP, so there is a risk of information leakage, which is not in line with ADX's neutral market position.

Both of these means have been applied in actual products. The RTB gives advertisers the maximum select space for traffic, presents higher requirements for the system, and brings some practical problems:

(1) Each presentation involves ADX server and multiple DSP servers, which greatly increase the cost of server and bandwidth. It can be easily calculated that if the size of each ad call is 1KB, 5,000 ad calls are generated per second, and each ad call is sent to 10 DSPs, then the bandwidth shall reach 400Mbit/s, yet it is only a small size for ADX.

(2) In the process of ad request, ADX has to wait for an agreed time slice (generally about 100ms), which increases the delay of ads and has a negative impact on CTR. However, in the case of the mobile app advertising, the impact of this problem is less significant since the customer can cache advertising creative.

(3) In principle, DSP can participate in the bidding at a very low price, so as to obtain the user behavior data of the media at a low cost although the traffic allocation is unavailable, yet there is a potential risk of information leakage.

There are two recipients of RTB's interface: the one at the side of ADX is known as the "RTB for demand" (RTBD); the one at the side of DSP is referred to as the "RTB for Supply" (RTBS). The details and parameters of the RTB interface vary greatly among ADXs. It is apparently adverse for advertisers to buy traffic uniformly from different ADXs. In order to solve this problem, after full market research and cooperation with enterprises, the IAB has developed an interface standard known as the "OpenRTB," which covers the RTB problems in video, Wi-Fi, text, banner, and other forms of advertising, and has been adopted by some exchanges. Readers who need further details on RTB execution can refer to this standard.

It should be noted that the "real-time" limit in RTB particularly refers to the process where the demand side joins in each bidding in real time and the supply side compares the bids of different ads. Such situation is also seen in general auction-based advertising. Therefore, we should not regard search ads and ADN as the RTB-based products.

6.2 OTHER MODES OF PROGRAMMED TRADE

After the advent of RTB, the advertising trade has become increasingly dependent on online communication between machines, rather than prearranged or through manual transactions, it is known as programmatic trade. The core purpose of programmatic trade is to allow the demand side to freely choose traffic and bid. In addition to RTB, there are a number of other types of programmatic trade in the market. In the IAB's report, according to the features of inventory and price type, the means of exchange related to programmatic trade are divided into four categories (see Table 6.2):

TABLE 6.2 Summary of IAB on programmatic trade

Means of exchange	Type of inventory	Type of price	Mode of participation	Exemplar terms
Automated guaranteed	Reserved	Fixed Price	One-to-one	**Programmatic direct**, programmatic premium
Unreserved fixed rate	Unreserved	Fixed Price	One-to-one	**Preferred deals**, private access, first right of refusal
Invitation-only auction	Unreserved	Bidding	One-to-few	**Private marketplace**, private auction, closed auction, private access
Open auction	Unreserved	Bidding	One-to-more	**Real-time bidding (RTB)**, open exchange, open marketplace

6.2.1 Preferred Deal

Preferred deal (PD) was born earlier than RTB. It can be seen as a programmatic trade only with demand side, see its trading process in Figure 6.3.

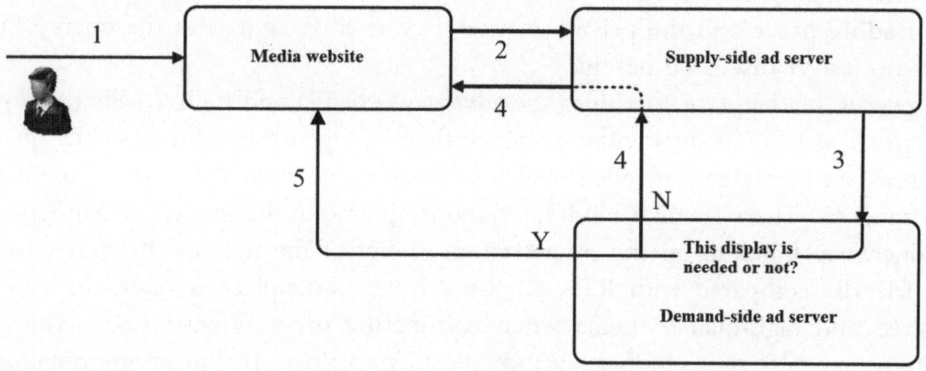

FIGURE 6.3 Process of preferred deal.

The PD allows a single demand side to select the traffic according to its own wish and avoid the complex bidding process. The PD process consists of the following five steps:

(1) A user visits the media page.

(2) The media page initiates an ad call to the supply-side ad server through JavaScript code or SDK. The supply-side ad server sometimes belongs to the media or sometimes belongs to other suppliers.

(3) The supply-side ad server initiates an ad call the demand-side ad server, inquiring whether it needs this advertising display opportunity.

(4) The demand-side ad server determines whether it needs the display opportunity. If so, it will return the corresponding advertising creative.

(5) If the demand-side does not need the display opportunity, it will notify the media ad server, and the supply-side ad server will choose the right creative from its own ad bank and return.

The PD process enables the demand side to choose the traffic freely, so it is also a programmatic trade. With only one demand side involved, it is easier for the media to control the quality and sources of advertising. The PD is generally settled by CPM, because there is no multi-party bidding, and the traffic selection is convenient, it often agrees on a unit CPM price higher than the market price. Compared with RTB, one of the disadvantages of PD is that there may be more round trips in the decision-making process: in extreme cases, it takes three round trips to get the final ad.

6.2.2 Private Marketplace

In addition to RTB – a public market auction mechanism – sometimes the media expect to limit the auction to a small range of the demand side, so as to guarantee the quality of advertisers. This type of programmatic trade is called "private marketplace." Since the online trading process in the private marketplace is consistent with the open RTB, this topic is no longer discussed herein.

The private marketplace combines the advantages of PD and RTB: (i) First, the private marketplace, like PD, is an invitation rather than an open transaction, so the quality of advertisers can be better controlled, which helps to ensure that the value of the media is not harmed. (ii) There is still a bidding relationship among the invited demanders, which is conducive to building up the monetization ability of the media. Of course, both are media friendly compared with RTB, so the private marketplace is often the choice for large-sized and high-quality media when considering programmatic trade. The private marketplace enables more high-quality media to participate in the programmatic trade, which in turn promotes the programming process of brand advertising.

Since 2014, the private marketplace has received more and more attention in the entire programmatic trade market. The mainstream ADX, which is represented by DoubleClick and Mopub, has been vigorously strengthening the products and services in the private marketplace. It is foreseeable that with the full development and integration of private and public marketplace, the programmatic trade will become increasingly mature in balancing the effect and brand, media interest and advertiser interest.

6.2.3 Programmatic Direct Buy

The programmatic direct buy (PDB) is a transitional trading mode between direct purchase and RTB. The characteristic of PDB is that the trade itself is still completed on basis of pricing, quantity guarantee or semi-quantity guarantee, but the demand side can make ad serving decisions for the purchased inventory by itself, and sometimes select a certain amount of traffic. Generally speaking, there are several application scenarios of PDB:

(1) Cross-media frequency capping. In the traditional agreement-based advertising, each media respectively signs an agreement with the advertiser, and the media is responsible for the execution of the agreement. When the same user appears on different media, frequency capping is carried out separately, which is adverse for effective use of budget. In the case of PDB, the DSP implements ad serving on behalf of advertisers, making it possible for cross-media frequency capping, which is one of the advantages of PDB.

(2) Traffic allocation for multiple sub-products. For some large group advertisers, such as P&G and Volkswagen, there is often more than one line of advertising needs. Therefore, the traffic reallocation for sub-products on the uniformly purchased traffic has become a real demand. In the case of PDB, the demand-side ad server can flexibly allocate traffic among sub-products according to its own CRM, DMP and self-determined strategies, which is equivalent to turning the purchased resources into an internal ADN, which is fairly important for increasing the use value of traffic.

(3) A certain proportion of restitution. Some media, when implement the PDB model, provide a certain amount of restitution to the DSP (return 20% of the ad call), which enables the DSP to obtain the traffic selection ability between the agreement-based purchase and RTB. When the frequency is too high or the audience segmentation does not match, the DSP can use the power of restitution to reject ad serving. However, this restitution is far from as complete as RTB, and it is still an optimization process with strong constraints, and the actual optimization effect is quite limited.

6.2.4 Spectrum of Advertising Transactions

Now let's make a summary of the mainstream transactions in the online advertising market (see Figure 6.4). The exclusive sales based on time frame and advertising positions and the quantity guaranteed agreement-based sales are the transaction models by which the sales staff and customers agree on their core requirements for ad serving, human factors play a considerable role in this process, but such kind of sales usually satisfies the brand advertising and boasts strong premium ability, they are preferred by the high-quality media, and referred to as "premium sale." On a technical level, the premium sale as a whole is not particularly computationally intensive, and the major technologies (e.g., online allocation and audience targeting) are more associated with the supply side.

In the case of auction-based ADN, the supply side can directly trust the ad spaces to ADN to achieve monetization, or takes advantage of multiple affiliates and chooses different ADN by segmenting the traffic according to some rules or models, which is known as "network optimization" (Section 6.4). For the demand side, they need to select the right crowd tag and make a reasonable bid to optimize the overall ROI. Although such transaction mode has been relatively computation dependent, the decision-making of both parties is not completed in real time and the efficiency has not reached the highest level. This type of trading can be called semi-programmatic trade.

In the case of RTB, the process of programmatic trade becomes simpler and more direct. Through the interfaces of RTB or PD, DSP directly docks with ADX and completes the refined traffic purchase. In addition to these two common trading

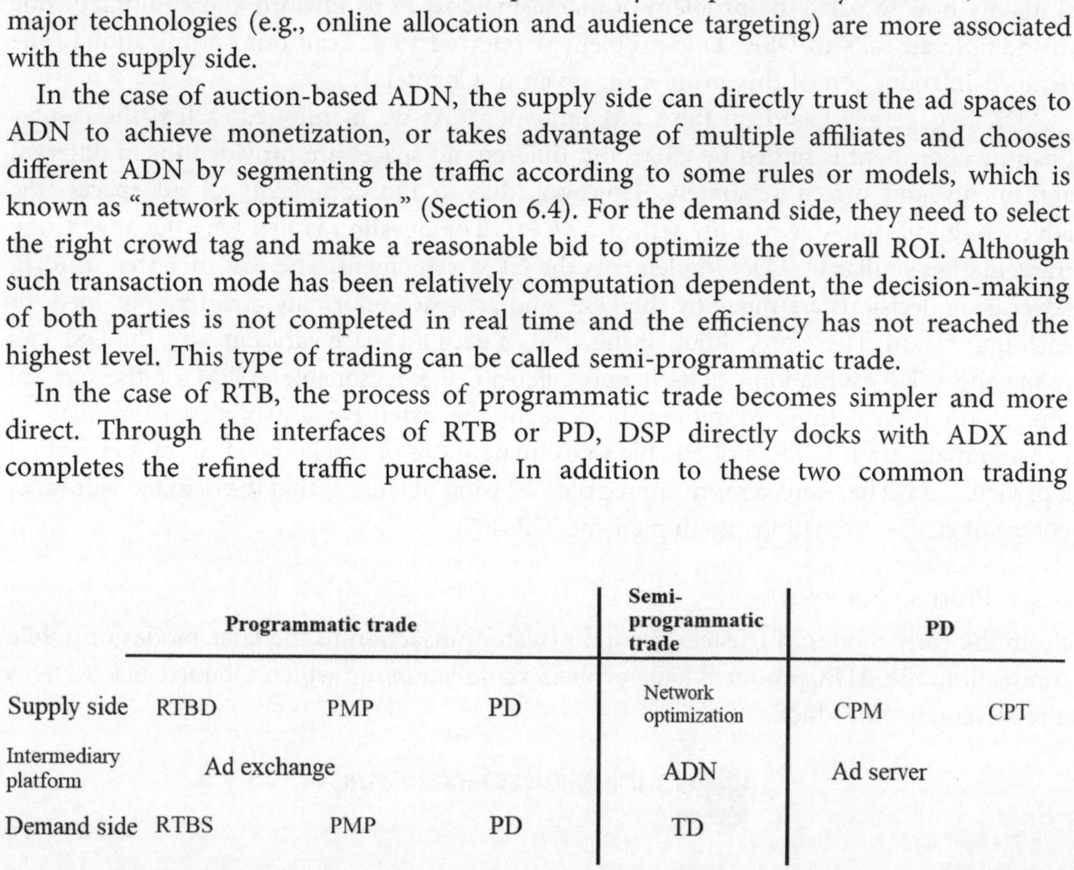

FIGURE 6.4 Main transaction modes in online advertising.

modes, the abovementioned PD and private marketplace are increasingly showing up in the market. In Figure 6.4, we list the main transaction modes of various online ads, including premium sale and programmatic trade.

6.3 AD EXCHANGE

The ad exchange (ADX) is a key product in the era of programmatic trade. It sells media traffic to DSP through auction, which is analogous to the exchange in the stock market. RightMedia, the original ADX product, was initially developed to exchange remnant traffic between advertising agencies in New York. As a result, the early RightMedia did not implement RTB, but adopted a trade mode similar to private marketplace and trusteeship. However, this private marketplace cannot meet the demand for large amount long-tail media traffic exchange, because the remnant traffic can only be exchanged in the most accurate and targeted way of the demand side to obtain the highest value. Consequently, when RTB came out, it quickly became the standard and even the main function of ADX.

The ADX product strategy is relatively simple. Because all advertising bidding is conducted in real time, there is no need for ad base or advertising retrieval, and the ranking process is very simple. The product strategy to be paid attention to in the ADX is mainly how to solve the problem of increasing cost in bandwidth and equipment due to multiple ad calls to DSP. This problem is referred to as "call out optimization." The detailed introduction of this problem is given in Chapter 15.

ADX is generally based on the CPM settlement. As we mentioned earlier, the display quantity agreement is settled by CPM, but different ad spaces are provided for in different agreements and priced separately. However, due to the complexity of ad spaces, the advertising sales in ADN is only settled by CPC. The question is that why the advertising trade market similar to ADN implements the CPM settlement. The reason is that in RTB, advertising decisions are made by the DSP, and ad space information can be obtained for each impression. Therefore, although the CTR of each ad space varies greatly, the DSP can refine the CTR estimation by itself and calculate the reasonable eCPM of the current impression in real time. Moreover, because of the extensive use of first-party data in programmatic trade, DSP is often able to estimate more precisely the effect of a crowd on a particular ad. Therefore, a more appropriate division of labor is that the demand side takes charge of eCPM estimation and implements CPM.

6.3.1 Product Samples

From the early modes of trusteeship and private transaction to the later modes of public transaction, the ADX products have evolved rapidly, among which DoubleClick ADX is a representative product.

doubleclick ad exchange
by Google

In 2007, Google bought DoubleClick at a price of US$3.1 billion. On this basis, Google launched its advertising trading platform DoubleClick ADX and connected it with AdWords and AdSense. Among them, AdSense is accessed from the supply side as an ADN, while AdWords is accessed from the demand side. The advertisers of Google AdWords can directly access ADX and have more media resources, while the publishers of AdSense will have a wider range of high-quality advertisers. As an advertising trading platform, DoubleClick connects numerous ADNs and DSPs. When an advertising display takes place, AdSense and AdWords are just two participants, the display won by AdWords is not necessarily on AdSense, and the ads displayed on AdSense are not necessarily from AdWords.

DoubleClick offers a fully transparent and open market in which any DSP can theoretically bid on any traffic. The media usually allow some or all of the demand side to access their traffic in this way. Usually there is no direct communication with the demand side, and media owners can participate in the open market traffic auction without knowing anything about it.

The open and transparent RTB model of DoubleClick overcomes some design flaws of RightMedia due to historical problems, and its ADX boasts a unique design in topological structure. As for the topological structure design of RightMedia, the traffic exchange between two media requires both parties to sign a contract, i.e., to connect the sides of the media that will exchange; with the increasing number of media, the connection between nodes is arbitrary and irregular, which brings the complexity of design. DoubleClick adopts the star-shaped topological structure, the direct exchange of traffic needs to go through Google at the first place, and directly sign a contract with Google. In this way, the complexity of ADX model is reduced, and the simple revenue sharing is split into revenue and cost in two contracts, which also increases the cash flow of Google.

Every day DoubleClick ADX manages the RTB for tens of billions of ad impressions around the world. It is also one of the most important ADXs in the Chinese market.

6.4 DEMAND-SIDE PLATFORM

Corresponding to ADX, the demand-side product in the programmatic trade is DSP. There are two core features of DSP products: one is RTB, PD, and other programmatic traffic purchase; the other is the ability to support demand-side customization of audience segmentation. These are the two core features, which are actually two aspects of the same problem: in order to divide ad purchase based on demand-side customized users, an open bidding interface is needed; if the purchase is made only on basis of supply-side audience segmentation, then the non-RTB like ADN will be sufficient.

What is customized audience segmentation?[2] From the perspective of audience targeting, those targeting methods like $t(a, u)$, i.e., the advertiser-related targeting

2 The term "customized" in this book expresses the different results of different customers, while the term "personalized" expresses the different results of different users.

methods, are customized user segmentation. Take two intuitive examples: (i) Assuming that an e-commerce site is to prepare for an ad serving for its old customers, then the "old customers" here is customized user segmentation, apparently it is the e-commerce site itself that is able to identify this user group, and any media or ADN, no matter how much data they have, they cannot work out this tag. (ii) A bank that expects to reach potential credit card holders through advertising. To find these potential customers, we need to take the existing customers of the bank as the basis, analyze the characteristics of their behavior and demographical attributes, and then expand the potential customers according to these characteristics. This process is in urgent need of demand-side data, the media or third-party data, and the processed crowd tag is still related to advertisers, so it also belongs to customized user segmentation.

Since it can be subdivided into each impression for making decisions and bidding, it enables the demand side to execute advertising campaigns as sophisticatedly as a recommendation system, and it also enables recommendation and advertising – two important Internet products – to find the perfect meeting point.

6.4.1 DSP Product Strategy

The advertising decision-making process of DSP (see Figure 6.5) is similar to that of ADN. It also goes through the stages of retrieval, ranking, and pricing, but there is a stage of bidding. In the RTB environment, bid directly determines the unit cost and profit of the DSP traffic, and bid is one of the key product strategies of DSP.

There is another difference between DSP and ADN, which lies in the audience targeting method. In ADN, the mainstream targeting is based on the tags processed by the second-party data; in DSP, the targeting $t(a, u)$ that stresses the first-party data and integrates with the second-party or third-party data is the focus of attention. Among all kinds of customized tags, the methods of retargeting and looking-alike have some universality, which is the product strategy that DSP needs to pay special attention to.

Let's discuss these strategies for the two key products in DSP.

6.4.2 Bidding Strategy

In the auction-based ADN, the purpose of eCPM estimation is to rank ads, and the absolute eCPM value does not need to be too accurate. But in DSP, it is critical to accurately estimate the eCPM, which is the basis of the bidding strategy for DSP, as the CPM is quoted to ADX for each impression.

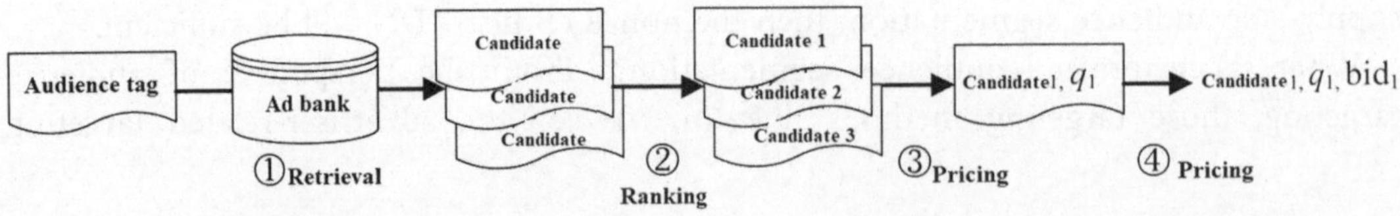

FIGURE 6.5 DSP decision-making process.

The intuitive bidding strategy for DSP is simple, as long as the eCPM estimation is accurate enough to bidding on its basis. Since ADX is also generally billed as a GSP, this strategy ensures of certain profit margin. If the bid is above this price, there may be risk of loss; if the bid is below this price, then the traffic is not fully utilized. Assuming there is no budget constraint, and then this bidding strategy could be an optimal one.

Why do budget constraints make a difference? Let's look at Figure 6.6. The curve in the figure marks the changes on the transaction price of an ADX in a day (bid landscape) [15]. We have found that the curve is not smooth or even drastically changes due to the changes on advertisers, budgets, and bids in DSP. In this market, assuming that our eCPM is a fixed value above the market level, we can compare two bidding strategies: (i) Strategy A: since the eCPM is higher than the market level, we can bid on all inquiries based on the eCPM, so that we can get all the traffic until the budget of the day is exhausted (i.e., Strategy A in Figure 6.6) (ii) Strategy B: we bid on some traffic with a lower market price, obtain this traffic until the budget of the day is exhausted (i.e., Strategy B in Figure 6.6). Obviously, the cost of the Strategy B is significantly lower than that of Strategy A, so we can make a higher profit that day.

In the above example, the bidding strategy optimized by DSP can be qualitatively described as follows: Firstly, draw a market price curve through observation and prediction of historical data. Secondly, allocate the budget for the day to the traffic with a lower market price. Of course, the actual practice is more complicated, because the eCPM changes over time, for example, the eCPM of game ads in leisure time is significantly higher than that in work time. Therefore, the traffic we expect is not the one with a low market price, but the one with a high ratio of eCPM to market price. As a result, the bidding strategy of DSP is based on two curves: a curve of eCPM and a curve of market price that change over time.

In addition to finding a right price range on the timeline, we can extend the pricing strategy to more dimensions. For example, the traffic of female users usually boasts a higher commercial value, so its market price is accordingly higher, if your DSP ads

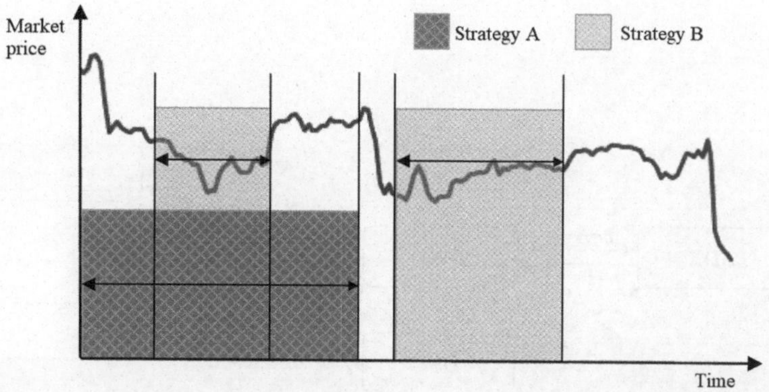

FIGURE 6.6 Different bidding strategies in DSP.

have little difference in the eCPM of male and female users, or even higher on male users (e.g., games), then you should try to allocate more traffic to male users to generate more profit. But adding more dimensions will complicate this matter, and other factors do not have a significance impact on the market price as time, so it is crucial to develop a proper bidding strategy on a timeline.

6.4.3 Bidding and Pricing Processes

DSP has an advertiser-oriented pricing process and an ADX-oriented bidding process, and these two processes are closely correlated. Although the principle is the same as the pricing model in auction-based advertising, people will have a great variety of questions in practice. Therefore, it is necessary to explain the DSP pricing process. We will take account of the scenarios where DSP charges advertisers by CPC, in this case, the bidding and pricing processes are illustrated in Figure 6.7.

DSP estimates and ranks the eCPM of each candidate ad. When charging the top advertiser (a_1 in Figure 6.7), it should be based on the CPC second price $p_1 = r_2/\mu_1$; therefore, the CPM bid on ADX shall be equal to r_2. It should be noted that since ADX also adopts the second price, r_2 is already the optimal bid strategy, although the specific strategy may vary with budget constraints (refer to Subsection 15.2.4).

If the DSP wins the RTB, then ADX will charge DSP based on the bid *b'* of the second-place DSP. In this case, the DSP gets the expected return of *b-b'*. However, in the case of DSP charging advertisers by CPC, this will be an expected rather than a definite revenue.

6.4.4 Retargeting

Retargeting is one of the earliest and most widely used customized tags in online advertising. Its concept is fairly simple: find the users who once showed a clear interest in an advertiser's service, and then deliver the ads of this advertiser to them. For different types of ads, retargeting mainly has two purposes:

(1) For brand awareness: when a user once selected the service or product of a brand, when noticing the ads of this brand in high-quality media, he/she will be more

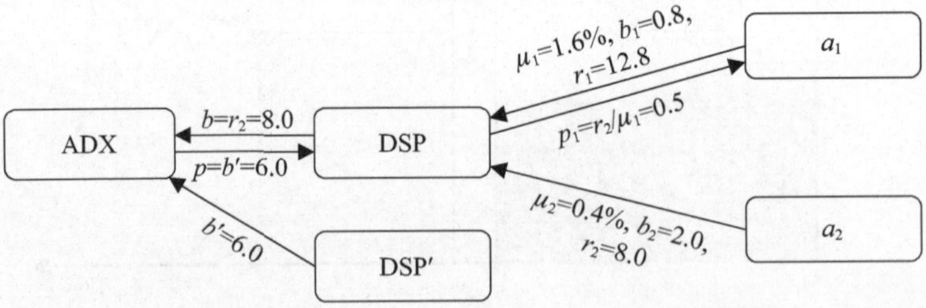

FIGURE 6.7 Bidding and pricing processes at DSP.

confident of his/her choice and more impressed of this brand. In this case, the main purpose should be promoting the brand instead of specific products.

(2) For direct response. If a user once considered a product but has not completed the final conversion, the CTR and conversion rate will be significantly higher than the average level. If a user has selected the product, then the recommendation technology can be used to push relevant product ads to him/her.

Retargeting is distinguished into site retargeting, personalized retargeting, and search retargeting by information source and sophistication of information use. See the details as follows:

I. Site retargeting and personalized retargeting

Site retargeting aims at the users who have reached the advertiser sites or applications for a certain period of time. The eCPM of such retargeting traffic is generally an order of magnitude higher than that of untargeted traffic, so the volume of traffic shall be input as much as possible. When buying this kind of retargeting traffic on the media, the amount that can be obtained has two main influencing factors, one is the advertisers' own visitor records, and the other is the degree of overlapping between their visitors and those of the media. The former factor cannot be expanded through advertising, while the latter requires purchasing retargeting traffic through various channels as much as possible. Well, DSP is apparently an appropriate channel.

Personalized retargeting is a special case of retargeting. The deep processing of the retargeting traffic, according to the category and the purchase stage and other factors on the depth of creative personalization, is personalized retargeting. Specifically, personalized retargeting can dig deeper in two areas: First, for users at different stages of purchase, appropriate creative should be adopted to push them to complete conversion as soon as possible. Second, for users who have some purchase records, the recommendation technology is used to show relevant products to them to improve the secondary purchase rate. In these two scenarios, this approach has a lot in common with recommendation. From the perspective of product recommendation, it can be considered as an off-site recommendation. In other words, it moves the recommendation module on the original advertiser website to off-site.

Figure 6.8 shows an example of personalized retargeting ad. The object of this ad is a user of Jingdong (JD. com) – another e-commerce giant in addition to Taobao. The user is likely to have followed some kind of mobile phones on JD. com, and also some technical books on PHP programming. Therefore, the advertising system recommends relevant mobile phones and technical books for him according to his personalized shopping interest and the commodity inventory of Jingdong. It is conceivable that such ad has a relatively higher CTR and conversion rate.

FIGURE 6.8 Example of ad based on personalized retargeting.

Personalized retargeting is notably different from traditional audience targeting, which manifests in the following three aspects:

(1) Dynamic creative. The core of personalized retargeting is the idea of using recommendations to determine what items to display in real time. Since advertisers tend to have a fairly large number of items, it is obviously not possible to prepare creative in advance for all the product combinations. Therefore, dynamic creative is the most important supporting technology for personalized retargeting, which is also an important step in the development of online advertising toward complete personalization and dynamic.

(2) Recommendation engine. Personalized retargeting can be thought of as off-site recommendation. But there are a few differences from the on-site recommendation: First, the recommendation on the product page of the website is mainly based on the context information, while the off-site recommendation is based on user information. In addition, because the on-site recommendation is in a specific purchase link, it does not need frequent adjustment to the creative stage according to the user purchase, while it is necessary for off-site recommendation to do so.

(3) Real-time interface of advertiser commodity inventory. For off-site product recommendation, if users click on a single product to reach the advertiser website, they find that the product has been sold out or removed from the shelves, or the price is inconsistent with the creative publicity, it will cause serious damage to the advertiser's brand image. To avoid this as much as possible, personalized retargeting services need to provide a real-time commodity inventory interface that allows advertisers to synchronize inventory and price information in a timely manner.

II. **Search retargeting**

Search retargeting aims at the groups of users who have searched for the keywords that are directly associated with advertisers. This approach can obtain an accurate user base, and its absolute quantity is also higher than site retargeting, but for non-major search engine providers, it is uncertain that search retargeting may cover a higher proportion of users than site retargeting.

Since search retargeting uses the second-party data from search engines, why should it be classified as a customized segmentation? This starts with how to get the word list used for search retargeting. Generally speaking, there are several ways to determine a suitable word list for search retargeting. The train of thought is as follows:

(1) Manual experience determines the word list.

(2) If advertisers also deliver ads in search engines, the same word list for delivery can be borrowed directly.

(3) Based on the advertiser traffic statistics, i.e., making statistics of the advertiser website traffic that comes from search engines, the high-frequency terms will enter the word list for search retargeting.

The last approach boasts two advantages in practice: first, because it is based on the actual traffic data, the effect is often better than other approaches; second, after obtaining the first-party data by placing codes on the advertiser website, the whole process becomes automated, simple, and easily operable. Therefore, we prefer the third strategy as the first choice for retargeting, while this strategy relies on the first-party, implying that it is also a customized tag.

6.4.5 Look-Alike

The retargeting is precise, but the amount is extremely limited. Moreover, for most advertisers, in addition to intensive cultivation of old users, they hope to have a way to reach those potential users who are "likely" to be interested in their products. This is especially true for e-commerce companies that are growing fast, or for offline advertisers (such as banks and automobiles) that don't have a lot of website traffic.

The tag "may be interested in their own products" is very clear in purpose, but vague in practice. The easy way to think about it is: some of the seed users are provided by the advertisers according to their first-party data, and then the advertising platform with more abundant second-party data analyzes the characteristics of these users' network behaviors, and finds the extended groups with similar characteristics according to these characteristics. Obviously, this is also a customized user tag. Such tag processing strategy is called "new customer recommendation," i.e., look-alike.

From the perspective of recommendation, look-alike can be considered as a way of "new customer recommendation," which focuses on promoting to potential users who do not pay attention to advertisers' products. Of course, since it is recommended, it is not aimless broadcast-type promotion. In addition, such recommendation technology takes into account the recommendation without the behavior on the advertiser website, which is an extension of the originally narrow-sensed recommendation problem.

Look-alike is a reasonable product idea targeted at audiences. However, it is possible to generate value only with certain data support. Besides, as it involves the acquisition and processing of the first-party data and the third-party data, it is technically challenging. When readers encounter such products, they should pay special attention to judge their real value from the perspective of data and technical solution rationality. To put it bluntly, in the Chinese market, the term "look-alike" has to some extent become a fig leaf for the targeting methods without explicit effect or clear-cut principles, and almost all advertising products claim to have this ability, which is described as "chaotic look-alike" in China.

6.4.6 Product Cases

The emergence of customized user segmentation and RTB technology has spawned many DSP companies that optimize ad buying in a technical way. Some of these companies focus on the arbitrage model of CPM acquisition and ROI optimization. Some focus on transparent purchasing and functional service optimization. We hereby give examples of these two types of DSP.

I. **Criteo**

criteo.

Criteo is an ad-tech company based in France. Judging from its historical business, Criteo uses a preferred way to buy traffic in addition to RTB. Unlike other DSPs, Criteo focuses on buying ads in a personalized and targeted way. The core technologies are already mentioned above: dynamic creative, recommendation engine, and real-time interface to commodity inventory. Some examples of Criteo's personalized retargeting creative are shown in Figure 6.9.

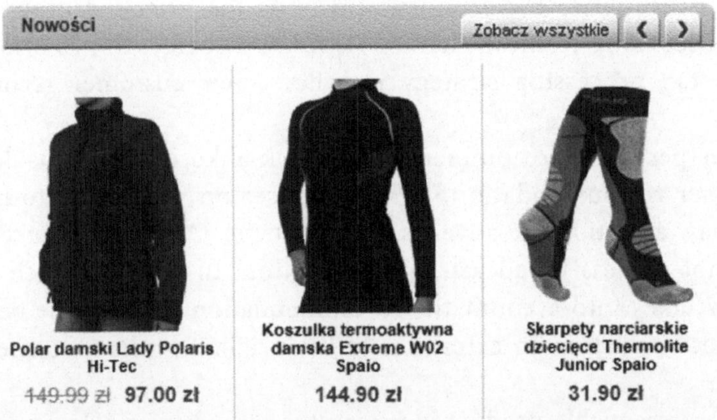

FIGURE 6.9 Example of Criteo personalized retargeting ad.

The settlement between Criteo and media is by CPM on basis of RTB or PD, but the settlement with advertisers is solely by CPC, so as to realize arbitrage and be more easily accepted by response advertisers. In the scheme framework of personalized retargeting, Criteo also provides flexible optimization functions in four dimensions as user, category, data, and banner, i.e., advertisers can set different click offers according to different user segments, product categories, specific data, and creative types, so as to achieve sophisticated ROI management and optimization. The sophistication degree of such display advertising operations and delivery is similar to that of search advertising: deliver response ads based on highly accurate subdivision of traffic, and control bidding based on fairly fine granularity. However, this approach has some inherent defects for display advertising: unlike search ads, personalized retargeting requires tracking codes to be pre-installed on the advertiser site, complicating the process for new advertisers to access. Therefore, the companies specialized in personalized retargeting will face the problem of insufficient demand at the initial stage, and it will take a lot of efforts and good record of operators to improve it gradually, Criteo also went through this process.

Currently valued at about US$3 billion, Criteo is one of the world most valuable independent third-party advertising platform.

II. **InviteMedia**

InviteMedia was originally an independent DSP company. It was acquired by Google in June 2010 at a price of about US$7 million. Now it has been integrated into DoubleClick's advertising series and renamed as DoubleClick Bid Manager. Although Google is integrated in all advertising products, InviteMedia remains relatively independent and there is still a game between it and DoubleClick ADX that represents media interests.

InviteMedia is one of the pioneers in the advertising trading market. Its business is to provide transparent RTB purchasing functions, such as setting some rules and optimization goals, helping advertisers to switch in relevant ADX, and collecting a fixed percentage of commission from doing so, in the hope of rapidly expanding the influence of advertisers. Of course, as the business grows, more and more ROI optimization services are being offered. At the same time, the domain name InviteMedia was switched to the domain name dc.com of DoubleClick in 2013. Therefore, InviteMedia does not need to conduct cookie mapping with DoubleClick ADX, which reduces the loss caused by cookie mapping and improves the purchase efficiency and the final delivery effect.

6.5 SUPPLY-SIDE PLATFORM

Let's take a look at the yield optimization scheme for the supply side after the programmatic trade is generated. For the media, it is not necessary to put all the traffic into one trading mode. They can not only sell brand ads at a high premium through direct sales, but use a variety of trading methods to pursue a higher filling rate.

Referring to the spectrum of advertising transaction mode in Section 6.2, the monetization platform of media can adopt such product logic: when the ad request arrives, first check whether there is demand for the order of priority sales, including the CPT and CPM contract. If there is no such sales contract, the bidding process is started: on the one hand, find the high eCPM from the self-operated ad base, and estimate the number of advertising network eCPM that can be called, find the high eCPM between the two, and then implement the ad request to each DSP through the RTB interface of MRP. It can be seen in this logic that the ad request is assigned to the operation of ad inventory (ad serving), or in the form of embedded JavaScript or SDK docking with other ADN, or docking with DSP via RTB, it is a dynamic decision according to their online yield, such scheme is called dynamic allocation. The corresponding product form is supply-side platform (SSP).

6.5.1 SSP Product Strategy

The multiple advertising sources in SSP are subject to dynamic allocation; the corresponding decision-making process is shown in Figure 6.10.

This process involves three crucial links:

(1) **Mediation:** To whom an ad request is sent? Make an online decision on this question by integrating with JavaScript code or SDK of multiple ADNs. The logic for selecting ADN is also an estimation of the eCPM of the candidate ads with a display opportunity (u, c), so as to optimize the reward. Since we do not have any specific advertising information at this time, we can only make a rough estimation of the eCPM. The practical strategy shall take account of two main factors: (i) the profit-share model and proportion of ADN or DSP, (ii) the ad return rate of ADN or DSP, of which the statistics is made by time frame and geographical location. If these partners themselves are engaged in delivering the ads on certain types of industry, then the crowd and environmental tags are also helpful.

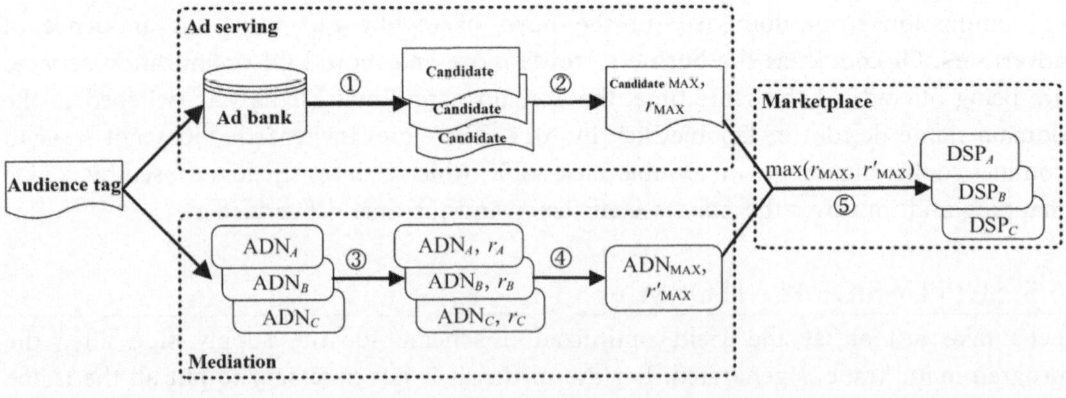

FIGURE 6.10 Decision-making process for dynamic allocation.

(2) **Ad serving:** In general, SSP will also provide the function of placing ads sold by the media itself, i.e., helping the media carry out ad serving. From this perspective, it's more like helping media implement a private ADN. The difference is that these internal ads need to be ranked together with the external ADN to decide whether to serve internal ads or external ADN ad request, while the only criterion is revenue optimization.

(3) **Marketplace:** After the programmatic trade, SSP will also request ads from DSP in the form of RTB, which forms a market. There is no essential difference between SSP and ADX, especially when the number of DSP is increasing and the number of ADN is decreasing, SSP and ADX have shown an increasingly strong homogenization trend.

In the above three demand sources, the general decision-making process is to firstly estimate the aggregated ADN the eCPM of internal advertising, ADN then selects the optimal price as the base price, sends an ad request to DSP. Sometimes, after delivering the ad request to the selected ADN, it is not for sure that the ADN will be able to fill the display opportunity, then the SSP will turn to the second demand side, if it is still an ADN, it needs to launch another ad request, and so on. This is known as the "waterfall model." Obviously, multiple requests will significantly increase the delay of the overall ad request, so this is quite an inefficient model. The following model Header Bidding will somewhat solve this problem.

6.5.2 Header Bidding

The formation and improvement of programmatic trade mechanism provides new imagination space for the effect of advertisers and the monetization of media. However, it is not just technology that is decisive in this market, but also the game of commercial interests. With the increasing monopoly of Google, Mopub, and other brands in the supply market, they will more or less prioritize their own internal advertisers in allocation of traffic, and charge relatively high fees (maybe as high as 40%), which harms the interests of advertisers and media to some extent. Driven by the maximization of earnings, the market forces advertisers and the media to work together to break the monopoly, which gives rise to the Header Bidding technology.

Let's firstly look at the statistics made by trends.builtwith.com to learn about the demand for Header Bidding from worldwide media websites. As shown in Figure 6.11, from February to September 2016, the number of the media websites that adopt Header Bidding almost exploded: in less than a year, more than 40% of the head websites started employing this technology.

Header Bidding is a way of establishing a direct connection between the Bidder and the media to bypass ADX. The Bidder has a chance to bid directly to the media prior to the start of real-time Bidding and the media determines the winning Bidder based on the Bidding level. Here the Bidder, for all can be quoted for the service, can be DSP, ADX, or other advertising participants. If not, ADX will bid in real time. But the direct quotation process, is occurs in the client side, namely, the browser or the application. Its advertising decision-making process is shown in Figure 6.11.

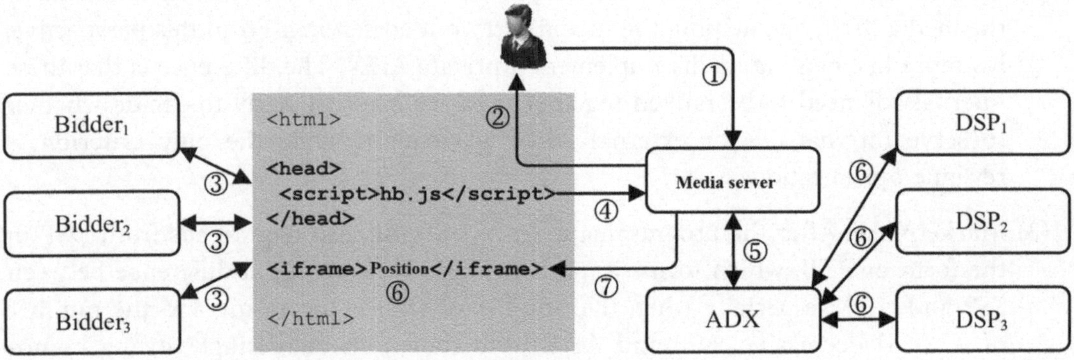

FIGURE 6.11 Decision-making process with Header Bidding.

(1) The user visits the media page and makes an HTTP request to the media server.

(2) The media server will put "hb.js" (script of the function of Header Bidding) into the "head" tag of HTML, which will be sent to user browser as an HTTP Response.

(3) When parsing the HTML, the user browser will download the hb.js, which is configured by the media website, to the local host. Under the control of the hb.js, the user browser will send the bid request for the exposure opportunity to the Bidders which is agreed with the media website, and then the Bidders will return the quote to the user browser.

(4) Under the control of hb.js, the user browser will send back the quote information of each Bidder to the media website.

(5) The media server sends ad request to ADX or SSP concurrently.

(6) ADX or SSP initiates the RTB process and receives candidate ads.

(7) The media server ranks the bidding results of Header Bidding and of RTB, the one offers a higher bid wins this display opportunity, and the user browser will request the bid winner to load the ads.

Header Bidding may also be regarded as a supply-side product or a special SSP. Compared with the abovementioned general SSP decision-making process, the uniqueness of Header Bidding is that it bypasses ADX and joins up the DSP that returns quoted price, rather than the ADN only capable of estimating eCPM, so as to optimize revenue in a simple and direct manner and obtain a higher eCPM more easily. But this approach has obvious technical problems: the most critical point is that the customer-side model brings along a relatively longer advertising delay, which reduces the actual exposure and affects the user experience. Therefore, we are prone to believe that the success of Header Bidding is a result of a commercial game rather than a technical progress.

6.5.3 Product Cases

In the era of ADN, SSP products are of great value to the media for their one-stop access to multiple ADNs. However, along with the development of programmatic trading, the market space of SSP products has been squeezed, since their functions are overlapping with ADX, which can be illustrated by the following products.

(1) **Admeld**

Admeld

Michael Barrett, founder of Admeld, had been holding senior positions at AOL and FOX, that's why the products of Admeld were designed from the start to manage advertising for portals and optimize the interests of media. Their early customers included AOL, FOX, and other large-sized web portals with significant traffic in the United States. Since 2008, Admeld has been leading the development of SSP-related technologies and product in the direction of network optimization and PMP.

Early AdMeld on revenue management, for the media access to the main traffic is not only from the RTB traffic in ADX, but mainly from major ADNs, such as the north American market has access to more than 50 ADNs, in other words the media, as long as they are embedded with a piece of AdMeld code, can dock with all of these ADNs, it has greatly made the remnant traffic to be monetized and optimized. While doing network optimization of these over 50 ADNs, as mentioned above, because of ADN own targeting and ad bank is not particularly clear, it is the use of such basic division as ad space and time frame that is fairly steady, so the eCPM estimation and traffic segmentation are made on such few dimensions as ad space, time frame, ad return rate, and profit-sharing proportion.

AdMeld will also purchase user data from DMP. On the one hand, it can further estimate the eCPM of each advertising network; on the other hand, it is convenient for DSP participating in bidding to understand the traffic quality, thus stimulating the bidding price and market liquidity of DSP.

After being acquired by Google at a price of US$400 million in 2011, AdMeld integrates DoubleClick's DoubleClick for Publishers (DFP) ad management system. After the acquisition by Google, Google can obtain some top content providers' traffic and good media relations that they cannot obtain, while the SSP-related technology of AdMeld is also integrated into DFP to improve the advertising ecological chain of Google.

(2) **Mopub**

mopub

In the field of PC and mobile Web, with the development of programming, the importance of ADN is gradually declining, so the SSP has also evolved into a product form similar to ADX that is based on RTB. However, in the field of mobile app monetization, with closed ADN-like FAN becoming more and more important, the traditional SSP, or the product called "aggregation platform," gradually occupies a place in the market, and one of the most typical representatives is Mopub.

Mopub is a platform for mobile media applications that optimizes media revenue by integrated management of various advertising sources. Corresponding to the product logic in Subsection 6.5.1, Mopub mainly provides the following liquidity functions.

(1) ADN mediation: ADN is generally embedded in the Mopub SDK in the form of an SDK. The media can manage the priority of each ADN in each region and time period by themselves, and use waterfall requests to make comprehensive use of each ADN. Mopub does not charge media for this part of liquidation.

    Because of the importance of Facebook, Admob, and others in monetizing mobile applications, this part is often the most important source of revenue for media. However, since ADNs do not bid for Mopub in real time, there is relatively little room for optimization. Generally speaking, SSP needs to pull reports from Facebook, Admob, and others in the way of API to optimize revenue. However, Admob currently uses the operation method of manually filling RPM of each ADN by media, which seems not particularly convenient or easy to achieve real-time optimization.

(2) Programmatic trade market: Mopub built its own program trading market for the traffic other than ADN monetization, acquiring advertising ADN monetization, from various DSPs. This part is not different from the functions of general ADX, but because it is a programmatic trade market within SSP, it needs to follow the dynamic allocation scheme detailed in Subsection 6.5.1 to comprehensively optimize the income.

    When concerning the programmatic trade, Mopub charges a relatively higher agency fee of up 30% to 40%.

(3) Ad serving: Mopub also allows the media to sell their own ads and to serve direct customers. In general, direct media sales may command the highest premium on some head traffic. Therefore, the SSP needs to deliver direct customer advertising at the top priority, ADN then transfers the remnant traffic to ADN mediation or trading market for monetization.

In September 2013, Twitter paid US$350 million for Mopub, which generated US$56 million in revenue in 2014. Revenue in recent years is unknown, but Mopub is undoubtedly one of the most important SSPs in mobile. However, Mopub has been slow to iterate since it was acquired by Twitter and has made little progress with new forms of advertising such as video, giving a huge market opportunity to several companies specializing in reward video ad.

CHAPTER 7

Data Processing and Exchange

Through a discussion in Chapter 6, we come to know that technology is not the predominant factor for raising the audience targeting accuracy and population coverage, then what is the decisive factor? The answer is source and quality of data – a crucial point of view for correct understanding of the precise advertising business. To highlight this point of view, we hereby take the petroleum processing industry for example (see Figure 7.1). In this industry, the crude oil is raw material for the whole industry, while refinery is to process this raw material into gasoline and other fuels and transmit them to the sales terminals like petrol station. In targeted advertising, we can liken user behavior to the raw material in the oil industry, while log collection and cleaning systems seem like the oil excavating equipment; the audience targeting platform processes the cleaned logs into user tags – just like the refinery processes crude oil, so that these user tags will become marketable and usable; the advertising position, although plays a key role in traditional advertising, is nothing more than a petrol station that consummates the process of product consumption.

How to correctly understand the role of technology in targeted advertising? The above analogy tells that technology is undoubtedly important, as indispensable as the extracting and refining equipment in the oil industry. The level of technology directly affects the effectiveness of data collection and monetization. But the role of technology should not be overstated. As the old Chinese saying goes, "one cannot make brick without straw," without high-quality raw materials (i.e., user data), even the most sophisticated technology is useless.

Historically, the data-related products and industries were used to serving the advertising industry at the very beginning. But to date, the data industry has developed into a relatively independent industry with great development potential. That's why we devote this chapter to data, hoping readers may reflect on the development law of the data products themselves beyond the scope of advertising.

In this chapter, we will firstly introduce the data assets with definite market value and how much is their value, which are important judgment bases for data collection, exchange, and processing. Upon possession of these data assets, we will process them into the directly available information and monetizable products – collectively referred

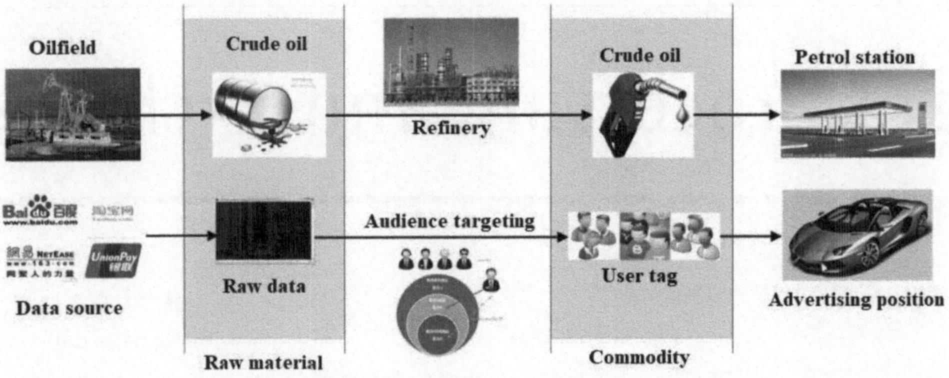

FIGURE 7.1 Data-driven computational advertising vs oil processing.

to as Data Management Platform (DMP). Of course, DMP is also split into the first-party DMP and third-party DMP. Their basic logic and business model will be introduced in this chapter. In addition, we'd like to discuss the frontier issues about data transaction and data privacy security, so as to help readers acquaint with these important concepts.

7.1 VALUABLE DATA SOURCES

Now that data are focal point of targeted advertising, their processing and trading is as significant as the ad serving technology. Which types of data directly contribute to the targeted advertising business? They mainly fall into the following six categories:

(1) User ID. To identify which behaviors belong to the same user is a critical issue for advertising, yet the importance of user ID to behavioral targeting is often overlooked. In fact, stable and precise user ID, which is as striking as the figure "1" prior to a string of figure 0, is critical to accurately define audience and use data. But note that no matter how much behavioral data you collect, they are unworkable unless you dock them with the ad serving system.

With regard to browser behavior, the most common user ID is cookies, but there may be cases where multiple browsers used at the same time, cookies expired or deleted by users, which weakens the long-term consistency of user ID. Fortunately for advertising, it is recent user behavior that plays a vital role, that's why cookies remain as the primary user ID that is widely accepted. If one domain name is shared by advertising and other services (e.g., email and SNS) holding permanent user identity, then the expired or deleted cookies can be recalled with this permanent identity, which will improve the consistency of user ID. On the contrary, if the domain name of an advertising business differs from that of other services holding permanent user identity, upon consent of the latter, we can employ cookie mapping to match up their IDs. The details in this regard will be discussed later when we talk about the ad trading technologies.

In the case of mobile Internet, the in-app advertising ID in iOS differs from that in Android: the former is an identifier for advertising (IDFA) specially developed by Apple Inc., which is in essence similar to cookie; while the latter does not have a proprietary advertising ID, but generally uses Android ID or international mobile equipment identity (IMEI).

High-quality user IDs are by themselves a type of valuable data, which are both exchangeable and marketable.

(2) User behavior. It is an industrial consensus that the following types of online behaviors can be widely collected and exert a definite effect on audience targeting: conversion, pre-conversion, sponsored search click, ad click, search click, search, share, page view, and ad view. According to their effect on direct response, these behaviors are divided into decision-making behavior, active behavior, semi-active behavior, and passive behavior.

The decision-making behavior consists of conversion and pre-conversion, both of them take place in the advertiser website and directs to definite user interest. For example, on e-commerce sites, the conversion corresponds to a confirmed order, while the pre-conversion involves search, browsing, price comparison, adding to shopping cart, and other preparations before placing an order. The data for decision-making behavior are the most valuable, yet not easily attainable for the supply side or advertising platforms. These data are most directly used for site retargeting or personalized retargeting. Though not in a large volume, these data play an unneglectable role in behavioral targeting.

Active behavior includes ad click, search, and search click. These behaviors take place online with definite user intention, meaning that they contain relatively rich information. In general, the amount of ad click is not large, so it cannot act as the main data source for behavioral targeting. In contrast, search behavior is able to generate massive and attainable data, which should be carefully explored and utilized.

Semi-active behavior mainly indicates sharing and page view. Both active and semi-active behaviors are generated in the process of content consumption with weak purpose of users. The interest areas involved are valuable for grasping user information, but the accuracy of details is discounted. Though semi-active behavior has limited guiding significance, its data size is the largest among all types of behaviors.

Passive behavior refers to ad view. Strictly speaking, ad view cannot be regarded as the basis for behavioral targeting, yet it is available for modeling of behavioral targeting, because its frequency is negatively correlated with the clicks of the ads in corresponding categories.

(3) Demographical attributes. Since this targeting tag is frequently used, its data sources are very important. Generally, such data are only available to the services that are tied to the identity of real-name users. We can use the online behavioral data to predict the tags for demographical attributes, but their accuracy is on the whole limited, and some calibration data are needed for training. For some demographical attributes, it may be easier to make accurate judgments based on special information, such as the voice signals recorded by voice service, which can correctly distinguish men from women.

(4) Geographical location. The use of geo-location information varies considerably depending on the degree of accuracy. If the mapping is made on basis of IP, we can only get a city-level location, yet it is still valuable for lots of ad serving. In the context of mobile Internet, GPS or cellular will provide a positioning as precise as a scope of only several hundred meters, which enables us to collect user interest in offline stores, and makes it possible for hyper-local advertisers (e.g., catering) to deliver targeted ads.

(5) Social relationship. The relationships on social networks reflect the interpersonal connections, and also imply a reasonable assumption of "similar interests" between people. Thus, social relationship can be used for smoothness of user interests: when the advertising system observes that the behaviors of a user are not enough for precise behavioral targeting, it may replicate the behaviors and interests of his/her social network friends. For example, if one's Weibo friends include lots of football fans, it is possible that he/she is also keen on football. We are not sure such guess is 100% correct, but at least it is statistically reasonable and helpful for guaranteeing the ad serving effect. It is important to note that this smoothness only applies to the long-term stable interests, not to instant buying interest. In this sense, the SNS of strong relation is more advantageous than that of weak relation.

(6) Equipment information. Mobile devices can provide far richer data than PCs, and the status information of some devices, such as the application installation list, model, age, gyroscope, and even battery power, is very helpful for scenario targeting. Therefore, mobile advertising is of special significance for the collection and deep processing of device information. See the discussion about scenarios in Section 8.4.

As for the significance of the above behavioral data in the advertising performance, we have extracted two basic rules as follows: (1) As the user intent becomes more active, the behavioral data tend to be increasingly valuable. (2) For the behaviors closer to conversion, they are more instructive to the response advertising. These rules will help us evaluate the value of all types of behavioral data. Please do not forget that the fundamental objective of advertising is to "reach prospective users at a low cost," if the behavioral data are only evaluated by the outcome of conversion, then it is the behaviors closer to conversion that are more accurate, because the users at this stage are about to make decisions, in other words, they are prone to be "real" buyers and no longer "prospective." Therefore, when concerning the problem of behavioral targeting, we should not only pursue ROI or conversion, but balance the advertising performance and coverage according to the specific user groups of advertisers.

7.2 DATA MANAGEMENT PLATFORM

The Data Management Platform (DMP) in marketplace is split into the first-party and third-party DMPs in two different scenarios. These two DMPs, despite of generally the same technical procedures, vary notably in their product direction and business model.

7.2.1 Tripartite Data Partitioning

The user data available for advertising are broken down into the first-party, second-party, and third-party data based on their varied sources (see Figure 7.2). In general, the first party and second party respectively refer to the advertiser and advertising platform. Other data providers that do not directly participate in ad trading are collectively known as the third party. In the case of ADN, it is the second-party data that prevail; while in the case of RTB, in addition to the first-party data, a large amount of third-party data has been subject to processing and trading. The first-party data, though in small amount, are the soul of all data. Making better use of the second-party and third-party data on basis of the first-party data is an important methodology in an age of RTB.

7.2.2 First-Party DMP

The data-processing product oriented to the first party is referred to as a DMP in a narrow sense. The collection and processing of the first-party data is a fairly important link in the advertising market. Though advertisers lack of technological accumulation in this regard, they don't have to set up a special work team for data processing, because there is a product specialized in management of data processing, i.e., the first-party DMP. It has the following core functions:

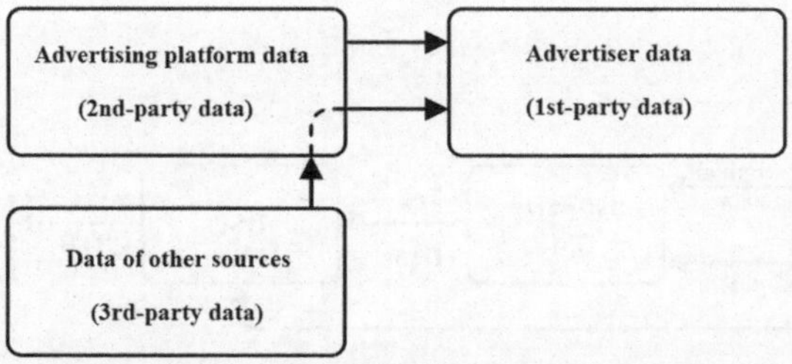

FIGURE 7.2 Tripartite data sources.

(1) It performs the audience targeting function for a website (either media or advertiser) and applies the resulting user tags to the website business. In this process, in addition to common tags, DMP shall flexibly process the audience data according to the user tags defined by the website.

(2) DMP enables the advertiser website to realize more convenient data docking with the ad purchase channels, which can be understood from the following application: if an advertiser enlists an external advertising platform to do retargeting, it shall inform the platform of its user set through certain technical means. If every advertising platform adds a tracking code to the advertiser website to collect user data, there will be two drawbacks: (i) when multiple advertising platforms add codes at the same time, the web page will become too heavy; (ii) the accumulation of visitors may take as long as several weeks, which lowers the retargeting efficiency of the advertising platform. If DMP the only one that that takes charge of accumulation and division of users for the advertiser website, and transmits the outcome via the data interface to the advertising platform, then the above drawbacks can be largely resolved.

The business model of the first-party DMP is shown in Figure 7.3. At the request of data provider (DP), DMP collects the first-party data and processes them into the user tags to meet the first-party needs. With these user tags, DP will conduct in-site operation or guide the ad serving of DSP. As shown in Figure 7.3, DSP uses these tag data to deliver ads in the ADX in the form of RTB. Of course, the first party shall pay the fees to DSP.

Since DMP collects and processes data at the request of DP, it will charge fees from DP, but it should never treat data as its own property for second monetization or mix the data from different DPs. The first-party DMP provides a data escrow and processing service, instead of data monetization, and its customers are mostly large- and medium-sized media and advertisers. Of course, they can build an exclusive DMP to serve their own business.

7.2.3 Third-Party DMP

The third-party DMP is also known as "data exchange." Its main function is to aggregate the online user behavioral data from diverse sources, process them into valuable user tags, and then sell these tags in advertising market for monetization. The product boundary

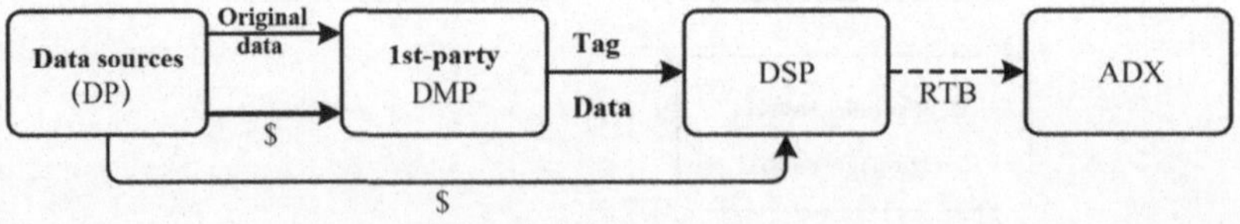

FIGURE 7.3 First-party DMP business model.

between the data exchange and DMP is not definite. Generally speaking, in addition to aggregating the formed user tags, the data exchange also performs the function of aggregating original behavioral data and self-processing of tags, i.e., it is able to perform some functions of DMP. But the data exchange usually develops their own tag systems and processes data according to their own logic, rather than at the request of media. In short, the data exchange mainly provides products with the third-party data, so it is referred to as the third-party DMP.

The business model of the third-party DMP is shown in Figure 7.4. DMP collects the original data from multiple DPs, processes them into user tags according to its own logic, sells the tag data to DSP, and then distributes a certain proportion of the resulting yield to DPs. Unlike the first-party DMP, the third-party DMP is a product for data monetization, and its DPs are mostly small- and medium-sized media and data owners.

7.2.4 Product Cases

The data management and trading products have been popular in the programmatic trading market, but not in full swing in the Chinese market, which may be attributed to a large number of cheating, traffic hijacking (see Section 16.4), and gray low-cost channels. In view of this, we will introduce some mature data products in the international market: BlueKai and AudienceScience.

(1) **BlueKai**

BlueKai is a typical third-party DMP and one of the bellwether companies that are devoted to data exchange.

bluekai

Omar Tawakol, CEO of BlueKai, believed that in the future the clients of display advertising would expect precise ad delivery to specific groups of consumers, which motivated him to build the "Data Exchange" in 2008: it is a database that on the one hand receives the information about traffic and membership from small- and medium-sized websites, and on

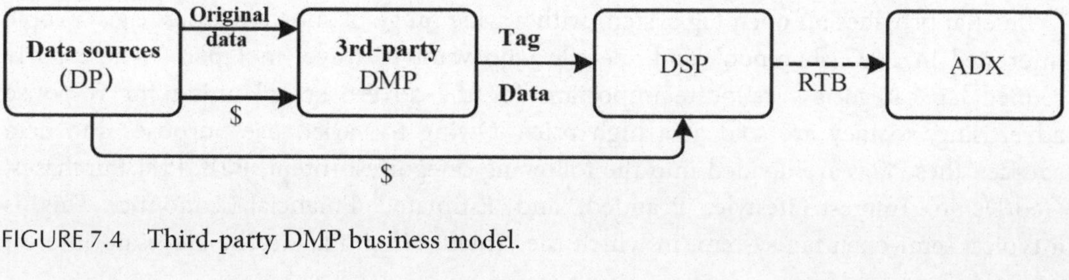

FIGURE 7.4 Third-party DMP business model.

the other hand processes and sells the information to small- and medium-sized advertisers. In 2009, BlueKai launched the "Software-as-a-Service" (SaaS) to help users distinguish audience buying behaviors. In 2011, BlueKai acquired TrackSimple to build up its data analysis capability and provide advertisers with a one-stop SaaS (including data analysis and data purchase). In recent years, BlueKai – a leading data exchange and DMP – has ushered in a new era of being an independent DMP with more than 300 million active users; the top 20 ADNs and 80% of portals are using BlueKai data.

Being an independent DMP, BlueKai refuses to integrate the DSP business like other DMPs, and never provides the bidding-based media procurement, since it insists on maintaining the neutrality of DMP, which enables it to dock and cooperate with diverse DSPs. In February 2014, BlueKai was acquired by Oracle at a price of US$400 million. Oracle does not have any media procurement business; it mainly provides marketing management services for enterprises, which is in line with BlueKai's market positioning as an independent DMP. Because of such positioning, BlueKai only earns a modest revenue annually, e.g., its total revenue in 2013 was merely about US$64 million.

The main business model of BlueKai is to aggregate the valuable behavioral data from a large number of small- and medium-sized media, develop user tags with the audience targeting technology, sell these tags to generate revenue, then return a large proportion of the revenue to DPs. BlueKai mainly deals with the websites of automotive, tourism, and shopping, because behind these websites there is a population with high homogeneity, and their advertisers (e.g., airlines and automobile manufacturers) are in need of precise marketing. Take a small online clothing shop for example, it has search and purchase data of users, but the data size is too small to be worthy of analysis and monetization. BlueKai tends to cooperate with these small- and medium-sized websites, aggregate their user information and behavioral data, and then process the data into user tags for sale. For example, some DSPs want to learn about the user tags, yet they have no user information, then they will resort to BlueKai (pay in advance or distribute profit), and BlueKai will return part of the revenue to the websites.

Through this kind of data exchange, the most valuable data resources in the advertising market are put to good use: data providers monetize their data without directly involved in the complex advertising business; data buyers find it easier to access to data sources and quickly improve the ad serving effect. BlueKai has also noticed the privacy issue, so it provides an interface for users to look up who is using their data or "donate their data to charity." But it is in fact a way to avoid risks, which does not affect the anticipated revenue of BlueKai and small- and medium-sized websites. For more information about privacy, please refer to Section 7.4.

BlueKai provides an open tag system with a wide range of sub-categories, e.g., "people interested in P&G shampoo" and "people who want to travel in Japan." These fairly refined tag categories are quite important for the advertisers planning for response advertising, so they are sold at a high price. Owing to varied use purposes and data sources, these tags are divided into the following categories: Intent, B2B, Past Purchases, Geo/Demo, Interest/Lifestyle, Branded, and Estimated Financial/Economic. This is a typical semi-open tag system, in which the "Intent" is similar to the aforesaid interest tag and processed by BlueKai with the user behavioral data collected by the data exchange. Among the remaining tags, some are directly provided by other DPs, like the "B2B" provided by Bizo; some are subject to the data fusion of more than one DPs, e.g., the "Demo/Geo" actually integrates the data sources from Bizo, Datalogix, Expedia, and other DPs.

The tag system of BlueKai is an open one, because it constantly expands and adjusts the category and content of tags according to the data sources and market demand, so as to meet the unique needs of as many advertisers as possible. The common tags, number of covered users, and major data sources of BlueKai are given in Table 7.1.

(2) **AudienceScience**

AudienceScience

In the advertising market, it was AudienceScience that took the lead in explicitly putting forward the idea of audience targeting, and the company has all along been committed to data processing and algorithmic construction in this regard. Its core business includes the following aspects:

i. It mainly acts as a first-party DMP to provide service to media and advertisers. For example, the *New York Times* has numerous readers and rich online data, but its core business is neither advertising nor data processing, so it is ready to hand over the data to AudienceScience; the company processes some meaningful user tags for the newspaper, such as financial users and sports users. The BI system of the *New York Times* will then analyze these tags to identify the readers of specific content, and decide how to optimize the content.

TABLE 7.1 Main categories in BlueKai's tag system

Category	Description	Data sources	User scale
Intent	Users whose recent word input shows their desire for certain product or service	BlueKai Intent	>1.6 billion
B2B	Users whose occupation closes to certain demand	Bizo	0.9 billion
Past Purchase	Users who are likely to buy certain product based on their past consumption habits	Addthis, Alliant	0.65 billion
Geo/Demo	Users who are geographically or demographically close to a tag	Bizo, Datalogix, Expedia	
Interest/LifeStyle	Users who may like a particular product or lifestyle	Forbes, i360, IXI …	>1.03 billion
Qualified Demo	The demographical attributes based on consensus and consistency on multiple data sources	Multiple sources	>0.9 billion
Estimated Financial	Categorization based on an estimate of users' financial situation	V12	

ii. AudienceScience directly runs a direct response ad network to help advertisers manage and optimize their ad serving; in this process it will employ the user tags it has processed. In terms of data aggregation and revenue sharing, AudienceScience has a lot in common with BlueKai; the main difference between the two is that the former does not rely on the revenue from tag sales, since the tags are exclusively used by the advertisers that enlist AudienceScience to do performance optimization. AudienceScience achieves monetization by running an ADN, the revenue from tag use is partially shared with the DPs (i.e., the media). AudienceScience does so is due to a small profit margin after deducting the profit share to the media, it has found a much larger space for arbitrage by running an ADN.

The specific business process of AudienceScience is as follows: the website (either advertiser or media website) firstly escrows its own traffic to AudienceScience and pays some technical service fee to it, then AudienceScience processes the data into tags and transfer them to the website for optimizing its traffic and user experience.

Unfortunately, AudienceScience closed down in May 2017, which reflects that in the current Internet advertising industry, it is hard for the pure data service to make headway with the constraints in limited scale and profitability.

3. **TalkingData**

TalkingData
移动 · 数据 · 价值

TalkingData is a well-known mobile data platform in the Chinese market. With the statistical analysis tools provided to developers as the entry point, TalkingData has accumulated about 700PB of independent device data every month. Based on these data, it launched the product "MarketingCloud," which is a DMP that combines third-party and first-party data for marketing, but it is more like a first-party DMP from the perspective of business model. The main functions of MarketingCloud are as follows:

i. User ID mapping and management. The first-party user data collected by the clients in various scenarios usually carry different IDs. For example, the data about CRM, offline stores, online browsing, and WeChat public accounts show different user IDs. In order to effectively manage users, it is necessary to unify the data with different IDs of the same user, which calls for solid third-party data accumulation, while the MarketingCloud is just capable of doing so.

ii. The third-party tag library open to clients. Since TalkingData has accumulated a large amount of third-party data, it enables clients to fully understand and use the entire network user data for audience targeting or look-alike marketing, in addition to their own first-party data. In contrast to the first-party DMP that mainly uses the first-party data, these third-party data may qualitatively enhance the marketing ability of the clients when dealing with new users. At present, the third-party user tags in MarketingCloud include demographical attributes, city, device property, application interest, consumer preference, etc., which could be segmented into over 800 dimensions.

iii. Geo-fencing-based audience targeting. Through GPS, Wi-Fi, Bluetooth, and other means, mobile devices can locate user geographic locations more accurately, and these locations are often used to restore the exact user scenarios. With the geo-location data accumulated by TalkingData, MarketingCloud is able to open the geo-fencing-based audience targeting to its clients.

iv. Monitoring and management of marketing process. One of the primary purposes of first-party data management and third-party data utilization is marketing. In this regard, MarketingCloud provides a series of functions for audience insight before marketing and data analysis after marketing, hoping to gradually realize automation of the marketing process.

In recent years, the data-driven automated marketing products, which are similar to MarketingCloud, have become a hotspot in the market. It is one of the major development trends in the future to realize basic automation of the marketing process (including user acquisition, remarketing, performance evaluation, and optimization) through integrated use of both first-party and third-party data.

7.3 BASIC PROCESS OF DATA TRADING

The data trading process (see Figure 7.5) is generally completed with ADX or SSP as a transit. Various user tags processed by DMP are delivered to ADX via batch transmission and sold to DSPs as an auxiliary product of ADX. The tags are usually priced by CPM. When a DSP intends to purchase a certain type of tag, ADX will send the requested user tags to this DSP during the ad call. In the end, the actual display quantity will be multiplied by CPM; their product will be the additional cost for DSP's data buying.

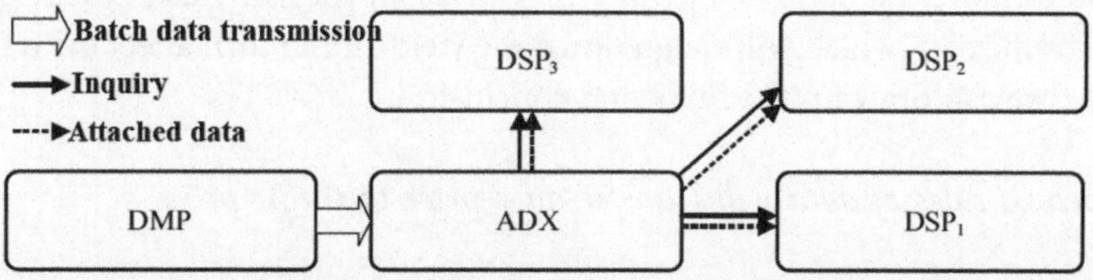

FIGURE 7.5 Data trading process.

Compared with the direct data exchange between DMP and DSP, the data exchange with advertising trade as the carrier seems more reasonable, such product solution boasts the following advantages:

(1) Where the magnitude of data is large, the cost of data transmission will be too high to be ignored. In the case of data exchange between DMP and DSP, the overall data transmission cost is very high. In contrast, if the user tags are attached to an ad request and then transmitted, there will be no additional service expense, meaning that the overall data exchange cost only stems from the one-off transmission between DMP and ADX.

(2) All DSPs and DPs only need cookie mapping with ADX, so the ADX-centered topological structure is obviously more convenient than the one in which DSPs directly map cookies with DPs. The user scale reached by ADX is usually much larger than that of a single DSP or DMP, which avoids the data loss from cookie mapping to the maximum extent.

(3) Another prominent advantage of this solution is partial exchange of data: it is seldom for a DSP to make use of all the data delivered by a DMP. By transmitting data in the advertising process, the DSP is free to control the scope of data to its needs. For example, if a DSP only deals with the Shanghai-based clients, it will no longer receive the data of other areas after selecting "Shanghai" in ADX.

(4) Between the data buyer and seller, ADX plays a role in monitoring and billing of data use.

But being an information product, data are repeatedly marketable, which is the biggest difference from other physical goods and even ads; moreover, data also distinguish from software – although the latter is also sold repeatedly, because software users are separated from each other, while data users fall into the same group where there exists a game relationship.

It is a trade of a special kind of commodity, our knowledge of it evolves step by step. At this point, some problems do exist in the data trading mechanisms as described above. For example: suppose a DMP is aware of a user being a golf fan, it sells this information to a DSP as a kind of data, so that the latter could make use of the data to create a rich economic benefit, of course it will agree to buy the data at a relatively high price. However, if the DMP sells the data to more than one DSP, when they direct at the same user, their biddings will push up the traffic cost, which will weigh down the yield and in turn affect the data price. To put it simply, we can draw up the following conclusion:

The repeated sales of data will transfer data price to traffic price.

The other problem with unlimited and repeated data sales is that it makes auction-based sales infeasible. It is known that the auction-based sales has remarkably increased the number of customers on the online advertising market and also improved its ability of monetization. In view of this, we expect such a sales model to apply to the data trade. Suppose the data are sold in limited quantity, then the auction-based sales will be possible, and the interests of DPs will also be guaranteed. The limited data sales is to sell each piece of information to a designated number of buyers. But for how to define the number of buyers and how to implement such a sales model, there is yet an industrial consensus.

7.4 PRIVACY PROTECTION AND DATA SECURITY

Advertising is a typical personalized system that needs a large number of user behavioral data for audience targeting. Moreover, in the advertising market there also exists data transaction. No matter it is audience targeting or data transaction, we shall be watchful for disclosing the privacy of users while using their behavioral data. At the same time, we shall care about the interests of data owners, especially the advertisers, because there is possibility that their vital business information is acquired or employed by other platforms or rivals in the advertising market.

7.4.1 Privacy Protection

The privacy problem discusses the security of personal information, but there have been some misunderstandings about this problem on the market. In fact, privacy protection focuses on two aspects of challenges: one is the leakage of user data in batches, and the other one (also the more important one) is the privacy snooping of acquaintances – the snooper attempts to dig more privacy information of the snoopee based on the background information that he already knows. The latter challenge poses the greatest risk to privacy, since it may be a combination of human and machine, and often insensitive to cost. Sometimes our privacy leaks even without our awareness, for example: a Tsinghua student once deduced the home address of Chinese artist Luodan Wang with her selfies: when Luodan Wang posted some selfies on her microblog, this Tsinghua student analyzed her texts and photo details to locate where she was dwelling. Now let's learn more about the problems in privacy protection and its principles.

(1) **Basic principles for privacy protection**

Great attention has been attached to privacy protection since the early stage of the Internet-based personalized services. The EU has organized in-depth researches in this regard and put into effect of several norms for privacy security. To date, the industrial community has reached consensus on the following principles for privacy protection:

i. **Try not to use the Personal Identifiable Information (PII).** PII is the most important private information, including ID number, phone number, e-mail address, and home address, which is easily traced back to the concerned users. If such information is maliciously obtained, it will cause great inconvenience and potential risks to the people concerned, so it needs to be protected strictly and unconditionally. It should be noted that the user IDs frequently used in the advertising system, such as cookies and IMEI, do not belong to the PII because they cannot directly identify the users.

ii. **Users deserve the right to ask the system to stop tracking and using their behavioral data.** When some behaviorally targeted ads are delivered to users, they shall be attached with an entry through which the users will know why they receive these ads, i.e., the "Ad Choices" at the right part of the ad as shown in Figure 7.6. If users are not happy at their behavioral data used in such way, they can access this entry, and then click the "Opt Out" on the description page to inform the system to stop tracking and using their behavioral data. Upon receipt of the user request, the system shall stop recording their behaviors and no longer deliver the behaviorally targeted ads to them. In short, such entry gives users the right to accept or reject the personalized ads, which is fairly important for privacy protection in specific situations.

iii. **User behavioral data should not be retained or used for a long time.** Even if users accept the behaviorally targeted ads, the advertising platform shall moderately use and store their data. Any long-term retention of such data is of limited significance for audience targeting, and at the same time increasing risks for data leakage. Therefore, the user behavioral data shall be kept only for a certain period, and the expired data, if not directly associated with the advertising business, shall be no longer physically stored.

iv. **Pay special attention to assignment of data access permission and minimum data access in engineering.** When they are debugging programs, the engineers shall use the sampled data subsets with key information anonymized, but access the original data sets with special secret keys during production. Despite of those that develop data handling programs, no one is entitled to access to the data, including the management personnel.

The above four principles are essential fundamentals that should be followed by advertising and recommendation systems as the top priority while accessing user behavioral data. But these principles are impotent when dealing with the underlying privacy leakage

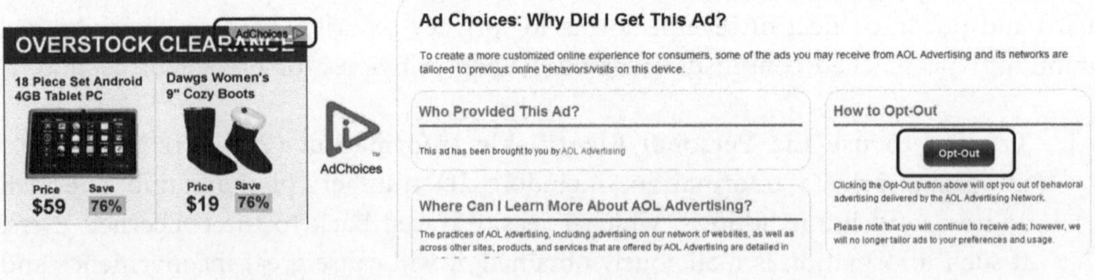

FIGURE 7.6 Example of Ad Choices.

Securing Cyber-Physical Systems

Securing Cyber-Physical Systems

Edited by Al-Sakib Khan Pathan

CRC Press
Taylor & Francis Group
Boca Raton London New York

CRC Press is an imprint of the
Taylor & Francis Group, an **informa** business

CRC Press
Taylor & Francis Group
6000 Broken Sound Parkway NW, Suite 300
Boca Raton, FL 33487-2742

Version Date: 20150805

International Standard Book Number-13: 978-1-4987-0098-6 (Hardback)

Library of Congress Cataloging-in-Publication Data

Securing cyber-physical systems / edited by Al-Sakib Khan Pathan.
pages cm
Includes bibliographical references and index.
ISBN 978-1-4987-0098-6
1. Computer security. 2. Cooperating objects (Computer systems)--Security measures. 3. Embedded computer systems--Security measures. 4. Infrastructure (Economics)--Security measures. I. Pathan, Al-Sakib Khan.

QA76.9.A25S37556 2016
005.8--dc23 2015016377

Visit the Taylor & Francis Web site at
http://www.taylorandfrancis.com

and the CRC Press Web site at
http://www.crcpress.com

Dedicated to my beloved daughter, Rumaysa.

Contents

Preface ix
Acknowledgment xi
Editor xiii
Contributors xv

1 Securing Power Systems 1
MARTIN SAINT, JUAN HOYOS, AND TIMOTHY X. BROWN

2 ICT Modeling for Cosimulation of Integrated Cyberpower Systems 27
ALEXANDRU STEFANOV, CHEN-CHING LIU, AND KITHSIRI LIYANAGE

3 Moving Target Defense Mechanisms in Cyber-Physical Systems 63
SHIH-WEI FANG, ANTHONY PORTANTE, AND MOHAMMAD IFTEKHAR HUSAIN

4 Ontological Framework–Assisted Embedded System Design with Security Consideration in a Cyber-Physical Power System Environment 91
BO XING

5 WSNProtectLayer: Security Middleware for Wireless Sensor Networks 119
VASHEK MATYÁŠ, PETR ŠVENDA, ANDRIY STETSKO, DUŠAN KLINEC, FILIP JURNEČKA, AND MARTIN STEHLÍK

6 Securing Transportation Cyber-Physical Systems 163
NNANNA EKEDEBE, HOUBING SONG, WEI YU, CHAO LU, AND YAN WAN

7 Securing the Future Autonomous Vehicle: A Cyber-Physical Systems Approach 197
MARIO GERLA AND PETER REIHER

8 A Study of Security Issues, Vulnerabilities, and Challenges in the Internet of Things 221
KASHIF LAEEQ AND JAWWAD A. SHAMSI

9 Security and Privacy in the IPv6-Connected Internet of Things 241
SHAHID RAZA, CHAMATH KEPPITIYAGAMA, AND THIEMO VOIGT

10 Security Issues and Approaches in M2M Communications 259
YUE QIU AND MAODE MA

11 Securing Embedded Systems: Cyberattacks, Countermeasures, and Challenges 279
MOHAMED AMINE FERRAG, NASSIRA CHEKKAI, AND MEHDI NAFA

12 Using Software-Defined Networking to Mitigate Cyberattacks in Industrial Control Systems 305
BÉLA GENGE, HUNOR SÁNDOR, PIROSKA HALLER, ADELA BEREŞ, AND ISTVÁN KISS

13 Tackling Cross-Site Scripting (XSS) Attacks in Cyberspace 331
AL-SAKIB KHAN PATHAN AND IMRAN YUSOF

14 Trojan-Resilient Circuits 349
JEAN-PIERRE SEIFERT AND CHRISTOPH BAYER

15 Intrusion Detection, Prevention, and Response System (IDPRS) for Cyber-Physical Systems (CPSs) 371
JIANGUO DING

16 Security-Integrated Quality-of-Service Paradigm for Cyber-Physical Systems 393
ZUBAIR MD. FADLULLAH

Index 409

Preface

Cyber-physical system (CPS) is a relatively new term, coined in the field of interconnected devices and networks that enhances the notion of cyberspace. It offers a kind of cyberspace based on several interconnected physical devices, each of which is run by sophisticated embedded systems and software. Checking the history, we find that the initial promoters of this idea had a strong background in software engineering technologies for embedded software, working on stand-alone systems. Hence, from their perspective, they focused on a single embedded system. When the idea of CPS was being developed, it considered how to make it possible for multiple embedded control systems to interact among themselves through communications and physical environments (e.g., from one's actuators to another one's sensors). Apart from this, many other networking and software development issues were raised, such as how to model, design, implement, and test software, how to consider and reflect uncertainty and heterogeneity due to the integration within the development phase, how to provide reliability and dependability on such systems, how to maintain such systems, and so on. Recently, security topics in CPS have emerged. The question, however, is whether a CPS's structure changes the security requirements of those present in the areas of the Internet of Things (IoT), machine to machine (M2M), and similar communications. With multiple definitions of CPS today, the security issue is still an open field and many link CPS security with their own field of research—some from a programming or software engineering point of view, some from a middleware/operating system (OS) point of view, and some with IoT, M2M, or similar technologies. In fact, the security techniques in other fields would also help CPS security. The term is indeed attractive, but the core of the technology is similar to that of other security technologies. General works on IoT, for instance, would also be relevant to such an interconnected system. This book aims to address these issues covering different mechanisms related to CPS security.

A total of 16 chapters have been included in this book. As expected, the authors have addressed different aspects of CPS, often with slightly different definitions. Most of the chapters were selected based on a rigorous review, while some were invited from the experts in the field. All these chapters are arranged within three parts in the book. Though each part does not address a common topic within (or related to) CPS, the sequence is such that readers should find it easy to understand the contents of the later chapters.

The concept and various facets of CPS are still being developed. Hence, this attempt to compile works specifically focused on the security issues of CPS has been difficult to accomplish. With multiple different meanings of the same term, the book still binds all the chapters with a single thread, which is supposed to be beneficial for the readers. The overall content may help researchers in finding future direction and scope for their research as well.

With best wishes,

Al-Sakib Khan Pathan
International Islamic University Malaysia

Acknowledgment

My sincere gratitude is to the Almighty Allah who once again allowed me to accomplish such a work with the time I needed in this transient life. The entire process has been, as usual, lengthy, requiring non-stop work and interactions with several people in various ways. I am indebted to all the authors, reviewers, and critics who helped me shape the book in a better way. Last, but not least, special thanks goes to CRC Press and all the staff who have worked professionally on the publication of this book.

Al-Sakib Khan Pathan
International Islamic University Malaysia

Acknowledgment

Editor

Al-Sakib Khan Pathan received his PhD degree (MS leading to PhD) in computer engineering in 2009 from Kyung Hee University, South Korea. He received a BSc degree in computer science and information technology from the Islamic University of Technology, Bangladesh, in 2003. He is currently an assistant professor in the Department of Computer Science at the International Islamic University Malaysia, Malaysia. Until June 2010, he served as an assistant professor in the Computer Science and Engineering Department at BRAC University, Bangladesh. Prior to holding this position, he worked as a researcher at the Networking Lab, Kyung Hee University, South Korea, until August 2009. His research interests include wireless sensor networks, network security, and e-services technologies. Currently, he is also working on some multidisciplinary issues. He is a recipient of several awards/best paper awards and has several publications in these areas. He has served as a chair, organizing committee member, and technical program committee member at numerous international conferences/workshops such as the Global Communications Conference, International Conference on Communications, International Conference on Green Computing and Communications (GreenCom), International Conference on Advanced Information Networking and Applications, Wireless Communications and Networking Conference, International Conference on High Performance Computing and Simulation, International Conference on Algorithms and Architectures for Parallel Processing, International Wireless Communications and Mobile Computing Conference, Vehicular Technology Conference, and International Conference on High Performance Computing and Communications. He was awarded the IEEE Outstanding Leadership Award and Certificate of Appreciation for his role at the Institute of Electrical and Electronics Engineers (IEEE) GreenCom 2013 conference. He is currently serving in various editorial positions, including as an associate technical editor of *IEEE Communications Magazine*, editor of *Ad Hoc and Sensor Wireless Networks* (Old City Publishing) and the *International Journal of Sensor Networks* (Inderscience Publishers), area editor of the *International Journal of Communication Networks and Information Security*, associate editor of the *International Journal of Computational Science and Engineering* (Inderscience), guest editor of many special issues of top-ranked journals, and editor/author of 12 published books. One of his books has been included twice in Intel Corporation's Recommended Reading List for Developers, in the second half of 2013 and first half of 2014; three other books were included in IEEE Communications Society's (IEEE ComSoc) Best Readings in Communications and Information Systems Security, 2013; and a fifth book is in the process of being translated into simplified Chinese from the English version. Also, two of his journal papers and one conference paper are included under different categories in IEEE ComSoc's Best Readings Topics on Communications and Information Systems Security, 2013. He also serves as a referee for numerous renowned journals. He has received awards for his reviewing activities: one of the most active reviewers of the *International Arab Journal of Information Technology* twice, for 2012 and 2014, and recognized reviewer status for *Computers and Electrical Engineering* (Elsevier; March 2014) and *Ad Hoc Networks* (Elsevier; April 2014). He is a senior member of the IEEE (United States).

Contributors

Christoph Bayer
Security in Telecommunications
TU Berlin and Deutsche Telekom Laboratories
Berlin, Germany

Adela Bereș
Department of Computer Science
Technical University of Cluj-Napoca
Cluj-Napoca, Romania

Timothy X. Brown
Interdisciplinary Telecommunications Program
University of Colorado
Boulder, Colorado

and

Department of Electrical and Computer Engineering
Carnegie Mellon University
Kigali, Rwanda

Nassira Chekkai
Department of Computer Science and Its Applications
Université Abdelhamid Mehri de Constantine
Constantine, Algeria

Jianguo Ding
School of Informatics
University of Skövde
Skövde, Sweden

Nnanna Ekedebe
Department of Computer and Information Sciences
Towson University
Towson, Maryland

Zubair Md. Fadlullah
Graduate School of Information Sciences
Tohoku University
Sendai, Japan

Shih-Wei Fang
Department of Computer Science
California State Polytechnic University, Pomona
Pomona, California

Mohamed Amine Ferrag
Department of Computer Science
Guelma University
Guelma, Algeria

Béla Genge
Department of Informatics
Petru Maior University
Târgu Mureș, Romania

Mario Gerla
Computer Science Department
University of California, Los Angeles
Los Angeles, California

Piroska Haller
Department of Informatics
Petru Maior University
Târgu Mureș, Romania

Juan Hoyos
Interdisciplinary Telecommunications Program
University of Colorado
Boulder, Colorado

and

Empresas Públicas de Medellín
Medellín, Colombia

Mohammad Iftekhar Husain
Department of Computer Science
California State Polytechnic University, Pomona
Pomona, California

Filip Jurnečka
Faculty of Informatics
Masaryk University
Brno, Czech Republic

Chamath Keppitiyagama
School of Computing
University of Colombo
Colombo, Sri Lanka

István Kiss
Department of Informatics
Petru Maior University
Târgu Mureş, Romania

and

Department of Computer Science
Technical University of Cluj-Napoca
Cluj-Napoca, Romania

Dušan Klinec
Faculty of Informatics
Masaryk University
Brno, Czech Republic

Kashif Laeeq
Department of Computer Science
National University of Computer and Emerging Sciences
Karachi, Pakistan

Chen-Ching Liu
School of Mechanical and Materials Engineering
University College Dublin
Dublin, Ireland

and

School of Electrical Engineering and Computer Science
Washington State University
Pullman, Washington

Kithsiri Liyanage
Department of Electrical and Electronic Engineering
University of Peradeniya
Peradeniya, Sri Lanka

Chao Lu
Department of Computer and Information Sciences
Towson University
Towson, Maryland

Maode Ma
School of Electrical and Electronic Engineering
Nanyang Technological University
Singapore

Vashek Matyáš
Faculty of Informatics
Masaryk University
Brno, Czech Republic

Mehdi Nafa
Department of Computer Science
Badji Mokhtar University
Sidi Amar-Annaba, Algeria

Al-Sakib Khan Pathan
Department of Computer Science
International Islamic University Malaysia
Gombak, Malaysia

Anthony Portante
Department of Computer Science
California State Polytechnic University, Pomona
Pomona, California

Yue Qiu
School of Electrical and Electronic Engineering
Nanyang Technological University
Singapore

Shahid Raza
Networked Embedded Systems Group
SICS Swedish ICT
Kista, Sweden

Peter Reiher
Computer Science Department
University of California, Los Angeles
Los Angeles, California

Martin Saint
Interdisciplinary Telecommunications Program
University of Colorado
Boulder, Colorado

and

Department of Information and Communication Technology
Carnegie Mellon University
Kigali, Rwanda

Hunor Sándor
Department of Computer Science
Technical University of Cluj-Napoca
Cluj-Napoca, Romania

Jean-Pierre Seifert
Security in Telecommunications
TU Berlin and Deutsche Telekom Laboratories
Berlin, Germany

Jawwad A. Shamsi
Department of Computer Science
National University of Computer and Emerging Sciences
Karachi, Pakistan

Houbing Song
Department of Electrical and Computer Engineering
West Virginia University
Montgomery, West Virginia

Alexandru Stefanov
School of Mechanical and Materials Engineering
University College Dublin
Dublin, Ireland

Martin Stehlík
Faculty of Informatics
Masaryk University
Brno, Czech Republic

Andriy Stetsko
Faculty of Informatics
Masaryk University
Brno, Czech Republic

Petr Švenda
Faculty of Informatics
Masaryk University
Brno, Czech Republic

Thiemo Voigt
Networked Embedded Systems Group
SICS Swedish ICT
Kista, Sweden

and

Department of Information Technology
Uppsala University
Uppsala, Sweden

Yan Wan
Department of Electrical Engineering
University of North Texas
Denton, Texas

Bo Xing
Department of Computer Science
University of Limpopo
Sovenga, South Africa

Wei Yu
Department of Computer and Information Sciences
Towson University
Towson, Maryland

Imran Yusof
Department of Computer Science
International Islamic University Malaysia
Kuala Lumpur, Malaysia

Chapter 1

Securing Power Systems

Martin Saint and Timothy X. Brown
University of Colorado and Carnegie Mellon University

Juan Hoyos
University of Colorado and Empresas Públicas de Medellín

Contents

1.1 Power System Overview 2
1.1.1 The Power System as Critical Infrastructure 3
1.1.2 Generation 4
1.1.3 Transmission 4
1.1.4 Distribution 5
1.1.5 Load 6
1.2 New Capabilities and Challenges for Modern Control Systems 6
1.2.1 Objectives 7
1.2.2 Performance 8
1.2.3 Culture 8
1.2.4 Cyber-Physical Coupling 8
1.2.5 Distributed Systems 8
1.2.6 Design Lifetime 8
1.2.7 Regulation and Standards 9
1.2.8 Risk Management 9
1.3 IEC 61850 Standard 9
1.3.1 Background 9
1.3.2 Overview of the Standard 11
1.3.3 Example IEC 61850 Functionality 12
1.3.4 Challenges and Vulnerabilities 13
1.3.4.1 Complexity 14
1.3.4.2 Cyber-Physical Security for IEC 61850 14
1.3.4.3 The Problem of Encryption and Message Authentication versus Latency 15
1.3.4.4 Other Issues 16

1.4 IEC 61850 Attack Vectors, Consequences, and Mitigation 17
1.4.1 Attack Vectors and Techniques 17
1.4.2 Attack Consequences 17
1.4.3 Mitigating Attacks 18
1.5 Exploiting IEC 61850 via GOOSE 18
1.5.1 Normal GOOSE Function 19
1.5.2 Building a Practical Cyberattack 20
1.5.2.1 Technical Details 20
1.5.2.2 Building the Script 21
1.5.2.3 The Results of the Attack 21
1.6 Conclusion 23
Acknowledgment 23
Author Biographies 23
References 24

Abstract: Security issues for the power industry have become increasingly relevant as it relies more than ever on networking and automation protocols. The next generation of electrical grid incorporates significant advances in communications and control that closely couple cyber and physical systems. This enables new capabilities, but also exposes new vulnerabilities. While modern control networks share many elements in common with traditional information technology networks, they must be designed, managed, and secured with different goals in mind. The IEC 61850 standard for power automation has been widely adopted, and the design concepts are being incorporated throughout the generation, transmission, and distribution areas of the power industry. The success of IEC 61850 for substation automation has led to adaptations developed for other applications such as hydroelectric plants, wind turbines, distribution feeders, and high-voltage switch gear. This chapter describes the IEC 61850 architecture and potential threats, existing security protections, and some remaining vulnerabilities. Challenges to implementing security for IEC 61850 are described. An example IEC 61850 exploit is implemented on real equipment to demonstrate what might be necessary for a successful attack capable of creating a widespread interruption in power generation and distribution. Mitigations for some current vulnerabilities are offered, and areas which require further solutions are highlighted.

Keywords: Cyber-physical security; GOOSE message; IEC 61850; Substation security; Critical infrastructure.

1.1 Power System Overview

Electricity is a key energy sector in modern society. Electricity is provided through a power system consisting of interconnected generation, transmission, distribution, and end-user load components. The electrical grid has been called the most important engineering achievement of the twentieth century, and the transmission and distribution system is the largest machine ever made [1]. However, it still uses technologies that have changed little in the last hundred years and are poised for a revolution in their physical, organizational, and conceptual structure. What began as a physical system governed by electromechanical controls is rapidly evolving to become a complex cyber-physical system that relies on the integration of sophisticated control and communication networks. At the same time, there is a new focus on the critical nature of key infrastructure that affects the function of society and the need to identify vulnerabilities and improve critical infrastructure security. The increasingly interdependent nature of infrastructure is also being recognized; for instance, telecommunications depend on electric power, and control of the electric grid depends increasingly upon telecommunications, creating the possibility for a negative feedback loop following a disturbance in either.

Electricity is a major industry in which service providers retail power that is provided by operator companies at prices that are set by a combination of markets and regulatory oversight. The electric power industry is a $385 billion (2013) industry in the United States [2] and tops $1882 billion (2012) worldwide [3]. Failures such as outages and voltage fluctuations lead to significant economic losses and impact societal health and safety. Reports written for the U.S. Department of Energy (DoE) by LaCommare and Eto in 2004 [4] and 2006 [5] place the cost of power outages at approximately $80 billion annually in the United States. They note, however, that there are significant gaps in the amount and quality of outage information gathered. They performed sensitivity analysis, which indicated costs could range from less than $30 billion to over $130 billion annually. Other work by Clemmensen et al. [6] in 1999 estimates losses of $26 billion per year, Swaminathan and Sen [7] in 1999 estimate $150 billion per year, and the Electric Power Research Institute in 2001 [8] reports an estimate of $119 billion per year. Even these comprehensive studies have their limits: LaCommare and Eto state that an extended power outage may have social impacts such as emergency response or public health costs, or the costs of inconvenience and anxiety, none of which are accounted for. Studies often do not take into account the effects of power quality disturbances, only outages.

1.1.1 The Power System as Critical Infrastructure

Critical infrastructure protection is becoming an increasingly important topic internationally, and particularly after the events of September 11, 2001 in the United States. Federal laws mandate that any virtual or physical assets whose incapacity or destruction would have a debilitating impact on security, national economics, or national public health or safety must be considered critical infrastructure [9]. The Department of Homeland Security defines a total of 18 sectors* for the United States, and each sector is assigned to a specific government agency, which is responsible for identifying risks and promoting rules or standards to protect its assigned critical infrastructure [10].

For energy-related critical infrastructure, the U.S. DoE has been assigned to identify and promote best practices and methodologies for protection and continuity of energy services. The DoE has designated the North American Electric Reliability Corporation (NERC) as the organization responsible for assuring security of the power grid and elevating awareness and understanding of threats and vulnerabilities to utility assets, systems, and networks. In May 2006, NERC released a set of Critical Infrastructure Protection (CIP) Cyber Security Standards, CIP-002 through CIP-009, applicable to users, owners, and operators of the power grid. The CIP standards are designed to minimize the risk of possible cyberattacks using the communications infrastructure, as well as potential physical attacks, either of which could compromise the integrity of the grid [11].

There are other organizations, such as the British Standards Institute (BSI), the U.S. National Institute of Standards and Technology (NIST), and the International Society of Automation

* The full list includes agriculture and food, banking and finance, chemical, commercial facilities, communications, critical manufacturing, dams, defense industrial base, emergency services, energy, government facilities, healthcare and public health, information technology, national monuments and icons, nuclear reactors and materials and waste, postal and shipping, transportation systems, and water.

(ISA), that are working on internationally applicable standards for cybersecurity for automation processes.

The rest of this section describes the key generation, transmission, distribution, and load components of the electrical grid system. A basic overview of the system is helpful for understanding how it is evolving, why there is a need for sophisticated communications and control, and where specific vulnerabilities exist.

1.1.2 Generation

Common generators are driven by hydro, wind, oil, or nuclear power and work on the principle of electromagnetic induction. When a conductor moves in relation to a magnetic field, voltage is induced in the conductor. Power plant generators are three phase, or constructed with three terminals, each producing power that is 120° out of phase with the others. This permits constant instantaneous power from the generator and reduces the overall size of conductors required for transmission. In North America, alternating current (AC) generators operate at 60 Hz, and in much of the rest of the world at 50 Hz. It is important that all generators connected to a common system be able to coordinate their output so that the sine waveforms produced are as nearly synchronous as possible.

Classic generators convert mechanical energy to electrical energy. The rotating shaft of the generator is driven by a prime mover, such as a steam turbine, or directly through hydropower. Most generation is thermally driven, which means that a fuel such as coal or natural gas is burned to produce steam, which drives a turbine. In the case of nuclear plants, it is the heat from the fission reaction that is used to create the steam for the turbine.

As it is impractical to store large quantities of electricity, at any instant the quantity of electricity generated must match the quantity demanded by the load. This leads to three types of generating plants: baseload, load-following, and peaking. Baseload generation, such as is provided by coal-fired and nuclear plants, is economical to operate but cannot be quickly modulated. It is used to meet the level of relatively constant loads that are determined to historically exist on a power system. Load-following units, such as combined-cycle gas turbine-driven generation, have the ability to run for long periods of time, but may be turned off and can vary their output more readily than baseload units. Peaking plants, such as gas turbine, may be started, stopped, and regulated quickly. They are normally only used when electricity demand is near its peak. The electricity generated from these plants is relatively expensive, as they may use more expensive fuels, and building the plants involves high fixed costs, even though they may be idle most of the time.

Environmental concerns, difficulty obtaining permits and approvals, and high cost all serve as impediments to constructing new traditional generation facilities. At the same time, increasing demand and aging infrastructure pose a threat to reliability and adequate capacity in the electric sector. Advances in sensing, communications, and control hold the promise of reducing and shifting demand, improving efficiency, enabling the incorporation of alternative generation, and providing for better monitoring and maintenance.

1.1.3 Transmission

Unlike the first generating stations, as power plants grew they began to be located outside of the population centers they served, necessitating the long-distance transmission of power to the local distribution networks. The transmission system is composed of transmission substations and transformers to boost the voltage from the level at which it can be safely generated to levels high enough to be efficient for long-distance transmission. It is also composed of high-voltage transmission lines, commonly between 138 and 765 kV, and shares distribution substations containing transformers that reduce the transmission voltages back down to distribution levels. Substations also contain related equipment, such as switchgear or circuit breakers, which are used to protect the system and disconnect parts of the network for maintenance. Measurement, metering, control, and communications equipment are also housed in substations and at points along the transmission network, allowing parameters such as voltage, current, and power quality to be remotely monitored and some equipment to be remotely controlled.

The amount of power that can be transmitted over a given conductor is limited by a number of factors, including the conductor's material, size, length, and distance from other conductors and potential ground elements. Transmission loads are also governed by *thermal limits*, *stability limits*, and *voltage limits*. *Thermal limits* are primarily a function of heating of the conductors due to resistance in the conductor material, leading to excessive power loss and sag in the line. While not the primary constraint, transmission thermal limits are affected by ambient temperature, and are part of the concept of *dynamic rating*, which permits the maximum carrying capacity of the line to be adjusted for factors such as ambient temperature and the amount of time the line has been heavily loaded. The *stability limit* refers to the difficulty of keeping remote generators in synchronism with each other, particularly as feedback is required due to ever-varying loads on each generator. *Voltage limits* affect power transmission because impedance in the transmission line causes a drop in voltage over its length, and for practical reasons, electrical systems generally do not permit a drop to less than 95% of the design voltage. Shorter transmission lines are usually constrained by the thermal limit and longer lines by the stability limit. Voltage limits may also constrain longer lines, although it is possible to install equipment that helps to boost or regulate voltage.

Transmission networks are typically connected in a grid or mesh topology, rather than point-to-point or hub-and-spoke. This creates redundancy and allows electricity to take multiple routes, bypassing generation and transmission resources which may be accidentally or intentionally taken off-line. As electricity follows the path of least resistance, affected by phase, amplitude, and impedance, it is difficult to predict the exact circuit it will follow between varying generation and loads when there is more than one possible route. Small changes in voltage and impedance may be made to influence the power path and hence the load on individual lines, but a great deal of state information and computation is required to monitor and control the system to prevent transmission line overloads. Increasingly, the U.S. electrical grid faces the issue of *congestion*, whereby loads cannot be matched to the most economical remote generation due to the lack of capacity and potential for overloads in the transmission system. Congestion, lack of incentive, and the difficulty of obtaining rights-of-way and permits to build new transmission lines present a significant threat to critical energy infrastructure.

Developments of new conductor materials that support high temperatures and have low sag are coming in the next decade to boost the capacity of existing transmission corridors, avoiding the environmental issues related to the construction of new lines. Until new conductors are viable in the market, utilities have taken the path of optimizing their existing infrastructure using existing technology. Current technologies include flexible AC transmission systems (FACTS), synchrophasors, Volt/VAR regulation/optimization, grid-scale energy storage, and installing utility-scale smart solar inverters. All of these techniques require high interdependence between telecommunication, control, and power system operation.

1.1.4 Distribution

Distribution networks begin at the distribution substation, which typically steps power down from transmission voltages to the 4–35 kV range. The substation may contain equipment similar to that found in transmission substations, although currently they are often less automated, providing an opportunity for improvement. Like transmission lines, distribution is three phase, although the conductors may be split near the load to serve individual neighborhoods. Residential and small commercial loads in the United States are typically served at 120 and 240 V, requiring another small transformer near the point of consumption. Distribution networks are often arranged in a radial topology, although ring and mesh are not uncommon. Even with ring and mesh configurations, a disconnect is usually left open so that the networks are operated as point-to-point connections with the ability to close the disconnect and failover to another route if necessary. While power flows have historically been from substation to load, this is changing with the introduction of distributed generation and microgrids, which will require more sophisticated monitoring and control.

1.1.5 Load

While it is an important element of the electric system, beyond the meter the grid becomes the domain of the consumer more than the regulator or the utilities. While this domain is generally not considered part of regulated critical infrastructure, if the goal is to deliver end-to-end reliable electricity, this link in the chain cannot be ignored. As "smart" buildings, homes, and systems become interconnected with the electrical grid, the potential for disruption of the grid increases, even if consumer systems are not directly interconnected with utility control and communications architecture.

Electrical loads are the reason the electrical grid exists, and they have important engineering implications for the way the grid functions. A charging plug-in electric vehicle (PEV) may draw as much power as an entire house, so the appearance of several within a neighborhood may easily exceed the original design for the neighborhood's distribution system unless they can be monitored and controlled. It is also important to monitor the load on the total system, both to plan for peak demand and to meet instantaneous requirements.

The type of load also has important implications for the way the grid functions, based upon its so-called impedance. In an AC system, voltage and current are sinusoidal, and both reverse their polarity at the same time if the load is strictly resistive, resulting in the transfer of only *real power*. If the load has capacitance and inductance elements, then voltage and current are out of phase and some current flows back to the source during each cycle. This *reactive power* does no useful work, but conductors, transformers, and generators must be sized to carry the total current and dissipate the heat generated.

Baseboard heaters and incandescent light bulbs are examples of purely resistive loads, which only consume real power. Many loads, such as motors, are a combination of resistive and inductive impedance, which effectively draws reactive power. The number of motors connected to the grid means that it is heavily skewed toward needing generators to supply both real and reactive power. It is possible to connect capacitor banks, which produce reactive power, to cancel inductive loads and reduce the demands on generation and transport, but this introduces the need for monitoring and control of power quality in the system.

1.2 New Capabilities and Challenges for Modern Control Systems

The requirements of the future smart grid communications infrastructure will create significant new challenges for control system cyber-physical security. High-speed, two-way communication will create more attack possibilities. The expansion of the network and more monitoring and control points will also increase the attack surface, as will the addition of customer interfaces. The interconnection of networks will present a greater number of vulnerabilities, particularly if communications use public data networks. The use of wireless devices and protocols will open new avenues for access, presenting challenges because the wireless spectrum cannot be physically secured. The control system trend is toward open software and protocols, but this also makes the source code and necessary knowledge to exploit these systems readily available. In addition to the increase in vulnerability, expanding the scope of systems and interconnection also increases the potential scale of any damage should a system be compromised.

As electric grid industrial control systems (ICSs) evolve, they are taking on many of the characteristics of enterprise information technology (IT) systems, such as running common enterprise operating systems like Microsoft Windows and Linux on personal computer-like architecture and the use of protocols such as the transmission control protocol and the Internet protocol (TCP/IP) using physical infrastructure such as Ethernet or public communication networks [12]. While IT systems pose their own ever-evolving security challenges, the environment and methods by which these challenges are addressed is more mature than for modern ICSs, and there is a need to develop a different approach to ICS security.

Although ICSs are starting to share some similar components and architectures, such as hardware, operating systems, and protocols, they are fundamentally different from enterprise IT systems. Some of the reasons for this are considered next, and additional differences are detailed in several documents from the National Institute of Standards and Technology [13] (updated in [14] and [15], among others).

1.2.1 Objectives

Information systems, including control systems, have three broad security goals:

Confidentiality. "Preserving authorized restrictions on information access and disclosure, including means for protecting personal privacy and proprietary information" [16].

A loss of confidentiality is the unauthorized disclosure of information [15].

Integrity. "Guarding against improper information modification or destruction, and includes ensuring information non-repudiation and authenticity" [16].

A loss of integrity is the unauthorized modification or destruction of information [15].

Availability. "Ensuring timely and reliable access to and use of information" [16].

A loss of availability is the disruption of access to or use of information or an information system [15].

ICSs manage processes that are integral to the functioning of critical national infrastructure, life safety, and the orderly functions of society. In ICSs, availability is the most critical metric, while IT systems prioritize confidentiality and integrity. As ICSs monitor continuous processes, they are not tolerant of interruptions, and any upgrades or maintenance must be tested and planned in advance to insure availability and continued reliability.

1.2.2 Performance

Peterson and Davie state that the two principal metrics of networking are throughput and delay [17]. ICSs are real time and may be sensitive to delay and jitter or require deterministic protocols. Though many applications do not require high sustained throughput [12], data burst rates can be very high in order to reduce packet latency in support of real-time control.

1.2.3 Culture

ICSs are often managed by control engineers, not IT specialists, and while control engineers may not have the same level of familiarity with modern IT infrastructure, they are more aware of the impact of communications and control on overall power system performance. A commitment to system reliability and availability may necessitate a compromise in other common IT objectives; for instance, rapid access to the control system by different operators in the event of an emergency may be more critical than strict access control or conformance to the principle of least privilege.

1.2.4 Cyber-Physical Coupling

ICSs typically control physical processes, and cyber-physical systems highlight the intersection of physical processes, computation, and communications. Unlike, for instance, embedded systems, where the focus is primarily on computation, cyber-physical systems recognize the important role of interaction with the physical world [18].

Security issues also have cyber-physical coupling. We focus here on cyberoriginated attacks that have physical consequences, so-called cyber-physical (CP) threats, rather than cyber-cyber (CC), physical-cyber (PC), or physical-physical (PP) threats [19]. CC threats include attacks on power system information management systems via network and other cyberavenues. CC attacks are addressed through traditional cybersecurity measures. PC threats include physical destruction of cyberassets or their supporting cabling and power supplies. These threats require proper physical security around cyberequipment. Further, we are more interested in attacks that impact the physical power grid. PP threats include causing physical faults in one part of the network, such as overloads, demand spikes, or loss of synchronization, that propagate to other parts of the power grid. These threats tend to lie within traditional grid stability and control systems. Here, we focus on CP attacks that cross the cyber to physical domain.

1.2.5 Distributed Systems

ICSs are often widely distributed, although they have centralized servers similar to IT systems. Unlike IT systems, which may only include a few types of distributed clients, ICSs often have a much greater variety of complex devices and systems at the edge of the network. It may also be difficult to physically access these systems for maintenance or troubleshooting, whereas IT systems tend to be more centralized and accessible.

1.2.6 Design Lifetime

Components in IT systems are often replaced on 3–5 year life cycles. ICSs may be expected to have a service life of 10–15 years. This impacts everything from multivendor support to available computational resources and capabilities. It is also often necessary to couple modern ICSs with legacy devices and protocols, which may have few security features or options.

1.2.7 Regulation and Standards

The electrical system is in many respects a natural monopoly in each local area. Due to economies of scope and scale, it is more efficient to build a single large power generation plant than two side-by-side competitors. Historically, with large coal, hydro, or nuclear generation plants, it made more sense to build a single transmission and distribution network than to provide multiple sets of wires between the producers and consumers of power. Because of their monopoly position and critical infrastructure status, these entities must be, and are, regulated. Most utilities are covered by a variety of regulations, which range from federal to local and govern all areas of the utility, from rates to reliability. Organizations such as the Institute of Electrical and Electronics Engineers (IEEE), NIST, and the International Society of Automation (ISA) all publish recommendations and standards that relate to the electric grid. Standards cover equipment specifications, safety, communications protocols, cybersecurity, and other topics that vary widely in their scope and focus. While standards are not in themselves regulations, they may be incorporated "by reference" such that compliance with the standard becomes a required part of the regulation [20].

1.2.8 Risk Management

Risk mitigation includes four categories of alternatives:

Retain. Accepting the chance of loss from a risk.
Avoid. Eliminating the vulnerability or consequence.
Reduce. Taking steps to reduce the impact of a threat acting on a vulnerability.
Transfer. Sharing some or all of the exposure or consequence.

Maintenance activities such as patch management are common in IT systems and may even be automated. Since it is not possible to patch or reboot a control element without advance testing and planning, the process is much more expensive and involved for ICSs. Security managers may need to retain risk for a period of time and balance the cost of avoidance or reduction against the potential impact of compromise or failure.

1.3 IEC 61850 Standard

1.3.1 Background

The International Electrotechnical Commission (IEC) standard 61850 was originally conceived for substation automation. It has been adopted by the industry, and its success in substation automation has led to adaptations developed for other applications such as hydroelectric plants, wind turbines, distribution feeders, and high-voltage switchgear. Table 1.1 lists some of these adaptations and shows both the depth of industry interest in this protocol and the need to understand the security implications of the IEC 61850 methodology. The operational benefits for utilities that have moved to IEC 61850 for substation automation are providing a visible incentive to innovate and create solutions outside of substation boundaries. The new target of utilities is to use modern

Table 1.1 Extensions to the IEC 61850 Protocol to Domains beyond Isolated Substation Automation

IEC 61850-7-410	Hydroelectric power plants—communication for monitoring and control
IEC 61850-7-420	Communications systems for Distributed Energy Resources (DER)—logical nodes
IEC 61850-90-1	Use of IEC 61850 for the communication between substations
IEC 61850-90-2	Use of IEC 61850 for the communication between control centres and substations
IEC 61850-90-3	Using IEC 61850 for condition monitoring
IEC 61850-90-4	IEC 61850—network engineering guidelines
IEC 61850-90-5	Use of IEC 61850 to transmit synchrophasor information according to IEEE C37.118
IEC 61850-90-6	Use of IEC 61850 for distribution feeder automation system
IEC 61850-90-7	Object models for photovoltaic, storage and other DER inverters
IEC 61850-90-8	Object models for electrical transportation (E-Mobility)
IEC 61850-90-9	Object models for batteries
IEC 61850-90-10	Object models for scheduling
IEC 61400-25	Application of the IEC 61850 methodology for wind turbines
IEC 62271-3	Communications for monitoring and control of high-voltage switchgear

telecommunications technologies such as long-term evolution (LTE), Worldwide Interoperability for Microwave Access (WiMAX), and spread spectrum in conjunction with IEC 61850 to create applications with benefits similar to those seen in substations. Applications such as distribution automation, microgrids, distributed generation, smart metering, wide area protections schemes, and synchrophasors are all possibilities.

The IEC 61850 design concepts are being incorporated throughout the generation, transmission, and distribution areas of the power industry and may even see adoption in the consumer/load component, as there is a proposal for hybrid PEV charging based on the standard. While not necessarily well known outside of the electric industry, the impact in this sector is similar to the introduction of the local area network (LAN) for corporate networks in the 1980s. Similar benefits and challenges may be ascribed to other automation networks in a variety of critical infrastructure and industrial automation applications. For the remainder of the chapter, IEC 61850 is discussed in the context of the original substation automation application, but it is applicable to any of its derivatives.

For more than 20 years, almost all communication between devices inside and outside of power substations has been implemented using copper wires and legacy communication protocols such as MODBUS, DNP 3.0, and IEC 60870-5-101/104 [21]. There were many disadvantages to this approach, including long implementation schedules, the high cost of copper wiring, relatively few parameters available for monitoring, proprietary implementations, lack of interoperability, and the need for substantial ongoing maintenance. Ethernet (IEEE 802.3)-based systems have overcome some of these problems by applying the same LAN solutions that have worked for more than 25 years in the IT industry [22], but a solution that addressed more than networking alone was needed. In response to these trends, disparate legacy protocols are being replaced by the more structured suite of protocols defined by the IEC 61850 standard.

Electric substations perform a number of different functions, including transforming voltage up or down, and in some cases monitoring voltage, via *transformers*. The substation can also switch electricity to different distribution circuits via *switches* or *disconnects* and provide overload or overcurrent protection via *circuit breakers*. In modern substations, this equipment is connected to microprocessor-based controllers called intelligent electronic devices (IEDs), which receive data from the power equipment and other sensors. They are also capable of issuing control commands, such as opening a circuit breaker. These devices are networked to perform protection, monitoring, automation, metering, and control of the substation.

1.3.2 Overview of the Standard

The first version of IEC 61850 was released in 2005 [6] with several broad goals. These included the desire to design a single complete standard for configuring, monitoring, reporting, storing, and communicating the equipment and related data in a substation. The standard also aimed to permit interoperability of equipment from different manufacturers. Data for configuration of all of the equipment in the substation can be stored in the substation configuration language (SCL). Physical devices such as circuit breakers are mapped to logical devices with specifically defined functions, data types, and attributes, such as their states and permitted functions.

In addition to a data model, IEC 61850 defined a communications model for methods and performance requirements related to data exchange. IEC 61850 was designed to run on top of a standard Ethernet LAN, usually implemented with ruggedized switches and routers. Cabling could be standard copper wire, but is almost always fiber optic to avoid electromagnetic interference, to prevent unplanned power conductors, and to permit high throughput should it be required. IEC 61850 defines two communication busses or LANs in the substation, a process bus and a station bus, although new trends can support one physical network with two logical networks. The process bus sends raw power system information such as status, voltage, or current from switchyard devices such as transformers to the IEDs, where the data is processed into reported measurements or logical decisions and actions. The process bus is very sensitive to delay, so it has high bandwidth to reduce packet insertion delay and eliminate any congestion-based losses which would incur retransmission delays. Due to its importance, the process bus often has redundant components to ensure high availability. The station bus connects all of the IEDs, switches, and other networked equipment to each other and to a router for external communications with the utility control center or any other entity that needs data from the substation. The station bus is used for less sensitive data compared with the process bus, but still uses high bandwidth and redundant and reliable networks to ensure proper substation operation.

A number of different communication protocols are defined by IEC 61850. They can be classified into three different groups: machine-to-machine (M2M), client-server, and configuration protocols. The M2M protocols are based on the Generic Substation Event (GSE), which is a peer-to-peer layer 2 protocol that multicasts events to multiple devices, typically IED to IEDs. The GSE protocol is further subdivided into Generic Substation State Events (GSSE) and Generic Object Oriented Substation Events (GOOSE). In GSSE, only status events can be transferred, and practically speaking it is seldom used, as the industry standardizes on GOOSE messages. Any data set, such as status or values, may be sent via GOOSE. The IEC 61850 standard specifies that certain GOOSE messages must be sent and received within 4 ms, which equates to roughly the time of one-quarter of a wavelength in a power system operating at 60 Hz, and is considered critical for actions such as tripping protection devices. To minimize the network and device processing time, GOOSE was designed to operate at layer 2 and not layer 3, minimizing the processing time associated with the upper layers of the Open Systems Interconnection (OSI) model.

Messages are sent via GOOSE as a publish-subscribe model, in which the publishing device sends to a class of subscribers without regard for their unique identity and without knowledge of whether or not the message was successfully received. For speed and reliability, GOOSE data is embedded directly in Ethernet packets and sent over a virtual LAN (VLAN) with IEEE 802.1Q priority tagging. Messages are also automatically retransmitted at varying intervals and automatically tagged as a new or retransmitted message. Sampled measured values (SMV) messages are similar to GOOSE messages, but optimized for interchanging sensitive analog data, such as measurements from current and voltage transformers.

The client-server protocols are based on the manufacturing message specification (MMS). MMS is used to communicate between equipment such as remote terminal units (RTU) or data concentrators and IEDs. The MMS works under a client-server architecture in which the client (RTU) requests information from a server (IED) that has the field data. MMS uses the complete TCP/IP protocol stack, including IP addresses and all the control fields, unlike the GOOSE protocol, which uses layer 2 media access control (MAC) addresses to deliver its packets. It is useful to think of GOOSE as operating in a horizontal fashion between devices across the substation and MMS messages traveling vertically between a sensor or actuator and a specific control element.

The configuration protocols define the interchange between engineering configuration tools and IEC 61850 substation components. The configuration is defined in the SCL, which is based on a structured XML file with specific elements that help represent the power grid systems.

1.3.3 Example IEC 61850 Functionality

A full description of IEC 61850 is beyond the scope of this chapter; however, an example of its functionality is provided in this section to better appreciate the operation of the protocol and the correspondence to physical hardware and network devices. A key element of the protocol is SMV and GOOSE messaging. The example below shows how the protocol behaves in a protection scenario. A hardware device in IEC 61850 may house one or more *logical devices*. A logical device is composed of one or more predefined *logical nodes*. For instance, a protection relay logical device could be composed of the logical nodes instantaneous overcurrent protection (predefined in IEC 61850 and denoted PIOC) and similarly protection trip condition (PTRC). The PIOC subscribes to SMV messages published on the process bus by devices such as a current transformer in the switchyard and reports when some overcurrent situation arises. From the IEC 61850 perspective, a PIOC is a data object, with predefined fields which have one or more attributes. The PTRC decides when the data in the PIOC warrants tripping the relay. A trip results in a GOOSE message being published to other logical devices, which may reside in the same hardware device, in the same equipment bay, or perhaps in a different bay or substation. For the purposes of this example, let the different logical devices be in different bays. Although there are no explicit commands defined in a GOOSE message, a state change of a Boolean value that represents a virtual trip is effectively a command for other devices. A circuit breaker (XCBR) will have been configured to subscribe to this relay. It receives the GOOSE message and physically trips a switch in the switchyard, possibly via a GOOSE message on the process bus. The trip open event is reported via a GOOSE message, to which the PTRC subscribes so that it can verify that the logical command has been physically carried out. This same message may also be subscribed to by an auto recloser (RREC). The recloser notes the circuit breaker tripping open, and after a waiting period, commands the circuit breaker to close. If the overcurrent fault has cleared, normal operation will continue (Figure 1.1).

1.3.4 Challenges and Vulnerabilities

The IEC 61850 standard uses abstraction of power elements, functions, services, and communication protocols to provide better device interoperability and simpler commissioning. While the foregoing description is brief, the standard itself and a number of other resources provide exhaustive detail, and so are not reproduced here. While IEC 61850 is a forward-thinking standard, not all future requirements were predicted, and the remainder of this section details some of the challenges we have experienced in the lab and the field.

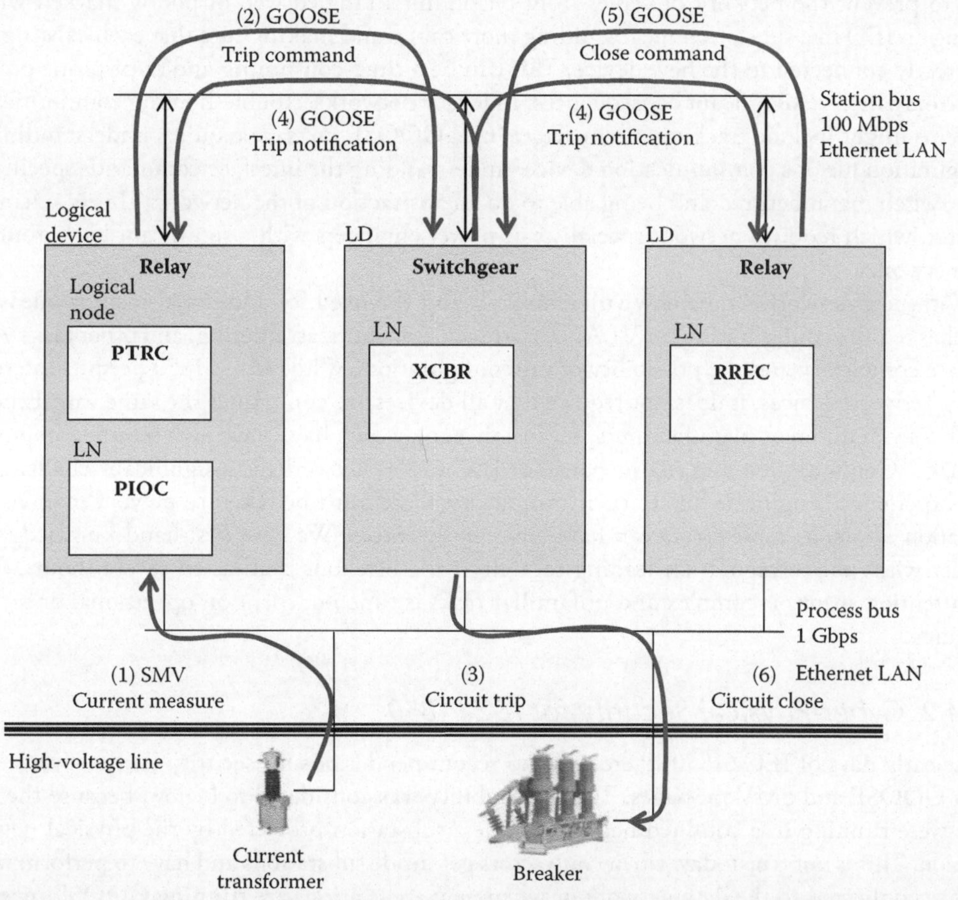

Figure 1.1 IEC 61850 Example: Steps (1) to (6) in a current overload condition.

1.3.4.1 Complexity

One downside of the move from legacy communications to IEC 61850 is the increased technical complexity, a situation which has operational and human consequences. While IEC 61850 is simpler than previous solutions that used dedicated wires between every device and its controller, nevertheless, as the demand for more electricity and new technologies on the grid increases, more and more IEDs are being integrated into the substations. As a result, the substation computer networks are ever more complex and more difficult to manage. Utilities may lack the right operational technology (OT) or IT engineers to support the new infrastructure, creating a reliance on outside consultants or requiring significant internal training. For at least a period of time, utilities may not fully understand or fully control their own networks.

The engineers configuring the computer network today are power engineers whose specialization is working with the electrical half of the electric grid, not the computer network half. They may lack the training to properly configure computer network devices such as switches and routers, which may result in minimal attention to computer network security or even skipping security configurations altogether.

The IEDs, devices that read information about the substation, have to be physically connected. The process of connecting each IED with every other IED requires significant cable management skills to prevent the network of cables from becoming a tangled web of poorly marked wiring. Adding an IED to a substation means adding more cables and making sure that each existing IED is correctly connected to the new device. This can be a time-consuming and error-prone process, and errors can have significant consequences. In legacy networks, troubleshooting communication problems might include tracking cables. Tracking a GOOSE message requires understanding the configuration file of a communication device, understanding the interface commands specific to a given switch manufacturer, and being able to do an abstraction of the network. This is a demanding task, which requires network specialists or power engineers with a significant background in data networks.

With new networks come new vulnerabilities and the need for additional security measures. Switches require configuration for VLANs, port security, multicast filtering, and other tasks which increase complexity and the possibility of misconfiguration. While IEC 61850 permits interoperability between devices, it does not require that all devices are configured the same way. Ethernet switches from different manufacturers, for instance, may each have their own interface command language. Configuration and maintenance of IEC 61850 networks is a significant challenge for even experienced engineers due to their complexity. Care must be taken to prevent manual configuration errors, as these errors can have real consequences. We have first-hand knowledge of a simple switch misconfiguration leading to a city-wide blackout that lasted several hours. Time and attention spent on complex and unfamiliar tasks is time not spent on operational or security measures.

1.3.4.2 Cyber-Physical Security for IEC 61850

In the early days of IEC 61850, there were no recommendations for security on the layer 2 multicast GOOSE and SMV messages. The vulnerability was considered to be low, because the messages were running in a confined network inside a substation protected by the physical network isolation. This is not true today, when contractors get inside substations and have to perform maintenance connected to the data network or when new applications are running GOOSE messages outside substations for wide-area transmission protection schemes and distribution automation schemes [23,24]. Further, substations have become more connected to external networks and often employ wireless networks, with the potential to expose their IEC 61850 network to outside attackers.

In 2007, the same technical committee that developed IEC 61850, the IEC Technical Committee 57 (TC57) in the Working Group 15 (WG15), released the IEC 62351 standard to provide security to a number of TC57 protocols, including IEC 61850 GOOSE messages. The objectives of IEC 62351 are authentication of data transfers through digital signatures, intrusion detection, and prevention of eavesdropping and spoofing [25]. This provides security enhancements for MMS, GOOSE messages, and SMV messages. Part 6 of the IEC 62351 standard covers data and communication security for IEC 61850 peer-to-peer profiles, Part 3 defines the communication network and system message authentication profiles including TCP/IP, and Part 4 specifies the mechanism of strong authentication to be used with MMS profiles. These definitions provide manufacturers and integrators with the tools necessary to implement security for IEC 61850 and the GOOSE stack [26]. Although IEC62351 addresses many security issues, problems remain.

1.3.4.3 The Problem of Encryption and Message Authentication versus Latency

Latency is one of the primary barriers to implementing security for peer-to-peer communications between IEDs. IEC 61850-5 specifies a 4 ms maximum delay for class P1 type 1A GOOSE messages related to breaker trip functions [27]. As a result, encryption or other security measures that increase delay or latency are avoided.

The IEC 62351 standard defines a mechanism that requires low computational power to authenticate data when adding a digital signature. The digital signature is created via mathematical techniques to validate the authenticity of a digital message using asymmetrical cryptography. This kind of scheme uses public and private keys to authenticate the message. The public key is shared with everyone to decrypt a hash of the message, while the private key is kept private by the publisher to sign the message. In the IEC 62351 standard, Part 6 states: "for applications using GOOSE and IEC 61850-9-2 and requiring 4 ms response times, multicast configurations and low CPU overhead, encryption is not recommended" [25]. Nevertheless, the standard does not say anything about authentication and its limitations. Based on the ambiguity of authentication or encryption requirements, some manufacturers do not implement any security in their IEDs, arguing that any security mechanism will increase the processing time, decreasing the speed of action against a fault.

At present, it is difficult to reconcile the needs for security and low latency. One study conducted by Cambridge University and ABB in 2010 showed that processing (encoding and decoding) digital signatures required intense central processing unit (CPU) consumption. Therefore, 32-bit Intel and ARM cores are generally incapable of computing and verifying a digital signature using the Rivest, Shamir and Adleman (RSA) algorithm with 1024-bit keys within 4 ms [28]. The time for a digital signature to be generated at the sender and verified at the receiver is shown in Table 1.2, as well as other similar algorithms such as the Digital Signature Algorithm (DSA), the Elliptic Curve DSA (ECSDA), and the Boneh, Lynn, Shacham (BLS) scheme [29]. Although RSA is the fastest (8.3 ms), this is not good enough to comply with the 4 ms time constraint. In a 2011 report, NIST qualified the RSA 1024-bits keys as acceptable through 2011, deprecated from 2011 through 2013, and disallowed after 2013. After 2013, it is recommended to use 2048-bit keys, which will make the 4 ms time restriction even more difficult to meet [30].

Table 1.2 Time to Generate and Verify a Digital Signature on a 1.0 GHz Pentium III Processor for Different Schemes

Algorithm	*Generation Time (ms)*	*Verification Time (ms)*	*Bandwidth (bits)*
RSA	7.9	0.4	1024
DSA	4.1	4.9	320
ECDSA F_2^{160}	5.7	7.2	320
ECDSA F_p	4.0	5.2	320
BLS F_3^{97}	3.5	23.0	170

Source: D. Dolezilek and L. Hussey, Requirements or recommendations? Sorting out NERC CIP, NIST, and DOE cybersecurity, in 64th Annual Conf. for Protective Relay Engineers, 2011. With permission.

The CPUs embedded in the IEDs have restrictions due to power dissipation. The IEDs are fanless, since they are commonly installed in closed cases to avoid environmental issues such as dust, water, or insects. Thus, many embedded processors are slower than the 1.0 GHz processor used in this table, and processing times will be even longer. New technologies such as multiple cores may enable faster computation within the same heat dissipation budget; however, there are many IEDs already installed with slower CPUs.

Currently, neither the IEC 62351 recommendation nor proprietary manufacturer solutions have been implemented extensively to improve the security of GOOSE messages. In November 2011, Siemens published a patent to implement a new method of group key generation and management for the GOOSE model that could help to address the need for low-latency security [31]. Meanwhile, there is little clarity on how to implement security for fast GOOSE messages without degrading the actual performance of the IEDs.

1.3.4.4 Other Issues

The rapid advance of technology and the lengthy standardization process can create gaps in needs, capabilities, or security that go unaddressed for a period of time. The IEC 61850 standard was originally designed for intra-substation communication on a LAN, and some of the protocols involve layer 2 multicasts that are not easily routable between different networks without compromising the integrity of the substation automation architecture and security. An amended standard, IEC 61850 90-1, was released to allow inter-substation communication [7], and IEC 61850-90-5 defines routable GOOSE and SMV protocols, but this took time.

A current issue is the lack of security within the substation network once a machine is physically connected. It has been shown that once connected, without authentication, a machine can inject traffic indicating the occurrence of a substation event, the results of which could be as severe as the substation going off-line or initiating a cascading failure [8]. While physical security at substations is relatively good, at least in the United States, many operate remotely and without staff. Controlling physical access is also not always straightforward, as power systems, substations, and equipment may be owned, installed, and maintained by a federation of partners or contractors.

While the transition from analog to digital data acquisition allows the power industry to innovate with new communications technologies and protocols such as IEC 61850, it also poses new cyber-physical security problems that can affect the stability and reliability of the power grid [9]. In the following section, we discuss IEC 61850 based attacks.

1.4 IEC 61850 Attack Vectors, Consequences, and Mitigation

1.4.1 Attack Vectors and Techniques

An attack is defined by the motivation, vectors, and techniques. For this work, we assumed a motivated attacker and focus on the attack vectors and techniques. The attack vector is a path or means by which an attacker gains access to a computer or network in order to achieve their ultimate goal. Attack vectors enable exploitation of system vulnerabilities, including human elements. Access to the network could be obtained via installation of malware on the computers of maintenance operators, engineers, or manufacturer support teams who access a GOOSE network and are unknowingly carrying the malware. A similar attack vector was used to allow the Stuxnet worm to gain access for an attack on Siemens industrial software and equipment in 2010 [32].

An attack vector can come from malicious persons among cleaning crews or substation personnel who have access to the IEC 61850 network. Another attack vector is through manufacturing facilities of producers of IEC 61850 IED equipment or other network equipment. Such equipment can be infected with malware at the time of manufacture and installed directly in a substation, bypassing physical protection and providing the malware with a host. The attacks that we describe can be hosted on even simple devices.

There are several layer 2 attack techniques that could be applied to GOOSE messages, since the underlying IEC 61850 network is Ethernet. Attacks on Ethernet include: address resolution protocol (ARP) attacks, MAC flooding attacks, spanning-tree attacks, multicast brute-force attacks, VLAN trunking protocol attacks, private VLAN attacks, identity theft, VLAN hopping attacks, MAC spoofing, and double-encapsulated 802.1Q/Nested VLAN attacks. An attack could be created using a variety of techniques described above, and the structure of protocols in the OSI model are such that the upper layers in the model could be unaware that layer 2 has been compromised [33].

1.4.2 Attack Consequences

There are several consequences if a layer 2 attack is executed in a substation. The main purpose of the GOOSE message is to carry vital information (alarms, status, and control) between devices. Any alteration of these values could create an automation breakdown, causing a circuit breaker to miss an operation, bypassing interlocks, or causing physical damages in field devices such as power transformers or circuit breakers. If the attack compromises a bus bar or differential protection, more than one distribution or transmission circuit could be affected, and as a result, one part of a city or an entire region would suffer an outage. If the same attack involved transmission or generation circuits, the outage could trigger cascading failures and become sufficiently large to affect complete cities or states.

As a specific example, the Palo Verde Nuclear Generating Station (PVNGS) and California ISO use GOOSE messaging between their substations to create a remedial action scheme (RAS) on the Salt River Project. The GOOSE messages are implemented in a flat Ethernet ring and carry analog and digital values to control the load at both sides. Measured changes in generation levels on one side of the system must affect load balance on the other side of the system over 150 miles away in less than 1 s. A GOOSE attack that appears to changes the values of generation levels could produce voltage dips, frequency excursions, and cascading problems throughout the Western Electricity Coordinating Council (WECC) region [24].

Recall also that the IEC 61850 architecture has been applied to hydroelectric plants, wind turbines, distribution feeders, and high-voltage switchgear (see Table 1.1). Thus, these domains are also vulnerable to the kinds of attacks described here.

1.4.3 Mitigating Attacks

Although some attack vectors could be reduced using physical security, there are others that are more difficult to control because they use trusted personnel or equipment. Some traditional IT techniques to prevent Ethernet layer 2 attacks could be applied to protect GOOSE messages. These practices include, but are not limited to: setting a dedicated VLAN ID for all trunk ports, disabling unused ports and putting them in an unused VLAN, using a VLAN other than the default (VLAN 1), setting all ports to nontrunking, creating an access or prefix list based on user/device credentials, and avoiding the use of shared Ethernet such as WLANs or hubs [34]. All of these techniques are well documented and known by IT staff.

Using the measures indicated provides some degree of protection against intrusion originating from outside of the organization. For trusted employees or compromised equipment with valid credentials inside the facility, most of the traditional IT techniques would be ineffective. Additional security measures would, therefore, be required. To prevent insider attacks, it is necessary that end devices have security algorithms implemented to encrypt packets or have a digital signature added so that they cannot be monitored by the attacker and authenticated, permitting spoofed packets to be sent. As noted previously, legacy and low-capability IEDs cannot support these cryptographic algorithms.

Solutions such as adding an external security module to network interfaces in each IED add expense and additional failure modes. These devices could be added just to the switches and some key equipment in the Ethernet to provide some limited protection. An alternative approach could use switches and routers that understand the IEC 61850 protocol and inspect GOOSE message content. In this approach, the network could discard or generate alarms when it detects logically inconsistent messages (such as packets with the same MAC address coming from different ports on a switch or messages not consistent with the IEC 61850 configuration).

Software-defined networking (SDN) is a recent innovation to address network complexity and vendor-specific protocols. SDN decouples the proprietary software running on each network device from the hardware that is responsible for forwarding the traffic according to the rules determined by the software on the network devices. With SDN, an open interface (currently led by the OpenFlow standard) abstracts the network from the applications by exposing the forwarding table as the interface to manage the devices. A centralized, logical server (or collection of servers) runs software (which can come from a variety of sources) that has a network-wide view and can monitor and configure the forwarding table. As it is an open standard, the software works across a variety of hardware, and likewise, the hardware can work across a variety of software. As a result, a more consistent environment can be presented for configuration and management of the network supporting IEC 61850.

1.5 Exploiting IEC 61850 via GOOSE

This section demonstrates how to create computer malware that can capture, alter, and reinject GOOSE messages into the network. By taking advantage of existing security holes in the GOOSE messaging protocol, we show how a malware could be used to significantly disrupt the power grid and highlight the need to apply security measures in this area.

1.5.1 Normal GOOSE Function

The main objective of GOOSE messaging is to provide a fast and reliable mechanism for the exchange of data between two or more IEDs over IEEE 802.3 networks. To exchange these datagrams, IEC 61850-8-1 describes a type of communication based on a publish-subscribe model, in which one IED (the publisher) creates a message that is delivered to a group of destination IEDs (the subscribers) simultaneously in a single transmission from the source [35]. GOOSE messages are periodically sent through the network. When there is no change in data set values, the retransmission time between messages is T_0 (see Figure 1.2).

If an event occurs, a message is generated immediately. After the first event message, the publisher retransmits (T_1, T_2, …, T_N) with a variable time separation between messages that is not defined by the standard, but is typically implemented following an exponential back-off until it reaches the stable retransmission time T_0. If T_0 is exceeded, the subscriber could declare a problem in the communication link or in the GOOSE message [35].

The GOOSE datagram has twelve fields that define the protocol data unit (PDU). The first two fields, *preamble* and *start* of frame, are equal to the first two fields of an Ethernet frame. The *destination* corresponds to an Ethernet MAC multicast address. IEC 61850 has been assigned Ethernet addresses that start with the three first octets (01-0C-CD). The fourth octet could be 01 for GOOSE, 02 for GSSE, or 04 for multicast SMV. The last two octets of the six are used as individual addresses for each GOOSE message. The *source address* is a unicast MAC address. The *VLAN priority tagging* is IEEE 802.1Q. The *Ether-type* of a GOOSE message is 88-B8. The *Application ID* is 00. The *length* indicates the total number of bytes in the frame less eight bytes. The *Reserved1* and *Reserved2* fields are reserved for future standardized applications and are set to 0 by default. The last two fields are the *Application PDU (APDU) length* and finally the *frame checksum sequence* [35]. The APDU has ten fields, described here. *DatSet* is a string that describes the name of the data set. *GoID* is the IED sender identifier. *T* is the "time stamp" at which the attribute *StNum* was incremented. *StNum* is the *state number*, a counter that increments each time

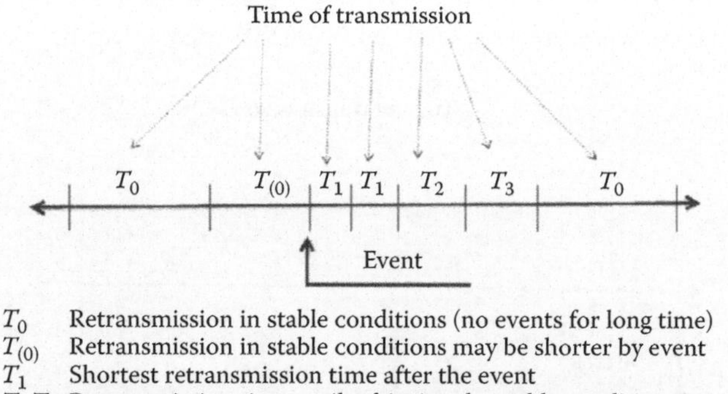

Figure 1.2 GOOSE transmission. (From IEC 61850-8, Communication networks and systems in substations: Specific communication service mapping [SCSM]. International Electrotechnical Commission, 2008. With permission.)

a GOOSE message has been sent with any change in the values of the data set. The *SqNum* is the *sequence number*, containing an incremental counter for each time a GOOSE message has been sent. The *Test* field indicates whether or not the message is a test. *TimeAllowedToLive* is the time that the receiver has to wait for the next message. *ConfRev* is the *configuration revision*, a count of the number of times that the configuration of the data set has been changed. *NumDatSetEntries* is the *number of data set entries*, the number of elements that comprise this specific data set [35].

1.5.2 Building a Practical Cyberattack

1.5.2.1 Technical Details

The following attack was implemented in the Digital Energy Laboratory at the University of Colorado, Boulder as an ethical demonstration of a security vulnerability, with details of the equipment and scripts intentionally omitted. A similar attack could move from the lab to the field in a matter of days.

Our attack uses a GOOSE exploit via spoofing, whereby an intruder publishes false layer 2 packets, and devices on the receiving side mistakenly believe they are receiving valid (true) packets sent by a trusted or secured entity. This attack is possible due to the unencrypted and unauthenticated nature of GOOSE messages, because of the latency issues on IED devices previously detailed.

A practical GOOSE message spoof attack can be divided into four steps. First, monitor packets on the physical ports looking for GOOSE messages based on Ether-type identification. Second, decode the GOOSE message using Abstract Syntax Notation One (ASN1) and Basic Encoding Rules (BER) [36]. Third, change the values inside each data set, keeping the sequence for the different counters and timers. Fourth, encode the packet using BER and send the packet through a physical port, cloning the source MAC address. The schematic in Figure 1.3 shows how the attacker has opportunities between valid messages to insert the spoofed messages with incorrect data.

There are several programs that can be used to do this: Scapy, Yersinia, Macof, TCPDump, Cain & Abel, EtterCap, and Wireshark are a few. This attack was created using Scapy in conjunction with Python scripts. Scapy is also a Python program that enables the user to sniff, dissect, forge, and send network packets. These capabilities allow the construction of tools that can probe, scan, or attack Ethernet networks.

To prove the vulnerability of the GOOSE networks, our attack script uses the network configuration shown in Figure 1.4, which represents a typical substation automation architecture. In addition, new scenarios were created, such as GOOSE messaging between substations using

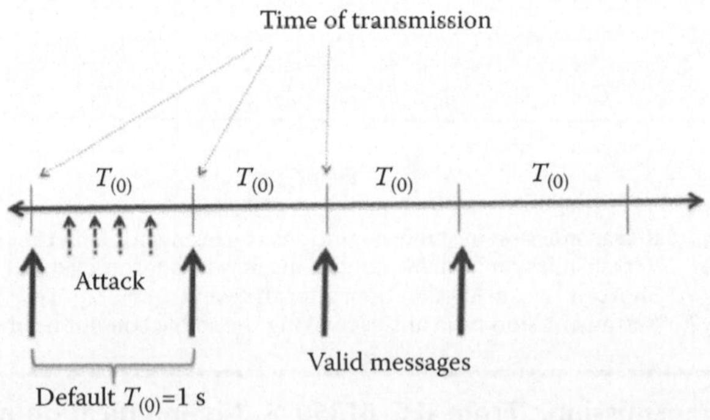

Figure 1.3 GOOSE attack schematic.

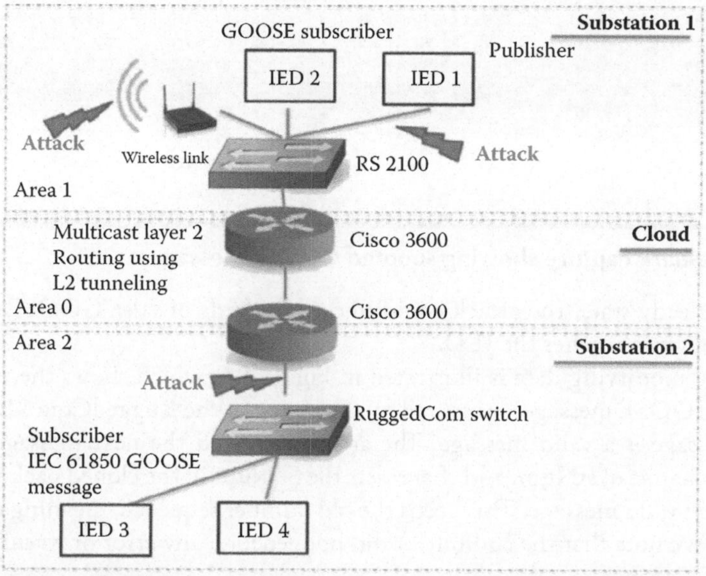

Figure 1.4 Network diagram.

Layer 2 tunneling and wireless communications inside the substation. The lightning bolts in Figure 1.4 represent the attack points. The attack was successful in all scenarios, and we describe one in detail below.

The hardware used for the test included two Cisco 3600 routers, one RuggedCom 2100 switch, one RuggedCom RS900, one Linksys wireless router, and four IEDs. The script ran on a MacBook Air 1.5 GHz Intel core i5 within a virtual machine running Xubuntu OS.

1.5.2.2 Building the Script

The first step to carry out the attack is to identify GOOSE messages in the network. After using Scapy to monitor all physical ports and capture the raw packets, the code parses the Ethernet frames looking for the specific GOOSE Ether-type, which in this case is 0x88B8. Second, it is necessary to decode the GOOSE message using the definition of ASN1 described in the IEC 61850-8-1. After decoding, the script looks for three specific fields: stNum, sqNum, and the Boolean values inside the data sets. For any Boolean value inside the data set, if the value is true the code overwrites a false, and vice versa. The last part of the code generates the spoofed messages and sends them through the network with the same source and destination MAC address as the valid user. To show that the attack can be successful, we implemented the above steps on the laptop described above.

1.5.2.3 The Results of the Attack

Figure 1.5 shows a Wireshark capture, where the topmost and the bottommost arrows are the true messages. The four middle arrows, events 194 to 197, are the spoofed messages. Looking at the time stamp of the packets 193 and 195, the time to generate spoofed GOOSE messages is less than 1 ms. This means that in a default GOOSE configuration, where the messages are sent at 1 s

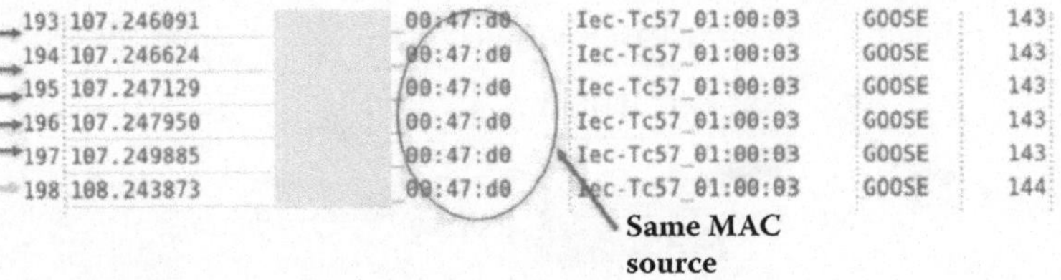

Figure 1.5 Wireshark capture showing spoofed GOOSE messages.

intervals during steady state, the attack could inject hundreds of false GOOSE messages before the next valid datagram reaches the IED.

The process of modifying data is illustrated in Figure 1.6, which shows the variable values in three successive GOOSE messages measured by the laptop at the RuggedCom 2100 in Figure 1.4. The leftmost message is a valid message. The attacker created the next message in the middle, which shows the change of stNum, and that resets the SqNum in the cloned packet. The rightmost message is the next valid message. This keeps the old number sequence, meaning that it is actually out of sequence. We note that the equipment did not generate any error or warning that the messages were out of sequence.

The attacker does not directly know the high-level meaning of this GOOSE message (e.g., that this is a command from a circuit-breaker controller to a circuit breaker). However, he can decode the message to find and change the data values. In Figure 1.6, the attacker changes the Boolean data value from False to True. To verify this has an effect, Figure 1.7 shows the sequence event recorder (SER) on the IED. The SER monitors the physical outputs and generates a time stamp of output events.

Event 4 (number on the left) shows the times when the valid message instructed the IED to deassert output 101. After 5 ms, a spoofed message is processed at the IED, asserting the output and generating event 3. Another 995 ms later, the next true message arrives, generating event 2, which again deasserts the output. In this case, the effect of this action is to cause the IED to trip the relay, which in a real substation could control a circuit breaker or switch. Thus, through spoofed messages we were able to cause actual IEC 61850 equipment that might reside

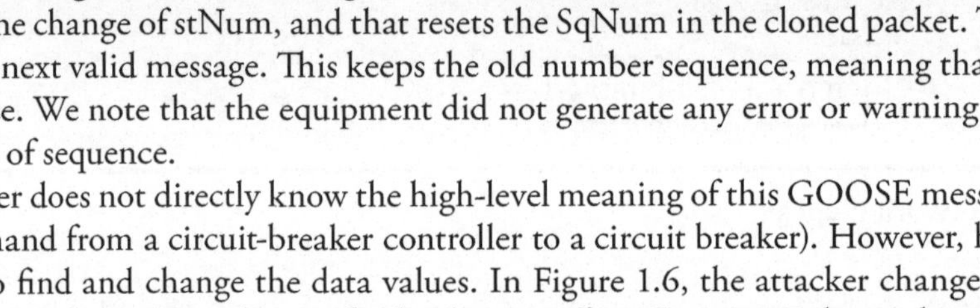

Figure 1.6 GOOSE exploit.

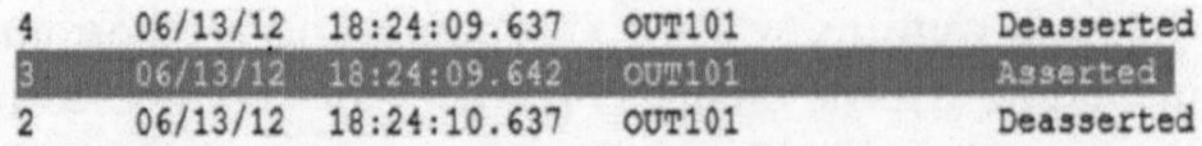

Figure 1.7 IED output status.

in a substation to change its state, with the potential to cause outages and other problems as described in Section 1.4.2.

There are many variants on this type of attack. For instance, a single GOOSE frame with a very high sequence number can be multicast to a subscriber. Once processed, any legitimate GOOSE message with a sequence number equal to or less than the spoofed message will not be processed by the subscriber.

1.6 Conclusion

Electric power systems pose unique challenges for cyber-physical security, and adverse events carry significant consequences due to the scale and importance of the industry. In this chapter we provided insight into the structure and function of the electric grid, the evolution of communications and control, and some of the challenges related to this evolution. We provide an introduction to the modern IEC 61850 grid automation standard, and discuss some of the issues and vulnerabilities which require further work. We demonstrated that a simple attack enables malware to control IEC 61850-enabled electrical equipment. This control has the potential to cause outages that range from a single feeder to cascading failure. While there is currently no clear definition of how to implement security for GOOSE messages, utilities and power companies must find ways to implement cyber-physical measures to prevent this kind of attack. We describe several techniques for improving security, as it is of vital importance that network switches and routers be configured to permit only trusted traffic and users inside the substation network.

Lack of clarity in the standards concerning security for IEC 61850 layer 2 messages with current technology opens the door for new research. This includes a search for security measures and development of standards that could be backward compatible, allowing thousands of IEDs to be made capable of running GOOSE securely.

Acknowledgment

This work was supported by U.S. Department of Energy grant DE-OE00436.

Author Biographies

Martin Saint is currently a visiting scholar at Carnegie Mellon University in Rwanda. His background includes network and telecommunications engineering, creating and managing facilities and infrastructure for data center and telecommunications clients, work in emergency planning and response, and corporate business management. He currently teaches and researches in the areas of complex networks, wireless networks, and cyber-physical systems. Martin holds an MS in telecommunications and is a PhD student in the Interdisciplinary Telecommunications Program at the University of Colorado. He has studied with the U.S. Federal Emergency Management Agency's Emergency Management Institute, the International Centre for Theoretical Physics in Italy, and Idaho National Laboratory, home to the U.S. Department of Homeland Security's Control System Security Program and the Industrial Control Systems Cyber Emergency Response Team. He is a member of the Department of Homeland Security Industrial Control Systems Joint Working Group.

Juan Hoyos has a decade of experience in advanced computer network communications, specializing in substation communications engineering and automation. He was most recently a lead hardware engineer at Empresas Públicas de Medellín (EPM), Colombia's largest utility, which provides electricity, gas, water, and telecommunications services. EPM's energy strategic business unit (SBU) provides over 4 million customers with over 3000 MW of capacity. Mr. Hoyos holds an MS in telecommunications (with a specialization in energy communication networks) from the University of Colorado at Boulder and a BS in electronics engineering from Universidad Pontificia Bolivariana, and is a certified project management specialist.

Timothy X. Brown is a professor in electrical, computer, and energy engineering in the Interdisciplinary Telecommunications Program at the University of Colorado, Boulder. He received his BS in physics from Pennsylvania State University and his PhD in electrical engineering from California Institute of Technology in 1990. His research interests include adaptive network control, machine learning, and wireless communication systems. His research funding includes National Science Foundation (NSF), Federal Aviation Administration, Department of Energy, and industry. He is a recipient of the NSF CAREER Award and the Global Wireless Education Consortium Wireless Educator of the Year Award. Since 2013, he has been a visiting professor in electrical and computer engineering at Carnegie Mellon University's campus in Rwanda.

References

1. G. Constable and B. Somerville, *A Century of Innovation: The Engineering That Transformed Our Lives*. Joseph Henry Press, Washington, DC, 2003.
2. U.S. Energy Information Administration, Electric power monthly. U.S. Energy Information Administration, Washington, DC, 2014.
3. MarketLine, Electricity: Global industry guide, Industry Guide ML00016-40. MarketLine, an Informa business, Manchester, UK, 2014.
4. K. H. LaCommare and J. H. Eto, Understanding the cost of power interruptions to U.S. electricity consumers, Final report LBNL-55718. Ernest Orlando Lawrence Berkeley National Laboratory, Berkeley, CA, 2004.
5. K. H. LaCommare and J. H. Eto, Cost of power interruptions to electricity consumers in the United States, Final report LBNL-58164. Ernest Orlando Lawrence Berkeley National Laboratory, Berkeley, CA, 2006.
6. J. Clemmensen, J. Bates, and S. Kraft, The top 50 equipment suppliers and service providers, *Power Qual. Assur. Mag.*, vol. 10, no. 4, pp. 13–25, 1999.
7. S. Swaminathan and R. K. Sen, Review of power quality applications of energy storage systems, Contractor report SAND98-1513, Sandia National Laboratories, Albuquerque, NM, and Livermore, CA, 1998.
8. D. Lineweber and S. McNulty, The cost of power disturbances to industrial and digital economy companies, Technical report TR-1006274. Electric Power Research Institute, Palo Alto, CA, 2001.
9. U.S. Code, Information analysis and infrastructure protection, critical infrastructure information act of 2002, Title 6 U.S. Code Section 121, 2002.
10. Department of Homeland Security, National infrastructure protection plan. Department of Homeland Security, Washington, DC, 2009.
11. Critical Infrastructure Protection Committee, NERC Standard CIP-002 through CIP-009. North American Electric Reliability Council, 2006.
12. W. Wang, Y. Xu, and M. Khanna, A survey on the communication architectures in smart grid, *Comput. Netw.*, vol. 55, no. 15, pp. 3604–3629, 2011.
13. K. Stouffer, J. Falco, and K. Scarfone, Guide to industrial control systems (ICS) security, Special Publication 800-82. National Institute of Standards and Technology, Gaithersburg, MD, 2011.

14. K. Stouffer, J. Falco, and K. Scarfone, Guide to industrial control systems (ICS) security, revision 1, Special Publication 800-82r1. National Institute of Standards and Technology, Gaithersburg, MD, 2013.
15. The Smart Grid Interoperability Panel Cyber Security Working Group, Guidelines for smart grid cyber security, NISTIR 7628. National Institute of Standards and Technology, Gaithersburg, MD, 2010.
16. U.S. Code, Definitions, Title 44 U.S. Code Section 3542, 2011.
17. L. L. Peterson and B. S. Davie, *Computer Networks: A Systems Approach*, 5th ed. Morgan Kaufmann, Boston, 2011.
18. E. A. Lee and S. A. Seshia, *Introduction to Embedded Systems: A Cyber-Physical Systems Approach*. LeeSeshia.org, Morrisville, NC, 2011.
19. C. Neuman and K. Tan, Mediating cyber and physical threat propagation in secure smart grid architectures, in *2011 IEEE International Conference on Smart Grid Communications (SmartGridComm)*, Brussels, 2011, pp. 238–243.
20. D. Dolezilek and L. Hussey, Requirements or recommendations? Sorting out NERC CIP, NIST, and DOE cybersecurity, in *64th Annual Conference for Protective Relay Engineers*, 2011, College Station, TX, 2011, pp. 328–333.
21. R. E. Mackiewicz, Overview of IEC 61850 and benefits, in *IEEE Power System Conference and Exposition (PSCE'06)*, Atlanta, GA, 2006, pp. 623–630.
22. G. W. Scheer and D. J. Dolezilek, Comparing the reliability of Ethernet network topologies in substation control and monitoring networks, in *Proceedings of 2nd Annual Western Power Delivery Automation Conference*, Spokane, WA, 2000.
23. M. Goraj, L. Lipes, and J. McGhee, IEC 61850 GOOSE over WiMAX for fast isolation and restoration of faults in distribution networks, presented at the Protection, Automation & Control World Conference (PAC World), Dublin, Ireland, June 2011.
24. J. Sykes, M. Adamiak, and G. Brunello, Implementation and operational experience of a wide area special protection scheme on the SRP system, presented at the Power System Conference: Advanced Metering, Protection, Control, Communication, and Distributed Resources (PS'06), 2006, pp. 145–158.
25. IEC 62351, Power systems management and associated information exchange, data and communication security. International Electrotechnical Commission, 2007.
26. H. Falk, Securing IEC 61850, in *2008 IEEE Power and Energy Society General Meeting: Conversion and Delivery of Electrical Energy in the 21st Century*, 2008, pp. 1–3.
27. IEC 61850-5, Communication networks and systems in substations: Communication requirements for functions and device models. International Electrotechnical Commission, 2008.
28. S. Fuloria, R. Anderson, K. McGrath, K. Hansen, and F. Alvarez, The protection of substation communications, in *Proceedings S4 2010: SCADA Security Scientific Symposium*, Miami, FL, 2010.
29. B. J. Matt, The cost of protection measures in tactical networks, in *Proceedings of the 24th Army Science Conference*, Orlando, FL, 2005.
30. E. Barker and A. Roginsky, Transitions: recommendation for transitioning the use of cryptographic algorithms and key lengths, Special Publication 800-831A. National Institute of Standards and Technology, Gaithersburg, MD, January 2011.
31. S. Fries and M. Seewald, Method of group key generation and management for generic object oriented substation event model, International Patent WO2011/141040A1, November 17, 2011.
32. R. McMillan, Siemens: Stuxnet worm hit industrial systems, *Computerworld*, September 14, 2010.
33. Y. Bhaiji, Understanding, preventing, and defending against layer 2 attacks, presented at the Cisco Expo 2009, Riyadh, Saudi Arabia, February 9, 2009.
34. Y. Bhaiji, *Network Security Technologies and Solutions*, 1st ed. Cisco Press, Indianapolis, IN, 2008.
35. IEC 61850-8, Communication networks and systems in substations: Specific communication service mapping (SCSM). International Electrotechnical Commission, 2008.
36. ITU Standard X.609, Information technology ASN.1 encoding rules: Specification of basic encoding rules (BER), canonical encoding rules (CER) and distinguished encoding rules (DER). International Telecommunication Union (ITU), 2002.

Chapter 2

ICT Modeling for Cosimulation of Integrated Cyberpower Systems

Alexandru Stefanov
University College Dublin

Chen-Ching Liu
University College Dublin and Washington State University

Kithsiri Liyanage
University of Peradeniya

Contents

2.1 Introduction 28
2.2 Cyberpower System Cosimulation 30
2.2.1 Coupling of Simulation Tools 31
2.2.1.1 Real-Time Simulation and HIL 32
2.2.1.2 Off-Line Simulation and HIL 33
2.2.2 Simulation Tools 36
2.2.2.1 Power System Tools 36
2.2.2.2 Communication Network Tools 40
2.2.2.3 Power System Communication Protocols 42
2.2.3 Example of Real-Time CPS Simulator 42
2.3 ICT Modeling of Integrated Cyberpower Systems 44
2.3.1 Power System Layer 46
2.3.2 Cybersystem and Transmission Operator Layers 47
2.3.2.1 ICT Device Modeling 48
2.3.2.2 Substation ICT Model 50

2.3.2.3 Control Center ICT Model 53
2.3.2.4 Transmission Operator ICT Model 54
2.3.3 Transmission Operator Console....55
2.4 CPS Performance 55
2.5 Simulation Results 56
Acknowledgment 58
Glossary 58
Author Biographies 59
References 59

Abstract: The supervisory control and data acquisition (SCADA) system is the primary infrastructure for online monitoring and control of power grids. SCADA systems have evolved from isolated structures into open and networked environments. The new communication systems for modern power grids present cybersecurity vulnerabilities. Cybersecurity studies for SCADA systems can be conducted effectively on an integrated cyberpower environment. The information and communication technologies (ICTs) supporting SCADA are coupled with the electric grids. Together, they form a cyber-physical system (CPS). Computer simulations of cyberattacks and impact analysis of the power grid help identify the vulnerable points of the SCADA system with a high impact on the grid's operation. The power and cybersystems must be modeled and integrated in a cosimulation environment. Tools are required to study simultaneously the dynamics of the electric grid and its data delivery infrastructure. This chapter is a tutorial for the development of a cosimulation model that integrates the cyber and power systems. The coupling techniques for software simulators for cybersystems and physical power systems are reviewed. The existing power system simulation tools and communication network simulators are presented. An example of the real-time coupling technique for industrial-grade simulation environments and SCADA software is provided. The chapter continues with a brief overview of power system models and their integration with the ICT model of SCADA for data exchange. The emphasis is on modeling of the information and communication system for power grids and the grid control hierarchy. Queuing theory is used for the ICT models. The integrated CPS model is validated with the IEEE 39-bus system.

Keywords: Communication; Cosimulation; Cybersystem; Cyber-physical system; Cyberpower system; ICT; IED; Power system; Queuing theory; RTU; SCADA

2.1 Introduction

The SCADA system is the primary infrastructure for online monitoring and control of power grids. SCADA is undergoing major changes as new requirements of the power grid arise, for example, large scale deployment of phasor measurement units (PMUs) that acquire a massive amount of data at high sampling rates. Both power and data delivery infrastructures must be considered for smart grid innovation at the transmission level [1].

SCADA systems have evolved from isolated structures into open and networked environments. SCADA connectivity has increased significantly over time. Transmission control protocol/Internet protocol (TCP/IP) and Ethernet technologies are widely used for smart grid communications. The new communication systems for modern power grids allow more data to be exchanged at higher transmission rates and reduced costs. However, they present cybersecurity vulnerabilities. The private communication networks used by power systems have become vulnerable with respect to cyberattacks [2]. It is widely recognized that IP-based attacks on the SCADA system of critical infrastructures have technical, financial, and societal implications. Cyberattacks on power grids may damage physical devices, for example, generators, and have an impact on the power system operation. Coordinated cyberattacks can cause cascading events in the power grid [3]. There is a significant risk of cascading events leading to a blackout [4]. Furthermore, intelligent cyberattacks can take the SCADA system out of service to impede power system restoration. Denial-of-service (DoS) attacks can disrupt the communications network of SCADA by compromising and disconnecting network nodes, for example, routers, switches, and hubs [5]. Hence, cybersecurity studies for SCADA systems and impact analysis for different cyberevents, including cyberattacks, device failures, and latency, are critical research subjects. They can be conducted effectively in an integrated cyberpower environment.

The ICTs supporting SCADA are coupled with the electric grids. The ICT infrastructure resides on top of the power grid for monitoring and control. Together, they form a CPS [6]. Solutions for planning future developments of power systems and ICT networks have been researched separately. However, as ICT and power devices become more interdependent, solutions are needed that explicitly model their interactions. ICT has greatly increased the connectivity of power systems. Potential threats from a broad range of cyberattacks have become a serious concern. Solutions to secure SCADA are needed. Computer simulations of cyberattacks and impact analysis of the power grid help identify the vulnerable points of the SCADA system with a high impact on the grid's operation [7]. Therefore, power and cybersystems must be modeled and integrated in a cosimulation environment. Tools are required to study simultaneously the dynamics of the electric grid and its data delivery infrastructure. A methodology for CPS cosimulation is needed for solutions to cybersecurity enhancement of future power grids.

A graph-theoretic model for the SCADA system of an integrated CPS is reported in [7]. Methods to model cyberintrusions and assess the CPS security are proposed. The ICT and cyberattack models are described from an analytical point of view. In this chapter, the focus is on the ICT software models and tools and their implementation for cosimulation of integrated cyberpower systems. This chapter is a tutorial for the development of a cosimulation model that integrates the cyber and power systems. The resulting CPS is a tool that enables communication and interaction between the power grid, its SCADA system, and the grid control hierarchy in an online simulation environment. In this chapter, the coupling techniques for software simulators for cybersystems and physical power systems are reviewed. The existing power system simulation tools and communication network simulators are presented. Their modeling capabilities are summarized. An example of the real-time coupling technique for industrial-grade simulation environments and SCADA software is provided using the object linking and embedding for process control (OPC) interoperability standard. A comprehensive and powerful tool for CPS modeling and simulation is created by integration of industrial-grade power and computer network simulation environments. The chapter continues with a brief overview of power system models and their integration with the ICT model of SCADA for data exchange. The emphasis is on modeling of the information and communication system for power grids and the grid control hierarchy. In the SCADA model of the power grid, critical ICT devices are incorporated. The ICT models are described from a software implementation point of view. Queuing theory is used for the ICT models. The SCADA system provides communication capabilities for the power grid. The ICT model of the SCADA system interacts with the grid model and transmission operator (TO) console. The TO console environment includes a real-time database and the SCADA mimics.

In this chapter, the term *physical system* refers specifically to the power grids. The tutorial presented for modeling of the ICT infrastructure and the control hierarchy can be applied to different physical infrastructures supervised via SCADA, for example, water systems and natural gas pipelines.

Five applications of the CPS are presented:

1. *Dispatcher training environment*: The CPS tool facilitates real-time monitoring and control of a power grid by system operators via SCADA in an integrated cosimulation environment. Power and ICT events are simulated, for example, load variations, faults, line tripping, ICT failures, and latency. Time domain simulations (TDS) are synchronized by the system's time. The status of the power grid is reported through SCADA in real time. System operators monitor the grid and take control actions. The impact and control efficiency are assessed by observing the grid dynamics.
2. *SCADA development planning and performance assessment*: The transition from the present grid to a smart grid environment requires extended communication, computation, and control capabilities. CPS is used to study development of the ICT infrastructure supporting SCADA to meet the smart grid requirements. Latency and the optimal update rate can be calculated. ICTs causing communication congestions are identified. The purpose is to improve the overall SCADA performance.
3. *Assessment of the communication security*: ICT events are defined, including buffer overflows, DoS, ICT failures, and packet losses. The monitoring and control capabilities of the power grid can be affected. The impact on power system operation is analyzed. Communication security is studied and improved.
4. *Enhancement of cybersecurity for SCADA systems*: Security controls that protect the ICTs are modeled. SCADA vulnerabilities are identified. The cyberpower system cosimulation tool is used to assess how malicious attacks on the cybersystem affect the stability of the power grid. Attacks are simulated at the cybersystem layer, and the impact analysis on grid dynamics is conducted at the power system layer in an integrated cosimulation environment. Different attack types are considered, for example, DoS, man-in-the-middle, and unauthorized access and control of physical devices. For example, attackers exploit the security vulnerabilities to gain unauthorized access to the substation communication network. They take unauthorized control actions on the power grid using the compromised remote terminal units (RTUs). The vulnerable ICTs of the SCADA system with potential impact on the power grid are identified. Attack and defense strategies are developed for cybersecurity enhancement.
5. *Testing environment for the energy management system (EMS) tools:* Prototype tools for the EMS are connected to the real-time database of the CPS. They are tested and validated before their deployment for operation. For example, extensive research is ongoing to develop decision support tools for power system restoration. The CPS is used as a testing platform. Power system blackout scenarios are defined. Scenarios where the SCADA system is partially unavailable are envisioned. The tool supports decision-making of system operators for power system restoration in an online environment. It computes the optimal/feasible solutions to restoration subproblems or checking the feasibility of operators' decision options based on the actual grid condition. Operators benefit from the adaptation of system restoration strategy to the changing system conditions.

2.2 Cyberpower System Cosimulation

Deployment of the ICT infrastructure transforms a power system into a CPS. Efficient operation of the CPS relies on close interactions between cyber and power systems. Consequently, inclusion of a cybersystem model with the power system models is important for the analysis of complex scenarios involving the dynamics of both systems.

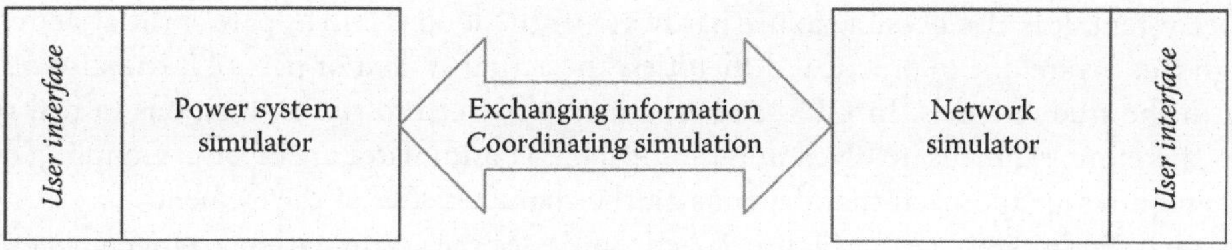

Figure 2.1 CPS simulator.

Model-based numerical simulation is a typical method to study systems. The use of actual hardware or emulators together with simulation models is also found in some studies.

Power system simulations include steady-state, for example, power flow studies, or dynamic, for example, transient stability studies. However, computer networks are represented as discrete event-driven systems using statistical models. The cybersystems can be represented by computer networks, and tools such as NS-2, OMNeT++, and OPNET are used for simulation. Therefore, CPS cosimulation requires a combination of diverse simulation tools and coordination of their execution. In developing cosimulators, there is a preference for the use of existing software tools. This is because they have familiar features and libraries that enable one to choose the most appropriate tools according to purpose and requirements. Figure 2.1 shows a CPS simulator formed by coupling power system and network simulation tools.

2.2.1 Coupling of Simulation Tools

Various types of tools and elements, as shown in Figure 2.2, can be combined to form a CPS cosimulator. For instance, it is possible to use only simulation tools to represent both power system

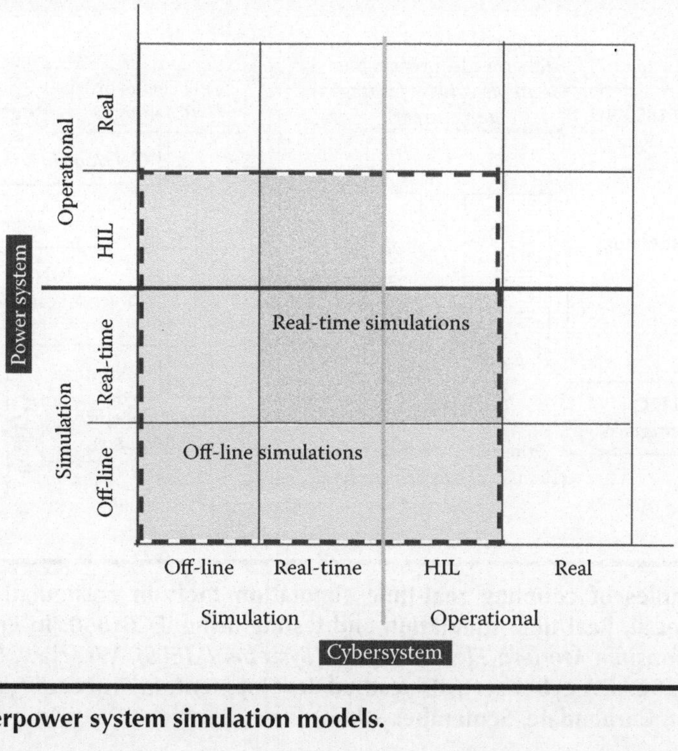

Figure 2.2 Cyberpower system simulation models.

and cybersystem. It is also possible to use hardware-in-the-loop (HIL) as part of the system model. Although this is rare due to practical difficulties, the actual system or part of it can also be incorporated in the study models. In CPS studies, a user may need to run simulations in real time or off-line. Therefore, elements involved in building a CPS cosimulator are diverse. Coupling of these elements requires an approach that depends on the characteristics of the elements.

The square in broken lines in Figure 2.2 encompasses the cosimulation arrangements that are commonly used. Due to the large scale of a power system and its cybersystems, a complete representation of either system using HIL alone is not usually feasible. Thus, HIL typically appears as HIL-simulation combinations.

2.2.1.1 Real-Time Simulation and HIL

Real-time simulation requires the same time as the study period to complete a simulation. Complex studies covering a large number of scenarios could take a prohibitively long time to complete simulations. As such, for lengthy multiscenario studies, off-line simulations are more realistic.

Coupling a real-time simulation tool with another real-time simulation tool or a piece of hardware requires compatible interfaces. An example of real-time cosimulation with HIL of a RTDS simulator is reported in [8]. In this example, a separately developed IEC61850-compatible interface for the RTDS simulator delivers data over Ethernet from and to IEC61850 compliant intelligent electronic devices (IEDs). In another example, power system simulator PowerServer and network simulator RINSE have been coupled to form a cosimulator [9]. A virtual private network (VPN) is created through the network simulator and used to connect the power system simulator to a network client in a control center. Cosimulation environments described in these two examples are shown in Figures 2.3a and 2.3b, respectively. Synchronization of real-time clocks of multiple computers and coupling delays are important issues when setting up the real-time simulators.

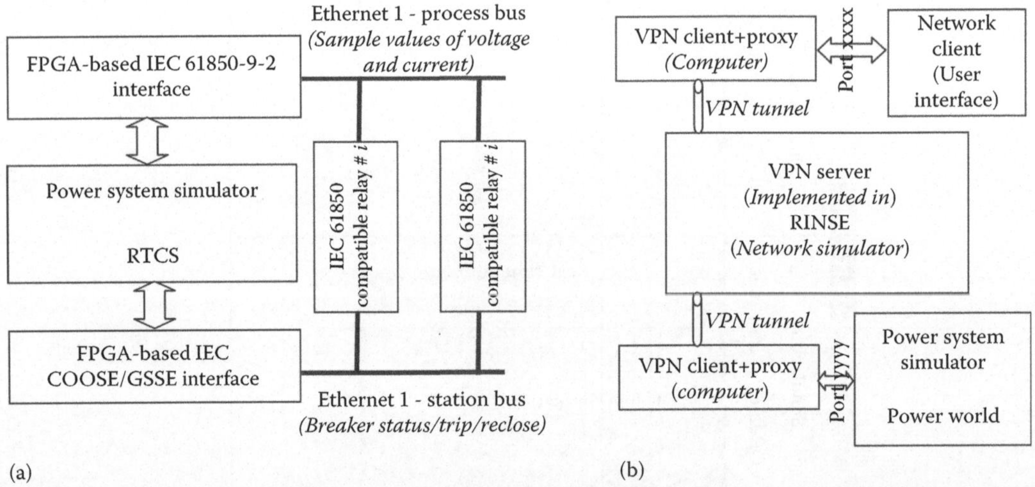

Figure 2.3 Examples of coupling real-time simulation tools in cosimulation environment. (From Kuffel, R., et al. Real time simulation and testing using IEC61850. In *Proceedings of the International Symposium Modern Electric Power Systems (MEPS)*, Wroclaw, September 2010; Davis, C. M., et al. SCADA cyber security testbed development. In *Proceedings North American Power Symposium*, Carbondale, September 2006.)

A detailed example of CPS simulation in real time is presented in Section 2.2.3. The communication network modeled in MATLAB® is coupled to DIgSILENT PowerFactory, an industrial-grade power system simulator. As indicated in this example, the OPC client-server models over TCP/IP and Ethernet connect the simulators to create the CPS cosimulation platform.

2.2.1.2 *Off-Line Simulation and HIL*

Coupling off-line power and cybersystem simulation tools needs different approaches depending upon the study objective. For instance, a study to understand the dynamic behavior of power systems due to malicious attacks on a cybersystem requires coupling of a cybersystem simulator with a time-domain simulator of the power system. Since the simulation is to determine the evolution of the system over time, synchronization of software execution in the time domain must be ensured in the coupling process. On the other hand, a study of the variation of power flow patterns due to malicious operations of circuit breakers only requires coupling of the power system simulator for power flow calculation. In this case, software tools for power system simulation and cybersystem simulation can be simply coupled.

2.2.1.2.1 Cosimulation without Time Synchronization

In this category of cosimulation, an example in which simulation tools and HIL communicate using standard protocols such as IEC 61850, DNP3, and IEC 60870 is reported in [6]. The simplified form of this system is shown in Figure 2.4.

2.2.1.2.2 Time Synchronization in Cosimulation

For continuous-time CPS simulations using off-line simulation tools, time synchronization is essential, and is achieved mainly by following three approaches:

1. Master-slave [10–13]
2. Time-stepped [14,15]
3. Global event-driven [16,17]

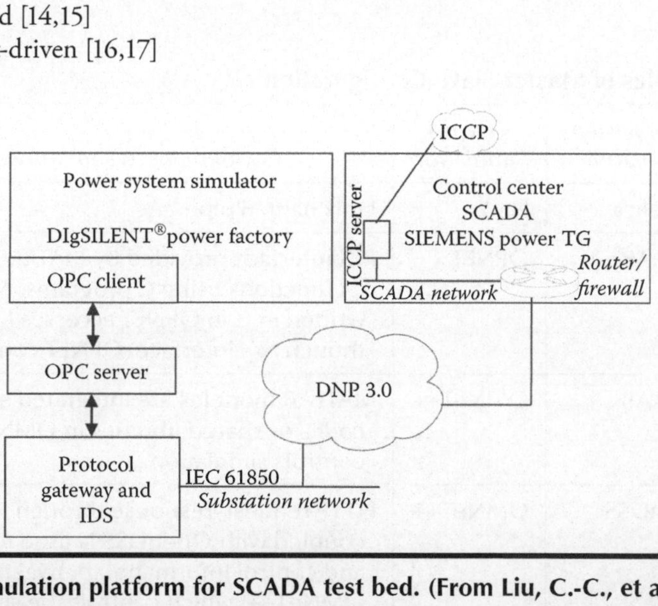

Figure 2.4 Cosimulation platform for SCADA test bed. (From Liu, C.-C., et al. *IEEE Power and Energy Magazine*, 10(1), 2012.)

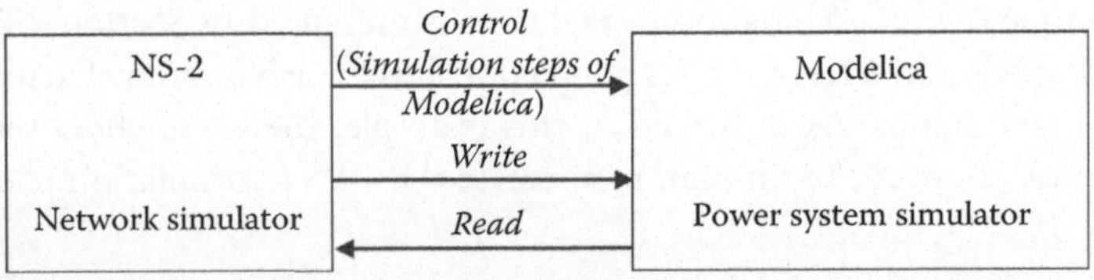

Figure 2.5 Typical master-slave configuration. (From Liberatore, V. and Al-Hammouri, A. Smart grid communication and co-simulation. In *Proceedings IEEE Energytech*, Cleveland, May 2011.)

2.2.1.2.2.1 Master-Slave Approach In the master-slave operation, one simulator acts as master and dictates the coordination of cosimulation steps. For instance, the cosimulation of voltage control of a generating plant using a remote controller over the network is presented in [10]. Both the network and the voltage sampling part are performed inside the network simulator (NS-2), and the plant is simulated using a modeling language (Modelica Association). The network simulator controls the simulation steps of the power system simulation as shown in Figure 2.5. The simulation is performed in time steps. NS-2 controls the Modelica simulation time steps such that Modelica simulation is carried out one time step after NS-2 carries out its simulations. In this example, Unix named pipes are used to exchange data between NS-2 and Modelica. Table 2.1 summarizes a few practical examples of this approach in the literature.

2.2.1.2.2.2 Time-Stepped Approach The time-stepped approach works by synchronizing simulations at preagreed points in time. The power system and communication network simulators run independently. They stop and exchange information at every synchronization point before advancing simulation to the next time step [14,15]. However, it is not possible to make the synchronization points coincide with the events occurring in the system. This is because the events are stochastic in nature. The drawback is that the events between two synchronization points have

Table 2.1 Examples of Master-Slave Configuration

Ref.	*Power System Simulation*	*Network Simulation*	*Coupling between Software Tools*
[10]	Modelica	NS-2	Unix named pipe
[11]	MATLAB	OPNET	MX interface provided by MATLAB is used to call its functions using C programs. A program written in C in OPNET accesses MATLAB models though MX interface. OPNET controls simulation.
[12,18,19]	MATLAB	OMNeT++	MATLAB modules are integrated either as source codes or shared libraries in OMNeT++, which controls simulation.
[13]	OpenDSS	OMNeT++	HTTP request–response through an HTTP server coupled with OpenDSS is used to exchange data and control information between OpenDSS and OMNeT++, which controls the simulation.

Table 2.2 Examples of Time-Stepped Synchronization in CPS Studies

Ref.	*Power System Simulator*	*Network Simulator*	*Coupling with Cosimulation Coordinator*
[14]	PSCAD/EMTDC and PSLF	NS-2	PSCAD/EMTDC uses an external programming interface to communicate with the coordinator. A gateway program written in EPLC in PSLF is used to communicate with the coordinator. On the NS-2 side, a new transport protocol serves as a link to the coordinator.
[15]	Virtual test bed (VTB)	OPNET	API based on COM standard allows coordinator to step the VTB solver. OPNET uses its external system module (Esys) through execution controller and Windows sockets to communicate with the coordinator.

to wait until the next synchronization point in time. The advantage of this method is the ability to run both simulators simultaneously. Hence, the simulations can be run quickly. Some examples of this approach are summarized in Table 2.2. The typical operation of time-stepped synchronization is depicted in Figure 2.6.

2.2.1.2.2.3 Global Event-Driven Approach Global event-driven synchronization uses a global event list and a global scheduler to synchronize simulators. It carries all events of the power system and communication system in a sequential order for the simulation period. Two simulation tools run according to the sequence of events defined in this list. This allows only one simulator to run at a given time. Although this will eliminate the drawback of a time-stepped approach mentioned in Section 2.2.1.2.2.2, the overall cosimulation speed may be affected. A few examples based on this approach are given in Table 2.3. The typical configuration of global event-driven systems is shown in Figure 2.7.

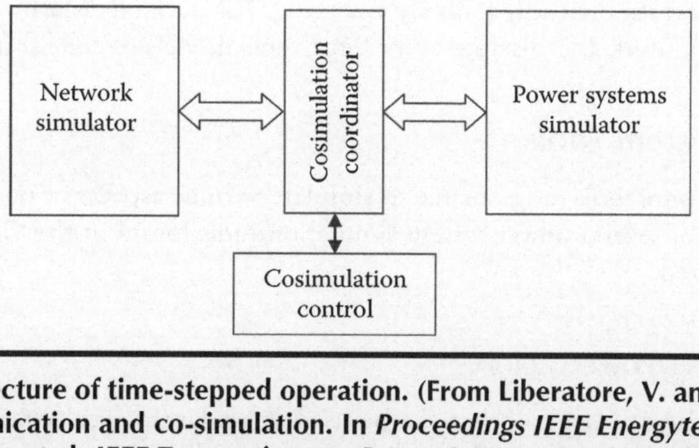

Figure 2.6 Architecture of time-stepped operation. (From Liberatore, V. and Al-Hammouri, A. Smart grid communication and co-simulation. In *Proceedings IEEE Energytech,* Cleveland, May 2011; Hopkinson, K., et al. *IEEE Transactions on Power Systems,* 21(2), 2006, IEEE.)

Table 2.3 Examples Using Global Event-Driven Approach

Ref.	*Power System Simulator*	*Network Simulator*	*Coupling with Cosimulation Coordinator*
[16]	*adevs*	NS-2	The models developed in adevs are linked to NS-2 using simulation control API, which is a part of *adevs software*. NS-2 accommodates *adevs* as a TclObject in simulation. NS-2 controls the simulation.
[17]	PSLF	NS-2	In PSLF, a dynamic model written in EPLC (scripting language) is used as port to NS-2 for communication. In NS-2, a C++ class is used to drive the simulation of PSLF and coordinate the actions in between. Global Event List and Global Scheduler are maintained in NS-2.

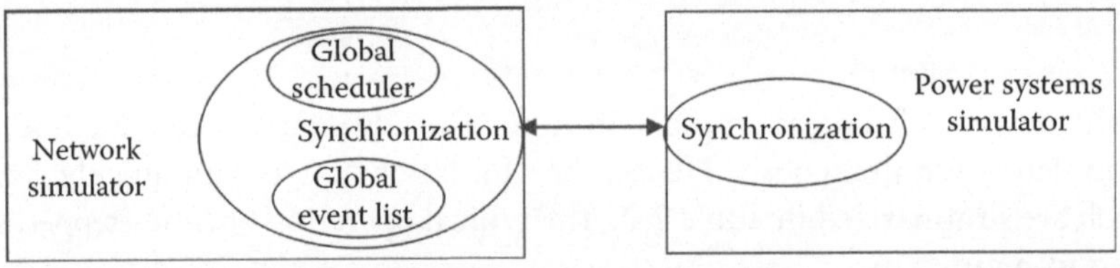

Figure 2.7 Global event-driven configuration. (From Nutaro, J., et al. Integrated hybrid-simulation of electric power and communications systems. In *Proceedings on IEEE Power Engineering Society General Meeting*, Tampa, June 2007, IEEE; Lin, H., et al. *IEEE Transactions Smart Grid*, 3(3), September 2012, IEEE; Mets, K., et al. Combining power and communication network simulation for cost-effective smart grid analysis. *IEEE Communications Surveys & Tutorials*, 16(3), March 2014, IEEE.)

2.2.2 Simulation Tools

Many industrial-grade software tools are available for power grid and communication network simulations. In this section, the features of the power and cybersystem simulation tools commonly found in CPS research are presented. It is worth noting that, with the rising importance of CPS cosimulation, new user-friendly tools are emerging. For example, Mathworks gateway blocks enable time-based Simulink and discrete-event SimEvents models to coexist in simulations [21].

2.2.2.1 Power System Tools

A wide range of software tools are available to simulate various aspects of power systems. In this section, the features of several power system simulation tools found in the CPS cosimulation literature are summarized.

2.2.2.1.1 DIgSILENT PowerFactory

DIgSILENT PowerFactory is a tool that can be used to analyze power generation, transmission, distribution, and industrial systems. Its capabilities for grid analysis include power flow, fault analysis, voltage stability, contingency analysis, protection functions, harmonic analysis, optimal power flow, state estimation, and quasi-dynamic simulation.

PowerFactory has mechanisms and options for interfacing with external applications. The DIgSILENT-GIS-SCADA interface is a bidirectional interface designed for data exchange with other applications, for example, GIS and SCADA. It supports Oracle, MS-SQL, and ODBC System DSN databases and ASCII Text (CSV), XML, MS-Excel, and MS Access file formats. OPC is another interface available for asynchronous communication and data exchange with SCADA and control systems [20,22]. Native implementation makes PowerFactory an OPC client communicating with an OPC server controlled through an external source. OPC server libraries are also available as third-party products [22]. An example of coupling between PowerFactory and MATLAB is presented in Section 2.2.3. The application programming interface (API) allows external applications to embed PowerFactory's functionality into their own program. It enables direct access to the PowerFactory data model and gives access to the calculations and results.

2.2.2.1.2 SIEMENS PSS®E

SIEMENS PSS®E is a software tool for analysis of power transmission networks. Its functionalities include power flow, contingency analysis, dynamic simulation, eigenvalue and modal analysis, and short-circuit calculations.

In PSS®E, the components implemented in languages such as FORTRAN, C, C++, and MATLAB/Simulink can be linked to the simulation process as external functions via appropriate user model interface mechanisms [23]. PSS®E can also interact with user-written scripts in Python [23]. PSS®SINCAL offers a method to integrate external programs through API and COM interfaces as presented in [20] and [24] and shown in Figure 2.8.

2.2.2.1.3 NEPLAN

NEPLAN is a commercial software tool for planning of transmission and distribution networks, renewable energy systems, smart grids, and generation/industrial plants. Its functions include power flow, energy loss calculation, short circuit, reliability analysis, harmonic analysis, overcurrent protection, flicker analysis, optimal capacitor placement, optimal separation point, optimal network restoration strategy, and low voltage calculation [25].

NEPLAN can act as a server that communicates via TCP/IP connectivity. All NEPLAN data and calculation functions can be controlled by a client program through TCP/IP connection. The calculation results are transmitted over TCP/IP to databases. Figure 2.9 [26] shows how to interface NEPLAN with the external client through TCP/IP.

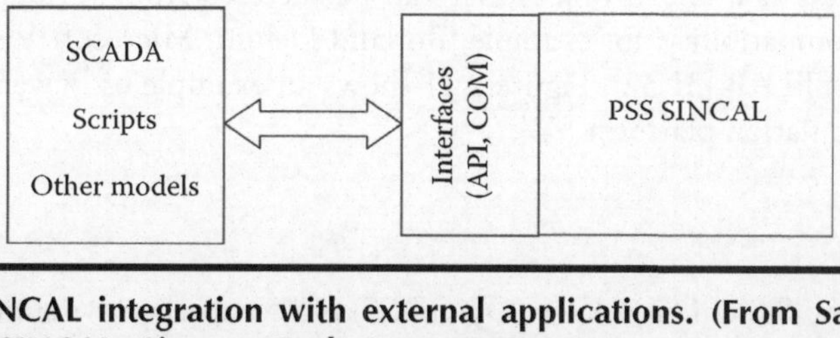

Figure 2.8 PSS®SINCAL integration with external applications. (From Sachs, U. Smart grid offering within PSS SINCAL. *Siemens Tech.* Rep., 2012.)

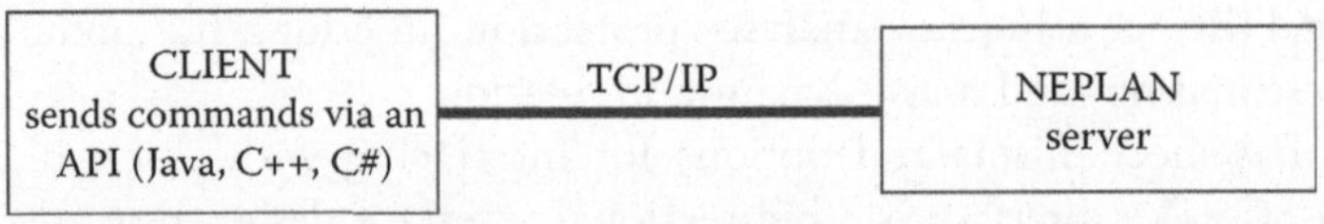

Figure 2.9 NEPLAN interface with external clients through TCP/IP. (From NEPLAN. NEPLAN—SmartGrid application. 2014.)

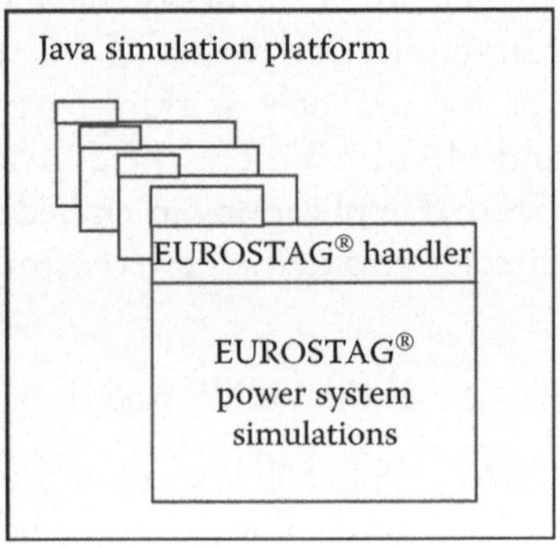

Figure 2.10 Coupling EUROSTAG with a Java simulation platform. (From Issicaba, D., et al. Islanding operation of active distribution grids using an agent-based architecture. In *Proceedings IEEE PES Innovative Smart Grid Technologies*, Gothenburg, October 2010, IEEE.)

2.2.2.1.4 EUROSTAG®

EUROSTAG is a software tool for simulations of power system dynamics. It is capable of modeling HVDC systems, SVC, and a variety of loads [27]. The functionality of EUROSTAG includes power flow, dynamic analysis, eigenvalue calculations, security assessment, and small signal analysis [27].

EUROSTAG supports the import and export of dynamic data in the CIM ENTSO-E profile Revision 2 [27]. The embedded API allows the integration of EUROSTAG into an external process through MATLAB, Python, C or C++, and JAVA [27–29]. Figure 2.10 shows an example of EUROSTAG's integration within external Java simulation platforms [29].

2.2.2.1.5 PowerWorld

PowerWorld is a power system simulation package designed to simulate high-voltage power system operation. The simulation capabilities of PowerWorld include contingency analysis, area generation control, time-step simulation, available transfer capability, voltage adequacy and stability, variety of power flow calculations, and transient stability [30].

A tool called Simulator Automation server (SimAuto) provides PowerWorld users with the ability to access PowerWorld Simulator functionality within a program written externally by the user. The SimAuto acts as a COM object that can be accessed from various programming languages with COM compatibility, for example, Borland Delphi, Microsoft Visual C++, Microsoft Visual Basic, and MATLAB [31,32]. Figure 2.11 shows an example of PowerWorld cosimulation with a Java-based simulation platform [33].

2.2.2.1.6 OpenDSS

The Open Distribution System Simulator (OpenDSS) is a comprehensive simulation tool for electric utility distribution systems developed by EPRI. OpenDSS is the open-source implementation

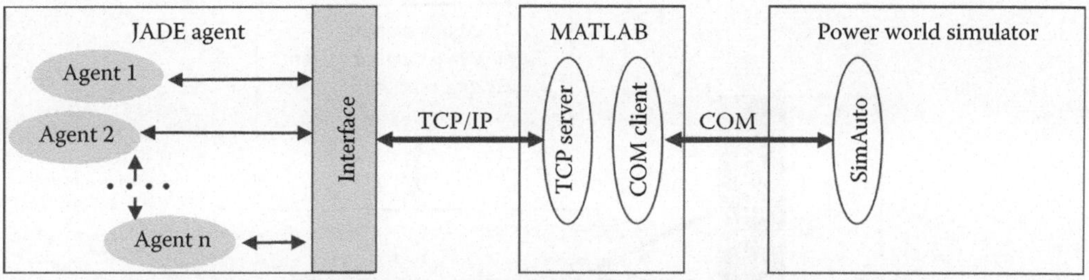

Figure 2.11 PowerWorld interfaced with Java simulation platform. (From Roche, R., et al. A framework for co-simulation of AI tools with power systems analysis software. In *Proceedings Database Expert Systems Applications,* Vienna, September 2012, IEEE.)

of the EPRI's Distribution System Simulator. OpenDSS can be used for many studies, such as power flow, faults, distribution planning and analysis, multiphase alternating current (AC) circuit analysis, distributed generation, wind power simulations, harmonic analysis, and voltage simulations.

OpenDSS has been implemented as a stand-alone executable program and COM DLL design in order to provide the facility to drive it from a variety of existing software platforms. The executable version has a basic user interface to assist users in developing their own scripts [13,34]. In the other implementation, through the COM interface, users are able to add other solution modes and features externally. OpenDSS is open-source; the source code is accessible to users. Therefore, users have the flexibility to modify the source code to suit special interfacing needs. The structure of OpenDSS is illustrated in Figure 2.12.

2.2.2.1.7 PSCAD®/EMTDC

PSCAD/EMTDC is a combination of a graphical user interface, that is, power systems computer-aided design (PSCAD), and a DC simulation engine, that is, electromagnetic transient (EMTDC). It is a TDS program for the study of transient behaviors of power systems. PSCAD enables the user to construct a circuit schematically, run a simulation, analyze the results, and manage the data in a graphical environment. Online features such as plotting, controls, and meters enable the user to alter system parameters during simulation. PSCAD comes with a library of preprogrammed and simulation models, ranging from passive elements and control functions to more complex models, for example, electric machines, flexible alternating current transmission system (FACTS) devices, and transmission lines and cables. PSCAD also provides users with the ability to build custom models [35,36].

PSCAD has the ability to interface with the functionality of MATLAB commands and toolboxes through a special interface. This is achieved by calling a special subroutine from within a

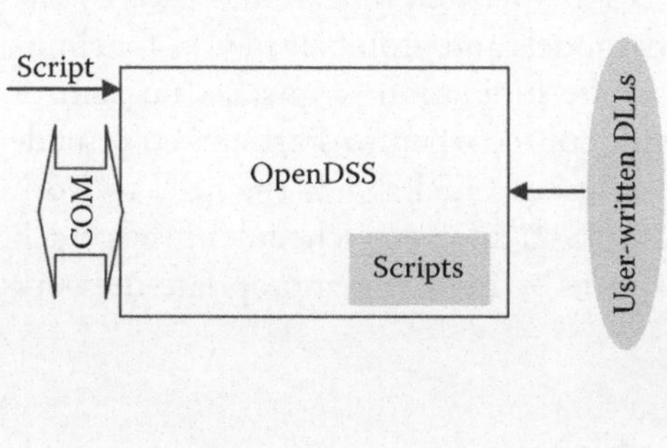

Figure 2.12 The structure of OpenDSS. (From EPRI. Simulation tool—OpenDSS. 2014.)

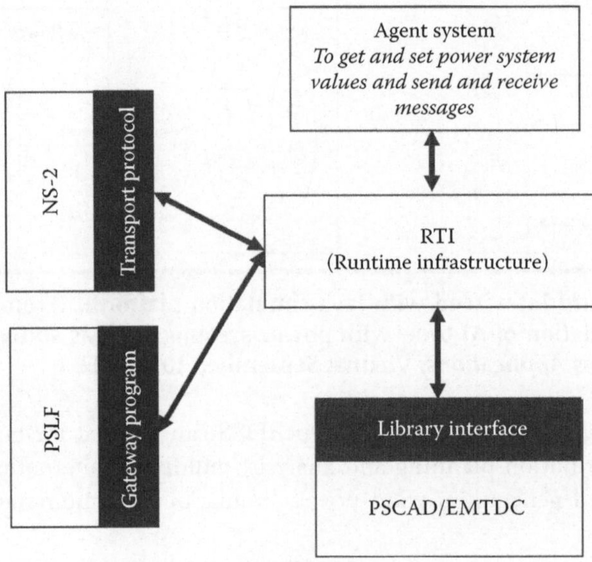

Figure 2.13 A cosimulation platform using PSCAD/EMTDC. (From Hopkinson, K., et al. *IEEE Transactions on Power Systems*, 21(2), 2006, IEEE.)

standard component in PSCAD. The user has to develop the specific MATLAB/Simulink component to be interfaced with PSCAD. Once designed, a component can be treated as a normal component in PSCAD and may be used interactively with other components [35]. The ability to combine PSCAD/EMTDC through external program interfaces is demonstrated in [14]. It is coupled with PSLF and NS-2 to produce a cosimulation platform. The system architecture is depicted in Figure 2.13.

2.2.2.2 Communication Network Tools

In a CPS, the cybersystem is generally modeled as a computer network for simulation purposes. Therefore, network simulation tools are used for cybersystem simulations due to their availability and familiarity. Users can choose open-source simulators, for example, NS-2, NS-3, and OMNeT++, or commercial simulators, for example, OPNET. Brief descriptions of these simulation tools, commonly found in the CPS cosimulation-related literature, are presented below.

2.2.2.2.1 Network Simulation Version 2 (NS-2)

NS-2 is a widely used open-source network simulator. NS-2 is written in C++ and used by the research community. Users of NS-2 can develop network models and protocols in C++ for simulations. NS-2 provides a scripting language (OTcl) to create simulation scripts, set up control configurations such as network topology, and tell a traffic source when to start and stop sending packets through an event scheduler [37]. The availability of OTcl avoids the need to work with C++ programming for simulation modification. In NS-2, an event scheduler keeps track of the simulation time and releases the events in the queue by invoking appropriate network components [37].

A network animator, called NAM, provides packet-level animation and protocol-specific graph for design and debugging of network protocols [38]. NS-2 provides good support for the simulation of Internet protocols.

2.2.2.2.2 Network Simulation Version 3 (NS-3)

NS-3 is an open-source discrete-event network simulator. NS-3 has been developed to overcome the deficiencies of NS-2. It is not backward compatible with NS-2.

The core of NS-3 is C++. However, in NS-3, instead of the OTcl interpreter, a Python scripting interface is made available for scripting. NS-3 supports the integration of real implementation code by providing standard APIs, such as Berkeley sockets or POSIX threads, which can be transparently mapped to the simulation [39].

2.2.2.2.3 OPNET Modeler®

OPNET Modeler is a commercial software tool that can be used to study communication networks, devices, protocols, and applications. It offers visual and graphical support for users. The graphical editor interface can be used to build network topologies and entities from the application layer to the physical layer. OPNET Modeler provides programming tools for users to define the packet format of the protocol. The programming tools are also required to define the network model and the process module.

OPNET Modeler has a high-level visual user interface offering access to a large library of C and C++ source code blocks. They represent different modes and functions. It has an open interface that allows integration of external object files, libraries, other simulators, and HIL to facilitate cosimulation. In addition, the smart grid communication assessment tool (SG-CAT) has been built on top of OPNET Modeler [20]. OPNET is capable of simulating the models of a variety of modern wireless networks, for example, LTE, WIMAX, UMTS, ZigBee, Wi-Fi, and path-loss models [20]. This feature makes OPNET suitable for the simulation of smart grid entities, for example, future distribution systems.

2.2.2.2.4 OMNeT++

OMNeT++ is a general-purpose discrete event-based simulation framework. Due to its capability to handle discrete-event systems, it is mostly applied to the domain of network simulation. Its INET package provides a comprehensive collection of Internet protocol models, for example, IPv4, IPV6, TCP, UDP, and Ethernet. In addition, model packages, for example, VNS, INET_MANET, and Castalia, facilitate the simulation of mobile ad hoc networks or wireless networks in OMNeT++ [20,39]. In the context of cosimulation, OMNEST, the commercial version of OMNeT++, provides federation support based on high-level architecture (HAL) [20].

OMNeT++ simulations consist of simple modules that realize the atomic behavior of a model, for example, a particular protocol. Multiple simple modules are combined together to form compound modules, for example, a host node. A network simulation in OMNeT++ is implemented as a compound module that is a combination of other compound modules [39]. OMNet++ uses C++ for the implementation of the simple modules. However, the composition of these simple modules into compound modules and the setup of network simulation take place in NED, the network description language of OMNeT++. NED supports the specification of variable parameters in the network description. This allows the number of nodes in a network to be configured at runtime [39]. OMNet++ has been used to simulate communication systems based on OFDM, PLC, IP over PLC, multihop wireless networks, and IEC 61850 [20].

2.2.2.3 Power System Communication Protocols

A variety of standard protocols have been developed and adopted over time for communications in power systems. Some commonly used communication protocols in power systems operation and control are Modbus, DNP 3, IEC 61850, and inter-control center communication protocol (ICCP)—IEC 60870-6 [40]. In the context of present data networks, these protocols are application-level protocols that concern end devices. The implementation of these protocols is crucial for HIL simulations that involve hardware using these protocols for communications [6,8]. Since the end devices are elements of power systems, the developers of power system simulation tools are in the process of upgrading their products to support these protocols [41]. Some tools exist [42].

2.2.3 Example of Real-Time CPS Simulator

The simulation tools for power systems and communication networks and their coupling techniques are summarized in Sections 2.2.1 and 2.2.2. An example of a real-time CPS simulator is presented. The coupling mechanism is the OPC interoperability standard. The CPS simulation environment and software tools used for this tutorial are shown in Figure 2.14. DIgSILENT PowerFactory was selected for power system simulation. The power grid dynamics are computed during the simulation runtime. Online power flow is used for steady-state analysis of the power grid. DIgSILENT PowerFactory has embedded OPC functionality. When it is enabled, DIgSILENT PowerFactory runs as an OPC client. It exchanges data with external OPC servers. Alternatively, any other commercial tools with OPC functionality can be used. Furthermore, technical computing tools are flexible options, for example, MATLAB/Simulink in combination with different toolboxes such as SimPowerSystems, voltage stability toolbox (VST), power system analysis tool (PSAT), MATPOWER, power system toolbox (PST), and power analysis toolbox (PAT). However, communication interfaces with the external OPC servers must be created for data exchange. MATLAB is used for the cybersystem simulation in combination with different toolboxes, that is, Simulink, SimEvents, and OPC. MATLAB/Simulink is chosen for its modeling flexibility of discrete-event systems using the queuing theory. SimEvents offers a component library for Simulink. It is a discrete-event simulation engine for modeling the communication processes between ICTs. The OPC toolbox in MATLAB offers the interface capability of the cybersystem model with external OPC servers. It includes function blocks to exchange data between OPC servers and the MATLAB/Simulink-SimEvents model. In this example, the cybersystem model incorporates two OPC clients for data exchange with the power system simulator and the TO's console. Industrial-grade SCADA software for control centers (CC) is used for the TO's console, that is, SIEMENS SICAM PAS and Spectrum Power TG. SICAM PAS is the SIEMENS software for the substation automation system. It is configured as an OPC client. Data is exchanged with the OPC server in real time. SICAM PAS communicates via DNP 3.0 over TCP/IP with the Spectrum Power TG software. SIEMENS Spectrum Power TG is the SCADA software for system operators. It includes a real-time database and the SCADA mimics for power system monitoring and control. The OPC protocol facilitates the connectivity between components of the CPS. The MatrikonOPC Simulation Server provides the coupling mechanism for real-time data exchange. It provides a simulated environment for OPC server-clients architectures. MatrikonOPC Simulation Server is a testing tool for OPC clients and connections before their

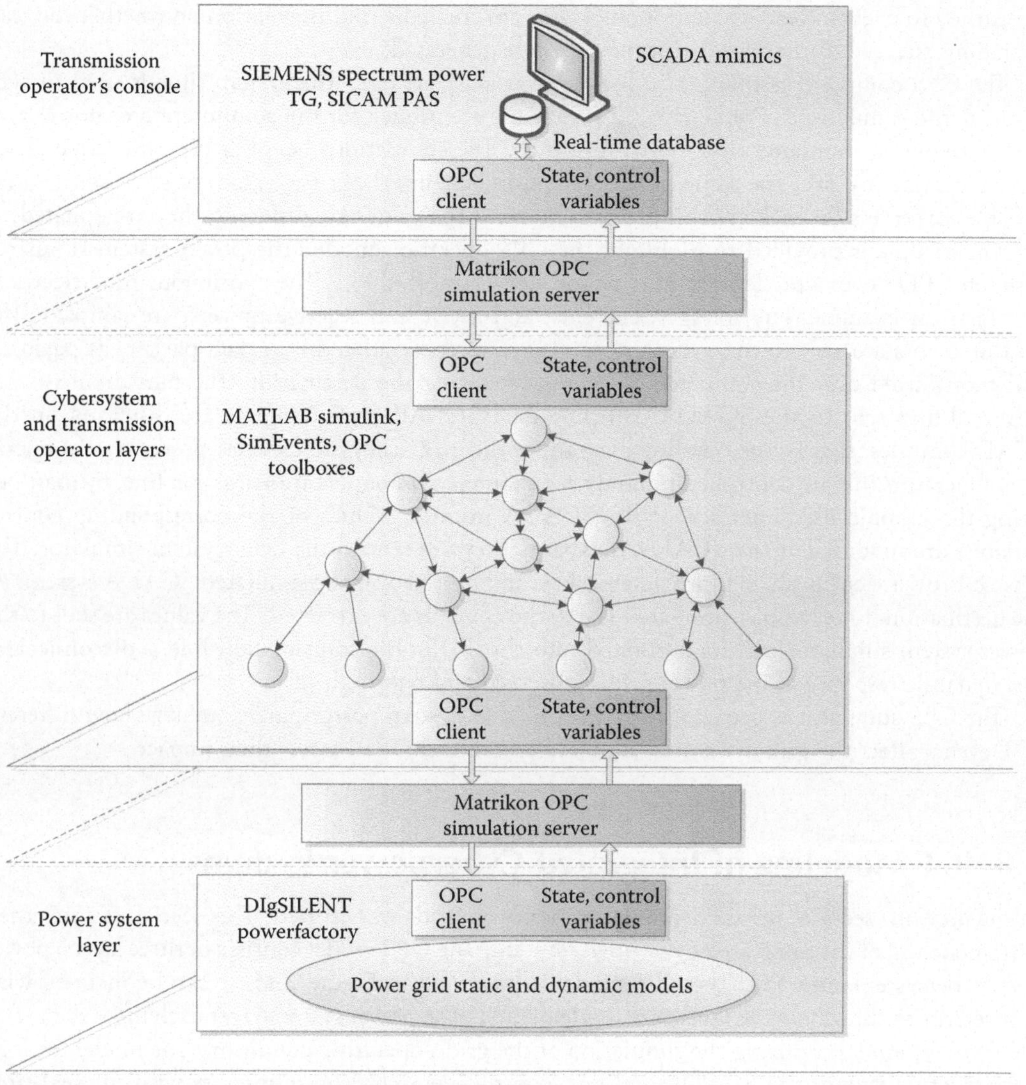

Figure 2.14 Integrated CPS simulation environment.

deployment for operation. Unlike the industrial-grade software used for this CPS example, that is, DIgSILENT PowerFactory, MATLAB, SIEMENS SICAM PAS, and SIEMENS Spectrum Power TG, the MatrikonOPC Simulation Server is free for nonproduction use and it can be distributed openly.

The CPS components are integrated using two client-server architectures. Two OPC servers and four clients are used, as represented in Figure 2.14. In this tutorial, an OPC server connects the power and cybersystems. The second OPC server communicates data between the cybersystem and the real-time database of the SCADA software. The OPC servers exchange state and control variables between the clients. The interactions take place at certain time intervals. The clients perform asynchronous read and write operations to exchange data bidirectionally through the OPC servers. For example, two clients place requests for data to servers. Their sessions continue processing the next instructions. The read operations occur in the background. The requested data is returned to clients. Read asynchronous events are created with information on whether the read operations succeed. Otherwise, error messages are generated.

The CPS components interact in real time at a 10 ms rate. The system time is used to synchronize the simulations. For clarity, 60 s real time are needed for the computation of power grid dynamics over a simulated time horizon of 60 s. The simulations begin at the same time. They run independently over the same period. The OPC clients check the values of state and control variables at servers for each synchronization point. If the values are different, they are updated.

An example is provided to highlight the CPS operation mode. The power system simulator computes TDS over a predefined time period, for example, 300 s. The continuous-time electrical variables, for example, bus voltages, currents, and active and reactive powers, are sampled. The measurements are sent to the cybersystem. They are encapsulated into data packets as payloads and transmitted over the simulated SCADA system. At the destination, the measurements are extracted and sent to the SCADA real-time database. All measurements are displayed on the SCADA mimics, that is, the one-line diagram of the grid. They are used for power system operation. Operators initiate control commands, for example, disconnect transmission line, by manipulating the graphic user interface of the SCADA mimics. Values of the corresponding control variables are modified at the SCADA database. They are sent to the cybersystem simulator. The new controls are encapsulated into data packets and routed over the simulated SCADA system. At the destination, for example, simulated IEDs, the controls are extracted. The values are sent to the power system simulator and incorporated into the TDS. The transmission line is disconnected. The dynamic response of the power grid is observed and reported.

The CPS simulator is used to study the SCADA system performance, analyze how different ICT events affect the grid dynamics, simulate cyberattacks, and assess their impact.

2.3 ICT Modeling of Integrated Cyberpower Systems

In the previous section, the CPS simulator for power grids was created. This section is concerned with modeling of the integrated cyberpower system. The CPS model consists of three layers: power grid, cybersystem, and TO. The CPS model is presented in Figure 2.15. It can be mapped with Figure 2.14 to show how the layers are implemented. The power system layer exchanges data with the cybersystem layer during the simulation of the grid's operating condition. The model for ICT infrastructure supporting SCADA and grid control hierarchy communicates with the real-time database of the SCADA software. Data is displayed on the TO's console. It supports power system monitoring and control.

The cyberpower system model in Figure 2.15 results from the modeling and preparation of each layer for real-time data exchange. The power grid is a continuous-time system. Both static and dynamic models for the power grid are implemented [43]. TDS is used for the grid's operating condition. The electric parameters are sent to the cybersystem layer at a sampling rate. Here, the ICT model of SCADA is created. It is a discrete-event system. Queuing theory is used for the SCADA model [44]. A queuing system describes the behavior of each ICT device. The information exchange capabilities are captured to evaluate communication performance and security. Measurements and breaker status are gathered by polling the RTUs. They are communicated using simulated data packets over the wide area network (WAN) to the TO console. Data is communicated bidirectionally with time delays between the system components at the cybersystem and TO layers. The SCADA model enables remote control of RTUs and IEDs from the TO console.

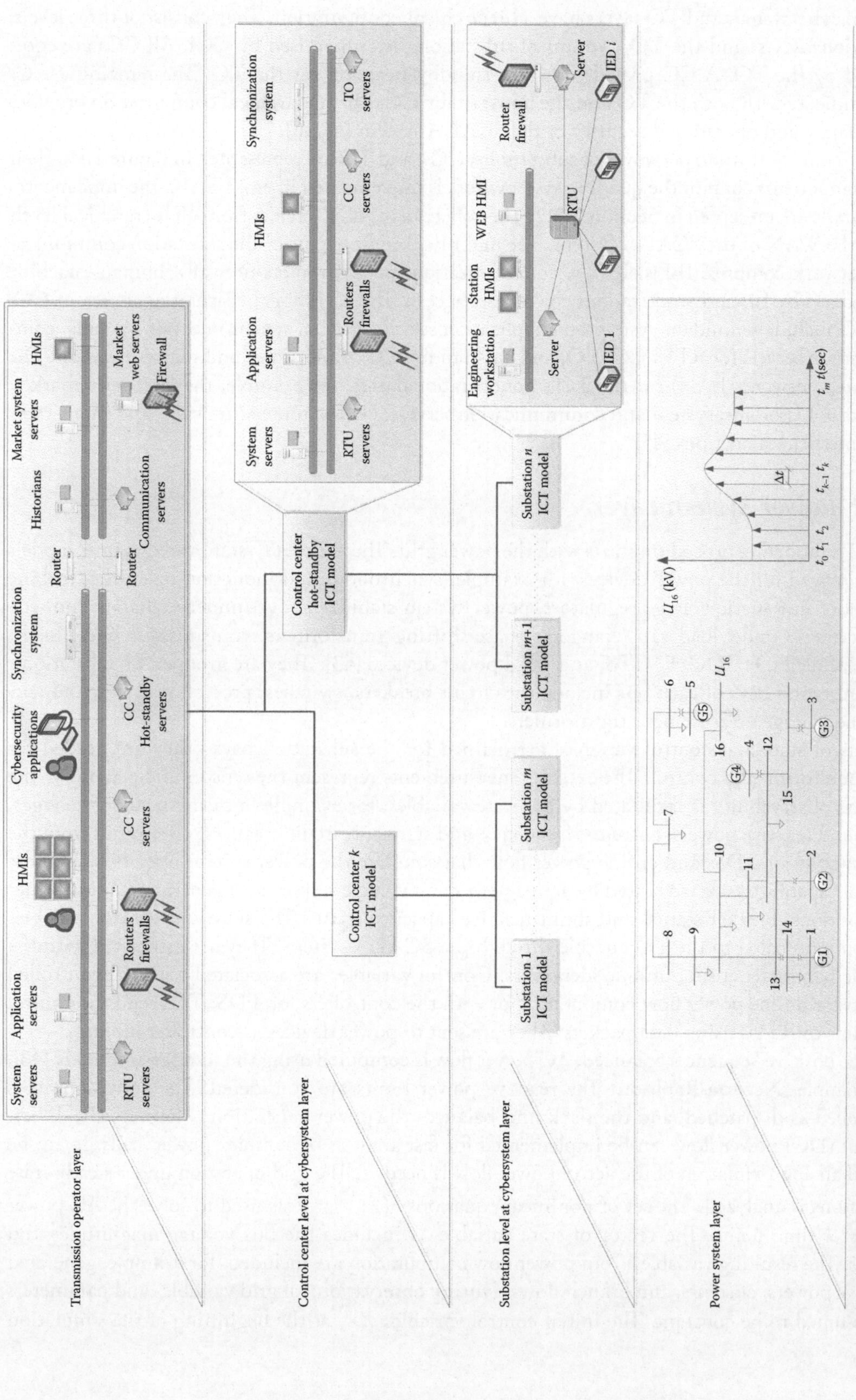

Figure 2.15 Cyberpower system model.

The cybersystem and TO layers have a hierarchical configuration. They consist of three levels: substations, CCs, and the TO. Groups of substations are supervised by CCs. All CCs are coordinated by the TO. A CC provides the hot-standby function for the TO. The remaining CCs communicate with both the TO and the hot-standby CC. The hierarchical configuration provides redundancy and operational security of the SCADA system [45,46].

The communication networks of substations, CCs, and TO are represented in Figure 2.15. Their ICT components contain the queuing system models implemented in MATLAB. The implementation details are presented in Section 2.3.2. The collection of ICT devices from all hierarchical levels forms the WAN of the SCADA system. The main ICT components of the substation communication network comprise IEDs, RTUs, communication servers, routers/firewalls, human–machine interfaces (HMIs), and workstations for remote access. The ICTs for the operational area of CCs and TO include redundant system and application servers, HMIs, synchronization systems, communication servers for RTU, CC, TO, and hot-standby CC connections, and routers/firewalls. The local area network (LAN) for the TO's nonoperational area, for example, the electricity market, consists of historians, system and communication servers, HMIs, routers/firewalls, and web servers with Internet connections [45].

2.3.1 Power System Layer

The CPS modeling procedure starts with the power grid. The AC steady-state and dynamic models are employed for the power devices, for example, synchronous and induction machines, turbine governors, automatic voltage regulators, power system stabilizers, over/under-excitation limiters, transformers, under-load tap changers, phase-shifting transformers, transmission lines, loads, shunt elements, HVDC, FACTS, and wind power devices [43]. They are grouped by substations. The substation bays of each bus include the circuit breakers, switches, protection relays, and current and voltage measurement transformers.

Sets of state and control variables are defined for the substation bays. They are needed for grid monitoring and control. The external measurements represent the sensors and actuators. The system's observability is facilitated by the state variables, for example, measurements of voltages, active and reactive powers, currents, frequency, and status of circuit breakers. They result from the computation of TDSs and online power flow that simulate the power system operation. Remote control capabilities are facilitated by active power and voltage setpoints of generators, transformer tap positions, breaker status, and shunt reactive/capacitor status. The state and control variables are communicated to the TO console through the SCADA system. They are associated with the electric parameters using unique identifiers. Control variables are associated with the controlled objects for online power flow computation or with the controllers for TDS. TOs send the control setpoints to RTUs using data packets. They are sent to power devices as controller inputs.

The positive-sequence, balanced, AC power flow is computed using the standard methods [43], for example, Newton-Raphson. The reactive power limits are considered. The active power is controlled as dispatched, and the slack unit balances the power generation. Alternatively, direct-current (DC) power flow can be implemented for fast analysis of complex power grids. It can be used if an approximation of the active power flow is needed. The grid operation under steady-state conditions is analyzed. The set of nonlinear equations $h(X_S^{(k)}) = 0$ is used to solve the AC power flow at k time point. The vector of state variable X_S includes the bus voltage magnitudes and angles. The resulting variables from power flow computation are included, for example, generated reactive powers, currents, and branch flows. During observation, all grid variables and parameters are assumed to be constant. The initial control variables $X_C^{(0)}$ at the beginning of the simulation correspond to the static data of the power system model. $X_S^{(0)}$ are computed and written to ICT devices at the cybersystem layer. At the current point k of simulation, the control variables $X_C^{(k)}$ are read from the ICTs. A new power flow is computed to find $X_S^{(k)}$ if the vector of control variables is different from the previous one, that is, $X_C^{(k)} \neq X_C^{(k-1)}$. The new state variables are reported. The system goes into an iterative loop whereby the modification of the values of control variables triggers the power flow computation.

TDS describes the dynamic behavior of the power grid. TDS provides a comprehensive impact analysis of ICT events, for example, cyberattacks or equipment failures. A set of differential algebraic equations is used for TDS computation [47]. They allow the exchange of state and control variables, with a sampling interval Δt, as shown in Figure 2.15. The time of writing/reading data to/from ICT devices, at sampling point k, is t_k. The user defines the sampling interval Δt. The power network representation type, for example, balanced positive sequence or unbalanced three phase, and the integration step size must be defined. A load profile can be simulated to describe the grid operating condition over a period of time. Power flow is used to compute the initial condition for TDS. The resulting state variables $X_S^{(0)}$ are reported. Computation of the electromechanical transients is performed by solving the differential algebraic equations over the simulation period. The simulation is synchronized by the system time. For example, it takes 60 s to compute the grid dynamics over a time period of 60 s. The state variables are continuous-time electrical parameters. They are sampled and reported to the cyberlayer. At each point k, the vector of control parameters $X_C^{(k)}$ is read at t_k from the cyberlayer. If the values are different from the previous reading, it indicates that the operators have sent control commands. They are integrated into the computation as parameter, switch, and tap position events. These external events represent variations of controller setpoints and enable remote tripping of network elements. The corresponding $X_S^{(k)}$ is reported, and the sampling point k is advanced.

The IEEE 39-bus system is used for model validation. It is described by the steady-state and dynamic models. The balanced, positive-sequence network representation is used. The test system is divided into 27 substations, as shown in Figure 2.16. Therefore, the OPC server for sensors and actuators contains 27 groups of data access items. Each group includes the items for all state and control variables defined for the corresponding substation. The power grid layer provides the measurement and status data to the 27 groups at the update rate and acquires the controls.

2.3.2 Cybersystem and Transmission Operator Layers

This section presents the models for the hierarchical structure of ICT networks at the cybersystem and TO layers (see Figure 2.15). They represent the SCADA model for the power grid. Data for power grid monitoring and control originates from the power system layer and the TO console, respectively. It is bidirectionally routed through the SCADA system in real time. However, there are time delays for data packets between the source and the destination. Queuing theory [44] is used to model the communication processes of ICT devices and the ICT communication networks of the SCADA system, that is, substations, CCs, and TO. A queuing system captures the packet generation, buffering, processing, and switching capabilities of the ICT device.

Data exchange capability between the ICTs of the SCADA system is modeled. The SCADA communication security is analyzed. It is affected by increased latency, throughput, packet loss, and cyberattacks. The queuing model for the general ICT device is described in Section 2.3.2.1. The ICT template based on queuing theory is customized in Sections 2.3.2.2–2.3.2.4 to model the networks of ICT devices at substations, CC, and TO. They are described from a software implementation point of view.

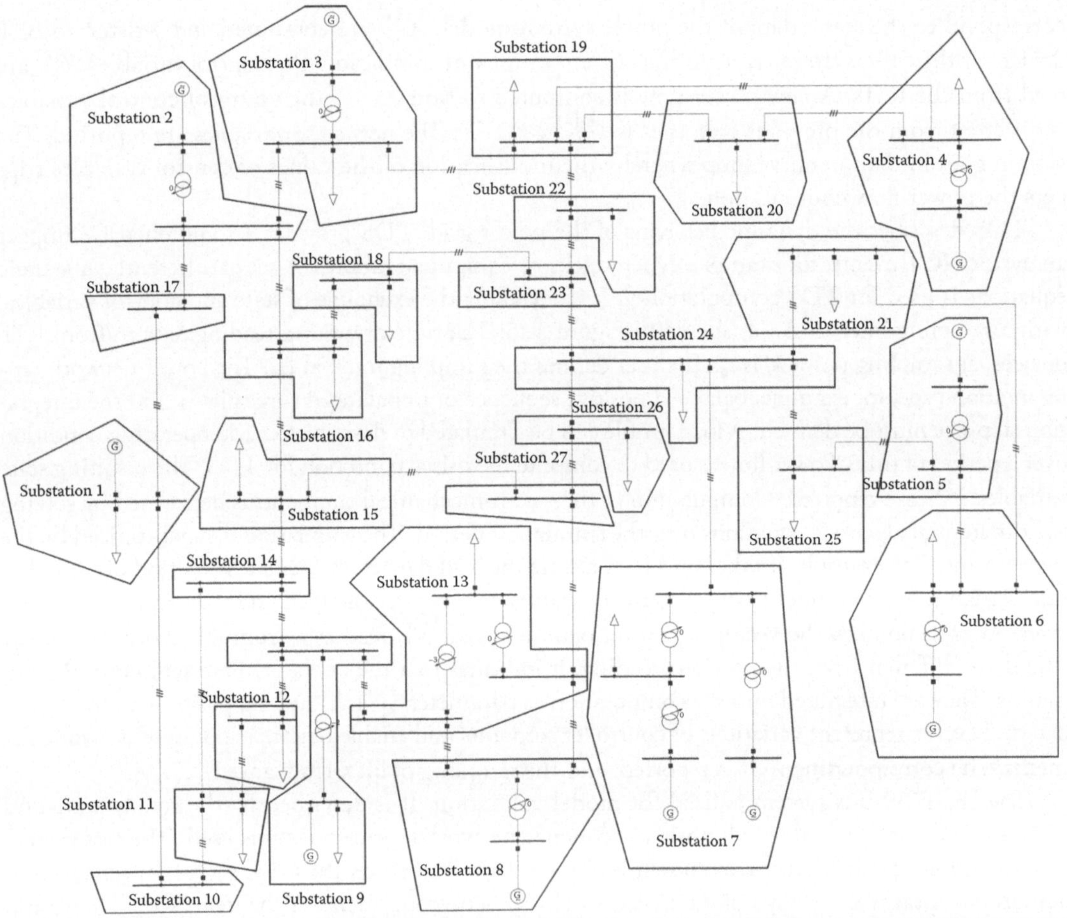

Figure 2.16 IEEE 39-bus system model at the power system layer.

All ICT devices are simulated using a combination of function blocks provided by Simulink, SimEvents, and OPC toolboxes in MATLAB. It can be envisioned that the ICT simulation models are masked and connected as shown in Figures 2.18, 2.23, and 2.24. They are networked as shown in Figure 2.15. Examples are provided in Figures 2.19 through 2.22 to create the simulation models for the IEDs, RTUs, and routers/firewalls. The function blocks are represented. The simulation models can be reproduced by selecting the corresponding function blocks from the libraries of Simulink, SimEvents, and OPC toolboxes in MATLAB. The remaining ICTs of the communication networks are modeled similarly. All simulation models have a common characteristic. They are based on the general model of the ICT device presented in Section 2.3.2.1.

2.3.2.1 ICT Device Modeling

The ICT device is modeled using the *D/D/m/K* queuing system as illustrated in Figure 2.17. The components are function blocks implemented in MATLAB. They can be found in the library of the SimEvents toolbox. The ICT simulation model is customized based on the functions of the SCADA components. The basic ICT model is described by m servers, for example, $m = 3$, and

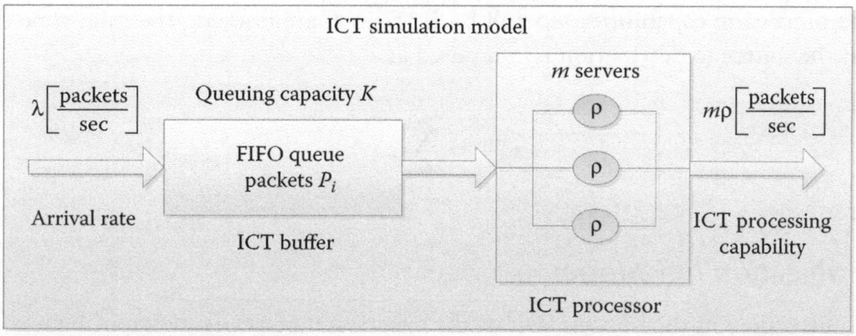

Figure 2.17 ***D/D/m/K* queuing system for the ICT model.**

one queue with finite K capacity. The queuing system is single class. The interarrival and service times are deterministic (D). The power system model is integrated with the ICT system model. It provides simulated real-time data at Δt rate. Therefore, the deterministic approach is possible. The arrival rates λ (packets/s) are known. They vary as $\lambda \in [\lambda_{\min}, \lambda_{\max}]$ depending on the number of packets generated by the power grid layer. The arrival rate for each ICT device is determined based on the number of state and control variables with different values from the previous reading. λ packets per second arrive at the queue. Each packet must access one of the m servers. A first in, first out (FIFO) queue models the ICT buffer. The ith packet in the queue is denoted by P_i. Each server has a limited processing rate ρ (packets/s). The ICT processing capability is $m\rho$.

The packets wait in the queue W_i (s) when all m servers are busy processing other data packets. Let i be the packet order number in the queue. q is the number of packets that must be served before the ith packet can access the same server. T is the monitoring period. The waiting time in the queue for packet i is $W_i = q \cdot 1/\rho$, where $q = 0,1,\ldots,(\lambda \cdot T/m) - 1$ and $i = qm + 1,\ldots,(q + 1)m$. After this time, the packet is processed by the system server. The service time is $G_i = 1/\rho$ s. When it is completed, the ith packet departs and the next packet in the queue will be served. The overall time delay for P_i in the ICT device is $t_{Pi}^{\text{delay}} = W_i + G_i = (q+1) \cdot 1/\rho$. All packets that have been admitted into the queue will be served as long as the servers are available. However, if the queuing capacity K is reached, the new packets arriving at the ICT device are dropped.

An example is provided to compute W_i for each packet in the queue. An ICT device has $m = 3$ empty servers. They process the packets in parallel as shown in Figure 2.17. $\lambda = 6$ packets per second arrive at the queue to be processed. The monitoring period is $T = 1$ s. In this case, the number of packets is divided into $\lambda \cdot T/m = 2$ groups. q takes the values of 0 and 1. For each group, the range of i is computed. For the first group, set $q = 0$. The corresponding packets are $i = 1,2,3$. In the second group, $q = 1$. The associated packets are $i = 4,5,6$. The first three packets in the queue are served immediately. The waiting time in the queue is $W_i = 0 \cdot 1/\rho$. Each packet in the second group waits for $W_i = 1 \cdot 1/\rho$ s. This is the service time for the packets in the first group. They are processed simultaneously.

The ICT template is customized to model the SCADA components, as shown in Figure 2.15. Additional SimEvents function blocks are used. Three examples are provided in Section 2.3.2.2. The SCADA system is a collection of queuing systems. ICT paths are formed by networking the ICT devices. They transmit over the WAN data packets carrying measurements from IEDs to the ICT device for the system server at the TO. At the TO, the arriving packets are processed and payloads are extracted. The communication is bidirectional. System operators send packets carrying control commands via the SCADA model. A packet is routed through an ICT path with n_{ICT}

devices. The processing capabilities $m\rho$ and buffer sizes K are known. The total time delay for a packet from the source to destination is computed as

$$t_P^{\text{delay}} = \sum_{i=1}^{n_{\text{ICT}}} t_{Pi}^{\text{delay}}$$

2.3.2.2 Substation ICT Model

The substations represent the bottom level at the cybersystem layer as shown in Figure 2.15. They model the communication processes. The substations simulated at the power system layer model the electrical processes. The integrated layers model the cyberpower substation.

The substation ICT model for simulation is presented in Figure 2.18. It includes the bay and station levels [45]. At the bay level, a local operating network (LON) connects different parts of the protection system. It enables communication with the station level. The LON connects the IEDs and RTUs that directly interact with the power devices. A start topology is used. The number of IEDs in a cybersubstation is the number of bays from the corresponding power substation. For example, substation 3 includes a generating unit, transformer, load, and two transmission lines, as shown in Figure 2.16. Six IEDs are assigned to each high-voltage (HV)/medium-voltage (MV) bay for sensing, telemetry, protection, and control. The RTU enables communication with the substation control room and the CC. The LAN at the station level is based on Ethernet. It connects ICTs such as communication servers, router/firewalls, HMIs, and workstations for remote access.

The IEDs acquire measurements from the power grid and send control commands to power controllers. The set of variables $X_{\text{var}}^{(k)} = \{X_S^{(k)}, X_C^{(k)}\}$ is exchanged at each point t_k between the power and cybersystem layers and between the TO layer and the TO console. The IEDs generate data packets carrying measurement values and status information as payloads. Packets are sent to the higher-level devices. They are delivered to the communication servers for the substation's control room and CCs. Controls can be initiated by operators remotely from the TO/CC or locally from the substation's control room.

The ICT template presented in Section 2.3.2.1 is customized to model the IED. The ICT simulation model for the IED is shown in Figures 2.19 and 2.20. The main IED components include the input/output ports, data packet generators, path combiners, buffers, processors, output switches, and network interfaces. They can be simulated using the library function blocks as shown in Figures 2.19 and 2.20. The simulation model includes the following SimEvents and

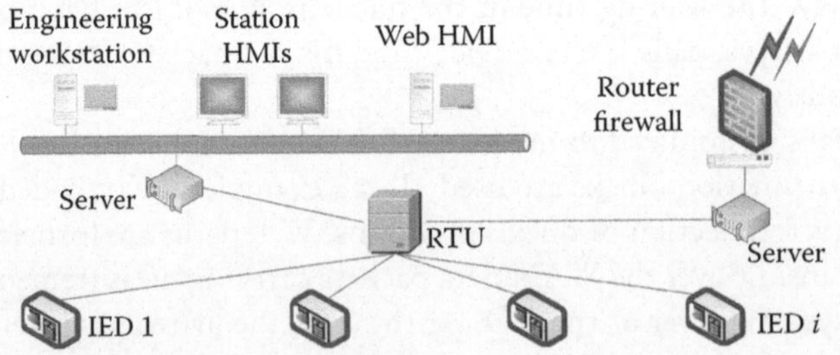

Figure 2.18 Substation ICT simulation model.

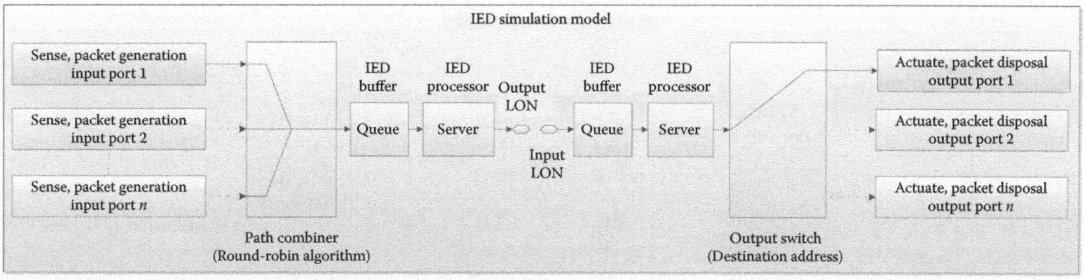

Figure 2.19 ICT simulation model for IED.

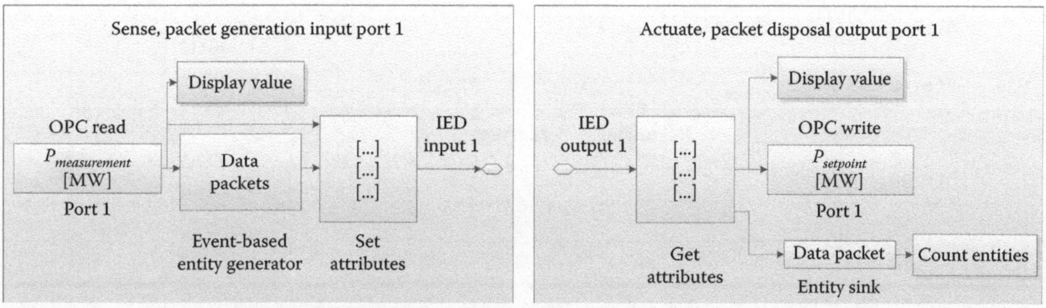

Figure 2.20 IED sensing and actuating capabilities.

OPC function blocks: OPC read and write, event-based entity generators, set and get attributes, combine and switch discrete events, queues, servers, and entity sinks.

The number of state variables defined for a substation bay corresponds to the number of IED input ports. OPC reading blocks acquire the measurement and status data from the OPC server for sensors and actuators (see Figure 2.20). The OPC server is connected to the power grid model. They exchange data with a Δt sampling interval. For each input port, the value of the corresponding state variable $X_{Si}^{(k)}$ is read asynchronously from the power device at sampling point k and displayed. An entity is created by the event-based entity generator when the new value is different from the previous reading $X_{Si}^{(k)} \neq X_{Si}^{(k-1)}$. Attributes are attached. The value of the state variable is attached as payload. It must be delivered across the SCADA system to the destination. The ICT's destination and source addresses are attached. The CC, substation, IED, and IED port numbers are used for the destination and source addresses. For example, 1.3.1.1 represents the source address for a packet incoming from CC 1, substation 3, IED 1, and the first IED port. Similarly, the destination address is defined and attached.

A data packet $p_i(X_{Si}^{(k)})$ is represented by the discrete entity carrying the associated attributes. A path combiner merges all generated packets from different input ports on the same path (see Figure 2.19). It uses a round-robin algorithm [48]. Packets access the FIFO queue and server. Time delays are introduced based on IED buffering and processing capabilities. All packets are outputted over the LON. Packets with control commands $p_j(X_{Cj}^{(k)})$ initiated by operators are incoming over the LON. They are stored and processed. The number of control variables defined for the substation bay corresponds to the number of IED output ports. Each packet is switched to the specific output port by its destination address. The payload, that is, control command, $X_{Cj}^{(k)}$ is

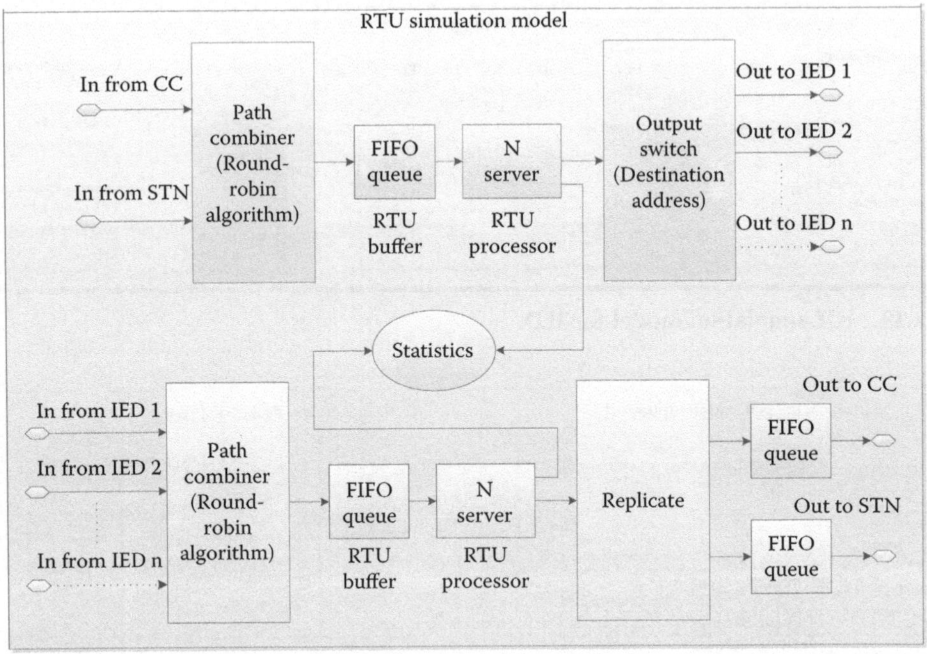

Figure 2.21 ICT simulation model for RTU.

extracted, displayed, and written asynchronously to the OPC server as shown in Figure 2.20. It is sent toward the corresponding control variable at the power system layer. The discrete event is discarded using the entity sink. The disposed entities are counted for statistical analysis. The grid dynamic behavior is observed and reported. The IED performances over time can be statistically computed.

The functions of the RTU are data acquisition, processing, local storage, and control. A single RTU is used for small- to medium-size substations [45]. In Figure 2.18, the RTU is networked with the communication servers and IEDs using the star topology. The ICT model for RTU simulation is shown in Figure 2.21. The function blocks used are two path combiners, four FIFO queues, two servers, an output switch, and a packet replication block.

Data packets carrying measurements and status information are received from the IEDs. The packets with control commands are inputs from the CC or substation control room. Incoming packets from either side are merged on the same path, stored in the RTU's buffer, and served by the processor. Time delays are introduced corresponding to the RTU's queuing and processing performance. The packets from IEDs are replicated and sent to both communication servers for connection with the CC and the substation control room, respectively. In case the substation communication server fails, system operators can control the RTU remotely from the CC or TO. Packets carrying the controls as payloads are assigned to the appropriate IEDs according to destination addresses, for example, IED number.

The router/firewall is an ICT device that enables secure communications with the CC and TO. It creates a network security perimeter for the substation. The ICT model for the router/firewall simulation is presented in Figure 2.22. The ports that are not needed are blocked for security. Data incoming from the RTU is queued, processed, and routed to the CC. Packets arriving from outside the substation communication network are inspected to prevent unauthorized

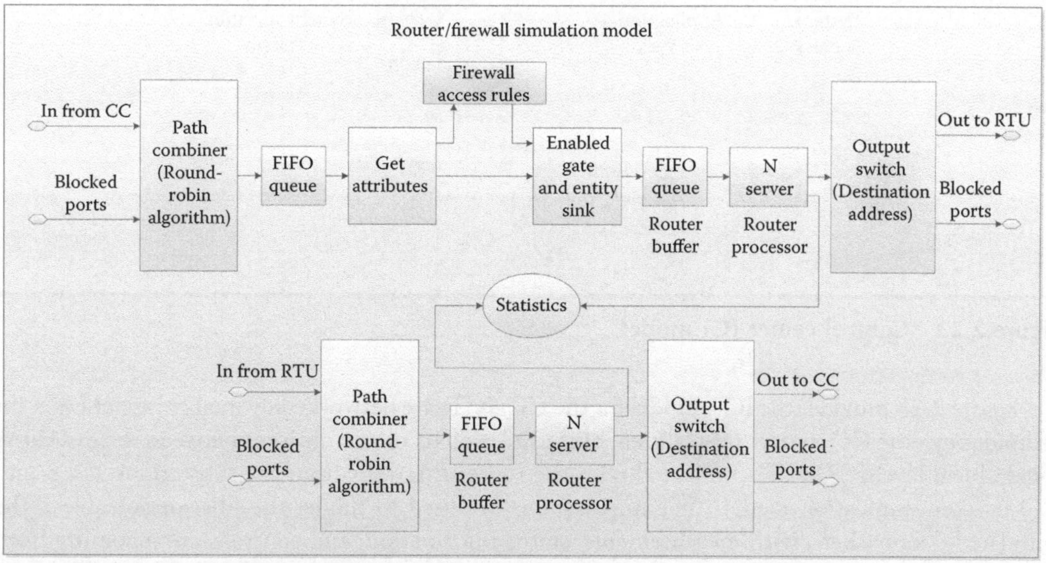

Figure 2.22 ICT simulation model for router/firewall.

access. The router/firewall protects the substation ICTs from outside traffic and malicious activities. Data packets from the CC are stored in the FIFO queue. Their attributes are extracted for inspection. Based on the firewall access rules, an enabling signal is computed for each packet. A function block simulates the gate. It is set to open or close. Legitimate packets are allowed to pass. Malicious packets are dropped using an entity sink without notifying the sender. Legitimate packets access the router's buffer and processor. They are routed toward the communication server and RTU (Figure 2.22).

Both communication servers shown in Figure 2.18 for the CC and substation control room connection are modeled. The simulation models presented for the IEDs, RTUs, and routers/firewalls can be modified and customized for the remaining ICT devices. For example, the Ethernet switch in Figure 2.18 is modeled using the function blocks for paths combining, servers, and packet replication. When a packet is received at one of the input ports, it is transmitted to all ports. Packet collisions are avoided if the Ethernet carrier sense multiple access with collision detection (CSMA/CD) protocol is implemented. An arriving packet is transmitted to all ICTs on the network. The destination address is inspected, and, if it is different from the ICT's network address, the packet is dropped.

The ICT template for the substation, shown in Figure 2.18, is customized to model the cybersystem of each substation. The number of ICT components depends on the substation size and configuration, for example, number of bays and state/control variables.

2.3.2.3 Control Center ICT Model

The CCs represent the second level of the hierarchical architecture for the grid control. CCs facilitate communication between substations and the TO layer. The CCs implement the operational regimes. They perform equipment maneuvers coordinated by the TO. The CCs have decision authority for their areas of control concerning voltage control [45].

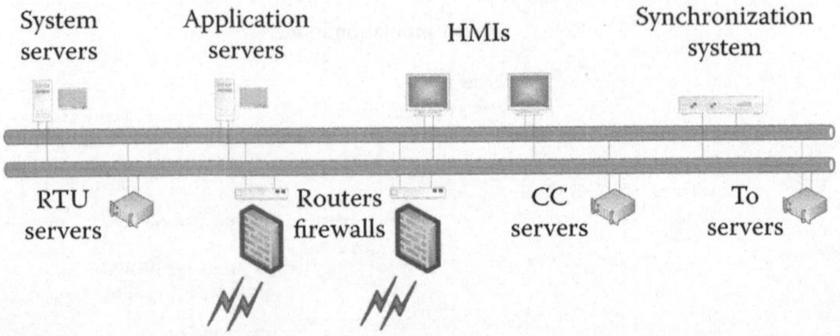

Figure 2.23 Control center ICT model.

Figure 2.23 provides the ICT model for the CC. ICTs are networked by dual Ethernet LAN for redundancy. The CC routers/firewalls enable bidirectional communication between the SCADA's hierarchical levels. They are connected with the routers/firewalls from the substations, CCs, and TO by communication media. Queuing systems are used to model the fiber-optic cables. The simulated data packets, with measurements, status information, and controls, are incoming from the substations and TO, respectively. Legitimate packets are sent over the LANs to the corresponding communication servers for the RTUs, CCs, and TO connections. Malicious packets are dropped. Data is accessible to the networked ICTs, for example, system and application servers and HMIs. Monitoring data is stored, processed, and displayed to operators. It is sent to the TO and hot-standby CC that supervise the entire power grid. Control data packets are routed to the destination substation.

2.3.2.4 Transmission Operator ICT Model

All CCs are supervised by the TO. TO is the first level in the grid control hierarchy, as represented in Figure 2.15. It is responsible for power generation, transmission coordination, and operational security.

The ICT simulation model of the TO is illustrated in Figure 2.24. The communication network is divided into the operational EMS and electricity market. The ICTs are networked by dual Ethernet LANs. All ICT components at the TO layer are redundant [45,46]. Data packets from CCs are inspected by the routers/firewalls on the operational side of the EMS/SCADA system. They are sent to the communication servers over LANs. The final destination of data packets is the system server. Here, the payloads are extracted, and the carrying entities are disposed. Data is processed by the EMS. The measurements, status information, and control commands are exchanged with the TO console. Control data packets are generated by the system server and

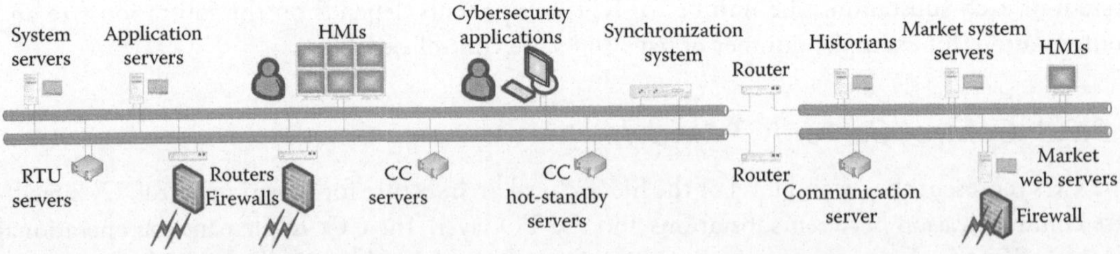

Figure 2.24 Transmission operator ICT model.

sent to the substations via the SCADA system. The operational ICT system interfaces with the electricity market system through routers/firewalls. The routers/firewalls are similar to the model given in Figure 2.22. However, for cybersecurity reasons, they are configured to send the real-time simulated data only from the operational to the nonoperational ICT system. The system servers send data packets with relevant information to the market system servers. They are processed and archived by the HMIs and historians. A router/firewall protects the communication and market web servers from malicious activities originated from the Internet.

The ICT templates for modeling the CCs and TO communication networks are customized based on the number and size of the supervised substations. For example, the 27 substations of the IEEE 39-bus system are supervised by four CCs and coordinated by the TO. The OPC server for the TO connection contains only a single group of data access items with all the state and control variables. The TO provides the measurement and status data to the group and acquires the controls.

2.3.3 Transmission Operator Console

Data is exchanged bidirectionally between the TO layer and the TO console. The measurements and status information are available through the TO console for real-time supervision of the power grid. A real-time database is created. The data points have unique telemetry and control addresses. Warning and alarm limits are defined for the telemetry data points. The one-line diagram display of the power system is created. Data points of the real-time database are linked with the display of the power grid.

Simulated real-time data is received from the cybersystem. It populates the real-time database and is displayed on the SCADA mimics. The console is used for power grid operation. System operators initiate control commands. They are sent from the SCADA mimics to the real-time database and toward the cybersystem. The control packets are routed through the simulated SCADA system and delivered to the power system. The controls are integrated into the computation of TDS or online power flow. The grid response is reported in real time.

2.4 CPS Performance

The foreground network traffic is considered for the SCADA model. It is represented by data communication between the RTUs at the substations and the TO. The network background traffic represents other communication activities in the ICT infrastructure supporting the SCADA system. It can be modeled in the form of standard distributions.

The buffering and processing capabilities for the ICTs are defined in [48] and [49]. Latency can be used to characterize the performance of the SCADA system. The time delay for a data packet from the source to the destination depends on the communication performance along the path. The performance of each ICT is known. However, the traffic on the communication network varies. The dynamics of the ICT system are influenced by the network traffic. This has an impact on the network latency. The update rate of the SCADA system at the TO is 2–4 s [50]. The ICT paths have a good performance if the latency is lower than an accepted tolerance $t_p^{delay} \leq t_\xi$. The time delay for a data packet on the same communication path varies. A performance index is computed for the *i*th ICT path. It is the mean value of the time delays on normal network traffic conditions

$$\Psi_{\text{index},i} = \frac{\overline{t_{p,i}^{delay}}}{t_\xi} \leq 1$$

The SCADA overall performance index is

$$\Psi_{\text{overall}} = \sum_{i=1}^{n_{\text{paths}}} \frac{\Psi_{\text{index},i}}{n_{\text{paths}}}$$

The sampling interval can also affect the CPS performance. A large interval disrupts monitoring of the measurements. The continuous-time electrical variables are sampled, encapsulated into data packets, transmitted through the SCADA system, and decoded at the destination. ICT congestions and traffic influence the time delays from the moment of sampling until the measurements are decoded. Packets are dropped when buffers overflow and packets collide. The stability assessment of the power system can be affected by the sampling interval, latency, and packet drop [51,52]. Time delays for the communication of control signals affect the power grid stability [47]. Reducing the latency, packet drops, and the sampling interval would be expected to solve the problem. However, the number of measurement samples increases when the sampling interval is reduced. More samples lead to larger numbers of data packets transmitted over the SCADA system. The stability of the queuing system can be affected. It depends on the packet arrival rates and ICT processing capabilities. A queuing system is stable when the processing capability is larger than the arrival rate $\lambda \leq m\mu$. All data packets are processed. Otherwise, the queuing system becomes unstable. The size of the queue is constantly increasing with the arrival of new packets until capacity is reached. When the buffer overflows, all the new packets arriving are dropped, and the network latency increases. Therefore, the sampling interval has a significant impact on the stability of both power and cybersystems. The appropriate upper and lower limits are determined based on the size and characteristics of the CPS.

2.5 Simulation Results

A SCADA test bed at University College Dublin (UCD) has been developed for cybersecurity studies [6]. A simplified version of the cosimulation platform for the SCADA test bed is illustrated in Figure 2.4. The CPS presented in this chapter is integrated with the test bed as reported in [53]. The integrated CPS model is validated on the UCD test bed with the IEEE 39-bus system. The test system is divided into 27 substations at the power layer, as shown in Figure 2.16. The dynamics of the power grid are computed for a predefined load profile. The communication networks of the substations, CCs, and TO are modeled at the cybersystem layer. Data packets carry measurements from the IEDs to the TO through the SCADA system. The cosimulation results indicate the communication performances of the SCADA model. The purpose is to assess and improve the overall SCADA performance.

A summary of results of cosimulation is presented in Table 2.4 for substations 5, 15, and 27. The time delay and communication performance are computed for each ICT path originated from the substation's IED toward the TO. An overall performance index for the substation is calculated as described in Section 2.4. Based on the substation performance indices, the SCADA communication performance is assessed. The update rate of the SCADA system at the TO is 2 s.

Table 2.4 CPS Communication Performances

Substation	ICT Path	Timestamp IED (s)	Timestamp TO (s)	Time Delay (s)	Performance Index	Overall Performance Index
5	1	00.561	01.840	1.279	0.640	0.643
	2	00.561	01.842	1.281	0.641	
	3	00.561	01.847	1.286	0.643	
	4	00.561	01.855	1.294	0.647	
15	1	00.503	01.903	1.400	0.700	0.702
	2	00.503	01.905	1.402	0.701	
	3	00.503	01.908	1.405	0.703	
	4	00.503	01.910	1.407	0.704	
27	1	00.555	01.811	1.256	0.628	0.631
	2	00.555	01.817	1.262	0.631	
	3	00.555	01.823	1.268	0.634	
SCADA Performance Index						0.677

The cosimulation results indicate that all time delays are less than the acceptable tolerance of 2 s. The ICT paths have good performance indices, being lower than 1. The performance indices for substations 5 and 27 have similar values. However, substation 15 has a value of 0.702, indicating a lower communication performance. The analysis shows that ICT path 4 in substation 15 has the highest time delay of 1.407 s. ICT upgrades are needed to improve the communication performance for substation 15.

The computational performance for the entire SCADA model is shown in Figure 2.25. The best performance index (0.58) is computed for substation 11, while the worst (0.81) is registered

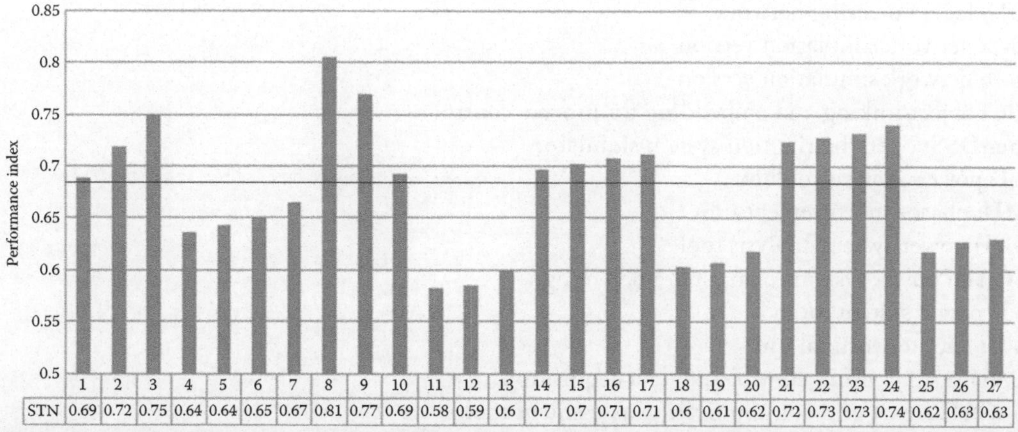

Figure 2.25 Performance indices for CPS communication.

for substation 8. The overall SCADA index is 0.677. This is calculated for all 27 substations. It suggests a good communication performance. The cosimulation results indicate that there are no communication issues in the SCADA model. However, they can be repeated for different buffering and processing capabilities of the ICTs.

Acknowledgment

This research is supported by EU Framework Program FP7 through the AFTER project, "A Framework for electrical power sysTems vulnerability identification, dEfense and Restoration," and partially supported by the U.S. National Science Foundation through grant 1202229, "Collaborative Research: Resiliency against Coordinated Cyber Attacks on Power Grid."

Glossary

API: application programming interface
CC: control center
CPS: cyber-physical system
CSMA/CD: carrier sense multiple access with collision detection
D: deterministic
DoS: denial-of-service
EMS: energy management system
EMTDC: electromagnetic transient
FIFO: first in first out
HAL: high-level architecture
HIL: hardware-in-the-loop
HMI: human–machine interface
ICCP: inter-control center communication protocol
ICT: information and communication technologies
IED: intelligent electronic device
LAN: local area network
LON: local operating network
NS-2: network simulation version 2
NS-3: network simulation version 3
OPC: object linking and embedding for process control
OpenDSS: open distribution system simulator
PAT: power analysis toolbox
PMU: phasor measurement unit
PSAT: power system analysis tool
PSCAD: power systems computer-aided design
PST: power system toolbox
RTU: remote terminal unit
SCADA: supervisory control and data acquisition
SG-CAT: smart grid communication assessment tool
SimAuto: simulator automation
TDS: time domain simulation

TO: transmission operator
UCD: University College Dublin
VPN: virtual private network
VST: voltage stability toolbox
WAN: wide area network

Author Biographies

Alexandru Stefanov received BSEE and MSEE degrees with honors from the University Politehnica of Bucharest, Romania, in 2009 and 2011, respectively. He graduated his PhD from University College Dublin, Ireland. His research interests include cyber-physical system modeling, cybersecurity in energy management system/supervisory control and data acquisition (EMS/SCADA) systems, and power system restoration strategies.

Chen-Ching Liu (Fellow 1994) received a PhD degree from the University of California, Berkeley, CA, United States. He is presently Boeing Distinguished Professor at Washington State University, Pullman, WA, USA, and professor of power systems at University College Dublin, Ireland. He was Palmer Chair Professor of Electrical Engineering at Iowa State University, Ames, IA, USA, and professor of electrical engineering at the University of Washington, Seattle, WA, USA. Dr. Liu received an Institute of Electrical and Electronics Engineers (IEEE) Third Millennium Medal in 2000 and the IEEE Power and Energy Society Outstanding Power Engineering Educator Award in 2004. He was recognized with a Doctor Honoris Causa from University Politehnica of Bucharest, Romania, in 2013. He served as chair of the Technical Committee on Power System Analysis, Computing and Economics, IEEE Power and Energy Society. Professor Liu is a fellow of the IEEE.

Kithsiri M. Liyanage is attached to the Department of Electrical and Electronic Engineering, University of Peradeniya, Sri Lanka, as a professor. He obtained his BSc Eng from the University of Peradeniya in 1983 and his DrEng from the University of Tokyo in 1991. He was a visiting scientist at the Department of Electrical Engineering, University of Washington, from 1993 to 1994; visiting research fellow at the Advanced Centre for Power and Environmental Technology, University of Tokyo, Japan, from 2008 to 2010; visiting faculty member at University Oulu, Finland in 2011 and 2012; and senior scientist at University College Dublin, Ireland, in 2014. He has authored or coauthored more than 40 papers related to smart grid applications and control since 2009. His research interest is mainly the application of information and communications technology for the realization of the smart grid.

References

1. A. Bose. Smart transmission grid applications and their supporting infrastructure. *IEEE Transactions Smart Grid*, 1(1), pp. 11–19, 2010.
2. Y. Mo, T. H.-J. Kim, K. Brancik, D. Dickinson, H. Lee, A. Perrig, and B. Sinopoli. Cyber-physical security of a smart grid infrastructure. *Proceedings of the IEEE*, 100(1), pp. 195–209, 2012.
3. S. Liu, B. Chen, T. Zourntos, D. Kundur, and K. Butler-Purry. A coordinated multi-switch attack for cascading failures in smart grid. *IEEE Transactions Smart Grid*, 5(3), pp. 1183–1195, 2014.
4. P. Henneaux, P. E. Labeau, and J. C. Maun. Blackout probabilistic risk assessment and thermal effects: Impacts of changes in generation. *IEEE Transactions Power Systems*, 28(4), pp. 4722–4731, 2013.

5. P.-Y. Chen, S.-M. Cheng, and K.-C. Chen. Smart attacks in smart grid communication networks. *IEEE Communications Magazine*, 50(8), pp. 24–29, 2012.
6. C.-C. Liu, A. Stefanov, J. Hong, and P. Panciatici. Intruders in the grid. *IEEE Power and Energy Magazine*, 10(1), pp. 58–66, 2012.
7. A. Stefanov, C.-C. Liu, M. Govindarasu, and S.-S. Wu. SCADA modeling for performance and vulnerability assessment of integrated cyber-physical systems. *International Transactions on Electrical Energy Systems*, 25(3), 2013.
8. R. Kuffel, D. Ouellette, and P. Forsyth. Real time simulation and testing using IEC61850. In *Proceedings of the International Symposium Modern Electric Power Systems (MEPS)*, Wroclaw, pp. 1–8, September 2010.
9. C. M. Davis, J. E. Tate, H. Okhravi, C. Grier, T. J. Overbye, and D. Nicol. SCADA cyber security testbed development. In *Proceedings North American Power Symposium*, Carbondale, pp. 483–488, September 2006.
10. V. Liberatore and A. Al-Hammouri. Smart grid communication and co-simulation. In *Proceedings IEEE Energytech*, Cleveland, pp. 1–5, May 2011.
11. W. Li, H. Li, and A. Monti. Using co-simulation method to analyze the communication delay impact in agent-based wide area power system stabilizing control. In *Proceedings of the 2011 Grand Challenges Modeling and Simulation Conference*, Vista, pp. 356–361, June 2011.
12. K. Mets, T. Verschueren, C. Develder, T. L. Vandoor, and L. Vandevelde. Integrated simulation of power and communication networks for smart grid applications. In *Proceedings on IEEE Computer Aided Modeling and Design of Communication Links and Networks*, Kyoto, pp. 61–65, June 2011, IEEE.
13. M. Lévesque, D. Q. Xu, G. Joos, and M. Maier. Communications and power distribution network co-simulation for multidisciplinary smart grid experimentations. In *Proceedings Spring Simulation Multiconference*, San Diego, pp. 1–7, March 2012.
14. K. Hopkinson, X. Wang, R. Giovanini, J. Thorp, K. Birman, and D. Coury. EPOCHS: A platform for agent-based electric power and communication simulation built from commercial off-the-shelf components. *IEEE Transactions on Power Systems*, 21(2), pp. 548–558, 2006.
15. W. Li, A. Monti, M. Luo, and R. A. Dougal. VPNET: A co-simulation framework for analyzing communication channel effects on power systems. In *Proc. IEEE Electric Ship Technologies Symposium*, Alexandria, pp. 143–149, April 2011, IEEE.
16. J. Nutaro, P. T. Kuruganti, L. Miller, S. Mullen, and M. Shankar. Integrated hybrid-simulation of electric power and communications systems. In *Proceedings on IEEE Power Engineering Society General Meeting*, Tampa, pp. 1–8, June 2007, IEEE.
17. H. Lin, S. S. Veda, S. S. Shukla, L. Mili, and J. Thorp. GECO: Global event-driven co-simulation framework for interconnected power system and communication networks. *IEEE Transactions Smart Grid*, 3(3), pp. 1444–1456, September 2012.
18. C. P. Mayer and T. Gamer. Integrating real world applications into OMNeT++. Institute of Telematics. [Online]. Available: http://doc.tm.uka.de/TM-2008-2.pdf, February 2008.
19. Z. Zhang, Z. Lu, Q. Chen, X. Yan, and L.-R. Zheng. COSMO: CO-simulation with MATLAB and OMNeT++ for indoor wireless networks. In *Proceedings IEEE Telecommunication Conference*, Miami, pp. 1–6, December 2010, IEEE.
20. K. Mets, J. A. Ojea, and C. Develder. Combining power and communication network simulation for cost-effective smart grid analysis. *IEEE Communications Surveys & Tutorials*, 16(3), pp. 1771–1796, March 2014, IEEE.
21. MathWorks. SimEvents. User's guide. March 2014 [Online]. Available: http://www.mathworks.com/help/pdf_doc/simevents/simevents_ug.pdf.
22. DIgSILENT GmbH. DIgSILENT PowerFactory version 15. User manual. 2013 [Online]. Available: http://digsilent.de/index.php/downloads.html.
23. P. E. Bjorklund, J. Pan, C. Yue, and K. Srivastava. A new approach for modeling complex power system components in different simulation tools. In *Proceedings PSCC*, Glasgow, pp. 1–6, July 2008.
24. U. Sachs. Smart grid offering within PSS SINCAL. Siemens Technical Report, 2012. [Online]. Available: http://w3.usa.siemens.com/datapool/us/SmartGrid/docs/pti/2011November/PDFs/Smart_Grid_Offering_within_SINCAL.pdf.

25. NEPLAN. NEPLAN 360 overview. 2014. [Online]. Available: http://support.neplan.ch/html/e/e_PowerSystems_Properties_default_web.htm.
26. NEPLAN. NEPLAN—SmartGrid application. 2014. [Online]. Available: http://support.neplan.ch/html/e/pdf_e/e_neplan-SmartGrid-v2-1.pdf.
27. TRACTABEL Engineering GDF Suez. New powerful features of EUROSTAG release 5.1. 2014. [Online]. Available: http://www.eurostag.be/en/products/eurostag/eurostag-release/eurostag-release.
28. European Commission CORDIS. ICOEUR Report summary. 2014. [Online]. Available: http://cordis.europa.eu/result/rcn/56212_en.html.
29. D. Issicaba, N. J. Gil, and J. A. P. Lopes. Islanding operation of active distribution grids using an agent-based architecture. In *Proceedings IEEE PES Innovative Smart Grid Technologies*, Gothenburg, pp. 1–8, October 2010, IEEE.
30. PowerWorld Corporation. PowerWorld Simulator. 2014. [Online]. Available: http://www.powerworld.com/products/simulator/overview.
31. M. U. Tariq, B. P. Swenson, A. P. Narasimhan, S. Grijalva, G. F. Riley, and M. Wolf. Cyber-physical co-simulation of smart grid applications using NS-3. In *Proceedings Innovative Database Research*, Georgia Tech., pp. 1–8, May 2007.
32. PowerWorld Corporation. Simulator automation server overview. 2014. [Online]. Available: http://www.powerworld.com/WebHelp/Content/html/Simulator_Automation_Server.htm#.
33. R. Roche, S. Natarajan, A. Bhattacharyya, and S. Suryanarayanan. A framework for co-simulation of AI tools with power systems analysis software. In *Proceedings Database Expert Systems Applications*, Vienna, pp. 350–354, September 2012, IEEE.
34. EPRI. Simulation tool—OpenDSS. 2014. [Online]. Available: http://smartgrid.epri.com/SimulationTool.aspx.
35. Manitoba-HVDC. PSCAD user's guide. February 2010. [Online]. Available: https://hvdc.ca/uploads/ck/files/reference_material/PSCAD_User_Guide_v4_3_1.pdf.
36. O. Anaya-Lara and E. Acha. Modeling and analysis of custom power systems by PSCAD/EMTDC. *IEEE Transactions on Power Delivery*, 17(1), pp. 266–272, 2002, IEEE.
37. J. Pan and R. Jain. A survey of network simulation tools: Current status and future developments. November 2008. [Online]. Available: http://www.cs.wustl.edu/~jain/cse567-08/ftp/simtools.pdf.
38. G. F. Lucio, M. Paredes-Farrera, E. Jammeh, M. Fleury, and M. J. Reed. OPNET modeler and Ns-2: Comparing the accuracy of network simulators for packet-level analysis using a network testbed. In *Proceedings International Conference on Simulation, Modeling, Optimization*, Rethymno, pp. 700–707, October 2003.
39. E. Weingartner, H. vom Lehn, and K. Wehrle. A performance comparison of recent network simulators. In *Proceedings IEEE International Conference Communications*, Dresden, pp. 1–5, June 2009, IEEE.
40. S. Mohagheghi, J. Stoupis, and Z. Wang. Communication protocols and networks for power systems—Current status and future trends. In *Proceedings Power Systems Conference Exposition*, Seattle, pp. 1–9, March 2009, IEEE.
41. DIgSILENT GmbH. Data integration. 2014. [Online]. Available: http://www.digsilent.de/index.php/products-stationware-data_integration.html#bottom.
42. OPAL-RT Technologies. New communication protocols. Applications and implementation. 2013. [Online]. Available: http://www.opal-rt.com/sites/default/files/RT13_New%20communication%20protocols.pdf.
43. F. Milano, *Power System Modelling and Scripting*, 1st edn. Springer, London, 2010.
44. C. G. Cassandras and S. Lafortune, *Introduction to Discrete Event Systems*, 2nd edn. Springer, New York, 2008.
45. S. C. Savulescu, *Real-Time Stability Assessment in Modern Power System Control Centers*, 1st edn. IEEE Press, Wiley, New York, 2009.
46. *IEEE Standard for SCADA and Automation Systems*, IEEE Standard C37.1-2007, May 2008.
47. F. Milano and M. Anghel. Impact of time delays on power system stability. *IEEE Transactions on Circuits and Systems I: Regular Papers*, 59(4), pp. 889–900, 2012.
48. A. Tanenbaum, *Computer Networks*, 4th edn. Prentice Hall, 2003.

49. T. S. Sidhu and Y. Yin. IED modeling for IEC61850 based substation automation system performance simulation. In *Proceedings of IEEE PES GM*, Montreal, pp. 1–7, June 2006.
50. K. Tomsovic, D. E. Bakken, V. Venkatasubramanian, and A. Bose. Designing the next generation of real-time control, communication, and computations for large power systems. *Proceedings of IEEE*, 93(5), pp. 965–979, 2005.
51. J. P. Hespanha, P. Naghshtabrizi, and Y. Xu. A survey of recent results in networked control systems. *Proceedings of IEEE*, 95(1), pp. 138–162, 2007.
52. J. Nutaro and V. Protopopescu. The impact of market clearing time and price signal delay on the stability of electric power markets. *IEEE Transactions of Power Systems*, 24(3), pp. 1337–1345, 2009.
53. A. Stefanov and C.-C. Liu. Cyber-physical system security and impact analysis. In *Proceedings of International Federation Automatic Control (IFAC)*, Cape Town, pp. 11238–11243, August 2014.

Chapter 3

Moving Target Defense Mechanisms in Cyber-Physical Systems

Shih-Wei Fang, Anthony Portante, and Mohammad Iftekhar Husain
California State Polytechnic University, Pomona

Contents

3.1 Introduction....64
3.2 MTD at Different Layers of a System....65
 3.2.1 Dynamic Runtime Environment....65
 3.2.2 Dynamic Software....65
 3.2.3 Dynamic Networks....66
 3.2.4 Dynamic Platforms....66
 3.2.5 Dynamic Data....67
3.3 Attacks on MTD Techniques....67
 3.3.1 Brute-Force or Bypass MTD Techniques....67
 3.3.2 Predict MTD Techniques....68
 3.3.3 Limiting the Choice of Movement....68
 3.3.4 Disabling Movement....68
3.4 Cyber-Physical System....68
3.5 MTD Techniques for Network Security....69
 3.5.1 Denial of Service....69
 3.5.2 Packet Scheduling....71
 3.5.3 Eavesdropping....73
3.6 MTD Techniques for Controller Security....75
 3.6.1 Deception Attack....76
 3.6.2 Worms and Viruses....77
 3.6.3 Buffer Overflow....80

3.7 MTD Techniques for Physical System Security....81
3.7.1 Deception Attacks....82
3.7.2 Buffer Overflow....82
3.7.3 Physical Attack....84
3.8 Conclusion....86
3.9 Future Research Direction....87
Author Biographies....87
References....88

Abstract: This chapter presents the importance and feasibility of applying moving target defense (MTD) techniques to cyber-physical systems (CPSs) as well as understanding what a malicious attacker may attempt to do to circumvent such defenses. MTD is a relatively new form of cybersecurity and, until recent years, it only consisted of Internet protocol (IP) hopping and address space randomization. It is a concept of changing the properties of a system. By randomizing and reconfiguring the system properties, MTD dynamically alters the attack surface in such a way that the cost for the attacker to locate and launch a successful attack on a target increases. A CPS is a combination of cyber and physical systems such as industrial control systems (ICSs) and the smart grid. MTD is a practical and powerful choice to improve the security of CPSs. This chapter provides a classification of MTD mechanisms and discusses how these mechanisms can be applied to thwart attacks in different parts of a CPS: network, controller, and physical system.

Keywords: Moving target defence; Cyber-physical systems; Security; Diversity; Smart grid; Industrial control system

3.1 Introduction

Moving target defense (MTD) is a game-changing cybersecurity concept that allows defenders to alter the attack surface of a particular system and makes system penetration difficult for attackers. Originating from the idea of address space randomization [1] and Internet protocol (IP) hopping [2], MTD has now evolved into more modern techniques such as software behavior encryption [3] and Internet protocol version 6 (IPv6) address randomization [4]. To access a system successfully, attackers need to collect specific information at every stage. MTD allows us to alter this information in either a random or a timed manner, significantly prolonging the time for a successful attack. With more and more vulnerabilities being discovered every day, having a robust defense is vital to secure sensitive systems, such as a cyber-physical system (CPS). A CPS is a system that facilitates the interaction between the cyberworld and the physical world, and it has rapidly emerged in the past decade. CPS security is a crucial challenge not only because of its rapid emergence, but also because of its importance. For example, many electricity distribution systems have recently been upgraded to a CPS, known as the *smart grid*. In [5], the authors state that a single bug in the smart grid could cause a loss of more than a billion dollars due to the immense size of this industry. To sum up, because of its growth and significance, a CPS requires a more advanced and robust defense technology, such as MTD.

In this chapter, we will discuss MTD basics and how MTD can be applied to a CPS. We will first dive into certain MTD techniques that are being applied to different layers of the system. After getting a firm grasp of the MTD basics, we will then explore security issues in the CPS domain and how the MTD techniques can be applied to different layers or parts of a CPS.

3.2 MTD at Different Layers of a System

MTD is one of the key components of a cybermaneuver that reshapes friendly networks and their associated assets to be resilient to cyberattacks. Every system has attack surfaces and the goal of MTD is to continually shift the attack surface in a planned way that makes every step to the attack more costly for the attacker. A real-world example of MTD was demonstrated by the Georgia government in 2008 when it came under large-scale cyberattack [6]. During the attack, Georgia sought cyberrefuge from the United States and other friendly countries such as Poland and Estonia by relocating its key government services to these countries. In making a defensive cybermaneuver, Georgia was able to maintain key government services in the face of a massive denial-of-service (DoS) attack and demonstrated the effectiveness of MTD. With the recent advances in technology, such as virtualization, process migration, redundant network connections, just-in-time compilers, instruction set randomization, and address space layout randomization, the realization of MTD has become feasible.

At the National Cyber Leap Year (NCLY) Summit 2009, MTD was chosen as one of the five game-changing techniques [7]. Although MTD has earned attention from researchers for only a decade, numerous research ventures have been developed. Based on the layer of the system that it is applied to, MTD can be grouped into five categories [8]:

3.2.1 Dynamic Runtime Environment

Dynamic runtime environment changes the environment during executions. There are two major techniques in this category: address space randomization and instruction set randomization. Address space randomization is the most known example of MTD, and has been developed for roughly a decade. This MTD mechanism protects the system from buffer or stack overflow attacks. By overrunning the static memory structure, buffer overflow attacks overwrite key data on a memory address and call specific functions to control the system. To obscure attackers from knowing the location of key data, address space randomization randomly selects memory addresses or sizes. There are different variations of memory randomization, such as randomizing the stack structure, the heap structure, or the function pointer structure [9]; each of these provides different levels of complexity for the attacker. For instance, in address space layout permutation (ASLP) [10], the kernel-level address permutation contains randomizations for the user stack, the *brk()*-managed heap, and the *mmap()* allocation.

The other technique is instruction set randomization [11], which prevents code-injection attacks, including buffer overflow attacks. Taking a buffer overflow attack as an example, the attacker overwrites the data with the address of specific functions in order to control the system. Instruction set randomization impedes the attack by constantly changing the location of the instruction sets, which means the function addresses are vague. Due to the uncertainty of locations, the attacker cannot correctly invoke the desired functions. This technique is implemented by manipulating the instruction structure, function name, or system call data. It can also be done by encrypting the instruction sets with an encryption scheme such as the Advanced Encryption Standard [12].

3.2.2 Dynamic Software

Dynamic software dynamically changes an application's code by modifying the program instructions, their order, their grouping, or their format. Software diversity techniques prevent code-injection attacks and worms by diversifying vulnerabilities. An execution system, such as a compiler or a server, holds distinct implementations with identical functionality and randomly allocates them to minimize the damages. One such example of this can be found in [3], where the authors describe the concept of software behavior encryption, dubbed *ChameleonSoft*. It changes the implementation sequence of complex services and programs even including the language of implementation that is used to thwart language-specific attacks. A more in-depth discussion on ChameleonSoft can be found in Section 3.3. O'Donnell and Sethu propose a software diversity technique to improve network security using distributed coloring algorithms [13]. To increase the diversity of the whole network, they show that randomizing individual systems is insufficient. They analyze network topologies of software packages with identical functionalities. Using distributed coloring algorithms, the system allocates software packages to prevent the spread of attacks. Since each package suffers from different vulnerabilities, the attacker needs to come up with unique attack schemes for each package. Moreover, by choosing diverse packages for servers or clients, the defense minimizes the damage from identical attacks. There are other implementations for software diversity. Fraser et al. [14] presented a defense that manipulates the security policies of servers. Roeder and Schneider [15] introduced a method for creating server replicas with less identical vulnerabilities.

3.2.3 Dynamic Networks

By reconfiguring network properties, MTD techniques in *dynamic networks* secure the integrity and availability of connections. Depending on the implementations, the defense can randomize distinct properties on the network, such as IP addresses, the transmission control protocol (TCP) port, and trust nodes. Kewley et al. [2] developed a gateway called DYNAT, which randomizes the IP address and the TCP port. In order to communicate with each other, DYNAT needs to be installed on both sides of the connection. Before the data transmits to the public network, DYNAT modifies the destination host address on an IP header and the destination port on a TCP header. The randomization of addresses is an encryption based on shared secrets between two DYNATs. The secrets are updated periodically. By constantly changing the addresses, the defense impedes attackers from observing the connections. In concealing the connections and the locations of both sides, DYNAT avoids attacks utilizing IP addresses, such as DoS, eavesdropping, and hijacking. Furthermore, depending on the purpose of the connection, there are different MTD techniques. To quickly and correctly update the information, Li [16] presented MTD randomizing trust nodes. By treelike connections, the source spreads the updates, and each node transmits to its child nodes. When joining to the network, this defense diversifies the parent and child nodes to avoid incorrect updates or the attacker's updates.

3.2.4 Dynamic Platforms

Dynamic platforms change the configuration of platforms, such as operating systems (OSs) and central processing units (CPUs). According to the requirements of the defense, the platform randomizes different properties, such as the OS version, OS instance, and CPU architecture. Holland and his team [17] proposed a virtual machine monitor that produces a large number of OSs with slight differences. To resist 100 attacks per second for a week requires 2^{27} distinct machines, which means 27 independent binary decisions. They analyzed possible properties for creating different machines, such as the number of registers, word size, and representations of a signed number. However, no practical experiment has proved the concept. Next, Okhravi [18] described a framework that can migrate applications on heterogeneous platforms, called the

Trusted Dynamic Logical Heterogeneity System (TALENT). Supporting programs that are written in C, TALENT is able to move to another OS and hardware while running the application. In order to move across the environment, TALENT uses OS-level virtualization to sandbox the application. This defense is able to prevent code-injection attacks that utilize the vulnerabilities of specific OSs or hardware.

3.2.5 Dynamic Data

Dynamic data changes the properties of data, such as data format, syntax, and representations. Ammann and Knight [19] proposed a data diversity technique that provides fault tolerance. By reexpressing an input to multiple inputs, they computed the function with a different implementation. For instance, with $\sin(x) = \sin(a)*\sin(\pi/2 - b) + \sin(\pi/2 - a)*\sin(b)$, the program is able to compute $\sin(x)$ using another implementation. When $a + b = x$, two implementations are expected to have identical results. By choosing a different a and b, the program is able to compute several answers to avoid faults from computations. They decomposed the input and recomposed the results by utilizing the representation of data. In [20], the authors present data randomization techniques, which provide probabilistic protection from attacks that exploit memory errors. Using XOR-ing data with random masks, the defense encrypts data before storing it in the memory. Because the data is decrypted before use, attackers cannot overwrite the memory with malicious data, which results in an error when decrypting. Similarly, attackers are unable to obtain confidential information from other classes, since the encrypted key is different.

Although MTD has been categorized into five categories, its techniques are not restricted to one single category. For instance, the software diversity technique falls under both the dynamic software and the dynamic platform since it can change both the codes and the properties of the platform simultaneously.

3.3 Attacks on MTD Techniques

In this section, we discuss the vulnerabilities of existing MTD techniques as identified in [8].

3.3.1 Brute-Force or Bypass MTD Techniques

If the space of randomization is not large enough, the attacker can brute-force the defense. By launching a large number of attacks simultaneously, the attacker can overwhelm a number of targets. Also, after analyzing MTD technique, an attacker can carefully craft an attack to bypass the protection.

For instance, rather than injecting codes in the systems, the return-to-libc attack utilizes the system-defined libraries where instruction set randomization does not have an effect [21]. With the existing libraries, the attacker bypasses the randomization of instruction sets. Introduced by Shacham [22], return-oriented programming (ROP) is an improvement of the return-to-libc attack, which again bypasses MTD. Instead of jumping to the beginning of the library, ROP chains the instructions in existing codes to execute the desired functions; however, there are also improvements in instruction set randomization. For instance, G-Free is a defense that protects from ROP attack [23]. Onarlioglu et al. discovered that ROP utilizes specific instructions in libraries, called free branch. By randomizing the locations of the instructions, G-Free impedes the attacker from chaining the instructions.

3.3.2 Predict MTD Techniques

In this category, the attacker predicts the choice of defender in an MTD technique. MTD mechanisms are not always random due to the restriction of the deployment environment. For example, in software diversity techniques, the software may not be installed on all types of OS, such as Windows and Mac OSs. The attacker can target the software on a specific OS. Moreover, even when MTD randomizes the choice, prediction is still possible through information leaked by side channels. In address space randomization, the attacker might predict the location of libraries by leaked addresses. Also, if MTD technique randomizes its choices by cryptography such as IP hopping, the attacker can predict IP addresses with the key leakage. So, based on information leakage of the system, it might be possible for the attacker to predict the technique applied by MTD.

3.3.3 Limiting the Choice of Movement

By limiting the choice of movement, the attacker is able to decrease defense options. For example, the adversary can fill up memory space to limit the randomization possibilities in address space randomization. Moreover, the limitation may not always be caused by attackers. In IPv4, the free space for IP addresses is scarce due to incremental usage. Thus, the IP hopping technique for IPv4 is not sufficient due to the shortage of IP addresses. Although the scope of IPv6 is very large, the IP hopping technique may also suffer from limited space in the future.

3.3.4 Disabling Movement

In this attack, the adversary disables the movement of MTD. In other words, the attacker turns off MTD or impedes MTD from operating. For instance, by pushing a bad configuration, attackers can disable the address space randomization in the OS. Shacham [21] introduces an attack against address space randomization that disables the server from reconstructing the object. Generally, when modifying the address, the system produces errors and restarts the function or system; however, Shacham found that the location is identical when restarting the system for specific functions. That is, the attacker is able to obtain the correct position without an attempt limit. For instance, if there are n possibilities of the position, without changing the position the attack will succeed before completing all n attempts.

Despite some existing vulnerabilities, MTD still provides sufficient defense because of the improvements in its design and flexibility. In the following sections, we examine the security of a CPS and discuss MTD applications in different parts of a CPS.

3.4 Cyber-Physical System

By definition, a CPS [14] can be viewed as the construction of a network, a physical system, and a controller, as shown in Figure 3.1. The network delivers feedback and controls the signals between controllers and physical systems. Physical systems include sensors and actuators. Sensors collect the physical information from the physical world, and actuators interact with the physical world by commands from controllers. Lastly, controllers make decisions and command actuators based on information from sensors. Each component faces its own security challenges not only as individual pieces, but also from the interaction as a whole. Due to the complexity of a CPS, we analyze its security by discussing MTD techniques that are being applied to each of the three components as well as possible attacks.

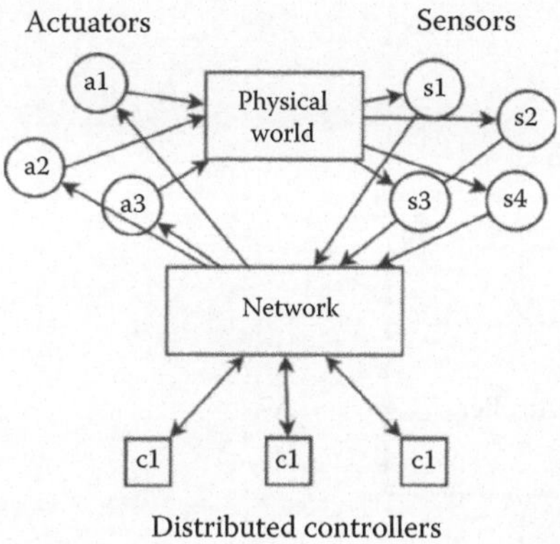

Figure 3.1 Components of a CPS. (From Petkac, M., et al. Security agility for dynamic execution environments. *DARPA Information Survivability Conference and Exposition, 2000. DISCEX '00. Proceedings*, 2000. With permission.)

3.5 MTD Techniques for Network Security

Confidentiality, integrity, and availability (CIA) are three basic requirements in cybersecurity. For a CPS there are several issues that makes the CIA requirements challenging. First of all, the network is connected to the public network, which is not only used by employees, but also by public users. A CPS should provide security schemes for external access based on the system requirements. Secondly, the network access is diverse. Depending on the environment, information is transmitted via a particular type of network: wired or wireless. For example, a CPS may transmit through near field communication (NFC), Bluetooth, or Wi-Fi in a wireless connection; and also cable, Ethernet, or other wired access. Due to the diversity of network access, each CPS faces a unique type of attack. Next, the amount of data transmission varies. Each CPS should be robust enough to address specific situations. A smart meter may only need to transmit data once per day; however, it may need to transmit data every second for a monitor. Lastly, there is a huge difference in computational power between the physical systems and the controllers. For instance, smart meters contain one processor, nonvolatile storage, and a communication interface [5]; however, control centers are combinations of computers. The extreme difference between the two sides of the network restricts a complex defense with heavy resources. Due to the abovementioned challenges, each CPS needs unconventional solutions for its security. To avoid the diversity of a CPS, we focus on the possible attacks that occur in a CPS.

Figure 3.2 shows attacks in a CPS, which are represented by tags: A1–A12. In this section, we introduce attacks on network security and discuss MTD techniques to address such attacks. Table 3.1 shows MTD techniques for each attack.

3.5.1 Denial of Service

Denial of service, or distributed denial of service (DDoS), is an attack that makes the service or network unavailable to users. Although the methods, targets, and resources vary, DoS temporally suspends use of the connection in general. For example, by flooding the network, jamming the connection, and attacking the protocols, DoS prevents users from reaching the service. DDoS is a DoS with multiple simultaneous attacks, usually performed by bots (or botnets), which are collections of Internet-connected programs that perform identical tasks. In this chapter, DoS represents both DoS and DDoS since the attack strategy is identical.

In a CPS, DoS attacks impede the connection between the controller and the physical system. As shown in Figure 3.2, A4 is a DoS attack that renders the controller unavailable to receive

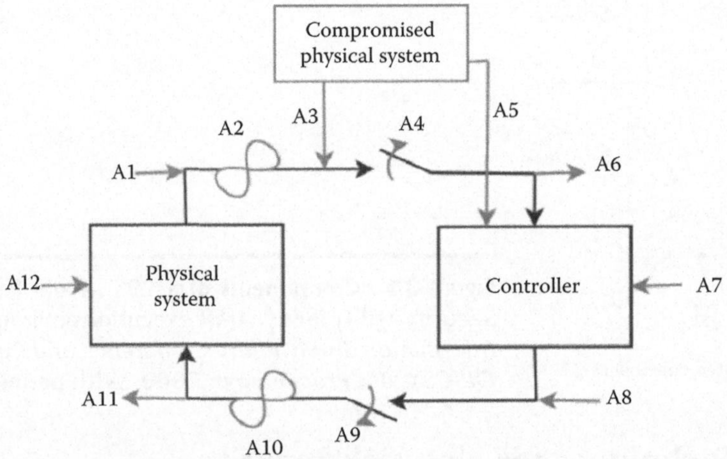

Figure 3.2 Attacks on a CPS.

Table 3.1 MTD Techniques to Address Network Security Attacks on CPS

Tag	*Attacks*	*MTD Category*	*Example*	*CPS Extension Exists?*
A4, A9	DOS	Dynamic network	DynaBone	No
			MT6D	Yes
A2, A10	Packet scheduling	Dynamic network	MT6D	Yes
A6, A11	Eavesdropping	Dynamic network	DynaBone	No
			MT6D	Yes
		Dynamic data	N-variant with data diversity	No

connections from physical systems. Without information collected from the physical world, the controller is unable to make decision; furthermore, the attacker can mislead the controller to perform unintended actions [27]. On the other hand, A9 is the DoS in the opposite direction. The data sent from controllers are control signals executed by the physical system. Without the signal, physical systems will not be able to perform the action signaled, which may be the intention of the attackers. For instance, by restricting the control signal, a smart meter will not turn off the home appliance, which will cause an inconvenience to users. Furthermore, physical systems face additional effects from DoS. Since embedded systems often have significant energy constraints, and many are battery powered, DoS may cause battery attacks in physical systems [33]. With power-hungry communications, DoS wastes the batteries of physical systems during interaction. By draining the battery power, the attacker turns off the physical device without even breaking into it.

Touch et al. [34] proposed an MTD against DDoS attacks among private groups of networked systems, called DynaBone. Using parallel interior overlays, known as *innerlays*, DynaBone provides multiple targets for attackers while maintaining a single network service, called the *outerlay*. To manipulate the outerlay and innerlays, Touch et al. propose a proactive/reactive multiplexer

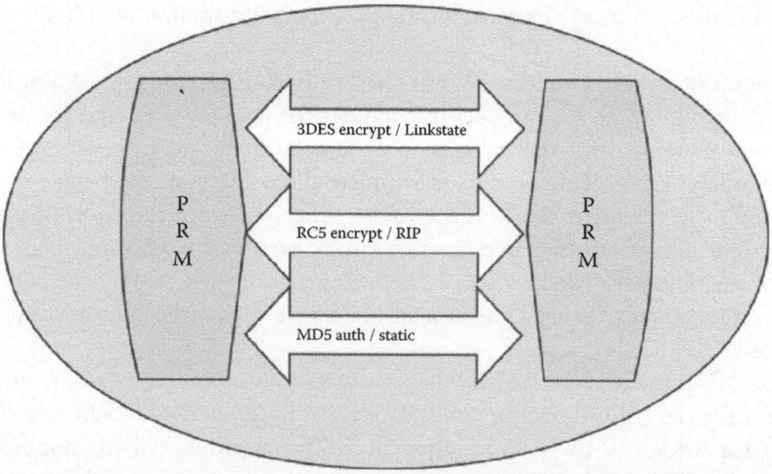

Figure 3.3 DynaBone design. (From Touch, J. D., et al. DynaBone: Dynamic defense using multi-layer Internet overlays. In *Proceedings 3rd DARPA Information Survivability Conference and Exposition (DISCEX-III)*, Washington, DC. 2003. With permission.)

(PRM) that decides the distribution of packets for each innerlay. Figure 3.3 shows the design of DynaBone. Each innerlay utilizes a distinct network protocol and security algorithms.

In general, the PRM distributes packets in the innerlays with attack statistics and scatters the damage from DoS. Since the PRM changes the packets in each innerlay, the attacker cannot understand the information of the blocked packets; that is, the attacker can only target specific packets by chance. On the other hand, when suffering DoS on some innerlays, the PRM transmits the packets with other innerlays. This approach detects DoS attacks from incorrectly received packets, and moves the attacked connection to a safe innerlay. Due to the combination of different approaches, DynaBone not only handles DoS attacks, but also escapes from future attacks.

The controller and the physical systems are private groups in some CPSs. For instance, the smart grid can be considered a private group of network systems, since smart meters are privately connected. In general, for smart meters the only communication is with the control center. While there may exist communications with other devices, such as cell phones and home appliances, smart meters can create a private connection with the control center [35]. The major issue with implementing DynaBone is the computational power of physical systems. The PRM, innerlays, and outerlay design can be simplified without using statistical analysis. While the security algorithms are intensive for physical systems, the application of this MTD technique is still feasible. By randomly distributing packets into overlays and disabling the attacked overlays, MTD can be simplified for a lesser amount of security guarantee.

3.5.2 Packet Scheduling

The second attack is a packet-scheduling attack that reorders the packets. Rather than blocking the entire network, such as DoS, packet-scheduling attacks delay some packets to in turn cause a system error. Packet-scheduling attacks can be mounted using several techniques. For example, by placing malicious software on the router on the path of the connection, the attacker reorders the packets without consent. Since the latency of the packets is minimal, it is difficult for a system to detect.

Packet-scheduling attacks can also be launched in both directions in a CPS. From physical systems to the controller (A2), the attacker reschedules the packets to exceed the deadline, which causes the system to retransmit the packets. The delay and the missing data on the controller cause a control analysis problem. Due to incomplete data, the controller may conclude with a false decision [30]. On the other hand, if the packets received from the controller are reordered, the physical system may perform the actions in same order (A10). This may cause errors in the performance of the physical system. Packet-scheduling attacks utilize only the connection information and not the content. Even if the attacker has no information on the content, the attack may still succeed.

Groat et al. [4] presented an MTD that protects the connection from attackers, called MT6D. Specifically, MT6D hides the communication by proactively changing the IP address in the IPv6 space, which is an IP hopping–type MTD method. IPv4 is not feasible for this scenario because of the high density and the ease of scanning the entire address space. In IPv6, however, the address space is huge and is time consuming to scan with current technology. In fact, scanning the whole address space in IPv6 would take 8.77×10^{10} years [36]. While there are several IP hopping techniques in IPv6, MT6D provides the implementation in the smart grid.

Similar to other IP hopping techniques, MT6D provides an MT6D gateway, which is installed in both sides of the connection. In this case, the controller and the physical system both need to implement an MT6D gateway. Figure 3.4 shows the third party's view after implementing the MT6D gateway for one controller and one physical system. Since the IP address is dynamically determined, there are numerous possibilities for the location of the physical system. On the other hand, the controller also hides in a subnet with a dynamic configuration. The attacker cannot even target the subnet, since the location is concealed.

To compute the IP address, which is an MT6D interface identifier (IID), MT6D provides a function using three components. The first component is the value of the host, such as a media

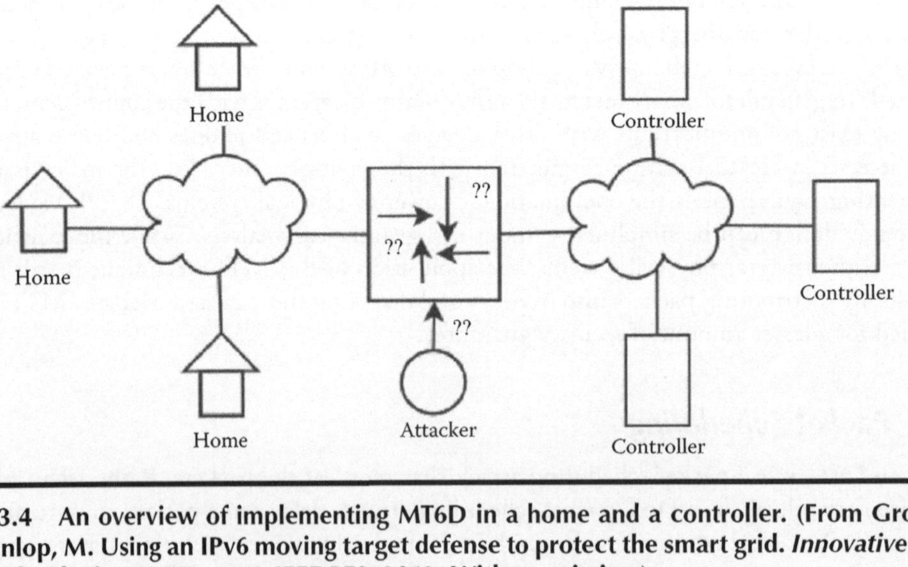

Figure 3.4 An overview of implementing MT6D in a home and a controller. (From Groat, S., and Dunlop, M. Using an IPv6 moving target defense to protect the smart grid. *Innovative Smart Grid Technologies (ISGT), 2012 IEEE PES,* 2012. With permission.)

access control (MAC) address. The second component is a key that is shared between the controller and the physical system, such as a symmetric key. The last component is a nonce value, such as time, which is known by both parties. Although there are three components in this function, the only component that needs to be secret is the shared key. The function is formed as

$$IID_{x'(i)} = f\{IV_x * S * CV_i\}_{64}$$

The output of this function is 64-bits. The IID represents the new location in a subnet for host x at instance i; IV_x is the first component that is unique to the host x; S is the shared secret key; and CV_i is the nonce value at instance i. The operation is denoted by * and the 64-bit function is denoted by $f\{.\}_{64}$. This function may be a computation of a MAC address, a shared symmetric key, and the current time. To proactively change with time, each MT6D computes both its IID and the other's IID with the next time value, which means that the IP address is not randomized, but is determined by the time variable; however, to the attacker, without knowing the shared secret key, the IID appears to be a random object. Moreover, MT6D provides the obfuscation without causing the additional overhead of reestablishing or breaking down during midsession. By computing the next IP address, MT6D automatically changes the destination address when needed. This protects against an attacker that is trying to collect all packets for a particular session.

Although MT6D secures the system with a varying address space, there are still limitations. First of all, this technique provides an additional shared key to randomize the IID. When constructing the connection, MT6D transmits the key over the network. So, the security of the key becomes another challenge in the system. Secondly, although the concept of MT6D also works for IPv4, it is not feasible to implement. The lack of free space in IPv4 and the ease of scanning a whole subnet are the major issues. Lastly, the latency and overhead are another challenge. MT6D utilizes an additional 62 bytes to encapsulate the connection. Since the smart gird transmits data with small pieces of information, the latency may not be affordable.

In [4], MT6D is targeted to smart grid systems; however, its application to other CPSs may also be feasible. Although each CPS needs specific modifications, the concept of IP hopping secures CPSs by hiding their connection. Moreover, MT6D may also be improved by using other existing techniques. For example, Kewley et al. [2] randomized not only the IP address, but also the TCP port.

3.5.3 Eavesdropping

An eavesdropping attack attempts to secretly listen to private conversations without consent. In computer science, all communication between devices, computers, and components can be defined as conversations. Eavesdropping can be done over wired and wireless connections. Attackers analyze the packets and obtain the targeted information. From an eavesdropped packet, the attacker can receive the information of an IP address, a TCP address, and even the content. Since eavesdropping is passive and does not modify data, its detection is difficult.

There are also two directions for an eavesdropping attack. In Figure 3.2, A6 represents the eavesdropping on the connection from physical systems to controllers. Although eavesdropping may not immediately harm the system, attackers are able to construct other attacks based on the information. By A6, attackers may understand the syntax of the data, analyze the packets of the connection, and gather the information of sensors. With the syntax of the data, attackers can transmit the artificial data to compromise the system; with the analysis of the packets, adversaries may break security encryptions; and with the sensor's data, the attacker understands factors that influence the decisions of controllers. On the other hand, A11 eavesdrops on the connection from the controller to the physical system, which is the control signal. By analyzing the control signal, attackers can spoof the physical system by modifying the data.

The MTD technique introduced in Section 3.5.1 is also sufficient to thwart eavesdropping. By distributing packets into overlays, the attackers can only partially understand the information. That is, even if the attackers break a specific innerlay, they may obtain the content on the innerlay, but not the whole connection. Moreover, with a different algorithm on innerlays, the attackers need to construct distinct attacks to compromise the data; however, the reactive technique is no longer useful. Since eavesdropping will not be detected, DynaBone cannot escape the eavesdropping attack reactively.

Furthermore, the IP hopping technique is also a solution to eavesdropping. Attackers cannot target the connection because of the obfuscation of the IP address. By proactively changing the IP address or protocols, attackers need to obtain the connection using other methods, such as a Domain Name System (DNS) server. The MTD techniques introduced so far are for securing the communication; however, since attackers can analyze content with eavesdropping, the system also needs to protect the data.

In the dynamic data category, there is an MTD technique for data diversity. Although research targets software fault tolerance and data intrusion, the concept is able to enhance the security of data. The previous design, called N-variant [37], provides software fault tolerance. By implementing redundant functions, the software obtains multiple outputs. Based on the comparison of outputs, the software is able to avoid false computation. The redundant functions have to be identical in functionality but distinct in implementation. With the same input, the functions cause different types of errors or false computations depending on the implementation. Since the errors are manifested differently, the system is able to choose the correct answer with the majority vote.

Furthermore, based on the N-variant defense, the researchers proposed an MTD technique for data intrusion, which protects the system from malicious inputs. By reexpressing the input, the system compares the output and rejects it if they are different. In this design, the functions also provide identical functionality but different input expressions. For each function, as shown in Figure 3.5, the system reexpresses the input, computes the function, and transforms the output based on the reverse

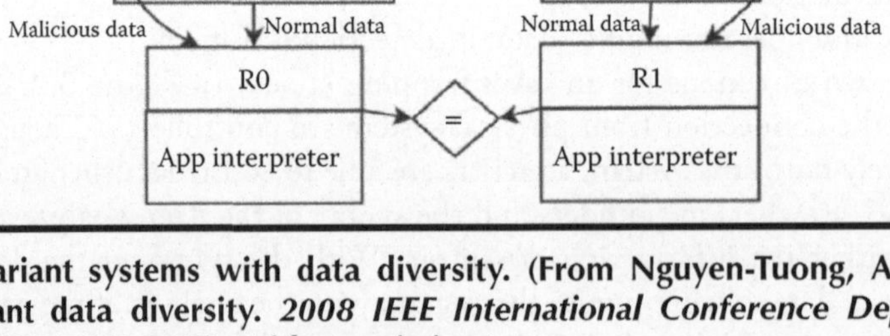

Figure 3.5 N-variant systems with data diversity. (From Nguyen-Tuong, A., et al. Security through redundant data diversity. *2008 IEEE International Conference Dependable System Networks with FTCS DCC*, 2008. With permission.)

of the reexpression function. The malicious inputs produce different outputs since the implementation of functions is distinct. To sum up, the concepts of the designs are redundancy and reexpression. N-variant utilizes the redundant functions to tolerate function faults; N-variant with data diversity, on the other hand, reexpresses the inputs to overcome the intrusion.

To apply the concept to eavesdropping on a network, we employ both redundancy and reexpression. By providing redundant transmission, the defender is able to confuse the attackers from understanding the content. Since the attackers are unable to know which packet contains useful information, they make a false decision based on the wrong information. Although this may provide certain security, the performance reduction due to the increment of traffic is a drawback. The reexpression can also be applied on the network. By reexpressing data before transmission, it may be difficult to understand the actual meaning of the transmission. The space of randomization varies based on the expressions of data.

Furthermore, by increasing the complexity of encryption and dynamically changing the encryption methods, the connection can also be protected. DynaBone distributes the packets in innerlays with different encryptions. With the concept of IP hopping, the encryptions can also be changed based on time, keys, or other factors. Since eavesdropping targets both connection and content, MTDs that hide the connection or complicate the content are protections to a certain level. In fact, by preventing eavesdropping, MTDs also impede other attacks, such as a deception attack, a command injection attack, and more. These attacks are launched based on the information from eavesdropping. Attackers cannot construct the attacks without collecting the information.

3.6 MTD Techniques for Controller Security

In the previous section, we introduced MTD techniques for network security. In this section, we discuss MTD techniques to secure controllers in a CPS.

Controllers are usually a combination of computing devices that are responsible for receiving data from sensors, analyzing the data, and sending feedback to actuators to interact with the physical world. Compared with the other two components, controllers have more computational power; however, there are still several issues in controller security [24].

In general, a CPS has a high reliability requirement, since the electric, gas, and water distribution systems as well as the Industrial Control Systems (ICSs) should remain safe and maintain the availability of resources as long as it is operating. As the brain of a CPS, controllers are responsible for the reliability of the whole system. Even if there is a compromised physical system, the CPS remains functional and is available for other users; however, the effect of compromised physical systems can lead to disasters with a small deviation in controller functionality [38].

Next, the network dynamics are simple. The packets transmitted between the physical systems and the controllers are data from sensors and control signals for actuators. Contrary to public production networks, the patterns of transmission are easier to analyze, which means that attackers can duplicate or modify the connection with less effort.

Lastly, the data is in real time and is collected from the physical world. Since events occurring in the real world are unpredictable, the data is composed with infinite possibilities. It is hard for controllers to differentiate the data from attackers and that from its own physical system. The trust in the data becomes a challenge for controllers. To summarize, the aforementioned challenges can cause the following attacks in controllers. Table 3.2 shows MTDs that are used to combat each attack.

Table 3.2 MTD Techniques to Address Controller Security Attacks on CPS

Tag	*Attacks*	*MTD Category*	*Example*	*CPS Extension Exists?*
A1	Deception	Dynamic network	DynaBone	No
			MT6D	Yes
		Dynamic data	N-variant with data diversity	No
			State estimation MTD	Yes
A3	False information from compromised sensors	Dynamic data	State estimation MTD	Yes
A5	Replay	Dynamic data	N-variant with data diversity	No
			State estimation MTD	Yes
A7	Worm and virus	Dynamic platform	Implementation Diversity	Yes
		Dynamic software	Software Diversity	No
A7	Buffer overflow	Dynamic runtime environment	Address space randomization	No
			Instruction set randomization	No

3.6.1 Deception Attack

Deception attacks are attacks that transmit false information. Figure 3.2 shows several deception attacks. To begin with, the first attack is A1, a deception attack from the physical system to the controller. By analyzing the information collected from an eavesdropping attack, the attacker creates a fake transmission or modifies the data. The fake data then deceives the controller and is used for decision. Based on the incorrect information, the controller analyzes data from sensors, and commands actuators to take the wrong actions. For instance, Amin et al. [39] introduced a deception attack for water Supervisory Control and Data Acquisition (SCADA) systems, which withdraws water from pools through offtakes. By modifying the parameter of the water partial differential equation (PDE) system, the controller is unable to detect when water is lost. Specifically, the adversary opens the offtake and deceives the controller with a fake water level to avoid detection. Since the water will rebalance after the offtake is closed, the attacker is able to restore the original environment without being noticed.

Another deception attack is A3, which transmits the data from compromised sensors. Although the consequence is identical to A1, A3 is more difficult to detect because of the trust from compromised sensors. The adversary can construct the connection as usual with the security identification, such as shared keys. For example, Kim et al. [40] proposed a deception attack from compromised components against a smart grid system. With a slightly and continuously changing electric volume, the attacker places the system in an extreme situation. In the event of a huge change, the system breaks down since the physical system cannot handle the excess electricity. The attack can be performed sequentially and is time costly due to the trust of compromised sensors.

Another attack in this category is a replay attack (A5). By replaying the transmission, the system receives redundant information and goes with the attacker's intention. In [41], the authors presented a replay attack to a smart grid system. The attack can steal the energy or even cause damage to the system. By simply replaying the data, the compromised smart meter reports fake usages to steal the electricity or, similar to A3, the artificial data may damage the system by replaying messages.

Since the characteristics of attack are different, there are specific MTD solutions for each deception attack. To perform the attack described under A1, the adversary needs to eavesdrop on the connection to construct the attack. So, the MTD techniques introduced in Section 3.5.3 can partially defend against deception attacks as well. IP hopping and DynaBone protect the connection from attackers. Since replay attacks do not need to understand the communication, the protection on the network has no influence on the attacker.

In addition, the data diversity technique reexpresses the content to prevent the reuse of the connection. For example, since there are different expressions with a single meaning, the system requires a specific expression and will not accept the replaying data.

A3 is an attack where compromised sensors transmit false information to the controller. The defenses on the network and the data cannot address these attacks. To secure from compromised sensors, trust is the crucial factor. Tang et al. [32] introduced a trustworthiness analysis of sensor data in a CPS, called *Tru-Alarm*. By comparing the data with neighboring sensors, the Tru-Alarm system may distinguish the deception attack. For example, in a water SCADA system, a Tru-Alarm can detect a malicious reporting of wrong water level by a sensor by comparing it with the water levels reported by neighboring sensors.

Furthermore, Rahman et al. [42] introduced an MTD that prevents state estimation (SE) from deception attacks. In a smart grid system, SE is a process of estimating the current state of systems using information from smart meters and other physical systems. With continuous false information, the attacker deceives the controller and places the system in an extreme situation as described in [40]. Rather than reexpressing data, this MTD changes the set of measurements and perturbs line admittances. Similar to the N-variant system, it develops multiple measurements of SE based on distinct attributes. By changing the estimation methods dynamically, attackers cannot be certain of the success of the deception attacks. On the other hand, it also dynamically modifies the topology of networks, such as an alternating current (ac) transmission system. This technique is similar to the DynaBone design, which provides multiple inner layers for transmissions. Since attackers may inject malicious codes in an ac transmission system, this MTD avoids the false data by changing the route.

3.6.2 Worms and Viruses

Worms and viruses are malicious programs that may damage a computer or a system. A virus attaches itself to a program or a file and infects others. Most viruses hide in executable files. That is, the virus will only start infecting other programs or files after running the program. On the other hand, worms are similar to viruses and are considered a subclass of a virus by some researchers. Contrary to viruses, worms spread from computer to computer without human action. From the file or data communication features, worms automatically exploit vulnerabilities in systems and infect other systems.

In 2009, a worm called Stuxnet [31] targeted an ICS and other similar systems. The final goal of Stuxnet is to compromise the programmable logic controllers (PLC) and change the operation of systems without notice. To accomplish this goal, the code contains a mass array of components, such as zero-day exploits, a Windows rootkit, PLC rootkits, and more. Each component is able to utilize certain functionalities or compromise specific vulnerabilities. In fact, Stuxnet is an extremely sophisticated worm, which includes different attack vectors. According to a Symantec report, as of September 29, 2010, there are approximately 100,000 infected hosts from 155 countries [31].

To address malicious software, the first MTD is *implementation diversity*. This MTD includes several different layers. For instance, similar to the N-variant, the function layer contains redundant implementations with identical functionalities; however, rather than running all functions, the system randomly chooses an implementation, which may be able to avoid an attack that is targeting a specific vulnerability. In other words, the adversary can only exploit the system with probability since the execution is nondetermined. Moreover, the technique can also be *build diversity* [43], which provides a similar concept in a different layer. From high-level language implementation, diverse binary images can be produced with different building tool chains. When an application is built, the system randomly selects code-generation template variants to provide a nondetermined binary image. Build diversity reduces the success probability of an attack designed for a specific image. The implementation diversity technique includes multiple layers, such as function, binary, structural, and more.

System diversity is another MTD technique that constantly changes the system's environment. By modifying runtime policies, the system is able to execute with different environmental configurations. Since attackers are able to observe the concurrent environment, system diversity changes periodically to avoid attacks. For attacks targeting a specific environment, this technique reduces the chance of a successful attack.

Azab and Eltoweissy [3] proposed an MTD technique called ChameleonSoft, incorporating the idea of implementation diversity and system diversity. Inspired by chameleons in biology, the system provides multilayer diversity for different purposes. ChameleonSoft is based on cell-oriented architecture (COA). COA utilizes active components termed *cells* that support the software development, deployment, execution, and maintenance. Separating logic, state, and physical resources, cells contain specific information about the system. Using a composition of cells, an organism is generated, representing complex multitasking applications. Figure 3.6 illustrates an abstract view of a COA cell at runtime. Containing a specific functionality, cells isolate the executable logic from the underlying physical resources.

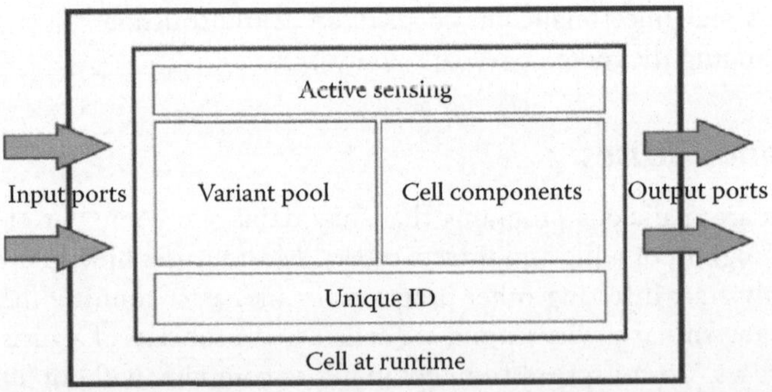

Figure 3.6 COA cell at runtime. (From Azab, M., and Eltoweissy, M. ChameleonSoft: Software behavior encryption for moving target defense. *Mobile Networks Applications,* 2012. With permission.)

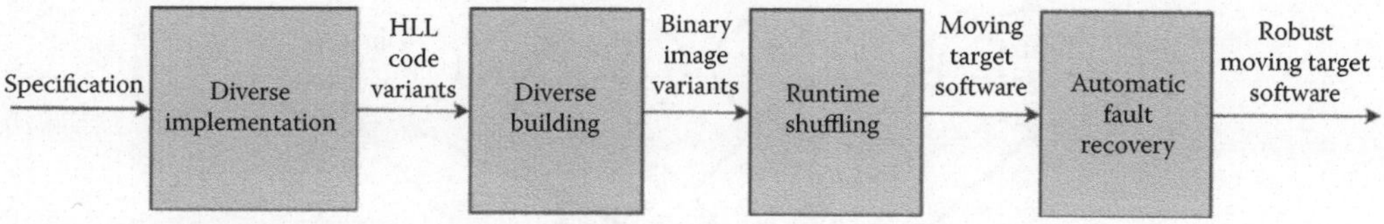

Figure 3.7 BioSENSE overview. (From Eltarras, R. M. Biosense: Biologically-inspired secure elastic networked sensor environment. Ph.D. dissertation, The Faculty of the Virginia Polytechnic Institute and State University. 2011. With permission.)

Furthermore, Eltarras introduced a system integrating MTD techniques for a CPS, called *BioSENSE* (Biologically Inspired Secure Elastic Networked Sensor Environment) [43]. Also based on the COA, BioSENSE provides an implementation diversity that includes more randomizations. Figure 3.7 depicts the MTD principles of BioSENSE. In the first two stages on the left, the system creates static randomizations for layers. The randomizations include not only structural diversity, but also fault, tough spot, and failure diversity. Fault diversity estimates the faults found among variants; tough spot diversity estimates the fault-proneness among the elements of variants; and failure diversity estimates the failure behavior among variants. These variants provide the system to be composed of organisms with more diversity. Moreover, the system also supports build diversity in randomizing binary images. In the third stage, BioSENSE provides several shuffles for organisms: periodic, random, event-driven, and application-initiated shuffling. The periodic and random shuffling changes the composition of organisms by time. Rather than changing with a static duration, random shuffling reconstructs over a random period. Event-driven shuffling changes when an event occurs, such as detection. Lastly, the system reconstructs the organisms when explicitly requested to by the running variant. For instance, when an unexpected error occurs, the system restarts the current stage and shuffles the cells.

Different from the aforementioned diversity techniques in considering a single system, software diversity considers a whole ecosystem. In Section 3.2.2, we briefly introduced two software diversity techniques targeting different variables: software and vulnerability. Using a distributed coloring algorithm, O'Donnell and Sethu diversify the software on the network [13]. Figure 3.8 illustrates a simple example of the difference between a homogeneous network and a diversified network. In Figure 3.8a, servers and clients all install Software 1; in Figure 3.8b, clients have Software 1 and servers install Software 2. With identical Software 1, a worm can infect all the computers on the network (a), since the vulnerabilities are identical; however, in network (b), due to the difference in vulnerability, servers X and Y will not be infected by a malware that exploits the vulnerability of Software 1, which means that there is no infection when any system is compromised.

Furthermore, Neti et al. [44] focused on diversifying vulnerabilities. If different hosts contain identical vulnerabilities, diversifying software cannot prevent an attack from exploiting the same vulnerability. Each piece of software contains different numbers of vulnerabilities. By computing the diversity entropy of software, Neti et al. calculate the diversity of the system, and improve the resilience of the network as a whole. This MTD technique can also reduce the numbers of systems that are compromised by worms or viruses, but it does not completely defend them.

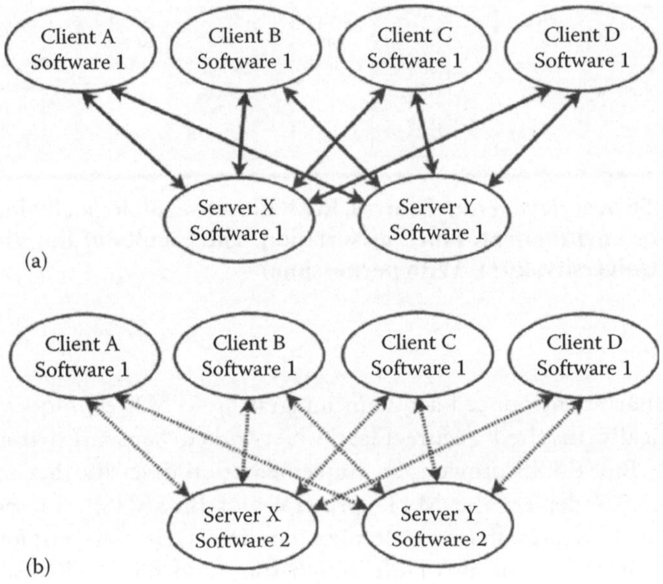

Figure 3.8 Homogeneous network and diversified network. (From O'Donnell, A. J., and Sethu, H. On achieving software diversity for improved network security using distributed coloring algorithms. In *Proceedings of the 11th ACM Conference on Computer and Communications Security*, ACM, New York. 2004. With permission.)

3.6.3 Buffer Overflow

Buffer overflow is an attack that manipulates the return address on a stack to execute a specific code. Depending on the execution of the attack on the stack or heap, this attack is also termed *stack overflow* and *heap overflow*. In controllers, the buffer overflow may reset passwords, modify content, and run malicious codes. To perform a buffer overflow attack, an attacker needs to execute several steps. First of all, attackers need the position of the return address in a stack and the position of the malicious function that it intends to execute. With the positions of the return address and the function known, the attackers modify the data on the return address with the function address. As a result, when the return address is called, the system will execute the function that the attackers intend to execute. The key components of this attack are the positions of the return address and the functions. Since a buffer overflow attack is a common attack within cybersecurity, there are several MTD techniques based on address space randomization and instruction set randomization.

Address space randomization has been around for roughly a decade. Its goal is to randomize the position of the return address. Without knowing the return address, attackers can also attack by guessing the address. Since there are numerous implementations with a similar concept, we introduce one specific example: ASLP [10]. Rather than randomizing the return address, ASLP modifies several structures. The changes can be classified into user level and kernel level. In user-level randomization, ASLP can modify the execution file to randomly relocate the static code, data segments, and other elements. Since the object file (e.g., *helloworld.o*) contains information, such as relocation records, the type of object file, and debugging-related information, attackers may construct attacks based on them. With a binary rewriting tool, ASLP transforms an executable and linking format (ELF) file into another layout. Specifically, the user level makes a coarse-grained permutation and a fine-grained permutation. By rewriting the ELF header, program header, and sections, the coarse-grained permutation shifts the code and segments according to a user-defined offset value, and the fine-grained permutation randomly reorders functions and variables within the code and data segment. With the permutations in the user level, ASLP impedes attackers from utilizing the compiled files.

On the other hand, the kernel level modifies the structure of data in runtime. There are three regions for permutations: the user-mode stack, the *brk()*-managed heap, and *mmap* allocations. In the early stage of process creation, ASLP randomizes the stack pointer of the user stack from 0 to 4 KB. In the later stage, the permutation randomly selects a start location of stacks between 128 MB and 3 GB. For the heap randomization, ASLP also performs in process creation. A page-aligned virtual address between 0 and 3 GB is generated and a subpage random value between 0 and 4 KB is determined. Lastly, *mmap()* is used to map objects into the memory. The *mmap* allocation also provides random, page-aligned addresses between 0 and 3 GB. With the permutations of stacks and heaps, ASLP prevents a buffer overflow attack.

Moreover, instruction set randomization can also protect the system from a buffer overflow attack. Rather than changing the stack and heap structure, this defense randomizes the location of functions. G-Free is an instruction set randomizer that protects from an ROP attack [23]. As introduced in Section 3.3.1, ROP is an improvement on utilizing function calls. Rather than transferring the program execution to the beginning of a library function, ROP chains specific functions, called *gadgets*, and executes them directly. Kornau discovered that each gadget has to end with a "free-branch" instruction, which changes the program to the attacker-defined destination. G-Free randomizes "free-branch" instructions causing false connections between gadgets. This prevents attackers from completing buffer overflow attacks.

3.7 MTD Techniques for Physical System Security

In this section, we discuss the security of physical systems in a CPS. Physical systems contain two subcomponents: sensors and actuators. Sensors collect information from the physical world and transmit it to controllers, while actuators receive commands from controllers and perform actions interacting with the physical world. Although there are differences in their design details, such as their sensing range and action target, physical systems generally communicate with controllers and interact with the physical world. There are two major challenges in physical systems: resource constraints and physical interaction.

Contrary to controllers, physical systems face tremendous limitations from computation, energy consumption, and budgets. Computational power is based on the quality and quantity of hardware; however, both of these are constrained for physical systems. For example, pacemakers and implantable cardiac defibrillators (ICD) are devices that maintain a normal heart rhythm [28]. Since these devices are implanted into the human body, their size, weight, and materials are restricted and their computation capability is low.

Moreover, the energy consumption of physical systems restricts their ability. Taking the same pacemakers and ICDs as examples, once the device is implanted in the body, the battery should support the device for the rest of its life. The more computation a physical system has to do, the more energy it will consume. In order to maintain the battery life, the computational capacity is restricted.

Last but not least, the cost of hardware is also a resource constraint on the physical system. For instance, smart meters are placed in buildings, such as homes, companies, and factories. Because of the huge demand of smart meters, a dollar increment causes an additional million dollars of budget. The hardware should be used completely and efficiently; however, smart meters should also remain functional for a long period of time. The huge number of devices not only causes an increment in the budget, but it is also difficult to replace and update them.

Furthermore, interaction with the physical world contains unexpected actions and physical security issues. Changes in the physical world can be unexpected, which means that the system cannot take all possible information into account. For example, noisy messages are common for sensors in the physical world. Physical security is one of the major attacks in a physical system. Due to the lack of resources and interaction with the physical world, the security of a physical system is a challenge for researchers. The MTD solutions for physical systems are shown in Table 3.3.

3.7.1 Deception Attacks

In Section 3.6, we introduced MTD techniques to address deception attacks. Since those MTDs are sufficient to address attacks in physical systems, we will not repeat them in this section. In contrast with the controller domain, physical systems face resource constraints and battery issues. Therefore, the design of controllers for physical systems should be more lightweight while providing a reasonable level of security. For example, Halperin [28] proposed a deception attack for pacemakers and ICDs. The adversary can obtain the personal information or modify the data on the device by eavesdropping on the connection with administrators and replaying the transmission. Since resources are limited, the defense should be designed with lightweight computation and low energy consumption.

3.7.2 Buffer Overflow

Although we also introduced the buffer overflow attack in Section 3.6, different MTD techniques exist for physical systems. Due to the lack of computational power, physical systems may not be able to implement address space randomization and instruction set randomization; however, physical systems also face buffer overflow attacks. To overcome these attacks, researchers proposed a different type of MTD technique for physical systems.

McLaughlin and Podkuiko [45] proposed an MTD technique for smart meters. This static MTD technique encrypts the data with several keys before saving, and checks the decryptions

Table 3.3 MTD Techniques to Address Physical System Security Attacks on CPS

Tag	*Attacks*	*MTD Category*	*Example*	*CPS Extension Exists?*
A8	Deception	Dynamic network	DynaBone	No
			MT6D	Yes
		Dynamic data	N-variant with data diversity	No
			N-variant	No
A12	Buffer overflow	Dynamic data	Data randomization	Yes
A12	Physical	Dynamic platform	Data migration	Yes
		Dynamic data	REA	No

before using them. The following codes illustrate the differences between original and instrumented executions:

Original function call:

```
push    A                 ; Save address
jmp     B                 ; Perform branch
```

Instrumented function call:

```
mov     D [key1_addr]     ; D = K_1
mov     C A               ; C = A
xor     C D               ; C = C XOR D
push    C                 ; Save encrypted address
mov     D [key2_addr]     ; D = K_2
mov     C A               ;
xor     C D               ; Second redundant encryption
push    C                 ;
mov     D [key3_addr]     ; D = K_3
mov     C A               ;
xor     C D               ; Third redundant encryption
push    C                 ;
jmp     B                 ; Perform branch
```

Original return call:

```
pop     A                 ; Load return address
jmp     A                 ; Perform branch
```

Instrumented return call:

```
mov     D [key3_addr]     ; D = K_3
pop     A                 ; Load third encrypted address
xor     A D               ; A = A XOR D
mov     D [key2_addr]     ; D = K_2
pop     B                 ; Load second encrypted address
xor     B D               ; B = B XOR D
mov     D [key1_addr]     ; D = K_1
pop     C                 ; Load first encrypted address
xor     C D               ; C = C XOR D
cmp     A B               ; Check A - B
jnz     fail_stop         ; Fail if A - B!= 0
cmp     B C               ; Check B - C
jnz     fail_stop         ; Fail if B - C!= 0
jmp     A                 ; Return to calling function
```

For function calls, the original code has only two operations: save address and jump to another branch. On the other hand, the instrumented function call encrypts (XOR) the address with three different keys and saves the three encrypted data. The encryption of a function call performs 11 more lines than the original and utilizes two more data spaces. On the other hand, the original return code also contains two operations: load address and jump to the address; however, the instrumented return code executes 14 operations. In the first nine lines, the system decrypts (XOR) the three pieces of data with corresponding keys, and on lines 10–13, it compares the three pieces of decrypted data with each other. If the data is different, the system will stop the execution. Although wasting two more data spaces and several lines of operations, this MTD is sufficient for smart meters. Since the computations of smart meters are small and lightweight, the performance that is lost is acceptable. This MTD provides a $1/2^{48}$ probability of guessing the data.

Rather than encrypting the return address, Cadar et al. [20] described an MTD for several situations: general case, function calls, instrumentation with fixed-size masks, load-time instrumentation, and more. Although this MTD provides only one encryption per data, its implementation secures more operations. For example, when performing a function call, such as `o1 = CALL & _ function, o2, o3`, it transforms into

```
t2 = BITXOR o2, m2
t3 = BITXOR o3, m3
t1 = CALL &_function t2, t3
o1 = BITXOR t1, m1
```

Where o1, o2, and o3 are unsafe operands; t1, t2, and t3 are new temporaries; and m1, m2, and m3 are constants with the mask values for the operands. In the first two lines, the system decrypts the two operands. Line 3 performs a normal function call. Then Line 4 encrypts the result before writing it into the memory. By encrypting the data, this defense prevents attacks from utilizing memory errors. This MTD is also suitable for physical systems since the performance overhead is low, with an 11% runtime overhead and a 1% space overhead on average.

3.7.3 Physical Attack

A physical attack is an attack that physically compromises or destroys the device. This attack can be achieved in multiple ways, such as smashing the device, reverse engineering the system, and disconnecting the transmission feature. For a CPS, controllers are safe from physical attacks because they are settled in an access-controlled area; however, physical systems are located in exposed locations. Each system may face different physical attacks.

Szefer et al. [46] presented an MTD against physical intrusions for data centers. The goal of the adversary is to obtain the data in the data center. To prevent physical intrusions, numerous mechanisms are implemented. These include security locks, crash barriers, two-factor authentication, surveillance cameras, security guards, and so on. Based on these sensors, MTD analyzes the statuses and moves, encrypts, or deletes the data in the data center. In order to implement MTD, they introduce three components to the data center: a physical security monitor, an application programming interface (API), and decision logic.

As Figure 3.9 shows, the physical security monitor collects information from sensors and transfers it to an API. For sensors that are not connected to the management system, the physical security monitor provides a conversion to use the API. The API is used as the standard since normal environmental controls should be able to communicate with it. The management infrastructure gathers all sensor information from the physical security monitor and environmental controls and analyzes it with decision logic. Although the architecture seems complicated, the concept is simple: collecting sensor information, analyzing the information, and then reconfiguring it if necessary. For this MTD, Szefer et al. provide three different MTD techniques: move, encrypt, and delete.

The move action refers to transmitting the sensitive data to another data center; the encrypt action refers to encrypting the data to prevent the attacker from knowing the data; and the delete action refers to deleting the data. These three different actions are decided by the remaining time

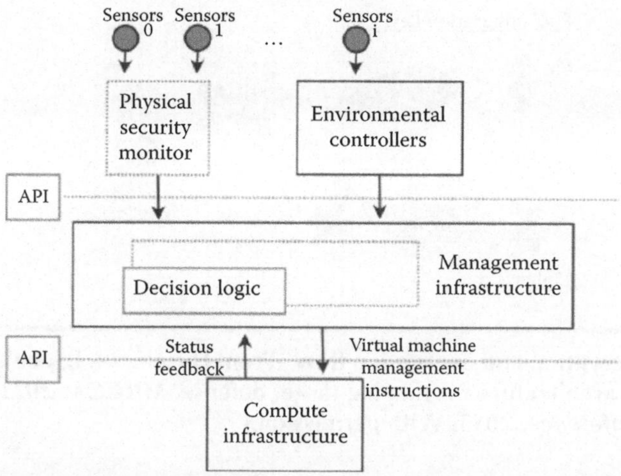

Figure 3.9 The components of the system by Szefer et al. (From Szefer, J., et al. Physical attack protection with human-secure virtualization in data centers. In *IEEE/IFIP International Conference Dependable Systems Networks Work.* [DSN'2012], 2012. With permission.)

of the attack. On detecting an intrusion, the system computes the remaining time before the attacker obtains the data, based on the status of the sensors. If there is enough time to transmit data to another data center, it chooses move; if the time is only enough to encrypt data, it chooses encrypt; and if the time is only enough to delete data, it chooses delete. Since the loss from each movement is different, the order of choice is move, encrypt, and then delete.

To adopt this MTD to a CPS domain, we discuss the data center in two perspectives. The management system can be considered as a controller, which collects information from sensors and commands the movement of data when detecting attacks. That is, this MTD approach can be viewed as a CPS. Rather than protecting physical systems, this MTD protects data (assets in controller) from intrusions. When physical devices are attacked, they transmit signals to the controller to prevent further attacks. With this perspective, the controller receives information and performs a dynamic-reactive MTD.

On the other hand, a data center can be considered a physical system. The physical system moves its sensitive data to another physical system or controller to escape physical attacks. This is similar to MTD used during the Russo-Georgian war. With a bird's-eye view, the data is hidden in multiple data centers. When a physical intrusion occurs, the controller moves or destroys the data. In this perspective, physical systems protect themselves if there is a physical attack. To sum up, although we consider this defense as an MTD with multiple perspectives, its goal is to escape damage, not to protect physical systems from physical attacks. In order to prevent physical attacks, we introduce another MTD.

Husain et al. [47] proposed lightweight reconfigurable symmetric encryption architecture (REA) to maintain data confidentiality on devices in a resource-constrained scenario. This MTD prevents cryptanalysis, which is based on knowledge of encryption architecture. REA supports the implementation of any symmetric encryption algorithm (substitution-permutation network). A substitution-permutation network is a substitution from a block of bits to another block of bits, and permutes to represent the input of the next round. Operations such as lookup table (LUT), XOR, and bitwise rotation can be efficiently performed with hardware. With multiple rounds, the

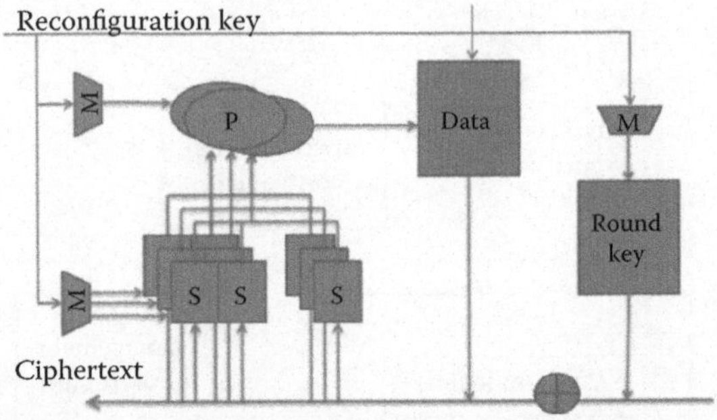

Figure 3.10 REA encryption and decryption flow. (From Husain, M. I., et al. Lightweight reconfigurable encryption architecture for moving target defense. *MILCOM 2013–2013 IEEE Military Communications Conference*, 2013. With permission.)

encryption provides a randomization, which is impossible to break with cryptanalysis. Figure 3.10 presents the architecture of REA.

The idea of the architecture is to load the S-boxes and permutations based on the key for each round. The S-box is a substitution box that substitutes bits for other bits. To begin the encryption, the key and plaintext are passed through the S-boxes and permutations to become the input of the next round. The symbol M indicates the choice of options. Repeating the encryption for a user-defined round, the architecture will produce an encrypted text in the final round. The decryption is executed using the same scenario since REA is a symmetric encryption architecture. Using REA, this MTD prevents the compromise of the data that is stored on physical systems.

3.8 Conclusion

In this chapter, we discussed MTD techniques for a CPS. MTD is the concept of moving attack surfaces in a system to obscure them from an attacker. As the technology has matured, various MTD techniques have been realized, such as address space randomization, instruction set randomization, software diversity, data randomization, and more. We described the taxonomy of MTD and showed how it is suitable for CPS security in different parts of a CPS: network, controller, and physical system.

In addressing network security, we introduced DoS, packet-scheduling attacks, and eavesdropping attacks. To address these attacks, a CPS may hide connections and diversify data from attackers. The implementations include transmission diversity, transmission partitioning, IP hopping, and data diversity. Secondly, controllers are vulnerable from deception attacks, false information from compromised sensors, replay attacks, buffer overflow attacks, worms, and viruses. The defenses in network security can also partially secure attacks through the network. The concepts used in controller security are implementation diversity, software diversity, address space randomization, and instruction set randomization. Each MTD impedes attackers at a unique layer.

The last component is the physical system. Due to the lack of resources, although facing the same attacks as controllers, MTD should be implemented with less computation and complexity. Moreover, physical attacks only exist in the physical system, such as smashing the device, reverse engineering the system, and disconnecting the transmission feature. Data randomization, data migration, and data encryption are techniques that ensure the integrity of the data on physical systems. Although some MTD concepts have no implementation in CPS as of yet, we have discussed how those can be used in the CPS domain.

3.9 Future Research Direction

In this chapter, we introduced different MTD concepts that can be applied to secure a CPS; however, some concepts have still not been implemented in the CPS domain. For example, REA can be applied for specific physical systems, data diversity can be implemented for controllers, and transmission diversity can be realized for networks. These implementations are possible research directions for the future. Also, since most of the MTD techniques we discussed here are for the ICS or the smart grid, we need to look at other types of CPSs, such as water distribution systems, gas distribution systems, or unmanned aerial vehicle (UAV) command systems, to see how the MTD techniques could be applied to those types of CPSs.

Furthermore, innovative MTD concepts can be developed. For instance, Zhu et al. [48] introduced an MTD for information technology (IT) systems. The reinforcement learning algorithm analyzes the current attack status and computes the best response. This MTD dynamically changes the policies of the intrusion detection system. Finally, the combination and modification of existing MTDs are also a possible research direction. For example, DynaBone [43] and *ChameleonSoft* [3] both contain multiple MTD strategies in single systems. More such composite MTD techniques can be developed.

Author Biographies

Shih-Wei Fang is currently a third-year graduate student in computer science at California State Polytechnic University, Pomona. He obtained his undergraduate degree in mathematical science from the National ChengChi University in Taiwan. His research interests include moving target defense, the cyber-physical system, and game theory. His thesis focuses on the interaction between moving target defense and game theory. He plans to continue his education and obtain a PhD.

Anthony Portante is a senior undergraduate student at California State Polytechnic University, Pomona. He is an Air Force Reserve Officers' Training Corps (ROTC) cadet and is scheduled to commission in June 2015 and join the air force as a cyberoperations officer. He has been conducting research in the area of moving target defense (MTD) since the fall of 2013, focusing on the application of MTD techniques within virtualized environments. Some other areas that he finds interesting are operating systems, human–agent teamwork systems, and cyber-physical systems. Anthony plans to continue his education within the Air Force and obtain his master's and PhD degrees.

Mohammad Iftekhar Husain has been a tenure-track assistant professor of computer science at California State Polytechnic University, Pomona, since 2012. His broad research interest is in the domain of security and forensics, specifically in the areas of cloud computing, cyber-physical systems, and unmanned aerial vehicles (UAV). Dr. Husain's academic activities are supported by the National Science Foundation (NSF), Northrop Grumman Corporation, and Microsoft Corporation. He graduated with a PhD in computer science and engineering from the University at Buffalo, The State University of New York, in 2012.

References

1. S. Forrest, A. Somayaji, and D. Ackley. 1997. Building diverse computer systems. In *Proceedings of the 6th Workshop on Hot Topics in Operating Systems (HotOS-VI) (HOTOS'97)*, IEEE Computer Society, Washington, DC, pp. 67–72.
2. D. Kewley, R. Fink, J. Lowry, and M. Dean. Dynamic approaches to thwart adversary intelligence gathering. In *Proceedings DARPA Information Survivability Conference & Exposition II. DISCEX'01*, Anaheim, CA, vol. 1, pp. 176–185.
3. M. Azab, and M. Eltoweissy. 2012. ChameleonSoft: Software behavior encryption for moving target defense. *Mobile Networks Applications*, 18(2), pp. 271–292.
4. S. Groat, and M. Dunlop. 2012. Using an IPv6 moving target defense to protect the smart grid. *Innovative Smart Grid Technologies (ISGT), 2012 IEEE PES*, pp. 1–7.
5. P. McDaniel, and S. McLaughlin. 2009. Security and privacy challenges in the smart grid. *IEEE Security & Privacy*, 7(3), pp. 75–77.
6. S. W. Korns. 2009. Botnets outmaneuvered. *Armed Forces Journal* [Online]. January 1. Available: http://www.armedforcesjournal.com/botnets-outmaneuvered/. Accessed August 8, 2014.
7. A. K. Ghosh, D. Pendarakis, and W. H. Sanders. 2009. National Cyber Leap Year Summit 2009 co-chairs' report. The Networking and Information Technology Research and Development (NITRD) Program.
8. H. Okhravi, M. Rabe, T. Mayberry, W. Leonard, T. Hobson, D. Bigelow, and W. Streilein. 2013. Survey of cyber moving targets. Technical report 1166, MIT Lincoln Laboratory.
9. H. Shacham, M. Page, B. Pfaff, E.-J. Goh, N. Modadugu, and D. Boneh. 2004. On the effectiveness of address-space randomization. In *Proceedings of the 11th ACM Conference on Computer and Communications Security (CCS '04)*, ACM, New York, pp. 298–307.
10. C. Kil, J. Jim, and C. Bookholt. 2006. Address space layout permutation (ASLP): Towards fine-grained randomization of commodity software. *Computer Security Applications Conference 2006. ACSAC'06. 22nd Annual IEEE, 2006*, pp. 339–348.
11. G. S. Kc, A. D. Keromytis, and V. Prevelakis. 2003. Countering code-injection attacks with instruction-set randomization. In *Proceedings of the 10th ACM conference on Computer and Communications Security (CCS '03)*, ACM, New York, pp. 272–280.
12. W. Hu, J. Hiser, D. Williams, A. Filipi, J. W. Davidson, D. Evans, J. C. Knight, A. Nguyen-Tuong, and J. Rowanhill. 2006. Secure and practical defense against code-injection attacks using software dynamic translation. In *Proceedings of the 2nd International Conference on Virtual Execution Environments – VEE'06*, Ottawa, Canada, p. 2.
13. A. J. O'Donnell and H. Sethu. 2004. On achieving software diversity for improved network security using distributed coloring algorithms. In *Proceedings of the 11th ACM Conference on Computer and Communications Security*, ACM, New York, pp. 121–131.
14. M. Petkac, L. Badger, and W. Morrison. 2000. Security agility for dynamic execution environments. In *DARPA Information Survivability Conference and Exposition, 2000. DISCEX '00 Proceedings*, vol. 1, pp. 377–390.
15. T. Roeder, and F. B. Schneider. 2010. Proactive obfuscation. *ACM Transactions on Computer Systems*, 28(2), Article 4.
16. J. Li, P. L. Reiher, and G. J. Popek. 2004. Resilient self-organizing overlay networks for security update delivery. *IEEE Journal on Selected Areas Communications*, 22(1), pp. 189–202.
17. D. A. Holland, A. T. Lim, and M. I. Seltzer. 2005. An architecture a day keeps the hacker away. *ACM SIGARCH Computer Architecture News*, 33(1), 34.
18. H. Okhravi, A. Comella, E. Robinson, and J. Haines. 2012. Creating a cyber moving target for critical infrastructure applications using platform diversity. *International Journal of Critical Infrastructure Protection*, 5(1), pp. 30–39.
19. P. E. Ammann, and J. C. Knight. 1988. Data diversity: An approach to software fault tolerance. *IEEE Transactions Computers*, 37(4), pp. 418–425.
20. C. Cadar, P. Akritidis, M. Costa, J.-P. Martin, and M. Castro. 2008. Data randomization. Technical report, Microsoft Research. MSR-TR-2008-120.

21. H. Shacham, M. Page, B. Pfaff, E.-J. Goh, N. Modadugu, and D. Boneh. 2004. On the effectiveness of address-space randomization. *Proceedings of the 11th ACM Conference on Computer and Communications Security – CCS'04*, New York, pp. 298–307.
22. H. Shacham. 2007. The geometry of innocent flesh on the bone: Return-into-LIBC without function calls (on the x86). In *Proceedings of the 14th ACM Conference on Computer and Communications Security (CCS '07)*, ACM, New York, pp. 552–561.
23. K. Onarlioglu, L. Bilge, A. Lanzi, D. Balzarotti, and E. Kirda. 2010. G-Free: Defeating return-oriented programming through gadget-less binaries. In *Proceedings of the 26th Annual Computer Security Applications Conference (ACSAC '10)*, ACM, New York, pp. 49–58.
24. A. Cardenas, S. Amin, and B. Sinopoli. 2009. Challenges for securing cyber physical systems. In *Workshop on Future Directions in Cyber-Physical Systems Security*, DHS, July 23, 2009.
25. Q. Shafi. 2012. Cyber physical systems security: A brief survey. *2012 12th International Conference Computational Science and Its Application*, pp. 146–150.
26. D. M. Nicol, C. M. Davis, and T. Overbye. 2009. A testbed for power system security evaluation. *International Journal of Information and Computer Security*, 3(2), pp. 1–18.
27. A. A. Cárdenas, S. Amin, and S. Sastry. 2008. Research challenges for the security of control systems. In *Proceedings of the 3rd Conference on Hot Topics in Security HotSec*, Berkeley, CA.
28. D. Halperin. 2008. Pacemakers and implantable cardiac defibrillators: Software radio attacks and zero-power defenses. *Security and Privacy, 2008. IEEE Symposium on SP 2008.*
29. Y. Mo, and B. Sinopoli. 2009. Secure control against replay attacks. In *47th Annual Allerton Conference Communication Control and Computing*, pp. 911–918.
30. Y. Shoukry, J. Araujo, and P. Tabuada. 2013. Minimax control for cyber-physical systems under network packet scheduling attacks. In *Proceedings of the 2nd ACM International Conference on High Confidence Networked Systems*, ACM, New York, pp. 93–100.
31. N. Falliere, L. Murchu, and E. Chien. 2011. W32. Stuxnet dossier. White paper, Symantec Corporation, Security Response, 4, pp. 1–69.
32. L.-A. Tang, X. Yu, S. Kim, Q. Gu, J. Han, A. Leung, and T. La Porta. 2013. Trustworthiness analysis of sensor data in cyber-physical systems. *Journal of Computer and System Sciences*, 79(3), pp. 383–401.
33. P. Koopman. 2004. Embedded system security. *IEEE Computer*, 37(7), pp. 95–97.
34. J. D. Touch, G. G. Finn, Y. Wang, and L. Eggert. 2003. DynaBone: Dynamic defense using multilayer Internet overlays. In *Proceedings of the 3rd DARPA Information Survivability Conference and Exposition (DISCEX-III)*, vol. 2, Washington, DC.
35. M. Weiss, F. Mattern, T. Graml, T. Staake, and E. Fleisch. 2009. Handy feedback: Connecting smart meters with mobile phones. In *Proceedings of the 8th International Conference on Mobile and Ubiquitous Multimedia (MUM'09)*, ACM, New York.
36. G. Stephen, D. Matthew, M. Randy, and T. Joseph. 2011. Using dynamic addressing for a moving target defense. In *Proceedings of the 6th International Conference on Information Warfare and Security (ICIW'11)*, Academic Conferences Limited.
37. A. Nguyen-Tuong, D. Evans, J. C. Knight, B. Cox, and J. W. Davidson. 2008. Security through redundant data diversity. *2008 IEEE International Conference Dependable System Networks with FTCS DCC*, pp. 187–196.
38. H. Khurana, M. Hadley, N. Lu, and D. A. Frincke. 2010. Smart-grid security issues. *IEEE Security & Privacy*, 8(1), pp. 81–85.
39. S. Amin, X. Litrico, S. S. Sastry, and A. M. Bayen. 2010. Stealthy deception attacks on water SCADA systems. In *Proceedings of the 13th ACM International Conference Hybrid Systems Computation and Control (HSCC'10)*, p. 161.
40. T. T. Kim, H. V. Poor. 2011. Strategic protection against data injection attacks on power grids. *IEEE Transactions on Smart Grid*, 2(2), pp. 326–333.
41. T.-T. Tran, O.-S. Shin, and J.-H. Lee. 2013. Detection of replay attacks in smart grid systems. *2013 International Conference Computing, Management and Telecommunications (ComManTel)*, pp. 298–302.
42. M. A. Rahman, E. Al-Shaer, and R. B. Bobba. 2014. Moving target defense for hardening the security of the power system state estimation. In *Proceedings of the First ACM Workshop on Moving Target Defense*, ACM, New York, pp. 59–68.

43. R. M. Eltarras. 2011. Biosense: Biologically inspired secure elastic networked sensor environment. PhD dissertation, The Faculty of the Virginia Polytechnic Institute and State University.
44. S. Neti, A. Somayaji, and M. Locasto. 2012. Software diversity: Security, entropy and game theory. In *Proceedings of the 7th USENIX HotSec*, Bellevue, WA.
45. S. McLaughlin, and D. Podkuiko. 2010. Embedded firmware diversity for smart electric meters. In *HotSec Proceedings of the 5th USENIX Conference on Hot Topics in Security*, Berkeley, CA.
46. J. Szefer, P. Jamkhedkar, and R. B. Lee. 2012. Physical attack protection with human-secure virtualization in data centers. In *IEEE/IFIP International Conference Dependable Systems Networks Work (DSN'2012)*, pp. 1–6.
47. M. I. Husain, K. Courtright, and R. Sridhar. 2013. Lightweight reconfigurable encryption architecture for moving target defense. *MILCOM 2013–2013 IEEE Military Communications Conference*, pp. 214–219.
48. M. Zhu, Z. Hu, and P. Liu. 2014. Reinforcement learning algorithms for adaptive cyber defense against heartbleed. *Proceedings of the First ACM Workshop on Moving Target Defense*, ACM, New York, pp. 51–58.

Chapter 4

Ontological Framework–Assisted Embedded System Design with Security Consideration in a Cyber-Physical Power System Environment

Bo Xing
University of Limpopo

Contents

4.1 Introduction 92
4.2 Motivation 93
4.3 Literature Review 93
4.3.1 Cyber-Physical System 93
4.3.2 Embedded System Design for In-Pipe Inspection 94
4.4 Hypothesized Solution: Cloud Robotics–Assisted In-Pipe Inspection 95
4.5 Security Challenges Relevant to Our Hypothetical Solution 96
4.5.1 Hardware Side 96
4.5.2 Software Side 96
4.5.3 Network Side 97
4.6 Other Design Challenges 98
4.6.1 Incompleteness of Design Knowledge 98
4.6.2 Dynamics of Design Knowledge 99
4.7 Proposed Methodology 99
4.7.1 What Is the PFWSB Framework? 100

4.7.1.1 Purpose.......... 100
4.7.1.2 Function.......... 101
4.7.1.3 Behavior.......... 101
4.7.1.4 Structure.......... 102
4.7.1.5 Environment.......... 102
4.7.1.6 Constraint.......... 102
4.7.1.7 Working Space.......... 103
4.7.1.8 Design Description.......... 103
4.7.2 Why PFWSB Framework?.......... 103
4.8 How to Use PFWSB to Understand and Represent the Knowledge.......... 105
4.9 Representing and Understanding the Knowledge Flow during the Conceptual Design Stage via PFWSB Framework.......... 107
4.10 Discussion.......... 111
4.10.1 Contributions.......... 111
4.10.2 Future Work.......... 113
4.11 Conclusions.......... 114
Author Biography.......... 114
References.......... 114

Abstract: A cyber-physical power system (CPPS), as the main energy source for other infrastructure, stands central and is essential to the operation of all other systems. In practice, various technologies are used to generate electricity, the combination of which is often referred to as the "plant mix." The utility is constantly investigating other forms of energy and renewable energy sources that could be used to expand its current plant mix and has initiated various research projects looking at wind, solar, tidal, wave, and biomass sources of energy. Nevertheless, with the rapid expansion of a country's power plant mix, the security of the CPPS (on both the cyber and the physical side) has become a crucial issue confronting practitioners. In this chapter, a knowledge-based representation, which is based on the purpose-function-working space-structure-behavior (PFWSB) paradigm, is adopted for designing a cloud-facilitated intelligent embedded system, which can be used for in-pipe security inspection. Since most of the cyber-physical system (CPS) security studies are mainly focused on the cyberside, the purpose of this study is to fill such a gap by adding the physical security issue. At the conclusion of this work, we outline the technical challenges in the PFWSB framework and provide some recommendations for future work.

Keywords: Cyber-physical power system (CPPS); Purpose-function-working space-structure-bahavior (PFWSB) framework; In-pipe inspection; Cloud robotics; Knowledge flow; Embedded system design

4.1 Introduction

The electric power system, as the main energy source for other infrastructure, stands central and is essential to the operation of all other systems. Ideally, an electric power system should be designed such that the required power to its customers can always be supplied as economically as possible and with an acceptable degree of continuity and reliability. However, in this new era of competition, electric utilities are confronted with many challenges, such as load forecasting, unit commitment, economic load dispatch, maintenance of system frequency, and declared voltage levels as well as interchanges among the interconnected systems in power pools. As a consequence, modern power systems are increasingly vulnerable to cascading failures in which a small series of events can lead to a major blackout. To deal with these threats, the introduction of the cyber-physical system (CPS) is a significant contributor, in which the embedded computing is integrated to gather information about the most relevant parameters to generate suitable control commands to achieve the desired application goals. In other words, to make power systems more efficient, we will have to depend heavily on the CPS, which will be able to monitor, share, and manage information and actions. Generally speaking, the cyber-physical power system (CPPS) is a next-generation infrastructure of the traditional power system, integrating physical-world devices, cyberworld computing, and communication capabilities, so as to make the operation of generating facilities more efficient and cost effective [1]. The possibilities of developing a CPPS are detailed in [2–4].

The remainder of this chapter is organized as follows. Subsequent to the introduction in Section 4.1, the motivation of this study is briefly outlined in Section 4.2, which is followed by a detailed corresponding literature review in Section 4.3. Next, a hypothetical solution to deal with our focal scenario is proposed in Section 4.4. The various challenges encountered are detailed in Sections 4.5 and 4.6. A detailed description of the employed design framework can be found in Section 4.7, which is followed by a concise explanation of how it can be used in Section 4.8. Section 4.9 presents an experimental study to demonstrate the feasibility of our proposed approach. Discussions regarding the contributions and future research directions are then provided in Section 4.10. Finally, the conclusions that are drawn in Section 4.11 close this study.

4.2 Motivation

This research was motivated by a design concept concerned with the inspection of pipeline infrastructures, which is considered the safest and most economical method for transporting fluids over long distances (e.g., oil [5,6], gas [7,8], and liquid [9,10]) and is thus found in various industrial environments. Taking the electricity-generating industry as an example, in each power plant, thousands of different kinds of pipes are used to ensure that the machinery runs properly. All these power plants together become a critical part of a country's CPPS. A brief review of the literature indicated that a number of studies have been conducted concerning the impacts of the condition of the pipelines on the overall performance of a power plant (e.g., [9,11]). Therefore, the inspection and the proactive maintenance of pipelines turns out to be an essential activity. In general, one of the most important inspection and securing tasks of pipelines is to identify the pipelines' interior status. Issues such as corrosion, fatigue, and even erosion significantly increase the danger of leaks or even bursting [12].

4.3 Literature Review

4.3.1 Cyber-Physical System

Generally speaking, the CPS can be defined as an integration of computational and physical characteristics [13]. Nowadays, the use of CPSs pervades all areas of our lives, from common household appliances such as microwave ovens, to complex applications such as automobiles, the power grid, and robots. Although they provide higher productivity and greater flexibility, it is inevitable that they are not fault-free. Some faults may be attributed to inaccuracy during the development phase, while others can stem from external causes such as the uncertainty and heterogeneity due to the cross-platform integration. Therefore, high dependability is a requirement for every CPS. Indeed, recent experience (e.g., the websites of Adobe and eBay have been attacked through cyberspace) has shown that the concerns of cybersecurity have become the new domain of warfare. Cybersecurity is challenging because the architecture of the cloud networking was designed to promote connectivity, not security. In this context, one of the major challenges is the confidentiality of CPSs, especially information flow security. Various security models that analyze multilevel security system behavior from different perspectives, such as the access, control, and execution sequence, have been discussed. Apart from these issues, however, physical security [14] is often oblivious of and thus is not always coordinated with cybersecurity so that the safety of the whole CPS can be ensured.

4.3.2 Embedded System Design for In-Pipe Inspection

An embedded system usually contains electronics and software that are embedded in an enclosed product that performs a dedicated function [15]. It was pioneered by the military for applications ranging from autopilots on aircraft to smart bombs and missiles. The core idea behind the design of such systems is to control real-time operations while meeting dependability requirements, such as reliability, maintainability, availability, safety, and security [13]. In practice, a typical CPS is normally formed when various building blocks, that is, embedded systems, are connected to the physical environment through sensors and actuators, using the fundamental techniques of communication technology (e.g., cloud networking) to have an immediate impact on their surrounding environments. Humans have been designing products for nearly 5000 years [16]. Among the wide variety of products, each must undergo a lengthy and challenging design process. This is particularly true in the case of robot design. Nowadays, researchers in the field of robotics are proposing a great variety of robots. Examples that can be found are crab-like robots [17], humanoid robots [18–20], and jumping robots [21–24]. Each individual design is characterized by unique configurations and functional capabilities. In this work, the author intends to perform a miniature robot conceptual design study with a focus on an in-pipe inspection scenario. Contrary to other robot categories, such as the entertainment robot [19], the inspection robot belongs to the class of industrial robots, which the Japanese Industrial Robot Association defines as follows [25]:

> Industrial robots are those devices providing versatile and flexible moving functions similar to those of human limbs and which provide flexible moving functions through their sensing and recognising capabilities.

In the context of our focal scenario, that is, CPPSs, depending on the size of the pipe diameter, the pipe inspection robots can be broadly divided into three categories: (1) for small size (10 mm or less), inchworm-like microrobots or helical-type robots, for example, [26,27], have been highlighted because of their advantage of moving in curved pipes; (2) for medium size (40–170 mm), wheeled or caterpillar robots, for example, [28,29], are a more efficient choice due to their strength in navigating pipeline branches; (3) for large pipes, legged walking robots, for example, [30,31], are usually adopted since they are able to step over obstacles and move faster. Research and development on the in-pipe inspection robot systems has been actively carried out based on different designs and the systems have been used in various domains. For example, Sabzehmeidani et al. [32] designed a wormlike microrobot with intelligent active force control capability, while Appelqvist [33] studied a swarm of small-sized, ball-shaped, underwater mobile robots, which were equipped with a microcontroller central processing unit (CPU), several sensors, tank actuators, and a short-range radio for communication. To inspect the urban gas pipeline system, a multifunction robot was proposed in [7] and [34]. In addition, Prasad et al. [29] proposed a mobile robot with the ability to move inside horizontal and vertical pipes. More recently, a review of the design of the hybrid locomotion of an in-pipe inspection robot (e.g., caterpillar wall-pressed type, wheeled wall-pressed type, and wheeled wall-pressing screw type) was reported in [35]. Additionally, the authors of [36] highlighted several major requirements for applying a robotic system when inspecting pipelines, which include visual inspection, magnetic leakage detection, eddy current inspection, and ultrasonic inspection, and an acoustical method.

To summarize, there are two significant reasons to adopt the smart embedded systems (or more specifically intelligent robots) for inspection activities. One is that there is little doubt that the primary motivation for introducing robots is economic. The other is that they are liked because of their technological efficiency and product quality. For example, robots offer the opportunity to achieve virtually complete quality inspection since they are not subject to variations in output as a consequence of errors or boredom, and they can perform repetitive, dirty, and dangerous tasks 24 h a day.

Although conceptually simple, designing an embedded system is a challenge. First of all, like most things in life, the process of designing an embedded system begins with a goal, that is, the system must meet the product requirements definition and functionality description. Second, the system should be self-starting, self-contained, and self-upgrading, that is, the system must be capable of interfacing with some piece of real-world hardware and controlling a specific real-time device or function. Third, the development costs for such a system must be considered. Last but not least, the evaluation of the dependability (e.g., reliability and security) of such systems plays a critical role. As can be seen from the literature review, the security test is often ignored when designing an embedded system, in particular when considering the in-pipe inspection robot designs.

4.4 Hypothesized Solution: Cloud Robotics–Assisted In-Pipe Inspection

As can be seen from the literature review conducted in Section 4.3.1, human intervention is often needed to facilitate the coordination between the cyber and the physical sides as intruders may simultaneously attack both sides to make them conflict with each other to bypass at least one of them. Returning to our CPPS environment, traditionally these types of routine inspection and securing activities are usually carried out by human beings based on maintenance plans and condition monitoring techniques. The inspection tools used are thus dominated by rather simple cable-based video technology that does not sufficiently comply with the qualified inspection demands. For example, the authors of [37] claimed that the bottlenecks of these inspection systems are the use of a wire and the limitation of the range of operation. In addition, the human errors that occur during inspection and maintenance tasks could lead to a high risk of accidents [38].

For all of these reasons, the application of robots for inspection and maintenance, or more generally, ubiquitous robotics [39], is considered a new technical means for complex working processes in hazardous environments. Nevertheless, based on the investigation conducted in Section 4.3.2, it can be concluded that the current in-pipe inspection robot design rarely takes security issues into consideration. Bearing this in mind, in this study, we intend to introduce cloud robotics as a potential solution.

The relationship between robots and cloud computing is the basis for the use of the phrase *cloud robotics* in describing the robots-in-the-cloud [40–42]. It is an emerging research area that aims to move parts of the robot control program into the cloud, but focusing on different aspects, such as storing and sharing knowledge [43], learning from each other via cooperation so as to adapt to their surrounding environment [44], off-loading complex computations, remotely operating partly autonomous robots [45], and so on. A recent survey by Goldberg gives a good overview of this topic [46].

4.5 Security Challenges Relevant to Our Hypothetical Solution

In general, the future of information and communication technologies (ICTs) can be characterized by terms such as *ubiquitous computing* [47], *pervasive computing* [48], *ambient intelligence* [49], and the *post-personal computer (PC) era* [13]. Essentially, these terms are the same with only slightly different aspects of future information technology. Overall, two fundamental technologies are necessary for next-generation ICT systems [13], namely, embedded systems and communication technologies. In line with this statement, the potential security challenges that confront our focal scenario are classified into the following three categories in which the first two groups are mainly linked to embedded systems, while the third group finds itself linked with communication technologies.

4.5.1 Hardware Side

A computer has three major hardware components: a CPU, internal memory, and input/output (I/O) devices [50]. In simple terms, the CPU is the brain of a computer, the memory is used to carry out arithmetic operations and store the intermediate results during the execution of a program, and the I/O devices refer to the devices that communicate with the outside world such as keyboards, mouses, and printers.

Generally, they are all directly or indirectly connected to the motherboard since they must all communicate with the CPU. In that regard, hardware security, which involves storing passwords on a chip, restricting unauthorized remote access, replacing vulnerable software with secure hardware, and so on, must be protected against damage or attack [50]. For example, in modern embedded systems, the memory plays an important role and therefore requires a stringent worst-case performance guarantee. To meet this goal, a well-known solution is to make some or all writable regions of memory nonexecutable to prevent attacks, such as Sasser and Blaster worms. Moreover, hardware encryption and protection can also help to protect unauthorized access to data stored on computers and flash drives or to remove data in the event that a hacker is trying to break the password. Also, if the cloud-computing concept is to be implemented, then the hardware security issue is the most common concern, since hackers may bring up their own virtual machine on the same physical hardware. In addition, cloud computing represents a major change to the definition of "good" security, since what is "secure" for one organization may be viewed as inadequate by another organization with a lower appetite for risk.

4.5.2 Software Side

In short, an operating system (OS) is a set of programs that work together to control a computer's hardware resources and provide common services for application software [13]. In an embedded computer system, the OS is thus often regarded as the most important type of system software. Normally, without a properly installed OS, an end user cannot run an application program on a computer. Nowadays, the security of an OS is often treated as one of the most important information security topics. Typically, there are two logical questions often asked by a layman [51]: Is there any possibility to build a fully secure OS? and If so, why has this not been done yet?

Theoretically, the answer to the first question is "yes," as long as the software itself is not too complicated. In terms of the second question, one has to take the following factors into account: First, the disposal cost of shifting from an old system to a new one. Second, features eat the system security. Unnecessary features of an OS mean more complexity, more lines of code, and more potential bugs, making it more prone to security failures.

In practice, there are two types of security policies related to an OS [51]:

- *Discretionary access control policy*: In general, the majority of OSs give individual users the option to determine who has the right to read and write their files and other objects. Although this model works fine in many environments, there are some situations where tighter security is required.
- *Mandatory access control policy*: Where the flow of information is regulated to ensure that it does not suffer from data breach.

In summary, the key to establishing the desired secure system is to keep the security model at the heart of an OS as simple as possible. By doing that, developers can actually grasp the whole system, and thus resist all deviations that lead to adding new features.

4.5.3 Network Side

Nowadays, data communication is regarded as one of the fastest-developing technology areas in the world. In short, the purpose of data communication is to provide an efficient and reliable data exchange method between two end nodes or hosts. Since the functionalities of many organizations are largely dependent on the effectiveness, efficiency, and power of the Internet, which likewise is affected by the efficient flow of data communications, the importance of developing a suitable computer network protocol cannot be overstated. In the literature, various types of protocol models can be employed to facilitate message composition or receiving. Among these, the most widely used model is transmission control protocol/Internet protocol (TCP/IP), which offers reliable software that enables communications between diverse vendor equipment, and is now the building block for a proper Internet operation.

The enabling components and the fundamental working principles of TCP/IP are out of the scope of this study. Here, we only outline the basic security concerns that are threatening the safe use of wired and wireless networks. With an ever-increasing number of computer systems constantly connected to the Internet, the number of malicious users and attackers has also grown rapidly. Under such circumstances, network administrators, who are responsible for keeping a system efficient and secure, are placed under a great deal of security-related pressure when their system (including confidential data and the networking infrastructure) is exposed to malicious users of the Internet. In practice, system developers adopt various network security standards and mechanisms to prevent their network from being attacked by different levels of hackers or malicious users. Among these approaches, one frequently used mechanism is an Internet firewall. A firewall refers to hardware or software or a combination of both, which can monitor and control the transmission of digital information packets as they pass through a certain boundary of a network. However, simply introducing firewalls does not mean that a network is fully protected. Although the firewall mechanism enjoys a vast amount of advantages, it still suffers some constraints and limitations as outlined next.

- A firewall is useless if attacks can bypass it. In other words, if attacks do not have to go through the firewall, the protection provided by firewalls will be very limited.
- Firewalls have difficulty dealing with the threats posed by betrayers, traitors, or unwitting network users.
- Firewalls are not effective in preventing corporate spies from stealing sensitive data.
- Firewalls fail to stop the transfer of virus-infected software or files.
- Data-driven attacks are beyond the scope of the protection of firewalls.

Essentially, there are two basic policies that can be employed in designing a firewall management program:

- Default-deny policy
- Default-allow policy

Of these two methods, the first one is the most secure approach; however, the second approach is the most widely used in practice. The designer has to find a trade-off between these two methodologies.

In summary, a firewall plays an important role in conventional network security architecture as it controls most of the network's ingoing and outgoing traffic. In principle, a firewall is a must-have for most network systems.

4.6 Other Design Challenges

Although in-pipe robot research has enjoyed great success over the past few years, one of the major challenges that is still faced by academicians and practitioners is that most of the existing inspection robots were constructed by the research institutions, which meant that their use by the end users was not fully explored. Their failure was due to the lack of understanding of the nature of multidisciplinary design and the lack of tools to support it. In addition, it is crucial to understand that design does not actually start with a drawing made on a kind of computer-aided design (CAD) package such as SolidWorks® [52], though with the rapid advancement of CAD packages [53], designers are capable of beginning their designs much earlier than ever before. Additionally, the more time and effort that designers spend on articulating the problem definition and understanding the consumer needs statement, the less frequent the need for iteration. Also, as designing is a highly creative and knowledge-intensive process, the designer will face a multitude of obstacles before coming up with a suitable design. Among these barriers, the incompleteness and the dynamics of design knowledge deserve a mention.

4.6.1 Incompleteness of Design Knowledge

When designers set off to accomplish a new design task, the usable knowledge set for them is often limited and incomplete. For example, the mixture of raw data, unclustered information, and meaningful knowledge often imposes immense pressure on designers' research ability to differentiate these influential factors from each other. In order to reduce the degree of incompleteness of design knowledge, one solution called Big6™ was given by Eisenburg and Berkowitz [54,55] in which six categories of research skills have to be developed, that is, (1) task definition such as what data or information or both need to be collected; (2) information-seeking strategies such as how will you go about seeking the information required; (3) location and access such as where you collect all the information; (4) use of information to extract the information that is needed; (5) synthesis, such as to process and present this information in the final knowledge; and (6) evaluation. However, this approach is only suitable to address problems with a low degree of complexity.

4.6.2 Dynamics of Design Knowledge

Apart from the incompleteness, another inevitable characteristic is the dynamic nature of knowledge structures. This challenge could raise the following research questions: What are the dynamics? What are the carriers of the dynamics? How should the dynamics be managed? How should the dynamics be adapted during the development? To answer these questions, a large amount of research work is being conducted, For example, the authors of [56] addressed the emerging trends in the collective dynamics found in knowledge networks. The study in [57] proposed a model for the information spreading process on dynamic social networks. However, the present results are far from satisfactory though some promising progress has been made.

4.7 Proposed Methodology

Bearing in mind the abovementioned study motivation and the various challenges encountered, there is an urgent need for a logical procedure that can be followed to meet a specific need. From the knowledge management point of view, several authors (e.g., [58–60]) are convinced that owning knowledge-based resources can influence the achievement of a successful design. As per this statement, the cloud robotics design for in-pipe inspection is no exception. As an embedded computer system, millions of integrated elementary electronic components make cloud robotics a complex system. In this situation, the inherent hierarchical nature of most complex systems can help us to understand their composition. Basically, a hierarchical system can be described as a set of interrelated subsystems, each of which, in turn, are hierarchical in structure until the lowest level of the elementary system can be reached [15]. In this study, we will follow this trend since the hierarchical description of a complex system is essential to its design. In the light of this statement, the system developer only needs to deal with one particular system level at a time. At each level, the designer is mainly concerned with the correlated structure, function, and the corresponding behavior:

- *Structure*: The interrelated way that components are connected.
- *Function*: The manner in which each individual component is operated as part of the structure.
- *Behavior*: Each level's behavior is dependent only on its lower level's simplified, abstracted characterization.

Since the control system, locomotion mechanisms, actuators, and suction structures involved in in-pipe inspection robot design are inevitably different and complex, it is necessary for designers to formulate customer requirements from the knowledge perspective to increase the retrievability of various types of knowledge. Bearing this in mind, in this chapter, we attempt to use a formal knowledge-level model, that is, the purpose-function-working space-structure-behavior (PFWSB) framework [61], as a vehicle to address our focal issues.

4.7.1 What Is the PFWSB Framework?

In the literature, a large body of integrated design knowledge modeling or frameworks or both has been proposed. For instance, one of the most famous design representative models is called the function-behavior-structure (FBS) framework, originally proposed by Gero [62] in 1990. Since then, different knowledge-based systems have been developed and used in various domains. One example is an integration modeling called *requirement-function-behavior-structure*, which was presented in [63] for improving Gero's FBS conceptual design framework. Meanwhile, a knowledge-based logistics strategy system was developed by [64], which is used to enhance the effectiveness of logistics. Interested readers are referred to [65] and [66] for more details regarding the previous studies and the current research status relative to the knowledge-intensive collaborative design modeling. Among various example frameworks, a recently proposed PFWSB framework [61] has drawn the author's attention due to its capability for systematically dealing with design. In other words, this framework can be utilized to represent and understand the nature of design from both the object- and the process-oriented perspective.

As we can see from Figure 4.1, a typical conceptual design process can be generalized, via the PFWSB framework, to the following factors:

- Three fundamental variables, that is, function (*F*), behavior (*B*), and structure (*S*)
- Four extended variables, that is, purpose (*P*), environment (*E*), constraint (*C*), and working space (*W*) and
- A bunch of design descriptions (*D*), which typically involve seven classes of design activities, for example, formulation, search, synthesis, analysis, evaluation, documentation, and reformulation.

In the following subsubsections, we provide a brief description of these factors.

4.7.1.1 Purpose

In general, purpose refers to a series of attempted actions, which will eventually lead to the all-round fulfillment of a client's (or agent's in general term) requirement(s). As mentioned in [61],

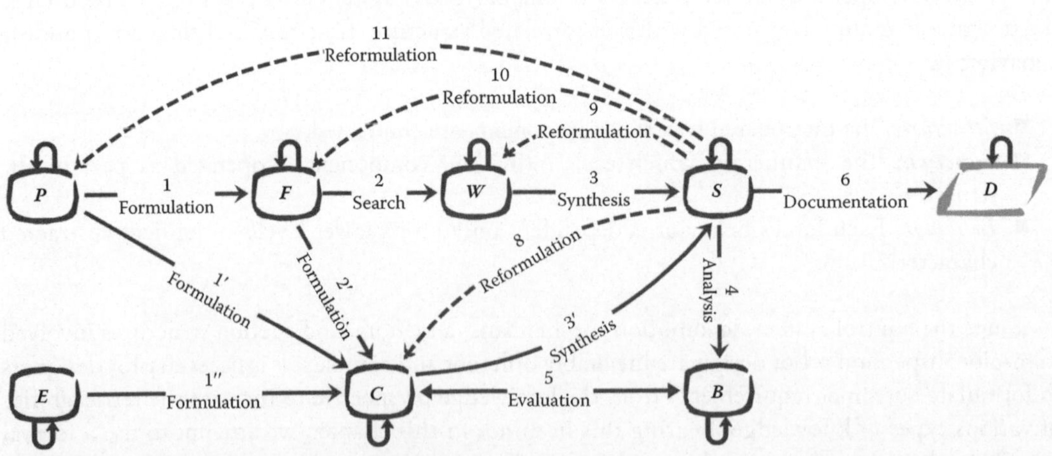

Figure 4.1 The general form of the PFWSB framework.

because the "purpose" is more action oriented, so it possesses a much clearer meaning than that of a "goal." This can also be witnessed from the psychological point of view [67].

In the PFWSB framework, a purpose is denoted via Equation 4.1 [61]:

$$P = (P_G, P_A, P_o), \tag{4.1}$$

where P_G (=(P_{GF}, P_{GC})) stands for the goal of an agent, in which P_{GF} refers to the technical function of an artifact (e.g., performing in-pipe inspection, which is the concern of this study), and P_{GC} is used to represent the nontechnical function (e.g., easy to be manipulated), while P_A refers to the actions sequentially performed by an agent for reaching the goal (e.g., start the power supply for an in-pipe inspection robot, send it through the targeted pipe, and identify the potential defected position), and P_o indicates the desired artifact, that is, a miniature in-pipe inspection robot, required by an agent.

4.7.1.2 Function

Once the purpose has been identified, you need to start developing an idea on how the product could function, that is, to convert your customer requirements into "functions." The overall function of a product is the relationship between its input and its output.

In the PFWSB framework, the function can be expressed via Equation 4.2 [61]:

$$F = (F_{VN}, F_{FLOW}), \tag{4.2}$$

where F_{VN} represents the name of a function in which a verb–noun pair is used for the purpose of formulating design problems in a solution-neutral term so that it can be turned into a function (e.g., rotating a camera), and F_{FLOW} refers to a system's input and output flow (e.g., data flow and image flow).

4.7.1.3 Behavior

The behavior is the characteristic that enables an artifact to achieve its function. In other words, the behavior describes how the function behaves to accomplish its function.

In the PFWSB framework, behavior is defined through Equation 4.3 [61]:

$$B = (B_D, B_U), \tag{4.3}$$

where B_D denotes a desirable behavior and B_U denotes an undesirable behavior. Normally, by following certain allocated working principles of a system, a desirable behavior refers to a welcomed state variation triggered by a given input flow. Under the umbrella of the current study theme, a typical example of such a desired behavior is the moving performance of a wheel (forward or backward driven by an appropriate type of motor) underneath the engineered robot platform. On the contrary, an undesirable behavior often implies the variation of a state that usually has unpleasant side effects on the overall performance of a system. When dealing with in-pipe robot inspection, a common example of such undesirable behavior is a robot scout getting stuck in a corner inside the inspected pipe.

4.7.1.4 Structure

The structure means the physical construction and the elements of a complex system, which include the features, attributes, and topological relations. In the PFWSB framework, structure is represented by Equation 4.4 [61]:

$$S = (S_E, S_P, S_H), \tag{4.4}$$

where S_E stands for the elements that together constitute a system; S_P denotes the property of each element found in such a system; and S_H represents the historical information relative to the system (as a whole) and the individual element, respectively.

4.7.1.5 Environment

This theme has many variations, but the basic idea is that every project has some elements of social, cultural, and legislative constraints and some type of natural phenomenon to overcome, and requires some amount of indispensable parts to support. For instance, remanufactured engines share a significant market segment in European countries such as Germany, due to their environmentally friendly and cost-saving benefits. Nevertheless, due to the lack of relevant knowledge from the customer side and the corresponding legislation from the government side, the market performance of the same product is very poor in other countries around the world, such as China and Southern African countries. Bearing this in mind, the introduction of the environment concept at the early design stage plays a vital role in accomplishing a successful artifact. Accordingly, in the PFWSB framework, instead of treating the environment as an ordinary design constraint, it is defined as a key variable via Equation 4.5 [61]:

$$E = (E_S, E_N, E_L, E_O), \tag{4.5}$$

where E_S stands for the constraints from social perspective (e.g., legislation, culture, and the composition of population groups); E_N represents the constrains from the natural perspective (e.g., weather, geographical location, and temperature); E_L denotes the constraints from a product life-cycle operations perspective (e.g., usage and maintenance); and finally, E_O is utilized to describe an environmental entity that is essential for an artifact to work properly (e.g., a power supply is crucial for a remotely controlled in-pipe inspection robot).

4.7.1.6 Constraint

Constraints are a set of specifications that have to be met by designers during the process of making their corresponding design decisions. In the PFWSB framework, the variable of constraint can be defined through Equation 4.6 [61]:

$$C = (C_{PF}, C_{PQ}, C_E, C_P), \tag{4.6}$$

where C_{PF} denotes the value of a certain functional property (e.g., moving forward at the speed of 10 cm/s during the course of in-pipe inspection), C_{PQ} indicates the variation of a product's function during its life cycle, C_E stands for the environment-related constraints (e.g., the height of an obstacle is less than 10 mm), and C_P represents the constraints relative to users' nontechnical functions such as the budget (e.g., no more than 5000 local currency) and the time line for the final deliverables (e.g., by the end of March 2014).

4.7.1.7 Working Space

In the proposed PFWSB framework, the working space is referred to as the accumulated knowledge for bolstering the search for the scientific consequences, disciplinary knowledge, and/or working principles that meet various functional needs. Mathematically, the variable of working space is interpreted via Equation 4.7 [61]:

$$W = \left(W_E, W_D, W_W\right), \tag{4.7}$$

where the effects disclosed through scientific investigations are denoted by W_E. In general, the effect is a description of the kinds of consequences that derive from the observation of certain phenomenon, for example, the singularities observed in analyzing parallel mechanisms. Briefly, when a manipulator reaches its singular configurations, different amounts of degrees of freedom will be lost, which can escalate the status of the manipulator to out of control [68]. A category of disciplinary knowledge (e.g., a brush-type direct-current [dc] motor), which is indicated by W_D, develops a torque when a current flows in the rotor coils through the magnetic field created by the stator. The torque is thus the result of two equal but opposite forces acting on the sides of the coil. Mathematically, this force can be expressed as $\mathbf{F} = \mathbf{I} \times \mathbf{B}$, where $\mathbf{I}$ represents the current vector, $\mathbf{B}$ [69] denotes the magnetic field vector, and W_W represents a group of working principles (e.g., the behavior of an ideal operational amplifier, a common component found in many control circuits, defined by three golden rules [70]).

4.7.1.8 Design Description

In the PFWSB, a design description is usually the result of a series of interactions among different variables (e.g., F, B, S, P, E, C, and W). By grouping these design activities as per their attributes, seven categories can be further defined as shown in Figure 4.2 [61].

4.7.2 Why PFWSB Framework?

In general, it is not difficult to observe from the design literature that a typical engineering design can be abstracted as either a function-effect-structure (FES) model (e.g., [71]) or the FBS (e.g., [62,72–74]). Under the umbrella of the FES model, one function is typically treated as a kind of effect, which in turn determines a certain working principle. Once a set of working principles is obtained, a form can be synthesized to construct the final structure of a desired artifact. In terms of the FBS, a conceptual schema (i.e., a design prototype) is used to provide a framework for storing and processing design knowledge according to four categories: function, behavior, structure, and their relations. However, implementations with both models are still limited to routine design. Other factors, such as environmental variables and the working principles, which the PFWSB framework pursues, need further investigation before the design prototype can be implemented in a system.

Another reason for employing the PFWSB is that it clearly shows designers the knowledge flow between the different involved parties, in particular the cooperation and collaboration required

Design activities	Variables involved	Design descriptions
Step 1: Formulation	$P \rightarrow F$ $P \rightarrow C$ $E \rightarrow C$ $F \rightarrow C$	Transforming the description of the customer's purpose and environment factors into the description of the designer agent's function and constraints.
Step 2: Search	$F \rightarrow W$	Searching the required effects and working principles that meet the function demands.
Step 3: Synthesis	$W \rightarrow S$ $C \rightarrow S$	Reflecting the effects, working principles, and constraints in the product structure design.
Step 4: Analysis	$S \rightarrow B$	Deducing the potential behavior from the designed structure.
Step 5: Evaluation	$B \leftrightarrow C$	Comparing the acquired behavior with the constraints and making a decision to generate the final design or to obtain new knowledge set.
Step 6: Documentation	$S \rightarrow D$	Recording the design description to assist the final design.
Step 7: Reformulation	$S \rightarrow S'$ $S \rightarrow C'$ $S \rightarrow W'$ $S \rightarrow F'$ $S \rightarrow P'$	Decision making of establishing a new S. Decision making of creating a new C. Decision making of composing a new W. Discussing and selecting a new F. Discussing and choosing a new P.

Figure 4.2 Design activities involved in the PFWSB framework.

between multidisciplinary design teams. Traditionally, because of a lack of common methodologies for representing and understanding the multidisciplinary knowledge, designers have had to overcome many inherent barriers, which prevent useful knowledge moving efficiently and effectively between different parties. However, with a unified knowledge framework that is representative and understanding, the PFWSB can help designers pinpoint the missing linkages of knowledge, which will in turn yield many benefits including communication time saving and design progress accelerating.

Additionally, during the design process, the status of the design knowledge keeps changing from scattered state to consolidated state, exhibiting a highly evolving feature. Through the use of the PFWSB framework, this process can be illustrated in a meaningful and efficient way, as shown in Figure 4.3.

As we can see in Figure 4.3, each variable group can be treated as a knowledge set. Initially, when designers start the design task, the knowledge status is incomplete and unorganized. For instance, in the PFWSB, the complete knowledge set regarding the constraint is expressed as $C = (C_{PF}, C_{PQ}, C_E, C_P)$ [61], while in the situation of knowledge incompleteness, some information may be unknown in advance, which makes the expression of constraint $C = (C_{PF}, ?, ?, C_P)$. As the project advances, an additional knowledge set, for example, $C^* = (?, C_{PQ}, C_E, ?)$, will be injected into the design-in-progress process. Once all of these knowledge sets are clustered and interrelated, a complete knowledge set will emerge.

4.8 How to Use PFWSB to Understand and Represent the Knowledge

As one can see from the abovementioned descriptions, the PFWSB framework paves the way for dealing with a complex engineering design problem from the perspective of a set of resolvable subcomponents. Under the umbrella of the PFWSB, the movement of knowledge and its corresponding evolution are both able to be described in an explicit manner. However, one may still wonder how the PFWSB can actually be used to understand and represent the knowledge. To clear up such confusions, for the rest of this section, we will apply the PFWSB to the task of understanding and representing design knowledge.

In the literature, a design activity, or more formally a decision node (DN), can be expressed as a knowledge-obtaining process [54]. This process is first triggered by a customer-required design task. Then, through implementing a series of relative information seeking, gathering, analyzing, and synthesizing strategies, the initial input of an incomplete form of knowledge is transformed to a more useful knowledge output form. The simplified version of this complex process is illustrated in Figure 4.4.

As shown in Figure 4.4, there are two types of knowledge streams flowing in and out of each DN, namely, the horizontal knowledge stream (HKS) and the vertical knowledge stream (VKS). In terms of HKSs, they often have a direct I/O relationship, while for VKSs, they often contain partially usable information, which means they can only help to increase the input knowledge stream's completeness degree.

As mentioned in [75], the intrinsic properties and the exhibited flowing characteristics are often differentiable among different knowledge categories. For instance, the implicit degree of tacit knowledge is very high and thus it cannot flow at a similar speed or travel at a comparable distance compared with its counterpart, that is, the explicit knowledge. Accordingly, the introduction of the PFWSB framework can help designers in this regard by representing design knowledge

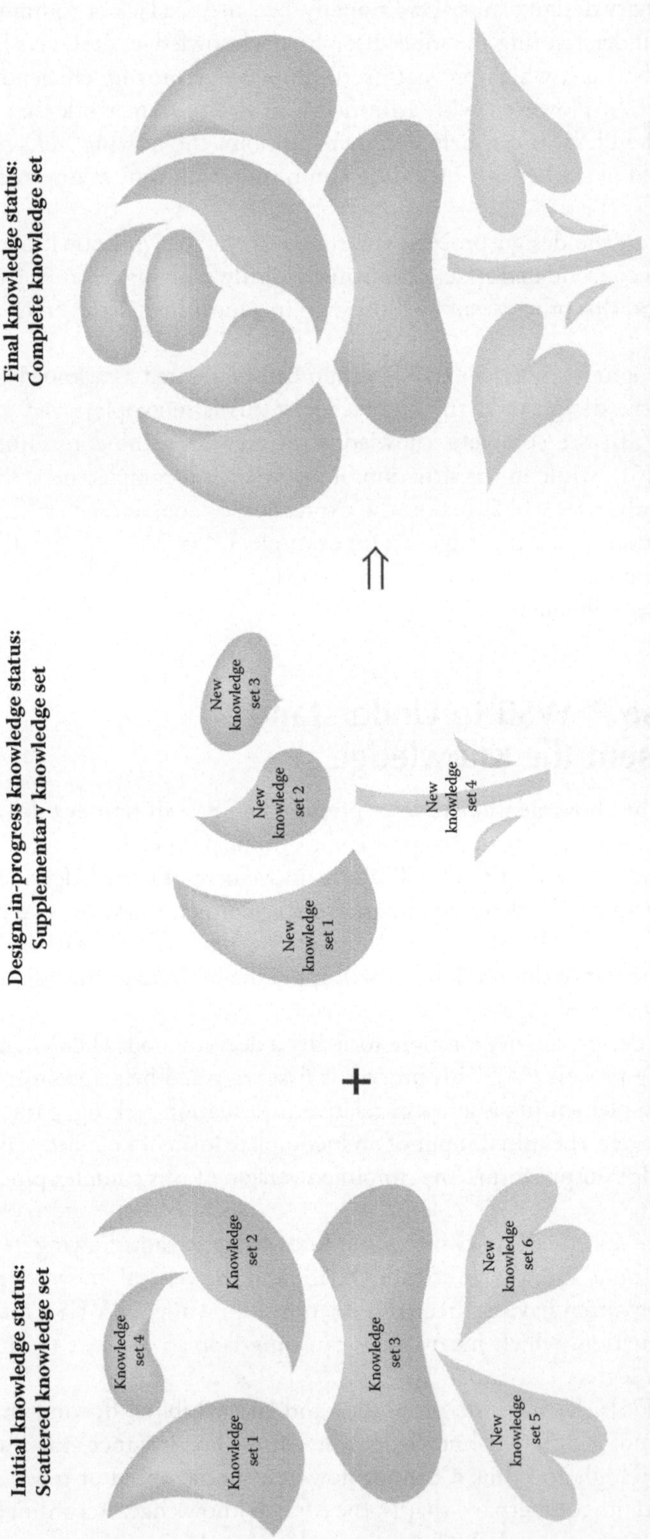

Figure 4.3 The evolution of the knowledge set status.

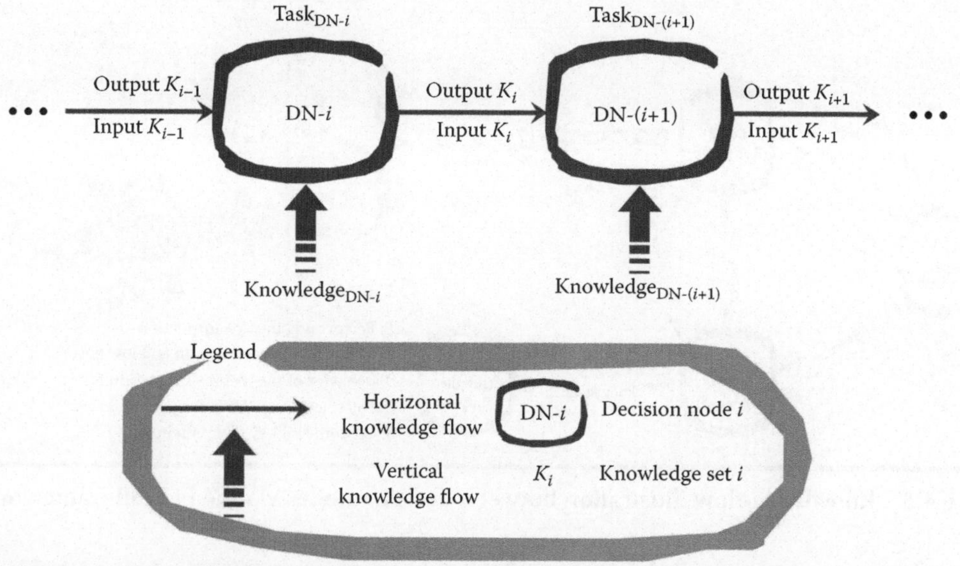

Figure 4.4 The knowledge stream between any two decision nodes.

in a more extensive and structured way. In the design literature, there is a common agreement that the knowledge sets relative to the design object and the design process, respectively, are two important knowledge categories, which often play a key role in leading to a final successful product design [76].

4.9 Representing and Understanding the Knowledge Flow during the Conceptual Design Stage via PFWSB Framework

In this work, a case study of an in-pipe inspection robot conceptual design process is introduced, while the PFWSB framework is utilized to show how the knowledge flow about a real-world design requirement can be successfully understood and described.

As depicted in Figure 4.5, some key steps of the knowledge transferring process can be summarized as follows.

- *Step 1*: A company (denoted by DN-1) has many pipeline infrastructures that have to be periodically maintained. Therefore, a responsible person from the company sends a request to a university research group (represented by DN-2) for a set of possible conceptual designs that can fulfill the company's requirements. An example of this kind of communication is illustrated in Figure 4.6a.

Figure 4.6 a shows the virtual (but reasonable) beginning of a robot design project that has been requested by a customer, Daniel. He highlights the purpose of building a robot platform, that is, in-pipe inspection. Daniel also suggests a cost requirement and the robot size specification. After going through this e-mail, Bo (the designer in this case) starts to think about the project plan proposal and the anticipated specifications for Daniel. The subsequent activities might include preliminary concepts, embodiment designs, key enabling components (both hardware

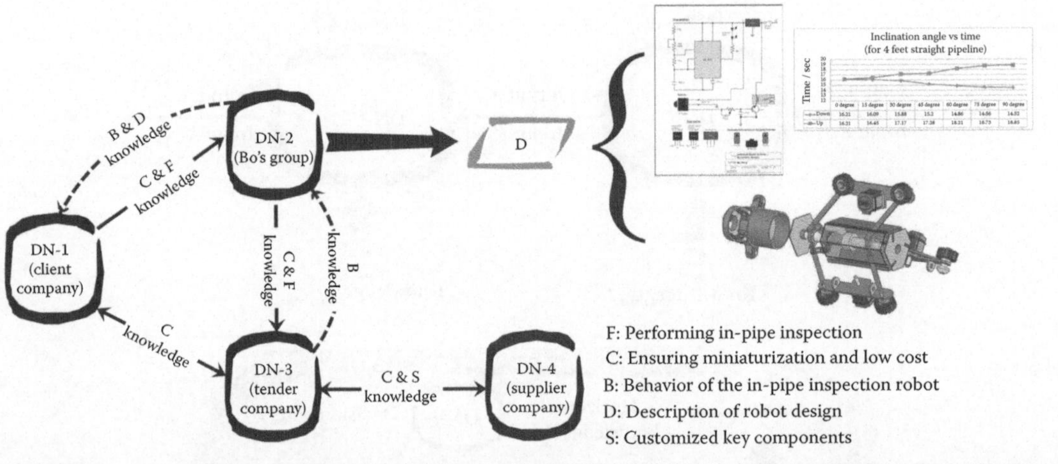

Figure 4.5 Knowledge-flow illustration between decision nodes via the PFWSB framework.

and software), and a quotation for Daniel. The detailed design, possible manufacturing options, and maintenance strategies are also on Bo's to-do list (see Figure 4.6b for an illustration).

In this initial stage, the process of knowledge transition occurs continuously during the course of several rounds of follow-up, face-to-face meetings and e-communications. A typical example that can be found is some accumulated knowledge such as inspecting the in-pipe condition (i.e., the knowledge of function) and ensuring the miniaturization and low cost (i.e., assigned constraints knowledge) flowing from DN-1 to DN-2. Also, design engineers may consult some sources to determine what is already available in the market and what they have to offer, such as technical and trade journals, research reports, and the Internet. This kind of knowledge flow can normally be viewed as "knowledge input."

For instance, computer architecture often refers to the structure and behavior of the various functional modules of the computer and how they interact to provide the processing needs of the user [15]. Over the past decades, electronic computers have gone through five generations of development. Although the division of generations is marked primarily by sharp changes in hardware and software technology, most of the features that were introduced in the earlier generations have been passed to the later generations, that is, evolutionary rather than revolutionary changes. Among others, the most remarkable milestones is a design (i.e., the architecture of a stored-program computer) proposed by John von Neumann and his colleagues at Princeton in 1946.

General speaking, the Neumann computer architecture involves a CPU (i.e., arithmetic logic unit and program control unit), memory and storage, I/O devices, and a bus with address, data, and control signals that connect the components [50]. Nowadays, the majority of computers still stick to this architecture. However, if we look at this dominant model from a security perspective, some drawbacks can easily be pinpointed. In a classical Neumann model, all components are connected to one single-system bus, which consists of a control-, data-, and address-bus. This type of structure means that as long as the intruders can break into a system from any network location, the whole system will be taken over.

To deal with these security threats, a recently introduced modified Neumann model [50], where an independent system bus is allocated to a computer system's network communication component, is introduced into our embedded system design. A detailed description of this new computer architecture model can be found in [50].

From: Daniel B. Dean
Date: Thu., Nov 7, 2013, at 5:01pm
To: Bo Xing <bo.xing@university.ac.za>
Subject: Meeting to discuss a robot system for in pipe inspection

Dear Dr. Xing,

Following the meeting with my line manager, I would like to meet with you so that we can agree on the possible in-pipe inspection robot designs that are needed for our company. Miniature and low cost are necessary.

Here are some dates that I am open (we probably need about 2 hrs, max 3):

Fri, 15 Nov at Rosherville from 10h00 to 12h00 (my office);
Fri, 22 Nov at Melo Park from 12h00 to 15h00 (we can meet at the reception);
Thu, 28 Nov any time at either Rosherville or Melo Park.

Best Regards,
Daniel

From: Bo Xing
Date: Fri., Nov 8, 2013, at 8:02am
To: Daniel B. Dean <ddean@powerplant.co.za>
Subject: Re: Meeting to discuss a robot system for in-pipe inspection

Dear Daniel,

I will drop over on Fri, 22 Nov at 12h00am. See you at the reception

Regards,
Bo

(a)

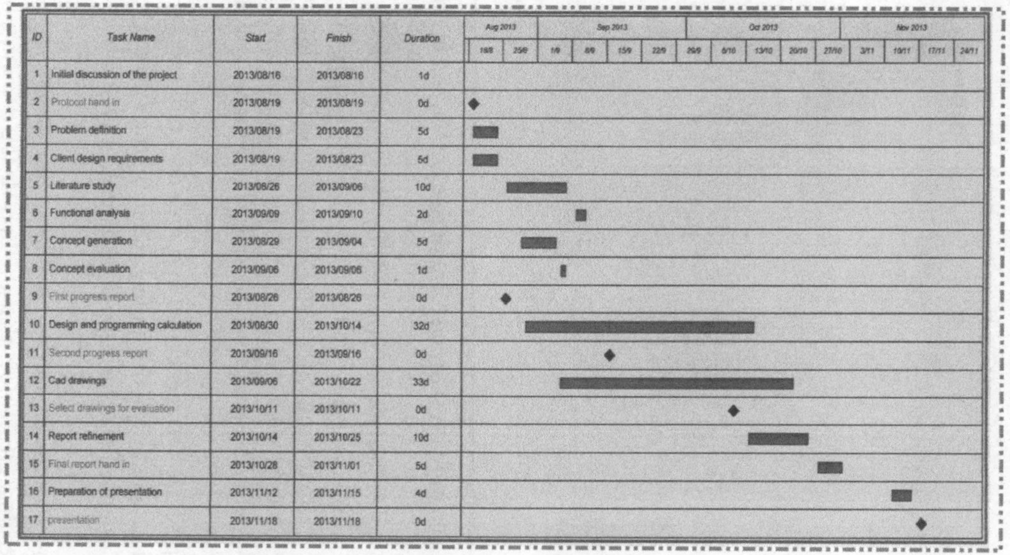

ID	Task Name	Start	Finish	Duration
1	Initial discussion of the project	2013/08/16	2013/08/16	1d
2	Protocol hand in	2013/08/19	2013/08/19	0d
3	Problem definition	2013/08/19	2013/08/23	5d
4	Client design requirements	2013/08/19	2013/08/23	5d
5	Literature study	2013/08/26	2013/09/06	10d
6	Functional analysis	2013/09/09	2013/09/10	2d
7	Concept generation	2013/08/29	2013/09/04	5d
8	Concept evaluation	2013/09/06	2013/09/06	1d
9	First progress report	2013/08/26	2013/08/26	0d
10	Design and programming calculation	2013/08/30	2013/10/14	32d
11	Second progress report	2013/09/16	2013/09/16	0d
12	Cad drawings	2013/09/06	2013/10/22	33d
13	Select drawings for evaluation	2013/10/11	2013/10/11	0d
14	Report refinement	2013/10/14	2013/10/25	10d
15	Final report hand in	2013/10/28	2013/11/01	5d
16	Preparation of presentation	2013/11/12	2013/11/15	4d
17	presentation	2013/11/18	2013/11/18	0d

(b)

Figure 4.6 (a) A fictional e-mail exchange scenario and (b) an imaginary Gantt chart regarding the expected design task breakdown.

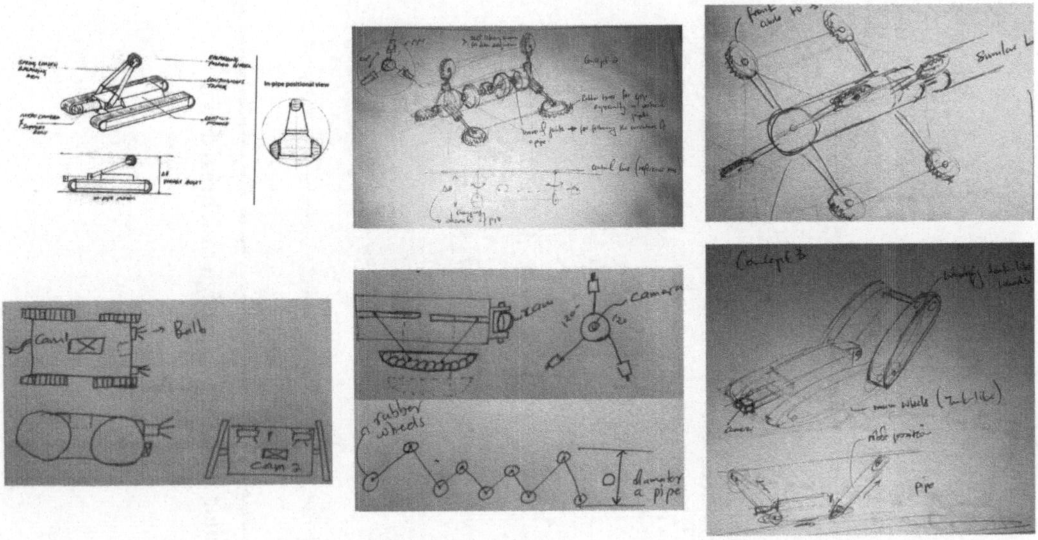

Figure 4.7 A glimpse of design activities: brainstorm designs delivered by Bo and his group.

Based on some preliminary requirements provided by the client, a series of literature studies, necessary calculations, and brainstorms (see Figure 4.7) are conducted by Bo and his group. For example, they will ask the following questions: What actions should the product perform during its lifetime and operation? What function do we try to accomplish with the inspection? These questions should not be defined too narrowly, because the designer will eliminate acceptable solutions.

Once a number of concepts have been generated in sufficient detail, a new query may arise: Are the components contained in these designs manufacturable by the selected tender? Under these circumstances, a further knowledge flow will happen as described in Step 2.

- *Step 2*: After consulting with the chosen tender company, Bo and his group can further tailor their conceptual designs. Please note that the knowledge exchange between DN-2 (i.e., Bo's group) and DN-3 (i.e., the tender company) are actually the anticipated robot design's structural and behavioral knowledge. This stage does not yet include any details (e.g., the tolerances or dimensions), but it will begin to illustrate a clear definition of a part, how it will work, and how it interfaces with the rest of the parts in the product assembly. Accordingly, if the DN-1 can notify DN-2 regarding the manufacturing capability of DN-3, the above-mentioned knowledge movement would simply disappear. In the case of a complex robot design, which may contain different mechanical, electrical, and electronics subassemblies, one or more nodes (e.g., DN-4) will be introduced as the supplier to provide the necessary knowledge in terms of part availability. The characteristics of these parts (e.g., customized or off-the-shelf; see Figure 4.8 for an illustration) will have a great influence on whether the final design can meet the customer's requirement.

After acquiring a sufficient amount of knowledge from DN-3, some initial conceptual designs will be eliminated and a further comparison among various selected designs will be carried out until a satisfactory conceptual design has been chosen. An example of the concept's design rating and selection is depicted in Figure 4.9a.

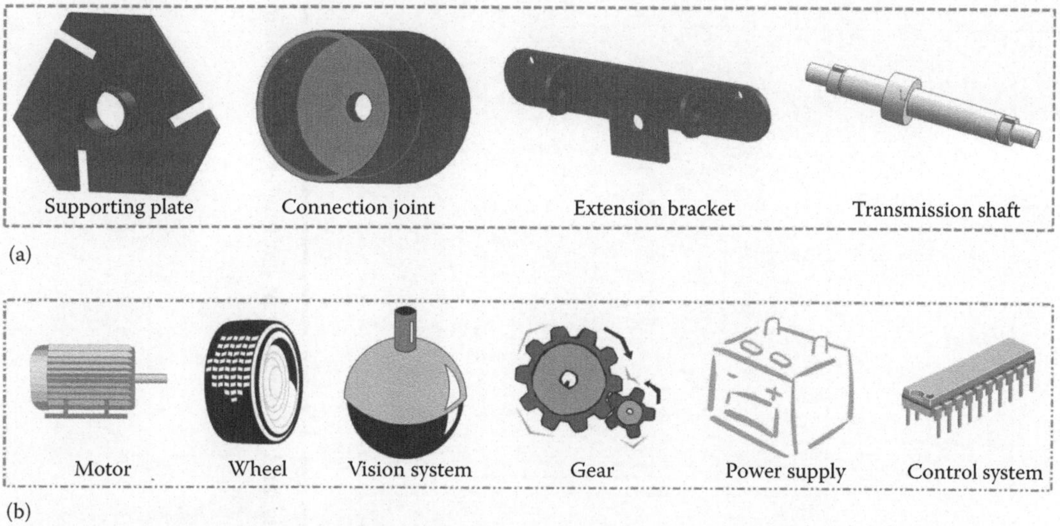

Figure 4.8 Examples of (a) customized parts and (b) off-the-shelf parts.

- *Step 3*: In the alternative scenario explained in Step 2 (i.e., the manufacturing capability of DN-3 is well known by DN-1), the PFWSB framework can also be utilized to represent the knowledge transfer between these two nodes. The knowledge categories involved in such an interchange include constraint and behavioral knowledge.
- *Step 4*: Once the DN-2 has acquired a certain amount of knowledge from downstream parties, the synthesis phase of the design will be completed and the analysis phase, for example, cost analysis and component parameter calculation (see Figure 4.9b and c for an illustration), will start.

Often, the analysis requires a concept design to be altered or redefined and then reanalyzed, which means that the activities involved at this stage are constantly shifting between synthesis and analysis. Finally, when a finalized conceptual design is generated, it will be submitted to the client company for a review. In this case study, a hybrid type of inspection robot is designed and its assembly drawing is depicted in Figure 4.10.

4.10 Discussion

In this study, a recently developed ontological framework, namely the PFWSB, has been employed to assist in the knowledge-flow representation and comprehension during the in-pipe inspection robot design process. The main contributions achieved by this research are summarized as follows, while the highlighted future work can also be found thereafter.

4.10.1 Contributions

One of the major contributions obtained via this research is that it creates a more detailed case study for demonstrating the suitability of the PFWSB framework. As mentioned in [61], more case studies are needed to further verify the feasibility of the PFWSB framework. The in-pipe inspection robot case presented in this study actually fills this research gap to some extent.

Criteria	Concept 1	Concept 2	Concept 3	Concept 4
Manufacturability	3	3	3	3
Compactness	4	3	4	4
Manufacturing less cost	3	3	3	3
Diameter adjusting	1	3	3	3
Maintainability	3	3	3	3
Robustness	2	3	4	3
Assembling ease	2	3	3	2
Size	3	3	3	2
Operation ease	2	3	3	3
Inclined pipes	2	3	4	4
Maneuverability	3	3	3	4
Total points	28	33	36	34

(a)

Part	Material	Unit price	Manufacturing	Quantity	Total cost
Shaft 1	30x130 rod	60	30	1	90
Link holder	5x60 plate	40	20	1	60
Link 1	40x5x2 plate	12	8	3	60
Link 2	20x5x2 plate	12	7	3	57
Spring 1	Wire 10 turns	6	4	1	10
Link 1 1	40x5x2 plate	10	4	3	42
Wheel shaft 1	1x2 rod	2	2	6	24
Wheel 1	17x1rod	6	4	6	60
Wheel rubber tire		13	7	6	120
Link 3	70x20x5 plate	9	6	3	45
Servo motor			150	3	390
Gear 1	Steel		30	2	60
Worm gear 1	Steel	30		1	30
Inspecting module	aluminium	90	60	1	150
Guide wheel holder	Aluminium	30	20		50
LED			70	4	280
Camera LED holder			400	1	400
Front wheel		10	5	6	90
Plate 2	30x7 rod	40	10	1	50
Plate 1	30x7 rod	40	10	1	50
Plate 3	42x80x5	40	10	3	50
Pins and split pin	iron		70		80
Universal joint	Steel	150	100	1	250
Key		7	3	2	20
Back plate	Aluminium	25	27	1	52
Total					R2570

(b)

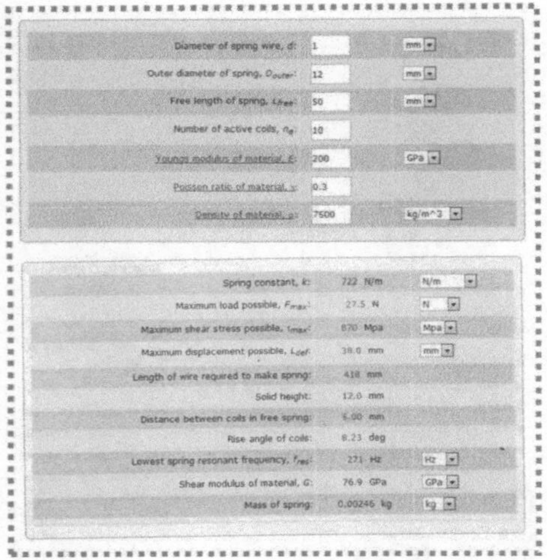

(c)

Figure 4.9 Example of a preliminary (a) concept design rating and selection, (b) cost analysis, and (c) component parameter calculation in terms of one particular design.

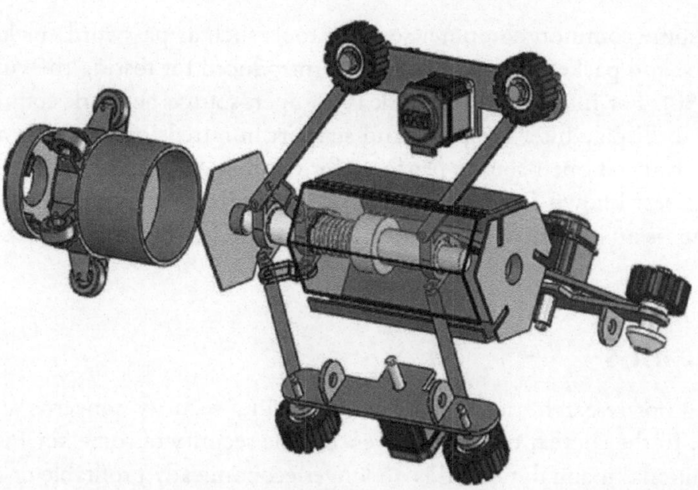

Figure 4.10 Final conceptual in-pipe inspection robot design.

In addition to this, most of the existing security-related CPS studies simply focus more on the cyberside. This study made an attempt to extend the effort to both the cyber and the physical sides. There are rather limited similar studies found in the literature.

Another contribution made by this work is that it discovered a drawback of the PFWSB framework. Robot design is a complicated process that requires its designers to take a large amount of objectives (maybe conflicting in many situations) into account for achieving an optimal final design, for example, budget limitation versus latest technology, security versus usability, and mobility versus payload requirement. These rapidly accumulating design variables often mean that designers face a multi-objective design optimization problem, which is difficult to handle. However, the employed PFWSB failed to address how to deal with this issue when too many clashing knowledge flows existed within the framework.

4.10.2 Future Work

In alignment with the suggestions given in [61], one study that could be carried out in the immediate future would be to build a working prototype of the designed miniature in-pipe inspection robot. Based on the established platform, we can physically test how the PFWSB can improve the representability and understandability of knowledge for such a design task. Since the robot is the kind of product that involves multidisciplinary knowledge inputs such as mechanical, electrical, electronics, and computer science, a mechatronics approach [77] could be used for fulfilling the interrelated requirements.

As mentioned in Section 4.7.1, we have to admit that the introduction of security considerations does increase the complexity of an already complicated embedded system design. The multiple design objectives are often in conflict or they even contradict each other. To deal with this multi-objective design optimization issue, the author suggests developing an improved version of the PFWSB that can tackle this problem class. Because most traditional optimization techniques fail to work, advanced optimization techniques such as innovative computation intelligence [78] and metaheuristics [79] methodologies can be introduced as a building block for an enhanced PFWSB framework.

Additionally, some common computer security tools such as password crackers, sniffers, vulnerability scanners, and packet crafters can also be introduced for testing the vulnerability of the involved system [50]. For instance, Wireshark is an open-source network communications protocol that is used to display filter language and support hundreds of protocols and media types; Metasploit is an advanced open-source platform for developing, testing, and using exploit code; Aircrack, which is best known for recovering wireless keys once enough encrypted packets have been gathered; Snot is an intrusion detection system for wireless networks; and so on.

4.11 Conclusions

CPS is currently a hot research area and its corresponding security concerns are drawing many people's attention. In the context of CPPSs, to ensure the security of some key infrastructure (e.g., pipeline), the traditional manual method is no longer economically profitable or feasibly practical. Under these circumstances, robot-assisted, in-pipe inspection has emerged as an alternative solution. Screening the literature, there is no shortage of studies [7,12,27,28,32,34,35,80–85] dedicated to this field, but designing a robot scout from the knowledge-flow perspective with security considerations is very rare. This study makes an attempt in this direction by applying a recently developed ontological framework, namely, the PFWSB model. Through the case study illustrated, the author believes that the PFWSB framework can indeed enable the synthesis of knowledge sets during the course of the cloud in-pipe robot conceptual design.

Author Biography

Bo Xing is an associate professor at the Department of Computer Science, School of Mathematical and Computer Science, University of Limpopo, South Africa. He was a senior lecturer in a division of the Center for Asset Integrity Management at the Department of Mechanical and Aeronautic Engineering, Faculty of Engineering, Built Environment and Information Technology, University of Pretoria, South Africa. Dr. Xing earned his doctorate in engineering with a focus on soft computing and remanufacturing in early 2013 from the University of Johannesburg, South Africa. He also obtained his BSc and MSc degrees both in mechanical engineering from the Tianjin University of Science and Technology, People's Republic of China, and the University of KwaZulu-Natal, South Africa, respectively. He was a scientific researcher at the Council for Scientific and Industrial Research, South Africa. He has published more than 50 research papers in books, international journals, and international conference proceedings. His current research interests lie in applying various nature-inspired computational intelligence methodologies to big data analysis, miniature robot design and analysis, advanced mechatronics systems, and e-maintenance.

References

1. K.-D. Kim and P. R. Kumar, Cyber-physical systems—A perspective at the centennial, *Proceedings of the IEEE*, 100, 1287–1308, 2012.
2. M. D. Ilić, L. Xie, U. A. Khan, and J. M. F. Moura, Modeling of future cyber-physical energy systems for distributed sensing and control, *IEEE Transactions on Systems, Man, and Cybernetics—Part A: Systems and Humans*, 40, 825–838, 2010.

3. R. R. Rajkumar, I. Lee, L. Sha, and J. Stankovic, Cyber-physical systems—The next computing revolution, in *Proceedings of the Design Automation Conference 2010*, Anaheim, CA, pp. 1–6, 2010.
4. K.-J. Park, R. Zheng, and X. Liu, Cyber-physical systems—Milestones and research challenges, *Computer Communications*, vol. 36, pp. 1–7, 2012.
5. B. Guo, S. Song, A. Ghalambor, and T. R. Lin, *Offshore Pipelines—Design, Installation, and Maintenance*, 2nd ed., Waltham, MA: Gulf Professional Publishing, 2014.
6. J. Okamoto, Jr, J. C. Adamowski, M. S. G. Tsuzuki, F. Buiochi, and C. S. Camerini, Autonomous system for oil pipelines inspection, *Mechatronics*, vol. 9, pp. 731–743, 1999.
7. S.-G. Roh and H. R. Choi, Differential-drive in-pipe robot for moving inside urban gas pipelines, *IEEE Transactions on Robotics*, vol. 21, pp. 1–17, 2005.
8. H. R. Choi and S. M. Ryew, Robotic system with active steering capability for internal inspection of urban gas pipelines, *Mechatronics*, vol. 12, pp. 713–736, 2002.
9. A. Vepsä, H. Haapaniemi, P. Luukkanen, P. Nurkkala, and A. Saarenheimo, Application of finite element model updating to a feed water pipeline of a nuclear power plant, *Nuclear Engineering and Design*, vol. 235, pp. 1849–1865, 2005.
10. H. C. W. Lau and R. A. Dwight, A fuzzy-based decision support model for engineering asset condition monitoring—A case study of examination of water pipelines, *Expert Systems with Applications*, vol. 38, pp. 13342–13350, 2011.
11. J. Lee, S. Han, K. Kim, H. Kim, and U. Lee, Failure analysis of carbon steel pipes used for underground condensate pipeline in the power station, *Engineering Failure Analysis*, vol. 34, pp. 300–307, 2013.
12. M. M. Moghaddam, M. Arbabtafti, and A. Hadi, In-pipe inspection crawler adaptable to the pipe interior diameter, *International Journal of Robotics and Automation*, vol. 26, pp. 135–145, 2011.
13. P. Marwedel, *Embedded System Design—Embedded Systems Foundations of Cyber-Physical Systems*, 2nd ed. Dordrecht: Springer, 2011.
14. A. E. Hassanien, T.-H. Kim, J. Kacprzyk, and A. I. Awad, eds, *Bio-Inspiring Cyber Security and Cloud Services—Trends and Innovations*. Heidelberg: Springer, 2014.
15. W. Stallings, *Computer Organization and Architecture—Designing for Performance*, 8th ed. Upper Saddle River, NJ: Pearson Education, 2010.
16. D. G. Ullman, *The Mechanical Design Process*. New York: McGraw-Hill, 2010.
17. X. Chen, L.-Q. Wang, X.-F. Ye, G. Wang, and H.-L. Wang, Prototype development and gait planning of biologically inspired multi-legged crablike robot, *Mechatronics*, vol. 23, pp. 429–444, 2013.
18. K. Hirai, The Honda humanoid robot—Development and future perspective, *Industrial Robot*, 26, pp. 260–266, 1999.
19. F. Mastrogiovanni and A. Sgorbissa, A behaviour sequencing and composition architecture based on ontologies for entertainment humanoid robots, *Robotics and Autonomous Systems*, vol. 61, pp. 170–183, 2013.
20. X.-Y. Wang, Y. Zhang, X.-J. Fu, and G.-S. Xiang, Design and kinematic analysis of a novel humanoid robot eye using pneumatic artificial muscles, *Journal of Bionic Engineering*, vol. 5, pp. 264–270, 2008.
21. D. H. Kim, J. H. Lee, I. Kim, S. H. Noh, and S. K. Oho, Mechanism, control, and visual management of a jumping robot, *Mechatronics*, 18, pp. 591–600, 2008.
22. S. M. Reilly and M. E. Jorgensen, The evolution of jumping in frogs—Morphological evidence for the basal anuran locomotor condition and the radiation of locomotor systems in crown group anurans, *Journal of Morphology*, vol. 272, pp. 149–168, 2011.
23. M. Wang, X.-Z. Zang, J.-Z. Fan, and J. Zhao, Biological jumping mechanism analysis and modeling for frog robot, *Journal of Bionic Engineering*, vol. 5, pp. 181–188, 2008.
24. J. Zhang, G. Song, Y. Li, G. Qiao, A. Song, and A. Wang, A bio-inspired jumping robot—Modeling, simulation, design, and experimental results, *Mechatronics*, vol. 23, pp. 1123–1140, 2013.
25. K. Yonemoto, *Robotization in Japanese Industires*. Toronto: Japan External Trade Organization, 1982.
26. J. Lim, H. Park, J. An, Y.-S. Hong, B. Kim, and B.-J. Yi, One pneumatic line based inchworm-like micro robot for half-inch pipe inspection, *Mechatronics*, vol. 18, pp. 315–322, 2008.
27. Q. Liu, T. Ren, and Y. Chen, Characteristic analysis of a novel in-pipe driving robot, *Mechatronics*, vol. 23, pp. 419–428, 2013.

28. M. Horodinca, I. Doroftei, E. Mignon, and A. Preumont, A simple architecture for in-pipe inspection robots, in *Proceedings of the International Colloquium on Mobile and Autonomous Systems*, Magdeburg, Germany, pp. 61–64, 2002.
29. E. N. Prasad, M. Kannan, A. Azarudeen, and N. Karuppasamy, Defect identification in pipe lines using pipe inspection robot, *International Journal of Mechanical Engineering and Robotics Research*, vol. 1, pp. 20–31, 2012.
30. J. A. Cobano, J. Estremera, and P. G. de Santos, Accurate tracking of legged robots on natural terrain, *Autonomous Robots*, vol. 28, pp. 231–244, 2010.
31. S. S. Roy and D. K. Pratihar, Dynamic modeling, stability and energy consumption analysis of a realistic six-legged walking robot, *Robotics and Computer-Integrated Manufacturing*, vol. 29, pp. 400–416, 2013.
32. Y. Sabzehmeidani, M. Mailah, M. Hussein, and A. R. Tavakolpour, Intelligent control and modelling of a micro robot for in-pipe application, *World Academy of Science, Engineering and Technology*, vol. 48, pp. 449–454, 2010.
33. P. Appelqvist, *Mechatronics Design of a Robot Society: A Case Study of Minimalist Underwater Robots for Distributed Perception and Task Execution*. Espoo: Helsinki University of Technology, 2000.
34. J.-S. Lee, S.-G. Roh, D. W. Kim, H. Moon, and H. R. Choi, In-pipe robot navigation based on the landmark recognition system using shadow images, in *Proceedings of IEEE International Conference on Robotics and Automation*, May 12–17, Kobe, Japan, pp. 1857–1862, 2009.
35. N. S. Roslin, A. Anuar, M. F. A. Jalal, and K. S. M. Sahari, A review—Hybrid locomotion of in-pipe inspection robot, *Procedia Engineering*, vol. 41, pp. 1456–1462, 2012.
36. H. Qi, X. Zhang, H. Chen, and J. Ye, Tracing and localization system for pipeline robot, *Mechatronics*, vol. 19, pp. 76–84, 2009.
37. S. Cordes, K. Berns, M. Eberl, W. Ilg, and R. Suna, Autonomous sewer inspection with a wheeled, multiarticulated robot, *Robotics and Autonomous Systems*, vol. 21, pp. 123–135, 1997.
38. G. Heo and J. Park, A framework for evaluating the effects of maintenance-related human errors in nuclear power plants, *Reliability Engineering and System Safety*, vol. 95, pp. 797–805, 2010.
39. A. Chibani, Y. Amirat, S. Mohammed, E. Matson, N. Hagita, and M. Barreto, Ubiquitous robotics—Recent challenges and future trends, *Robotics and Autonomous Systems*, vol. 61, pp. 1162–1172, 2013.
40. U. Pagallo, Robots in the cloud with privacy—A new threat to data protection?, *Computer Law & Security Review*, vol. 29, pp. 501–508, 2013.
41. S. Tian, D. Saitov, and S. G. Lee, Cloud robot with real-time face recognition ability, *Advanced Science and Technology Letters*, vol. 51, pp. 77–80, 2014.
42. E. Guizzo, Robots with their heads in the clouds, *Spectrum*, vol. 48, pp. 16–18, 2011.
43. M. Waibel, M. Beetz, J. Civera, R. D'Andrea, J. Elfring, D. Gálvez-López, et al., RoboEarth. *IEEE Robotics & Automation Magazine*, vol. 18, pp. 69–82, 2011.
44. K. Kamei, T. Ikeda, M. Shiomi, H. Kidokoro, A. Utsumi, K. Shinozawa, et al., Cooperative customer navigation between robots outside and inside a retail shop—An implementation on the ubiquitous market platform, *Telecommunications*, vol. 67, pp. 329–340, 2012.
45. K. Kamei, S. Nishio, N. Hagita, and M. Sato, Cloud networked robotics. *IEEE Network Magazine*, vol. 26, pp. 28–34, 2012.
46. K. Goldberg, B. Kehoe, S. Patil, and P. Abbeel, Cloud robotics and automation—A survey of related work, Technical Report UCB/EECS-2013-52013. EECS Department, University of California, Berkeley, 2013.
47. C.-H. Hsu, Ubiquitous intelligence and computing—Building smart environment in real and cyber space, *Journal of Ambient Intelligence and Humanized Computing*, vol. 3, pp. 83–85, 2012.
48. D. J. Cook and S. K. Das, Pervasive computing at scale—Transforming the state of the art, *Pervasive and Mobile Computing*, vol. 8, pp. 22–35, 2012.
49. D. J. Cook, J. C. Augusto, and V. R. Jakkula, Ambient intelligence—Technologies, applications, and opportunities, *Pervasive and Mobile Computing*, vol. 5, pp. 277–298, 2009.
50. S. P. Wang and R. S. Ledley, *Computer Architecture and Security—Fundamentals of Designing Secure Computer Systems*. Singapore: Wiley, 2013.
51. A. S. Tanenbaum and H. Bos, *Modern Operating Systems*, 4th ed. Upper Saddle River, NJ: Pearson, 2015.

52. J. D. Bethune, *Engineering Design and Graphics with SolidWorks*. Upper Saddle River, NJ: Pearson, 2010.
53. A. K. Goel, S. Vattam, B. Wiltgen, and M. Helmsa, Cognitive, collaborative, conceptual and creative—Four characteristics of the next generation of knowledge-based CAD systems: A study in biologically inspired design, *Computer-Aided Design*, vol. 44, pp. 879–900, 2012.
54. Y. Haik and T. Shahin, *Engineering Design Process*. Stamford, CT: Cengage Learning, 2011.
55. M. B. Eisenberg and R. E. Berkowitz. Big6: More relevant and important than ever. www.big6.com.
56. X. Liu, T. Jiang, and F. Ma, Collective dynamics in knowledge networks—Emerging trends analysis, *Journal of Informetrics*, vol. 7, pp. 425–438, 2013.
57. C. Liu and Z.-K. Zhang, Information spreading on dynamic social networks, *Communication on Nonlinear Science and Numerical Simulation*, vol. 19, pp. 896–904, 2014.
58. I. M. Prieto, E. Revilla, and B. Rodríguez-Prado, Building dynamic capabilities in product development—How to contextual antecedents matter?, *Scandinavian Journal of Management*, vol. 25, pp. 313–326, 2009.
59. G. Verona and D. Ravasi, Unbundling dynamic capabilities—An exploratory study of continuous product innovation, *Industrial and Corporate Change*, vol. 12, pp. 577–606, 2003.
60. M. Zollo and S. G. Winter, Deliberate learning and the evolution of dynamics capabilities, *Organization Science*, vol. 13, pp. 339–351, 2002.
61. Z.-N. Zhang, Z.-L. Liu, Y. Chen, and Y.-B. Xie, Knowledge flow in engineering design—An ontological framework, *Proceedings of the Institution of Mechanical Engineers, Part C: Journal of Mechanical Engineering Science*, vol. 227, pp. 760–770, 2013.
62. J. S. Gero, Design prototypes—A knowledge representation schema for design. *AI Magazine*, vol. 26, pp. 26–36, 1990.
63. F. Christophe, A. Bernard, and É. Coatanéa, RFBS—A model for knowledge representation of conceptual design, *CIRP Annals—Manufacturing Technology*, vol. 59, pp. 155–158, 2010.
64. H. K. H. Chow, K. L. Choy, W. B. Lee, and F. T. S. Chan, Design of a knowledge-based logistics strategy system, *Expert Systems with Applications*, vol. 29, pp. 272–290, 2005.
65. X. F. Zha and H. Du, Knowledge-intensive collaborative design modeling and support. Part I: Review, distributed models and framework, *Computers in Industry*, vol. 57, pp. 39–55, 2006.
66. X. F. Zha and H. Du, Knowledge-intensive collaborative design modeling and support—Part II: System implementation and application, *Computer in Industry*, vol. 57, pp. 56–71, 2006.
67. R. Gross, *Psychology—The Science of Mind and Behaviour*, 6th ed. London: Hodder Education, 2014.
68. X.-J. Liu and J. Wang, *Parallel Kinematics—Type, Kinematics, and Optimal Design*. Berlin: Springer, 2014.
69. M. Jouaneh, *Fundamentals of Mechatronics*. Stamford, CT: Cengage Learning, 2013.
70. A. Smaili and F. Mrad, *Mechatronics—Integrated Technologies for Intelligent Machines*. New York: Oxford University Press, 2008.
71. G. Pahl and W. Beitz, *Engineering Design—A Systematic Approach*, 3rd ed. Berlin: Springer, 2007.
72. J. S. Gero and M. A. Rosenman, A conceptual framework for knowledge-based design research at Sydney University's Design Computing Unit, *Artificial Intelligence in Engineering*, vol. 5, pp. 363–382, 1990.
73. J. S. Gero and U. Kannengiesser, The situated function-behaviour-structure framework, *Design Studies*, vol. 25, pp. 373–391, 2004.
74. J. S. Gero and U. Kannengiesser, A function-behavior-structure ontology of process, *Artificial Intelligence for Engineering Design, Analysis and Manufacturing*, vol. 21, pp. 379–391, 2007.
75. M. E. Nissen, *Harnessing Knowledge Dynamics: Principled Organizational Knowing & Learning*. Hershey, PA: IRM Press, 2006.
76. Y. Ishino and Y. Jin, Acquiring engineering knowledge from design processes, *Artificial Intelligence for Engineering Design, Analysis and Manufacturing*, vol. 16, pp. 73–91, 2002.
77. C. W. de Silva, *Mechatronics—An Integrated Approach*. Boca Raton: CRC Press, 2005.
78. B. Xing and W.-J. Gao, *Innovative Computational Intelligence—A Rough Guide to 134 Clever Algorithms*. Heidelberg: Springer, 2014.

79. X.-S. Yang, *Nature-Inspired Metaheuristic Algorithms*, 2nd ed. Frome: Luniver Press, 2008.
80. H. R. Choi and S.-G. Roh, In-pipe robot with active steering capability for moving inside of pipelines, in *Bioinspiration and Robotics Walking and Climbing Robots*, ed. M. K. Habib, Rijeka, Croatia: InTech, Chapter 23, pp. 375–402, 2007.
81. C. Jun, Z. Deng, and S. Jiang, Study of locomotion control characteristics for six wheels driven in-pipe robot, Presented at the *IEEE International Conference on Robotics and Biomimetics*, 22–26 August, Shenyang, China, pp. 119–124, 2004.
82. Y. K. Kang, J. W. Park, and H. S. Yang, Analytical approach of the in-pipe robot on branched pipe navigation and its solution, *World Academy of Science, Engineering and Technology*, vol. 77, pp. 449–453, 2013.
83. D. Lee, J. Park, D. Hyun, G. Yook, and H.-S. Yang, Novel mechanisms and simple locomotion strategies for an in-pipe robot that can inspect various pipe types, *Mechanism and Machine Theory*, vol. 56, pp. 52–68, 2012.
84. J. K. Ong, K. Bouazza-Marouf, and D. Kerr, Fuzzy logic control for use in in-pipe mobile robotic system navigation, *Proceedings of the Institution of Mechanical Engineers Part I: Journal of Systems and Control Engineering*, vol. 217, pp. 401–419, 2003.
85. Y. Zhang and G. Yan, In-pipe inspection robot with active pipe-diameter adaptability and automatic tractive force adjusting, *Mechanism and Machine Theory*, vol. 42, pp. 1618–1631, 2007.

Chapter 5

WSNProtectLayer: Security Middleware for Wireless Sensor Networks

Vashek Matyáš, Petr Švenda, Andriy Stetsko,
Dušan Klinec, Filip Jurnečka, and Martin Stehlík
Masaryk University

Contents

5.1 Introduction 120
  5.1.1 Chapter Roadmap 121
5.2 Description of Scenarios 122
  5.2.1 Types of Devices 122
  5.2.2 Common Assumptions 122
  5.2.3 Attacker Model 123
  5.2.4 Scenario Analysis 124
    5.2.4.1 Warehouse Monitoring 124
    5.2.4.2 Mobile Emergency Unit 127
    5.2.4.3 Building Monitoring 128
  5.2.5 Summary of Attacks 131
5.3 Middleware WSNProtectLayer: General Principles 131
  5.3.1 Main Components 132
    5.3.1.1 Privacy Component 133
    5.3.1.2 Intrusion Detection Component 133
    5.3.1.3 Key Establishment Component 134
    5.3.1.4 Cryptography Component 135
  5.3.2 WSNProtectLayer Middleware Lifecycle 135
5.4 Implementation Details 136
  5.4.1 ProtectLayerC Component 137
  5.4.2 Configuration Component 137

5.4.3 Logging 137
5.4.4 Uploader and ProtectLayerConfigurator 138
5.4.5 Packet Acknowledgments 139
5.4.6 TelosB and MICAz Performance Platform Comparison 139
5.5 Experiments 140
5.5.1 How to Build a Development Test Bed 140
5.5.2 Supporting Experiments 143
5.5.2.1 RSSI Radio Signal Strength Experiment 143
5.5.2.2 CTP Routing Tree Discovery 143
5.5.2.3 IDS and Jamming Experiment 146
5.5.2.4 Localization Experiment 146
5.5.3 Complex Experiments 151
5.5.3.1 Cikhaj 2012: Social Interactions 151
5.5.3.2 Cikhaj 2013: Attacker Detection 152
5.5.3.3 Test Bed 2013: Movement and Item Detection 154
5.5.3.4 Mirov 2014 155
5.5.3.5 Test Bed 2014 156
5.4 Future Work 157
5.5 Conclusion 158
Acknowledgments 158
Author Biographies 159
References 160

Abstract: This chapter presents a case study addressing the problem of achieving transparent privacy protection, intrusion detection, and key distribution in the area of wireless sensor networks (WSNs) when used for critical infrastructures. We first analyzed the functional and security needs of three different usage scenarios and then designed and tested (a prototype of) our security middleware in the form of virtual radio for the wireless sensor nodes. Multiple supporting experiments with our implementations of middleware for the TinyOS platform are discussed, together with typical problems we encountered and addressed.

Keywords: Building monitoring; Critical infrastructure; Intrusion detection; Key distribution; Mobile emergency unit; Open-source privacy protection

5.1 Introduction

A wireless sensor network (WSN) consists of resource-constrained wireless devices called sensor nodes. When deployed in an area, they monitor some physical phenomena (e.g., humidity, temperature, pressure, light) and send measurements to a base station (BS) using hop-by-hop communication. WSNs are a prominent example of systems that interact among themselves through communications and physical environments. WSNs become a critical part of cyber-physical systems, especially since their area of deployment is rarely protected physically, which implies a higher risk of both internal and external attacks. The external attacks are carried out by devices that do not belong to the network. The internal attacks are carried out by devices that are authenticated to the network. A sensor node usually does not have a secure storage for keys that are deployed at the node. An adversary, who has physical access to the deployment area (usually the case), can capture a node, read the keys and deploy her* own devices in the area. The internal and external attacks can be further divided into active (that affect communication) and passive (that focus on eavesdropping and usually remain undetected).

Detection and prevention mechanisms are used to protect a WSN from the attacks, thus protecting the cyber-physical infrastructure this WSN is part of. Sensitive information (such as location of subjects being monitored by the sensor nodes or a BS placement) that can be revealed by attacks, in most cases, can be protected by secure cryptographic protocols (privacy protection mechanisms). Active attacks (such as jamming or packet dropping) on a network can usually be detected by intrusion detection systems (IDSs).

While working on our recent applied research project (sponsored by the Czech Ministry of the Interior, under the project code VG20102014031) in the area of security for critical infrastructures (final report available [1]) with the use of a WSN, we considered three potentially interesting applications: *warehouse monitoring*, *mobile emergency units*, and *building monitoring*.

The development of a secure platform for a WSN is a challenging task due to severe constraints put on sensor nodes. The specifics of the target platform and the lack of real-world examples call for novel approaches. The following text summarizes the experimental development of the *WSNProtectLayer*—an open-source middleware for security and privacy support. This middleware, we believe, will decrease development time (for developers of end applications) and decrease the risk of design/code security errors. WSNProtectLayer is a middleware for TinyOS [2]—the most widely used operating system for sensor nodes. Our middleware consists of three components: privacy protection, intrusion detection, and a key distribution component.

5.1.1 Chapter Roadmap

Section 5.2 discusses the subsequent analyses of these scenarios. The analysis was necessary to better understand their security, privacy, and functional requirements. It helped to render the functionality of the developed platform.

Section 5.3 describes the final architecture of the WNSProtectLayer. It provides an overall picture of the architecture and a description of the major components—privacy, key distribution, and intrusion detection. For every component, we state its basic functionality and connection to other components. Besides these major components, this section contains a description of additional components and applications that we designed and implemented for the management of a WSN as well as the WSNProtectLayer itself.

Section 5.4 contains information on the implementation details of the WSNProtectLayer. It provides information on licensing and on a repository with the source codes together with a description of the main components. The designed architecture is implemented for the widely used TinyOS operating system, so that existing applications can continue using the radio interface. Our middleware is designed in such a way as to make incorporation of the entire security architecture as easy as possible, requiring only minimal changes to an original application source code by simple rewiring of a few components.

Section 5.5 describes experiments conducted as a part of the design and development of the WSNProtectLayer platform. We conducted several supporting experiments and tests of the partly or fully developed platform. The behavior of the wireless radio transmission (packet loss ratio, communication range, speed of routing topology convergence) was examined during the experiments, which ran over a time span of several days. Based on the results of the experiments, we

* The gender of our attacker was independently decided by a toss of an unbiased coin.

set the default parameters of the platform. During more complex experiments, we evaluated the behavior of the whole platform.

Section 5.6 concludes the chapter.

5.2 Description of Scenarios

In the first stage of our work, we have to carefully assess the application scenarios, the set of devices used in the final system, the attacker model, and various other general assumptions that play a role further along the development process.

5.2.1 Types of Devices

We consider five types of devices that may be part of a network:

- *The central point* is the center of the system. It communicates with BSs. The central point evaluates events coming from the BSs. It has computational resources similar to a server computer. It is not limited in energy consumption as it is connected to an electrical system. The central point is physically protected and only a limited number of people have physical access to the central point.
- *A base station* (BS) is a data collection sink and a gateway between the central point and the rest of a network. There is a wired connection between a BS and the central point. A BS is also equipped with motion sensors to detect any movement in its locality. A BS is not limited in energy consumption—it is connected to an electrical system.
- *Static sensor nodes* are equipped with motion sensors to detect any movement in their locality.
- *Mobile sensor nodes* can detect their own position (GPS, triangulation) and their own movement. They are usually carried by authorized persons.
- *Tags* are simple devices (e.g., radio-frequency identification [RFID]) that only respond to queries from static sensor nodes and BSs. They can be uniquely identified.

5.2.2 Common Assumptions

It is important to note that our final system focuses purely on the software and communication security. Therefore, we point out that we do not directly aim to make the system robust against hardware faults.

We consider these facts to hold:

- The central point
  - Knows the identifiers (pseudonyms) of all static sensor nodes and their location (either absolute or relative).
  - Is powerful enough to perform analysis of incoming messages almost in real time.
  - Can also be a part of other networks (e.g., the Internet). We do not consider attacks coming from such networks.
- The base station
  - The communication between a BS and a central point is secured and the activity itself is publicly unobservable.
  - We consider BSs as secured.

- Static sensor nodes
  - Static sensor nodes are equipped with motion detection sensors and any moving person in their neighborhood will be immediately detected.
  - Motion detection sensors are assumed to be accurate enough to detect both fast- and slow-moving person, yet able to distinguish from ordinary background noise.
  - No mobile/static sensor node is isolated; there is always a communication path from the sensor node to a BS.
  - Static sensor nodes and BSs are placed in such way that protected parts of the area are covered by static sensor nodes.
  - Measurements done by sensors are correct. We do not consider attacks on sensors themselves (e.g., disabling, removing or replacing sensors).
- The tags
  - We do not consider attacks on tags.
- The application
  - Software running on a network device is free of vulnerabilities, which can be exploited by an attacker to gain remote access to a device.
  - We do not consider attacks on the application layer. Hence, our protection system does not analyze the content of a packet.
- The attacker
  - The attacker is able to capture at most 10% of sensor nodes in the network. This holds, because the network may be temporal or under partial physical control and a missing node can be detected quickly.

5.2.3 Attacker Model

An attacker can be

- *Passive*: An attacker does not inject/modify messages and does not jam.
- *Active*: An attacker may inject/modify messages or perform jamming.
- *External*: An attacker is not a legitimate member of a network (has not compromised any node and does not possess any key material).
- *Internal*: An attacker is a legitimate member of a network (has compromised a single/few static/mobile sensor node(s) and/or possesses a single/few key(s)).
- *Local*: An attacker can overhear only a local area (only a single/few hop(s)).
- *Global*: An attacker can overhear all node-to-node and node-to-base station communication simultaneously all the time.

We consider four basic classes of attackers with respect to attack costs, equipment needed, and their impact on a network. These were selected to be sufficiently diverse and to be characteristic for a given attacker class.

A *Level 1 attacker* represents a low-cost attacker with minimum equipment requirements. An ordinary person can easily become a Level 1 attacker. As such, she can be considered as

- Passive
- External
- Local

A *Level 2 attacker* represents a medium-cost attacker with a distributed eavesdropping and transmitting device. The attacker does not compromise any node. Typically, a Level 2 attacker is a group of people with radio devices. This level can be considered as

- Active
- External
- Global

A *Level 3 attacker* represents a medium-cost attacker with common or special equipment and knowledge. This kind of attacker is the most common as far as intentional serious attacks on a network are concerned. An organization conducting industrial espionage is a typical Level 3 attacker. An attacker on this level can be considered as

- Active
- Internal
- Local

A *Level 4 attacker* represents a high-cost attacker class. The attacker has special equipment and knowledge. A typical Level 4 attacker is a well-funded organization with high motivation. This, the most powerful attacker, can be considered as:

- Active
- Internal
- Global

5.2.4 Scenario Analysis

In this section, we describe additional details of the scenario applications. We discuss the application setting, type of traffic in the network, the threat under assumptions, and aims and strategies of an attacker.

5.2.4.1 Warehouse Monitoring

The aim of this scenario is to monitor movement of employees within the protected area, monitor movement of protected objects, and generally support the work of employees and management of the warehouse.

The warehouse contains objects of different importance:

- *Very important objects.* We want to know the precise position of these objects and we want to be informed whenever any of these objects are moved. The number of such objects is not high (e.g., hundreds).
- *Less important objects.* We want to be informed whenever any of these objects leaves a corridor/enters a corridor.

We envision the protected area to be of typical rectangular shape with evenly distributed shelves. We consider all five types of devices to form the network:

- *A central point* is placed outside the space with shelves.
- *Base stations* are placed at entrances to corridors. In Figure 5.1, these are depicted as black circles.
- *Static sensor nodes* are placed in the corridors of a warehouse. In Figure 5.1, these are depicted as white circles. They are equipped with sensors for *tag* recognition.
- *Mobile sensor nodes* are attached to very important objects.
- *Tags* are attached to less important objects.

The assumed application traffic consists of the following messages:

- Central point → static sensor node
  - "What objects do you have in your communication range?" The list may contain IDs of neighboring static sensor nodes. Several static sensor nodes may observe the same tags/mobile sensor nodes.
  - "Do you have Object X in your communication range?"
- Static sensor node → central point
  - "Someone/something without a tag/a mobile sensor node passed near me."
  - "An object/employee with ID passed me."
  - A list of objects in its locality.
  - "Queried Object X is (not) in my communication range."
- Mobile sensor node→ static sensor node
  - A periodical message: "I am alive, and my position is X."
  - A message "I am being moved now, and my current position is X."
- Static sensor node → mobile sensor node
  - A message: "Reply if you are Object X."
  - A message: "Send me your ID."

In this scenario, we consider the four attacker levels defined in Section 5.2.3. We further extend these levels:

- *Insider attacker* is a staff member.
- *Outsider attacker* is not a staff member.

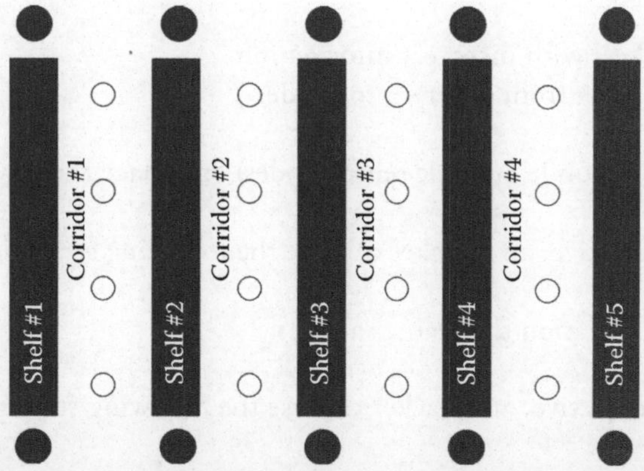

Figure 5.1 Device setup in the warehouse.

Finally, the attacker objective is to

1. Collect sensitive information (on movement of people and objects, placement and quantity of objects, and current mode of network operation)
2. Inject incorrect information (on movement of people and objects and placement and quantity of objects)
3. Cause false alarms
4. Prevent/suppress/delay legitimate alarms regarding
   a. An unauthorized movement of people in a warehouse.
   b. An unauthorized movement of objects in a warehouse by an unauthorized person.(The central point will detect that the employee came too close to the object.)
   c. A person who is authorized to take an object but moves it to an unauthorized place. (The central point will detect an object that is in a place in which it is not authorized to be.)

To fulfill the first objective, an attacker can use the following strategies:

- Deploy (outside or inside the warehouse) her own device to eavesdrop communication in the network and to infer (sensitive) information, e.g., by traffic analysis techniques.
- Get (direct or remote) access to a legitimate device of the network, to collect (sensitive) information forwarded (stored) by (on) the device, or to query the network on sensitive information (e.g., placement/quantity of objects, location of employees). To gain physical access to a device, an *outsider attacker must move in the warehouse undetected*. To do the same, an *insider has to take an object he/she is not authorized to take*. To gain remote access to a device, an attacker can exploit vulnerabilities in the software running on the device.
- Steal the identity of a device and deploy a new malicious device that imitates the legitimate device (central point, BS, sensor node) and collects (sensitive) information arriving from other devices.

To increase the efficiency of (sensitive) information collection, an attacker may perform sinkhole, packet injection, and packet replay attacks.

To fulfill the second objective, an attacker can use the following strategies:

- Inject her own packets with incorrect information.
- Modify packets coming from other sensor nodes.
- Replay old packets.
- Damage sensors (on mobile or static sensor nodes) or replace them with faulty sensors.

To fulfill the third objective, an attacker can use the following strategies:

- Inject incorrect information that causes alarms.

To fulfill the fourth objective, an attacker can use the following strategies:

- Get a valid mobile sensor node (it can be used only in the day mode).
- Destroy, disable, or remove sensor nodes (or sensors).

- Gain access (direct or remote) to a network device (e.g., sensor node, BS) so as to reprogram it in such a way that the device will not react to motion detection and will drop, modify,* or delay packets (with alerts) from other devices. To attract more traffic to the captured device, the attacker may perform a sinkhole attack. The attacker may exploit the routing metric and/or use sensor nodes with several identities (Sybil nodes).
- Jam a (part of) network. The attacker can use a device with hardware characteristics similar to a sensor node or a more powerful one.
- Perform a hello flood attack so important and less important packets will be lost.
- Inject packets to increase network latency (could be seen as a special case of jamming).

5.2.4.2 Mobile Emergency Unit

The network would be deployed ad hoc either around an emergency unit to protect the unit itself or around a site foreseen for engagement, to monitor the activity coming in and out of the protected area. An attacker (unidentified person) moving inside the protected area should be recognized, and the emergency squad members should be notified. Similarly, the position of the squad members should be monitored to improve the management of the force.

We consider two entities in the network:

- *Legitimate person* (e.g., a squad member): a moving entity inside the protected area who should be alarmed when an attacker enters the area
- *Attacker*: whose primary goal is to move inside the protected area undetected or monitor the movement of a legitimate person

We consider four types of devices that form a network:

- *Central point* provides the emergency squad members with information about the movement of relevant entities in the network. It shall be positioned in a physically secure environment and may be distant from the WSN target area.
- *Base station* is a device positioned in a WSN target area and responsible for transferring information collected from sensor nodes to the *central point*.
- *Static sensor nodes* sense movement in the area via motion sensors and facilitate communication in the network. Static sensor nodes may be deployed around a protected point (e.g., emergency car) or around a building with several entrances (e.g., to protect an operating unit inside). Static sensor nodes are placed with sufficient density over the protected area.
- *Mobile sensor nodes* (MSN) are carried by every legitimate person.

The assumed application traffic consists of the following messages:

- Static sensor node → central point
- Channel: Messages from static sensor nodes are transmitted by multihop fashion via other nodes to a BS and then to the central point.
- Static sensor node with ID "X" was alive at time T.
- Network nodes may aggregate "X alive" messages to lower the amount of traffic in the network.

---

* In such a way that other sensor nodes will drop the modified packets, e.g., by modifying a cyclic redundancy check (CRC).

- Static sensor node with ID "X" is close to (communicating distance) MSN with ID 'P.'
- Motion on a sensor on the node with ID "X" was triggered by movement.
- Central point → MSN
  - Channel: Message transmission is realized via direct communication channel from the central point (or a BS, if more suitable) to a squad member's MSN.
  - Alert about proximity of a detected attacker.
  - Alert about proximity of a geographically close squad member.

We consider the three attacker levels defined in Section 5.2.3. We do not consider an insider attacker. The attacker objectives are to

1. Prevent/suppress/delay legitimate alarms.
2. Collect sensitive information (about the current position and movement of the squad member).
3. Inject incorrect information (on the current position of the squad members or monitored objects).
4. Cause a false alarm.

To fulfill the first objective, an attacker can use the following strategies:

- Equip herself with a jamming device and try to reach a squad member undetected.
- Jam part of the network from a static jamming device and try to move undetected and mimic as a squad member to prevent the alarm, even when movement detection was successful (e.g., by MSN).
- Destroy part of the network and try to move undetected.
- Try to capture some nodes undetected, modify their behavior, and return them malfunctioning.
- Flood the network with fake messages to increase network latency to prevent delivery of the movement detection event in a required timeframe.
- Obtain information about the network topology and coverage to analyze possible unprotected areas suitable for undetected movement.

To fulfill the second objective, an attacker can use the following strategies:

- Passively monitor communication and infer information about the legitimate persons or successful detection of the attacker based on traffic analysis of transmitted packets.

To fulfill the third objective, an attacker can use the following strategies:

- Use communication relay equipment (wormhole) to
  - Create the perception of a legitimate moving person in a distant area (a squad member's MSN is relayed).
  - Create the perception of a close neighbor for sensor nodes in the field.

5.2.4.3 Building Monitoring

The scenario aim is to build a static network in a building without a wired option or with one that is not excessively costly. The building scenario would enable movement monitoring of visitors, enabling access to protected areas the visitor is authorized to enter, and protecting armed areas by notifying the operating personnel of a breach.

We recognize two kinds of (authorized) visitors:

- *Regular visitor.* We want to monitor the movements and location of these visitors. These are regular people, whose privacy should be protected to some extent. However, protection of their privacy is not critical since there is little motivation to compromise it. The vast majority of the people in the building are regular visitors. The number of regular visitors depends on the size of the building.
- *VIP visitor.* Privacy of VIP visitors is critical. We want to protect the information on their location and movements. This information should not be available even to the network supervisor unless she has proper clearance (e.g., bodyguards of the VIP visitor).

We consider two kinds of network supervisors:

- A *supervisor* has access to network data, except the data on VIP visitors.
- A *hypervisor* has access to all network data.

We consider four types of devices that form a network:

- *Central point.*
- *Base stations.*
- *Static sensor nodes* are placed in corridors and rooms of the protected building and on the building itself. They are equipped with sensors for *tag* recognition.
- *Tags* are attached to badges that are worn by visitors.

The assumed application traffic consists of these messages:

- Static sensor node → central point
  - Data reports from static nodes to the central point.
  - "There is a motion near me and no tag was detected."
  - "A tag with specified ID is near me."
- Static sensor node → central point
  - If a node successfully detects jamming, it broadcasts an alarm message into the network. All nodes that overhear the alarm message start to send confirmation messages ("still alive") every (short) time period (e.g., every 1 s) to the central point. This state of the network is enabled for a certain safety period until the central point disables the state.

Furthermore, we can tolerate latency of messages within single seconds. Unlike the warehouse scenario, this scenario does not support queries from a central point to nodes.

We consider the four attacker levels defined in Section 5.2.3. We further extend these levels: the attacker may have access to a supervisor interface; in such a case, the attacker becomes an *insider supervisor attacker.* The attacker objectives are to

- Collect information on people movement and track individuals (including VIPs).
- Collect information on the current privacy-preserving mode of network operation.
- Collect information on VIP visitor presence in the building.

- Collect information on the security state of areas.
- Achieve unobservable movement in the building.
- Inject bogus movement reports in the building.

To fulfill the first to fourth objectives, an attacker can use the following strategies:

- Using *passive attacks*,
  - Equip himself with an eavesdropping device (quality, range, and number of these devices depend on the attacker level), eavesdrop the communication, and analyze the content of eavesdropped packets or perform a traffic analysis.
- Using *active attacks*,
  - Capture some nodes and modify their behavior (an attacker approaches the nodes while jamming or wearing a proper tag). Having the nodes under control, the attacker can mount network-level attacks to support the traffic analysis or analysis of the packet content, e.g., an attacker can extract encryption keys from captured nodes or increase the number of messages available for analysis.
  - Deploy own devices and mount network-level attacks to support the traffic analysis or analysis of the packet content.
  - Deploy false BS and attract as much traffic as possible.

To fulfill the fourth objective, an attacker can use the following strategy:

- Use *active attacks* to disturb an area and observe the reaction of the network and building guards.

To fulfill the fifth objective, an attacker can use the following strategies:

- Using *active attacks*,
  - Equip himself with a jamming device and jam part of the network.
  - Jam part of the network from a static jamming device.
  - Destroy part of the network.
  - Capture some nodes and modify their behavior (an attacker approaches the nodes while jamming or wearing a proper tag). Having the nodes under control, the attacker can mount network-level attacks to suppress delivery of message on motion detection. Such attacks may include selective forwarding, sinkhole attack, hello floods, Sybil attacks, and so on.
  - Deploy own devices and mount network-level attacks to suppress the delivery of messages on motion detection.
  - Create a false BS and attract as much traffic as possible.
  - Trigger large numbers of false alarms to render an alarm ineffective, for example, by special equipment or by damaging tags of legitimate visitors.

To fulfill the sixth objective, an attacker can use the following strategies:

- Using *active attacks*,
  - Capture some nodes and modify their behavior. The nodes then inject bogus messages. Their activity may be supported by other network-level attacks, such as Sybil attacks, to increase the impact of the bogus messages.

– Replay eavesdropped packets.
– Inject packets into the network traffic with a special radio device with a large communication range. Thus, she can deliver the packets to distant nodes from a static place.

5.2.5 Summary of Attacks

After analyzing the scenarios, we can divide the attacks into three groups. When we mention a network device, we mean either a sensor node or a BS.

1. Physical attacks
   a. Destroy or remove (temporarily or permanently) a network device.
   b. Capture a network device and reprogram it.
   c. Deploy a new malicious node that becomes an authenticated participant of the network.
2. Attacks on communication stack
   a. Jam a (part of) network. Different strategies can be used, for example, constant, deceptive, random, or reactive jamming.
   b. (Selectively) drop packets.
   c. Inject new (not legitimate) packets into the network.
   d. Modify packets.
   e. Replay packets.
   f. Delay packets.
   g. Relay packets (wormhole attack).
   h. Attract traffic to a certain network device (sinkhole attack).
   i. Hello flood attack.
3. Eavesdropping attacks
   a. Eavesdrop packets.
   b. Do traffic analysis
      i. While there is a legitimate query to the network.
      ii. While the network responds to some external events.
      iii. While none of the previous conditions hold.

5.3 Middleware WSNProtectLayer: General Principles

The main design goal of the WSNProtectLayer middleware is to provide advanced security functions that can be utilized by already existing applications in a transparent manner. To achieve this goal, we identified the core required security functions, based on an analysis of the usage scenarios described in Section 5.2 and relevant attacker models. The following categories of security functionality were identified:

- Protection of exchanged messages (encryption, authentication, resilience against traffic analysis [3])
- A sufficient packet delivery probability by combination of broadcast and flooding
- Early detection of an active attacker inside the network(packet dropper, jammer, routing protocol manipulator [4–6])
- Management of a current privacy level resilient against an active attacker [7]
- Key exchange and establishment of cryptographic material (keys shared between direct neighbors and remote parties)

As described in the usage scenarios, a proposed solution must be scalable from tens to thousands of nodes, sometimes without prior knowledge about their deployment pattern and position. No tamper resilience is assumed, although usage of the contact and contactless smart cards was explored and can be eventually used as a trusted computational element [8].

Additionally, the WSNProtectLayer middleware is accompanied by a set of software components, modules, and applications for practical implementation of the usage scenarios:

- Node-state persistency management resilient against occasional node reboots
- Identification of an entity based on contactless smart cards
- Monitoring of movement based on ePIR technology [9]
- Batch configuration management tools for mass programming of tens or hundreds of nodes
- Proximity detection based on radio transmissions of the neighboring devices

5.3.1 Main Components

The three main parts from the security point of view are the intrusion detection component, privacy protection component, and key establishment component (see Figure 5.2), providing the functionality necessary to fulfill design goals. These core components are accompanied by several other components responsible for routing, internal memory management and backup, unified cryptographic providers, and others, as described in more detail in Section 5.4.

Due to the significantly limited amount of RAM memory available on current hardware platforms (e.g., TelosB has 10 kB only [10]), optimizations and memory trade-offs must be performed. Although multiple components exist inside the WSNProtectLayer middleware, necessary data are shared as much as possible in a central memory structure. This also makes an internal state backup easier. To maintain high transmission throughput even when longer operations (e.g., establishment of keys with all neighbors) needs to be executed, a split-phase style [11] of implementation is used, combined with an automata-based programming style.

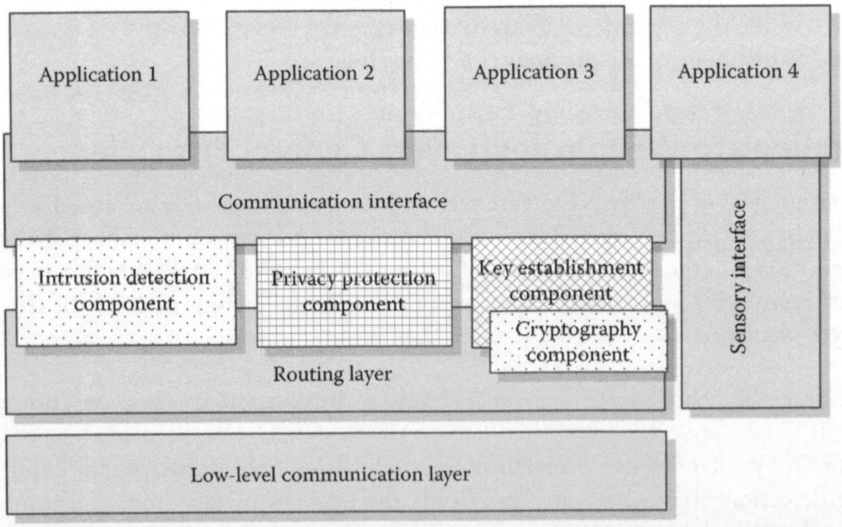

Figure 5.2 Basic scheme of the WSNProtectLayer middleware. The WSNProtectLayer components in the center (excluding the sensory interface) are with a grid background. A user application communicates with a manipulated interface providing message exchange functionality.

5.3.1.1 Privacy Component

The privacy component is paramount to the protection of exchanged packets both on the link level between direct neighbors and at the end-to-end level between a node and a BS. An operator of the network is responsible for setting a proper privacy level based on internal (e.g., information from an IDS component or movement detection) or external events (e.g., transient situation with an elevated sensitivity). Based on a current privacy level, different protection mechanisms are employed by the network nodes, allowing for different trade-offs between network protection and resource consumption.

For packet transmissions, three basic privacy levels are available: (1) no protection, (2) integrity protection (MAC) only, and (3) integrity protection and encryption. Additionally, the routing protocol is configurable based on a current privacy level. When required, the Collection Tree Protocol (CTP) [12] is replaced by phantom routing [13] with a source sender protection. When phantom routing is used, locating the originator of a message is significantly more difficult.

A broadcast authentication scheme for low entropy messages such as low-entropy authentication (LEA) [3] can be employed. Yet LEA is still unnecessarily costly, as we need to authenticate very low entropy messages, for example, 2 bits is enough to encode four different privacy levels. We have proposed [7] a lightweight mechanism for privacy level interchange (which is a low-entropy message) based on Lamport's one-time passwords [14]. In our platform, four privacy levels can be set up. Thus, a BS generates four one-way hash chains of length n and assigns each chain to a single privacy level. The flooding nature of the scheme ensures a robust propagation of the level interchange information. Thus, after the flood, the network should be in a consistent state.

To enable possible receiver identity protection, packets on a radio layer are not sent via unicast, but are broadcasted by the sender by default, received by all neighbors, and only later discarded by all other than the intended recipient. Alternatively, packet transmission to the next hop can be unicasted (this is a more common practice). Both options have security and performance implications. When a packet is broadcasted, the intended packet's recipient can be hidden inside the encrypted header, providing additional protection against a passive eavesdropper and traffic analysis. However, the packet must be then processed by all neighbors only later to be discarded by most of them. Ina harsh environment with a lot of noise, it may also lead to higher packet loss, as packets are not actively acknowledged because the intended recipient is hidden. Depending on the level of transmission channel usage, frequency of packet collisions, and background noise, less-efficient higher-layer acknowledgments may be necessary. To avoid potential negative impact, we have also implemented a variant of WSNProtectLayer that relies on unicast and uses per-packet acknowledgments. This improves the packet delivery ratio, even in difficult radio transmission conditions, but the IDS functionality in this mode is limited and receiver identity cannot be fully protected. Such protection would be possible in theory using broadcast with acknowledgments from all the receivers, but this would be prohibitively costly in terms of additional communication overhead.

The privacy component tries to protect mainly against the passive attacker, which performs packet eavesdropping or source localization attacks.

5.3.1.2 Intrusion Detection Component

The intrusion detection component allows for the monitoring and detection of an active attacker, which influences the network communication to some extent (e.g., packet modification or dropping, jamming). The IDS design builds on our latest results in the field [15–17]. All packets received on the low-level radio layer are monitored; packet characteristics are saved and compared with the packets retransmitted later. When the modified packet is received or the target node fails to transmit at all, the reputation score for that particular node is decreased. When a predefined threshold is reached, a high-priority IDS event is sent to a BS. The BS is responsible for evaluation of these events and providing a response. For example, the network-wide privacy level can be changed (increased security protection), or time-limited "suicide" can be performed to block the offending node[18].

Note that the overall accuracy of such a local detection is limited by multiple factors. A monitoring node may be close enough to receive an original packet, but too far to also receive a retransmitted packet. Network collisions or parallel transmission scan prevent the monitoring node from receiving the packet or the node itself may be occupied by other operations when the transmission is performed. Therefore, false IDS events may be generated, especially in a harsh environment. But as the IDS runs on every node in a network, a BS can evaluate and aggregate IDS events from multiple nodes and react accordingly.

The intrusion detection component tries to protect mainly against the active attacker manipulating communication traffic.

5.3.1.3 Key Establishment Component

The key distribution component is responsible for the handling of predistributed keys, creation of session keys between direct neighbors, and lifetime management of keys (e.g., backup and recovery from flash memory). Its design is based on our extensive experience in the field of key distribution for WSNs [19–23].

The key distribution component will ensure unique pairwise secrets between the following parties:

- A node to its direct neighbor (used for hop-by-hop encryption and message authentication)
- A node to a BS (for periodical collection of sensed data and network control messages)
- A node to a newly deployed node (used for later redeployment of new nodes)

Our scenarios assume a maximum of dozens of up to a few thousand nodes. With a common key length of 128 bits, every node is expected to store key material with a total size ranging from 4 KB (for 250 nodes in a network, emergency unit scenario) to 32 KB (for 2000 nodes in a network, building monitoring scenario). Even the scenario with a maximum of 2000 nodes occupies only a fraction of the memory available on commonly used nodes like TelosB (48 KB flash, 1024 KB EEPROM). Predistributed keys are generated in a trusted environment and stored into configuration files, uploaded via a dedicated Uploader application during a node personalization phase.

Performance overhead related to the key establishment is small, as session keys for all active neighbor nodes are kept in the RAM memory. The EEPROM memory with longer access times is utilized only for occasionally used keys (initial establishment, redeployment).

Alternatively, less common techniques like "key infection" [24] followed by a secrecy amplification phase can be used [25]. We implemented this approach, but keep it as an optional component due to node limited program memory resources.

The key distribution component uses the cryptography component for its core cryptographic functionality and maintains available cryptographic material even when the node is unexpectedly rebooted.

5.3.1.4 Cryptography Component

The cryptography component is responsible for the provision of higher-level cryptographic functions utilized by the other components. Its design and provided functionality is based on our recent discoveries in this field [26]. Due to an abstraction of the used cryptographic algorithms, higher-level components can change underlying concrete cryptographic algorithms, if necessary. For the prototype implementation, an advanced encryption standard (AES) algorithm in multiple different modes of operation was used. Furthermore, we investigated the performance of various encryption algorithms and multiple AES implementations in [27].

The following operations are provided by the cryptography component:

- Protection of a message: Based on the current privacy level, a message is encrypted and/or integrity protected. Encryption is performed using the AES algorithm in the counter (CTR) mode [28]. To decrease an overall application memory footprint, the integrity protection is implemented using the same underlying AES engine in the MAC mode [29]. The privacy component is the primary user of this functionality.
- Handling of an authenticated broadcast: ABS can change the network-wide privacy level via a special message distributed as an authenticated broadcast. As ordinary nodes can be compromised by an attacker, an authenticated broadcast cannot be simply protected by symmetric cryptography keys. The cryptography component provides the broadcast verification and related key update based on authenticated hash chains (see Section 5.3.1.1).
- Key derivation: When required, new cryptographic material is derived from long-term predistributed secrets stored in the EEPROM memory. Key derivation is a core functionality used by the key distribution component.
- Hash computation: An efficient hash function is required by the intrusion detection component to monitor and extract characteristics of received packets for neighbor monitoring.

To limit the memory and performance overhead, objects like cryptographic keys are not retrieved as a raw copy of value, but used via handles in a copy-free manner instead. To further limit the memory overhead, a single cryptographic primitive (AES) in different modes of operation is used to build other cryptographic primitives like a hash function and an integrity checksum. Software implementation of the AES was utilized, but if the underlying hardware platform supports hardware acceleration of a suitable algorithm, transparent exchange for the accelerated one can be performed.

5.3.2 WSNProtectLayer Middleware Lifecycle

The WSNProtectLayer middleware lifecycle contains multiple steps, depicted in Figure 5.3. Initially, a physical node is uploaded with a user application enhanced with the WSNProtectLayer middleware. Personalization data like pre-shared keys, initial values of the authentication hash chain, or sensitivity settings for the intrusion detection component are uploaded. The node is then ready for deployment.

Once physically deployed, the boot sequence is executed and low-level radio is started. The node is waiting for a command transmitted via an authenticated broadcast from the BS, which is propagated by the simple flooding algorithm. Once received, the node performs the neighbor discovery process, establishes unique shared cryptographic session keys, and initiates the CTP algorithm for routing tree discovery toward a BS. The CTP algorithm can be continuously executed

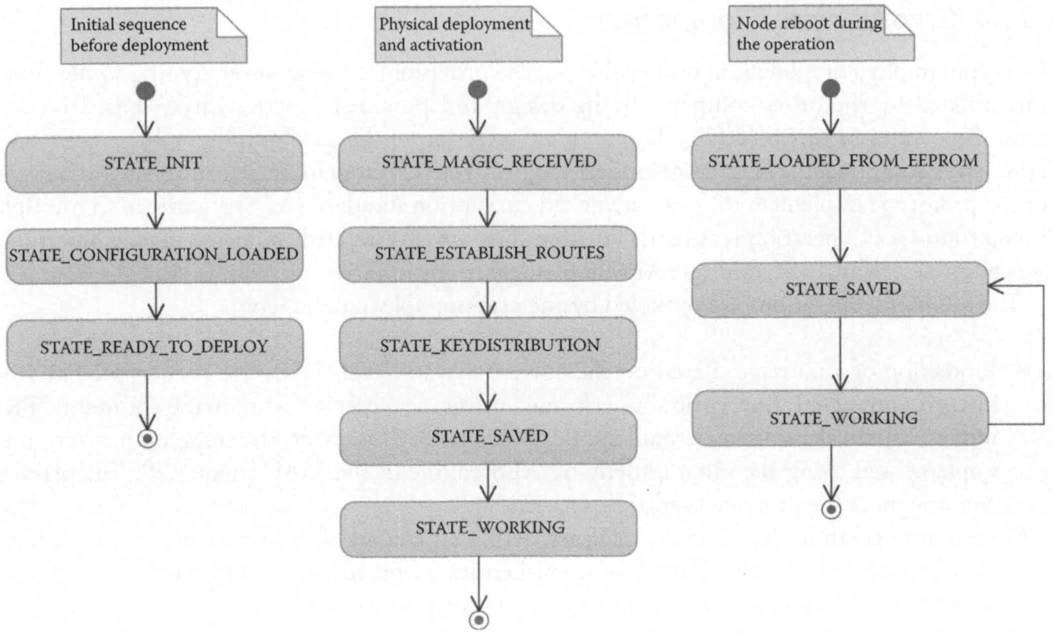

Figure 5.3 WSNProtectLayer middleware lifecycle.

with the network topology adapting on the current network configuration or executed only occasionally. When a secure connection with the neighbor nodes is established, the node backs up relevant internal data from the transient RAM into the persistent EEPROM memory as a precaution against an unintended rebooting event. When the initialization phase is finished, the node is ready for normal operation and control is given to the user application. The persistent backup is performed periodically (e.g., every minute) during the whole lifetime of the node.

If a node reboot eventually occurs (power glitch, user reset, etc.), the content of the backup from the EEPROM is restored into working transient structures stored in the RAM memory (shared keys, routing table, etc.) and checked for consistency. Once verified, the node continues to operate as usual. The restore operation takes less than 5 s to complete.

5.4 Implementation Details

The designed architecture is implemented for the widely used TinyOS operating system and is available as an open-source code under the FreeBSD license [30]. Already existing applications using radio interface were targeted. The design was performed to make incorporation of the architecture as easy as possible, requiring only minimal changes to the original application source code. As radio interfaces (AMSend, AMReceive, AMControl in TinyOS) are already in use by a user application, the WSNProtectLayer is inserted as another intermediate layer (middleware) between the user application and physical radio-related routines. For the user application, the WSNProtectLayer has exactly the same interfaces as the original AMSend, AMReceive, and AMControl, and therefore only a simple change in linking (called wiring in TinyOS) is required. The WSNProtectLayer itself utilizes original radio components for packet send and receive, but manipulates packets (encryption, integrity, routing path) in between. The complexity of all

```
configuration BlinkToRadioAppC {

---> Original Components
components ActiveMessageC;
components new AMSenderC();
components new AMReceiverC();

---> Replaced by ProtectLayerC

---> Original wirings
App.Packet -> AMSenderC;
App.AMPacket -> AMSenderC;
App.AMControl -> ActiveMessageC;
App.AMSend -> AMSenderC;
App.Receive -> AMReceiverC;

---> Rewired to ProtectLayerC

}
```

```
configuration BlinkToRadioAppC {


components ProtectLayerC;



App.Packet -> ProtectLayerC.Packet;
App.AMControl -> ProtectLayerC.AMControl;
App.AMSend -> ProtectLayerC.AMSend;
App.Receive -> ProtectLayerC.Receive;


}
```

Figure 5.4 Source code changes required to incorporate packet encryption, authentication, phantom routing, and intrusion detection provided by WSNProtectLayer middleware into Blink2Radio application are limited to a single wiring file (source code is edited for better visibility, with unimportant parts omitted).

components is therefore completely hidden from the user application. For example, a well-known TinyOS example application, Blink2Radio, requires only the changes depicted in Figure 5.4.

5.4.1 ProtectLayerC Component

The ProtectLayerC component is the main high-level interface for user application. To support easy integration, ProtectLayerC implements TinyOS standard radio interfaces that are usually used by the user application to facilitate wireless transmissions. As shown on the model of components of WSNProtectLayer middleware in Figure 5.5, the user application binds to ProtectLayerC instead of common radio interfaces where ProtectLayerC provides exactly the same methods (start of radio, transmission of message, etc.), but with additional protection transparently added. Once rewired, all packets are protected and routed according to the current privacy level, the necessary cryptographic keys are established, and monitoring for packet-dropping neighbors is performed.

5.4.2 Configuration Component

Components used in WSNProtectLayer define their own configuration structures to store their internal state. These structures are aggregated in one central configuration structure called *combinedData* that is stored in the SharedData component. SharedData acts as a central point for configuration, providing easy access to individual parts of the configuration structure. It also manages backup to EEPROM and restore from EEPROM to RAM upon node restart. Easy backup and recovery lead to a centralized configuration design.

5.4.3 Logging

To minimize the negative effects of logging and debugging (radio noise, collisions) on a real network, logs are collected using the UART (serial USB) interface over wire. The core of our logging mechanism is the TinyOS printf component, which internally buffers ASCII messages and sends them in a packet of a fixed size to the connected listener over UART. This design solution was easy to implement and use during development. Moreover, our logging mechanism uses severity of the

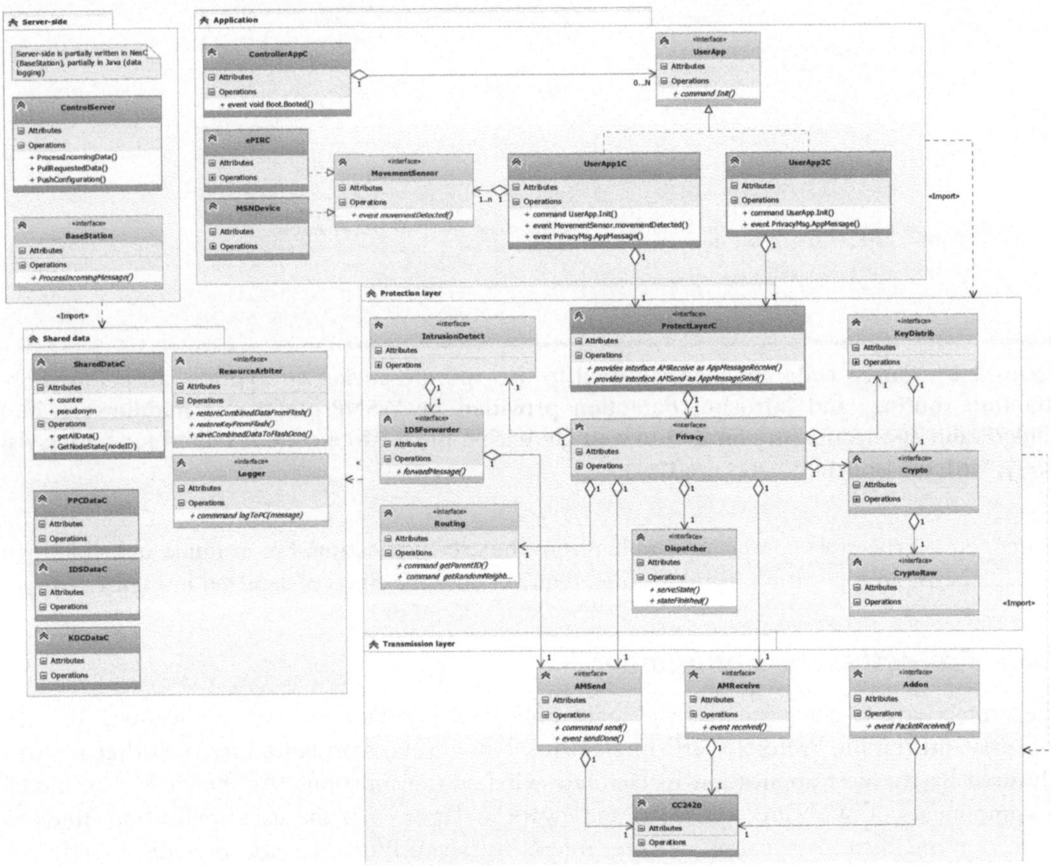

Figure 5.5 Overall architecture (only selected operations and attributes are shown).

log message and it is possible to disable certain severity levels at compile time and thus save both program memory and speed at runtime.

5.4.4 Uploader and ProtectLayerConfigurator

The entire project is composed of multiple applications. Uploader and *ProtectLayerConfigurator* are stand-alone applications meant for node initialization or preparation by preloading required data to the node prior to installation of the main application. Since the main application rewrites the ROM and RAM memory of the node, all preloaded information has to be stored within wiped EEPROM memory.

We separated unrelated functionality for the sake of the application design but also for practical reasons, so the production code is separated from the initial setup tasks. During the implementation process, the limits for both RAM and program storage were often hit, so the approach was to minimize the size of the running sensor node code.

Uploader is a Java application that, after successful connection to the a node, reads data, redistributes keys from configuration files, and sends them one by one to the node via USB.

The anode receiving the preloaded information has to store its information in the EEPROM memory. That is the purpose of ProtectLayerConfigurator. It is a TinyOS application installed on the node that, upon first reception of a key to be stored, erases the EEPROM, changing all bits to 1s, and then continually stores each incoming key in the designated memory block.

The application is designed in such a way that WSNProtectLayer configuration data (combinedData) can be uploaded to nodes' EEPROMs via Configurator, but in the actual implementation this was not used as it turned out to be unnecessary.

5.4.5 Packet Acknowledgments

We utilized multiple experiences with radio signal propagation obtained before (e.g., [31]) and during active development of the protect layer and focused on this aspect thoroughly. Development of secure middleware brings some overhead that can be limiting for an application and overall WSN performance.

To enable possible receiver identity protection, packets on the AM radio layer are not sent via unicast, but are broadcasted by a sender. Thus, a packet is received by all the neighbors and passed to the *Privacy* component that, based on possibly encrypted content (*SPHeader*), decides on further processing (or dropping) of the packet. However, this approach makes active acknowledging by the original receiver and retransmission by the sender of the packets impossible. Since the wireless communication is unreliable, this countermeasure may significantly decrease the number of received packets (up to 30%–40% in our indoor experiments). Thus, we decided to provide a possibility to switch the protect layer into "acknowledging" mode at the cost of limited identity protection and IDS functionality. Another approach would be to provide acknowledging on a "higher" *Privacy* component, but the hardware parameters of the sensor nodes are very limiting for any further extension.

We also performed some experiments on throughput of the WSN. We found out that sending a packet by each of the 28 nodes in a ragged laboratory environment more frequently than every5 s can increase the packet loss rate.

The IDS component is limited when privacy protection is used by the WSN. Thus, all overheard packets are passed decrypted by the *Privacy* component to the *IntrusionDetect* component. Using the decrypted content of the *SPHeader*, the IDS is able to monitor whether each monitored sensor node forwards packets as expected (i.e., to the expected receiver with the expected content).

5.4.6 TelosB and MICAz Performance Platform Comparison

We considered the two most popular WSN platforms for WSNProtectLayer implementation—TelosB and MICAz [10,32–34].

WSNProtectLayer compilation with the TinyOS tool chain states the following system requirements: 39,314 bytes in program flash and 8,120 bytes in RAM (compiled with gcc v4.8.1 and nescc v1.3.3 for TinyOS v2.1.2). On the TelosB, we almost hit the flash memory limit. The main difference in platforms is the size of the available RAM. WSNProtectLayer would not fit in the memory of the MicaZ, and thus TelosB was the platform of choice. WSNProtectLayer is supposed to be middleware, and thus there should be enough space for another application using WSNProtectLayer on the platform. Also, the convenience of the programming and collecting data from the network contributed to the selection of TelosB. MICAz needs a special programming board to be connected to the node to program it and communicate with it via a UART interface, while TelosB is equipped with a USB interface for this purpose (Table 5.1).

Table 5.1 Relevant Features of the TelosB and MikaZ Platforms from the Perspective of WSNProtectLayer

Properties	*MICAz*	*TelosB*
Processor	ATMega128L	MSP430 F1611
Clock frequency (MHz)	8	8
Bus (bit)	8	16
RAM (kB0	4	10
Program Flash	128	48
Flash memory (kB)	512	1024
Wake-up time	4.1 ms	6 μs
Radio chip	CC2420	CC2420
Flashing	Programming board needed	Directly with USB
Consumption active	8 mA @ 8 MHz, 3 V	4 mA @ 8 MHz, 3 V
Consumption idle	5 μA @ power down mode	2.6 μA

5.5 Experiments

The wireless transmission medium is notoriously unreliable and any idea, protocol, or application needs to be thoroughly tested in a real environment, especially when dealing with resource-constrained platform-like sensor nodes that can create additional computational or transmission bottlenecks and influence the functionality in an unanticipated way. We performed a significant number of various experiments with a network of real nodes, complementing our previous experiments inside the simulators [31]. Some experiments were focused on evaluation of basic features like radio propagation, packet drop rate, or received signal strength indicator (RSSI) variability, with the results being used to configure components of the WSNProtectLayer. The rest of the experiments were carried out during the development of the WSNProtectLayer and used to verify functionality, test additional hardware extensions (ePIR, RFID reader), and identify usability issues. We built the dedicated laboratory test bed with 30 TelosB nodes on top of nine connected offices and used it extensively during development and testing (see Section 5.5.1 for more details). We also moved the test-bed nodes outdoors and performed more complex tests with various network topologies (see Section 5.5.3) in normal and also more extreme (snow) conditions.

5.5.1 How to Build a Development Test Bed

Inspecting the network behavior is not a simple task. In an ad hoc wireless network, we have the following options:

- Collect information from a BS. The problem with this is that we only receive information that is successfully delivered to the BS and not other information, for example information on lost packets.

- Have entire network wired. This is only applicable in controlled and limited environments, such as our test bed in the laboratory, where we can afford to have the entire network connected via a USB interface, enabling the nodes to be powered and communication with them.
- Collect independent information from the wireless medium using nodes listening in promiscuous mode, aka sniffers connected to a laptop.
- Have all required information stored on the devices' flash memory. The disadvantage here is the manual labor related to following up the readout and the significant time penalty of the write operation.
- Use the visible output interface of the nodes, namely its red, blue, and green diodes. This has obvious disadvantages.

During our experiments, we used all these options. From our experience, the best option for application development is the wired option. A wired test bed can perform its functionality via the wireless medium while logging all required information for debugging purposes via the USB. We used active USB cables and separately powered USB hubs to obtain reliable communication over a distance of more than 30 m (Figure 5.6). Furthermore, sending debugging information via a wireless medium is unreliable and can cause collisions with normal WSN traffic, influencing statistics of delivery ratio and so on.

When performing an outdoor experiment, the sniffers option combined with the devices' flash memory option was deemed as the best fitting. An important issue for both options is the time synchronization of multiple nodes. Our solution for the sniffers consists of time-stamping each received message with the local time of the laptop(s) connected to the sniffers. However, we are only able to collect intercepted communication and do not get additional information on the nodes' inner state. Furthermore, covering the entire network can be just as expensive as connecting the network via a cable.

The flash memory option requires backward synchronization by finding same intercepted messages on multiple nodes. Moreover, the memory access is a very slow operation, taking about

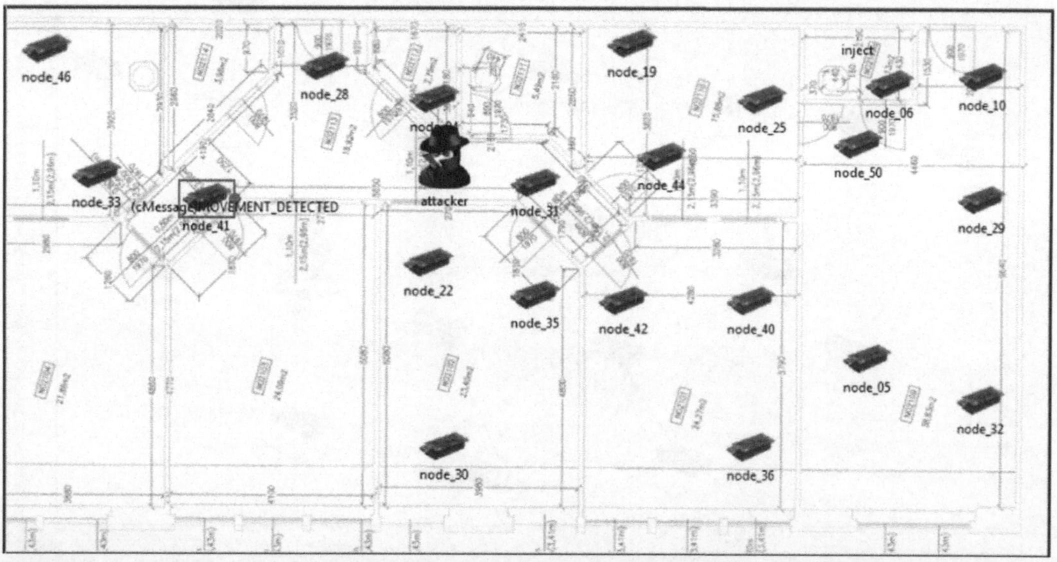

Figure 5.6 The replay of captured network traffic inside OmNET++ simulator (indoor test-bed experiment).

2.13 ms to write 16 bytes, while blocking additional functionality of the node. In comparison, from [27], sending a message of 16 bytes takes 8.02 ms. Furthermore, it can be expected that we would like to acquire and save more information during the experiment than just incoming or outgoing packets, thus significantly reducing the available computational time of the node.

When visualizing a passed experiment, we take advantage of the visual environment of the OmNET++ simulator as shown in Figure 5.7. We log the successfully sent messages from each node via USB to a separate file on the server, time-stamping each incoming message. These files are then serialized by the timestamps creating a single file with all logged messages and/or events. This file is then read by our application and line by line processed in the simulator, generating a depiction of the network's behavior.

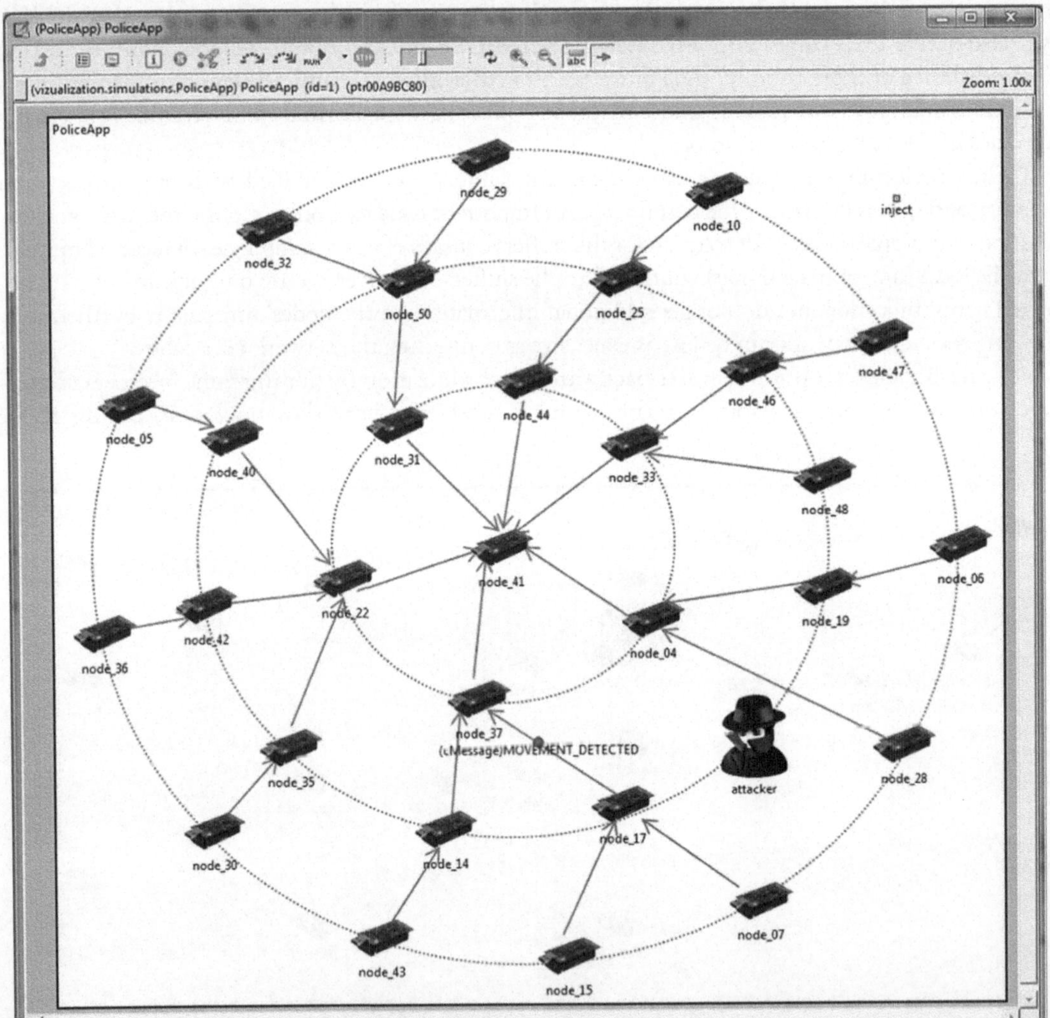

Figure 5.7 The replay of captured network traffic inside OmNET++ simulator (outdoor experiment).

The general communication pattern in WSNs is hop by hop. For visualization purposes, we do not take into account messages lost during transmission, as we can directly spot failure between hops by not forwarding the message.

5.5.2 Supporting Experiments

5.5.2.1 RSSI Radio Signal Strength Experiment

The aim of this experiment was to reconstruct the radio propagation map in the test bed. The experiment used RSSI of received packets to build an RSSI map for the whole test bed during the long time (days).

The whole experiment was controlled by a server application that periodically selected one node to transmit. There was only one transmitting node at a time; the node selection was round-robin to cover the whole test bed. All other nodes were silently listening to the incoming broadcast packets and monitored their RSSI, reporting measurements to the server application. The server stored the measured data (e.g., RSSI, packet loss) to the database. The length of a message being transmitted was set to a different size to study the possible correlation of packet loss and message length due to collisions.

The process is prone to errors. Some nodes may malfunction or hang from time to time. For this reason, we have to employ self-recovering mechanisms in the controlling application since in the long term the test bed could end up half-frozen. Every sensor node was periodically sending "I am still alive" packets to the server application (besides measured data) to declare its state and health. In case of a long interruption of these messages, the node was considered dead, automatically restarted, and reconfigured by the server application.

Configuration of this experiment was a tuple (txnode, txpower, msglength).

- The domain txnode (transmitting node) consisted of all nodes in the test bed.
- The domain txpower (transmit power) consisted of all TX power levels (transmission powers). Namely, for the TelosB platform, it is set {31,27,23,19,15,11,7,3}, from strongest to weakest.
- The domain msglength (extra message payload length) consisted of manually selected message sizes (0, 16, or 64 bytes).

The experiment ran on our test bed for 2 weeks. The results of this experiment were preprocessed in comma-separated values (CSV) format and RSSI maps were generated for each transmitting node, for each configuration. Figure 5.8 shows an example of such an RSSI map.

5.5.2.2 CTP Routing Tree Discovery

Having a complete RSSI map of the test bed, the question is how real routing protocols behave with respect to the collected data. The aim of this experiment was to collect statistics about legitimate CTP traffic.

One node (near the server that was collecting the results) was manually picked as a root of the CTP tree. Since almost every two nodes could in principle communicate on one hop in our test bed (see the signal propagation experiment discussed in Section 5.5.2.1), the CTP tree was scaled-down by reducing the TX power for all CTP-related frames. As a consequence, beacons and routing information were transmitted at lower power, resulting in a higher number of hops to the root node (a BS).

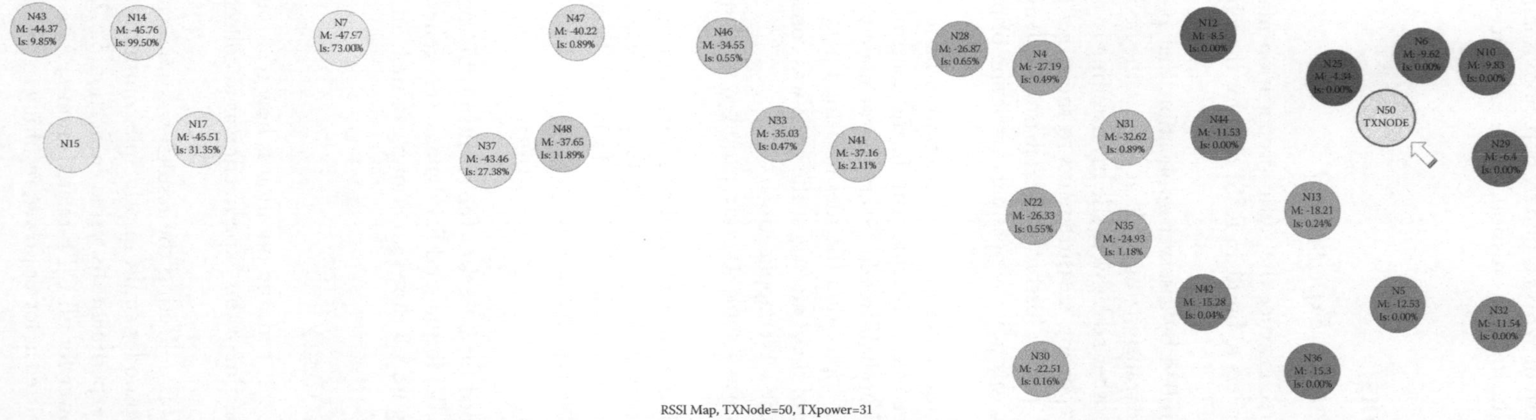

Figure 5.8 Example of RSSI received by nodes. The transmitting node is shown by an arrow. For all other nodes, the darker the color, the higher the RSSI of the received packet. There was intuition that during working hours, there should be more noise in the radio channel than at the weekend, for example. However, this cannot be proven for every node (see Figure 5.9). We found that RX–TX node pairs had a very stable RSSI channel, but, in contrast, there were nodes with very unstable channels (stability is better with higher average RSSI values).

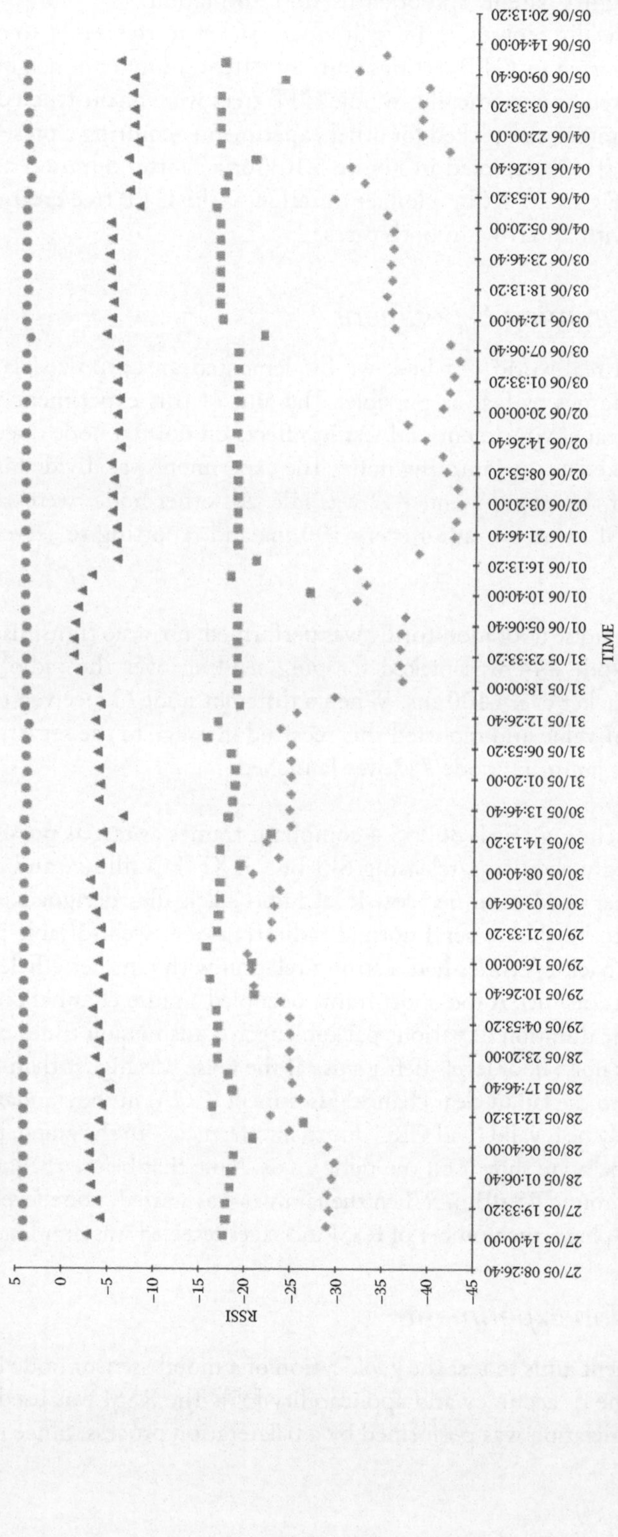

Figure 5.9 Variation of RSSI for various selected RX–TX node pairs.

A timer was running on every node (independently on every other node) that was triggering in the period of 10 s (±5 s variability, uniform distribution to avoid synchronized collisions). In the case of a timer fire event, a new CTP message sending was started. The CTP message contained a message origin, the origin's parent, and other useful information.

Every node periodically sent an "I am still alive" packet to the server to declare its state and health. Every node reported its CTP settings (current parent, number of neighbors, etc.) when the CTP timer was triggered or periodically. Whole CTP trees were reconstructed from these reports off-line and the most stable were picked for other experiments requiring a preset network topology.

An example CTP tree is depicted in Figure 5.10 (for a shorter duration of the CTP tree creation process) and in Figure 5.11 (for a longer duration of the CTP tree creation process). The BS (root) is pointed out with an arrow in both cases.

5.5.2.3 IDS and Jamming Experiment

To test jamming in a real-world test bed, we implemented an optimized jammer for TinyOS, sending application frames as fast as possible. The aim of this experiment was to test jammer implementation in a real environment and test its effects on normal node operation.

Node #42 was picked as the jamming node. The experiment was divided into three phases. In the first two phases of this experiment, #42 was idle. All other nodes were sampling radio noise floor level (actual RSSI value on radio) every 100 ms and reporting to server. Every phase took approx. 10 min.

- *First phase.* Only noise floor monitoring was performed; no radio transmission was performed.
- *Second phase.* Node #44 was picked for ping sending over the radio channel. The node broadcasted a packet every 100 ms. When a different node C received this ping message, it sampled its RSSI value and reported this received message to the server.
- *Third phase.* The jamming node #42 was launched.

The jammer was sending IEEE 802.15.4 compliant frames as fast as possible (fast retransmissions without repeatedly acquiring/releasing SPI bus, TXFIFO filling, and another packet sent overhead). The jammer used modified low-level radio stack files designed to be able to switch jamming on/off and to be able to send normal radio frames as well (disable jamming).We found that packet sizes and back-off times had a strong relation with jammer efficiency (a longer frame needed more time to transmit). A too-short frame occupied a radio channel only for a short period of time. A study on the duration of various packet length transmission times can be found in [27].

Figure 5.12 shows noise floor levels (left *y* axis). If the noise was higher than 80, a node could not send any message due to the fail in clear channel assessment (CCA) in the standard setting. A received message would probably be invalid (bad CRC due to interferences). In the graph, the RSSI of the packets received in 10 s blocks are shown on the right *y* axis. Note that before the jammer was launched, the noise values were around 75 dBm. When the jammer was started, noise levels rose to high values (80–130). In the third phase, the number of RSSI messages received was dramatically reduced.

5.5.2.4 Localization Experiment

This support experiment aims to test the geolocation of a mobile sensor node in a static real-world test bed and determine its accuracy and applicability [35]. The RSSI was used to measure the signal strength. The localization was performed by a trilateration process. Since trilateration involves

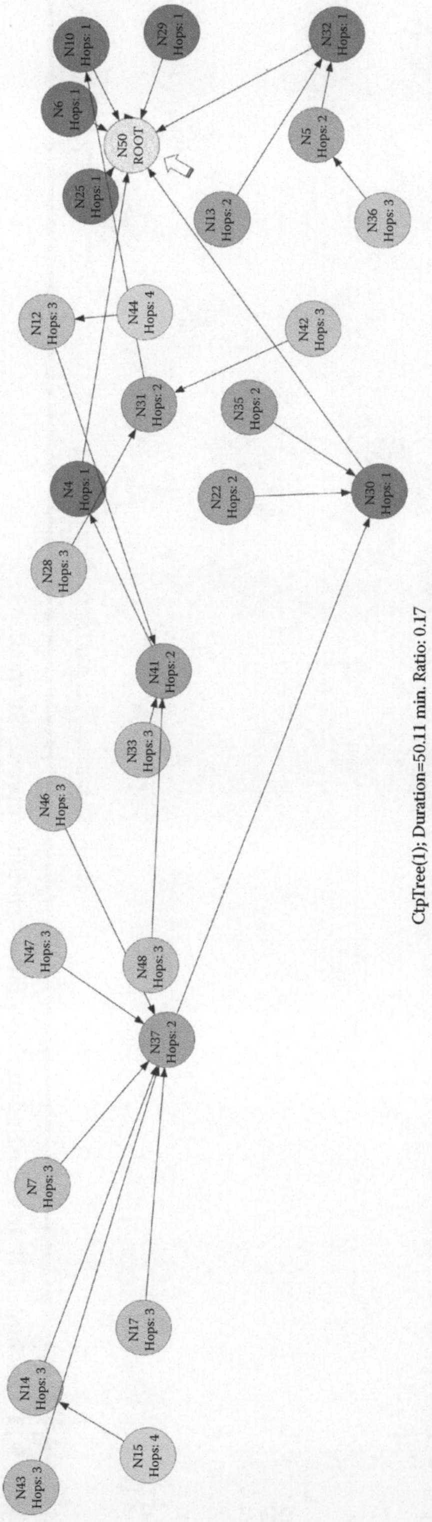

Figure 5.10 Example CTP tree created during a shorter period (approx. 50 min).

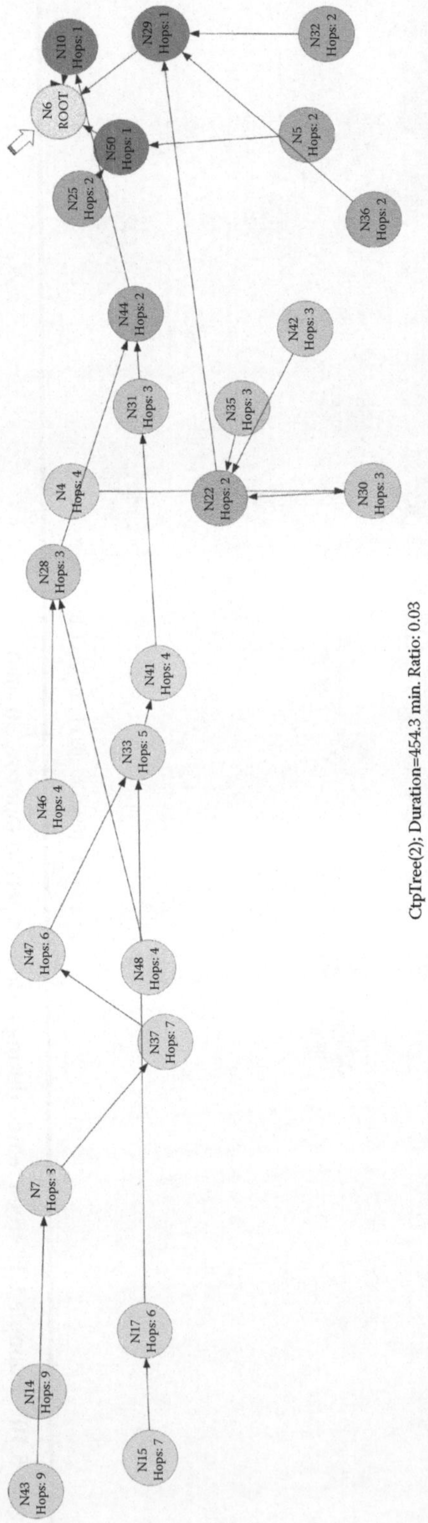

Figure 5.11 Example CTP tree created during a longer period (approx. 450 min).

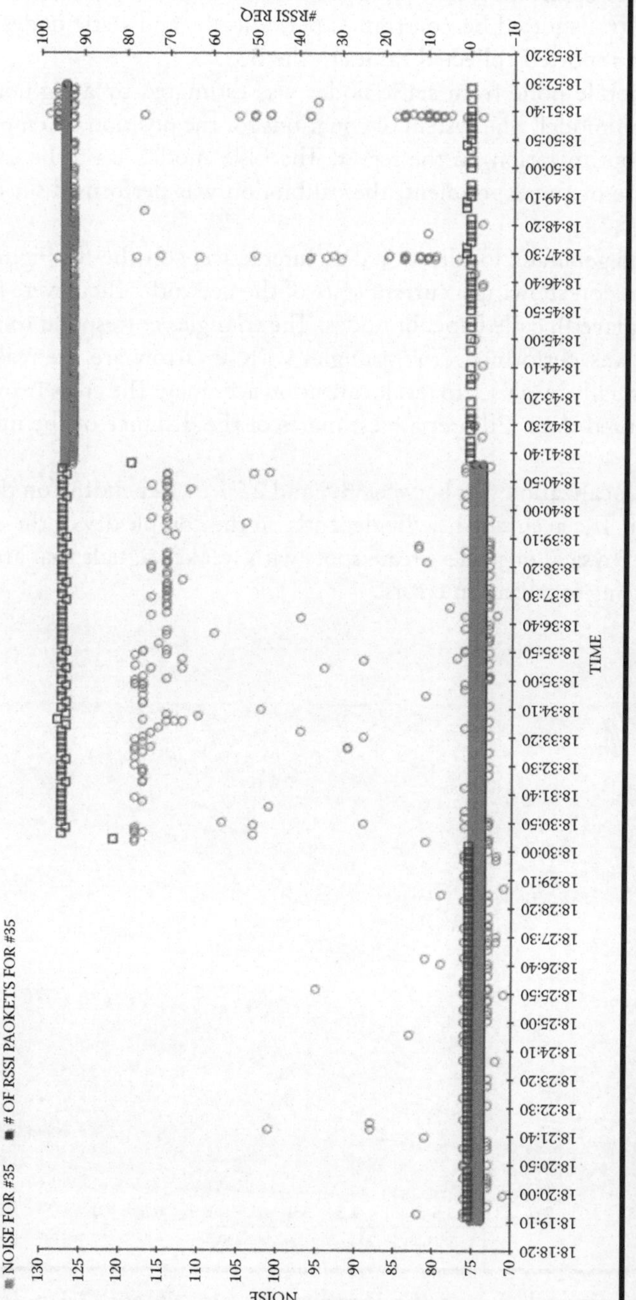

Figure 5.12 Noise floor in all three phases during the jamming experiment. Time is on the horizontal axis. Each phase of the experiment lasted for 10 min. Yellow circles denote noise floor radio measurement on node #35. Purple squares denote the number of ping packets received on node #35.

solving a system of nonlinear equations, the computation is expensive. Thus, it was carried out on the server.

Static test-bed nodes operated on batteries, deployed in one room. The test bed was connected via a BS node to the server application that managed the test bed and performed the localization. The mobile sensor node transmitted beacon frames periodically, and static nodes measured RSSI of incoming packets and reported collected values to the BS.

The distance of a mobile node from static nodes was estimated by a log-normal shadowing (LNS) signal propagation model. The system of equations for the position of a mobile sensor node was solved by numeric optimization on the server. The LNS model has to be calibrated at first. Thus, in the initial phase of the experiment, the calibration was performed for each static node separately.

The server application generates localization data interactively on-the-fly. Figure 5.13 is a snapshot of the application region showing a current state of the network. There were four static nodes in the network (two displayed), called anchor nodes. The triangles correspond to the places where the calibration of LNS was performed. The triangles with an arrow are the real position of the mobile node, added manually by a user to test localization accuracy. The cross is an estimated node position from the measured data. Ellipses are estimates of the distance of the mobile node from static nodes.

The accuracy of the localization was between 3.5 and 2.77 m, depending on the heuristic used during the computation. The accuracy heavily depends on the complexity of the environment the test bed is deployed in. Physical obstacles create spots with weaker signals that are not covered by the model properly, causing localization errors.

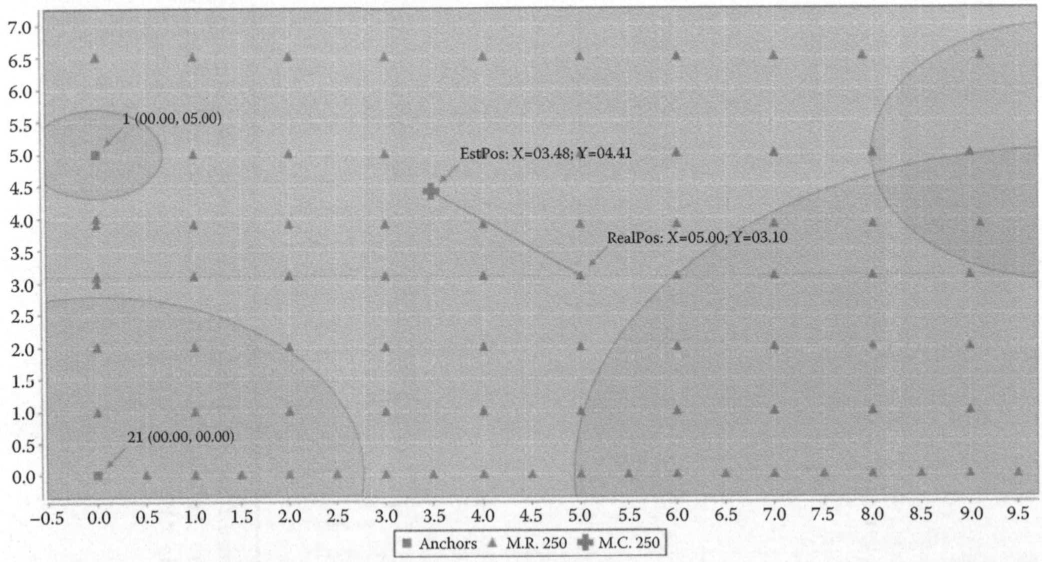

Figure 5.13 Map of a network during the localization experiment. Triangles denote points at which the system was calibrated. Squares are static WSN nodes performing localization measurements. Ellipses around them denote estimation of the distance from a mobile node. Crosses denote final estimated position, connected to a real position of the mobile node by line.

5.5.3 Complex Experiments

We performed five complex experiments during the WSNProtectLayer development period. Each of them is discussed in this section, including motivation for them, such as observations that we used for the subsequent development. Three of the experiments were performed during our project workshops in Cikhaj 2012 and2013 and Mirov 2014.

5.5.3.1 Cikhaj 2012: Social Interactions

The goal of this experiment was to analyze the accuracy of geographic localization using radio communication of sensor nodes. We also analyzed social interactions of the participants. The observations were beneficial, especially for the scenario of the building monitoring.

Each participant of the Cikhaj 2012 meeting was equipped with a TelosB sensor node positioned on their chest and programmed to observe nodes in its close proximity. While most of the nodes were mobile nodes worn by a person, six other nodes were positioned statically in strategic places like the meeting room, sleeping rooms, doors, and so on. The goal of the static sensor nodes was to record the geographical location of the participants. The static sensor nodes are depicted in Figure 5.14.

The application developed for the experiment worked in the following way. Every node broadcasted a *hello* packet every 5 s and listened for broadcasts from other nodes. Every time a node received a broadcast message, RSSI together with local time was stored into the EEPROM memory of the node. Additionally, the master time from one special statically placed node was periodically broadcasted and also stored in the EEPROM memory to enable exact log synchronization later during the evaluation.

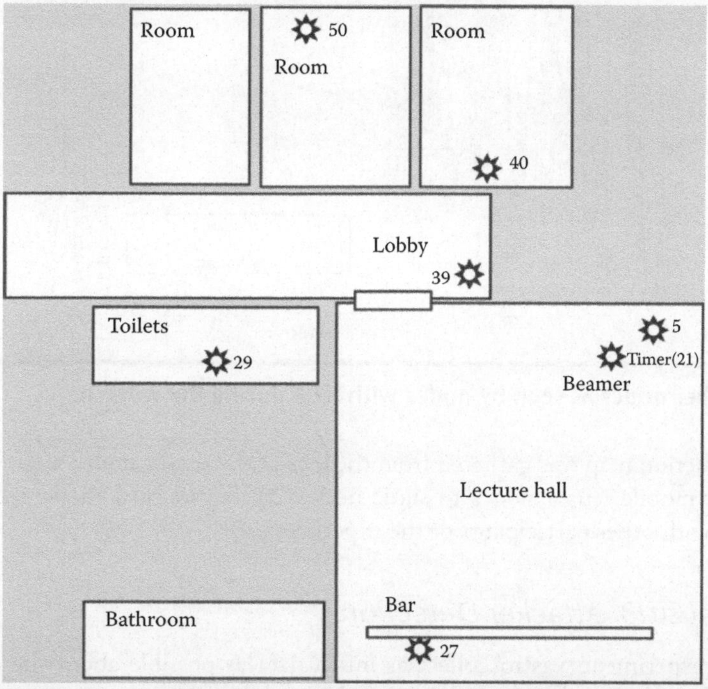

Figure 5.14 Placement of the static sensor nodes in the Cikhaj 2012 social experiment.

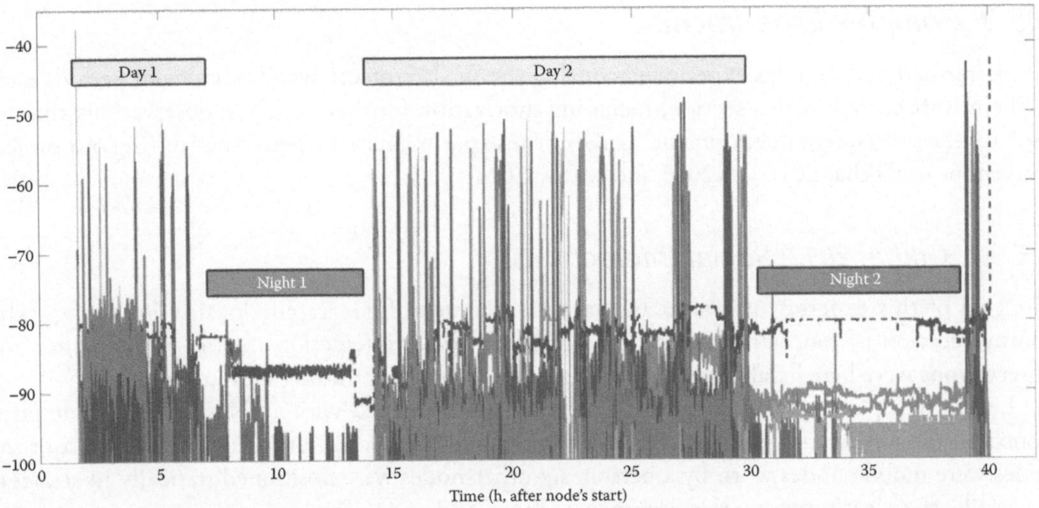

Figure 5.15 Proximity of mobile sensor nodes to static node # 29 during the workshop.

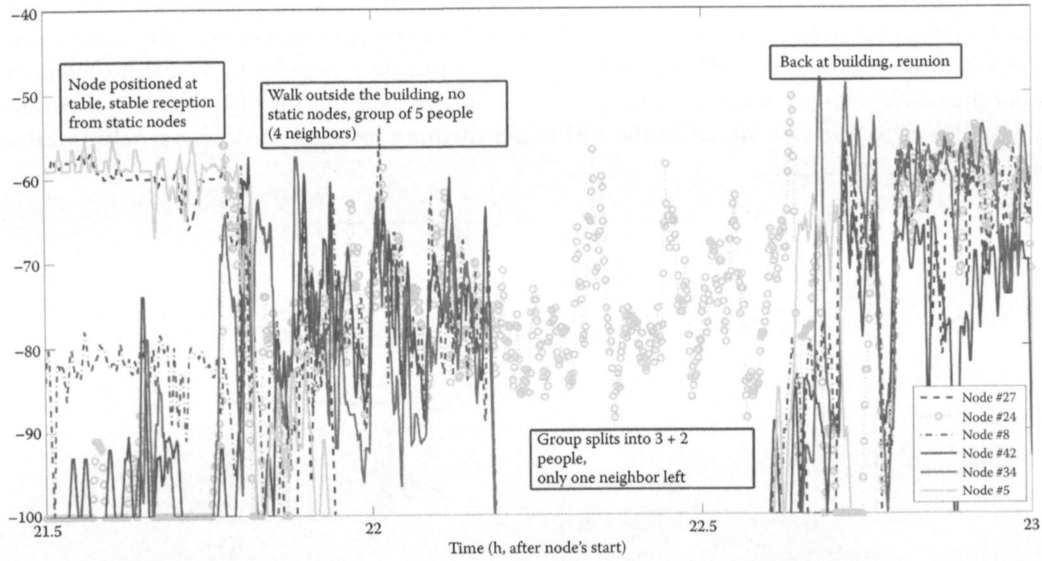

Figure 5.16 Other nodes as seen by nodes with ID 8 during the workshop.

A social interaction map was gathered from the logs of the sensor nodes. Figure 5.15 illustrates the proximity of mobile sensor nodes to static node #29. Figure 5.16 shows the interactions of mobile node #8 with other participants of the experiment.

5.5.3.2 Cikhaj 2013: Attacker Detection

The goal of the experiment was to collect as much data as possible about the behavior of real sensor nodes when deployed as described by the mobile emergency unit scenario with the WSNProtectLayer application enabled. The main goal was to field-test an intermediate version of

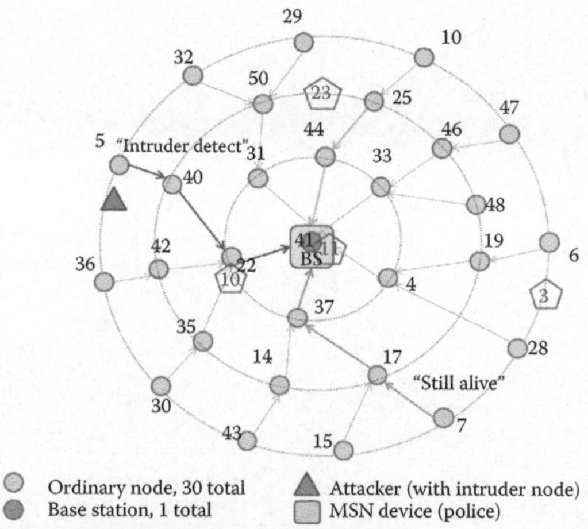

Figure 5.17 Topology for emergency unit scenario.

the prototype application. We also focused on the detection of movement of an attacker through the sensed area.

A network for the experiment was composed of 29 wireless sensor nodes placed on snow towers. Each node had more application components deployed and running: user application, WSNProtectLayer middleware, logger (serving as an IDS), and application for simulation of motion detection. Nodes were physically organized into three concentric circles in whose center a BS was located. Figure 5.17 shows the emergency unit scenario WSN topology. Sniffers that we used for monitoring the WSN communication are depicted by pentagons. The sniffers were not part of the WSN and did not actively participate in the communication.

The duration of the whole experiment was approximately 65 min. In the first 60 min, the network performed without the presence of an attacker, recording only ordinary communication. In the remaining time, there were four attacks simulated.

The task of each node was to inform the BS with two types of messages:

- Still alive message (SA): Generated regularly every 5 s informing the BS that the node is still actively connected to the network.
- Movement detected message (MD): Generated once whenever the node detects attacker's movement.

Nodes did not address their messages to the BS directly. Both SA and MD messages were delivered along a fixed static routing tree whose structure is indicated by the arrows in Figure 5.17. The sensor nodes logged network information. Every node was required to store every received (either addressed for this or a different node) message into the EEPROM memory.

The experiment was designed as a simulation of a sensor network for motion detection. Attacker movement detection was simulated by radio proximity. Whenever any node in the network captured a special packet produced by an attacker, it informed the BS by sending an MD message. During the experiment, there were four attacks simulated. Each attack differed in direction and speed (the attacker was moving slowly in the first case and fast in the others) of the attacker's movement. All of the intrusion scenarios are shown in Figure 5.18.

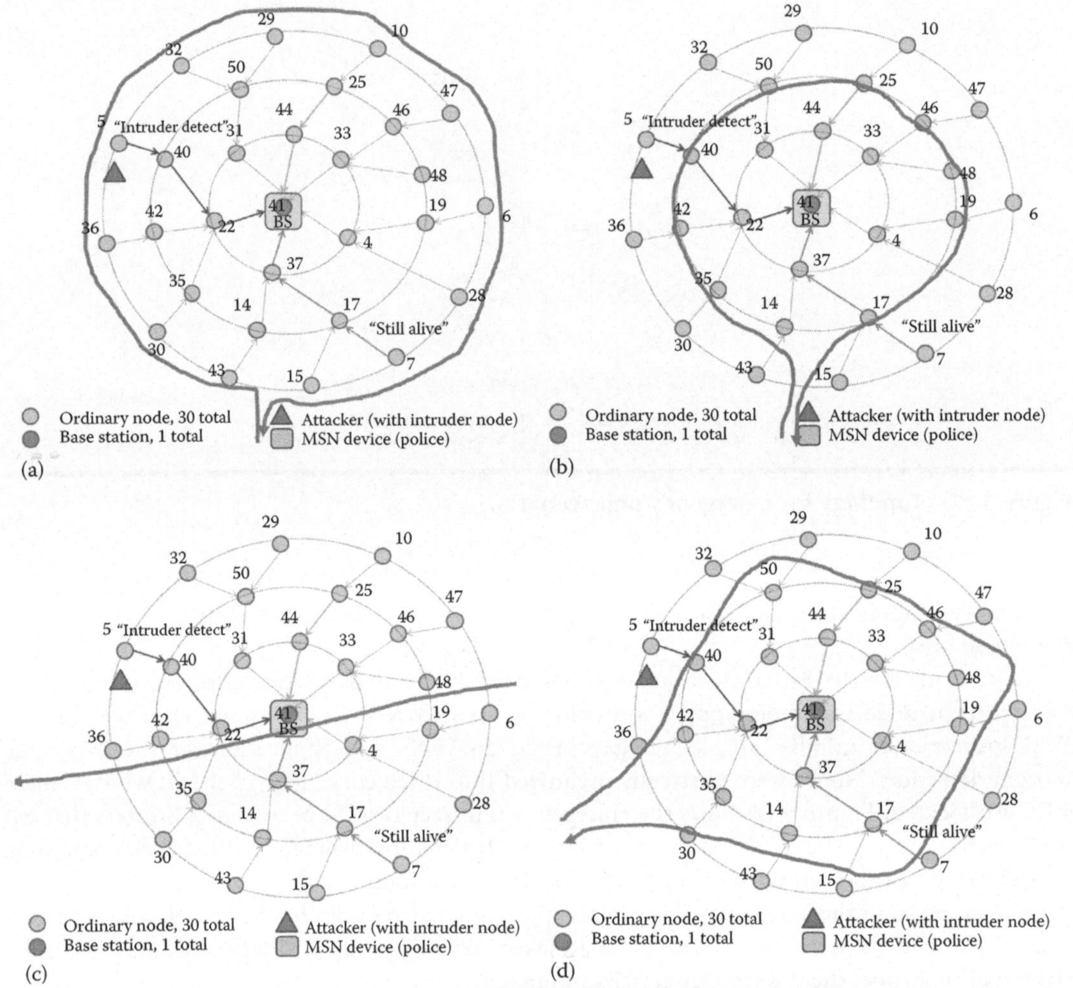

Figure 5.18 Movements of the attacker that was simulated during the experiment.

Valuable information about the area covered by sniffer nodes is depicted in Figure 5.19. The data it contains were collected from all sniffers together with duplicate logs removed (the same messages could be captured by more sniffers). Data coming from this analysis were later used for analyzing fractions of packets lost and also for describing the attacker's movement in time.

The main observation of this experiment was the fact that the ratio of successfully delivered packets should be increased. However, this experiment was an important milestone of our WSNProtectLayer development, as all relevant components were field-tested together.

5.5.3.3 Test Bed 2013: Movement and Item Detection

The main goal of the experiment performed in our laboratory test bed was to evaluate movement detection using sensor nodes equipped with movement detection and a contactless card reader (RFID). The hardware-enhanced sensor nodes are depicted in Figure 5.20. The test lasted 22 days, and a large amount of data was gathered. From the data, we were able to reconstruct the

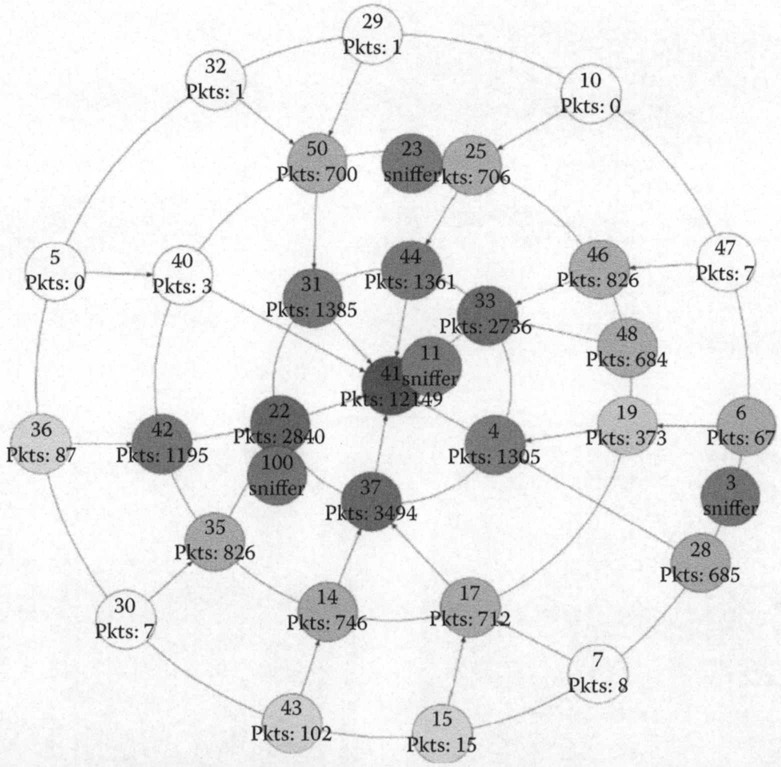

Figure 5.19 Description of what section of network was captured by sniffers. Graph contains data collected from all sniffers with duplicate logs removed.

movement paths of individuals. However, once more than five individuals were in the monitored area simultaneously, the system was not able to successfully identify all the individuals and their paths. This could be significantly improved with more nodes and more specific placement of the movement-detection nodes. Other results show that our EPIR module can be used for movement detection; the lifetime of the node's battery with a movement detector installed drops to 74%, which is acceptable and usable in practice.

5.5.3.4 Mirov 2014

The plan of the experiment was to get as much data as possible about the behavior of real nodes when deployed as described by the emergency unit scenario with WSNProtectLayer application with full implementation enabled. The main goal was to field-test the (then) latest version of the prototype application.

The topology of the WSN was the same as described in Section 5.5.3.2. However, the sensor nodes were placed on wooden towers instead of snow towers. During the experiment, we evaluated the following four aspects:

- Attacker movement reporting
- Network discovery, phantom routing
- All privacy levels and change via authenticated broadcast
- Intrusion detection system

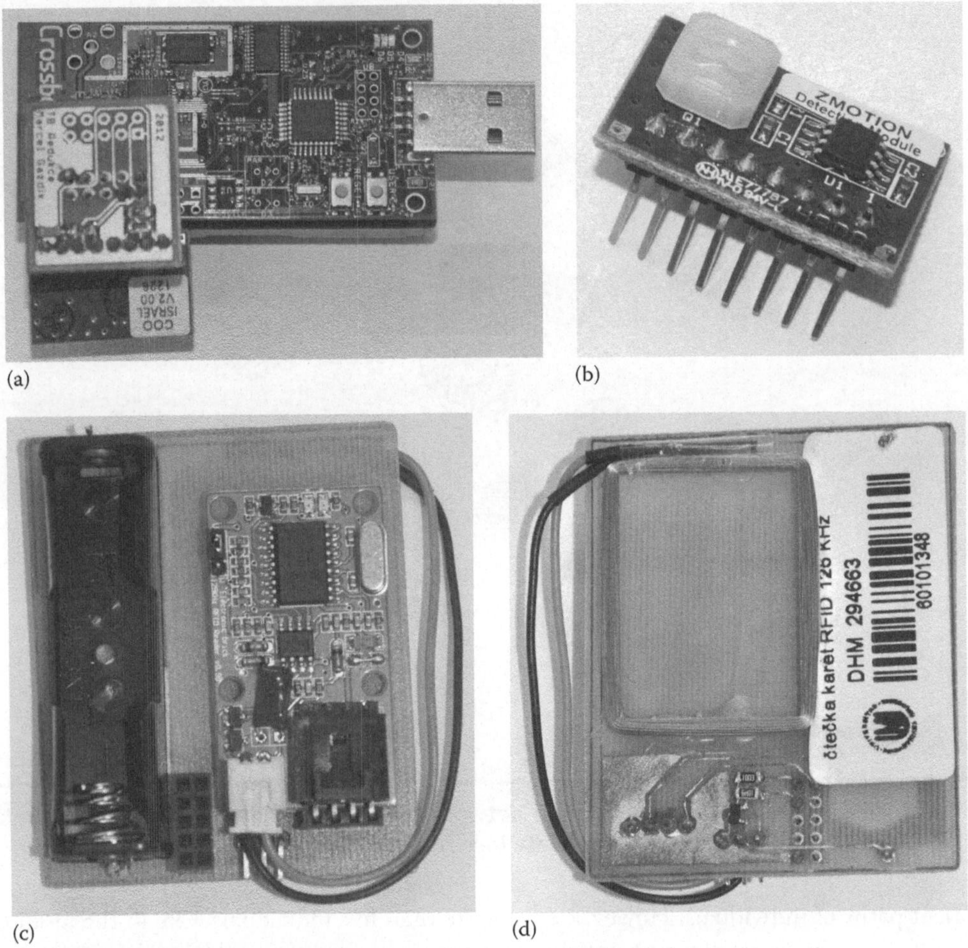

Figure 5.20 Sensor node equipped with movement detection (EPIR) sensor (left) and RFID reader (right).

Figure 5.21 shows the number of packets that were sent and forwarded by each of the nodes at the highest privacy level. Note that enabling acknowledgment would increase the number of delivered messages, as described in Section 5.5.3.5.

The IDS has to be calibrated properly for a given environment to optimize the trade-off between false-positive and false-negative alerts. For such optimization, we recommend using our optimization framework [4,6,17]. In addition, the frequency of alert sending can be decreased easily, as described in Section 5.3.1.2.

The main observation of the experiment was the fact that the WSN with WSNProtectLayer successfully worked in all assumed privacy modes.

5.5.3.5 Test Bed 2014

The final prototype was continuously and thoroughly tested in our laboratory test bed. The test bed tests played a critical role in debugging WSNProtectLayer. During these tests, various properties of the network were monitored and evaluated. The most important outcome is that the

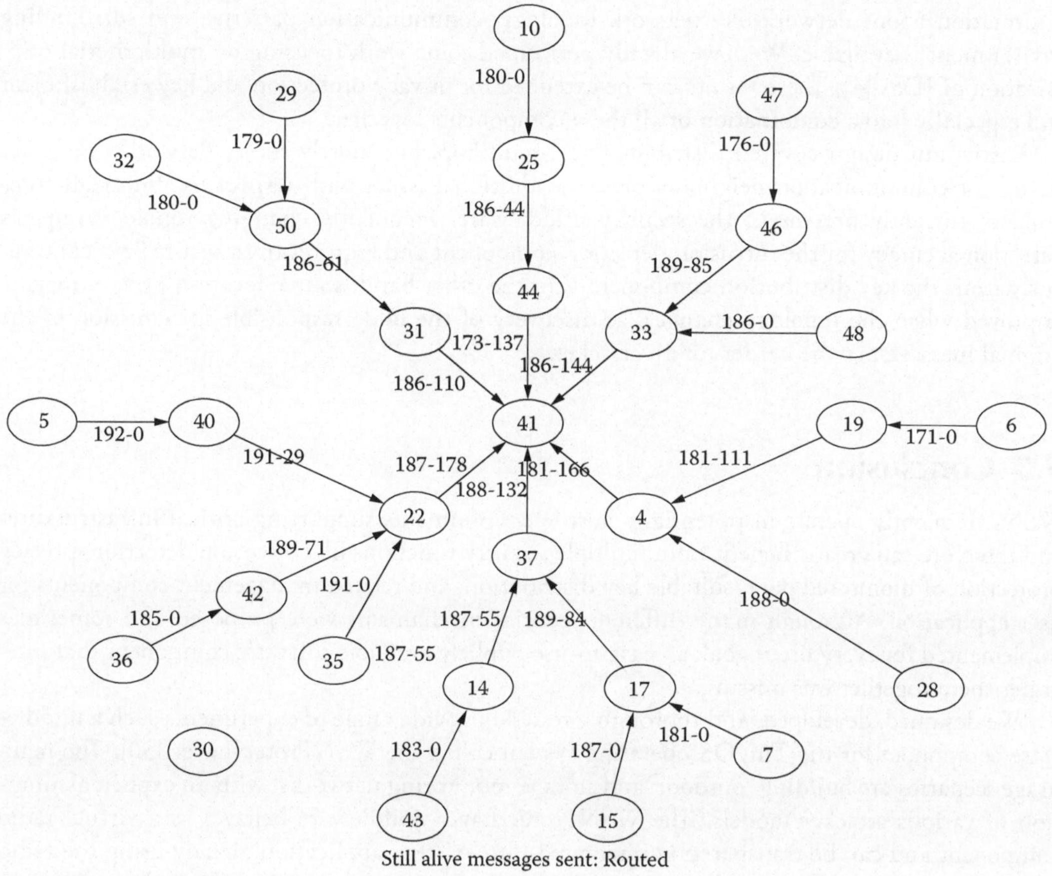

Figure 5.21 Number of packets sent and forwarded by each of the nodes.

final version of WSNProtectLayer works transparently and correctly. With the final platform, we observed that more than 90% of packets were successfully delivered to the BS with enabled acknowledgments (as described in Section 5.3.1.1). About 60% of packets were delivered in broadcasting (but more privacy friendly) mode with no acknowledgments enabled. These are expected numbers with respect to the indoor conditions of an office environment and the traffic pattern generated and require an application design that is able to cope with packet loss.

5.4 Future Work

The future course of work will focus on at least the three following areas. Firstly, we will incorporate additional security features in the current design not addressed so far, like secure routing or secure data aggregation. These features can be performed without (or with limited) input from the application itself and are therefore suitable for inclusion in the virtual radio middleware concept.

Secondly, our implementation aims to address parameterization of security middleware based on the different network characteristics provided by a network owner. Better security to resources trade-offs can be performed and incorporated into the security middleware where more precise information about network-like network topology, communication patterns, and surrounding environment is available. We have already performed some work focusing on multicriterial optimization of IDSs [4]. These results can be extended for privacy protection and key establishment and especially into a combination of all these components together.

Lastly, our design covered distributed and multihop, but mostly static, networks. Frequent change of communication neighbors presents additional issues with respect to almost all components currently present in the security middleware. Frequently changing topology impacts detection accuracy for the intrusion detection component and requires fresh secure keys continuously from the key distribution component. On the other hand, source-location privacy may be improved when the topology changes, as discovery of the node responsible for emission of the original message may be harder for an attacker.

5.5 Conclusion

WSNs frequently operate in potentially hostile environments supporting critical infrastructures and therefore can greatly benefit from multiple security functions like intrusion detection, privacy protection of monitored data, suitable key distribution, and related management components for user application. Although many different security mechanisms were proposed and sometimes implemented for every listed goal, an easy-to-use publicly available software component that integrates them together was missing.

We designed, developed, and thoroughly tested in a wide range of experiments such a middleware component for the TinyOS operating system called the WSNProtectLayer [30]. The main usage scenarios are building, outdoor, and storage monitoring networks, with an explicit assumption of various attacker models. The WSNProtectLayer middleware behaves as a virtual radio component and can be transparently integrated into existing application already using the radio stack. Exchanged packets are then transparently protected, routed, and monitored according to the current privacy level controlled from the central BS, together with security-related events. The WSNProtectLayer middleware is released under the open BSD 2-Clause License [30].

To facilitate development and testing, various supporting tools were built, including a dedicated laboratory test bed with 30 TelosB nodes, a fully automated deployment environment, and visualization of traffic logs in an OmNET++ simulator—with experience obtained shared in the relevant sections.

Various trade-offs have also been discussed, as some security requirements conflicts with others—for example, natural packet loss solved commonly with packet acknowledgments interfere with source protection in the privacy-preserving mechanism.

The WSNProtectLayer middleware was tested in various indoor and outdoor scenarios, with experience incorporated into the final design and implementation.

Acknowledgments

Research, design, and implementation were supported by project VG20102014031 of the Ministry of the Interior, Czech Republic: "Experimental Development of a Security Software Platform for Wireless Sensor Networks with Intrusion Detection and Privacy Support." We would also like to thank all the people involved in the discussions, development, and experiments throughout the project, particularly Jiří Kůr, Tobiáš Smolka, Ondřej Koutský, Marcel Gazdík, Lukáš Němec, and Radim Ošťádal.

Author Biographies

Vashek Matyáš is a professor at Masaryk University, Brno, Czech Republic, and vice-dean for foreign affairs and external relations at the Faculty of Informatics. His research interests relate to applied cryptography and security, in which he has had over 150 peer-reviewed papers and articles published and coauthored several books. He was a Fulbright-Masaryk Visiting Scholar with Harvard University's Center for Research on Computation and Society in 2011–12, and previously he worked with Microsoft Research Cambridge, University College Dublin, and Ubilab at UBS, and was a Royal Society postdoctoral fellow with the Cambridge University Computer Lab. Vashek edited *Computer and Communications Security Reviews* and worked on the development of Common Criteria and with ISO/IEC JTC1 SC27. He received his PhD degree from Masaryk University, Brno, and can be contacted at matyas@fi.muni.cz.

Petr Švenda is an assistant professor at Masaryk University, Brno, Czech Republic. He engages in research in the field of authentication and key establishment protocols for distributed architectures with multiple communicating parties or users, for example, wireless sensor networks. He also analyzes the practical security of cryptographic smartcards including the development of secure applications on this platform. His research focuses on the possibilities of using evolution algorithms for the analysis of cryptographic primitives. He devotes himself to the issues of secure programming using tools for static and dynamic code analysis. He has participated in consultations and development for academic, state, and industrial organizations in the Czech Republic and abroad. He received his PhD degree from Masaryk University, Brno, and can be contacted at svenda@fi.muni.cz.

Andriy Stetsko is a researcher at the Centre for Research on Cryptography and Security, Masaryk University, Czech Republic. Andriy also works for Y Soft Corporation a.s., where he is responsible for selected research activities and cooperation with academia. Andriy is interested in security and distributed systems. He has been involved in several research projects with different complexities and timeframes. These projects focused on security aspects of wireless sensor networks, payment systems, spam detection, authentication tokens, software security, and secure programming. Andriy received his PhD degree from Masaryk University, Brno, for his dissertation on intrusion detection in wireless sensor networks. He has over 15 peer-reviewed publications and occasionally helps with manuscript reviews for international journals and conferences. He can be contacted at xstetsko@fi.muni.cz.

Dušan Klinec is a PhD student at the Centre for Research on Cryptography and Security, Masaryk University, Czech Republic. Dušan also works as a chief technical officer with PhoneX Security, developing a system for secure end-to-end protected communication. He is interested in cryptanalysis, white-box cryptography, software security, Android and VoIP security, neural networks, and distributed systems. He has also participated in projects focused on wireless sensor networks and cryptanalysis using genetic algorithms. Dušan received his master's degree from Masaryk University, with his master's thesis on white-box attack-resistant cryptography. He was an intern at CERN, where he worked on projects related to grid computing and IPv6 compliance. He can be contacted at dusan.klinec@gmail.com.

Filip Jurnečka is a PhD student at Masaryk University and software developer at Solarwinds Czech, both located in Brno, Czech Republic. His area of interest covers many security and application development-related topics. During his studies, he has focused mainly on topics related to wireless sensor networks security. His main project was extending a simulator with functionality for automated evaluation of key management schemes specifically designed for wireless sensor networks. Currently, he focuses on improving his skills in application development for commercial environments. He received his master's degree from Masaryk University, Brno, and can be contacted at xjurn@fi.muni.cz.

Martin Stehlík is a PhD student at Masaryk University, Brno, Czech Republic. His research is focused on security in wireless sensor networks. He continues the work that Andriy Stetsko started during his PhD studies, namely optimization of intrusion detection systems using evolutionary algorithms and distributed computation. Apart from wireless sensor networks, he is also interested in computer and network security, network simulators, and wireless communication. He has participated in several projects with industrial partners, for example, on spam detection. Martin can be contacted at xstehl2@fi.muni.cz.

References

1. Jurnečka, F.; Klinec, D.; Kůr, J.; Matyáš, V.; Stehlík, M.; Stetsko, A.; Švenda, P.: Final report on WSNProtectLayer development: Experimental development of a security platform for wireless sensor networks encompassing an intrusion detection system and privacy preserving modes of operation, Czech Ministry of the Interior, VG20102014031,2014.
2. Levis, P.; Madden, S.; Polastre, J.; Szewczyk, R.; Whitehouse, K.; Woo, A.; Gay, D.; Hill, J.; Welsh, M.; Brewer, E.; Culler, D.: *TinyOS: An Operating System for Sensor Networks, Ambient Intelligence.* Berlin: Springer, 2005, pp. 115–148.
3. Luk, M.; Perrig, A.; Whillock, B.: Seven cardinal properties of sensor network broadcast authentication. In *Proceedings of the Fourth ACM Workshop on Security of Ad Hoc and Sensor Networks, SASN '06*, New York: ACM, 2006, pp. 147–156.
4. Stehlík, M.; Saleh,A.; Stetsko, A.; Matyáš, V.: Multi-objective optimization of intrusion detection systems for wireless sensor networks. In *Advances in Artificial Life, ECAL 2013, Proceedings of the Twelfth European Conference on the Synthesis and Simulation of Living Systems.* Cambridge, MA: MIT Press, 2013.
5. Stetsko, A.; Folkman, L.; Matyáš, V.: Neighbor-based intrusion detection for wireless sensor networks. In *ICWMC 2010: The Sixth International Conference on Wireless and Mobile Communications.* Los Alamitos, CA: IEEE Computer Society, 2010.
6. Stetsko, A.; Smolka, T.; Matyáš, V.; Stehlík, M.: Improving intrusion detection systems for wireless sensor networks. FIMU-RS-2014-01. Technical report. Faculty of Informatics, Masaryk University, 2014.
7. Kůr, J.; Matyáš, V.: Multi-level privacy protection framework for wireless sensor networks. In *MEMICS 2012, Eighth Doctoral Workshop on Mathematical and Engineering Methods in Computer Science.* 1st ed. Brno: NOVPRESS s.r.o., 2012, pp. 38–48.
8. Pecho, P; Nagy, J; Hanacek, P.: Power consumption of hardware cryptography platform for wireless sensors. In *International Conference on Parallel and Distributed Computing Applications and Technologies.* Higashi Hiroshima: IEEE, 2009.
9. Zilog: ZilogePIR Motion Detection Zdots, Product Specification PS028402-1008. https://www.sparkfun.com/datasheets/Sensors/Proximity/SEN-09587-PS0284.pdf, 2008. Last access: 2014-12-04.
10. MEMSIC, Inc.: MEMSIC TelosB mote platform, http://www.memsic.com/userfiles/files/Datasheets/WSN/telosb_datasheet.pdf. Last access: 2014-12-04.
11. Levis, P.; Sharp, C.: TEP106, schedulers and tasks. http://www.tinyos.net/tinyos-2.1.0/doc/html/tep106.html. Last access: 2014-12-04.
12. Gnawali, O.; Fonseca, R.; Jamieson, K.; Moss, D.; Levis, P.: Collection tree protocol. In *Proceedings of the 7th ACM Conference on Embedded Networked Sensor Systems.* New York: ACM, 2009.

13. Kamat, P.; Zhang, Y.; Trappe, W.; Ozturk, C.: Enhancing source-location privacy in sensor network routing. In *ICDCS '05*, Washington, DC: IEEE Computer Society, 2005, pp. 599–608.
14. Lamport, L.: Password authentication with insecure communication. *Communications of the ACM*, 24(11):770–772, 1981.
15. Bukač, V.; Matyáš V.: Host-based intrusion detection systems: Architectures, solutions, and challenges. In A. Ruiz-Martinez, R. Marin-Lopez, F. Pereniguez-Garcia (eds). *Architectures and Protocols for Secure Information Technology Infrastructures*. Hershey, PA: IGI Global, 2013, pp. 184–214, Advances in Information Security, Privacy, and Ethics (AISPE).
16. Bukač, V.; Tuček, P.; Deutsch, M.: Advances and challenges in standalone host-based intrusion detection systems. In S. Fischer-Hübner, S. Katsikas, G. Quirchmayr (eds). *Lecture Notes in Computer Science 7449: Proceedings of the 9th International Conference on Trust, Privacy and Security in Digital Business*. Berlin: Springer, 2012, pp. 105–117.
17. Stehlík M.: Optimization of intrusion detection systems for wireless sensor networks using evolutionary algorithms. In *Security and Protection of Information 2013*. Brno: University of Defence, 2013, pp. 119–124.
18. Clulow, J.; Moore, T.: Suicide for the common good: A new strategy for credential revocation in self-organizing systems. ACM SIGOPS Operating Systems Review, 2006.
19. Cvrček, D.; Švenda, P.: Smart dust security: Key infection revisited. *Proceedings of the First International Workshop on Security and Trust Management*, Italy, ENTCS, vol. 157, pp. 10–23, 2005.
20. Jurnečka, F.; Matyáš, V.: A better way towards key establishment and authentication in wireless sensor networks. In *Selected papers from MEMICS 2012, Eighth Doctoral Workshop on Mathematical and Engineering Methods in Computer Science*, Znojmo, Czech Republic, October 25–28. Lecture Notes in Computer Science, vol. 7721, Berlin: Springer, 2013, pp. 135–148.
21. Kůr, J.; Matyáš, V.; Švenda, P.: Two improvements of random key predistribution for wireless sensor networks: Revised version. *Infocommunications Journal*, IV(4):28–35, 2012.
22. Kůr, J.; Matyáš, V.; Švenda, P.: Two improvements of random key predistribution for wireless sensor networks. In *Security and Privacy in Communication Networks*, vol. 106 of Lecture Notes of the Institute for Computer Sciences, Social Informatics and Telecommunications Engineering. Berlin: Springer, 2013, pp. 61–75.
23. Švenda, P.; Sekanina, L.; Matyáš, V.: Evolutionary design of secrecy amplification protocols for wireless sensor networks. In *Second ACM Conference on Wireless Network Security (WiSec'09)*, Zurich, Switzerland,2009.
24. Anderson, R.; Chan, H.; Perrig, A.: Key infection: Smart trust for smart dust. In *Proceedings of the Network Protocols (ICNP'04)*. Berlin: IEEE Computer Society, 2004, pp. 206–215.
25. Oštádal, R.; Švenda, P.; Vashek, M.: A new approach to secrecy amplification in partially compromised networks. In *SPACE 2014*, LNCS 8804, Heidelberg: Springer, 2014.
26. Hanáček, P.; Švenda, P.: Cryptography for (partially) compromised sensor networks. Information Security Summit, Prague, Tate International, s.r.o., 2011, pp. 103–109.
27. Jurnečka, F.; Matyáš, V.: Using encryption for authentication: Wireless sensor network case. In *10th Annual IEEE Communications Society Conference on Sensor, Mesh and Ad Hoc Communications and Networks (SECON)*, New York, June. IEEE Communications Society, pp. 59–64.
28. Dworkin, M.: Recommendation for Block Cipher modes of operation: Methods and techniques. NIST Special Publication 800-38A, NIST, 2001.
29. Preneel, B.; Govaerts, R.; Vandewalle, J.: Hash functions based on block ciphers: A synthetic approach. In *Proceedings of the 13th Annual International Cryptology Conference on Advances in Cryptology, CRYPTO 93*. London: Springer, 1994, pp. 368–378.
30. Matyáš, V.; Gazdík, M.; Jurnečka, F.; Klinec, D.; Kůr, J.; Němec, L.; Smolka, T.; Stehlík, M.; Stetsko, A.; Švenda, P.: WSNProtectLayer1.0. Software. Available at: https://github.com/crocs-muni/WSNProtectLayer. 2014.
31. Stetsko, A.; Stehlik, M.; Matyas, V.: Calibrating and comparing simulators for wireless sensor networks. In *2011 IEEE 8th International Conference on Mobile Adhoc and Sensor Systems (MASS)*. Los Alamitos, CA: IEEE Computer Society, 2011, pp. 733–738.
32. Atmel Corporation: 8-bit Atmel microcontroller with 128KBytes in-system programmable flash, ATmega128, ATmega128L. http://www.atmel.com/images/doc2467.pdf. Last access: 2014-12-04.

33. Crossbow Technology, Inc.: MICAz: wireless measurement system. http://courses.ece.ubc.ca/494/files/MICAz_Datasheet.pdf. Last access: 2014-12-04.
34. Texas Instruments, Inc.: MSP430F15x, MSP430F16x, MSP430F161x mixed signal microcontroller. http://www.ti.com/lit/ds/symlink/msp430f1611.pdf. Last access: 2014-12-04.
35. Klinec, D.: Application for localization of sensor nodes in wireless sensor network. Bachelor thesis. Masaryk University, 2011. http://is.muni.cz/th/325219/fi_b/. Last access: 2014-12-04.

Chapter 6

Securing Transportation Cyber-Physical Systems

Nnanna Ekedebe, Wei Yu and Chao Lu
Towson University

Houbing Song
West Virginia University

Yan Wan
University of North Texas

Contents

6.1 Introduction....164
6.2 Transportation Cyber-Physical Systems....165
6.2.1 Architecture....166
6.2.2 Applications....166
6.2.3 Standards....167
6.2.4 Characteristics....167
6.3 Security and Privacy Issues in Transportation Cyber-Physical Systems....168
6.3.1 Security and Privacy Requirements....168
6.3.2 Security and Privacy Challenges....169
6.3.2.1 Security Actors and Entities....171
6.3.2.2 Attacker Profiles....171
6.3.2.3 Attack Classifications....171
6.4 Countermeasures for Security and Privacy in Transportation Cyber-Physical Systems....174
6.4.1 Cryptography Mechanisms....175
6.4.2 Cryptography Protections....175
6.4.3 Public Key Infrastructure....176
6.4.3.1 VANET Public Key Infrastructure....176
6.4.3.2 Group Signature....176

6.4.4 Security Countermeasures for Securing VANETs 176
6.4.4.1 Generic Security Mechanisms 177
6.4.4.2 Specific Security Solutions for VANETs 177
6.4.5 VANET Security Architectures 178
6.4.5.1 Global Security Architecture 178
6.4.5.2 VANET Privacy 178
6.5 Case Study 180
6.5.1 Test-Bed Setup 180
6.5.1.1 V2X Simulation Framework: VSimRTI Architecture 180
6.5.1.2 Real-World Data Set 183
6.5.1.3 Simulation Inputs and Parameters 183
6.5.2 Evaluation Scenarios 186
6.5.2.1 Scenario A (Traffic Efficiency) 186
6.5.2.2 Scenario B (Safety) 186
6.5.2.3 Scenario C (Jamming Attack) 186
6.5.3 Evaluation Results 187
6.6 Future Research 190
6.7 Final Remarks 191
Author Biographies 191
References 193

Abstract: Our world is facing serious transportation challenges, including safety, mobility, and environmental challenges, which can potentially be addressed by cyber-physical systems (CPS). Generally speaking, CPSs are engineered systems, which are built from the effective integration of a modern computational core, communication networks, and physical components. The application of CPS technology in the transportation domain will transform the way people interact with highway transportation systems, just as the Internet has transformed the way people interact with information. In particular, intelligent transportation systems (ITS), vehicular ad hoc networks (VANETs), and the Internet of Vehicles (IoV) are the networking infrastructure of transportation CPSs. Nonetheless, transportation CPSs are subject to cyberthreats, stemming from increasing reliance on computing and communication technologies. Cyberthreats exploit the increased complexity and connectivity of transportation CPSs, placing security, economy, public safety, and health at risk. In this chapter, we discuss various security and privacy issues in transportation CPSs, review various defense mechanisms to improve security and privacy in transportation CPSs, and present a case study on our test bed.

6.1 Introduction

Our world is facing serious transportation challenges, including safety, mobility, and environmental challenges. There are over 5.8 million collisions per year on U.S. roadways, resulting in 37,000 deaths annually. These crashes have a direct economic cost of $230.6 billion and are the main cause of death for the age group 4–34. Traffic congestion is an $87.2 billion annual drain on the U.S. economy, with 4.2 billion hours and 2.8 billion gallons of fuel spent sitting in traffic—the equivalent of one work week and three weeks' worth of gas per year. In addition, tailpipe emissions from vehicles are the single largest man-made source of carbon dioxide (CO_2), nitrous oxides (NO_x), and methane [1]. Hence, there is an urgent need to improve safety, efficiency, and environmental protection in highway transportation.

These challenges can potentially be addressed by cyber-physical systems (CPSs), which are (a) next-generation integrated systems with sensors, actuators, and a computation/control core, designed to sense and interact with the physical world (including human users) and support real-time, guaranteed performance in safety-critical applications [2] and (b) engineered systems that are built on the seamless integration of a computational core, communication networks, and physical components [3]. Advances in CPSs will improve capability, adaptability, scalability, resiliency, safety, security, and usability. The design of CPSs will drive innovation and competition in various sectors, including agriculture, energy, transportation, building design and automation, health care, manufacturing, and so on.

The application of CPSs in the transportation sector, that is, transportation CPSs, will transform the way people interact with highway transportation systems, just as the Internet has transformed the way people interact with information. In this way, the necessary foundation will be provided for a safe, efficient highway transportation system, which connects vehicles, infrastructure, drivers, and goods carried in vehicles. It is expected that transportation CPSs can potentially reduce accidents caused by human error, which currently account for 93% of the approximately 6 million annual automotive crashes. Vehicular ad hoc networks (VANETs) or Internet of Vehicles (IoV) are the networking infrastructure of transportation CPSs.

Nonetheless, transportation CPSs are subject to threats, stemming from increasing reliance on computer and communication technologies. Cyberthreats exploit the increased complexity and connectivity of transportation CPS, placing negative impact on security, economy, public safety, and health. In this chapter, we discuss various security and privacy issues in transportation CPSs, review various defense mechanisms to improve the security and privacy in transportation CPSs, and present a case study on our developed test bed.

The organization of this chapter is as follows: In Section 6.2, we present the state of the art and practice of transportation CPSs based on VANETs. In Section 6.3, we give an overview of security and privacy issues in transportation CPSs. In Section 6.4, we present various possible countermeasures to improve the security and privacy of transportation CPSs. In Section 6.5, we present one case study based on our test bed. In Section 6.6, we outline our envisioned future research directions of the ITS/VANET domain. Finally, in Section 6.7, we conclude the chapter with final remarks.

6.2 Transportation Cyber-Physical Systems

VANETs or IoV are the networking infrastructure of transportation CPSs. VANETs are based on the use of dedicated short-range communications (DSRC) technology, which is a two-way short-to-medium-range wireless communications capability with a high data transmission performance. In Report and Order FCC-03-324, the Federal Communications Commission (FCC) allocated 75 MHz of spectrum in the 5.9 GHz band for use by intelligent transportation systems (ITS)-related vehicle safety and mobility applications.

Smart vehicles [4] are able to process and record information from vehicle-to-vehicle (V2V) and vehicle-to-infrastructure (V2I) communications. The VANET consists of entities such as onboard units (OBUs), roadside units (RSUs), trusted platform modules (TPMs), and so on. These entities communicate with one another using V2V and/or V2I communication (i.e., vehicle-to-wireless infrastructure). V2I communication requires more bandwidth and is less susceptible to attacks. Some of the wireless communication standards that can be used with V2I communication

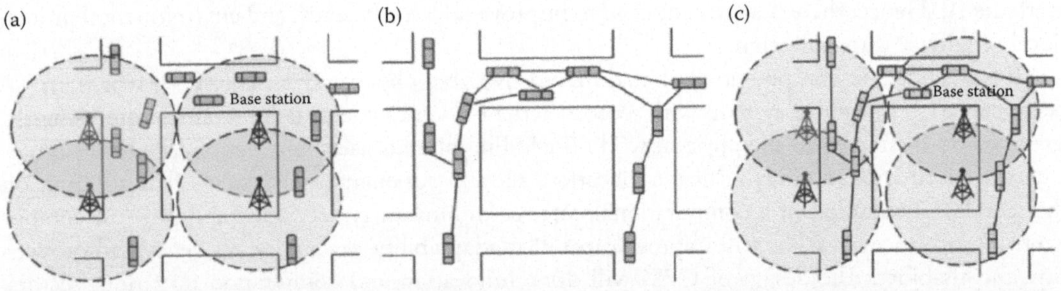

Figure 6.1 VANET network architectures: (a) pure cellular (V2I), (b) pure ad hoc (V2V), and (c) hybrid (V2V and V2I). (From Sharef, B.T., et al., *J. Netw. Comput. Applic.*, 40, 363–396, 2014. With permission.)

include, but are not limited to, global system for mobile communications (GSM), universal mobile telecommunications system (UMTS), and WiMAX.

In VANETs, two main routing methods have been identified: a source/centralized/V2I routing protocol on single hop and hop-by-hop/decentralized/V2V routing protocol on multihop. The seven main classifications of V2V routing protocols in VANETs are topology-based (which can be proactive/table-driven, reactive/on-demand, or hybrid), position-based, multicast-based, cluster-based, broadcast-based, geocast-based, and infrastructure-based routing protocols. On the other hand, static and dynamic infrastructure-based routing protocols are examples of V2I routing protocols [5–11].

In the following, we review the architecture, applications, standards, and characteristics of VANETs.

6.2.1 Architecture

The main types of architectures in VANETs are cellular/wireless LAN/centralized/V2I communication architecture, ad hoc/decentralized/V2V communication architecture (either single-hop, used for safety-related messages/communication, or multihop, used for non-safety-related messages), depending on the position of the receiver relative to the sender, and a combination of both (hybrid). A more elaborate view of VANET architecture is depicted in Figure 6.1. In addition, in VANETs, message transmissions can be performed through broadcast (V2I), unicast/ad hoc (V2V), or a combination of both (V2V2I), which are shown in Figure 6.1 [12–14].

6.2.2 Applications

VANET applications can be categorized under the following headings: safety, comfort/infotainment, and traffic efficiency applications. Traffic efficiency and safety can be enhanced through cooperative driving and traffic monitoring applications. The examples of safety applications of VANETs include, but are not limited to, electronic brake light warnings, and cooperative collision avoidance. Examples of traffic efficiency applications of VANETs include, but are not limited to, road congestion notifications and parking availability notification. VANET applications can also be used for warning, traffic management, and provision of value-added applications. Payment, infotainment, and location-based services are examples of applications of VANETs as well. Maintenance applications in VANETs can be performed through remote vehicle diagnosis [5–6,10,12,14–18].

6.2.3 Standards

In the VANET domain, DSRC and wireless access in vehicular environments (WAVE) are the vehicular communication standards in use. DSRC and WAVE are both based on IEEE 802.11p and IEEE 1609. In addition to DSRC (IEEE 802.11p) and WAVE (IEEE 1609), WiMAX, satellite, and cellular wireless technologies can be used in VANETs as well. Using the WAVE or the DSRC protocol/communication standard, V2V and V2I communication is secured against many attacks, including spoofing, eavesdropping, and modification attacks, and so on. It protects against these attacks using public key, hybrid key, and elliptical curve cryptography (ECC) techniques. For DSRC, there are seven channels in the United States and five channels in Europe. Some more detailed expositions of DSRC and WAVE are listed as follows:

- *DSRC*: The 5.850–5.925 GHz spectrum has been reserved by the U.S. FCC for vehicular communications. DSRC (IEEE 802.11p originating from IEEE 802.11) is the wireless communication standard for VANETs having a data rate of between 3 and 27 Mbps using a 10 MHz channel with a maximum transmission range of 1000 m. DSRC has low communication latency with high data transfer ranges. For situational awareness, vehicles constantly send beacon packets among one another with a frequency of 10 messages per second at a maximum communication range of 150 m.
- *WAVE*: The WAVE design and architecture address several features such as security, safety, automatic tolls, and traffic efficiency. IEEE 1609.2 reduces message overhead by half when the Elliptic Curve Digital Signature Algorithm (ECDSA) is used for signature generation and validation. Verification on demand (VoD), used in IEEE 1609.2, is an approach to reduce the computational/processing overhead of each connected vehicle by selecting a subset of the entire message for processing based on their threat level instead of the entire population [5,6,10,19–25].

6.2.4 Characteristics

VANETs are a subset of mobile ad hoc networks (MANETs) and other ad hoc networks, which have similar characteristics to autonomous devices (vehicles/OBUs, RSUs, traffic lights) acting as routers with frequently changing topologies. VANETs have a number prominent features that distinguish them from MANETs, including higher mobility and speeds, more scalability, frequently dynamic network topologies, predictable mobility, regular disconnections, transmission medium availability (air), support for anonymity, bandwidth limitations, susceptibility to attenuations, and limited transmission power. In addition, VANETs have higher privacy, safety, and security requirements than MANETs [5,6,10,15,17]. Some of the aforementioned unique features in VANET are as follows: (i) *Dynamic topology*: Nodes in VANETs usually move at very high speeds, resulting in short connection times—especially for nodes moving in opposite directions—together with susceptibility to interferences as a result of reflections from multipath propagations, weather (natural interferences), and so on. (ii) *Bandwidth limitations*: Reflections, signal fading, delays, diffractions, and so on all limit the effectiveness of exchanged messages in V2X communication with a maximum theoretical throughput of 27 Mbps. (iii) *Transmission power limitations*: VANETs have limited transmission powers (for up to a maximum of 1000 m). (iv) *Energy efficiency*: Because of steady power supply from batteries and other resources, VANETs do not normally suffer from energy limitations as experienced in other mobile devices such as smartphones. In addition, energy constraints might be neglected for VANETs, especially with respect to energy used by cryptographic algorithms because of efficient and effective energy utilization [5,6,10].

6.3 Security and Privacy Issues in Transportation Cyber-Physical Systems

In this section, we will review the security and privacy issues in transportation CPSs. We will begin with the security and privacy requirements and then discuss the challenges of ensuring adequate security and privacy.

6.3.1 Security and Privacy Requirements

Security, safety, and privacy are major requirements of VANETs. Security requirements in VANETs include, but are not limited to, integrity (data trust), confidentiality, nonrepudiation, access control, real-time operational constraints/demands, availability, and privacy protection. Some of these security requirements are unique to VANETs, but others are applicable to general security measures. In the following, we show some requirements for VANET security and privacy [5,10,12,14,15,17,23,26,27]:

- *Identification and authentication*: All OBUs, connected vehicles, RSUs, and every other participating entity must be properly authenticated before joining the network. Authenticating a vehicle (a sender) by the receiver is important in order to determine whether the sender is legitimate, especially with respect to safety and life-critical messages. This is true because false data injection (a typical type of data integrity attack) in VANETs can be used to disrupt traffic flow, cause accidents or other life-threatening injuries, and so on. Authentication prevents privilege escalation and increase in a node (vehicle or RSU) authorization level. It also prevents Sybil attacks, that is, one vehicle cannot take over the entire road by claiming that there is an accident or congestion ahead using many network identification numbers, because a vehicle can only possess one unique network identification number at any given time.
- *Data consistency verification*: The system must give the same results (as output) given a specified input.
- *Confidentiality*: Not every message in VANETs should be encrypted. For example, because of their low latency, safety-/life-critical requirements, safety-related messages should not be encrypted in order to obviate the often attendant/inevitable delays/latencies occasioned by the encryption and decryption process. Other message exchanges between RSUs that are sensitive in nature (e.g., toll payments, Internet connections through RSUs, and so on) must be encrypted. Secure communication can be realized using cryptography mechanisms such as asymmetric and symmetric cryptographical schemes.
- *Message integrity and data trust*: The system must not permit modifications in transit.
- *Nonrepudiation*: Although a driver's privacy must not be compromised, offending parties must be reliably made liable for their actions. Nonrepudiation is dependent on proper authentication, which ensures that a sender (vehicle or infrastructure such as RSU, and so on) cannot feign ignorance of all or part of its action(s) because auditability and accountability are enforced by maintaining evidence (e.g., vehicle's route, time stamps, speed, and other actions/violations) in a safe and secure tamperproof device (TPD). Consequently, a sender cannot refute sending a message, thus providing evidence for eventual prosecution.

- *Availability*: The system must not experience unscheduled downtime. Availability ensures continuous operation by designing fault-tolerant, resilient systems and using devices with high survivability such that normal operations continue even while under attack and/or parts of the network (devices) have failed or become unavailable. In other words, continuous availability must be maintained with respect to both anticipated and unanticipated usage.
- *Traceability and revocation*: The system must maintain a valid and verifiable record of all activities associated with participating nodes in order to enforce nonrepudiation and auditability condition. Nonetheless, maintaining a balance between auditability/accountability and privacy in VANETs is a major challenge.
- *Privacy*: The system must not collect unauthorized personally identifiable information. A major challenge ensues in trying to balance the need for privacy and the need for security. Nonetheless, with respect to privacy, unauthorized persons must not track a driver's behavior and location (past and/or present movements), and so on. In other words, personally identifiable information must not be traceable to an actual user, except by properly authorized persons [5,10,12].
- *Satisfaction of real-time constraints*: The safety and life-critical nature of VANET safety applications mandates 100% reliability and dependability with no tolerance for errors. With respect to VANET safety applications, real-time delivery, reliability, latency, security, and trust should be guaranteed.
- *Access control*: Using access policies, unauthorized access to privileged and sensitive information is forbidden by preventing privilege/role escalations.

To summarize, a balance or trade-off must be reached between ensuring security and ensuring privacy. This is true because some emergency situations may require law enforcement officers to know where a vehicle is located and who owns it in order to be able to respond appropriately. In addition, the desire for privacy and security must not jeopardize real-time operations. It is also imperative to note that the above list of security and privacy requirements of VANETs is not intended to be a comprehensive one because new requirements usually emanate upon actual deployments/implementations.

6.3.2 Security and Privacy Challenges

Just as security, safety, and privacy are major VANET requirements, they are VANET challenges as well [5,6,10,12,13,15,17]. Security compromises in VANETs can be fatal because of their safety-critical nature. Generally speaking, factors such as real-time communication requirements for responding to safety-critical messages before it becomes too late, increase in network size as the number of connected vehicles increase, frequent changes in network topology, transient authentication/security mechanisms, diverse definitions of security, safety, and privacy with respect to different jurisdictions, centralized storage/management of keys (who should be responsible for this and why), lack of user buy-in, and others are some of the constraints that must be addressed before VANETs can be widely adopted. In more detail, some of the security challenges respecting VANETs include, but are not limited to,

1. *High mobility*: It is more difficult to ensure security and nonrepudiation because of the transient nature of V2V and V2I communication interactions owing to frequently changing network topology and the high mobility of communicating/participating entities.

2. *Conflict between privacy and security requirements*: Generally speaking, more security usually means less privacy and vice versa. Many drivers will be unwilling to give up their privacy for some perceived/illusive security benefit. In addition, another major challenge is to balance strong security with good performance.
3. *Availability*: A high availability requirement is mandated in VANETs especially because of its safety-critical nature by providing fail-safe, resilient, and fault-tolerant operations.
4. *Low tolerance for errors*: Especially for safety and life-critical applications, with respect to VANETs, more focus must be placed on preventative security measures rather than corrective or detective ones. This is true because in a safety-critical scenario, for example, any infinitesimal delay in the dissemination of messages to intended recipients can prove fatal. Bandwidth saturation and communication overheads are some of the drawbacks of real-time or near real-time communications in VANETs.
5. *Key distribution*: With lots of participating stakeholders (e.g., government, vehicle manufacturers, and so on.), it is difficult to ascertain who should be the certificate authority (CA) responsible for public key distribution such that attacks manifesting in the form of Sybil or spoofing attacks can be inherently thwarted. In addition, interoperability among these different participating entities is a major challenge. For example, interoperability among different CAs residing or situated in different geographic jurisdictions and governed by varying laws and liabilities is a major problem in addition to the privacy problem of vehicle tracking, user profiling, and vehicle identification through linking.
6. *Cooperation*: Aligning the interests of different vehicle and automobile manufacturers, consumers, governments, and others is challenging because of their often divergent interests and goals. For example, users and consumers may offer fierce resistance to VANET use and will be reluctant to adopt it because they perceive that they are being monitored by the technology.

More specifically, before VANET technology can be fully embraced by all stakeholders (direct and/or indirect), it must address three major areas of challenge: social, economic, and technical. Some of these challenges are summarized as follows [5,12,19]:

1. *Privacy*: Driver and vehicle anonymity militates against privacy violations; however, an offending driver can feign ignorance of committing a crime. Consequently, a trade-off between privacy and security is imperative.
2. *Trust*: Abuse may become inevitable if authorities are given unmitigated or unabridged powers. Consequently, the misuse of authority by an authorized entity such as the police is a major privacy concern. Nonetheless, if appropriate security and privacy measures are implemented, the challenge of not having enthusiastic users of the technology because of security and privacy concerns can be allayed by focusing on the benefits of the technology (e.g., the reduction of road traffic accidents [safety], traffic efficiency, provision of infotainment services, and so on.). This is true because although there are risks in the use of cell phones or the Internet, people still use them today because they are convinced that their benefits far outweigh the risks.

The above list of possible VANET challenges is not intended to be exhaustive. This is true because new challenges usually manifest on actual real-world deployments and implementations.

6.3.2.1 Security Actors and Entities

Some actors who are directly or indirectly involved in VANET security include, but are not limited to, vehicle drivers, OBUs, RSUs, third parties (e.g., CAs [trusted] and untrusted stakeholders), and the adversary (who can be internal and/or authenticated vs. external, rational vs. irrational, active vs. passive, and local vs. extended). It is important to note from the outset that the OBU/vehicle, the RSU, and all order legitimate entities (or nodes) can be normal or malicious [6]. In other words, in addition to vehicles, other entities or nodes such as RSUs and traffic lights are also susceptible to attacks based on identified vulnerabilities [5].

6.3.2.2 Attacker Profiles

As mentioned, the adversaries in a VANET environment can be categorized as outsider versus insider, malicious versus rational, active versus passive, and local versus extended [5,10,12].

1. *Outsider versus insider*: It is very difficult for an outsider to execute devastating attacks. Insiders, however, unleash more damage than outsiders because they are legitimate members of the network, and they have been fully authenticated. Insiders can also be in the form of industrial insiders who can intentionally inject destructive code into a system.
2. *Malicious versus rational*: Malicious adversaries are undirected—they derive no specific gain or benefit from attacking or bringing down the system. As an example of malicious adversaries, pranksters can cause accidents or illusions of them such that other following vehicles are forced to slow down. Rational adversaries, however, are more focused or goal-directed and seek a specific result. The rational adversary can use eavesdropping, impersonation, message delay, or suppression to attack a targeted system.
3. *Active versus passive*: Active nodes (insiders) have network authorization, whereas passive nodes (outsiders) can only do things such as eavesdropping as they are not authenticated to operate within the network.
4. *Local versus extended*: Local adversaries are restricted in geographical influence or coverage, while extended adversaries reach to relatively larger geographical areas.

6.3.2.3 Attack Classifications

Some VANET security vulnerabilities or possible attacks can be conducted through jamming, interference, eavesdropping attacks, and so on [6,11]. Figure 6.2 illustrates an incomprehensive list of possible threats and attacks against some VANET system/security requirements.

It is pertinent to note that developing a comprehensive threat model on possible VANET attacks is a prerequisite for developing effective countermeasures against them [19]. Consequently, VANET security attacks can be classified as follows [5,6,10,19,21,22,28]:

- *Availability attacks*: Availability in VANETs can be compromised by denial of service (DoS), replay, communication channel jamming attacks, and so on. Availability attacks aim for the disruption of network operation. For example, they may focus on safety, and payment-related applications leading to wireless channel jamming. They can take the form of DoS attacks aiming to prevent the network from performing its normal functions, resulting in network downtime or unavailability. In other words, they can manifest in the form of DoS attacks that can be perpetrated by a malicious internal or external node; they can be used to prevent vehicles from

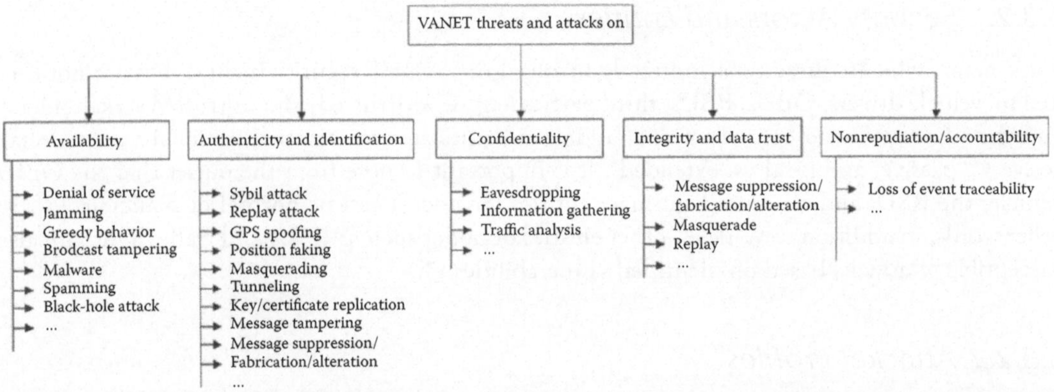

Figure 6.2 Examples of VANET threats and attacks. (From Mejri, M.N., et al. Survey on VANET security challenges and possible cryptographic solutions. *Vehicular Communications*, 04/2014.)

getting critical safety-related messages by jamming the communication channel. For example, a DoS attack can be used to prevent real-time verification of legitimate or critical message signatures because of replay attacks from spurious or noncritical messages used to overwhelm the system. Some examples of DoS attacks can be executed through jamming, greedy behavior, and black-hole attacks, and others, which are further elaborated as follows: (a) *Jamming attack*: Usually an intentional attack aimed at communication channel disruption. Jamming aims to preclude and starve other nodes from utilizing available resources. (b) *Greedy behavior attack*: Greedy drivers can give the illusion of an accident on a lane or road in order to take over the entire roadway or lane by causing following vehicles to use alternative routes, lanes, or paths. (c) *Black-hole attack*: This is an attack on availability where a malicious node hoards received packets or messages and refuses to participate in routing it from source to destination. This type of attack can also lead to a man-in-the-middle attack. (d) *Grayhole attack*: This is a malicious attack that selectively deletes or excludes some data packets meant for certain applications. (e) *Sinkhole attack*: A malicious node tries to redirect data packets to pass through it. A sinkhole attack can be the first step in executing a grayhole and/or black-hole attack. (f) *Malware attack*: This can be perpetrated, for example, during software updates where malicious software can be installed either advertently or inadvertently [6]. (g) *Wormhole attack*: This is a DoS attack that creates the illusion that two far apart or widely separated malicious nodes are close to each other's communication range. Consequently, other neighboring nodes falsely believe that both nodes are adjacent to each other when this is not so [6,10,13]. (h) *Broadcast tampering attack*: This can be executed by legitimate nodes that hide safety-related messages leading to accidents. (i) *Spamming attack*: This has the effect of consuming precious bandwidth, leading to collisions.

- *Authentication and identification attacks*: These attacks manifest themselves through the following examples: (i) *Sybil attack*: This has the effect of causing a malicious node to possess more than one (many) identity at the same time, which can be used to create a fallacious sense of congestion. Adequate authentication (security) guards against Sybil or spoofing attacks where a single vehicle can create a false notion of the presence of an accident, for example, when there is none [10,13]. (ii) *GPS spoofing/position faking attack*: This can be used to deceptively provide a position or location of a node that is untrue. Cheating with positioning, speed, and identity information applies to both safety- and payment-related applications such that an adversary can feign knowledge or ignorance of committing a malicious attack [19]. (iii) *Node impersonation attack*: Impersonation involves cheating with another person's or entity's (vehicles, RSUs, or traffic lights) identity [19]. It violates authentication by allowing one or more nodes in the network to have the same network identification number, which, in normal circumstances, must be unique. Consequently, the impersonating malicious node can feign ignorance of an attack because the nonrepudiation security requirement has been violated with impunity. To be useful as evidence (postcollision), traffic and other related incidents must use digital signatures that support nonrepudiation with no support for anonymity [6,13,22]. Property (e.g., vehicle or RSU), location or position, and identity authentication mechanisms can be used to prevent impersonation attacks. These make sure that the communicating entities are authorized together with their positions (location authentication) [10,12,29]. Impersonation attacks can be conducted by insiders to the network and they are normally rational and active [12]. (iv) *Tunneling attack*: In this attack, the adversary establishes a tunnel to another part of the network using a different communication channel—this is very similar to a wormhole attack. (v) *Key and/or certificate replication attack*: Duplicates unique keys or certificates, making unique identification of nodes/vehicles difficult, especially in disputes or accident resolutions because of the ambiguity created.

- *Confidentiality attacks*: Confidentiality ensures that only authorized persons have access to data or resources. An attack on confidentiality manifests itself through eavesdropping and traffic analysis (passive) attacks. This type of attack can not only lead to confidentiality violations, but also lead to violations of privacy. As an example, through eavesdropping, the adversary tries to obtain access to secret or confidential data through a vehicle (moving or stationary) or a compromised infrastructure or RSU. Implementing confidentiality requirements can be used to mitigate this type of attack via encryption.
- *Integrity and data trust attacks*: Ensures that data has not been modified in transit, that is, it makes sure that what was sent is the same as what was received. These attacks manifest themselves in the following ways: (i) *Masquerading attack*: In this attack, the adversary hides under a false identity that has the appearance of emanating from a legitimately authenticated node and uses this to generate untrue or lying messages or to execute black-hole attacks. (ii) *Replay attack*: A unique feature of replay attacks is that, unlike other types of attacks, they can be perpetrated by illegitimate nodes. Message replay has the negative effect of consuming or occupying precious bandwidth, resulting in the dropping of priority messages from the queue when full. Message deletion and replay are used to bring down the efficiency of the system; they cannot be prevented by using digital signatures like message forgery, and modification can [6,22]. (iii) *Suppressing/fabricating/modifying/tampering messages*: These violate the integrity/nonrepudiation security requirement. Fabrication attacks manifest themselves through the dissemination of false or bogus information, cheating with sensed information, tunneling, masquerading, and hidden vehicle attacks [10]. Hidden vehicle attacks prevent vehicles from participating in traffic condition information dissemination, thus breaking the multihop message distribution path; it is usually active and perpetrated by an insider [13]. By deleting, forging, replaying, or modifying a message containing parameters (e.g., vehicle speed, time stamp, location, or direction), the receiving entity or vehicle can over- or underestimate the severity of the message, leading to collisions and other negative consequences [22]. Specifically, message modification can trigger a false sense of security when a critical message that should trigger collision avoidance mechanisms or applications is downgraded and vice versa. This attack is perpetrated by a rational attacker [13]. (iv) *Illusion attack*: In this attack, voluntary sensors that generate false data are placed in the network. Because these

malicious sensors are properly authenticated, they cannot be prevented by authentication mechanisms [6]. It is important to note that illusion, modification, masquerading, and replay or broadcast attacks are also considered attacks on authentication and identification.

- *Nonrepudiation/accountability attacks*: These attacks manifest themselves in the form of loss of traceability/auditability of events or activities.
- *Other VANET attacks*: Other attacks in VANETs include, but are not limited to the following: (i) *Privacy attacks*: These attacks manifest themselves as (a) *tracking* by identity disclosure attack conducted through tracking of vehicles [19] and (b) *social engineering* by taking advantage of attacks based on various social engineering techniques (e.g., human drivers' naivety and so on.). (ii) *Timing attack*: In this attack, critical messages are intentionally delayed so that they arrive out of sync and cannot be subsequently used [6]. It can involve adding a delay to a sent message or not sending the message at all; this has the effect of negatively affecting availability and delaying time- and safety-critical information from promptly getting to its intended destination. It is worth noting that message integrity is not compromised—it only arrives out of sync or might not even arrive at all. With safety-critical messages, the consequences of this attack can be calamitous [10,12,13]. (iii) *Hardware tampering*: This can be done by the manufacturer and can be mitigated by physical inspection and the use of the TPMs. Here, availability must be maintained. The adversary can be from the inside or outside; rational and active [5,12]. (iii) *Brute-force attacks*: These can be committed or executed against message confidentiality, encryption keys, or identification and authentication. For example, a brute-force or dictionary attack can be performed in order to discover the network identification (ID) number of a node (e.g., vehicle, RSU, traffic light, and so on.) [6]. (v) *Man-in-the-middle attack*: This attack violates authentication, integrity, and nonrepudiation mechanisms. It is executed by having an intermediate or middle node or vehicle relay messages to or from one vehicle to another, while the transmitting vehicle falsely assumes that it is in direct communication with the receiving vehicle or node. Consequently, an innocent sending node can be falsely accused of a malicious activity or action they are not responsible for. Nonrepudiation and use of digital signatures and certificates can be used to mitigate against this type of attack [12].

In addition, with respect to the security requirements of a system, we can also categorize attacks in VANETs as *attacks on authentication and secrecy*, *network availability attacks*, and *stealthy attacks on integrity of service(s)* [10]. Raya and Hubaux [19] identified three major areas or classifications of security attacks in VANETs—namely, safety application, payment-based application, and attacks on privacy. With respect to VANET safety applications, because of the safety-critical nature of VANETs, they are normally accompanied by high levels of liability. Respecting privacy, because of V2V and V2I (V2X) communication, it is thus easier to track vehicles and/or their drivers because of their predominantly wireless nature. Nonetheless, an exhaustive/comprehensive list of all possible adversaries, requirements, and countermeasures in a security system is unrealistic and impractical, especially prior to adequate (full/partial) real-world implementations/deployments—as is the case with VANETs [10]. To this end, the various attacks and threats presented here are only, at best, an incomprehensive list.

6.4 Countermeasures for Security and Privacy in Transportation Cyber-Physical Systems

We now list the corresponding countermeasures for ensuring security and privacy in transportation CPSs. We will begin with reviewing cryptography mechanisms, cryptography protections,

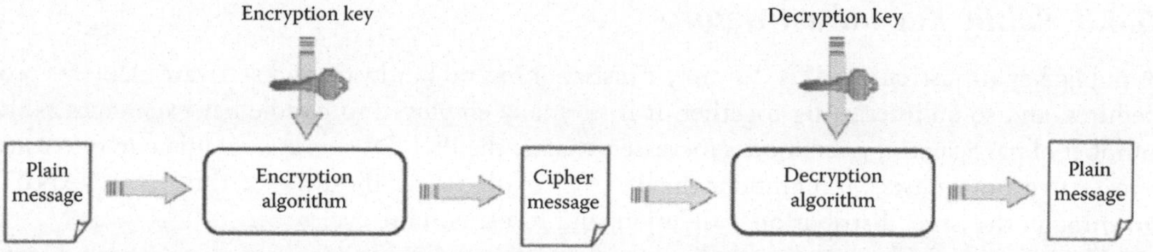

Figure 6.3 Encryption and decryption processes. (From Mejri, M.N., et al. Survey on VANET security challenges and possible cryptographic solutions. *Vehicular Communications*, 04/2014.)

and public key infrastructure and then discuss some countermeasures and architectures employed to improve/ensure security and privacy in transportation CPSs.

6.4.1 Cryptography Mechanisms

Figure 6.3 illustrates a pictorial view of the encryption and decryption process. Respecting cryptography mechanisms, the following types are employed:

- *Symmetric or private key cryptography* uses the encryption key to easily obtain the decryption key. It thrives on the fact that the secret key is never revealed to outsiders other than the communicating entities. Nonetheless, the requirement that both parties possess the secret key is a drawback of symmetric key cryptosystems in relation to their asymmetric/public key counterparts [6]. Symmetric or private key cryptography is no longer used for VANETs and most other domains because of its scalability issues and/or high overhead in key distribution, and maintenance cost, especially when network size increases [5].
- *Asymmetric or public key cryptography*: Here, the public key—which as the name implies is made public—is used for encrypting the message, while the private key (not made public) is used for message decryption. Public key or asymmetric cryptography is used in digital signatures through digital certificates issued by CAs. It is, however, slower and less efficient than the symmetric or private key cryptography counterpart. In addition, the process of verifying the digital signature of the sender by the receiver in order to verify that the message is authentic is not very amenable to real-time and safety-critical applications requiring little or no latency [22].

6.4.2 Cryptography Protections

With the use of cryptography, the following security requirements can be attained: (i) *Confidentiality*: Most exchanged VANET messages are transmitted unencrypted or unprotected excepting sensitive security- and privacy-related ones such as electronic toll payments [6]. For example, in general, safety-related messages are normally not secured by encryption or other security mechanisms because of the absence of critical/private data/information [10]. (ii) *Authentication*: It is implemented through digital signatures. (iii) *Integrity*: It is implemented through one-way hash functions. (iv) *Nonrepudiation*: It ensures that no participating node can feign ignorance of all or part of its legitimate activities.

6.4.3 Public Key Infrastructure

A public key infrastructure (PKI) simply consists of several hardware and software elements procedures, and so on interacting together. It is normally employed to handle key exchanges as the number of participating users/nodes increases, that is, the PKI CA acts as a middleman or trusted third party among users. It maintains the life cycle of digital certificates—certificates in VANETs go through the issue, distribution, validation, and revocation life cycles [6].

Identification, authentication, authorization, confidentiality, and nonrepudiation are achieved using PKIs and digital certificates. It is, however, imperative to note that interoperability, privacy, and the need to constantly update the certificate revocation list (CRL) in real time or near real time are major challenges in VANETs [5]. It is also germane to note that using PKIs alone cannot protect against privacy attacks or breaches, as they were not originally designed to provide privacy [5,20,30].

6.4.3.1 VANET Public Key Infrastructure

Similarly, VANET/vehicular public key infrastructure (VPKI) is used to efficiently authenticate communicating entities or nodes in a VANET environment using digital certificates or IDs issued by the CA such that each vehicle on the road is validated by a CA trusted by both parties [6,22]. Key management in VANETs requires anonymously installing, certifying, and revoking a public/private key pair by a CA [10]. Nonetheless, interoperability, interdomain authentication, and authorization between and among CAs located in different geographical jurisdictions and boundaries is challenging. For example, how can authentication and authorization be performed between two or among many intersecting CA domains (in real time or near real time)? One possible solution to the interoperability and authentication problems identified in VANETs is the interdomain authentication system (AS) proposed in [5]. As mentioned earlier, although the use of PKIs alone provides countermeasures against security compromises, they are helpless against privacy issues or compromises [5]. Privacy can, however, be maintained by using a centralized PKI together with a trusted third party [5,12]; cryptography is also used to maintain privacy [12]. A disadvantage of using VPKI is that it introduces extra delays in terms of signature generation, transmission, and verification, especially regarding safety- or life-critical messages [19]. In addition, because of the large number of PKIs and the number of instructions required to be executed, real-time digital signature verification suffers from significant performance or message overheads requiring expensive computational or power resources [22].

6.4.3.2 Group Signature

Group-based signatures, an alternative to using PKIs, reduce the number of exchanged keys in VANETs [5]. Nonetheless, group-based signature and identity-based signature approaches can suffer from scalability problems, especially as the number of vehicles in the group/cluster continually increases (i.e., computational complexity increases as scalability increases) [5].

6.4.4 Security Countermeasures for Securing VANETs

Most VANET implementations only start addressing security issues when a breach has occurred, as security is not built or designed into most implementations. This is also true of many other IT domains besides VANETs [19].

6.4.4.1 Generic Security Mechanisms

In VANETs, like many other security domains, proactive (preventative) security mechanisms supersede reactive (detective) ones [10,12], which are further elucidated as follows:

- *Prevention techniques*: Preventative security techniques are analogous to intrusion prevention mechanisms in other network security domains. The mechanisms include the following: (a) *Digital signature-based techniques*: These techniques ensure authentication, integrity, and nonrepudiation of participating entities. They can be certificate-based or certificate-void. The efficiency of digital signatures especially as scalability increases has not been sufficiently studied and ascertained. (b) *Proprietary system design*: This is aimed at making it difficult for an adversary to penetrate the system using known vulnerabilities. (c) *Tamperproof hardware*: This technique can securely store evidence from malicious modification attacks using a tamper-resistant/tamperproof device (TPD).
- *Detection techniques*: Reactive security measures are synonymous with intrusion detection techniques in other network security domains [10]. When preventive security mechanisms fail to deter an attack, detective security measures must be triggered as a fallback mechanism. Efficiently and reliably implementing detective security measures can go a long way in even preventing collisions and other safety-critical compromises or disasters [10,31]. Typical techniques include the following: (a) *Signature-based detection*: Compares current network traffic with previously known attack signatures; hence, this technique is effective only against known attacks or exploits. On the one hand, some of its advantages include simplicity and fast attack detection. On the other hand, one of its disadvantages is incapacitation against new attacks because it depends on regular updates to the attack signature database. (b) *Anomaly-based detection*: Detects unusual network activity based on predefined thresholds. One of its features is that it does not require frequent updates of the attack signature database. However, a downside is that it is susceptible to producing many false-positive results as a result of the vague and equivocal definition of normal versus abnormal use or behavior. (c) *Context verification*: The normal operation of entities in a VANET (e.g., RSUs, vehicles, and traffic lights), together with their environmental interactions, can be used to infer the presence or absence of attacks/abnormal operation [5].

6.4.4.2 Specific Security Solutions for VANETs

In the following, we list some specific security techniques for VANETs from the existing literature:

- *Specific attack-based solutions*: Privacy-preserving detection of abuses of pseudonyms (P2DAP) militates against Sybil attacks in VANETs. It is, however, incapacitated with respect to collusion attacks [10]. Channel, communication technology, and key switches or changes are some security solutions against attacks such as DoS.
- *Use of digital signatures*: This mechanism ensures message security that can be used to provide authentication, integrity, and nonrepudiation security requirements. Message security can also be protected or ensured using vehicular PKI. With respect to vehicular PKI, each vehicle uses its public and private key pairs to sign and verify all transmitted broadcasted messages [12].
- *Electronic license plates (ELPs)*: ELPs can be issued by transportation authorities to uniquely identify vehicles [19].

- *Encryption*: Confidentiality is ensured by encrypting all messages before sending them [12].
- *Event data recording*: Ensures that all events or incidents among participating entities (e.g., vehicles, RSUs, and traffic lights) are meticulously logged or stored for audit purposes, which may be used for establishing liability/exonerating from liability.
- *Use of tamperproof device or hardware*: This is a physical security mechanism used to secure messages (incoming and outgoing), keys, and so on. ELPs and VPKI can be kept safe or secured using tamperproof hardware [19]. In addition, all events in VANETs must be logged using event data recording, which can subsequently be retrieved and analyzed for audit purposes.
- *Data correlation*: As a protection against false data injection attacks, data correlation verifies the relevance, credibility, and consistency of data/information emanating from various sources before making actionable decisions with them [19].
- *Secure positioning*: This mechanism can be maintained using GPS security measures.
- *Secure routing*: Secure routing or communication can be identity-based—unicast (sent to an individual node), and/or geography-based—multicast (sent to two or more nodes [a group of nodes]) [10]. Secure routing protocols (SRP) [32] and secure beaconing [33] fall under the category of ID-based routing protocols because they are susceptible to privacy breaches/violations [10]. Generally speaking, because security is commonly included as an afterthought, most SRPs violate privacy requirements [10].
- *Secure MAC*: In addition to securing routing, securing medium access control (MAC) is also pertinent [10,34,35].

6.4.5 VANET Security Architectures

In the VANET literature, a number of researchers have studied VANET security architectures, primarily dealing with security and privacy concerns/requirement. Some of these architectures include, but are not limited to the following:

6.4.5.1 Global Security Architecture

Because privacy, safety, and security are some of the main deliverables of VANETs, a number of research efforts have sought to address these and other issues. For example, Engoulou et al. [12,17] proposed a security architecture for dealing with the security requirements, threats, and challenges of VANETs. This global security architecture consists of five levels—namely, cryptographic, message/data, trust, authentication, and security material levels. These levels are further categorized into three stages—namely, security material and authentication level (prevention stage); trust and message/data level (detection and correction stage); and cryptographic level (privacy stage) [12,17]. In addition, attacks in VANETs were described with respect to their nature, scope, consequences/impact, and target, as shown in the security architecture for VANET (SAV). It consists of basic security elements (PKI, positioning, and time), single-hop security (integrity, nonrepudiation, authentication, and confidentiality), multihop security (end-to-end security mechanisms for confidentiality, authentication, and nonrepudiation), and services protection (routing, location services, warning alarms, etc.) [12].

6.4.5.2 VANET Privacy

Privacy risks escalate when participating entities (vehicles, RSUs, and traffic lights) give out more information than is absolutely necessary [5]. Identity privacy, location privacy, and data privacy are the three main domains of privacy in VANETs. Anonymity can be used to ensure privacy using pseudonyms; pseudonyms are generic aliases or identifiers used to avoid the use of real or personally identifiable information [5]. Most pseudonymity techniques can successfully guarantee location and identity privacy; pseudonyms can also be used to prevent a malicious vehicle or individual from carrying out unauthorized activities manifesting in the form of node linking (user profiling) and tracking [5]. CAs manage a node's (vehicle, traffic light, or RSU) identity using public and private key encryption [12]. There have been a number of research efforts in this direction. For example, as shown in Figure 6.4 in [5], Serna-Olvera proposed a privacy-aware security framework, which consists of the following: (i) *Authentication system (AS)*: Using policy mapping, the AS enables interoperability of PKIs and certificate validation across untrusted domains. (ii) *Anonymous information retrieval (AIR)* uses query permutation and query forgery to prevent node/vehicle tracking that can be used for user profiling. (iii) *Attribute-based privacy (ABP)* uses incomplete/selective attribute/parameter disclosures to prevent vehicle tracking. (iv) *Trust Validation Model (TVM)*: As shown in Figure 6.4, TVM uses trust levels/sensitivity levels to avoid unauthorized access to a vehicle's private information that can cause a vehicle to believe a lie in order to deceive or manipulate it [5]. The online certificate status protocol (OCSP) is used to increase the efficiency of the verification of the status of a vehicle based on the CRL in a situation where you have many CAs. It also reduces network traffic resulting in better bandwidth management.

To summarize, the privacy-enhancing model (PEM), which consists of the ABP protocol—using attribute-based credentials (ABC) and the AIR protocol—can be used to ensure that a vehicle cannot be tracked or linked with an identifier. By doing so, privacy and anonymity is preserved [5]. The danger of possible leaks of personally identifiable information—a privacy concern—can be mitigated using a privacy enhancement feature to encrypt the hash of the sender's public key, which can only be decrypted by authorized parties/entities [22]. In other words, encryption can be used to ensure privacy [22].

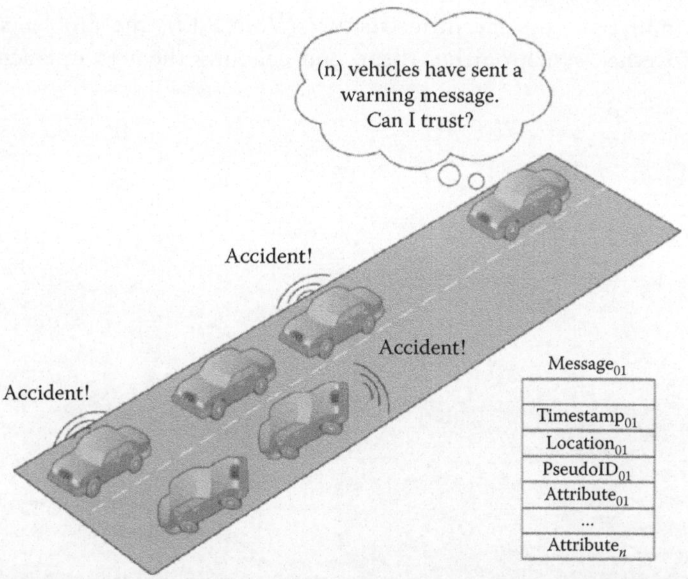

Figure 6.4 Using a TVM to avoid acting on malicious message dissemination that can compromise both security and privacy. (From Serna-Olvera, J.M., A trust-driven privacy architecture for vehicular ad-hoc networks, Universitat Politecnica de Catalunya, 2012. With permission.)

Finally, security and reliability are major prerequisites for dependable and wide usage of VANET safety-critical applications [10]. As has already been lucidly established, more security means less privacy and vice versa. Hence, a trade-off must be made because in order to enhance security, some privacy must be sacrificed [10]. Conflicts between security and efficiency, security and quality of service (QoS), together with other conflicting actors/requirements must be resolved in order to increase the real-world adoption of VANETs [10]. A holistic view of security from the ground up is essential, but lacking in VANETs—more research is needed in this area [10,36].

6.5 Case Study

In this section, we present a case study to demonstrate how to improve security of transportation CPSs. We will first present the test-bed setup and then the evaluation scenarios, followed by the evaluation results.

6.5.1 Test-Bed Setup

Here, we give a detailed description of our simulation architecture, platform, input, parameters, and evaluation scenarios toward the attainment of our research goals and objectives. A number of research efforts have endeavored to address the privacy and security challenges of VANETs. Nonetheless, most existing efforts are quite abstract or theoretical, without the use of real-world data, realistic road networks, or both [6,10,34,35]. To bridge this gap, we used both a real-world data set and road networks in our study. Figures 6.5 and 6.6 show pictorial views of our study area in MapQuest and Google Map.

6.5.1.1 V2X Simulation Framework: VSimRTI Architecture

Using the V2X simulation runtime infrastructure (VSimRTI), the problems of flexibly coupling simulators together, synchronizing them, and enabling them to interact with each other

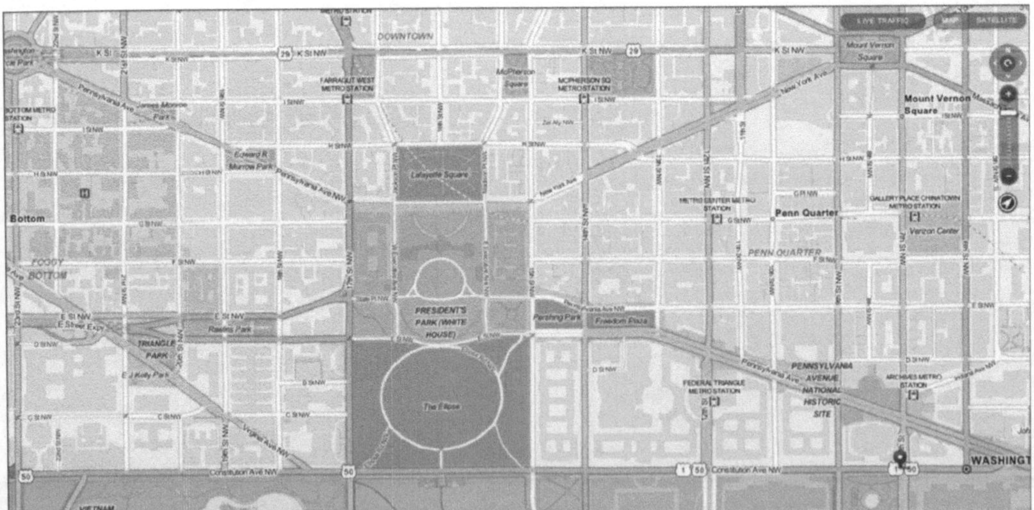

Figure 6.5 Study area in MapQuest.

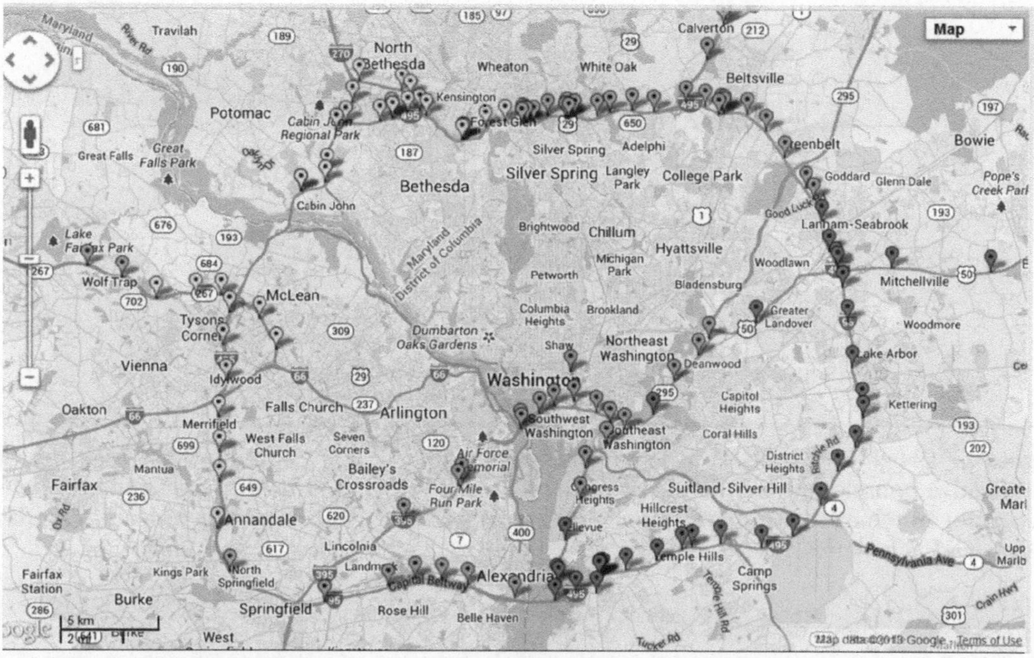

Figure 6.6 Selected study area.

have been solved without requiring changes to the underlying infrastructure, which is a major downside of fixed coupling approaches [37]. Deriving from the IEEE standard for Modeling and Simulation (M&S) High Level Architecture (HLA), the VSimRTI was developed and has been used for evaluating various types of V2X scenarios [37–46]. It enables flexible and loose coupling of various simulators, including traffic, network or communication, environment, and so on, which can be easily modified based on the simulation goals or objectives [1,35,40,41]. Several traffic simulators (e.g., SUMO and VISSIM), communication network simulations (e.g., JIST/SWANS, OMNeT++ [47], ns-3), and application simulators (e.g., VSimRTI_App), besides other data visualization/analysis and development tools have been successfully coupled with VSimRTI [37,38,42,44,46,48–50]. Upon starting a federate/simulator (e.g., the SUMO traffic simulator), a bidirectional communication is established between the federates ambassador and the VSimRTI. Figures 6.7 and 6.8 [51,52] show the VSimRTI architecture together with its interacting federates. The VSimRTI architecture consists of components responsible for federation, vehicle data, time and synchronization, and interaction and communication management [37,39,41,43,45].

Similar to VSimRTI, other frameworks have attempted to enable/establish bidirectional coupling of traffic, and communications simulators mostly in a fixed manner—attended by their pros and cons. Some of these frameworks include, but are not limited to, TraNS couples the open-source SUMO traffic simulator with ns-2 [34,35,43,48]; the Multiple Simulator Interlinking Environment for C2CC in VANETs (MSIECV) couples the commercial traffic simulator VISSIM and the ns-2 network simulator with MATLAB/Simulink responsible for application-level simulation [35,48]; iTETRIS couples the SUMO traffic simulator and ns-3 network simulator—it is particularly suited for large-scale simulation scenarios; veins [53] couples SUMO with the OMNeT++ network simulator [46,49–56]; and Paramics & ns-2, as the name indicates, couples the Paramics traffic simulator with the ns-2 network simulator. At a minimum, traffic, application, and communication/network

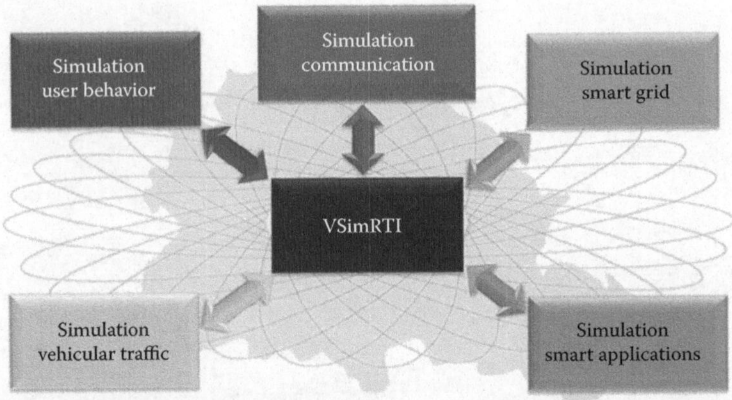

Figure 6.7 High-level VSimRTI architecture with coupled federates. (From Daimler Center for Automotive Information Technology Innovations. VSimRTI: Smart mobility simulation, Daimler Center for Automotive Information Technology Innovations, 2014. http://www.dcaiti.tu-berlin.de/research/simulation/. With permission.)

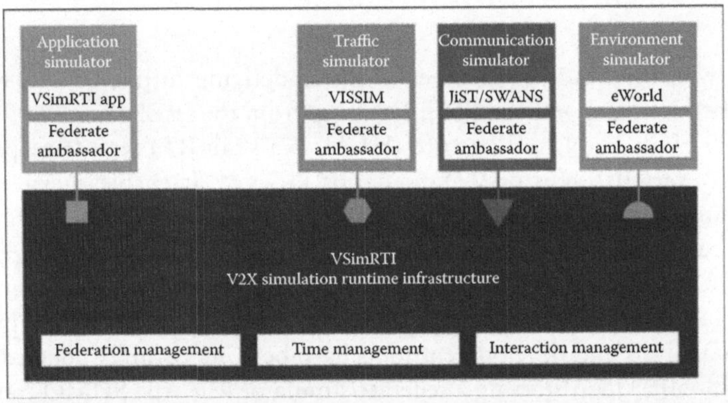

Figure 6.8 Basic federates necessary for successful V2X simulation using VSimRTI. (From VSimRTI: Smart mobility simulation, Daimler Center for Automotive Information Technology Innovations, 2014. http://www.dcaiti.tu-berlin.de/research/simulation/. With permission.)

simulator interactions/couplings are required for successful V2X communication using most V2X frameworks/infrastructure such as iTETRIS—this is also true with VSimRTI [37,41,42,45].

Because of the expensive nature of field tests and studies, simulation studies are normally carried out first [31]. Consequently, in order to perform the cybersecurity threats on a transportation CPS (e.g., our investigated V2X jamming attack scenario), we used the VSimRTI cosimulation platform, which comprises traffic, application, communication, and environment simulators as shown in Figure 6.8. The reason for this is because the use of traffic simulators alone is inadequate in fulfilling the requirements of V2X simulation [31]. To simulate V2X communication, all participating equipped vehicles must be running an application. In our scenario, our equipped vehicles were running our developed incident warning application (IWA).

6.5.1.2 Real-World Data Set

Our use of real-world traffic data was born from the fact that many existing studies [40] are void of them. In our study, 6 weeks of weekday traffic volume data patterns were collected and analyzed before feeding the output to the SUMO traffic simulator [57]. Our data consists of several fields/attributes such as lane number, zone number, lane type, vehicle speed, volume, occupancy, measurement time stamps and intervals, and so on. Figure 6.9 shows our entire data coverage area in Google Maps. Because most traffic congestions are experienced in the morning (5:00 a.m./7:00 a.m. to 10:00 a.m.) and evening (4:00 p.m. to 7:00 p.m.) rush hours, we chose the morning traffic condition as our primary simulation focus [56,58,59].

6.5.1.3 Simulation Inputs and Parameters

We used the VSimRTI for the purposes of our study because of its unique capability to couple various types of simulators together in a flexible manner [44]. Using road network data from OpenStreetMap [60] as input, eWorld [61] was used to generate events such as ice, road accidents/obstacles, and so on which were subsequently exported as inputs to the SUMO traffic simulator [39,43]. SUMO-generated vehicular traffic was then used as input to the Java in simulation time/scalable wireless ad hoc network simulator (JiST/SWANS) [41,43], which handles the exchange of messages among nodes such as vehicles, RSUs, and traffic lights. It can also modify a vehicle's position, speed, direction, and so on through a socket interface at runtime using the traffic

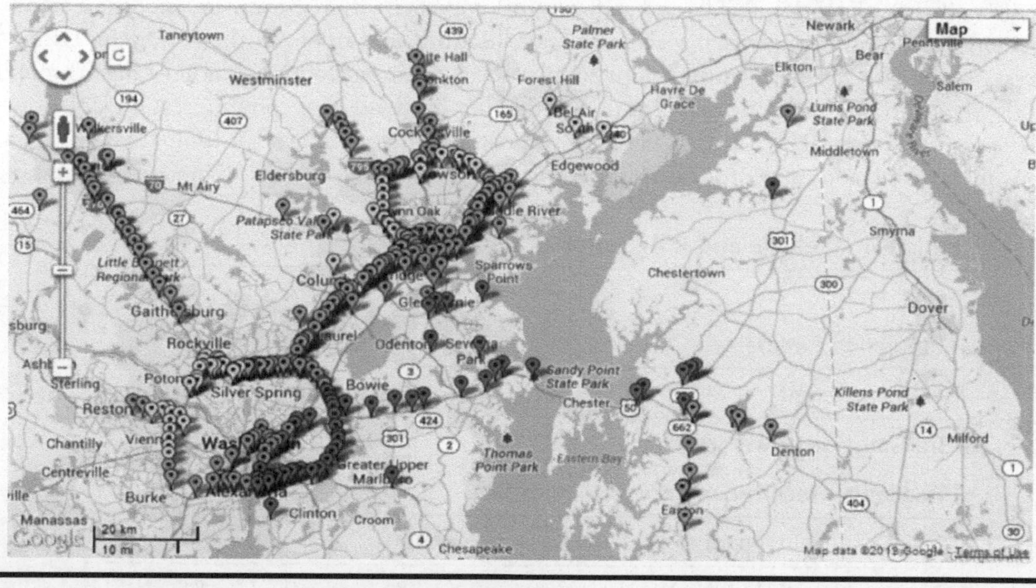

Figure 6.9 Coverage area of our field data set.

control interface (TraCI) [62]. The communication simulator (JiST/SWANS) is responsible for relaying vehicular situational awareness messages with cooperative awareness messages (CAM), messages that trigger rerouting with decentralized environment notification messages (DENM), and so on upon detecting roadway congestions caused by ice, accident, and fog. Both CAM and DENM have message lengths of 1500 bytes [41,44,49]. Some of the JiST/SWANs network simulator parameters used in our simulation study include, but are not limited to, simulation area (77,000 × 67,000 m), communication range (300 m), frequency (5.9 GHz), protocol (Cached Greedy Geo-cast [CGGC] geo-broadcasting protocol), wireless communication protocol/standard (IEEE 802.11p), and bandwidth (10 Mbps); our total simulation runtime/duration was set at 7000 s. The JiST/SWANs network simulator parameters shown in Table 6.1 regarding our IWA-equipped vehicles and RSUs were used in our simulation; these typically reflect real-world conditions.

A more detailed exposition at the VSimRTI framework and its coupled federates and simulators requisite for successful V2X simulation ensues.

6.5.1.3.1 Traffic Simulator (SUMO)

We used the open-source microscopic simulation for urban mobility (SUMO) [63] simulator as our traffic simulator. Some of its features include, but are not limited to, support for lane changing, overtaking, simulating vehicles individually, modeling of driver imperfections, collision-free vehicle movements, and multi- and single-lane roadway support. Road networks (streets/edges) and navigation routes were generated in SUMO using the *netconvert.exe* and *duarouter.exe* tools [31,39,57].

6.5.1.3.2 Network Simulator (JiST/SWANS)

The Java in simulation time (JiST) [64], a virtual machine-based simulator, was used together with its SWANS adjunct as our chosen network simulator. Using JiST/SWANS, CAMs are used to identify all nodes (vehicles, RSUs, and traffic lights), together with their transmission time stamp, position (latitude and longitude), speed, direction/heading, and so on. In the same vein, DENM messages are used for event notifications to all nodes within its communication range through single-hop/centralized (broadcast) or multihop/decentralized (ad hoc) communication [31]. Some of the features of the JiST/SWANS network simulator include, but are not limited to, specifications for transmission range, transmission power, bandwidth, receiver sensitivity, and geographic

Table 6.1 Vehicle and RSU Simulation Parameters

	Value	
Simulation Parameter	*Vehicle*	*RSU*
Antenna height (m)	1.5	10.0
Transmission power (dbm)	18.5	17
Transmitter/receiver antenna gain (dbm)	0	0
Receiver sensitivity (dbm)	−91	−91
Receiver threshold (dbm)	−81	−81

routing protocol. A major advantage of the JiST/SWANS communication simulator is that it is highly scalable with increasing network size. Its network layer supports IPv4 and the transport layer supports both UDP and TCP [39,65–68].

6.5.1.3.3 Application Simulator (VSimRTI_App)

Using the application simulator/federate, applications can be implemented that control nodes (vehicles, RSUs, and traffic lights) in a simulation [31,45]. Specifically, we developed and implemented an application called incident warning application (IWA). Vehicles running this application are able to use it to bypass identified traffic incidents with the propensity and proclivity of leading to traffic congestions, and other precarious driving conditions [39].

6.5.1.3.4 Event Simulator (eWorld)

The eWorld framework allows for the importation of OpenStreetMap files—both online and off-line—in which environmental events such as traffic jams, fogs, icy/slippery roads, rain, road work/construction, and so on can be incorporated. The map enriched with environmental events can subsequently be either exported to the SUMO traffic simulator as input or databases or saved within eWorld's file format. Other eWorld environmental events that can be added to the road networks include, but are not limited to, glazed frost, snow, ozone, smog, CO_2, and temperature. In addition, the duration of these events relative to the entire simulation runtime can be configured. After adding environmental events to a map, eWorld can export it directly into SUMO-specific file formats, which consist of SUMO network, edge or street, node, route, event definitions, traffic light definitions, variable speed sign (VSS) definitions, rerouting definitions, and other configuration definition files. In addition, traffic lights, vehicle routes, and points of interest (PoIs) can be added and modified using eWorld. Also, SUMO dump files, simulation outputs, and results can be imported into eWorld in order to compute and analyze some simulation statistics and parameters such as total travel time, vehicular density, occupancy, average speed, and so on. Simulation results can also be visualized within eWorld with capabilities of high occupancy lanes, street colorings, and width visualizations [39,61]. Figure 6.10 shows a slippery and frozen ice event being added to our reference study area—Constitution Avenue NW, Washington DC—using eWorld.

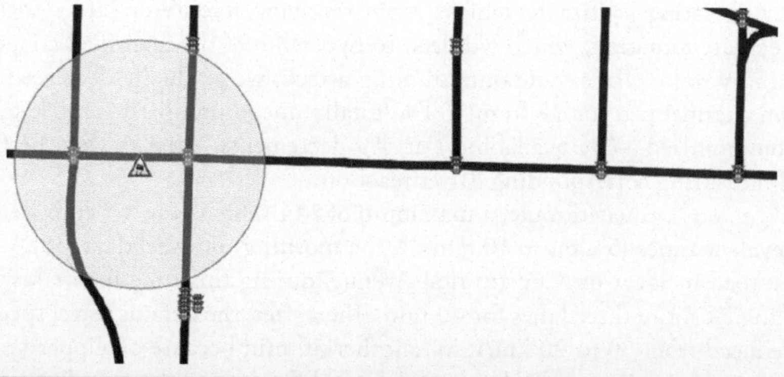

Figure 6.10 Slippery ice event added to Constitution Avenue NW using eWorld.

6.5.2 Evaluation Scenarios

In seeking to ascertain the traffic efficiency, safety, effectiveness, and resilience to attacks of V2V communication, the following scenarios were employed:

6.5.2.1 Scenario A (Traffic Efficiency)

In this scenario, vehicles using our developed IWA are notified to reroute because of the detected road traffic congestion ahead. Because classic or nonequipped vehicles do not receive or respond to these reroute messages, they drive heedlessly or blindly to meet the congested situation. As a consequence, our IWA-equipped vehicles bypass this incident while unequipped/classic vehicles suffer the consequences especially manifesting in aggravated/exacerbated trip time (TT), fuel consumption (FC), and CO_2 emission.

6.5.2.2 Scenario B (Safety)

In this scenario, the metric we used to evaluate safety was with respect to the total number of IWA-equipped vehicles that actually rerouted/heeded the reroute message to take an alternative route to their destinations in relation to the entire population equipped to reroute. Accordingly 100% safety can be attained if all vehicles that got the reroute request actually heeded it and vice versa. We assume that all IWA-equipped vehicles that received the message or directive to reroute actually heeded it. Using the human–machine interface (HMI), V2X-equipped vehicle drivers are notified of traffic incidents/events [31,42,46].

6.5.2.3 Scenario C (Jamming Attack)

In this scenario, we implemented a radio/communication channel jamming attack, which has a negative effect on Scenarios A, and B. In this attack, we disrupted the wireless communication channel's ability to disseminate traffic-related information to intended recipients in a progressive manner. As previously stated, a jamming attack is usually an intentional attack, which is aimed at communication channel disruption. Jamming aims to preclude or starve other nodes from utilizing available resources, which is a type of DoS attack in a physical layer that is active and malicious in nature [6]. To evaluate the effect of a jamming attack on our simulation setup, we simulated a situation in which a malicious insider overwhelms the communication channel with spurious signals, thereby obviating legitimate vehicles from receiving reroute or safety-critical messages in order to effectuate rerouting, which will lead to bypassing of the identified congestion on the original or primary route. To execute our jamming attack, we gradually decreased the available communication channel percentage from 100% (totally uncompromised—100% availability) to 0% (totally compromised—0% availability) at 5% decrements. Attacks were performed while observing and measuring corresponding driver reactions.

Specifically, on our evaluated route, a maximum of 144 vehicles every 5 min were recorded at congestion prevalent times (5 a.m. to 10 a.m. in the morning) on weekdays [38]. Consequently, we simulated a road incident on Constitution Avenue, during this time interval, which had the effect of blocking its entire three lanes for 40 min. Thereafter, the default travel speed limit of all vehicles was reduced from 50 to 20 km/h for another 50 min because of slippery road segments caused by frozen ice and compounded by the presence of fog around the area that resulted in poor driving visibility; the length of the affected roadway is 82.3 m [30]. Without the traffic incident on Constitution Avenue NW, every vehicle emanating from John Hanson Hwy from the West (source) through New York Ave NE and finally to Dulles Toll Road in the East (destination) will traverse/enter Constitution Avenue via 9th Street. Nonetheless, because of the traffic incident on Constitution Avenue, on getting to 9th Street, our IWA-equipped vehicles will receive reroute messages/directives from the RSU, located on 9th Street, to bypass Constitution Avenue. As a result, the IWA-equipped vehicles avoid the congestion on Constitution Avenue, by talking an alternative route via H. Street NW to Custis Memorial Pkwy before finally arriving at the final destination—Dulles Toll Rd. On the other hand, unequipped/classic vehicles suffer the consequences of the congestion on Constitution Avenue NW because they are uninformed and unintelligent.

Using the Handbook Emission Factors for Road Transport (HBEFA) version 3.1 database [69,70], which is similar to the Passenger car and Heavy duty vehicle Emission Model (PHEM), we modeled the pollutant and emission levels of our simulation by coupling its database to our simulation with the SUMO traffic simulator [57,69], using the passenger and light duty/delivery category (HBEFA3/PC_G_EU4) emission class. In addition to passenger cars (PC), light commercial vehicles (LCV) and heavy-duty vehicles (HDV) are some other vehicle categories that can be modeled with the HBEFA [71,57,69,72–74]. The following pollutants were considered for the purposes of our study: CO_2, carbon monoxide (CO), —hydrocarbons (HC; consisting of methane [CH_4], nonmethane hydrocarbons [NMHC], benzene, toluene, and xylene), NO_x (consisting of nitrogen dioxide [NO_2], and nitrogen monoxide [NO]), particulate matters/particulate mass value (PM_x), and fuel consumption (FC). Each driver's emission footprint is displayed via the vehicle's on board diagnostics display (OBD).

6.5.3 Evaluation Results

In this section, the results of our jamming attack and its effect on traffic efficiency and safety applications of V2V communication are presented. Figure 6.11a–f show the results of our 21 simulation runs with respect to some of our evaluated performance metrics from 0 to 100% communication channel availability at each 5% step/increment.

The ratio of IWA-equipped vehicles to classic/unequipped vehicles was kept constant at 50% each throughout the entire simulation. The suffixes _a, _n, and _r shown in Figure 6.11a–f refer to the evaluated performance metrics with respect to vehicles that are running our IWA used to bypass the road traffic congestion on Constitution Avenue by circumnavigating through other alternative/secondary routes (_a)—these vehicles are suffering from the adverse effects of the jamming attack scenario, vehicles that are running our IWA, but are not negatively affected/influenced by the jamming attack, that is, the normal scenario (_n), and vehicles that travel through the primary/original route through Constitution Avenue NW free of congestions, that is, the reference scenario (_r).

In addition to rerouting vehicles away from the primary roadway to the alternative ones in order to avoid congestion, our IWA-equipped vehicles also have prior knowledge of the congested states of these alternative routes such that vehicles are not blindly rerouted from one congested roadway to another; this is true when using V2V communication, but not V2I communication [15,75].

With respect to traffic efficiency (shown in Figure 6.11a–d), our average best-case result—with respect to travel time (TT)—was obtained at 100% communication channel availability with little or no difference observed among the evaluated performance metrics. In the same vein, the average worst-case scenario was, evidently, observed at 0% available communication channel

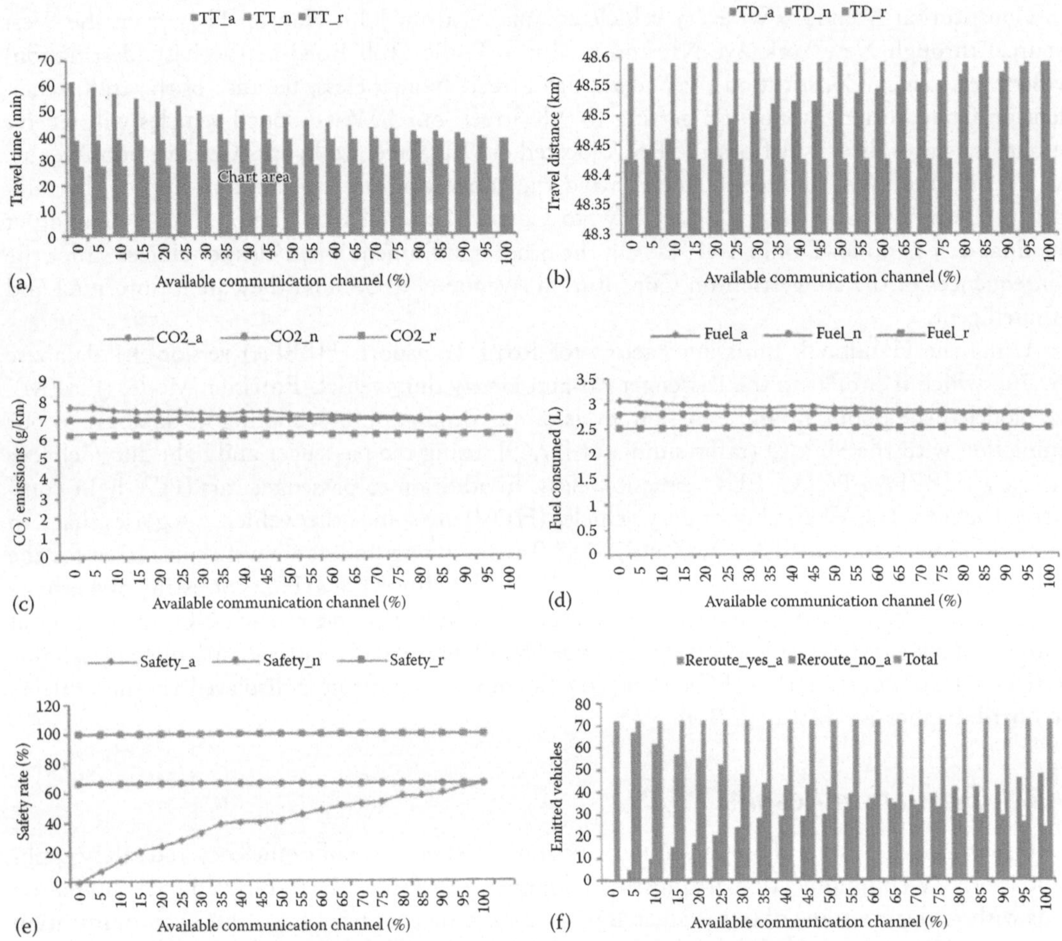

Figure 6.11 Performance of some evaluated metrics in relation to available communication channel as a result of jamming attack.

with the following recorded losses: TT (60.92%), 3655.56 s; average speed (38.06%), 29.01 km/h; PMx (3.16%), 0.02 g; CO (4.18%), 5.81 g/m; CO_2 (9.28%), 0.65 g/km; NO_x (5.68%), 8.06 g; HC (15.76%), 0.37 g; and fuel consumed (9.28%), 0.25 L. The only improvement was observed respecting travel distance [TD] at (0.33%): 161.5 m. Similarly, with respect to the average second-worst-case result obtained at 5% available communication channel, the following losses were observed: TT (54.92%), 1260.63 s; average speed (35.64%), 27.16 km/h; NO_x (5.51%), 0.84 g; PM_x (3.25%), 0.02 g; CO (4.07%), 5.65 g/m; CO_2 (8.81%), 0.61 g/km; HC (14.66%), 0.34 g; and fuel consumed (8.81%), 0.24 L. The only improvement was observed with respect to travel distance [TD] at 144.68 m (0.29%). Generally; IWA-equipped vehicles under the influence of the communication channel jamming attack (_a) travelled at an average speed of 61.66 km/h from source to destination while IWA-supported/equipped vehicles, free from the jamming attack (_n), maintained an average speed of 76.2 km/h. Consequently, because attacked vehicles travelled at lower and less uniform speeds owing to congestion, more fuel was utilized in the attack scenario than in the attack-free scenario.

Similarly, with respect to safety (Figure 6.11e–f), the average best-case safety performance was observed at 100% available communication channel having a safety rate of 66.66%, that is, only 48 out of 72 equipped vehicles heeded the reroute/change route directive—24 equipped vehicles did not. On the other hand, the average worst-case safety performance was observed at 0% available communication channel resulting in a 0% safety rate because none of the 72 IWA-equipped vehicles got the reroute/change route directive due to the completely jammed radio/communication channel. Similarly, the average second worst-case safety performance was observed at 5% available communication channel with a safety rate of 6.94%. This means that only 5 out of 72 equipped vehicles heeded the change route directive, that is, 67 equipped vehicles did not.

The overall poor performance (with respect to the evaluated metrics) of V2V communication is attributable to the fact that not all IWA-equipped vehicles that received the reroute directive actually heeded them. Other possible reasons why these reroute or change route directives were not heeded by IWA-equipped vehicles could be because they got the message a little bit too late to utilize it to bypass the incident on time (relative to their current travel speed) [25]. It is also evident that as the available communication channel of IWA-equipped (V2X) vehicles increased, the number of vehicles that responded to the change route request also increased. This is true because unlike V2I communication, which is primarily single-hop communication, V2V communication relies on multihop communication with leading vehicles transmitting messages such as road conditions and congested states to trailing or following vehicles. In a situation where more classic vehicles outnumber V2X vehicles within a given communication range (i.e., 300 m), these safety-critical messages may stop midway, as there are not enough relays and equipped vehicles to convey these messages beyond this communication range. This is one reason why safety-critical messages are best disseminated through single-hop/centralized (V2I communication) rather than multihop/decentralized (V2V communication). In addition, because of the high number of V2X message exchanges, especially at high communication channel availability and increased travel speeds (especially in a highway scenario), packet and message collisions can result in packet and message drops, corruption, and/or delays as a result of bandwidth saturation, and so on. Another possible reason why V2V communication did not perform as well as expected is man-made and natural interferences. Man-made interferences such as obstacles, high-rise buildings, and so on and natural interferences such as fog, heavy rain, tornadoes, and so on diminish the efficiency, effectiveness, and accuracy of V2V communications. This is especially true because V2V communication simulations performed on highway scenarios tend to produce more effective and predictable results than those done in other rural and city scenarios because of the infrequent interferences from high-rise buildings and other obstacles that limit and interfere with the V2V multihop communication path. This is the reason why, often, V2V/ad hoc communication is complemented with V2I/broadcast communication as a hybrid—hence the name V2X communication [64].

A jamming attack can also be executed via a timing attack. As already mentioned, in light of a timing attack, critical messages are intentionally delayed such that they arrive out of sync and cannot be subsequently used/useful [6]. It can involve adding a delay to a sent message or not sending the message at all; this has the effect of negatively affecting availability and delaying time-critical/safety-critical information from promptly arriving at its intended destination. Regarding safety-critical messages, the consequences of this type of attack, as we have clearly seen, can be calamitous [10,12,13].

As previously mentioned, DoS attacks compromise availability by jamming/flooding the network with overwhelming data. This type of attack can be carried out by an insider/outsider and rational/malicious attacker; however, more devastating attacks usually emanate from an insider. Some mitigation techniques against DoS attacks in VANETs include, but are not limited to, frequency hopping and communication channel and key switches/changes by the OBU [10,12].

In closing, our results concur with existing studies that assert that safety-critical messages are best disseminated using single-hop communication, especially in a complex, heterogeneous driving environment having a mixture of classic and V2X vehicles in equal or unequal proportions. As shown by the results, V2X communication indeed results in improved safety and traffic efficiency; however, these improvements are mostly dependent on factors that can be man-made (internal), natural (external), or a combination of both. Overall, as the communication channel available to IWA-equipped vehicles increases, performance with respect to TT, safety, and other performance metrics also increases [15,42,46].

6.6 Future Research

In the future, we will endeavor to investigate the following interesting and challenging research areas regarding the VANET/ITS domain:

- *VANET architecture*: The effect of jamming attacks, together with other types of security, and privacy attacks on V2I/broadcast/centralized communication needs to be further evaluated and studied. To this end, we plan to extend our current research work to both the V2I and the hybrid VANET/ITS architectures.
- *Electric vehicles (EVs)*: With the advent of electric vehicles, their comprehensive impact on the available power grid capacity is worthy of further evaluation studies—especially in more realistic scenarios like ours. This is true because most existing studies cannot be directly used in the real world because they are either void of real-world data (which is very difficult to obtain/secure based on our experience), real-world road networks, or both.
- *Human factors (HF)*: Safety, traffic efficiency, security, privacy, and so on are only as effective as the weakest link in the chain—this is often the unpredictable human driver, hence the name human-in-the-loop (HITL). Consequently, the influence of human factor characteristics such as perceptual, motor, and cognitive skills/capabilities on the aforementioned parameters is very much requisite in both field and simulation studies. In addition, as more self-driving cars are currently being promulgated by more companies such as Google, it will be quite interesting to study their effects in a heterogeneous driving environment consisting of other types of driving models such as completely human driven and semiautomatic (hybrid) driving.
- *Cryptography*: Because of the safety- and life-critical nature of ITS and its strict requirement of little or no tolerance for delays/errors in message dissemination, the influence of various cryptographic algorithms on timely and accurate message dissemination is imperative, especially as the network size begins to increase.

In addition, overcoming other challenges with respect to cloud storage, big data management of both historical and streaming/dynamic data, and application of various machine learning algorithms toward reliable and realistic traffic pattern prediction, and so on is imperative and they require more studies in order to further the VANET/ITS domain.

6.7 Final Remarks

Various transportation challenges, including safety, mobility, and environmental challenges, can potentially be addressed by transportation CPSs, where the networking infrastructure is a VANET. The application of advanced VANET technologies will bring connectivity to transportation, and transportation CPSs will enable transformative change in the transportation sector. Nonetheless, transportation CPSs are subject to threats stemming from increasing reliance on computer and communication technologies. Cyberthreats exploit the increased complexity and connectivity of transportation CPSs, placing security, economy, public safety, and health at risk. In this chapter, we have systematically discussed various security and privacy issues in transportation CPSs, reviewed various defense strategies and mechanisms to improve cybersecurity and privacy in transportation CPSs, and presented a case study on our test bed.

Author Biographies

Nnanna Ekedebe is currently a doctoral candidate in information technology (IT) at the Computer and Information Sciences Department at Towson University. He has a BEng in electrical and electronic engineering specializing in communication engineering from the Federal University of Technology Owerri (Nigeria) and an MS in management information systems from Bowie State University (Maryland). He has been a certified Project Management Professional (PMP) since August, 2010. He has also successfully passed the following prestigious information security certifications and will be fully certified in a couple of years: Certified Information Systems Auditor (CISA), Certified Information Security Manager (CISM), and Certified Information Systems Security Professional (CISSP), together with several Oracle database certifications. His research interests encompass all facets of computer networks together with their attendant human factors challenges, some of which include, but are not limited to, cyber-physical systems (CPS), artificial intelligence, computer/information systems audits, and forensic investigations.

Houbing Song received a PhD in electrical engineering from the University of Virginia, Charlottesville, in 2012, and an MS degree in civil engineering from the University of Texas, El Paso, in 2006. Currently, he is an assistant professor with the Department of Electrical and Computer Engineering, West Virginia University, Montgomery, where he is the founding director of both the West Virginia Center of Excellence for Cyber-Physical Systems (WVCECPS), sponsored by the West Virginia Higher Education Policy Commission, and the Security and Optimization for Networked Globe Laboratory (SONG Lab). He worked with the Texas A&M Transportation Institute (TTI) as an engineering research associate in 2007. He is an associate/area editor or a guest editor for several international journals. He has served as the general chair of five international workshops and on the technical program committee for more than 40 conferences or workshops. He has authored or coauthored more than 40 academic papers in peer-reviewed international journals and conferences. His research interests include cyber-physical systems and the Internet of Things.

Wei Yu is currently an associate professor in the Department of Computer and Information Sciences at Towson University. Before joining Towson University, he worked as a networking software developer for Cisco Systems, Inc., for over 9 years. He received his PhD degree in computer engineering from the Department of Computer Science and Engineering at Texas A&M University in May 2008. His research interests include cybersecurity, computer networks, and cyber-physical systems. His research is currently supported by federal agencies, including the National Science Foundation (NSF), Army Research Laboratory, National Institute of Standards and Technology, Air Force Research Laboratory, and so on. He has published over 140 papers, including articles in premier security and networking conferences such as Institute of Electrical and Electronics Engineers (IEEE) Symposium on Security and Privacy, Association for Computing Machinery Conference on Computer and Communications Security, IEEE INFOCOM, and International Conference on Distributed Computing Systems and journals such as *IEEE/ACM Transactions on Networking*, *IEEE Transactions on Dependable and Secure Computing*, *IEEE Transactions on Computers*, *IEEE Transactions on Parallel and Distributed Systems*, *IEEE Transactions on Mobile Computing*, and *IEEE Transactions on Vehicular Technology*. He received the NSF Faculty Early Career Development (CAREER) award in 2014, the 2012 Excellence in Scholarship Award from Fisher College of Science and Mathematics at Towson University, and the Best Paper Award at the 2013 and 2008 IEEE International Conferences on Communications.

Chao Lu has been a professor of computer science at Towson University since 1990. He took sabbatical leave at the US Naval Research Laboratory (NRL) in 1996 and was a consultant on micro-Doppler radar and computer vision for NRL1997-2010. He received the U.S. Federal Laboratories Excellence in Technology Transfer Award and Alan Berman Research Publications Award in 2001. Dr. Lu has coauthored two books: *Algorithms for Discrete Fourier Transform and Convolutions*, Springer, 1989, 2nd edition 1997; *Mathematics of Multidimensional Fourier Transform Algorithms*, Springer, 1993, 2nd edition 1997; 2 book chapters; and more than 80 journal and conference papers. He received a PhD in engineering (E.E.) in 1988 from the City University of New York. His research has been funded by the National Science Foundation, Naval Research Laboratory, Air Force Office of Scientific Research, Defense Advanced Research Projects Agency, Office of Naval Research, Army Research Laboratory, and National Institute of Standards and Technology. He has been conference general chair for four international conferences: the IEEE/ACIS International Conference on Software Engineering, Artificial Intelligence, Networking and Parallel/Distributed Computing (2005 and 2006), IEEE International Conference on Software Engineering Research, Management and Applications (2011), and Association for Computing Machinery Research in Adaptive and Convergent Systems Conference (2014), and has been invited by a number of international conferences as a keynote speaker.

Yan Wan received a BS degree from the Nanjing University of Aeronautics and Astronautics, Nanjing, China, in 2001; an MS degree from the University of Alabama, Tuscaloosa, in 2004; and a PhD degree from Washington State University, Pullman, in 2009. She is currently an assistant professor with the Department of Electrical Engineering, at the University of North Texas, Denton. Before that, she was a postdoctoral scholar with the Control Systems program at the University of California, Santa Barbara. Her research interests lie in developing solutions for decision-making tasks in large-scale networks, with applications to (air) traffic management, sensor networking, biological systems, and so on. Dr. Wan received the prestigious William E. Jackson Award (excellence in aviation electronics and communication) in 2009, which was presented by the Radio Technical Commission for Aeronautics.

References

1. U.S. Department of Transportation (US DOT), ITS Strategic Research Plan, 2009. http://www.its.dot.gov/strategic_plan2010_2014/2010_factsheet.htm.
2. Networking and Information Technology Research and Development Program, Cyber physical systems vision statement. NITRD, 2014. https://www.nitrd.gov/nitrdgroups/images/6/6a/Cyber_Physical_Systems_(CPS)_Vision_Statement.pdf.
3. National Science Foundation, Cyber-physical systems (CPS), NSF, 2015. https://www.nsf.gov/funding/pgm_summ.jsp?pims_id=503286.
4. J. P. Hubaux, S. Capkun, and L. Jun. The security and privacy of smart vehicles. *IEEE Security & Privacy*, vol. 2, pp. 49–55, 2004.
5. J. M. Serna-Olvera. A trust-driven privacy architecture for vehicular ad-hoc networks. PhD thesis, Computer Architecture, Universitat Politecnica de Catalunya (UPC), 2012.
6. M. N. Mejri, J. Ben-Othman, and M. Hamdi. Survey on VANET security challenges and possible cryptographic solutions. *Vehicular Communications*, 04/2014.
7. J. Kakarla, S. S. Sathya, and B. G. Laxmi. A survey on routing protocols and its issues in VANET. *International Journal of Computer Applications*, vol. 28, 0975-8887, 2011.
8. L. K. Qabajeh, M. L. M. Kiah, and M. M. Qabajeh. A scalable and secure position-based routing protocols for ad-hoc networks. *Malaysian Journal of Computer Science*, vol. 22, pp. 99–120, 2009.
9. A. G. Dludla, N. Ntlatlapa, T. Nyandeni, and M. Adigun. Towards designing energy-efficient routing protocol for wireless mesh networks, Southern Africa Telecommunication Networks and Applications Conference (SATNAC), Swaziland, 2009.
10. M. Razzaque, A. Salehi, and S. M. Cheraghi. Security and privacy in vehicular ad-hoc networks: Survey and the road ahead. In S. Khan and A.-S. Khan Pathan (eds) *Wireless Networks and Security*, Springer, 2013, pp. 107–132.
11. A. Dhamgaye and N. Chavhan. Survey on security challenges in VANET. *International Journal of Computer Science and Network (IJCSN)*, vol. 2, 2013.
12. R. G. Engoulou, M. Bellaïche, S. Pierre, and A. Quintero. VANET security surveys. *Computer Communications*, vol. 44, pp. 1–13, 2014.
13. J. Molina-Gil, P. Caballero-Gil, and C. Caballero-Gil. Aggregation and probabilistic verification for data authentication in VANETs. *Information Sciences*, vol. 262, pp. 172–189, 2014.
14. M. Kakkasageri and S. Manvi. Information management in vehicular ad hoc networks: A review. *Journal of Network and Computer Applications*, vol. 39, pp. 334–350, 2014.
15. B. T. Sharef, R. A. Alsaqour, and M. Ismail. Vehicular communication ad hoc routing protocols: A survey. *Journal of Network and Computer Applications*, vol. 40, pp. 363–396, 2014.
16. A. Boukerche, H. A. B. F. Oliveira, E. F. Nakamura, and A. A. F. Loureiro. Vehicular ad hoc networks: A new challenge for localization-based systems. *Computer Communications*, vol. 31, pp. 2838–2849, 2008.
17. S. Al-Sultan, M. M. Al-Doori, A. H. Al-Bayatti, and H. Zedan. A comprehensive survey on vehicular ad hoc network. *Journal of Network and Computer Applications*, vol. 37, pp. 380–392, 2014.
18. M. Faezipour, M. Nourani, A. Saeed, and S. Addepalli. Progress and challenges in intelligent vehicle area networks. *Communications of the ACM*, vol. 55, pp. 90–100, 2012.
19. M. Raya and J.-P. Hubaux. Security aspects of inter-vehicle communications. In *Proceedings of 5th Swiss Transport Research Conference (STRC)*, 2005.
20. D. Gantsou. Invited paper: VANET security: Going beyond cryptographic-centric solutions. In A. Laouiti, A. Qayyum, M. N. M. Saad (eds), *Vehicular Ad-Hoc Networks for Smart Cities*, Springer, Science+Business Media, Singapore, 2015, pp. 43–49.
21. Gridaptive. Smart cities, intelligent transportation and the smart grid. alternergy.mag, August 31, 2012. http://altenergymag.com/emagazine/2012/08/smart-cities-intelligent-transportation-and-smart-grid-standards--part-1/1954.
22. M. Zhao, J. Walker, and C.-C. Wang. Security challenges for the intelligent transportation system. In *Proceedings of the First International Conference on Security of Internet of Things*, 2012.

23. C. V. S. C. Consortium. Vehicle safety communications project: Task 3 final report: Identify intelligent vehicle safety applications enabled by DSRC. National Highway Traffic Safety Administration, US Department of Transportation, Washington DC, 2005.
24. IEEE Standards Association. Dedicated short range communication. Available: https://standards.ieee.org/develop/wg/1609_WG.html.
25. D. Jiang and L. Delgrossi. 802.11p: Towards an international standard for wireless access in vehicular environments. In *Proceedings of IEEE Vehicular Technology Conference (VTC)*, 2008.
26. M. Raya and J.-P. Hubaux. Securing vehicular ad hoc networks. *Journal of Computer Security*, vol. 15, pp. 39–68, 2007.
27. B. Parno and A. Perrig. Challenges in securing vehicular networks. In *Proceedigns of International Workshop on Hot Topics in Networks (HotNets-IV)*, 2005.
28. I. K. Azogu, M. T. Ferreira, J. A. Larcom, and H. Liu. A new anti-jamming strategy for VANET metrics-directed security defense. In *Proceedings of IEEE Globecom Workshops (GC Wkshps)*, 2013.
29. A. Stampoulis and Z. Chai. A survey of security in vehicular networks, Yale University, 2007. Technical report. Project CPSC 534. http://zoo.cs.yale.edu/~ams257/projects/wireless-survey.pdf (accessed Nov 28, 2011).
30. A. Laouiti, A. Qayyum, and M. N. M. Saad (eds), *Vehicular Ad-Hoc Networks for Smart Cities*, Springer Science+Business Media, Singapore, 2014.
31. N. Bißmeyer, B. Schünemann, I. Radusch, and C. Schmidt. Simulation of attacks and corresponding driver behavior in vehicular ad hoc networks with VSimRTI. In *Proceedings of the 4th International ICST Conference on Simulation Tools and Techniques*, 2011.
32. P. Papadimitratos and Z. J. Haas. Secure routing for mobile ad hoc networks. In *Proceedings of the SCS Commnication Networks and Distributed Systems Modeling and Simulation Conference (CNDS)*, 2002.
33. E. Schoch and F. Kargl. On the efficiency of secure beaconing in VANETs. In *Proceedings of the Third ACM Conference on Wireless Network Security*, pp. 111–116, 2010.
34. T. Zhou, R. R. Choudhury, P. Ning, and K. Chakrabarty. P2DAP—Sybil attacks detection in vehicular ad hoc networks. *IEEE Journal of Selected Areas on Communications (JSAC)*, vol. 29, pp. 582–594, 2011.
35. H. Hasbullah, I. A. Soomro, and J. Manan. Denial of service (DoS) attack and its possible solutions in VANET. *World Academy of Science, Engineering and Technology*, vol. 65, p. 20, 2010.
36. H. Dijiang, S. Misra, M. Verma, and X. Guoliang. PACP: An efficient pseudonymous authentication-based conditional privacy protocol for VANETs. *IEEE Transactions on Intelligent Transportation Systems*, vol. 12, pp. 736–746, 2011.
37. T. Queck, B. Schüenemann, and I. Radusch. Runtime infrastructure for simulating vehicle-2-x communication scenarios. In *Proceedings of the Fifth ACM International Workshop on VehiculAr InterNETworking*, 2008.
38. N. N. Ekedebe, Z. Chen, G. Xu, C. Lu, and W. Yu. On an efficient and effective intelligent transportation system (ITS) using field and simulation data. In *Proceedings of SPIE Sensing Technology+ Applications*, Baltimore, 2014, pp. 91210B–91210B-12.
39. T. Queck, B. Schunemann, I. Radusch, and C. Meinel. Realistic simulation of V2X communication scenarios. In *Proceedings of IEEE 2008 Asia-Pacific Services Computing Conference (APSCC)*, 2008.
40. IEEE. IEEE standard for modeling and simulation (M&S) high level architecture (HLA)—Federate interface specification. IEEE Std 1516.1-2010 (Revision of IEEE Std 1516.1-2000), pp. 1–378, 2010.
41. B. Schünemann. V2X simulation runtime infrastructure VSimRTI: An assessment tool to design smart traffic management systems. *Computer Network*, vol. 55, pp. 3189–3198, 2011.
42. K. Katsaros, R. Kernchen, M. Dianati, D. Rieck, and C. Zinoviou. Application of vehicular communications for improving the efficiency of traffic in urban areas. *Wireless Communication Mobile Compututing*, vol. 11, pp. 1657–1667, 2011.
43. D. Rieck, B. Schünemann, I. Radusch, and C. Meinel. Efficient traffic simulator coupling in a distributed V2X simulation environment. In *Proceedings of the 3rd International ICST Conference on Simulation Tools and Techniques*, 2010.

44. B. Schunemann, D. Rieck, and I. Radusch. Performance and scalability analyses of federation-based V2X simulation systems. In *Proceedings of the 11th Annual Mediterranean Ad Hoc Networking Workshop (Med-Hoc-Net)*, 2012.
45. D. Chuang, B. Schuenemann, D. Rieck, and I. Radusch. GRIND: A generic interface for coupling power grid simulators with traffic, communication and application simulation tools. In *Proceedigns of the Fifth International Conference on Advances in System Simulation (SIMUL)*, 2013.
46. K. Katsaros, R. Kernchen, M. Dianati, and D. Rieck. Performance study of a green light optimized speed advisory (GLOSA) application using an integrated cooperative ITS simulation platform. In *Proceedings of IEEE 2011 Wireless Communications and Mobile Computing Conference (IWCMC)*, 2011.
47. OMNeT++. (OMNeT++ 4.2 ed.). http://www.omnetpp.org/.
48. R. Protzmann, B. Schunemann, and I. Radusch. The influences of communication models on the simulated effectiveness of V2X applications. *IEEE Communications Magazine*, vol. 49, pp. 149–155, 2011.
49. K. Gajananan, S. Sontisirikit, J. Zhang, M. Miska, E. Chung, S. Guha, and H. Prendinger. A cooperative ITS study on green light optimisation using an integrated traffic, driving, and communication simulator. In *Proceedings of the 36th Australasian Transport Research Forum (ATRF)*, 2013.
50. B. Schünemann. The V2X simulation runtime infrastructure: VSimRTI, PhD thesis, Universität Potsdam, Germany, 2011.
51. T. Queck, B. Schunemann, I. Radusch. Runtime infrastructure for simulating vehicle-2-X communication scenarios. Daimler Center for Automotive Information Technology Innovations. http://www.sigmobile.org/workshops/vanet2008/slides/Posters/queck.pdf.
52. Daimler Center for Automotive Information Technology Innovations. VSimRTI: Smart mobility simulation, Daimler Center for Automotive Information Technology Innovations, 2014. http://www.dcaiti.tu-berlin.de/research/simulation/.
53. Veins. Vehicles in network simulation. http://veins.car2x.org/.
54. M. Piorkowski, M. Raya, A. L. Lugo, P. Papadimitratos, M. Grossglauser, and J.-P. Hubaux. TraNS: realistic joint traffic and network simulator for VANETs. *SIGMOBILE Mobile Computing Communication Review*, vol. 12, pp. 31–33, 2008.
55. I. Leontiadis, G. Marfia, D. Mack, G. Pau, C. Mascolo, and M. Gerla. On the effectiveness of an opportunistic traffic management system for vehicular networks. *IEEE Transactions on Intelligent Transportation Systems*, vol. 12, pp. 1537–1548, 2011.
56. C. Sommer, R. German, and F. Dressler. Bidirectionally coupled network and road traffic simulation for improved IVC analysis. *IEEE Transactions on Mobile Computing*, vol. 10, pp. 3–15, 2011.
57. D. Krajzewicz, J. Erdmann, M. Behrisch, and L. Bieker. Recent development and applications of SUMO—Simulation of Urban MObility. *International Journal on Advances in Systems and Measurements*, vol. 5, pp. 128–138, 2012.
58. M. J. Khabbaz, W. F. Fawaz, and C. M. Assi. A simple free-flow traffic model for vehicular intermittently connected networks. *IEEE Transactions on Intelligent Transportation Systems*, vol. 13, pp. 1312–1326, 2012.
59. M. Yongchang, M. Chowdhury, A. Sadek, and M. Jeihani. Integrated traffic and communication performance evaluation of an intelligent vehicle infrastructure integration (VII) system for online travel-time prediction. *IEEE Transactions on Intelligent Transportation Systems*, vol. 13, pp. 1369–1382, 2012.
60. OSM. OpenStreetMaps. http://www.openstreetmap.org, 2015.
61. Hasso Plattner Institute. eWorld. Hasso Plattner Institute, Potsdam, 2013. http://eworld.sourceforge.net/.
62. B. Schunemann, J. W. Wedel, and I. Radusch. V2X-based traffic congestion recognition and avoidance. *Tamkang Journal of Science and Engineering*, vol. 13, pp. 63–70, 2010.
63. SUMO. Simulation of Urban MObility, 2015. http://www.dlr.de/ts/en/desktopdefault.aspx/tabid-9883/16931_read-41000/.
64. JiST/SWANS. Java in simulation time/scalable wireless ad hoc network simulator, 2015. http://vanet.info/jist-swans.
65. R. Barr. SWANS: Scalable wireless ad hoc network simulator. March, 2004. http://jist.ece.cornell.edu/docs.html.

66. R. Barr, Z. J. Haas, and R. v. Renesse. JiST: An efficient approach to simulation using virtual machines: Research articles. *Software: Practice and Experience*, vol. 35, pp. 539–576, 2005.
67. N. Naumann, B. Schünemann, and I. Radusch. VSimRTI: Simulation runtime infrastructure for V2x communication scenarios. In *Proceedings of the 16th World Congress and Exhibition on Intelligent Transport Systems and Services (ITS Stockholm)*, 2009.
68. N. Naumann, B. Schunemann, I. Radusch, and C. Meinel. Improving V2X simulation performance with optimistic synchronization. In *Proceedings of IEEE Asia-Pacific International Conference on Services Computing Conference (APSCC)*, 2009.
69. J. C. Herrera and A. M. Bayen. Traffic flow reconstruction using mobile sensors and loop detector data, 2007.
70. J. Kühlwein, M. Rexeis, R. Luz, and S. Hausberger. Update of emission factors for EURO 5 and EURO 6 vehicles for the HBEFA version 3.2, 2013.
71. SUMO. Simulation of Urban MObility (0.17.0 ed.). http://sumo-sim.org/.
72. S. f. U. M. (SUMO). PHEM (Passenger car and heavy duty emission model), 2014.
73. S. f. U. M. (SUMO). Models/emissions, August 23, 2014.
74. P. D. S. Hausberger, D. I. M. Rexeis, D. I. M. Zallinger, D. I. R. Luz, and P. D. H. Eichlseder. Emission factors from the model PHEM for HBEFA version 3, 2009. Institute for Internal Combustion Engines and Thermodynamics, 2009. http://www.hbefa.net/e/documents/HBEFA_31_Docu_hot_emission-factors_PC_LCV_HDV.pdf.
75. M. P. Hunter, W. Seung Kook, K. Hoe Kyoung, and S. Wonho. A probe-vehicle-based evaluation of adaptive traffic signal control. *IEEE Transactions on Intelligent Transportation Systems*, vol. 13, pp. 704–713, 2012.

Chapter 7

Securing the Future Autonomous Vehicle: A Cyber-Physical Systems Approach

Mario Gerla and Peter Reiher
University of California, Los Angeles

Contents

7.1 Introduction 198
7.2 Vehicular Cyber-Physical Systems 199
  7.2.1 Architectures for Vehicular Computing 199
  7.2.2 Vehicular Computing Scenarios 201
    7.2.2.1 Scenario 1: Driving Safety 201
    7.2.2.2 Scenario 2: Congestion Avoidance 201
    7.2.2.3 Scenario 3: Platooning 202
  7.2.3 Basic Elements of Vehicular Computing 202
7.3 Security Challenges for Autonomous Vehicles and Vehicular Networks 204
  7.3.1 Confidentiality Risks 204
  7.3.2 Integrity Risks 205
  7.3.3 Availability Risks 205
  7.3.4 Mixed Risks 206
7.4 Security Mechanisms for Vehicular Networks 207
  7.4.1 Authenticating Vehicle Messages 207
  7.4.2 Tamper-Resistant Hardware for Vehicles 208
  7.4.3 Determining Trustworthiness of Vehicles and Their Messages 209
  7.4.4 Hardening Vehicles against Compromise 210
  7.4.5 Access Control to Vehicle-Generated Data 211

7.5 Emerging Areas for Research in Vehicular Security........213
7.6 Conclusion........214
Author Biographies........215
Glossary........215
References........217

Abstract: Automobiles rely increasingly on cybercontrol. In the near future, we expect to see fully autonomous vehicles that will depend on wireless networking and computer control of their physical systems, including systems handling steering, braking, acceleration, signaling, and essentially all other physical activities of the vehicle. Experience has shown that networked control systems are susceptible to cyberattacks, which can manifest themselves in the systems' physical-world activities. In the case of cars, these attacks could lead to collisions, intentionally caused congestion, and many other undesirable or even fatal consequences. This chapter surveys how autonomous vehicles are predicted to operate, what cyberbased attacks are likely to be performed on them, and the various defensive approaches already being used or under investigation to counter those attacks.

Keywrods: Autonomous vehicles; Vehicular ad hoc networks; VANETs

7.1 Introduction

The modern automobile is itself a cyber-physical system, and the multiple interacting vehicles on a road are a cyber-physical system of systems. The sophistication of the cybercomponents of vehicular systems is increasing radically, going from simple computers that monitored engine operations to internal local area networks carrying information between multiple processing units within a car. In the near future, cars will communicate with each other over vehicular networks. In the longer term (perhaps by 2020?) truly autonomous vehicles will do the driving, controlled by computers and supported by wireless networks. Our highways are poised to become managed by cyber-physical systems [1].

These cybercontrolled vehicular networks and systems will be exposed to new security threats, since they will manage hurtling multiton masses of metal capable of doing tremendous damage to people and property if improperly driven. Further, they are inherently expensive, making them desirable targets for theft. Their high mobility also makes them useful targets for attackers, who could exploit them as platforms for cybersurveillance and possible attacks.

Although this use of computers and networks in vehicles is at an early stage, researchers have already found serious vulnerabilities in a number of real vehicles. These vulnerabilities can allow locked cars to be opened from a distance [2], information about the car's systems to be divulged [3], and, most disturbingly, critical systems such as braking and steering to be commandeered by an attacker [4]. Thus, the security issue for vehicular systems is already well beyond the realm of speculation and theory; it is a clear and present danger.

We begin by briefly presenting the current status of vehicular cyber-physical systems and their expected evolution in the future of autonomous vehicles. We discuss security challenges in this environment, followed by the presentation of proposed security solutions. We then present areas requiring further attention and research to secure these systems as they become increasingly common and powerful. We complete the chapter with a summary of the security status of vehicular cyber-physical systems.

7.2 Vehicular Cyber-Physical Systems

Automobiles have always been a technological phenomenon that tends to embrace new advances to improve the performance, safety, and comfort provided to drivers and passengers. It is unsurprising that computer and network technologies have been incorporated into automobiles and that these technologies will become increasingly intertwined with all of a car's operations. From largely hidden control of the engine and other automotive systems, to wireless networking for improved communications and entertainment, to the use of such systems to enhance safety and take over some routine elements of driving, computers and networks play increasing roles in today's automobiles. Tomorrow's automobiles, according to many predictions, may be entirely controlled by computers, based on sensors and networked information from other vehicles, road devices, and even the wider Internet.

The new cybercapabilities of automobiles offer many advantages. Certain routine tasks (such as parallel parking) can already be done automatically, and fully autonomous vehicles that rely on cybercapabilities to drive safely and effectively without human assistance are expected to be on the roads in a few years. Research has clearly demonstrated that proper use of vehicular networking can reduce congestion, allow traffic to move safely at higher speeds, and prevent many accidents. Other research has demonstrated that proper use of cybercapabilities might lower emissions of polluting gases. Less dramatically, vehicular networking extends the Internet into the automobile, offering passengers and drivers the ability to perform all kinds of networking tasks, some related to their trip and others less so. Videos can be played for children, voice over IP (VoIP) calls can be made, gas stations and restaurants can be searched for, and the total power of the Internet can be at the fingertips of every driver.

7.2.1 Architectures for Vehicular Computing

The core technological advance required to achieve this vision is vehicular networking. This form of networking is challenging. It clearly must be wireless, it must work in environments of unusually rapid mobility, and traffic congestion on streets could obviously be mirrored by network congestion due to a high density of communicating cars in one area. In recent years, a wealth of research has studied how to handle these problems and optimize the internetworking of vehicles and other systems using short-range radios, for example, Wi-Fi and dedicated short-range communications (DSRC) to support a wide range of services. A fundamental question in this research has been how much infrastructure outside of the automobiles themselves is required to support vehicular operations. Clearly, systems that require substantial new deployment of sensors, communications equipment, and computational capabilities embedded into the roads are much more expensive than systems that require relatively few such new installations.

Since we anticipate that future vehicles will certainly contain embedded sensors, computing, and communications capabilities, relying primarily on those already deployed capabilities would reduce the costs of vehicular cybersystems. Thus, the use of vehicular ad hoc networks (VANETs) in metropolitan areas enables each vehicle to act as a traffic probe that measures and shares traffic-related information with neighbors [5]. This information can then be used by other vehicles to efficiently select their routes to avoid congested areas and improve traffic safety. In essence, an intelligent transport system can use the vehicles themselves to crowdsource traffic information. This form of vehicular networking is often referred to as V2V, or vehicle-to-vehicle.

On the other hand, augmenting vehicular capabilities with roadside functionalities may offer many advantages that offset the extra costs. These services would tend to be fixed (while the automobiles are inherently mobile), simplifying many problems. They could be run by trusted entities (such as local governments), alleviating some security concerns. They could be more readily updated and managed. Perhaps most importantly, they can more easily achieve a global picture of overall traffic conditions than any single car could. This form of vehicular networking is often referred to as V2I, or vehicle-to-infrastructure.

In the last decade, the U.S. Department of Transportation (DOT) sponsored the VII program (Vehicle Infrastructure Integration). At that time, there was a great expectation that vehicles could be "integrated" into the Internet infrastructure via roadside units (RSUs). Unfortunately, at the end of the VII program, the conclusion was that over 200,000 RSUs would be required on U.S. roads and highways to achieve that dream. The RSU business model is not mature yet and thus cannot provide answers to many important questions, such as *who pays for the RSU*? The new DOT program "Connected Vehicle" puts more emphasis on V2V communications (as the name hints), reducing the role of RSUs and encouraging users and manufacturers to instead consider commercial alternatives such as third-generation (3G) and long-term evolution (LTE) technologies to provide Internet connectivity.

Regardless of the future destiny and potential benefits of powerful roadside services, the advantages deriving from the deployment of a peer-to-peer-based VANET-based system are manifold. Currently, only major urban areas can afford monitoring infrastructures, and the costs of adding these everywhere would be great. The costs of creating a VANET, on the other hand, are spread evenly among all buyers of new cars, with each paying only a modest price that is bundled into the overall cost of the vehicle. Unless roadside infrastructure is totally deployed, vehicular cybersystems will sometimes need to rely only on VANET-based capabilities anyway, implying that we must be willing to pay the research and development costs for those services. Also, there may be privacy benefits to avoiding an overarching powerful traffic system that sees all and knows all.

While a system that relies purely on a VANET is clearly desirable and perhaps required, research in vehicular networking has continued in both directions: pure VANETs and vehicles making use of roadside infrastructures. Some technologies are developed to work well in both V2V and V2I modes. Such technologies are often referred to as V2X.

In recent years, the increased power and capacity of wireless networks and mobile computing devices have led to another option, a *vehicular cloud*, in which a group of vehicles in one general area combine their resources and information to produce powerful services for all [6]. Instead of paying a high cost to upload all traffic minutiae to the Internet, or limiting a car's abilities to merely what it can do on its own, cars dynamically cooperate for mutual benefit. The increasing storage and processing capacity of the cars' computers, on the one hand, and the scarcity of urban spectrum, on the other, make it more effective to communicate and keep the locally relevant content on the cars' computers instead of uploading it to the Internet.

There are also security benefits to the vehicular cloud approach. In such a system, vehicular security can be provided as a service of the *vehicular cloud platform*, offering the major advantage of standardization. Vehicular security is complex, consisting of many processing tasks and communications protocols intertwined together that must operate seamlessly to deliver a reliable service. The auto manufacturers understand the urgency of security and, left to their own devices, will come up with security and privacy procedures different from one another. Unfortunately, efficient security in the face of sophisticated attacks will require V2V cooperation. Stovepipe systems built separately by manufacturers will sadly fail the test, as similar examples from other computing and communications domains have repeatedly demonstrated.

7.2.2 Vehicular Computing Scenarios

Vehicular networks will be ubiquitous and powerful in the future, and it is impossible to foresee all the uses that will be made of them. Clearly, they will be used to improve the safety of driving, to reduce the burdens on human drivers, to assist drivers in finding routes to their destinations, to reduce congestion and pollution associated with vehicles, and to provide various kinds of connectivity from a vehicle to the larger Internet. Future uses of vehicular computing will determine the security threats they face, which implies that our incomplete knowledge of those uses also limits our ability to predict the eventual range of threats against them.

Rather than try to exhaustively describe all possible uses that might be made of vehicular computing, we will describe a few scenarios that make use of the new technologies that are commonly discussed by researchers and developers. The eventual uses of vehicular computing will certainly be broader than these scenarios, but they are also highly likely to include them.

7.2.2.1 Scenario 1: Driving Safety

In Figure 7.1, car 3 is traveling two cars behind the lead car, car 1. Car 1's driver, seeing a road hazard, slams on the brakes. Car 1's safety system automatically sends a broadcast message over the vehicular network indicating the sudden application of its brakes. When car 3 receives that message, milliseconds later, its safety system engages its brakes, much faster than human reaction times would allow. Since car 3 might be unable to see the brake lights of car 1 due to car 2, which is between them, this automatic brake engagement is surer and certainly faster than relying on car 3's driver to react. Even if the driver of car 3 was momentarily distracted, his car will stop in time to avoid running into car 2 ahead of him.

7.2.2.2 Scenario 2: Congestion Avoidance

In this scenario, car X is planning to take a particular route to destination D. Out of car X's line of sight, severe congestion clogs this route. If car X takes the planned route, the trip will be long and slow. However, the cars that can observe the congestion send out messages indicating their view of road conditions. When car X receives those messages, its navigation system plots a different route that avoids the congestion. If car X is an autonomous vehicle, it then automatically turns onto the new route. If not, perhaps it alerts the human driver that his planned route will be slow and offers a suggestion for an alternative.

Figure 7.1 Scenario 1: Driving safety.

Figure 7.2 Scenario 2: Platooning.

7.2.2.3 Scenario 3: Platooning

A group of cars traveling along the same stretch of a road can move more efficiently and rapidly if they work in close concert. More cars can fit into a given space, reducing congestion, and drag on the nonlead vehicles can be reduced. This method of driving is called *platooning*. Given that wireless networking has a limited range, tightly packed platoons will also have better network connectivity than loosely spaced individual vehicles. But safe and effective platooning requires tight coordination between all members. Changes that any member makes in his speed or direction will have a great impact on the necessary behavior of all other members, which implies quick, reliable communication of both planned alterations in behavior and observed road conditions. Figure 7.2 shows an example of platooning.

In this scenario, a driver traveling down the highway realizes that he is running out of gas and needs to fill his gas tank soon. He communicates via the vehicular network to query a map service for the location of the closest gas station. Meanwhile, he continues to stream a video for his children in the back seat, transferring the data across the same network. Of course, all of the more critical vehicular networking activities, such as sending and receiving safety messages, are also going on in the background at the same time.

These few scenarios are by no means exhaustive of the uses we expect vehicular computation and communications to be put to in the future. But they do suggest some of the important characteristics we need to be concerned about from a security perspective. Safety and speed are critical. Less critically, but still importantly, drivers and their cars will use these cyberfacilities to make decisions about where the car goes and how it gets there. These decisions will have a major impact on the driving experience. New modes of road use will rely on the vehicular network behaving properly, and the vehicular network and cars' computational assets will be used for many different purposes, some of which may have security implications themselves.

7.2.3 Basic Elements of Vehicular Computing

Modern vehicles suitable for vehicular computing will typically contain one or several computers controlling various aspects of a car's behavior. These include control of the engine's performance, gathering of data from various sensors located on the car, control of important automotive systems (such as steering and braking), presentation of data to the driver or passengers, and delivery of entertainment (radio or video). These systems are likely to be connected by a local network, typically a controller area network (CAN) bus, which also allows wireless connectivity by one or more links to the outside world. In some cases, these links allow vehicles to broadcast to other nearby cars. In others, they may permit communications with roadside infrastructure or even satellites.

As in other computing realms, connectivity between the Internet and system components offers opportunities to attackers. There have been highly publicized attacks on automotive components (e.g., brakes) from malware injected into the CAN bus from Internet entertainment applications. So, today the CAN bus allows Internet access only to manufacturer computers or to OnStar satellite service for diagnostics purposes. This restriction, however, does not prevent attackers from compromising the vehicle in other, less direct ways, sometimes even via the CAN bus. For example, [7] describes methods of attacking other devices attached to the CAN bus given that one already controls a device on that bus.

A number of standards have been developed for the networking components of the systems. Among these are 802.11p and DSRC. 802.11p is an extension of the existing IEEE 802.11 wireless network standards specifically designed to meet the special characteristics of vehicular networks, such as communication between fast-moving senders and receivers. DSRC is a standard developed by the U.S. DOT for transmitting safety information between vehicles at a high rate.

In V2V systems, each vehicle will use a short- to medium-range wireless broadcast to send information to all other properly equipped cars in range. This broadcast will contain information about the sending vehicle's position, speed, and other attributes and may also contain information about conditions observed by the vehicle's sensors. As will be discussed in Section 7.4.1, most proposals for securing vehicular networks expect such broadcasts to be signed digitally by the sending vehicle, ensuring that only the vehicle itself can make direct claims about its condition.

Some proposals call for fully autonomous vehicles, which can drive themselves without human intervention. This autonomy can only be achieved by complete cybercontrol of all the important vehicular systems, from acceleration to steering to braking. Thus, such vehicles will have actuators that permit the car's computers to order all required actions for safe and effective driving. Even some nonautonomous vehicles may include features such as collision avoidance systems that can intervene faster than human reaction permits.

Already, many vehicles have substantial informative and entertainment systems with cybercomponents. These allow Internet browsing, access to map and guidance systems, downloading and playing of music and videos, making telephone calls, and more. In principle, these activities could be supported by networks and computers entirely separate from those used for more critical activities. In practice, they will often share such systems to some degree.

Modern vehicles are also likely to have special cyberfeatures to assist in their maintenance and repair. These allow mechanics to diagnose problems and optimize the performance of the vehicle. They often require some degree of access to some of the other cybercontrolled elements of the vehicle, and would generally obtain that access using the same networking elements that are used for other purposes. For example, the wireless network might be used to provide information about the engine or the brake system to a mechanic. While such systems are intended for use only during service periods, they may be more generally accessible to anyone with sufficient knowledge and a reasonable degree of locality to the vehicle.

Speaking generally, the history of including cyberelements into physical systems has shown that for reasons of economy, simplicity, and better design, networks and computers will be connected and shared by multiple different services. This trend is likely to prove true for future vehicles as well and has certainly been common in vehicle design to date. While sharing the same network and computer for both critical safety systems and trivial entertainment offers many advantages, it also introduces serious security vulnerabilities. Preventing some of the car's own systems from using the local area network minimizes some dangers, but any interconnectivity among those systems introduces some vulnerabilities, as will be discussed in more detail in Section 7.4.4.

7.3 Security Challenges for Autonomous Vehicles and Vehicular Networks

As with other systems, the security challenges of autonomous vehicles and vehicular networks can be broadly categorized under attacks on confidentiality, integrity, privacy, and availability.

7.3.1 Confidentiality Risks

Vehicular networks rely on wireless networking. Thus, any party that puts up an antenna in the proper place can listen to their signals. Therefore, maintaining secrecy of information will be difficult for vehicular networks. For many purposes, however, secrecy is not a desirable goal for vehicular communications. Messages sent to transmit information about road conditions, hazards, traffic characteristics, and the current speed and position of a vehicle are not typically regarded as private. Indeed, many vehicular network designs benefit from wide sharing of precisely this kind of information. The more different participants in the vehicular network that know such information, the better they can adjust their behavior to optimize their own goals and the overall goals of the entire system.

One obvious exception is that messages sent by vehicles, especially those that pinpoint the vehicle's location, have privacy implications. If care is not taken, the regular safety messages sent by a vehicle can be used to track the movements of the vehicle's owner. Since such signals are sent out for anyone to hear, arbitrary parties can learn of his location. In particular, in architectures with roadside elements, those roadside receivers could forward everything they hear to a centralized system, perhaps run by the government, which would allow total surveillance of everyone who uses a vehicle. Techniques can be used to anonymize the messages sent by vehicles, but to the extent that other participants in the network take critical actions based on those messages, being able to verify the authenticity of the messages is important. If a malicious message causes a traffic accident, we want to be able to tie the message to the true sender (which implies that we need the security property of nonrepudiation for these messages). And if we hope to detect cheating participants who lie to gain advantages in the vehicular system at the expense of others, we need to tie their deceitful messages to a single identity. Therefore, simple anonymization techniques may prove insufficient. Balancing the security and privacy of the signals sent by individual vehicles is a serious challenge for vehicular networking and has received much research attention.

Cars contain increasing numbers of sensors, which sometimes include microphones, cameras, or other devices capable of picking up sensitive information. An attacker who has successfully compromised a car's internal systems could order these sensors to eavesdrop on the car's occupants. Another possibility is that a compromised car could be used as a surveillance platform to watch other cars or locations that the car is driving by. While using a car as a surveillance platform usually does not imply loss of truly secret information (except perhaps for cars that are in areas with restricted access, such as military bases), it does suggest security-related issues. For example, criminals could use such platforms to observe stores or individuals from a safe distance when planning a robbery.

The proliferation of sensors on autonomous vehicles and the increasingly rich uses of their communications and computational capabilities will lead to a wider range of information stored temporarily or permanently in such vehicles. Some of this information is likely to have confidentiality requirements. Since the autonomous vehicle is itself a distributed system whose components are subject to compromise, and the entire vehicle is also part of a larger communicating distributed system whose other members may sometimes be hostile, there will be confidentiality risks associated with protecting this information.

7.3.2 Integrity Risks

Antennas put up by malicious parties to intercept signals can also transmit their own signals into the wireless medium. These parties might not be vehicles at all, nor need they be legitimate parts of the roadside infrastructure. Again, proper authentication can detect such misbehavior, but with the potential privacy risks outlined above.

Another major integrity risk is that the cars themselves are now run by computers. Their software might be compromised, allowing the malware or the remote party who controls that malware to change the behavior of the car in critical ways. The car could be suddenly steered into a tree; hitting the brakes suddenly in heavy traffic could cause a major multicar accident; or any number of other dangerous attacks could be performed. If the car is not networked, compromises to its internal computer controls are only possible if the attacker obtains physical access to the car. Networking opens the possibility that flaws in the software that interacts with the network might give a remote attacker a foothold on the system, which then would allow him to perform such attacks. There have already been demonstrations of flaws leading to vulnerabilities in real cars, and there is good reason to believe more will be discovered in the future.

7.3.3 Availability Risks

There is a risk to availability related to the integrity issue described above. If a compromise to the car's cybersystems does not allow misuse of the car's physical controls, it might still prevent the car from sending or receiving the messages that it should. In essence, the car disappears from the cyberspace of the vehicular network. That is likely to have implications, at least for the car in question, and possibly for other cars in the vicinity. Generally, vehicular systems should be designed to be immune to a small number of vehicles behaving improperly, so a good vehicular network might not suffer much from an availability attack on a single car, though that vehicle itself would certainly lose any benefits of the network.

A broader attack on availability would be a distributed denial-of-service (DDoS) attack on the wireless network. Such attacks are easy to perpetrate, assuming the ability to inject messages into the network. As discussed above, any adversary who can raise his antenna within the area he wishes to congest can easily inject noise or false messages to cause trouble. If there is a roadside infrastructure that communicates to, and perhaps forwards messages from, the Internet, the attacker might not even need physical proximity to perform his DDoS attack. Instead, he could merely request enough messages to be forwarded to vehicles in his target area to overwhelm their network.

The vehicles in this network are themselves valuable items, worth perhaps tens of thousands of dollars or more. Car theft, which is essentially an attack on the physical availability of a vehicle for its owner, has been a serious problem since long before cars were cybercontrolled. For autonomous vehicles, particularly, the computer control and network availability suggests a new approach to auto theft. The attacker can use remote exploits to take over a car's cybersystem, and the car can then be ordered to drive itself to the chop shop, where the thieves merely await its arrival. More basic forms of car theft based on cybercapabilities are already known, such as using cybercapabilities to cause cars to unlock themselves.

7.3.4 Mixed Risks

Some risks faced by autonomous vehicles do not perfectly fit into the simple categories of confidentiality, integrity, or availability, sharing some aspects of more than one of these properties.

Given that we must expect some vehicles in this network to be compromised or to be owned by dishonest actors, we will be faced with situations in which some data the vehicle receives over V2V channels is poisonous. Authentication can tie such data to its creator, but it is equally necessary to determine which messages or requests are the bad ones. Ideally, the receiving vehicle's systems should be able to identify such bad inputs before acting upon them, but at worst they must eventually determine that some particular message caused a malicious effect and tie it back to its creator. With some further effort, the bad actors can be identified and, in the future, monitored for suspicious behavior. In essence, this is a problem similar to intrusion detection in the more traditional form of a computer network. Here, the bad actors are not intruders per se, since they may have all their authentication credentials in order and thus have as much right to use the highways and the vehicular network as anyone else. But, unless they are tagged as malicious, their bad behavior will continue to cause problems (which could attack any security property, confidentiality, integrity, or availability) indefinitely. If we are extremely effective in tying such bad behavior to the vehicle that caused it, and if we can take punitive action against bad actors (such as traffic tickets, loss of vehicle registration or driver's license, civil or criminal liability, and so on), we may introduce a sufficiently strong deterrent to provide substantial protection against such bad behavior happening at all.

The lessons of security in the Internet teach us that attacks that involve a single compromised or malicious node are soon followed by more sophisticated attacks involving multiple attack nodes. We should expect the same to be true in VANET security. In the future, some attacks will involve coordinated action by multiple vehicles, probably vehicles that attackers have compromised and organized specifically to carry out such attacks. Botnets are commonplace on today's Internet, and vehicular botnets may well be commonplace on our smart highways of the future. Many defensive mechanisms rely on assumptions about attacks coming from a single node, or, at worst, from a small minority of nodes, often with the additional assumption that the dishonest minority is not carefully synchronized in its misbehavior. Such mechanisms will not stand up well to attacks based on vehicular botnets.

As the use of vehicular networks increases, more sophisticated architectures will become possible and offer new opportunities. The vehicular cloud, referred to in Section 7.2.1, is an example. It will use the joint communications, computational, and sensing capabilities of all the vehicles in a particular area (plus possibly some roadside infrastructure, where available) to offer more powerful, yet locally oriented, services. All such new architectures are likely to introduce new security issues. For example, the vehicular cloud will perform distributed computations and will gather and use data from many different vehicles, some of which might be untrustworthy. The algorithms to be used in this architecture must thus be resilient to some forms of partial corruption of their data and computation and perhaps will need to be able to identify bad actors in the cloud, discounting or ignoring their contributions. The field of autonomous vehicles, vehicular networks, and mobile vehicular clouds is both new and fast moving, suggesting that we will see more new approaches that will introduce equally new security challenges.

Finally, the vehicle of the future is, in part, just another computer. So, any attack that can be perpetrated with a typical computer can also be perpetrated with a compromised car. Using a compromised Lexus to send spam might seem like underutilization of a valuable asset, but many attack mechanisms are highly automated and pay little attention to the special characteristics of the machine they infect. If a typical botnet can propagate more or less accidentally onto a car, that car's computer and communication systems are likely to be enlisted into normal botnet service, perhaps with the botnet owner never realizing he has obtained control of an autonomous vehicle. Such ordinary botnets have been known to make their way into elements of cyber-physical systems [8], apparently with no particular intention of specifically attacking those systems, so this possibility is not far-fetched.

7.4 Security Mechanisms for Vehicular Networks

A considerable amount of research has already been performed on suitable security mechanisms to address the problems outlined above [9], and research will continue. We discuss major areas of research on security mechanisms related to VANETs and cyberenhanced vehicles below. Beyond the material presented here, some research on more general problems in mobile wireless network security is of relevance to VANETs. For example, just like other forms of mobile ad hoc networks, VANETs are subject to wormhole and Sybil attacks. However, the general topic of mobile ad hoc network security has been widely investigated elsewhere, so we refer readers to [10] for a survey of this work and confine this chapter to issues more specific to future autonomous vehicles and VANETs.

7.4.1 Authenticating Vehicle Messages

In vehicular networks, most or all vehicles will send messages telling each other about their positions, velocities, and observed road conditions. A dishonest or malicious vehicle could inject false messages purporting to come from a different vehicle. If not detected, these messages could mislead honest vehicles and cause many kinds of problems. Thus, a large body of research has focused on authenticating the messages sent by vehicles.

By and large, this research has used public key cryptography as the core technology for authentication. If message authentication were the only issue, public key cryptography would offer a relatively simple and well-tested solution to the problem: assign a unique public/private key pair to each vehicle and digitally sign messages using the private key. With a suitable key distribution infrastructure (which might be more practical for vehicular systems than it has proven to be for general computing, given that vehicles are already legally registered and inspected by government authorities in many locales), all other vehicles could use the correct public key to verify the digital signatures.

While straightforward in principle, proper use of public key cryptography for message signature has some complexities (such as key distribution and revocation), but the fundamental approach could be made to work if these complexities are properly addressed. Different proposals have been made for the detailed use of public key cryptography for vehicular purposes, covering issues such as which public key algorithm to use, how to distribute the public keys, and how to limit the communications and processing costs associated with the approach. Reference [11] addresses the issue of computational costs by using a method derived from the TESLA approach, which involves hash chains of keys that are anchored by a more standard authority's signature. Checking messages signed with these keys can be substantially cheaper than standard use of public key cryptography. Reference [12] deals with the same issue by combining a TESLA approach with elliptic-curve cryptography, which is computationally cheaper than RSA, the most commonly used public key (PK) algorithm. Reference [13] addresses the problem of certificate revocation in VANETs by using an epidemic-based distribution algorithm for revocation lists. Reference [14] also addresses revocation issues using support from roadside units, and [15] discusses several approaches to the revocation problem, including compression of revocation lists, use of tamper-resistant hardware, and distributed systems techniques to deliver the lists.

VANET researchers realized early on, however, that signature-based approaches to authentication have a major drawback: they create a serious compromise of the privacy of the individual vehicle. Each vehicle was expected to send out signed messages very frequently, for safety purposes, and each such message would necessarily pinpoint the vehicle's location. Any party able to hear a sufficient number of these messages could track the vehicle's location wherever it went. One could also encrypt the signed messages, concealing the vehicle's identity, but since the purpose of the broadcast messages was primarily vehicle safety, any other vehicle that heard the messages needed to be able to decrypt them. The eavesdropper, by plausibly establishing his own need to read the messages, would very likely be able to obtain the decryption key and then use the signed messages to track the vehicle.

One widely investigated approach to ensuring authentication, while also providing privacy, is to sign messages using a pseudonym of some sort rather than the vehicle's true permanent identity. The pseudonym will typically persist for some period of time, so a series of safety messages, all sent by the same vehicle during a particular trip, might all be signed by the same pseudonym. But the pseudonym will also be changed regularly, perhaps per trip, perhaps at some other frequency, so that over the long term, the set of messages sent by the vehicle are not all signed by the same identity and cannot be used to track the vehicle. The trick in such approaches is to provide authentication that can be checked when and to the degree necessary, while not allowing relationships between different pseudonyms or their keys to permit tracking of the vehicle in the long run.

Several different approaches to handling the pseudonym issue have been suggested. [16] uses a technique relying on a trusted central authority to maintain such pseudonyms. Reference [17] proposes storing a large number of pseudonyms in each car, with other mechanisms for tying a pseudonym to an actual vehicle in critical situations. Reference [18] also uses a set of presigned pseudonyms to sign ongoing messages, changing them periodically. Their CARAVAN system also limits the use of particular pseudonyms by forming vehicles into groups and having group leaders authenticate their group members' messages to the infrastructure. Reference [19] uses a scheme in which vehicles generate their own pseudonyms as needed, using a group signature mechanism.

7.4.2 Tamper-Resistant Hardware for Vehicles

A major benefit of proposed vehicular networks is improved safety for all. This safety is achieved by broadcasting messages that inform nearby vehicles (and other interested parties) about important information, such as the sending vehicle's speed, position, and direction of travel. If the sender could simply lie about such information, he could compromise the safety of all who hear his messages. Correlating information from multiple sources can sometimes detect the lies, but it would be far better if lying about such fundamental safety information was impossible.

To that end, researchers have investigated the use of tamperproof hardware installed in cars to ensure that the messages they send contain true information, even if the car is controlled by a malicious party. Such tamperproof hardware would need to extend to the sensors that gather the raw data, the computational unit that interprets the data and formats the messages to be sent, and possibly some or all of the hardware involved in actually sending the messages.

Creating truly tamperproof hardware that cannot possibly be overcome is difficult, perhaps even impossible [20,21]. System designers typical speak of *tamper-resistant* hardware, by which they mean that the difficulty and cost for an attacker to cause the hardware to behave badly is likely to be larger than the benefit he would receive from subverting it. General system developers have designed and built some real tamper-resistant hardware that is widely deployed, such as TPM [22] and Secure Boot [23]. Vehicular network researchers tend to rely primarily on these existing systems, rather than postulate or design brand new tamper-resistant systems [24,25]. In some cases, researchers have postulated tamper-resistant hardware surrounding important components, such as global positioning systems (GPS) [16,26,27]. Using tamper-resistant devices to perform cryptographic operations or safely store cryptographic keys is also a popular approach, sometimes using TPM, sometimes using some other tamper-resistant device [9,17,28].

7.4.3 Determining Trustworthiness of Vehicles and Their Messages

The authentication mechanisms described in Section 7.4.1 only provide assurance that the message was created by a particular party. If that party lies, the authentication merely verifies that the lie you were told did indeed come from that party. If a tamper-resistant system is in place, one gets some additional assurance that whatever is covered by that hardware is indeed truthful, but not all systems contain tamper-resistant hardware, not all messages will be related to the sensors and subsystems tamper-resistant hardware protects, and tamper resistance is never perfect. Ideally, given the safety goals of a cybervehicular system, we would prefer to have better defense in depth than strong authentication, even if backed up with some tamper-resistant hardware, can provide. We want to have some method of knowing whether the message that we are sure was sent by some particular party is the truth or a lie.

A number of researchers have considered this issue. Reference [29], for example, examines trust mechanisms proposed for other types of networks, discussing their suitability for the VANET environment. One common approach many VANET researchers have taken is a mutation of the concept of intrusion detection from general computer systems. Intrusion detection systems analyze the nature and content of messages sent to a system to determine whether those messages represent a threat. In vehicular networks, analysis of the messages can give some indication of the probability that a message is truthful or deceitful.

The techniques used vary widely. Generally, the concept is to compare information obtained from each message with any other available information. This other information could include earlier messages sent by the same vehicle, messages sent by others, sensor readings (obtained either locally or in messages from other vehicles or roadside units), static information (such as road maps), and knowledge of physics and vehicle properties (e.g., to determine the plausibility of messages indicating drastic changes in speed). Algorithms of different types are then applied to this information to determine whether to trust a particular message.

Reference [30], for example, assumes availability of an onboard short-range radar system, which is indeed installed on some vehicles. By combining radar signals showing locations of other vehicles, observing the radar signals those vehicles send, and sharing such information between cars using wireless networking, this approach allows tracking of vehicle movements, which in turn permits detection of vehicles that lie about their speed and position.

Reference [31] concentrates on evaluating the truthfulness of messages reporting traffic congestion. A particle filter approach is used to evaluate a message concerning congestion using information from the receiving vehicle's own sensors and messages about the same situation from other vehicles.

Some researchers propose building trust-based systems that, over the longer term, maintain trust values for vehicles they encounter during their travels. Vehicles that send many implausible messages would develop low trustworthiness values over time, while vehicles that scrupulously tell the truth would have high values. These trust values could then be used to evaluate future messages from various senders. Reference [32] also introduces the notion of situational trust, suggesting that different entities might be trusted more or less depending on the situation being considered, such as determining congestion versus processing a safety message. Reference [33] proposes using information gathered over the long term by roadside infrastructure to help vehicles evaluate the trustworthiness of messages while also considering the trustworthiness of other vehicles that endorse those messages.

The general expectation is that such systems would provide advice or orders on whether to take actions based on a message due to its trustworthiness. A message from a known liar indicating congestion nearby might be ignored, while a message stating that a trusted vehicle has just slammed on its brakes to avoid an accident would likely be heeded.

7.4.4 Hardening Vehicles against Compromise

To date, more attention has been paid to the questions surrounding the security of the VANET connecting vehicles than to how to secure the vehicles themselves. Reference [34] went further, discussing some of the security characteristics that "nodes" in a VANET required, where the term "node" referred primarily to a vehicle participating in the VANET. To some extent, some of the approaches involving tamper-resistant hardware discussed in Section 7.4.2 touch on issues of protecting the vehicle, more in the sense of ensuring proper behavior of the vehicle's systems despite compromise of some elements of its computers and networks than in preventing such compromises in the first place.

Some work has more directly addressed the issue of individual vehicle compromise, however, especially in more recent years.

Reference [35] considered a wide range of potential problems with vehicle security and discussed cryptographic methods, backed with tamper-resistant hardware, to combat them. But much of the other early work described methods by which such compromises could be performed, echoing the general trend in cybersecurity research. (System builders tend to assert that attacks on their systems are impossible until such attacks are actually demonstrated.) Often such work on vehicular compromises is highly specific to one type of vehicle (e.g., [2] described attacks on Teslas) or one particular component that can be attacked, such as [36]'s attack on the passive keyless entry and start system and [3], which demonstrated compromising a vehicle through a wireless tire pressure gauge subsystem.

References [7,37–39] and others have investigated many different methods by which modern cyberequipped vehicles might be compromised. Often these rely on a legitimate device connected to the vehicle's CAN bus that itself can be compromised, offering an already trusted entry point into the larger system. This class of vulnerabilities is somewhat analogous to classic Internet attack techniques that compromise a trusted service on a target computer, then use that compromised service to attack the system as a whole.

One promising approach to protect vehicles from compromise is intrusion detection, in the more classic sense of the term than for analyzing VANET messages, as described in Section 7.4.3. Reference [40] describes use of an anomaly detection system to pinpoint attacks in CAN bus traffic. Their paper suggests that the predictability and regularity of legitimate CAN bus traffic largely eliminates false positives, which are a major drawback of anomaly detection systems in many Internet contexts. Reference [41] suggests using a stateful intrusion detection system (IDS) to observe and analyze traffic on the CAN bus. Reference [42] investigates a specification-based IDS system for the CAN bus, relying, like Muter et al., on the regularity and limited range of legitimate CAN bus traffic.

7.4.5 Access Control to Vehicle-Generated Data

Traditionally, the main concern in vehicular security has been to protect the vehicle from malicious messages that can cause unwanted reactions by drivers, or more recently by automated cars. However, with the increasing number of sensors on vehicles, it becomes necessary to protect access to the actual data residing on the cars. One possible approach is the tamper-resistant hardware described in Section 7.4.2. However, that approach is rather cumbersome and special purpose. It was originally intended to prevent a vehicle from lying about its own data (e.g., reporting incorrect sensor values to its neighbors). Also, in any computer, there is a fundamental problem of access control when some software components can be compromised: if the compromised component is legitimately allowed access to the data to be protected, no hardware or software mechanism can protect that data. In particular, if all software in all computing components of a vehicle is granted equal access rights, any compromise to any software divulges all sensitive data.

Real protection for sensitive data in a vehicle (e.g., sensor data or personal driver data stored on the vehicle, or even data that is broadcast in the neighborhood) requires that such data is made available only to an authorized class of software. For example, the car has various sensors that report engine parameters such as oil levels, state of brakes, pollution values, and so on. This data is carried on the CAN bus and is accessible via the onboard diagnostic (OBD) system. Remote access to this data should be allowed only to service stations and to manufacturers (e.g., via OnStar satellite). The car's music delivery system should not be able to access it. As another example, the car collects data about road accidents and other events of interest through its cameras. This data can be used in forensic investigations. Because of its potential sensitivity, this data should be accessible only to police agents with a proper court order. Pollution sensor data, on the other hand, should be accessible to Environmental Protection Agency agents and authorized researchers. One can easily understand how such data could be manipulated if it fell into the hands of unscrupulous observers and caused panic in certain residential areas exposed to pollution. As another example, suppose that the police department has received a bomb threat for a downtown location. It issues a warning that urges all vehicles within 1 mile of location X to get out as fast as they can. At the same time, it orders paramedics and first responders to converge on the area. If the message is read by all drivers in the city, it may cause unnecessary panic, especially if it is a false alarm. Again, only qualified vehicles should be able to read the message.

All these examples point to the need to provide strong access control for data that resides on a vehicle or emanates from the vehicle. Many mechanisms have been developed over the years for access control in standard computer systems [43], but even in such systems, proper use of access control has proven challenging. In some sense, though, the problem for vehicular systems might prove somewhat simpler than the general problem, since it may prove easier to specify the total set of parties involved in the use of vehicular data (drivers, mechanics, police, and so on) and the proper settings for each piece of data kept or created by the vehicle.

One possible approach is to use the vehicular cloud and exploit the ability to define virtual partitions in the car routers that allow access to restricted sets of sensors. These virtual partitions map to virtual networks within the cloud. For example, a virtual network of police agents can access only certain virtual partitions of sensors. Likewise, a virtual network of vehicles in a certain area and belonging to a certain class can read certain types of messages. Recall that the vehicular cloud was motivated by the need for on-vehicle storage and processing of data that could not be sent into the Internet cloud for background processing (because of tight real-time constraints of the application or because of excessive data volumes to transfer to the Internet). Virtualization support is a key property of the cloud that can be exploited here. However, the virtual network deployment overhead limits its feasibility only to a few major, well-defined applications and classes (e.g., law enforcement agents or taxi cabs). Using the vehicular cloud does introduce its own security issues, which researchers have begun to address [44].

A more flexible and scalable method to control access to data is offered by attribute-based encryption (ABE) [32]. In ABE, the user query carries private encryption material that includes a policy tree with a set of attributes that qualifies it to access data with a matching policy tree. For example, a taxi patron issues a query with policy tree (*YellowTaxi AND Westwood AND $20 AND 10 miles*), that specifies a taxi now located in Westwood, charging at most $20 and taking rides up to 10 miles. If a taxi with the proper credential (i.e., the taxi has obtained a public crypto key with that policy tree) receives the query, it can open the message and can contact the potential customer. The major advantage of ABE in this case is scalability. There is no need to set up key pairs a priori, nor is there a restriction on how many.

Consider an example more relevant to vehicular applications [32]. A taxi driver works for a small company A, which does not have an operator to distribute information to its drivers. The driver wants to tell other drivers in the same company that there are many guests waiting for taxis on a particular road segment of Washington Street. In this situation, the data privacy and the origin integrity are required to ensure the business secret. Then, the driver can send the following message through VNETs:

$$Attributes(companyAANDtaxiANDWashingtonSt.AND10-11am:3/28/08)||cipher||sigcompanyA.$$

In this example, attributes (*companyA AND taxi AND Washington Street*) specify the policy enforced on vehicles interested in decrypting the message; that is, if a taxi belongs to Company A and it happens to be on Washington Street, it can decrypt the message. The message is encrypted by the presented attributes (using an attribute-based encryption scheme [45]). The message is valid in the time interval 10–11am, 3/28/2008.

Here, the message is required to be validated by the company's name through the identity-based signature *sigcompanyA*. This also provides a certain level of anonymity for the sender (using an identity-based signature [IBS] scheme [46]). This example presents a concise and integrated approach to deal with policy group formation and key management.

The formation of a policy group is different from traditional security group formation in that no clear definition and enforcement of a group boundary is required. This property is very useful in a vehicular communication system, since a vehicle usually does not care which entity it communicates with. In Figure 7.3, a policy tree (PT) is presented, where all attributes are leaves and the logic operators are internal nodes. As long as the receivers can satisfy the security/privacy policies, they will be able to decrypt the message (i.e., decrypt the root).

Note that the policy in this example combines a static policy and a dynamic policy. Dynamic policies are typical in vehicular networks, where one's authorization to access data often depends on space/time parameters. The dynamic tree policy requires frequent certification on the user and allows efficient key revocation.

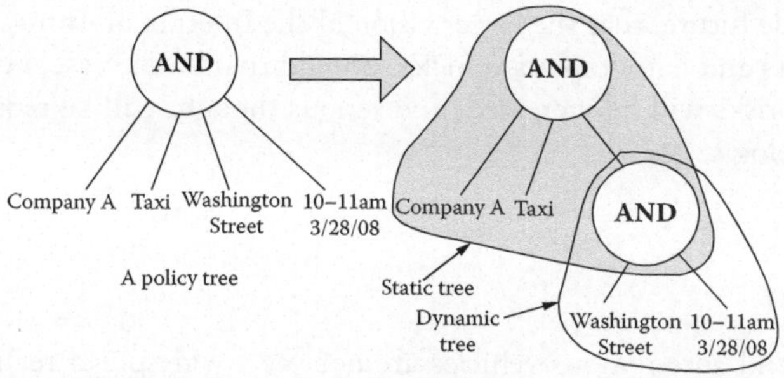

Figure 7.3 Policy tree example.

7.5 Emerging Areas for Research in Vehicular Security

Experience with the Internet's security problems suggests at least some areas in which future research in the security of autonomous vehicles and VANETs would be beneficial.

First, more research is required on vulnerabilities, particularly of systems either in deployment or being standardized. While research geared toward exposing system vulnerabilities seems counterproductive to those not familiar with the computer security field, experience has shown that vulnerabilities not discovered by the good guys probably will be discovered by the bad guys. Such research performed before the unalterable deployment of a widely used system or, worse, long-term standardization of something that will last for decades is vastly better than finding out one morning that an attacker has taken over your car or VANET by some previously unsuspected means.

We can also expect that attackers of these systems will learn from the lessons of attackers on the Internet. For example, denial of service has proven popular on the Internet. Wireless networks are particularly easy to attack this way, so we can expect denial-of-service attacks on VANETs. Whether they will look much like those on the Internet or have unique characteristics specific to the vehicular environment is a matter for research, as is the question of how to handle such attacks.

Another popular attacker trend on the Internet is to combine the capabilities of large numbers of compromised computers into malicious distributed systems commonly called botnets. Attackers of VANETs are likely to learn from this experience. Research should consider how attackers who control significant numbers of compromised autonomous vehicles might make use of them for malicious purposes. Once that is known, efforts should be directed toward detecting and responding to such attacks.

If the vehicular cloud becomes a key part of the future, its security will also be crucial. While it shares characteristics with ordinary cloud computing, it also has unique features based on its reliance on ever-changing sets of participating vehicles and high mobility. The vehicular cloud is thus likely to have some unusual security challenges. But it may also offer some new security possibilities, which certainly should be investigated.

In the past decade, much more information about individuals has been gathered than ever before. This wealth of information has led to innovative ways to make use of it, some of which have disturbing privacy implications. When our cars are equipped with rich sensors that might be providing off-vehicle updates to various sources, even more information will become available. We should spend much effort on understanding the privacy implications of collecting and sharing each piece of data that our vehicles might provide. We also should think about new privacy-enhancing mechanisms to allow vehicle owners, drivers, and passengers to better protect their privacy.

It is possible, in the future, that the larger vision of the Internet of Things will become tightly connected to VANETs and autonomous vehicles. Should that be the case, both the possible benefits and the security risks will be increased, and serious thought will be required to best protect this combined technology.

7.6 Conclusion

Vehicular networks and autonomous vehicles are not yet a widespread reality, though they are clearly on the horizon. Thus, it is impossible to fully predict the threats these future technologies will face and the measures that will be required to protect them. Based on the existing state of the research and on the history of the use of cybercapabilities in other arenas, however, we can confidently predict that cybersecurity will be a serious issue for autonomous vehicles and the networks they use. Some of the threats outlined here are likely to become reality as these technologies are adopted, and some of the security measures already researched and presented here are likely to be helpful in protecting our cars and roadways.

Certainly, though, more thought and research will be required. We are at a relatively fortunate state in terms of the security of autonomous vehicles and VANETs. There is time to improve their security before we become locked into particular choices, forcing us to live with the kind of insecure systems so prevalent in other networked technologies. Designers of these vehicles and supporting networks need to give serious consideration to security issues when they make important design decisions, particularly decisions that will be difficult to change later. When new computer-controlled functionality is added to a vehicle, for example, the designer should always consider what might happen if a malicious individual were able to use that functionality. Would he be able to crash the vehicle? Prevent the vehicle from starting? Steal the vehicle? Spy on the occupants of the vehicle? The worse the answers to such questions are, the more care must be taken in protecting systems providing the functionality.

Providing security in computer systems is always a trade-off between better security and other desirable system characteristics. Automotive engineers are very familiar with making design trade-offs—performance versus fuel efficiency, comfort versus price, and so forth. They now must consider another dimension: cybersecurity. As with other trade-offs, they will only be able to properly consider their options if they understand the dimensions of the trade-offs. Thus, automotive engineers, especially those working with the computer and networking components of the vehicles, must develop a thorough understanding of the basics of cybersecurity if they hope to make wise decisions.

A single book chapter is not sufficient to build such understanding, but perhaps it can provide a good starting point. Briefly, here are a few key points for automotive researchers and designers to remember in building safer systems:

- Be suspicious of outside information: it is always best not to trust information coming across a network unless you have positive reasons to do so. Consider trying to confirm critical information through multiple independent sources, perhaps based on different sensors or message origins.
- Bits are easy to copy: and all information processed by computers and carried on networks are merely patterns of bits. Cryptography can provide some degree of protection, but proper use of cryptography is not trivial and requires serious attention to detail.
- Practice defense in depth: do not assume that a single defensive mechanism will protect your vehicle.

- Avoid reliance on secrets: if some secrets (such as cryptographic keys) are unavoidable, minimize them, protect them well, and make sure you can easily change them if they are compromised.
- Prioritize your efforts: focus attention on the greatest dangers you face, which in the case of vehicles must include the physical safety of drivers, passengers, and other people they encounter.
- Be prepared for errors: even the best-designed, most carefully written software has been known to contain security flaws, so understand that yours might, too, and be prepared to fix problems. Avoid building systems that have no reasonable upgrade mechanism, and consider how you will handle the inevitable security flaws when they pop up.

The future of autonomous vehicles offers tremendous promise in so many ways that it seems almost an inevitable reality. The increased reliance on cybertechnology in such vehicles will equally inevitably lead to security problems. Our goal should not be to make such problems utterly impossible, since the only way to do so would be to forgo the benefits of autonomous vehicles, thus avoiding their risks. Instead, we should arm ourselves with knowledge and understanding of the systems we are using and the cyberthreats that face them, and design and build our autonomous vehicles and vehicular networks to combat those threats effectively and efficiently.

Author Biographies

Mario Gerla was born in Milan, Italy. He received a graduate degree in engineering from the Politecnico di Milano, in 1966, and MS and PhD degrees in engineering from the University of California, Los Angeles in 1970 and 1973, respectively. He joined the University of California, Los Angeles Computer Science Department in 1977. His research interests cover the performance evaluation, design, and control of distributed computer communication systems and high-speed computer networks (broadband integrated services digital networks and optical networks).

Peter Reiher received his BS from the University of Notre Dame in 1979, his MS from University of California, Los Angeles in 1984, and his PhD in computer science from the University of California, Los Angeles in 1987. He worked on the time warp operating system at the Jet Propulsion Laboratory until 1992, after which he returned to University of California, Los Angeles, where he is an adjunct professor in the Computer Science Department. Dr. Reiher has performed research on many topics in networks and systems, including network and system security (particularly distributed denial-of-service attacks), file systems, operating systems, wireless networks, mobility, active networks, and ubiquitous computing. He has coauthored books and published over 120 papers on these subjects in journals and conferences. He is a member of the Association for Computing Machinery, the Institute of Electrical and Electronics Engineers, and the Usenix Association; served as vice-chair of the Institute of Electrical and Electronics Engineers Computer Society from 2005 to 2007; and is an associate editor for *ACM Transactions on Internet Technologies*.

Glossary

802.11p: a variant on the IEEE's 802.11 standard for wireless communication specifically designed to support vehicular networking

ABE: attribute-based encryption. A form of cryptography in which only entities with suitable attributes are able to decrypt information

anonymization: an approach to providing some elements of confidentiality based on concealing the identity of a party creating or using certain information

autonomous vehicle: a vehicle capable of using computer control to handle all or most of the tasks required to drive it

botnets: an organized collection of computers that have been compromised by a malicious party, allowing all of them to work in concert on various forms of attacks

CAN bus: a standard type of computing bus used to connect internally networked elements of a single vehicle

DDoS: distributed denial of service. A form of attack on availability in which multiple entities work in concert to deny service to some targeted victim

DSRC: dedicated short-range communications. A communications standard developed by the U.S. Department of Transportation using dedicated spectrum to transmit safety information between vehicles

OBD: onboard diagnostic system. A system that allows internal or suitably attached external devices to obtain access to information about a vehicle's status

platooning: a driving strategy for autonomous vehicles in which groups of such vehicles drive closely together, gaining various benefits by so doing. Platooning is only possible with some vehicle autonomy and rather tight and reliable wireless networking communications

pseudonyms: in the context of VANETs, an approach to providing anonymization while still allowing proper attribution of actions, based on assigning temporary false identities to vehicles that can, under certain circumstances, be traced to the actual vehicle

RSU: roadside unit. An infrastructure element in a vehicular network that is typically located in a fixed place in or near the side of a road. Roadside units are usually intended to provide service to vehicles in their near vicinity. Often, but not always, roadside units are expected to have Internet connectivity

secure boot: a hardware standard developed by Microsoft for providing tamper-resistant capabilities, especially secure booting

TPM: a hardware standard for providing tamper-resistant capabilities, including secure booting and key storage

V2I: vehicle-to-infrastructure. A term describing communications in vehicular networks in which a vehicle sends messages to a (typically fixed) infrastructure element, either to communicate to that element or for further forwarding

V2V: vehicle-to-vehicle. A term describing communications in vehicular networks in which one vehicle sends messages directly to another vehicle without using any infrastructure for delivery

V2X: vehicle-to-any. A term describing communications in vehicular networks that subsumes both V2I and V2V communications

VANET: vehicular ad hoc network. A wireless network formed between vehicles (and possibly roadside units and other network elements) to support the activities of those vehicles and to deal with overall traffic issues

vehicular cloud: a vehicular networking approach in which a group of intercommunicating vehicles in a particular area pool their resources to provide services to each other

References

1. M. Gerla and L. Kleinrock, Vehicular networks and the future of the mobile internet. *Computer Networks*, Vol. 55, No. 2, pp. 457–469, 2011.
2. A. Tutu, Tesla model S vulnerable to cyber attacks, autoevolution. http://www.autoevolution.com/news/tesla-model-s-vulnerable-to-cyber-attacks-79407.html, 2014.
3. I. Rouf, R. Mustafa, T. Taylor, S. Xu, W. Gruteser, M. Trappe, and I. Seskar, Security and privacy vulnerabilities of in-car wireless networks: A tire pressure monitoring system case study, *19th USENIX Security Symposium*, Washington, D.C., 2010.
4. S. Rosenblatt, Car hacking code released at Defcon, *Cnet News*, August 2, 2013.
5. S. Yousefi, M. Mousavi, and M. Fathy, Vehicular ad hoc networks (VANETs): Challenges and perspectives, *6th International Conference on ITS Telecommunications Proceedings*, pp. 57–60, IEEE, Chengdu, China, 2006.
6. M. Gerla, Vehicular cloud computing, *The 11th Annual Mediterranean Ad Hoc Networking Workshop (Med-Hoc-Net)*, pp. 152–155, IEEE, Ayia Napa, 2012.
7. T. Hoppe, S. Kiltz, and J. Dittmann, Automotive IT-security as a challenge: Basic attacks from the black box perspective on the example of privacy threats, *Computer Safety, Reliability, and Security*, pp. 145–158, Springer, Berlin, 2009.
8. D. Goodin, Guerilla researcher created epic botnet to scan billions of IP addresses, *Ars Technica*, http://arstechnica.com/security/2013/03/guerilla-researcher-created-epic-botnet-to-scan-billions-of-ip-addresses/, March 20, 2013.
9. M. Raya and J. Hubaux, Securing vehicular ad hoc networks, *Journal of Computer Security*, Vol. 15, No. 1, pp. 39–68, 2007.
10. D. Djenouri, L. Khelladi, and N. Badache, A survey of security issues in mobile ad hoc networks, *IEEE Communications Surveys*, Vol. 7, pp. 2–28, 2005.
11. Y. Hu and K. Laberteaux, Strong VANET security on a budget, *Proceedings of Workshop on Embedded Security in Cars (ESCAR)*, Vol. 6, pp. 1–9, 2006.
12. A. Studer, F. Bai, B. Bellur, and A. Perrig, Flexible, extensible, and efficient VANET authentication, *Communications and Networks*, Vol. 11, No. 6, pp. 574–588, 2009.
13. K. Laberteaux, J. Haas, and Y.Hu, Security certificate revocation list distribution for VANET, *Proceedings of the Fifth ACM International Workshop on VehiculAr Inter-NETworking*, pp. 88–89, ACM, New York, 2008.
14. X. Lin, R. Lu, C. Zhang, H. Zhu, P. Ho, and X. Shen, Security in vehicular ad hoc networks, *IEEE Communications Magazine*, Vol. 46, No. 4, pp. 88–95, 2008.
15. M. Raya and J. Hubaux, The security of VANETs, *Proceedings of the 2nd ACM International Workshop on Vehicular Ad Hoc Networks*, Cologne, Germany, 2005.
16. F. Dötzer, Privacy issues in vehicular ad hoc networks, *Privacy Enhancing Technologies*, pp. 197–209, Springer, Berlin, 2006.
17. M. Raya, P. Papadimitratos, and J. Hubaux, Securing vehicular communications, *IEEE Wireless Communications Magazine, Special Issue on Inter-Vehicular Communications*, Vol. 13, pp. 8–15, 2006.
18. K. Sampigethaya, L. Huang, M. Li, R. Poovendran, K. Matsuura, and K. Sezaki, *CARAVAN: Providing Location Privacy for VANET*, Contract Report, Electrical Engineering Department, University of Washington, 2005.
19. G. Calandriello, P. Papadimitratos, J. Hubaux, and A. Lioy, Efficient and robust pseudonymous authentication in VANET, *Proceedings of the Fourth ACM International Workshop on Vehicular Ad Hoc Networks*, pp. 19–28, ACM, Montreal, 2007.
20. R. Anderson and M. Kuhn, Tamper resistance: A cautionary note, *Proceedings of the 2nd Usenix Workshop on Electronic Commerce*, pp. 1–11, Usenix Association, 1996.
21. R. Anderson and M. Kuhn, Low cost attacks on tamper resistant devices, In B. Christianson, B. Crispo, M. Lomas, and M. Roe (eds), *Security Protocols*, pp. 125–136, Springer, Berlin, 1998.
22. TPM Main Specification, http://www.trustedcomputinggroup.org/resources/tpm_main_specification, 2014.

23. Microsoft, Secure boot overview, http://technet.microsoft.com/en-us/library/hh824987.aspx, May 5, 2014.
24. G. Guette, and C. Bryce, Using TPMs to secure vehicular ad-hoc networks (VANETs). In J. A. Onieva, D. Sauveron, S. Chaumette, D. Gollmann, and K. Markantonakis (eds) *Information Security Theory and Practices. Smart Devices, Convergence and Next Generation Networks*, pp. 106–116, Springer, Berlin, 2008.
25. A. Wagan, B. Mughal, and H. Hasbullah, VANET security framework for trusted grouping using TPM hardware, *Second International Conference on Communication Software and Networks (ICCSN'10)*, IEEE, Washington, D.C., 2010.
26. J. Hubaux, and S. Capkun, The security and privacy of smart vehicles, *IEEE Security & Privacy*, Vol. 2, No. 3, pp. 49–55, 2004.
27. A. Weimerskirch, C. Paar, and M. Wolf, Cryptographic component identification: Enabler for secure vehicles, *IEEE Vehicular Technology Conference*, IEEE, Dallas, Texas, 2005.
28. T. Leinmüller, L. Buttyan, J. Hubaux, F. Kargl, R. Kroh, P. Papadimitratos, M. Raya, and E. Schoch, Sevecom-Secure vehicle communication, *Proceedings of IST Mobile Summit*, Mykonos, Greece, European Information Society, pp. 1–5, 2006.
29. P. Wex, J. Breuer, A. Held, T. Leinmuller, and L. Delgrossi, Trust issues for vehicular ad hoc networks, *IEEE Vehicular Technology Conference (VTC)*, Calgary, pp. 2800–2804, 2008.
30. G. Yan, S. Olariu, and M. Weigle, Providing VANET security through active position detection, *Computer Communications*, Vol. 31, No. 12, 2883–2897, 2008.
31. N. Bismeyer, S. Mauthofer, K. Bayarou, and F. Kargl. Assessment of node trustworthiness in vanets using data plausibility checks with particle filters, In *Proceedings of the IEEE VNC*, pp. 78–85, IEEE, Seoul, Korea, 2012.
32. X. Hong, D. Huang, M. Gerla, and Z. Cao, SAT: Situation-aware trust architecture for vehicular networks, *Proceedings of the 3rd International Workshop on Mobility in the Evolving Internet Architecture*, pp. 31–36, New York, 2008.
33. C. Liao, J. Chang, I. Lee, and K. K. Venkatasubramanian, A trust model for vehicular network-based incident reports, In *Proceeding of the IEEE 5th International Symposium on Wireless Vehicular Communications*, Dresden, Germany, 2013.
34. S. Eichler, A security architecture concept for vehicular network nodes, In *Proceeding of the 6th International Conference on Information, Communications & Signal Processing*, Singapore, 2007.
35. M. Wolf, A. Weimerskirch, and T. Wollinger, State of the art: Embedding security in vehicles, *EURASIP Journal on Embedded Systems*, 2007.
36. A. Francillon, B. Danev, and S. Capkun, Relay attacks on passive keyless entry and start systems in modern cars, IACR ePrint Report 2010/332, 2010.
37. T. Hoppe and J. Dittman, Sniffing/replay attacks on CAN buses: A simulated attack on the electric window lift classified using an adapted CERT taxonomy, *Proceedings of the 2nd Workshop on Embedded Systems Security* (*WESS*), Salzburg, Austria, 2007.
38. K. Koscher, A. Czeskis, F. Roesner, S. Patel, T. Kohno, S. Checkoway, D. McCoy, B. Kantor, D. Anderson, H. Shacham, and S. Savage. Experimental security analysis of a modern automobile, *2010 IEEE Symposium on Security and Privacy* (*SP*), pp. 447–462, San Diego, 2010.
39. S. Checkoway, D. McCoy, B. Kantor, D. Anderson, H. Shacham, S. Savage, K. Koscher, A. Czeskis, F. Roesner, and T. Kohno, Comprehensive experimental analyses of automotive attack surfaces, *USENIX Security Symposium*, San Francisco, CA, 2011.
40. M. Muter, A. Groll, and F. Freiling, A structured approach to anomaly detection for in-vehicle networks, *6th International Conference on Information Assurance and Security* (*IAS*), pp. 92–98, IEEE, Atlanta, 2010.
41. I. Studnia, V. Nicomette, E. Alata, Y. Deswarte, M. Kaâniche, and Y. Laarouchi, Security of embedded automotive networks: State of the art and a research proposal, *Proceedings of Workshop CARS (2nd Workshop on Critical Automotive Applications: Robustness & Safety) of the 32nd International Conference on Computer Safety, Reliability and Security*, Toulouse, France, 2013.
42. U. Larson, D. Nilsson, and E. Jonsson, An approach to specification-based attack detection for in-vehicle networks, In *Proceedings of the 12th IEEE Intelligent Vehicles Symposium*, Eindhoven, the Netherlands, 2008.

43. M. Bishop, *Computer Security: Art and Science*, Boston: Addison-Wesley, 2003.
44. G. Yan, D. Wen, S. Olariu, and M. Weigle, Security challenges in vehicular cloud computing, *IEEE Transactions on Intelligent Transport Systems*, Vol. 14, No. 1, pp. 284–294, 2013.
45. J. Bethencourt, A. Sahai, and B. Waters, Ciphertext-policy attribute-based encryption, *Proceedings of the 28th IEEE Symposium on Security and Privacy*, Oakland, CA, 2007.
46. A. Shamir, Identity-based cryptosystems and signature schemes, In T. Beth, N. Cot, and I. Ingemarsson (eds) *Advances in Cryptology*, Springer, Berlin, 1985.

Chapter 8

A Study of Security Issues, Vulnerabilities, and Challenges in the Internet of Things

Kashif Laeeq and Jawwad A. Shamsi

National University of Computer and Emerging Sciences

Contents

8.1 Introduction ... 223
8.2 IoT Technologies ... 223
8.3 Core IoT Technologies ... 224
8.3.1 Radio-Frequency Identification ... 224
8.3.1.1 Passive RFID ... 224
8.3.1.2 Active RFID ... 224
8.3.2 Wireless Sensor Networks ... 224
8.3.3 Near Field Communication ... 224
8.4 Supporting IoT Technologies ... 225
8.5 Security Issues in IoT ... 225
8.5.1 Insecure Architecture ... 226
8.5.1.1 Security Issues in Perception Layer ... 226
8.5.1.2 Security Issues in Network Layer ... 226
8.5.1.3 Security Issues in Application Layer ... 227
8.6 Vulnerabilities in ICT Technologies ... 227
8.6.1 Eavesdropping Attacks ... 227
8.6.2 Spoofing Attacks ... 227
8.6.3 Denial-of-Service Attacks ... 228
8.6.4 Distributed Denial-of-Service Attacks ... 228
8.7 Vulnerabilities in IoT Protocols ... 229
8.7.1 DoS Attacks on L1-L3 Communication Protocol ... 229

8.7.2 Generic Attacks 229
8.7.3 Redirection Attacks 230
8.8 Security Threats in Core IoT Technologies 230
8.9 Security Threats in IoT Devices 230
8.10 Privacy Issues in IoT 231
8.11 Security Requirements for IoT 232
8.11.1 User Authentication 232
8.11.2 Tamper Resistance 233
8.11.3 Secure Execution 233
8.11.4 Secure Data Communication 233
8.11.5 Identity Management 233
8.11.6 Confidentiality 233
8.11.7 Auditing 233
8.11.8 Integrity 234
8.12 Approaches to Mitigate IoT Issues 234
8.12.1 How Can We Protect IoT Architecture? 234
8.12.1.1 Perception Layer 235
8.12.1.2 Network Layer 235
8.12.1.3 Application Layer 235
8.12.2 Protecting IoT Protocols against Security Threats 235
8.12.3 Protecting RFID 235
8.12.4 Protecting NFC 236
8.12.5 Preventive Measures against Privacy Issues 236
8.13 Open Research Issues 237
8.14 Conclusion 237
Acknowledgments 238
Author Biographies 238
References 238

Abstract: A new concept that has changed the basic ideology of the traditional Internet by connecting things on a global scale is the Internet of Things (IoT). It is an extension of the Internet by the inclusion of world objects blended with a power to offer smart services to this global village. The core idea of this technology is closely related to the cyber-physical system (CPS) that allows the physical world to amalgamate with the virtual world leading to an IoT. In different ways, the IoT technology is involved either directly or indirectly in human daily life. The connection of billions of heterogeneous things in an always-on fashion makes this technology vulnerable and a high security risk. The increasing dependence on this omnipresent technology also highlights major security issues. Security is one of the biggest challenges facing this technology and no practical implementation can prevail if security issues are not handled properly. In this chapter, we highlight the principal security issues, vulnerabilities, and challenges related to the IoT devices. The chapter also explores the available methods and solutions in the IoT technology.

Keywords: IoT challenges; IoT security; IoT technologies; Internet of Things (IoT)

8.1 Introduction

Kevin Ashton, one of the founders of the Auto-ID research center at MIT, was the first person to realize that the world is not getting the most out of the current Internet infrastructure. In 1998, he introduced a novel term, *Internet of Things* (IoT), which is why he is considered the founder of the term *IoT* [1]. The IoT technology is proof of Marshall McLuhan's concept of the "global village," in which the whole world is treated as a small community where every person is connected and knows each other. The conceptual vision behind this technology is that the world's objects are now part of the Internet, and that each object is distinctively identified and can be accessed from anywhere at any time knowing its current status or position. Some intelligent and smart services are added to this advanced Internet, amalgamating physical and digital world, eventually impacting on our personal, professional, and social life [2]. These objects might be a small device such as a door of a house or a huge object such as an aircraft. The size of things is not an issue for this technology, anything that has mass or weight could be an object of the IoT. Just think of trillions of heterogeneous objects (tiny to huge) connected together in an always-on manner: then we can realize the immensity of this technology. In 2005, the International Telecommunication Union (ITU) defined the term *Internet of Things* as "Internet of Things will connect the world's objects in both a sensory and intelligent manner" [3]. The advancements and inventions of new technologies like radio-frequency identification (RFID) tags [4], quick response codes (QR codes) [5], and so on are expending the limitations of today's Internet. New devices, physical objects, and even human beings can easily be a part of the future Internet. Due to limited resources, the key management or authentication is one of the biggest challenges for these devices. The future IoT, as a smart association of tiny sensors, creates new issues of security, trust, and privacy.

As the ITU has defined [6], one of the biggest challenges for the IoT is protecting user data while ensuring privacy. Due to its diverse aspects, security for the IoT is a critical concern that must be addressed. The research on the IoT, particularly on security-related issues, is inadequate [7]. The inherent openness, terminal vulnerabilities, and heterogeneity of things pose enormous risks to the IoT operations. A single holistic security scheme for the IoT seems impractical, so the need for vital security mechanisms must be promptly recognized to ensure IoT security.

In this chapter, we have divided the IoT into four subdomains: architecture, technologies, protocols, and devices. The main contribution of this chapter is to elaborate on the IoT technology with respect to security, privacy, and vulnerability, and also to offer helpful solutions to improve the technology. Finally, this chapter concludes with some open research issues and challenges that will provide a new research direction for researchers in this domain.

The rest of the chapter is organized as follows: initially an overview of the IoT technology is provided and then IoT security issues and challenges are described. The main security requirements for the IoT are then underlined and some suggestions toward improving the IoT are provided. In addition, some open research issues are highlighted before the chapter is concluded.

8.2 IoT Technologies

The world is getting smarter; everything and everyone is connected with each other. The IoT technology claims that every person, animal, and even every object all over the world can communicate with each other via a unique identifier (UID). Object tracking can be performed using sensors, chips, and Internet protocol (IP) addresses. The IoT has emerged from three key technologies: wireless technologies, the Internet, and microelectromechanical systems (MEMS).

The ITU described four major IoT areas: item identification, embedded systems, sensor networks, and nanotechnology [2]. The tagging of things is an important feature of the IoT, and is mainly handled by RFIDs. Apart from RFID, objects can be tagged using different technologies such as near field communication (NFC), QR codes, bar codes, and digital watermarking. In other words, we can say that the IoT comprises and utilizes various technologies to facilitate a variety of its jobs. In general, we can classify these technologies into four main technologies that enable IoT operations: RFIDs are used for object identification, sensor technologies are used for feeling objects, smart technologies are used for thinking objects, and nanotechnologies are used for shrinking objects.

For a greater understanding, we separate IoT technologies into two broader categories: core IoT technologies and supporting IoT technologies. The following sections provide a brief overview of these technologies.

8.3 Core IoT Technologies

RFID, wireless sensor networks (WSNs), and NFC might be considered core technologies for the IoT.

8.3.1 Radio-Frequency Identification

RFID is a key technology for the IoT; it is also used for microchip designing, an essential part of wireless communications. RFIDs act like an electronic bar code [8] and are intended for the automatic detection or recognition of any Thing. There are two categories of RFIDs: passive and active RFIDs.

8.3.1.1 Passive RFID

The passive RFIDs are not powered by any external power supply or battery. They utilize the power of a reader's interrogation signals for any response. A variety of passive RFIDs are used in supply chain management, retail, access control, bank cards, and so on.

8.3.1.2 Active RFID

The basic difference between active and passive RFIDs is their power. Active RFIDs use their own battery power and passive RFIDs, as they have no embedded battery, use the RFID reader's signals for a response. Active RFID tags are widely used for monitoring purposes such as monitoring cargo [9,10].

8.3.2 Wireless Sensor Networks

Due to their low cost, efficiency, and low power consumption, WSNs are a vital technology of the IoT. They are typically used for remote sensing applications and information gathering [11]. WSNs and active RFIDs have many common features, but WSNs are more intelligent and have processing capabilities.

8.3.3 Near Field Communication

NFC is a widely used IoT technology that helps two electronic things to communicate within a 10 cm range with a data rate of a few 100 Kbps and a low power consumption. In the IoT, this technology supports multiple services such as access control, transport, smartphones, and smart cards [12]. By default, NFC is a vulnerable technology and does not support a security framework.

8.4 Supporting IoT Technologies

In addition to the core IoT technologies, numerous technologies participate in the general operations of the IoT. For example, the ability to uniquely identify Things is vital for the practical implementation of the IoT. Billions of unique items can be connected via the IoT. The IP version 4 (IPv4) addressing scheme can fail to provide unique identification to every participating Thing in the IoT; however, fortunately, we have IP version 6 (IPv6), which is more than capable of providing a UID to every object, exceeding its expectations [13]. Uniform resource name (URN) is another technology that produces replicas of the resources and can be accessed in the course of the URL. URN considers the basic technology for the IoT. The IP for Smart Object Alliance (IPSO) [14] highlighted that a lightweight protocol that connects various small, battery-operated devices in an IP stack with IPv6 over low-power personal area network (6LoWPAN) and 802.15.4 standard protocol makes IoT technology a true reality. Table 8.1 presents a summary of the major technologies that are used in the IoT.

8.5 Security Issues in IoT

In reality, it can be observed that academic research on the security issues of the IoT is still at an early stage. Various parts of the IoT are undergoing significant research; however, security issues require more academic as well as industrial research. Security could be one of the major constraints to implementing the IoT in the real-world environment. Protecting the IoT from various

Table 8.1 IoT Technologies

Communication Technologies	
Short range	NFC, RFID, ANT, Bluetooth, ZigBee, Z-Wave, IEEE802.15.4, Wi-Fi
Medium range	WiMAX, Weightless, DASH7, EnOcean, PLC, QR Code, Ethernet
Long range	GPRS, GSM, GPS, 3G/4G, LTE, Satellite
Prototype Hardware	
Raspberry Pi, Hackberry, Arduino Yun, Arduino Uno, PCDuino, The Rascal, Cubie Board, BeagleBone Black, OpenPicus Flyport Wi-Fi, Pinoccio	
Operating System	
Tiny OS, Contiki, Mantis, Nano-RK, LiteOS, FreeRTOS, Riot OS, SNAP OS, Abacus OS, Sapphire OS	
Protocol	
REST, IPv6, 6LoWPAN, UDP, Chirp, DTLS, XMPP-IoT, SSI, NanoIP, MQTT	

threats, malicious attacks, identity fabrication, denial of services (DoS), and so on, is a complex task and requires intensive research. The term *security* refers to the provision of security services incorporating authentication, confidentiality, authorization, nonrepudiation, integrity, and availability. Security solutions based on cryptographic schemes, such as hash function, block ciphers, and signature algorithms, are still under research for the IoT environment. With these security solutions, strong key management infrastructure is required to manage the essential cryptographic keys [15]. In the context of the IoT, security is the biggest challenge because of the billions of heterogeneous connections. The major components that participate in the IoT connections are sensors, actuators, RFID tags, smartphones, and other smart devices. Every attached component in the IoT acts like a node or a terminal of a wide area network (WAN). Securing IoT connections and its components from numerous malicious attacks is a very challenging task for researchers in this domain. In fact, the security domain of the IoT technology is still in a premature state and no in-hand solutions or schemes claim to protect this technology completely.

In this chapter, we emphasize the security issues and the challenges related to the IoT. For clarity, we have categorized the IoT into four subdomains: architecture, supporting technologies, core technologies, and protocols. The following section illustrates the security issues in various subdomains of the IoT.

8.5.1 Insecure Architecture

During the design and execution phase of the IoT, security must be guaranteed [16]. The most basic IoT architecture has been divided into three layers: the application layer, the network layer, and the perception layer [13,17,18]. The following sections elaborate the security threats in the IoT architecture.

8.5.1.1 Security Issues in Perception Layer

The perception layer aims to sense, collect, and recognize the physical world's information. This layer seamlessly transforms the physical world's objects into the digital or cyberworld. It has universal methodologies to access worldwide hetrogeneous objects. The key security issues at this layer are external attacks, DoS attacks, authentication, confidentiality, and integrity.

The following are some of the major security issues of the perception layer.

1. Due to the limited power and computation capability of sensor nodes, the chances of attacks are high, especially brute-force attacks.
2. Comprehensive authentication in the perception layer is very difficult; by utilizing this weakness, any malicious user can use a fake identity and perform a collusion attack.
3. This layer could be affected by routing attacks, particularly during the data forwarding process.

8.5.1.2 Security Issues in Network Layer

The network layer is responsible for securing the transmission of information and data communication across large, remote geographical locations. A few of the common technologies in this layer are the general packet radio service (GPRS), WiMAX, Wi-Fi, Bluetooth, local area network (LAN), WAN, 3G, and 4G. Man-in-the-middle attacks, distributed DoS (DDoS) attacks, and data confidentiality are common security threats at this layer [19].

The following are some of the security concerns at this layer.

1. The routing attack is the most fundamental attack at this layer, particularly at the time of data or message forwarding.
2. Since many different types of objects are communicating with each other, they simultaneously send huge data; at this time, DoS-type attackers can easily be camouflaged with a legitimate node, which increases the chances of DoS-type attacks.

8.5.1.3 Security Issues in Application Layer

The major task of the application layer is to set up connections between the user and the IoT. Providing IoT services to the user and processing the data are also the concern of this layer. This layer analyzes the services and, if required, it splits them into smaller subservices. Access control, data privacy, and information disclosure are common issues at this layer [20]. The following are some of the security issues at the application layer.

1. In the application layer, an attacker can easily hack secret data such as passwords.
2. Privacy could be one of the biggest challenges, especially in the application layer.
3. A data injection attack can easily be launched in the application layer.

Table 8.2 summarizes the key features, the security threats, and the security requirements of the IoT architecture layers.

8.6 Vulnerabilities in ICT Technologies

Information and Communication Technology (ICT) is the key infrastructure of the IoT. ICT is insecure and vulnerable to security attacks. The existing threats to ICT must be countered in the future IoT. The biggest challenge is to transform the existing solutions for securing ICT into IoT technology. Due to the limited energy and the resource constraints of the IoT components, it is difficult to shift in-hand security schemes into the future IoT. In the following section, we discuss some of the major attacks and threats to ICT technologies.

8.6.1 Eavesdropping Attacks

An eavesdropping attack is a passive attack, in which an attacker listens and uncovers useful information during communications. This information further exploits many malicious activities.

8.6.2 Spoofing Attacks

In this type of attack, the attacker changes the source address or hides his or her own identity to perform malicious activities. The attacker masks his or her own identity to gain illegal advantages. A man-in-the-middle attack is an example of this type of attack. The probability of spoofing attacks may be reduced by utilizing the extensible authentication protocol (EAP) [21].

Table 8.2 Key Features of IoT Architecture

Perception
Responsibility: To sense and recognize the physical world object and act as if they are digital world objects.
Key component: Sensor.
Limitations: Limited storage capacity and power.
Security threats: Malicious attacks particularly an external DoS attack.
Security needs: Node authentication, data encryption, lightweight cryptographic algorithms.
Network
Responsibility: To ensure the reliable transmission of information and data communications.
Key component: Internet.
Limitations: Bandwidth or throughput.
Security threats: Computer virus, malicious attacks particularly a man-in-the-middle attack. Vulnerable network servers.
Security needs: To establish an intelligent data confidentiality and integrity system. Requires smart intrusion detection systems (IDS).
Application
Responsibility: To establish a connection between the user and the IoT. Fulfill the application needs of IoT users.
Key component: Application and administrative protocols.
Limitations: User dependency.
Security threats: Information disclosure and security, data privacy protection.
Security needs: Authentication and key management across the heterogeneous networks. Users' and data privacy protection. Password implementation.

8.6.3 Denial-of-Service Attacks

DoS is a type of jamming attack, in which a malicious attacker sends a bulk of useless packets to the network, which impedes the network from executing the legitimate packets, ultimately resulting in a jamming or a denial of service problem. There are various solutions for DoS attacks in the literature. These types of DoS attacks may be reduced by utilizing any good intrusion detection system (IDS).

8.6.4 Distributed Denial-of-Service Attacks

This is the same as a DoS attack but in a DDoS attack, malicious attackers, from the same network, simultaneously send bulk packets or flood the target [21]. Ultimately, the resources of the target nodes are consumed to process these illegitimate packets and are unable to process any legitimate request.

8.7 Vulnerabilities in IoT Protocols

The IoT is an overlay type of network that utilizes the infrastructure and typical communication protocols of the traditional Internet. In other words, it is thought that the IoT is an extension of the Internet and that the protocols that are used in the Internet could be used in the IoT. However, the security requirements of the IoT are different from the conventional Internet, which could be one of the reasons for the separation of both technologies. IoT security solutions demand new energy-efficient security protocols without taking into account their interoperability with current IPs.

Actually, researchers are intensively investigating the available IPs in an effort to find any possibilities to alter them or use them as future IoT protocols. Researchers have also developed a set of protocols that can work properly with the IoT environment. Currently, Internet Engineering Task Force (IETF) working groups are developing protocols especially for smart objects. The 6LoWPAN group is working on the efficient communication and management of an IEEE 802.15.4 type of network with IPv6 addressing schemes. The Constrained Restful Environments (CoRE) group is working on a lightweight adaptation of the hypertext transfer protocol (HTTP) and the constrained application protocol (CoAP) for resource-constrained IoT devices.

Due to limited resources of devises, the threats to IoT protocols are more severe than those to the traditional Internet. The IoT environment is a heterogeneous distributed environment where one device can immediately communicate with other near or remote devices that mostly have limited computing or energy resources. In this situation, key management is a big challenge [22]. As public key cryptography algorithms require some processing resources and in the IoT scenario trillions of bytes of data are communicating, this type of cryptography is difficult in IoT; it may require huge communication resources. When we open a secure channel, communication demands secure parameters (such as AES-256 and AES-128 communication), but considering device constraints, how can these parameters work? Hui and Zou [23] claimed that the use of in-hand cryptographic and security techniques in the IoT is still an open issue, and needs further research to ensure that within the limited processor, memory, and power constraints, the traditional cryptographic and other security algorithms can be implemented in the IoT. A few of the most perilous attacks that aim to disrupt IoT protocols are discussed next.

8.7.1 DoS Attacks on L1-L3 Communication Protocol

In such types of attacks, an attacker specifically targets Layer 1 or Layer 3, and sends unwanted data, in bulk, over the radio carrier to disrupt wireless communications. On the media access control (MAC) layer, the attacker specifically sends his or her own packets to mix with the legitimate packets, thereby stopping the proper communication of the packets. IoT routing protocols, such as the routing information protocol (RIP), the border gateway protocol (BGP), open shortest path first (OSPF), and so on, are prone to security attacks such as impersonating attacks, spoofing attacks, falsification of routing packets, or selective forwarding [24].

8.7.2 Generic Attacks

The Internet has many schemes to combat the attacks launched by attackers targeting its upper-layer protocols. In such schemes, security architecture, intelligent firewall systems, and IDS are used; however, due to its low resources, the IoT system cannot use these in-hand schemes to secure its upper-layer protocols. So, the design of a robust security scheme to protect upper-layer protocols is vital.

8.7.3 Redirection Attacks

Internet control message protocol (ICMP) redirect, address resolution protocol (ARP) poisoning, and domain name system (DNS) poisoning are a few of the dangerous redirection attacks that mostly aim to disrupt the communication protocols stack. In this type of attack, the attacker first controls the communication packets and then changes the data or injects false data with devastating consequences for both the receiver and the sender.

8.8 Security Threats in Core IoT Technologies

The IoT is a combination of various novel and older technologies. Among these technologies, the most elementary and core technologies are RFID, NFC, and WSN. Due to their extremely open nature, these technologies are highly insecure and prone to security attacks. RFIDs are a widely used sensor technology that are vulnerable to malicious attacks. An attacker can simply jam or block a legitimate communication by producing malicious signals, such as radio signals, at the same frequency as the system. One of the major attacks on RFIDs is a relay attack, which utilizes the technique of fake tagging to communicate with the real reader. The information that the attacker receives is further used in illegal malicious activities. This type of attack may flourish if the range of RFIDs increases; therefore, the simplest solution to overcome this type of attack is to reduce the RFID range. However, a short-range tag is not a good solution to avoid a relay attack, as it may limit the scope of RFIDs. The RFIDs' communications are always under eavesdropping attack with the aim to disclose the communication between the RFID tag and the reader. To avoid these malicious activities, the RFIDs should be smart enough to detect and handle these intruders. A traditional IDS may not fit into this scenario because of its limited resources, energy, and computing power. Either the computing power of an IDS is increased or a new energy-efficient IDS is designed, which must utilize its limited resources of computing as well as energy.

WSNs could be one of the most widely used sensor networks for the IoT environment. Inherently, WSNs are insecure, their nodes are organized close to the start of the action, and they employ a wireless communication path for trading their messages. Consequently, any malicious attacker can control the WSN nodes, the communication channel, or the environment, and utilize all the resources for his or her benefit. Moreover, if that malicious attacker achieves right of entry to any node of the WSN, it might be possible to alter the flow of information that passes through the node. Hence, a sensor network, especially the WSN, should be equipped with the hardware or software to prevent or mitigate the consequences of such attacks. Table 8.3 reviews some of the most hazardous threats that can disrupt the most fundamental IoT technologies.

8.9 Security Threats in IoT Devices

As more and more devices are connecting to the IoT, there is a greater security risk and a higher chance of attacks. In the IoT environment, trillions of small and large devices are connecting to the IoT, but who is responsible for their security? Even an IoT device that acts like a node in a network can perform malicious activities. There is no guarantee that these devices will never carry out any malicious activity.

IoT devices are particularly vulnerable to physical attacks, software attacks, side-channel attacks, and so on. These types of perilous security attacks can easily disrupt the legitimate activity of IoT communicating devices [25].

Table 8.3 Security Threats in Core IoT Technologies

	Threats	*Key Component*	*Security Need*
RFID	DoS attacks	RFID tags and reader communications	Encryption
	Eavesdropping	User private data	Encryption
	Skimming	User private data	Shielding, blocking tags
	Relay attack	Authentication result	Synchronization
	Side-channel attack	User private data	Authentication
	Hardware destruction	Tags	Protective electronic component
	Software destruction	Commands	Key, password
NFC	Phishing attack	Application processor	Interfaces authentication
	User tracking	User privacy	Random UIDs
	Relay attacks	Tag/reader	Synchronization
	Confidentiality/data-forging attack	User data	SSL communication
	Malicious host	Application processor	Interfaces authentication
WSN	Wormhole	Multihop wireless network	Time limit on packets delivery
	Black-hole	Multihop wireless network	Protocol with good IDS
	Neighbor discovery	Network discovery protocol	Authentication supported protocol
	Spoofing	Wireless network	Packet authentication
	Ping Flood, ICMP Flood, Syn Flood	Network nodes	Use of IDS

Devices should be capable of guarding against network stoppages and attacks. The protocols should integrate mechanisms that counter anomalous conditions and permit the device to gracefully put down its service. Devices should be intelligent to bring into play the smart intrusion detection method and other protective mechanisms to combact malicious intruders. Table 8.4 provides a summary of the major attacks on IoT devices.

8.10 Privacy Issues in IoT

Billions of things are connected to the IoT and they produce huge amounts of public and private data. Public data does not require privacy, but in the case of private or secret data, comprehensive privacy is critical. IoT privacy protection seems an unavoidable dilemma. There is a thin line

Table 8.4 Security Threats in IoT Devices

Threats	*Attack Procedure*	*Security Requirement*	*Examples*
Physical attacks	Temper the hardware and other components.	Tamper resistance	Layout reconstruction, microprobing
Environment attacks	The devices encryption key can be known by the attacker by recovering the encryption information.	Secure encryption scheme	Timing attack, side-channel attack, fault analysis attack
Cryptanalysis attacks	Find ciphertext to break the encryption.	Secure encryption scheme	Known-plaintext attack, chosen plaintext attack
Software attacks	Exploit vulnerabilities in the system during its own communication interface and inject malicious codes.	Proper antivirus update	Trojan horse, worms, or viruses

between security and privacy, with security protecting against the exchange and processing of personal information. The main security parameters are authentication, confidentiality, and integrity, but privacy is mostly defined as transparency, verifiability, and right purpose.

Privacy directly conflicts with the basic ideology of the IoT, which is that anyone can be recognized anywhere at any time in an always-live fashion. The misuse of the omnipresent nature of the IoT may create immense privacy issues. Riahi et al. [26] discussed privacy as three parameters, that is, privacy in data sharing, collections, and management. Roman et al. [27] defined privacy in four ways: physical privacy, mental privacy, decision privacy, and information privacy. Actually, privacy in the IoT is a complex sociotechnical and legal issue. Privacy is sometimes linked with restrictions on individual liberty. Excessive implementation of privacy policies may create restrictions for IoT users that may limit the scope of the IoT. In point of fact, we can say that privacy is one of the most challenging and risky issues facing the IoT technology.

8.11 Security Requirements for IoT

The following sections outline the security needs or requirements of the IoT technology. The open nature of the IoT requires a comprehensive and concrete security solution for various security threats and attacks. As the technology grows, its security requirements will also become more demanding, challenging, and complex. The growing complexity of the IoT environment will also swell the number of security necessities. The following are a few of the most common security requirements for the IoT.

8.11.1 User Authentication

This security requirement is for every user who wants to communicate with the IoT system. The verification of one user among billions of users is a challenging security requirement of the IoT as a user's validity is critical for secure communication. Secure IoT communications should require mutual authentication between service provider and service user. For secure communications, the service providers and the service users must be authenticated, otherwise the security risks increase. The traditional registration or key authentication mechanism might not be good practice for the IoT because it may increase the delay in communication.

8.11.2 Tamper Resistance

This refers to the physical or logical security of IoT devices that must have high resilience against security attacks or any malicious activity. Tamper resistance from both physical damage or any malicious attack is one of the most fundamental security requirements of the IoT.

8.11.3 Secure Execution

The program or application execution environment in either hardware or software should be secure and well-designed to resist any unwanted action.

8.11.4 Secure Data Communication

A major security requirement for the IoT is to ensure secure data communication between and among various devices. Key management, authentication, identification, and security checks are the concern of secure data communications.

8.11.5 Identity Management

The conceptual idea behind the IoT is that the world's Things are becoming part of the Internet, where each object is distinctively or uniquely identified. The secure management of its identity is one of the fundamental IoT requirements.

8.11.6 Confidentiality

Confidentiality means that only authorized users have access permission to particular information [21]. The IoT system, particularly RFIDs, should not reveal any secret or sensitive information to illegal or unauthorized readers. IoT communications may contain sensitive data and the confidentiality of these data should be guaranteed. Traditionally, confidentiality is achieved through data encryption or through using cryptographic algorithms. It is debatable whether these in-hand confidentiality solutions can be utilized in the upcoming IoT. Mostly, encryption schemes are highly resource or device dependent, and IoT communications utilize numerous tiny sensors with limited resources; from this point of view, achieving confidentiality is a hard challenge for IoT researchers.

8.11.7 Auditing

The concept of auditing is to keep a record of the path of a user's interaction with the system. Complete data information, service utilization, and users and providers details can be achieved in auditing. Sometimes, auditing may look like a useless task, but during a security breach, auditing information is helpful to manage a security issue and to find out the reason for the security failure. Since IoT communication involves billions of Things, keeping an audit trail in such an environment is a challenging task.

8.11.8 Integrity

Integrity ensures that messages that are being conveyed are never despoiled. Integrity can be compromised primarily in two ways, either through malicious or accidental altering. In malicious altering, a malicious attacker interrupts a communication and changes, replays, removes, or revises the messages, but a transmission error is an accidental altering. The integrity of sensor data security is vital for designing trustworthy and reliable IoT applications (Figure 8.1).

8.12 Approaches to Mitigate IoT Issues

The following sections explicate the key solutions toward mitigating the issues of security, privacy, and vulnerabilities in the IoT.

8.12.1 How Can We Protect IoT Architecture?

The available architecture of the IoT is quite vulnerable and has various security issues and challenges. The following sections describe the key schemes to mitigate these security issues and challenges.

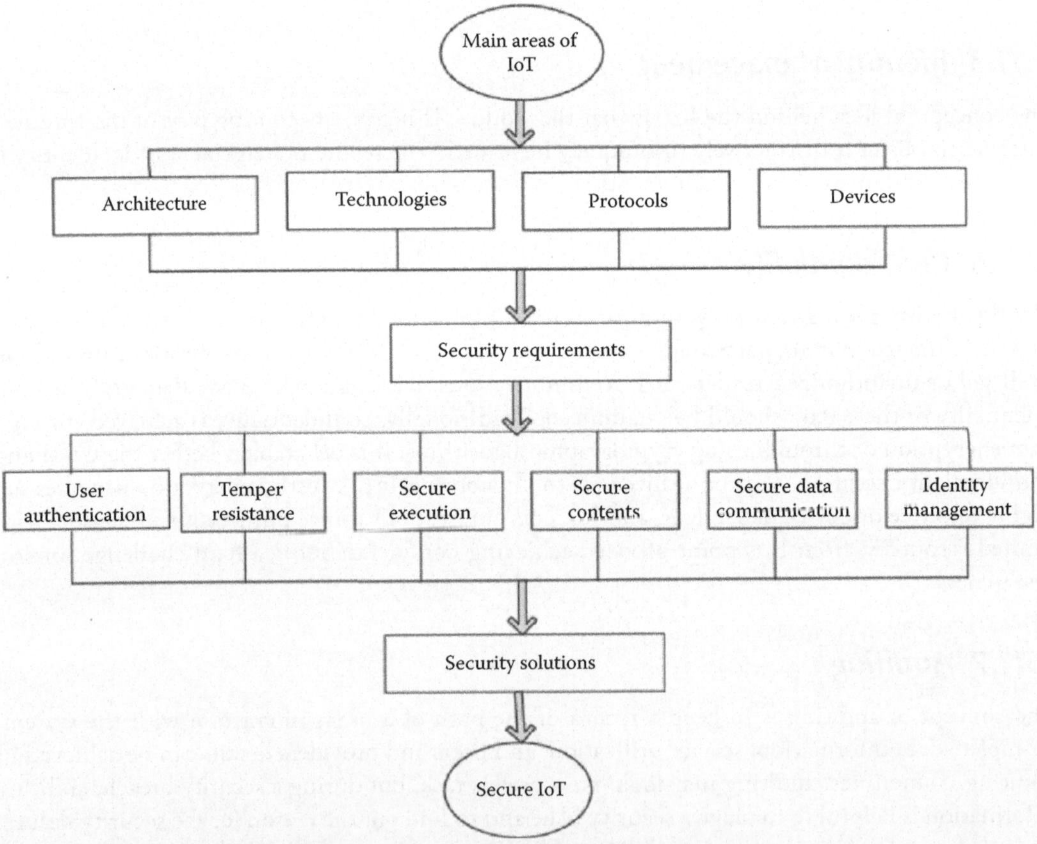

Figure 8.1 Security requirement for the IoT.

8.12.1.1 Perception Layer

1. Try to maintain *powerful* authentication with limited resources, because the perception layer has limited power and storage capacity.
2. Utilize lightweight cryptographic protocols and algorithms [23].
3. Node authentication, data encryption, and key management are absolute necessities for this layer.

8.12.1.2 Network Layer

1. A comprehensive study is required to determine whether existing communication security schemes should or should not be implemented.
2. For network node security, identity authentication mechanisms should be introduced [23].
3. A scheme should be introduced that ensures user data protection, confidentiality, integrity, and privacy.
4. The most common threat to this layer is the DDoS-type attack, so this layer should be secured with any intelligent IDS.

8.12.1.3 Application Layer

1. Privacy protection is one of the key elements of this layer (see previous section, "preventive measure against privacy issues").
2. Education about the disclosure of sensitive data and data management is vital to information security, particularly password management [28].
3. To prevent unauthorized access to the application layer, limit the rights of users [29].
4. For secure data communications, cryptography algorithms such as RSA must be used [30].

8.12.2 Protecting IoT Protocols against Security Threats

The IoT is a collection of various technologies, and to support their functions with seamless communication, protocols are vital. Robust, secure, and lightweight protocols are the true requirement for today's IoT.

The following are a few suggestions for enhancing the security of IoT protocols.

1. Use authentication with protocols, especially mutual authentication [22].
2. A comprehensive study is required to determine whether in-hand Internet security protocols should or should not be implemented in the IoT.
3. Can be utilized specially for IoT-designed web transfer protocols, for example, CoAP [31].
4. For constrained devices, commercial datagram transport layer security (DTLS) implementations are available [32].
5. Symmetric key–based protocols have high resilience to security attacks [33].

8.12.3 Protecting RFID

The communication between the network and RFID readers is considered a secure communication; however, communication between an RFID tag and reader is considered full of threats. Various malicious attacks could be possible during RFID tag and reader communication.

The following are a few schemes or methods that can mitigate the security risk of RFID communications.

1. The RFID Guardian is a gadget that can be utilized to prevent any invasive ciphering by actively generating jamming signals in the sidebands of a classic RFID tag, and monitoring the RFID environment for any attackers, especially eavesdroppers [34].
2. The RFID Guardian requires batteries to generate its own signal with a radius of about 50 cm; this signal protects the RFID [34]. In the literature [35], there is a simple solution to prevent a reader from examining RFID tags. To protect them, the RFID tags should be placed in a wallet made of metallic sheet. This strong wallet will obstruct malicious intruders by shielding the RFID tags from the high-frequency and the ultrahigh-frequency radio signals of eavesdropping attackers.

8.12.4 Protecting NFC

The following are a few schemes that can improve the security of NFC.

1. The UID of NFC can be tracked by malicious users; this issue can be mitigated by utilizing random UIDs.
2. To improve the confidentiality in NFC, provide security, such as secure sockets layer (SSL) communications, at the highest level.

8.12.5 Preventive Measures against Privacy Issues

The IoT technology has various challenges and issues and among them privacy is the most sensitive issue. Since the IoT technology claims that it is "always on," any and every object in the world can communicate at any time with each other. This claim generates many questions regarding users and the privacy of their private data. Users' information can be fetched automatically; this feature may increase privacy issues. To enhance privacy, transparency needs to be increased across the whole system, where users know who is managing their data and they have knowledge of stakeholders.

The biggest challenge for IoT researchers is to provide satisfactory answers about the users and their data privacy. In reality, privacy in the IoT (user, data, and object) is still an open research issue and needs more attention.

The following are a few suggestions for enhancing the privacy of IoT communications.

1. Entities that are involved in the IoT directly supervise their own data [36].
2. A specific privacy policy is required [22].
3. Ensure that privacy-enhancing technologies (PETs) present various communications, like multiparty computations prepared with PETs [37].
4. The author [38] has introduced a privacy coach, which seems to work well to improve privacy.
5. Urien and Elrharbi [39] discussed HIP-tag, which ensures privacy during object-to-object communications.
6. Kim et al. [40] proposed PAN Privacy Protection in Hand (PPPH) to protect consumer privacy.
7. For privacy improvement and robustness against privacy attacks, Fung and Al-Hussaeni proposed a novel model, named LKC-Privacy [41]. This is considered a vigorous scheme that combats privacy attacks.

8. A cryptographic solution and blocking scheme are introduced in [42], which describes the privacy issues in data collection modes.
9. The author [43] defines the Platform for Privacy Preferences (P3P) semantic web and some other privacy-preservation schemes such as t-closeness, 1-diversity, and k-anonymity.

8.13 Open Research Issues

The concept of the IoT is immense; billions of things talk to each other simultaneously, generating trillions of gigabytes of data in a fraction of a second. To manage such big data, heterogeneous networking environments, and secure ICTs, is a very big research challenge.

The following list presents some open research issues that could prevail in the IoT technology.

1. The main open research issue is how to achieve complete interoperability among interconnected devices with a high degree of intelligence and omnipresence, ensuring users' and their data's security, trust, and privacy [44].
2. One of the main open research issues is to design an encryption algorithm that consumes less energy and runs fast [45].
3. In the IoT, each object must have a unique identification, and to maintain and store this UID is the most challenging open research issue [45].
4. The enormous IoT framework will not support a single hardware and software platform. The practical implementation of the IoT requires smart and intelligent diverse systems, which are still an open research issue.
5. A model that supports decentralized authentication and trust is vital for the future IoT, which is still a challenge.
6. In the IoT, the data and the user's authentication use security keys, but the symmetric key management scheme validation, generation, and distribution is in its infancy, so further research is needed in this direction.
7. A privacy-preserving framework for a heterogeneous set of devices is a requirement for the IoT that is still missing.
8. IoT devices have limited power and resources, which points toward the need for power and resource-efficient encryption as well as a data protection scheme.
9. An artificial immune system for the IoT is still an open research issue.
10. In the IoT technology, the wireless security solution, particularly at the physical layer, is still vulnerable and prone to security attacks, so more research is required on this open issue.
11. Some of the open issues in the IoT architecture that require more consideration are: the proposed disseminated open-nature framework that has back-to-back characteristics through the interoperability of varied systems, fair access, unambiguous layering, and temper-resistance to a range of physical network attacks [45].
12. There is a need to design a power-saving communication using new protocol, frequency allocation, and a software-defined radio (SDR) that negates the requirements for recurrent upgrading of hardware for every new protocol.

8.14 Conclusion

This chapter provided a comprehensive study of the IoT security issues and challenges. The chapter was divided into four subdomains of the IoT: architecture, supporting technologies, core technologies, and protocols, to spell out their security, vulnerability, and challenges. The IoT services require the integration of several domains and each domain has its own security features, privacy, challenges, and constraints. To facilitate secure communication with billions of "Things" connections, ensuring security is the biggest challenge for this technology. With the intention of addressing these challenges, this chapter first explicated various security threats that could prevail in the IoT and also provided helpful solutions that mitigate security and vulnerability issues in this technology. This chapter also identified several open issues that may offer a new way of thinking about ways to enhance the IoT services. An exceptional distributed security framework for the IoT is urgently needed to secure the IoT technology.

Acknowledgments

We are grateful for the extended support of the Center for Research in Ubiquitous Computing, National University of Computer & Emerging Sciences, FAST-National University, Karachi, and the Federal Urdu University of Arts, Science and Technology, Karachi. A special thanks to Professor Dr. Zubair A. Shaikh, director of FAST-National University, for his valuable guidance in the completion of this study.

Author Biographies

Kashif Laeeq is currently pursuing a PhD in computer science in FAST-National University of Computer and Emerging Sciences, Karachi. He is an assistant professor in the Department of Computer Science at the Federal Urdu University of Arts, Science, and Technology, Karachi. He has published various research papers in journals and conferences. His research interests include cybersecurity, the Internet of Things, and wireless routing issues.

Jawwad A. Shamsi is an associate professor and head of the Computer Science Department at FAST-National University of Computer and Emerging Sciences, Karachi. He received his PhD from Wayne State University, Michigan, in 2009. His research interests include distributed systems, cloud computing, high-performance computing, and cyber and network security.

References

1. G. Santucci. From Internet to data to Internet of things. In *Proceedings of the International Conference on Future Trends of the Internet*, 2009.
2. L. Coetzee and J. Eksteen. The Internet of things—Promise for the future: An introduction. In *IST-Africa Conference Proceedings*, pp. 1–9, May 11–13, 2011.
3. ITU. Internet reports 2005: The Internet of things, ITU Internet report, 2005.
4. T. Obrien. In a nutshell: What are QR codes? Available: http://www.switched.com/2010/06/21/in-anutshell-what-are-r-codes/, 2010.
5. W. Zhang and B. Qu. Security architecture of the Internet of things oriented to perceptual layer. *International Journal on Computer, Consumer and Control (IJ3C)*, 2(2), pp. 37–45, 2013.
6. K. Bonsor and C. Keener. How RFID works, HowStuffWorks, 2010 http://electronics.howstuffworks.com/gadgets/high-tech-gadgets/rfid.htm.

7. International Telecommunication Union (ITU). *ITU Internet Report 2005: The Internet of Things*. Geneva: ITU, November 2005.
8. E. Welbourne, L. Battle, G. Cole, K. Gould, K. Rector, and S. Raymer. Building the Internet of things using RFID: The RFID ecosystem experience. *IEEE Internet Computing*, 13(3), pp. 48–55, 2009.
9. A. Juels. RFID security and privacy: A research survey. *IEEE Journal on Selected Areas Communications*, 24(2), pp. 381–394, 2006.
10. J. Yiek, D. Ghosal, and B. Mukherjee. Wireless sensor network survey. *Computer Networks*, 52(12), pp. 2292–2330, 2008.
11. H. Alemdar and C. Ersoy. Wireless sensor networks for healthcare: A survey. *Computer Networks*, 54(15), pp. 2688–2710, 2010.
12. D. Bandyopadhyay and J. Sen. Internet of things: Applications and challenges in technology and standardization. *Wireless Personal Communications*, 58(1), pp. 49–69, 2011.
13. P. Urien. LLCPS: A new security framework based on TLS for NFC P2P applications in the Internet of things. In *Proceedings of the IEEE Consumer Communications and Networking Conference (CCNC 2013)*, pp. 845–846, Las Vegas: IEEE, 2013.
14. M. Wu, T. Lu, and F. Ling. Research on the architecture of Internet of things. In *2010 3rd International Conference on Advanced Computer Theory and Engineering (ICACTE)*, vol. 5, pp. V5-484, V5-487.
15. O. Said. Development of an innovative Internet of things security system. *International Journal of Computer Science Issues (IJCSI)*, 10(6), pp. 155–161, 2013.
16. H. Suo, J. Wan, C. Zou, and J. Liu. Security in the Internet of things: A review. In *2012 International Conference on Computer Science and Electronics Engineering (ICCSEE)*, Vol. 3, pp. 648–651, Hangzhou: IEEE, March 23–25, 2012.
17. R. Roman, J. Zhou, and J. López. On the features and challenges of security and privacy in distributed Internet of Things. *Computer Networks*, 57(10), pp. 2266–2279, 2013.
18. A. Dunkels and J. P. Vasseur. IP for smart objects, Internet Protocol For Smart Objects (IPSO) Alliance, White Paper #1. URL: www.ipso-alliance.org/downloads/Security+Introduction, 2009.
19. A. Riahi, Y. Challal, E. Natalizio, Z. Chtourou, and A. Bouabdallah. A systemic approach for IoT security. In *2013 IEEE International Conference on Distributed Computing in Sensor Systems (DCOSS)*, pp. 351–355. Cambridge: IEEE, May 20–23, 2013.
20. Internet of Things Architecture (IoT-A). Project Deliverable D1.1—SOTA report on existing integration frameworks/architectures for WSN, RFID and other emerging IoT related technologies. Available: www.iot-a.eu/public/public-documents/d1.5/at_download/file.
21. A. Pescape and G. Ventre. Experimental analysis of attacks against intradomain routing protocols. *Journal of Computer Security*, 13(6), pp. 877–903, 2005.
22. M. R. Rieback, G. N. Gaydadjiev, B. Crispo, R. F. H. Hofman, and A. S. Tanenbaum. A platform for RFID security and privacy administration. In *20th USENIX/SAGE Large Installation System Administration Conference (LISA 2006)*, Washington, DC, December 2006.
23. M. C Domingo. An overview of the Internet of things for people with disabilities. *Journal of Network and Computer Applications*, 35(2), pp. 584–596, 2012.
24. T. Heer and O. Garcia. Security challenges in the IP-based Internet of things. *Wireless Personal Communication*, 61(3), pp. 527–542, 2011.
25. M. Brachmann, S. L. Keoh, O. G. Morchon, and S. S. Kumar. End-to-end transport security in the IP-based Internet of things. In *21st International Conference on Computer Communications and Networks (IC-CCN'12)*, pp. 1–5, Munich: IEEE, 2012.
26. Mocana–NanoDTLS. https://mocana.com/products.html. Accessed November, 2012.
27. R. Roman, C. Alcaraz, J. Lopez, and N. Sklavos. Key management systems for sensor networks in the context of the Internet of things. *Computers & Electrical Engineering*, 37(2), pp. 147–159, 2011.
28. A. Cavoukian. *Privacy by Design... Take the Challenge*. Canada: Information and Privacy Commissioner of Ontario, 2009.
29. V. Oleshchuk. Internet of things and privacy preserving technologies. In *1st International Conference on Wireless Communication, Vehicular Technology, Information Theory and Aerospace & Electronics Systems Technology (WirelessVITAE'09)*, pp. 336–340, Aalborg: IEEE, 2009.

30. G. Broenink, J.-H. Hoepman, C. van't Hof, R. van Kranenburg, D. Smits, and T. Wisman. The privacy coach: Supporting customer privacy in the Internet of things. In *Pervasive 2010 Conference Workshop on What Can the Internet of Things Do for the Citizen? (CIoT'10)*, Helsinki, Finland, pp. 72–81, 2010.
31. P. Urien and S. Elrharbi. HIP-Tags architecture implementation for the Internet of things. In *First Asian Himalayas International Conference on Internet*, pp. 1–5, Kathmandu: IEEE, November 2009.
32. E. Kim, T. Kwon, and J. H. Yi. A study of mobile proxy for privacy enhancement. In *2010 Digest of Technical Papers International Conference on Consumer Electronics (ICCE 10)*, pp. 177–178, January 2010.
33. B. Fung and Al-Hussaeni. Preserving RFID data privacy. In *IEEE International Conference on RFID*, pp. 200–207, Orlando: IEEE, April 2009.
34. SmartProducts. Available: http://www.smartproducts-project.eu.
35. QR code.com. Available: http://www.qrcode.com.
36. C. Ding, L. J. Yang, and M. Wu. Security architecture and key technologies for IoT/CPS. *ZTE Technology Journal*, 17(1), 2011.
37. Q. Gou and L. Yan. Construction and strategies in IoT security system. In *IEEE Conference on Green Computing and Communications and IEEE Internet of Things and IEEE Cyber, Physical and Social Computing*, pp. 1129–1132. Beijing: IEEE, 2013.
38. S. Babar, A. Stango, N. Prasad, J. Sen, and R. Prasad. Proposed embedded security framework for Internet of Things (IoT). In *Wireless Communication, Vehicular Technology, Information Theory and Aerospace and Electronic Systems Technology*, pp. 1–5, Chennai: IEEE, February 2011.
39. D. Bandyopadhyay and J. Sen. The Internet of Things: Applications and challenges in technology and standardization. *Springer International Journal of Wireless Personal Communications*, 58(1), pp. 49–69, 2011.
40. L. Heuser, Z. Nochta, N.-C. Trunk. *ICT Shaping the World: A Scientific View, ETSI*. New York: Wiley, 2008.
41. M. Shivlal and S. U. Kumar. Performance analysis of secure wireless mesh networks. *Research Journal of Recent Sciences*, 1(3), pp. 80–85, 2012.
42. P. Ali, M. Kambiz, and S. S. Mohammad. Fault-tolerant and information security in networks using multi-level redundant residue number system. *Research Journal of Recent Sciences*, 3(3), pp. 89–92, 2014.
43. H. Suo, J. Wan, C. Zou, and J. Liu. Security in the Internet of things: A review. In *Proceedings of International Conference on Computer Science and Electronics Engineering*, Hangzhou, China, pp. 648–651, 2012.
44. D. Chen, G. Chang, and L. Jin. A novel secure architecture for the Internet of things. In *Proceedings International Conference on Genetic and Evolutionary Computing (ICGEC)*, Washington, DC, pp. 311–314, 2011.
45. X. Sun, C. Wang, D. Jin, and S. Lin. The research of security technology in the Internet of things. *Advances in Computer Science, Intelligent System and Environment. Advances in Intelligent and Soft Computing*, Volume 105. Berlin: Springer, pp. 113–119, 2011.

Chapter 9

Security and Privacy in the IPv6-Connected Internet of Things

Shahid Raza
SICS Swedish ICT

Chamath Keppitiyagama
University of Colombo

Thiemo Voigt
SICS Swedish ICT and Uppsala University

Contents

9.1 Introduction 242
9.2 Background: IoT Protocols 244
9.2.1 IPv6 over Low-Power Personal Area Network 244
9.2.2 Constrained Application Protocol 245
9.2.3 Routing Protocol for Low-Power and Lossy Network 245
9.3 Security in Constrained Environments 245
9.3.1 Message Security 246
9.3.1.1 Per-Hop Security 247
9.3.1.2 E2E Security at the Network Layer 248
9.3.1.3 E2E Security at the Transport Layer 248
9.3.2 Network Security 249
9.3.3 Data Security 250
9.3.4 Standardization of IoT Security 250
9.3.4.1 Internet Engineering Task Force 251
9.3.4.2 Open Management Group 251

9.3.4.3 Bluetooth Low Energy 251
9.4 Privacy Challenges in the IoT 251
9.4.1 Things and Privacy 252
9.4.1.1 Scale and Ubiquity 252
9.4.1.2 Sensing Capabilities 252
9.4.1.3 Resource Constraints 253
9.4.1.4 Radio Signals 253
9.4.2 Internet Protocols and Privacy 253
9.4.2.1 Third-Party Services 253
9.4.2.2 Cookies 253
9.4.2.3 Media Access Control Protection 254
9.4.2.4 Network Address Translation 254
9.4.2.5 Semantics and Annotations 254
9.4.3 Promising Privacy Solutions 254
9.4.3.1 Privacy Aware Design 254
9.4.3.2 Privacy Preserving with Homomorphic Encryption 255
9.4.3.3 k-Anonymity 255
9.4.3.4 Legal Frameworks 255
9.4.3.5 Education 255
9.5 Conclusions 256
Author Biographies 256
References 257

Abstract: With the standardization of the Internet of Things (IoT) protocols, the development of new sensor hardware, the proliferation of smart cities solutions, and interest from governments and funding organizations, the vision of 50 billion connected devices by 2020 is becoming a reality. The Internet protocol version 6 (IPv6) and the standardization of novel IoT protocols such as IPv6 over low-power personal area network (6LoWPAN) are driving forces toward the IoT. On the one hand, the IoT offers tremendous possibilities to develop new applications; on the other hand, it poses new security and privacy threats. Also, unlike conventional resource-constrained networks such as wireless sensor networks (WSNs), security is one of the main requirements in the IoT. Providing security and privacy is a challenge in the conventional Internet and it is even more challenging in the IPv6-connected IoT because of global connectivity, heterogeneous and resource-constrained devices, and direct human intervention. In this chapter, we highlight the security and privacy requirements of the IoT, review the current security and privacy solutions that fit the IoT, and discuss the possibilities and research challenges of developing novel security and privacy solutions for the IoT.

9.1 Introduction

The Internet of Things (IoT) is a global network of uniquely identifiable physical objects, their interconnection with the Internet, and their representation in the digital or virtual world. Therefore, the IoT is a heterogeneous mix of constrained devices such as sensor nodes, smartphones, and conventional Internet hosts such as standard computers. Ericsson and Cisco's vision of 50 billion connected devices by 2020 is becoming a reality. A wide range of technologies form the IoT and enable identification, localization, networking, web support, and so on. The Internet protocol version 6 (IPv6) with potentially unlimited address space offers unique identification and the interconnection of almost every physical object with the Internet. Most IoT devices (called *things*) are battery-powered nodes with limited processing and storage capabilities. With IPv6 over low-power personal area networks (6LoWPANs) [1,2], it is possible to efficiently use IP in constrained environments such as wireless sensor networks (WSNs). IPv6/6LoWPAN offers interoperability and scalability, it eliminates the need for complex gateways between constrained devices and the Internet, and it has readily available software and a pool of experts, which lead to ease of programming. Further, the constrained application protocol (CoAP) [3], a variant of the hypertext transfer protocol (HTTP) for constrained environments, provides web support for the IoT. The recently standardized IPv6 routing protocol for low-power and lossy networks (RPL) [4] is a routing protocol for constrained networks in the IoT. With these novel technologies, the IoT enables new applications such as smart energy, item and shipment tracking, health monitoring, logistics management, home automation, and smart cities. Figure 9.1 shows an IoT setup using these recently standardized technologies.

Unlike conventional WSNs where security is mostly ignored in real deployments, security in the IoT is a requirement [5]. We would be happy to remotely turn on/off our thermostat using a smartphone application, but we would certainly not allow any random Internet-connected device to control the thermostat. Providing security is challenging in WSNs and in the Internet, but it is even more challenging in the IoT as the devices are expected to have IPv6 and web support,

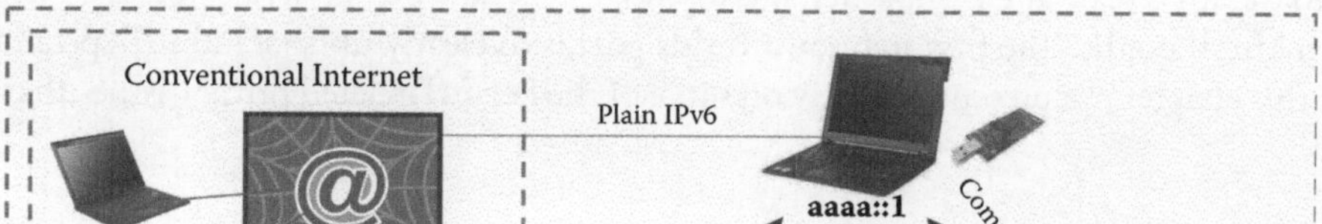

Figure 9.1 An interconnection between the Internet and constrained networks using the novel IoT technologies 6LoWPAN, CoAP, and RPL, which provide IPv6 support, web capabilities, and routing, respectively.

be globally accessible, heterogeneous (consisting of things, smartphones, standard computers, clouds), often deployed in unguarded environments, and use recent, less-tested IoT protocols such as 6LoWPAN, CoAP, and RPL. In addition, constrained environments in the IoT inherit the restraints of WSNs, such as limited energy, processing resources, lossy wireless links, and multi-hop communication.

In addition to (i) the communication security that ensures end-to-end (E2E) confidentiality and the integrity of messages in the IoT, it is essential to enable (ii) network security to protect constrained networks/nodes against trespass from the Internet or vice versa. Today, hackers are quite successful in compromising physically protected Internet hosts and creating fake networks (called *botnets*); it would be relatively easy to compromise tiny things to create so-called thingbots. In the IoT, it is also vital to (iii) safeguard the data that is stored inside constrained devices. In this chapter, we will discuss the state-of-the-art security solutions for the conventional Internet and their applicability and feasibility in billions of resource-constrained connected IoT devices.

Internet privacy, which is often neglected, should go hand in hand with security. The tools and technology for privacy in the conventional Internet are yet to mature. The prevalence of the large number of things in the IoT makes privacy an even more challenging issue than in the conventional Internet. The large number of devices that are intimately associated with a person, such as mobile phones, are already connected to the IoT. In addition, more and more devices that collect data on environments that people inhabit are also being deployed. So far, we do not have a clear understanding of the privacy issues related to these devices or mature technology to deal with these privacy issues.

Due to the IoT's scale and complexity, it is essential to handle privacy as a core design issue rather than as an afterthought. The first step toward this goal is to clearly understand IoT-specific privacy issues. In this chapter, we present our view on some of the key IoT-related privacy issues that we have identified.

9.2 Background: IoT Protocols

This section highlights the novel IoT technologies that have been designed primarily for the IPv6-connected IoT.

9.2.1 IPv6 over Low-Power Personal Area Network

6LoWPAN incorporates IP-based infrastructures and WSNs by specifying how IPv6 packets are to be transmitted in constrained networks such as IEEE 802.15.4 networks. To achieve this, the 6LoWPAN standard proposes context-aware header compression mechanisms: the IP header compression (IPHC) for the IPv6 header, next header compression (NHC) for the IPv6 extension headers, and the user datagram protocol (UDP) header. Due to the limited payload size of the link layer in 6LoWPANs, the 6LoWPAN standard also defines fragmentation and reassembly of a datagram. 6LoWPAN defines a fragmentation scheme in which every fragment contains a reassembly tag and an offset. When security is enabled or for large amounts of application data, the IEEE 802.15.4 frame size may exceed the maximum transmission unit (MTU) size of 127 bytes; in that case, additional fragment(s) are needed.

In order to allow compression of header-like structures in the UDP payload and the layers above, an extension to the 6LoWPAN header compression, called generic header compression (GHC), is also defined [5]. 6LoWPANs are connected to the Internet through the 6LoWPAN border router (6BR) that is analogous to a sink in a WSN. The 6BR performs compression/decompression and fragmentation/assembly of IPv6 datagrams.

9.2.2 Constrained Application Protocol

Due to the low power and lossy nature of 6LoWPANs in the IoT, the connectionless UDP instead of the stream-oriented transmission control protocol (TCP) is mostly used in the IoT. The synchronous HTTP is designed for the TCP and it is not feasible to use in the UDP-based IoT. Therefore, CoAP, a subset of the HTTP, is standardized as a web protocol for the IoT. Although CoAP specifies a representational state transfer (REST) interface analogous to HTTP, it is tailored for constrained devices and for machine-to-machine communication, and focuses on being more lightweight and commercially viable than its variant for today's Internet.

9.2.3 Routing Protocol for Low-Power and Lossy Network

Routing in constrained networks in the IoT, with limited energy and channel capacity, is achieved using the recently standardized IPv6 RPL. The RPL protocol creates a destination-oriented directed acyclic graph (DODAG) that aims to prune path cost to the directed acyclic graph (DAG) root. RPL supports both unidirectional traffic to a DODAG root (typically the 6BR) and bidirectional traffic between constrained nodes and a DODAG root. Each node in the DODAG has a node ID (an IPv6 address), one or more parents (except for the DODAG root), and a list of neighbors. Nodes have a rank that determines their location relative to their neighbors and with respect to the DODAG root. The rank should always increase from the DODAG root toward the nodes. In-network routing tables are maintained to separate packets that are heading upward and packets that are heading downward in the network; this is called the *storing mode.* RPL also supports the nonstoring mode where intermediate nodes do not store any routes.

9.3 Security in Constrained Environments

IoT technologies are getting ready to transform the way that we work and live; however, one problem that can hinder this transition is sag in security and privacy. IPv6 offers the interconnection of almost every physical object with the Internet. This leads to tremendous possibilities to develop new applications for the IoT, such as home automation and home security management, smart energy monitoring and management, item and shipment tracking, surveillance and the military, smart cities, health monitoring, and logistics monitoring and management. Due to the global connectivity and sensitivity of applications, security in real deployments in the IoT is a requirement [5]. Confidentiality, data integrity, source integrity or authentication, availability, and replay protection are necessary security services in the IoT.

Confidentiality or Data Privacy: An attacker could easily intercept messages that flow between a source and a destination and reveal secret contents. Therefore, these messages should be hidden from the intermediate entities; in other words, E2E message secrecy is required in the IoT. Also, the stored data inside an IoT device should be hidden from unauthorized entities. Confidentiality services ensure this through encryption/decryption.

Data Integrity: No intermediary between a source and a destination should be able to change the secret contents of messages, for example, the medical data of a patient, without being detected.

Also, stored data should not be modified without being detected. Message integrity codes (MIC) are mostly used to provide this service.

Source Integrity or Authentication: Communicating end points should be able to verify the identity of each other to ensure that they are communicating with the entities that they claim to be. Different authentication schemes exist [6].

Availability: For the smooth working of the IoT and access to data whenever needed, it is also important that the services that applications offer should always be available and work properly. In other words, intrusions and malicious activities should be detected. Intrusion detection systems (IDSs) and firewalls, in addition to the abovementioned security mechanisms, are used to ensure the availability of security services.

Replay Protection: Last but not least, a compromised intermediate node can store a data packet and replay it at a later stage. The replayed packet can contain a typical sensor reading (e.g., a temperature reading) or a paid service request. It is therefore important that there should be mechanisms to detect duplicate or replayed messages. Replay protection or freshness security services provide these mechanisms through integrity-protected time stamps, sequence numbers, nonce, and so on.

In order to provide multifaceted security, we must ensure E2E message (communication) security in the IoT, network security in constrained IoT domains such as 6LoWPANs, and data-at-rest security to protect stored secrets and data in things. Figure 9.2 depicts multifaceted security in the IoT.

9.3.1 Message Security

The IoT is a hybrid network comprising the Internet and constrained networks. Communication in the IoT can be secured with (i) lightweight security protocols that are proposed for constrained environments such as WSNs, (ii) novel security protocols that meet the specific requirements of the IoT, or (iii) established security protocols that are already used in the Internet.

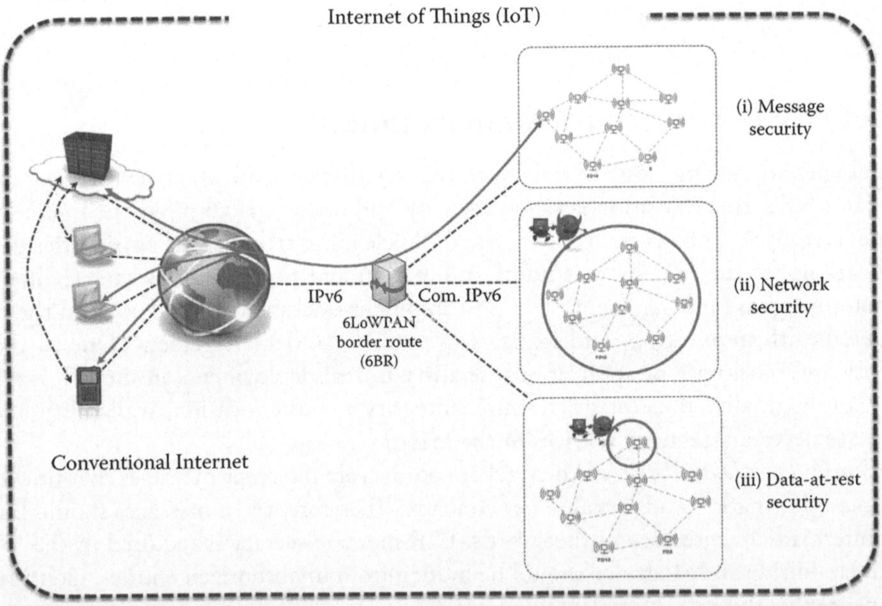

Figure 9.2 Multifaceted security is needed for the IoT: (i) message security, (ii) network security, (iii) and protection of stored secrets.

The security protocols that are proposed for WSNs are not designed for IP networks. Therefore, their use in the IoT requires a modification of these protocols and corresponding provisioning in the current Internet. Designing novel security protocols for the IoT may result in more efficient and lightweight solutions; however, such protocols would require changes in the Internet. As the current Internet consists of billions of hosts, any security solution that requires modifications to the current Internet is not practical. It is, however, worth investigating the applicability of established Internet security technologies in the IoT. Standards are important to achieve interoperability among devices from different vendors. A problem that may hinder the use of these security solutions in the IoT is that IP is not designed for resource-constrained devices but for more powerful computers. In this section, we review the current work on communication security in the IoT with a special focus on standard-based security solutions.

Messages in the IoT must be E2E protected with confidentiality and integrity services. Also, integrity protection should be employed on a per-hop base in wirelessly connected, constrained networks. Toward this end, network and upper-layer security solutions can ensure E2E security between constrained IoT devices and conventional Internet hosts, whereas security at the data-link layer protects messages on a per-hop base between two neighboring devices. Figure 9.3 shows an IoT stack with standardized IoT protocols and the corresponding security solutions at different layers.

9.3.1.1 Per-Hop Security

Security solutions at the link layer protect communications on a per-hop base. They require that every node on the communication path is trusted. 6LoWPAN uses the IEEE 802.15.4 protocol [8] at the link layer. Its security mechanisms [9] present the current state-of-the-art per-hop security solution for the IoT. A single pre-shared key is used to protect all communications. An attacker who compromises one device by gaining access to the key, can compromise the security of the whole network. Unlike E2E solutions, per-hop security can detect message modifications on each hop. Therefore, per-hop security with at least integrity protection should be used in 6LoWPANs to prevent unauthorized access through the radio medium, and to defend against attacks that are launched to waste constrained resources. Although link-layer security is limited to securing the communication link between two neighboring devices, it is a flexible option that can operate with multiple protocols at

E2E security ↑ Flexibility ↓

Stack layer	Communication protocol	Security protocol	Implications
Application	CoAP, HTTP	CoAPs, HTTPs	E2E (e.g, object security)
Transport/ session	UDP, TCP	DTLS, TLS	E2E
Network	IPv6, RPL	IPsec (RPL security)	Node level E2E (IPsec is mandatory in IPv6)
6LoWPAN	6LoWPAN	-	Compression and fragmentation of upper-layer header
Data link	IEEE 802.15.4	IEEE 802.15.4 security	Per hop

Figure 9.3 Security solutions at different layers of the IoT stack: Upper-layer security protocols are E2E but are less flexible as they are bound to specific communication protocols.

the layers above. For example, with link-layer security enabled, we can run both IP and non-IP at the network layer. In our previous work, we implemented and evaluated IEEE 802.15.4 security for the Contiki operating system (OS) on real hardware in an IoT setup [10]. Wood et al. [11] also proposed a solution to secure link-layer communication in TinyOS for IEEE 802.15.4-based WSN.

9.3.1.2 E2E Security at the Network Layer

In the Internet and hence in the IoT, security at the network layer is provided by the IP security (IPsec) protocol suite [12–14]. IPsec in transport mode provides E2E security with authentication and replay protection services in addition to confidentiality and integrity. By operating at the network layer, IPsec can be used with any upper-layer protocol including TCP, UDP, HTTP, and CoAP. IPsec ensures the confidentiality and integrity of the IP payload using the encapsulated security payload (ESP) protocol [14], and the integrity of the IP header plus payload using the authentication header (AH) protocol [12]. IPsec is mandatory in the IPv6 protocol [15], meaning that all IPv6-ready devices by default have IPsec support, which may be enabled at any time. Being a network layer solution, IPsec security services are shared among all applications running on a device, that is, IPsec is not a per-application unique security solution. Although the Internet key exchange (IKE) [16] protocol can be used to establish application-specific security associations, it is a chatty protocol and is based on certificate-based cryptography that is heavy for resource-constrained nodes. Since IPsec is lighter than datagram transport layer security (DTLS) and is mandatory in IPv6, and application developers do not need to take care of security if IPsec is used, IPsec is one of the most suitable options for E2E security in the IoT, as mostly only one application runs on a constrained device and the default security policies, without IKE processing, are enough for such scenarios. Furthermore, application developers need to make comparatively little effort to enable IPsec on IPv6 hosts, as it can be implemented at the network layer by device vendors.

To make IPsec feasible for the IoT, we have developed a lightweight IPsec for resource-constrained devices [17]. By applying 6LoWPAN header compression, we reduce the number of transmitted bits and hence decrease the IPsec header size, which results in a lower number of bits being transmitted and more space for application data, and may avoid 6LoWPAN fragmentation; ultimately, we reduce the total energy consumption by trading expensive radio communication for cheaper central processing unit (CPU) processing. Granjal et al. also investigate the use of IPsec for 6LoWPAN [18]. However, they do not provide the exact specifications of the required 6LoWPAN headers. Furthermore, no implementation is provided and no detailed evaluation of the possible communication performance is given. In their study, they analyze the execution times and memory requirements of the cryptographic algorithms that they propose for 6LoWPAN/IPsec integration. Recently, Jorge et al. [19] have extended our 6LoWPAN compressed IPsec and included support for IPsec in tunnel mode. They have implemented and evaluated their proposal in TinyOS.

9.3.1.3 E2E Security at the Transport Layer

Transport layer security (TLS) guarantees E2E security of different applications on one machine by operating between the transport and the application layers. Although IPsec can be used in the IoT, it is not primarily designed for web protocols such as HTTP or CoAP. For web protocols, TLS or its predecessor secure sockets layer (SSL) is the most common security solution. The connection-oriented TLS protocol can only be used over a stream-oriented TCP, which is not the preferred method of communication for smart objects; due to the lossy nature of low-power wireless networks, it is hard to maintain a continuous connection in 6LoWPANs. An adaptation of TLS for UDP, called DTLS [20], is available. DTLS in addition to TLS, which provides authentication, confidentiality, integrity, and replay protection, also provides protection against denial-of-service (DoS) attacks with the use of cookies. Although DTLS provides application-level E2E security, it can only be used in addition to the UDP; TLS is used over the TCP. The secure web protocol for the IoT, secure CoAP (CoAPs), mandates the use of DTLS as the underlying security solution for the CoAP. Therefore, it is necessary to enable DTLS support in the secure CoAP-based IoT.

Like IPsec, DTLS was developed for the conventional Internet, but researchers have optimized DTLS for constrained devices. Foulagar et al. [21] propose a TLS implementation for smart objects that involves the BR to reduce the cryptographic computational effort on smart objects. The introduction of a trusted BR breaks full E2E security. One could simply propose to use DTLS in 6LoWPANs and TLS in the Internet; Brachmann et al. [22] propose TLS–DTLS mapping to protect the IoT. Their solution also requires the presence of a trusted BR that breaks E2E security. In scenarios where it is possible to trust BRs, the two abovementioned solutions are viable to protect the IoT. Kothmayr et al. [23] investigate DTLS in 6LoWPANs with a trusted platform module (TPM); this solution requires specialized hardware. Granjal et al. [24] evaluate the use of DTLS as it is with CoAP for secure communication. They note that payload space scarcity would be problematic with applications that require larger payloads. As an alternative, they suggest to employ security at other networking layers such as a compressed form of IPsec. Brachmann et al. [25] provide an overview of state-of-the-art security solutions for CoAP-based applications, and discuss the feasibility of DTSL, TLS, IPsec, or a combination of these for E2E security and secure multicast communication. They assume pre-shared keys in their proposals due to the resource-constrained nature of the nodes. These solutions either review the use of (D)TLS in the IoT or they propose architectures that break E2E security.

We have reduced the overhead of DTLS in a CoAP-based IoT by employing 6LoWPAN header compression mechanisms, and implemented and evaluated it in an IoT setup on real hardware [26]. Our solution is DTLS standard compliant and ensures E2E security between CoAP applications. However, we rely on symmetric pre-shared keys for the initial authentication during the handshake. Recently [27], we have proposed solutions to optimize the heavyweight asymmetric cryptographic operations to reduce the overhead of the two-way certificate-based DTLS handshake. We have developed and evaluated (i) prevalidation of certificates at the trusted 6BR, (ii) session resumption to avoid the overhead of a full handshake, and (iii) handshake delegation to the owner of the resource-constrained device. This work in making certificate-based authentication viable for the IoT is complementary to our work on compressed DTLS.

Summary: IoT devices are resource constrained and we need to achieve a trade-off between performance and security. For that, it is necessary to employ optimization mechanisms at different layers and phases of security protocols. We proposed to use (i) 6LoWPAN header compression for security protocols too, such as at the network (IPsec) [10] or transport (TLS/DTLS) [26] layers; (ii) session resumption and DTLS handshake delegation mechanisms [27]; (iii) lightweight cryptography such as short public key infrastructure (PKI) certificates; and/or (iv) crypto chips [23].

9.3.2 Network Security

Although communication security protects messages with confidentiality and integrity services, attacks to breach network availability are possible. These attacks aim to disrupt networks, for example, by launching DoS attacks or by trashing the routing topology. In the IoT, 6LoWPANs are vulnerable to attacks both from the Internet and from inside the network. Also, 6LoWPANs with E2E connectivity with the Internet pose a serious threat to the current Internet as it is relatively easier to compromise resource-constrained wireless nodes than conventional Internet hosts, in particular when the nodes are deployed in unattended areas. IDSs are required to detect impostors and malicious activities in IoT networks, and firewalls are necessary to block unauthorized access to them.

RPL, a standardized IoT routing protocol [4], is prone to several routing attacks [28,29]. The IoT with 6LoWPANs running RPL, as shown in Figure 9.1, forms a network setup that is different from the typical WSNs. In conventional WSNs, there is usually no central control point and nodes are uniquely identified only within the WSN. In IoT networks, as in Figure 9.1, a 6BR is always accessible and sensor nodes are globally identified by a unique IP address. Considering the novel characteristics of the IoT, one can investigate the applicability of current IDSs and firewall techniques in the IoT, or design a novel IDS and firewall exploiting the contemporary IoT features and protocols. We have designed, implemented, and evaluated a lightweight firewall and an IDS for the RPL-connected 6LoWPANs, called SVELTE [30]. Our IDS can detect sinkhole, selective-forwarding, and spoofing attacks. This work needs further investigation to decrease the number of false positives and to detect other attacks such as wormholes. Recently, Matsunaga et al. [31] proposed a solution to improve the false-positive rate of SVELTE.

9.3.3 Data Security

It is important not only to protect communication and networks but also to safeguard the stored sensitive data in an IoT device. Most IoT devices are wirelessly connected, resource-constrained nodes. It is neither possible to physically guard all devices nor practical to protect them with hardware-based, tamper-resistant technologies such as smart cards or TPMs [32]. Moreover, IoT devices are supposed to be cheap and can be deployed in large quantities. It can be expected that devices will be thrown away at the end of their lifespan and that a proper decommissioning process in which data would be securely erased will not be commercially viable.

Various software-based solutions exist that can be used to cryptographically secure stored data on nodes [33–35]. These solutions use traditional secure storage models where data is encrypted and stored along with its hash. When a remote host requests stored data, the data is decrypted, its hash is verified, reencrypted, and hashed with communication security protocols, and sent. For resource-constrained IoT devices, these double cryptographic operations can be reduced to single encryption/decryption operations by securing the data with communication security protocols before storing it. This leads to several challenges such as the consideration of IP datagram header contents of future transmissions; we have investigated these challenges in combined secure storage and communication in the IoT [36]. Our evaluation with the IPsec protocol suite shows that 70% of a device's security-related processing can be reduced with a combined secure storage and communication approach. Future research should extend this approach to other IoT security protocols such as DTLS.

9.3.4 Standardization of IoT Security

Standards ensure superior product quality, an open competitive market, safety and reliability, interoperability among vendors, and so on. For billions of interconnected IoT devices, it is very important that the devices and networks are built on an open standardized protocol. Different IoT standardization efforts are underway and we highlight some of the important activities.

9.3.4.1 Internet Engineering Task Force

The Internet Engineering Task Force (IETF) is a major force behind the standardization of IoT protocols. The IETF's Constrained Restful Environments (CoRE), Routing Over Low-Power and Lossy Networks (ROLL), and 6LoWPAN working groups (WGs) have already standardized 6LoWPAN, CoAP, RPL, and a bunch of other supporting standards for the IoT. Currently, the IPv6 Over Networks of Resource-Constrained Nodes (6Lo), IPv6 Over the TSCH Mode of IEEE 802.15.4e (6TiSCH), and Lightweight Implementation Guidance (LWIG) WGs are working on further standardization of IoT protocols.

The DTLS in Constrained Environments (DICE) and Authentication and Authorization for Constrained Environments (ACE) WGs are primarily working on the standardization of security protocols for the IoT. The DICE WG is focusing on the adaptation of DTLS in constrained environments, and the ACE WG is working on authentication and authorization in constrained devices.

9.3.4.2 Open Management Group

In the IoT security domain, the Open Management Group (OMG), using the IETF security protocols, primarily develops solutions for security management. A unique contribution of the OMG in the IoT security domain is the secure bootstrapping of IoT devices where the IETF is not very active.

9.3.4.3 Bluetooth Low Energy

Bluetooth Low Energy (BLE)-enabled devices are expected to get a considerable share in future IoT domains. The Bluetooth 4.1 standard incorporates BLE, meaning that all upcoming Bluetooth devices are going to support and will be interoperable with low-powered Bluetooth-enabled IoT devices (Bluetooth things). Security is in-built in BLE; however, it is not using asymmetric cryptography. This makes BLE things less secure than things that can use asymmetric cryptography such as DTLS. The latest BLE standard, Bluetooth 4.2, introduces the Bluetooth IP support profile (IPSP) that can enable IPv6 and 6LoWPAN support in BLE.

Other standardization efforts for the IoT protocols with built-in security are also being carried out, for example, in ZigBee-IP, ISA100.11a, and WirelessHART.

9.4 Privacy Challenges in the IoT

The right to privacy is enshrined in Article 12 of The Universal Declaration of Human Rights. However, this right is increasingly threatened by the rapid growth of networked devices. Web usage, especially online social networking, has well-known privacy implications. Privacy concerns are more serious for mobile users as mobile devices are tightly coupled with individuals. In the IoT, the threat to users' privacy is even more severe because of the ubiquitous sensing of the everyday activities of individuals who often do not even notice when sensitive personal information is being sent over the Internet. This results in massive active and passive digital footprints tightly coupled with humans, which pose a serious threat to personal privacy.

IoT devices are diverse in many aspects, but by definition they all have an IP stack. Hence, the privacy issues related to the conventional Internet are also applicable to the IoT. For example, privacy issues related to the HTTP, such as the use of cookies and third-party services, impact smartphones as well. Some IoT devices push data onto the cloud and from that point onward any privacy issue related to the cloud also affects them. In addition, IoT devices also pose some peculiar privacy issues. Therefore, it is convenient to discuss the privacy issues related to IP and things-specific privacy issues separately.

9.4.1 Things and Privacy

According to the EU directive on privacy, a privacy concern arises when information can be related to the identifiable or identified natural person (Regulation 45/2001). The envisaged 50 billion devices by 2020 make the task of ascertaining whether a piece of information violates this directive or not extremely challenging. It is convenient to present these challenges with reference to some salient features of the IoT that have an important impact on privacy: scale and ubiquity, sensing capabilities, resource constraints, and the use of radio signals.

9.4.1.1 Scale and Ubiquity

The current numbers of connected things are not far from the predicted size of the IoT. According to a counter maintained by CISCO [37], there are already more than 13.5 billion such devices as of October 2014 and this number is growing rapidly. The scale of the problem is much bigger than the number of available devices since devices such as smartphones are capable of running millions of applications. As of September 2014, there were more than one million applications available for Android and Apple iPhones. Most of the publicly available applications are distributed through centrally controlled markets. Yet, it is not scalable to monitor all these applications and certify them as conforming to privacy guidelines. To make matters worse, these applications run on devices that have the highest capability to violate personal privacy: smartphones equipped with sensors.

The already deployed applications pose a challenging problem for privacy. Most of the applications that are running in billions of connected devices are designed without taking privacy into consideration. It is a daunting task to deploy any privacy solution on these devices. There are also devices that have been discarded by their owners and yet still function in some form, collect data, and transmit it. We also need to take these orphaned devices into account when devising comprehensive privacy solutions. Privacy by design is an often-promoted paradigm to deal with privacy issues, yet it cannot be applied retrospectively to already deployed systems. This also highlights the need to have proper procedures to decommission devices such as sensor nodes.

9.4.1.2 Sensing Capabilities

More and more things are equipped with sensors, for example, smartphones have accelerometers, global positioning systems (GPS), cameras, and gyroscopes, which are used by many applications. Often, the owners of these devices are not aware of the sensors' impact on their personal privacy. The ubiquity of these sensor-packed devices means that in addition to the smartphone that one owns and has control over, there are many other devices beyond one's control that collect potentially privacy-violating information. Even if a person is careful in selecting the correct privacy settings and taking appropriate actions in terms of privacy controls regarding his or her own devices, it is impossible to control or take precautionary measures against these ubiquitous devices.

9.4.1.3 Resource Constraints

While the capabilities in terms of sensing increase in sensor nodes, they also have to deal with the decrease in their capabilities in terms of energy, memory, and CPU due to their miniaturization. This is a highly undesirable situation with respect to privacy. These IoT devices can sense the environment and hence affect the privacy of individuals, yet they lack the capacity to implement privacy policies due to the abovementioned constraints. Most devices in the IoT are untethered, wireless, battery-powered devices. Therefore, conserving energy has become the main concern when developing and deploying long-running applications on these devices.

9.4.1.4 Radio Signals

The majority of IoT devices use radio for communication. Recent research on radio tomography has shown that a radio's signals can be used to track and locate people [37], with purpose-deployed wireless networks. However, an attacker can use the same principles to be a passive observer on wireless signals emitted by a legitimate IoT infrastructure to gather information on the location and movement of people, thus violating their privacy. In this case, the owners of the IoT devices cannot be held responsible for the privacy violations since they do not have any control over rogue elements using the wireless signals for privacy violation.

9.4.2 Internet Protocols and Privacy

The IoT has become a reality with the implementation of the IPv6 protocol stack on tiny devices, which has made it possible to extend the Internet to the things. The latter have truly become a part of the Internet, enabling them to directly interact with other services running on the Internet. This means that the things also inherit the privacy issues related to the IP stack and are also affected by privacy issues related to the services on the Internet. We discuss some of these issues in the following subsections, highlighting their impact on the IoT.

9.4.2.1 Third-Party Services

Third-party services such as Google analytics pose a threat to user privacy. These services are hosted on third-party servers and the main site has little or no control over these services, which results in a lack of transparency. Even if the IoT does not adopt the conventional HTTP-based web model, a cloud-based service may in turn rely on other third-party services. For example, a smart parking service may use a third-party weather service. This interlinked service-oriented model is expected to be a foundation of the future cloud-connected IoT. To avoid privacy breaches, privacy should be considered an important feature at the design stage when novel IoT architectures should decouple third-party services from end-users' identities.

9.4.2.2 Cookies

Cookies are benign unless they are generated based on personal data and used for tracking. CoAP-enabled devices do not use cookies; IoT devices using HTTP 2.0 may use cookies. To control privacy, users should protect cookies with a secure HTTP that uses SSL/TLS. The use of security protocols also protects other identity information in the packet, such as key/value pairs, device IDs, and session IDs.

9.4.2.3 Media Access Control Protection

The 64-bit interface address (mostly IEEE 64-bit Extended Unique Identifier [EUI-64™]) in the IPv6 address is often derived from the device's 48-bit media access control (MAC) address. This couples the identity of the device (and hence the user) with the IPv6 address. Attackers can exploit the use of a MAC address for privacy breaches. During IPv6 address autoconfiguration, the use of MAC addresses makes the device-bind public IP address unique. IPv6 privacy extensions (RFC3041) are proposed and should be enabled when using address autoconfiguration in the IoT; this can be done with regulations that force the Internet service providers (ISPs) to assign dynamically changing IPv6 prefixes. However, this can make the overall system more complex especially in the case of home networks where users have little understanding of the underlying network protocols. Delegating privacy rights to individual users and at the same time not demanding technical skills from them is a challenging research problem.

9.4.2.4 Network Address Translation

Network address translation (NAT) provides a mechanism to masquerade an entire IP address space behind a public IP address. With the depletion of IPv4 addresses, more and more NATs have been developed. The use of NATs increases complexity but enhances privacy as personal devices in local networks are hidden from the outside world. IPv6 addresses are potentially unlimited and each thing in the IoT is expected to get a unique IP address, which makes it more exposed to the outside world. Having a unique IPv6 address for each IoT device is useful for authentication but is more prone to privacy breaches. New, personally unidentifiable authentication protocols for the IoT are another open research problem.

9.4.2.5 Semantics and Annotations

IoT devices are expected to produce a huge amount of data. Annotation models and semantic technologies make this data searchable and hence more identifiable, which poses a threat to privacy. New semantic technologies should incorporate privacy provisions at the design stage. Privacy-preserved semantic annotations for the IoT are an open research problem.

9.4.3 Promising Privacy Solutions

IoT devices are diverse in terms of their capabilities, limitations, sizes, and use. Therefore, it is unlikely that a one-size-fits-all solution can address all privacy issues related to the IoT. Privacy issues can be best understood and addressed by segmenting this landscape. The following subsections detail some of the promising solutions that have the potential to be applied to protect privacy in the IoT.

9.4.3.1 Privacy Aware Design

Wicker and Shrader [39] propose several design principals to guide the design and deployment of information networks. They also demonstrate the application of these design principles by developing a privacy aware power-metering infrastructure. Their guidelines are a positive step toward protecting privacy. These guidelines require that the design makes it possible for the user to give explicit consent in collecting data. However, some IoT devices do not interact with users at all: they are embedded in our environment and hence people are not even aware of them. Moreover, it is not scalable to announce the presence and the functionality of each individual device. A repertoire of techniques, such as k-anonymity, homomorphic encryption, and virtual identities, are available to deal with privacy issues.

9.4.3.2 Privacy Preserving with Homomorphic Encryption

Data gathered from IoT devices, especially WSNs, is usually processed elsewhere; for example, in a cloud. To make sure that the data is protected from the source onward, the cloud should get only the minimal amount of information required to process the data. This can be achieved by encrypting the data at the source using homomorphic encryption. Homomorphic encryption allows an operation to be applied to cipher text in such a way that when the result is decrypted, it is equivalent to the result of applying another operation to the plain text. Riggio et al. [40] have presented a homomorphic encryption-based data aggregation system for WSNs, which is a good example of the use of homomorphic encryption in the IoT.

9.4.3.3 k-Anonymity

Anonymizing data is an essential step toward privacy protection. k-Anonymity [41] is a property of a data set that ensures that the information on any individual that is revealed by the data set (release) cannot be distinguished from at least other $k - 1$ individuals in the same set. The large scale of the IoT can be leveraged to provide k-anonymity with a large k, thereby ensuring better privacy protection.

9.4.3.4 Legal Frameworks

There is a market value for data that reveals personal information: target marketing is a multimillion-dollar industry that depends heavily on personal information. Therefore, market forces often discourage privacy protection unless compelled by law, in particular since there is a cost associated with implementing privacy-preserving safeguards in IoT applications. Hence, it is essential to have a legal framework to counterbalance these market forces.

Wicker and Shrader [39] describe the history and the current practice of laws related to privacy in the United States. The European Union Regulation 45/2001 protects the individual's right to privacy. Such laws and regulations are, however, not enacted everywhere and it is unclear how privacy can be preserved when IoT systems span multiple jurisdictions.

It often takes a long time for new laws to be enacted. Wicker and Shrader [39] highlight the time it has taken for privacy laws to come to terms with the telephone system in the United States. The IoT changes more rapidly than the telephone system did and hence legal frameworks may not be able to keep up with this rapid pace.

9.4.3.5 Education

Privacy always has a personal dimension. Therefore, solutions should allow interested parties to control the data that IoT devices have collected on them. To be effective, privacy controls must make people aware of privacy violations. Therefore, solutions that are confined to software and hardware are doomed to fail without the proper education of the users of IoT devices as well as the people who can potentially be affected by the data collected by them. With the growth of the IoT, this becomes important since it is becoming almost impossible to live a normal life without being sensed by IoT devices that one is not even aware of.

9.5 Conclusions

The IoT is expected to be the next computing revolution; however, before its massive rollout, security and privacy issues must be solved since the extension of the Internet to billions of connected devices poses new security and privacy threats. Our review of the state-of-the-art security solutions shows that security for the IoT has made some progress, in particular with respect to message security, whereas there are more open problems in the area of network and data security. Providing privacy is more difficult due to the sensing capabilities of many IoT devices and hence there are more open problems related to privacy than to security. Moreover, technical progress alone cannot solve all IoT-related privacy issues; legal frameworks and education are also required.

Author Biographies

Shahid Raza is a senior researcher at the SICS Swedish ICT Stockholm, where he has been working since 2008. Shahid completed his industrial PhD at Mälardalen University Västerås and SICS Stockholm in 2013. He also holds a technology of licentiate degree (PhLic) from Mälardalen University Västerås and a master of science degree from KTH The Royal Institute of Technology, Stockholm. He received a bachelor's degree in information technology from Arid Agriculture University of Rawalpindi, Pakistan, where he was awarded a gold medal for his extraordinary performance. Raza's research interests include security issues in wireless sensor networks in general and the Internet of Things in particular. For publications and other details, visit Shahid's homepage: www.ShahidRaza.info.

Thiemo Voigt is a professor at Uppsala University from where he received his PhD in 2002. He also leads the Networked Embedded Systems Group at SICS Swedish ICT, formerly the Swedish Institute of Computer Science. His research interests include networking, systems and security issues in wireless networks, and the Internet of Things. He is author or coauthor of more than 100 publications including award-winning papers at premium conferences such as the Institute of Electrical and Electronics Engineers/Association for Computing Machinery Information Processing in Sensor Networks and the ACM Conference on Embedded Networked Sensor Systems. His publications have received more than 6000 citations.

Chamath Keppitiyagama is a senior lecturer at the University of Colombo School of Computing, Colombo, Sri Lanka. He teaches undergraduate and postgraduate courses on operating systems, computer networks, and cryptography. He obtained his bachelor of science in computer science from the University of Colombo with first-class honors in 1997. Chamath was a graduate student and a teaching assistant at the University of British Columbia, Vancouver, Canada, from 1998 to 2005. He obtained his MSc and PhD degrees in computer science from the University of British Columbia in 2000 and 2005, respectively. Chamath spent a year at the SICS Swedish ICT as a European Research Consortium for Informatics and Mathematics/Marie Curie research fellow, conducting research on the environmental effects on sensor network communication. Chamath has research interests in distributed systems, sensor networks, and network security and privacy.

References

1. N. Kushalnagar, G. Montenegro, and C. Schumacher. 2007. IPv6 over low-power wireless personal area networks (6LoWPANs): Overview, assumptions, problem statement, and goals. RFC 4919, Internet Engineering Task Force, August. http://www.ietf.org/rfc/rfc4919.txt.
2. J. Hui and P. Thubert. 2011. Compression format for IPv6 datagrams over IEEE 802.15.4-based networks. RFC 6282, Internet Engineering Task Force, September. http://www.ietf.org/rfc/rfc6282.txt.
3. Z. Shelby, K. Hartke, and C. Bormann. 2014. The constrained application protocol (CoAP). RFC 7252, Internet Engineering Task Force. http://tools.ietf.org/html/rfc7252.
4. T. Winter, P. Thubert, A. Brandt, J. Hui, R. Kelsey, P. Levis, K. Pister, R. Struik, J. Vasseur, and R. Alexander. 2012. RPL: IPv6 routing protocol for low-power and lossy networks. RFC 6550, Internet Engineering Task Force, March. http://tools.ietf.org/html/rfc6550.
5. H. Yu, J. He, T. Zhang, P. Xiao, and Y. Zhang. 2012. Enabling end-to-end secure communication between wireless sensor networks and the Internet. *World Wide Web*, 16, 515–540.
6. C. Bormann. 2014. 6LoWPAN-GHC: Generic header compression for IPv6 over low-power wireless personal area networks (6LoWPANs). RFC 7400, Internet Engineering Task Force. https://tools.ietf.org/html/rfc7400.
7. R. E. Smith. 2001. *Authentication: From Passwords to Public Keys*. Addison-Wesley Longman, Boston.
8. I. C. Society, 2006. Wireless medium access control (MAC) and physical layer (PHY) specifications for low-rate wireless personal area networks (WPANs). IEEE std. 802.15.4-2006.
9. N. Sastry and D. Wagner. 2004. Security considerations for IEEE 802.15. 4 networks. In *Proceedings of the 3rd ACM Workshop on Wireless Security*, ACM, Philadelphia, pp. 32–42.
10. S. Raza, S. Duquennoy, J. Höglund, U. Roedig, and T. Voigt. 2014. Secure communication for the Internet of Things—A comparison of link-layer security and IPsec for 6LoWPAN. *Security and Communication Networks*, 7(12), 2654–2668.
11. A. Wood and J. Stankovic. 2006. Poster abstract: AMSecure—Secure link-layer communication in TinyOS for IEEE 802.15.4-based wireless sensor networks. In *ACM SenSys'06*, Boulder, CO.
12. S. Kent and R. Atkinson. 1998. Security architecture for the Internet protocol. RFC 2401, Internet Engineering Task Force. http://www.ietf.org/rfc/rfc2401.txt.
13. S. Kent. 2005. IP authentication header. RFC 4302, Internet Engineering Task Force. http://tools.ietf.org/html/rfc4302.
14. S. Kent. 2005. IP encapsulating security payload. RFC 4303, Internet Engineering Task Force. http://tools.ietf.org/html/rfc4303.
15. S. Deering and R. Hinden. 1995. Internet protocol, version 6 (IPv6) specification. RFC 1883 (Proposed Standard), Internet Engineering Task Force, December, obsoleted by RFC 2460. http://www.ietf.org/rfc/rfc1883.txt.
16. C. Kaufman, P. Hoffman, Y. Nir, and P. Eronen. 2010. Internet key exchange protocol version 2 (IKEv2). RFC 5996 (Proposed Standard), Internet Engineering Task Force, September. http://www.ietf.org/rfc/rfc5996.txt.
17. S. Raza, S. Duquennoy, T. Chung, D. Yazar, T. Voigt, and U. Roedig. 2011. Securing communication in 6LoWPAN with compressed IPsec. In *Proceedings of the 7th IEEE International Conference on Distributed Computing in Sensor Systems (IEEE DCOSS 2011)*, Barcelona, Spain, June.
18. J. Granjal, E. Monteiro, and J. S. Silva. 2010. Enabling network-layer security on IPv6 wireless sensor networks. In *IEEE GLOBECOM'10*, Miami, FL.
19. J. Granjal, E. Monteiro, and J. S. Silva. 2014. Network-layer security for the Internet of things using TinyOS and BLIP. *International Journal of Communication Systems*, 27(10), 1938–1963.
20. E. Rescorla and N. Modadugu. 2012. Datagram transport layer security version 1.2. RFC 6347, Internet Engineering Task Force, January. http://www.ietf.org/rfc/rfc6347.txt.
21. S. Fouladgar, B. Mainaud, K. Masmoudi, and H. Afifi. 2006. Tiny 3-TLS: A trust delegation protocol for wireless sensor networks. In *3rd European Workshop on Security and Privacy in Ad Hoc and Sensor Networks (ESAS'03)*, Hamburg, Germany.

22. M. Brachmann, S. L. Keoh, O. G. Morchon, and S. S. Kumar. 2012. End-to-end transport security in the IP-based Internet of things. In *2012 21st International Conference on Computer Communications and Networks (ICCCN)*, August, pp. 1–5.
23. Kothmayr, T. et al. 2012. A DTLS based end-to-end security architecture for the Internet of things with two-way authentication. In *37th IEEE Conference on Local Computer Networks Workshops*, pp. 956–963.
24. J. Granjal, E. Monteiro, and J. Sa Silva. 2012. On the feasibility of secure application-layer communications on the web of things. In *2012 IEEE 37th Conference on Local Computer Networks (LCN)*, IEEE, pp. 228–231.
25. M. Brachmann, O. Garcia-Morchon, and M. Kirsche. 2011. Security for practical CoAP applications: Issues and solution approaches. In *GI/ITG KuVS Fachgesprch Sensornetze (FGSN)*, Universitt Stuttgart, Stuttgart.
26. S. Raza, H. Shafagh, K. Hewage, R. Hummen, and T. Voigt. 2013. Lithe: Lightweight secure CoAP for the Internet of things. *IEEE Sensors Journal*, 13(10), 3711–3720.
27. R. Hummen et al. 2014. Delegation-based authentication and authorization for the IP-based Internet of things. In *IEEE SECON'14*, Singapore, June.
28. L. Wallgren, S. Raza, and T. Voigt. 2013. Routing attacks and countermeasures in the RPL-based Internet of Things. *International Journal of Distributed Sensor Networks*, 13(794326), 1–11.
29. A. Le, J. Loo, Y. Luo, and A. Lasebae. 2011. Specification-based IDS for securing RPL from topology attacks. In *Wireless Days (WD), 2011 IFIP*, IEEE, pp. 1–3.
30. S. Raza, L. Wallgren, and T. Voigt. 2013. SVELTE: Real-time intrusion detection in the Internet of things. *Ad Hoc Networks*, 11(8), 2661–2674.
31. T. Matsunaga, K. Toyoda, and I. Sasase. 2014. Low false alarm rate RPL network monitoring system by considering timing inconstancy between the rank measurements. In 2014 *11th International Symposium on Wireless Communications Systems (ISWCS)*, IEEE, pp. 427–431.
32. T. P. M. T. W. Group. 2007. TCG specification architecture overview (TPM 2007). http://www.trustedcomputinggroup.org.
33. I. E. Bagci, M. R. Pourmirza, S. Raza, U. Roedig, and T. Voigt. 2012. Codo: Confidential data storage for wireless sensor networks. In *8th IEEE International Workshop on Wireless and Sensor Networks Security (WSNS 2012)*, Las Vegas, NV, October.
34. N. Bhatnagar and E. L. Miller. 2007. Designing a secure reliable file system for sensor networks. In *Proceedings of the 2007 ACM Workshop on Storage Security and Survivability*, New York, pp. 19–24.
35. W. Ren, Y. Ren, and H. Zhang. 2008. Hybrids: A scheme for secure distributed data storage in WSNs. In *Proceedings of the 2008 IEEE/IFIP International Conference on Embedded and Ubiquitous Computing: Volume 02*, IEEE Computer Society, pp. 318–323.
36. I. E. Bagci, S. Raza, T. Chung, U. Roedig, and T. Voigt. 2013. Combined secure storage and communication for the internet of things. In *10th IEEE International Conference on Sensing, Communication, and Net-working (SECON'13)*, New Orleans, LA, June.
37. CISCO. 2014. Connections counter: The Internet of everything in motion. Accessed January 9, 2015. http://newsroom.cisco.com/ioe.
38. Y. Zhao, N. Patwari, J. M. Phillips, and S. Venkatasubramanian. 2013. Radio tomographic imaging and tracking of stationary and moving people via kernel distance. In *ACM/IEEE IPSN'13*, New York.
39. S. B. Wicker and D. E. Schrader. 2011. Privacy-aware design principles for information networks. *Proceedings of the IEEE*, 99(2), 330–350.
40. R. Riggio, T. Rasheed, and S. Sicari. 2011. Performance evaluation of an hybrid mesh and sensor network. In *IEEE GLOBECOM'11*, Houston, TX, December.
41. L. Sweeney. 2002. K-anonymity: A model for protecting privacy. *International Journal of Uncertainty Fuzziness Knowledge-Based Systems*, 10(5), 557–570.

Chapter 10

Security Issues and Approaches in M2M Communications

Yue Qiu and Maode Ma
Nanyang Technological University

Contents

10.1 Introduction 260
10.2 Security of M2M Communication 262
10.2.1 Security Requirements 263
10.2.2 Security Threats 263
10.3 Review of Solutions 264
10.3.1 Solutions for the M2M Device and Gateway Domain 265
10.3.1.1 Detection Schemes 265
10.3.1.2 Authentication Algorithms 265
10.3.1.3 Key Management 270
10.3.2 Solutions for Network Domain 271
10.3.2.1 Security in 6LoWPAN 271
10.3.2.2 Security in CoAP 272
10.4 Future Research Directions 274
10.5 Conclusion 275
Author Biographies 275
References 276

Abstract: The cyber-physical system (CPS), which forms the edges of the Internet of Things (IoT), seamlessly connecting the virtual world and the physical world, has become an emerging technology in recent years. Integrated with computational resources, networking, and physical process, CPSs could make our lives more convenient and comfortable by linking together mobile phones, networked appliances, and other intelligent devices. Machine-to-machine (M2M) communication, which allows wireless and wired systems to monitor different environmental and physical conditions without human intervention, is one of the most promising technologies in the CPS or IoT. In future, M2M communication could make possible many applications, such as e-health, smart grids, industrial automation and environmental monitoring, to produce various wide markets with many opportunities and to bring many more benefits to humans. Along with its development, M2M communication still faces various security threats and trust crises. Due to the large numbers of interconnected devices in the communication network, security is a critical issue in M2M systems. M2M nodes are generally deployed in the unattended M2M domain. They are vulnerable to malicious attacks and may be compromised by attackers. Though many solutions have already been proposed to address various security issues, research is still needed to overcome the vulnerabilities and provide intelligent solutions to protect M2M communication from various malicious attacks. In this chapter, we first introduce the background, architecture, security issues, and vulnerabilities of M2M communication systems. Then, we review the state-of-the-art security solutions and classify them into three major categories: detection, authentication, and key management schemes. New security threats and corresponding security solutions that could be applied to M2M communication in future will be discussed. Finally, some potential open research issues will be suggested to promote further research on the security of M2M communications.

Keywords: Security; M2M; CPS; 6LoWPAN; CoAP

10.1 Introduction

With the rapid development of computer networks, electronic technology, and control technology as well as increased requirements for intelligence in modern industry, the need for physical devices to become more compatible with information and the Internet is growing fast [1]. However, there is still a serious gap between the cyberworld, where information is exchanged and transformed, and the physical world in which we live [2]. The cyberworld and the physical world have been considered as two different entities in the past decades. In line with this issue, the cyber-physical system (CPS), which can seamlessly integrate the functions of computing, communication, and control, has developed as an intelligent system that performs computing and physical processes as a single entity. CPSs can be used in a wide range of applications, including intelligent transportation, precision agriculture, e-health, water and mine monitoring, aerospace, and so on, which undeniably demonstrates that in future, many service providers will implement CPS technologies for their customers [3].

A CPS mainly consists of two subsystems, a physical processing system and a cybersystem, which are usually composed of a set of networked agents including sensors, actuators, control processing units, and communication devices, as shown in Figure 10.1 [4].

The physical process system is controlled and monitored by the cybersystem, which consists of small devices with basic computation and wireless communication capabilities. While functioning, all the units within the system cooperate with each other over the CPS network, which links the cybersystem and the physical system, forming a large-scale heterogeneous distributed real-time system [1].

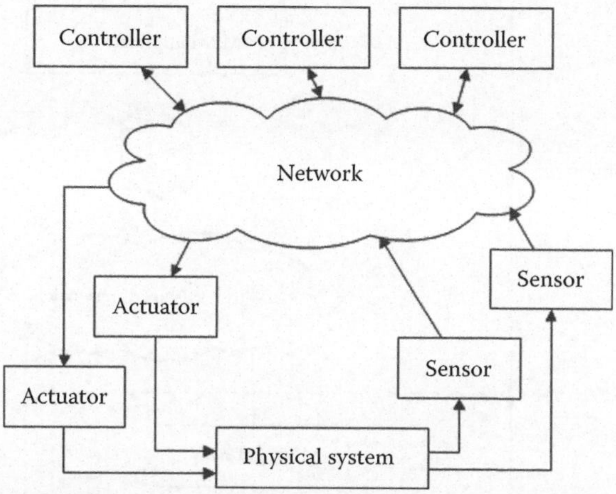

Figure 10.1 General architecture of a CPS.

Machine-to-machine (M2M) communication, which allows wireless and wired systems to monitor different environmental and physical conditions without human intervention, is the major communication technology used in most existing CPSs. In M2M, each device, such as a sensor or a smart meter, captures an event as it happens, such as a change of temperature or inventory level, which will be relayed through a wireless, wired, or hybrid network to an application that translates the captured event into meaningful information to trigger an actuation [5].

Since M2M devices are linked and managed through communication technologies that require integration and convergence among many different communication systems, architectures for M2M have been proposed and developed in different standards organizations. The European Telecommunications Standards Institute (ETSI) has formed a technical committee (TC) to perform the standardization work on M2M communication. The main goal of the committee is to develop an end-to-end architecture for M2M systems with outstanding features such as sensor network integration, quality of service (QoS), security, discovery and localization, and so on [6]. Figure 10.2 shows the high-level architecture of the M2M communications paradigm, which mainly consists of two domains: (1) M2M device and gateway domain and (2) network domain.

In the M2M device and gateway domain, the M2M devices can collect monitoring data from different sensors and transmit the collected information or reply to the requests for the information automatically. The M2M devices can be connected to the network domain via an access network (AN) or an M2M gateway, which acts as a proxy between the M2M devices and the network domain. An M2M area network can provide the connectivity between the M2M devices and the M2M gateways. The implementation of the M2M area networks will rely on wireless personal area network technologies such as Zigbee, Bluetooth, and so on, or other local networks such as Power Line Communications (PLC), Meter-Bus (M-BUS), Wireless M-BUS, and the international standard ISO/IEC 14543 (KNX) [7].

The major function of the M2M network domain is to provide reliable wired or wireless channels to enable transmission of sensory data from the M2M device and the gateway domain to M2M applications. The connectivity between the M2M device and gateway domain and M2M applications can be implemented by an that allows the M2M device domain to communicate with the core network [8], such as xDSL (digital subscriber line technologies), hybrid fiber-coaxial (HFC), satellite, global system for mobile communications (GSM) enhanced data rates for GSM

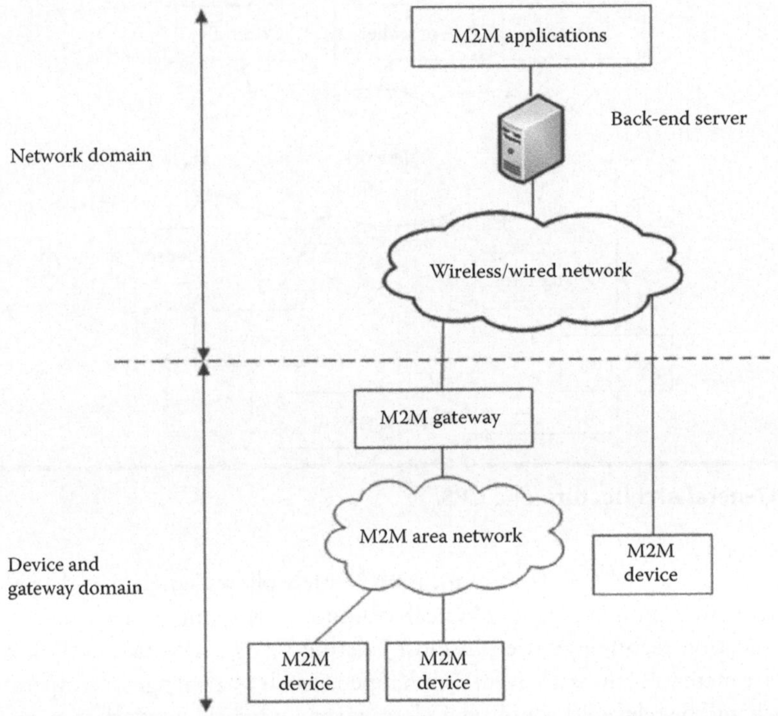

Figure 10.2 High-level architecture for M2M.

evolution (EDGE) radio access network (GERAN), universal terrestrial radio access network (UTRAN), evolved UTRAN (EUTRAN), wireless local area network (W-LAN), and worldwide interoperability for microwave access (WiMAX). The M2M core network (CN) provides the Internet protocol (IP) connectivity, service and network control functions, roaming, and interconnection with other networks. The M2M service capabilities (SCs) provide the M2M functions, which are exposed through a set of open interfaces. The M2M SCs can also use core network functionalities to simplify and optimize the development and deployment of various applications through hiding the network specificities [7]. The network management functions are formed by all the functions required to manage the ANs and CNs. These are all the functions required to manage M2M SCs in the network domain.

The reminder of this chapter is organized as follows. In Section 10.2, the security requirements and security vulnerabilities in M2M are introduced. In Section 10.3, the current security solutions are reviewed with the introduction of the key technologies applied in M2M communication. The future research direction is explored in Section 10.4. Finally, the chapter is concluded in Section 10.5.

10.2 Security of M2M Communication

The M2M communication networks in a CPS have several insecure features [9]. First, an M2M network is easily eavesdropped due to the broadcast nature of the communication medium. Second, sensor nodes can be easily compromised by malicious attacks due to limited energy capabilities and computing resources. In addition, there could be a protocol gap among wired/wireless devices integrated in the M2M communication systems. The above mentioned insecure features make the M2M system vulnerable to malicious adversaries. There is great demand for exploring solutions to effectively protect M2M communications.

10.2.1 Security Requirements

To establish a secure M2M communication, security mechanisms should meet the following requirements [10]:

- *Confidentiality*: Confidentiality prevents private sensory data from being eavesdropped by passive attackers, which can be achieved by using authentication and cryptographic encryption to ensure that the information transmitted in the M2M communications can be viewed only by authorized parties.
- *Integrity*: Data transmitted in the M2M communication system cannot be illegally altered by unauthorized participants before reaching the right recipient. Integrity, which can be achieved by employing cryptographic integrity checks, is critical in M2M communications, since tampering with the information could result in severe consequences.
- *Authentication*: Though integrity ensures that the data cannot be illegally altered in a transmission, it cannot know whether the recipient is authorized to access the private information. As a prerequisite for secure M2M communications, authentication allows the authenticator to identify whether the M2M nodes are trustworthy in the M2M domain.
- *Nonrepudiation*: Nonrepudiation guarantees that M2M devices cannot deny information which they have previously originated and sent.
- *Access control*: Access control mechanisms built on identification and authentication ensure that access to critical and sensitive information is restricted to authorized M2M parties.
- *Availability*: Since wireless radio communication is often used in M2M communication systems, communication availability can be affected by jamming attacks. To defend against jamming attacks, a mechanism should be applied in the system to provide availability, which ensures that data should be available whenever the authorized M2M parties access the authenticator.
- *Privacy*: For some privacy-sensitive M2M applications, the protection of privacy information is important. For example, in e-healthcare systems, if the patients' health files are illegally obtained by unauthorized third parties, it could lead to undesirable negative effects on patients' lives.

10.2.2 Security Threats

The abovementioned security requirements are also the requirements for the M2M communications to overcome vulnerability to various security threats [9], which have been specified by the Third Generation Partnership Project (3GPP) Security Workgroup (SA3). The resource-constrained M2M devices are usually placed in unattended and accessible locations without specific supervision and are more easily tampered with by unauthorized people compared with traditional equipment that has enough resources and is carefully protected. Thus, the security issues faced by the M2M system are challenging. In addition to the security issues encountered in general scenarios, the following security threats should be considered in M2M communication.

- Physical attacks, including physically moving a M2M device from an authorized place, theft of the communication module or security keys, side-channel attacks, denial of service (DoS) attacks, and so on, are difficult to detect due to the unattended nature of M2M devices. For M2M equipment with the universal integrated circuit card (UICC), which stores security credentials and functions, removing a UICC and inserting it into unauthorized M2M equipment in order to use a subscription to get network access could cause damage to the whole system. These possibilities require certain mechanisms to make the UICC either unmovable or unusable if it is removed.

- Compromise of credentials includes modifying existing credentials and obtaining the administrator or device credentials for use by the attacker. In addition to the physical attacks mentioned above, an attacker could launch brute-force attacks on authentication tokens and algorithms, as well as using malicious software to obtain sensitive information or corrupt a machine communication identity module (MCIM). Furthermore, compromise of credentials of an M2M device may not be quickly detected and reported, which enables attackers to get access to the network device and obtain critical data.
- Configuration attacks include configuration changes; misconfiguration by the owner, subscriber, or user; and misconfiguration or compromise of the access control lists. For example, malicious device triggering may result in battery draining, while M2M equipment usually needs to operate for a long time supplied by a single battery, unlike normal devices.
- Attacks on the core network are the main threats to the mobile network operator (MNO), including the impersonation of devices, traffic tunneling among the impersonated devices, misconfiguration of the firewall in the modem/router/gateways, and DoS attacks against the core network. An attacker could impersonate a legitimate M2M device by replicating credentials and MCIM and compromising the original device to obtain data and services, which are billed to the legitimate M2M equipment (M2ME) subscriber.
- User data and identity privacy attacks include monitoring/eavesdropping data transmitted in the network by other users' devices, masquerading as devices of other users/subscribers, and revealing users' network identity or other confidential data to unauthorized third parties. In the context of machine type communication (MTC), identity, location, and sensory information can be considered as privacy. If the user data and identity privacy information of a M2M device is eavesdropped and used by attackers over a period of time, this will seriously affect the confidentiality of privacy-sensitive information of the M2M system.

As well as the specification by the 3GPP security workgroup, the main security requirements of M2M sensing applications in different M2M application areas have been discussed by Granjal et al., in which the main security threats, corresponding approaches, and future directions in the context of the reference stack of M2M wireless communication technologies have also been explored [11]. The vulnerabilities of the M2M communication system will be exhibited under all of the abovementioned malicious attacks. These vulnerabilities may lead to M2M communication being destroyed under those attacks. It is vital to construct secure and efficient M2M communication systems with strong countermeasures against various malicious attacks [10].

10.3 Review of Solutions

Security is the major concern of most M2M applications, with a high demand for appropriate security mechanisms to protect the M2M communication systems. In this section, we introduce the key security technologies and solutions currently available in the M2M device and gateway domain and the network domain.

10.3.1 Solutions for the M2M Device and Gateway Domain

Many solutions applied in the M2M device and gateway domain are available to overcome the vulnerabilities in the M2M device and gateway domain caused by the security threats of the M2M communications. These security solutions can be classified as detection, authentication, and key management schemes.

10.3.1.1 Detection Schemes

In M2M communications systems, M2M nodes are generally deployed in the unattended M2M device and gateway domain. These nodes are vulnerable to some malicious attacks and could be compromised by the attackers. An early warning system for forecasting malicious events in the smart grid (SG) system has been proposed [12]. In the SG system scenario, an attacker can eavesdrop, inject, and modify the information transmitted in the SG network with the ability to access at least one smart meter and exploit multiple smart meters to launch distributed DoS attacks concurrently. Based on the designed attack model, a Gaussian process regression scheme has been adopted to predict the malicious activities which may disrupt SG communication. The performance evaluation demonstrates that the SG control center can forecast the time when the memory of the gateway will be exhausted by the algorithm with the input of a certain number of malicious authentications. However, this detection system can only predict the time of memory exhaustion. Further security mechanisms are needed to protect the appliances in SG from being compromised. Furthermore, M2M devices are also vulnerable to hijacking attacks in cellular networks, because a large number of the M2M devices deployed in physically inaccessible locations are static. In order to defend against hijacking attacks, a novel, efficient framework to not only detect but also prevent hijacking attacks on M2M devices has been proposed [13]. Detection of two particular types of hijacking attacks has been studied: attacks to spoof the identity credentials of the M2MEs and attacks to physically remove the UICC from the M2MEs. Designed with IP address filtering and traffic monitoring techniques, specific hijacking attacks can detected and prevented in a high rate packet data (HRPD) AN and other cellular networks such as the universal mobile telecommunications system (UMTS) and long-term evolution (LTE) networks. The novel solution is shown as a network-centric and lightweight detection scheme. Though some attacks can be blocked early by the proposed detection mechanism, attacks cannot be prevented if the adversary hacks into a legitimate M2ME and obtains the IP address and temporary identities in order to attack the M2M web server by launching a DoS attack.

Since M2M technologies are still immature, the existing detection mechanisms made a good start on developing new techniques for forecasting and preventing the malicious attacks early. Due to the limited capability of M2M devices, attackers can launch various attacks to compromise the functionality of these devices and obtain their credentials or secret keys. Further detection mechanisms are needed to detect malicious attacks early, before any severe damage to the network is caused. As well as attacks that are easy to detect, attacks such as eavesdropping and traffic analysis, which are difficult to detect, should also be prevented. Since a number of M2M devices are resource constrained, detection mechanisms should be lightweight and easy to expand.

10.3.1.2 Authentication Algorithms

10.3.1.2.1 Cryptography

Authentication is a prerequisite for M2M communication security. Cryptography, which can be used for user authentication, is essential to hide information transmitted over any untrusted medium. An encryption mechanism for short message service (SMS) applications over M2M communication networks has been proposed [14]. The signature of a message is a hashing value calculated by using the international mobile station equipment identity (IMEI), secret key, and payload at the devices. To further reduce the size of the encrypted short message, GNU zip, which works based on the Deflate algorithm, has been used to compress the payload. The evaluation shows that the proposed mechanism has no negative effect on the delivery time of the SMS service in comparison with the conventional SMS service on M2M communication networks. An identity-based encryption (IBE) using elliptic-curve cryptography (ECC), named IBE-ECC, has been proposed for secure M2M communication [15]. Identity-based encryption and decryption schemes based on Tate pairings have been implemented in JAVA and MATLAB to demonstrate the feasibility of the proposed scheme. The technique of zero correlation zone (ZCZ) code has been employed for the design of a mutual authentication scheme in the M2M communication system with the aim of achieving efficient security functionality [16]. The physical layer (PHY) security supported by the ZCZ code can minimize the traffic overhead and the overall cost of the data aggregation and the management message distribution in M2M communication systems.

Due to the vast quantities of information exchanged over the M2M network, the need for security should be considered. Cryptographic techniques provide a security foundation for exchanging messages over an insecure channel to guarantee the confidentiality and integrity of the exchanged information. For resource-constrained M2M devices, the computational cost of cryptographic algorithms should be lower.

10.3.1.2.2 General Authentication Schemes

To support secure connection between the legitimate users and the server, different authentication approaches have been proposed to support security and try to meet the security requirements of M2M communication systems. Authentication procedures can ensure the information transmitted to the legitimate users and prevent the M2M communications from compromised attacks.

The rapid development of M2M technology in the health-care industry raises new security concerns. In the scenario of health-care services, changes in action and contexts of patients need to be addressed quickly. However, it is also important to ensure that the privacy of the patients is preserved. To this end, an authentication scheme has been proposed to protect the communication between doctors and patients from disclosure to illegitimate users [17]. A dynamic ID-based authentication, which uses a pairwise key predistribution to establish a pairwise key between the mobile sink and any sensor node, is applied by the proposed scheme. Though the proposed security mechanism is novel in using a dynamic identity-based authentication to support mobile devices for health-care applications, this scheme has not exploited timestamps or nonce to prevent replay attacks. With the motivation of improving the security functionality of M2M communication, a low-cost dynamic-encryption authentication between mobile devices and the M2M service provider has been designed [18]. As with the scheme described above [17], four parties are involved in the proposed authentication scheme: a mobile device, a sensor node, a gateway, and an M2M service provider. In addition, the security aspect is significantly improved by applying time stamps and lightweight encryption algorithm [18]. It is more suitable for medical applications and can be expanded to other application scenarios. The analysis indicates that mutual authentication and the ability to withstand multiple attacks could be accomplished by the proposed solution. However, the security of these two schemes depends on pre-shared key space and noncompromised sensor nodes.

While health care is a promising application for using M2M communication, application to the home is also a likely prospect. Today, it is possible to remotely monitor the conditions at any distance from the house. With the convenience of a home network, the security issues of M2M applications need much more attention. A protocol consisting of an efficient password-based authentication scheme and a process of key agreement among the communicating parties has been proposed to protect the privacy and security of the home network service over the M2M communication system [19]. The goal of the proposed solution is to allow a mobile user to access his/her home network to communicate with specific home devices via the existing time division synchronous code division multiple access (TD-SCDMA) network. In this solution, a mobile user can register with the M2M server using his password and his home gateway ID. After receiving the user request, the M2M server will validate the applicant to provide permission to the user. Then, the corresponding home gateway will be allowed to communicate with the M2M server and get the encryption key. Subsequently, the user can get into the service system via a mutual authentication process and access his home network through the secure channel established between the M2M server and the home gateway. Security analysis shows that the proposed solution can prevent many malicious attacks and has some practical merit. Hash function and advanced encryption standard (AES) function are adopted to encrypt messages during the authentication process, which makes this proposed scheme suitable for resource-constrained systems. Besides remote user authentication, the home network, as a kind of heterogeneous network, contains various digital devices and terminals such as laptops, smartphones, printers, and so on. There are two modes for home applications based on device management: decentralized mode and centralized mode. To increase efficiency and security, a resource management framework based on the centralized mode has been proposed to protect the identities of the devices and meet the requirement for user anonymity in home M2M networks [20]. It can efficiently manage the keys for the authentication and the resources in the M2M network due to the adoption of an available bandwidth measurement algorithm. The algorithm can adaptively measure the bandwidth and dynamically adjust the resource used such that the authentication has a less negative effect on the performance of the M2M network.

With the development of wireless Internet, the number of smartphone users is rapidly growing. They will also have security problems that will need to be solved. A context-aware access control system has been proposed that uses context-awareness, integrated authentication, access control, and an open service gateway initiative service platform in the smartphone environment [21]. The security level is determined by fuzzy logic algorithm and multiattribute utility theory (MAUT) algorithm based on user location and access time. The proposed context-aware security system can provide a flexible, secure, and seamless security service by adopting diverse contexts. Being a widespread application of smartphones, mobile payment has become an important component in mobile e-commerce. An authentication mechanism for mobile payment including two-way authentication, reauthentication, roaming authentication, and inside authentication has been proposed [22]. Two-way authentication allows the mobile device and the center system to trust each other, which is the foundation of the other three mechanisms. Reauthentication reestablishes active communication after mobile subscribers change their points of attachment to the network. Inside authentication prevents attackers from obtaining privacy via attacking mobile devices that have been captured by an attacker. Roaming authentication proves the mobile subscriber's legitimate identity to the foreign agency when he/she roams into a foreign network, which can be regarded as the integration of the above three. The authors have summarized the abovementioned authentication mechanisms and the encryption mechanism to establish the integration of the security framework of mobile payment. Although this proposed mechanism can prevent existing drawbacks and compromises, the eavesdropping issue remains to be solved.

Generic authentication architecture (GAA) is a standard made by 3GPP and has two types of authentication mechanisms: one works based on a secret shared between the communicating entities and generic bootstrapping architecture (GBA); the other one works based on public-private key pairs, digital certificates, and support for subscriber certificates (SSC). An end-to-end security scheme has been proposed based on the GAA and with a shared key for the authentication at the application layer [23]. The proposed scheme is suitable for MTC and has good scalability. The function of the lifetime of the master session key against the expected number of bootstrapping requests has been described with an approach to identifying the lifetime of the optimized master session key. The standard GBA specified by 3GPP is a technology that provides a client and an application server with a common shared secret. A novel solution for the over-the-air automated authentication and verification of M2M wireless sensor networks using the existing authentication assets of a cellular network has been proposed [24]. This proposed scheme focuses on verifying the authenticity of the coordinator node in a ZigBee network, not in a generic scenario as in Zhang et al. [23]. The GBA standard has been extended to implement the solution with minimal additional hardware and software requirements. The proposed solution has two procedures: bootstrapping authentication using GBA and subsequent bootstrapping usage. One of the key benefits of the approach is that it eschews expensive add-ons to the existing operator infrastructure but addresses checking the integrity of remotely deployed wireless sensor networks.

In M2M systems, various types of sensitive information are transmitted through the network. Thus, security mechanisms targeted to the protection of privacy information should be in place in order to prevent these confidential data from being eavesdropped, tracked, or obtained. A privacy problem solution using a device and user authentication (PSDUA) scheme that can solve privacy and node-tracing problems has been proposed [25]. The PSDUA design certification service is in two steps. In the first step, the node is authenticated by the authentication server (AS) using various certification procedures. Each involved node must have authentication in an initial procedure. The procedure processes device authentication to the servers that supply the user-requested services and the gateway that sends any process step beforehand. When the node collects information, the PSDUA acquires authentication for the node. In the second step, the service that the user requested will be checked for authentication by AS and the certification provided to the server. If a user requests service to a server, the user authentication and the service certification procedure should be executed in advance. Thus, PSDUA can offer access control for the nodes in the network and permit service when a user wants to access the nodes, the gateway, and the server. If a user requests the service unfairly or launches masquerade attacks in the middle, it can prevent these from happening. A new communication protocol has been proposed to protect the confidentiality and integrity of the messages delivered through M2M communication networks by using attribute-based cryptography (ABC) [26]. ABC is a kind of public key encryption in which the encryption and decryption of the messages depend on attributes (e.g., users' location, nationalities, etc.). Though the proposed protocol can increase safety by protecting the right of access to the device and message privacy, the encryption and key-generation computational costs of ABC could make it unsuitable for resource-sensitive systems.

With the development of M2M communication, many applications may become possible, such as e-health, smart home, industrial automation, environmental monitoring, and so on. Health care is one of the major application fields in M2M service. Health-care systems, which comprise sensor nodes, mobile devices, and a server, should support real-time queries on information such as the location and medical data of patients. Thus, doctors or nurses can easily access this information to check the physical condition of every patient. However, despite the potential benefits of health-care systems, new security issues are raised. Authentication mechanisms, which can prevent personal medical information from being obtained by illegitimate users, should be adopted in the system. Home networks, including various home appliances, sensors, and monitoring devices, are also an important application of M2M service. A user can remotely control home devices and monitor his or her home conditions through an M2M home network, but personal information could be exposed without an authentication mechanism. A proper authentication scheme should be applied in case an adversary launches malicious attacks to obtain users privacy information. In addition to research on health-care and home networks, industrial automation and other application fields are also very important for the M2M network as a whole. Future research could focus on these application domains. What is more, since the devices in the M2M network are so diverse, proper authentication mechanisms should be adopted to ensure that the system can operate safely and efficiently.

10.3.1.2.3 Group Authentication

With the increasing development of M2M networks, emerging security issues, especially group authentication, should be addressed. Due to the large number of M2M devices, the network will be overloaded if each device needs to implement an authentication process independently. A group authentication scheme applied to M2M communications in LTE networks has been proposed [27]. Instead of using message authentication codes (MACs), the proposed scheme exploits the aggregate signature and the elliptic curve digital signature algorithm (ECDSA) to achieve mutual authentication and key agreement (AKA) between each M2M device in the same group and the mobile management entity (MME) at the same time. However, the asymmetric cryptography used in this scheme makes it unsuitable for resource-constrained devices in 3GPP LTE networks. In order to further reduce the authentication overhead, a lightweight group authentication protocol has been proposed for the authentication of resource-constrained M2M devices in the M2M communication system under the LTE platform, called LGTH [28]. The LGTH protocol has an initialization phase and a group authentication and key agreement phase. During the group authentication phase, a group leader will be selected based on the communication capability, storage status, and battery status among all the M2M devices. The MME can authenticate all M2M devices in a group simultaneously with the aggregate MACs. Therefore, the access networks can simultaneously set up a trust relationship with a group of M2M devices in a single authentication procedure. Compared with Cao et al. [27], the security analysis and performance evaluation demonstrate that LGTH can not only provide robust security but also reduce computation and signaling overhead. To enhance users' privacy protection, a secure and efficient authentication and key agreement protocol, named SE-AKA, is proposed for LTE networks [29]. Key forward/backward secrecy (KFS/KBS) can be guaranteed by adopting elliptic curve Diffie-Hellman (ECDH). But within this scheme, the first device should implement a full AKA procedure before the execution of an authentication protocol for the remaining devices in the same group. After successful authentication, a pairwise symmetric key used to encrypt/decrypt messages for future exchange is calculated by ECDH. To further optimize the group authentication for M2M networks, a new, secure and efficient group roaming scheme for group-based MTC, called SEGR, is proposed based on certificate-less aggregate signature [30]. By SEGR, all MTC devices of the same group can be authenticated simultaneously between 3GPP and WiMAX networks. As in Cao et al. [27], a key generate center (KGC) is required to provide private keys for authenticated MTC devices. A comparison of the proposed group authentication schemes is shown in Table 10.1.

With the increasing number of devices in M2M networks, group authentication is introduced to authenticate a group of devices simultaneously instead of authenticating these devices one by

Table 10.1 Comparison among Group Authentication Schemes

	Type of Cryptosystem	*Authenticating a Group of Devices at the Same Time*	*Total Signaling Overhead*	*Total Authentication Transmission Overhead*
Cao et al. [27]	Asymmetric	Yes	$2n + 6ms$	$(2n + 2m)a + 4mb$
LGTH [28]	Symmetric	Yes	$6m$	$2ma + 4mb$
SE-AKA [29]	Symmetric+ECDH	No	$6n + 2mdf$	$6na + 2mb$
SEGR [30]	Asymmetric+ECDH	Yes	$4m$	$4ma$

Note: n,m: n MTC devices form m groups; a: the units of the authentication transmission overhead between the MTC devices and the MME; b: the units of the authentication transmission overhead between the MME and the home subscriber server (HSS).

one. In future, group authentication should be able to provide an efficient and secure authentication and key agreement process with less computational cost, network latency, and bandwidth consumption.

10.3.1.2.4 Physical Layer Authentication

A simple but viable aggregation protocol has been designed to provide physical layer security by authenticating the PHY authentication preamble (AP) [31]. Taking into account various fading and shadowing conditions of the wireless channels, PHY configurations, media access control (MAC) layer configurations, and networking characteristics, the developed protocol, being secure in providing per-hop authentication and end-to-end confidentiality, becomes really reliable and energy efficient. However, since there is the possibility of desynchronization due to poor wireless channel conditions, a synchronization window is required. An innovative authentication verification approach has been presented to verify the authentication at the physical layer to deal with exhaustion attacks [32]. The proposed method is composed of a physical-layer AP that consists of a hash function of 32 or even 20 bits. The performance of the authentication verification test has been optimized at the physical layer by calculating the optimum synchronization window length with a consideration of the error rates. The work has been extended by proposing a novel synchronization scheme to further provide energy efficiency at the physical layer for M2M networks [33].

M2M devices usually deploy in an unattended environment, full of threats, and can be easily attacked by adversaries. Physical layer authentication, which is an effective way to prevent the M2M system from various malicious attacks, can be applied to provide end-to-end and hop-by-hop security for the system. Compared with the traditional authentication methods, M2M physical layer authentication should be fast, lightweight, and energy efficient due to limitations on the memory and computational capacity of M2M devices.

10.3.1.3 Key Management

Key management is the management of various cryptographic keys in a cryptosystem, which includes dealing with the generation, exchange, storage, use, and replacement of various keys. A novel collaborative protocol for key establishment has been presented in a heterogeneous M2M environment [34]. An efficient cooperative key establishment system could establish end-to-end secure communications between nodes with different resource capabilities. Heavy computation of cryptographic operations can be delegated to less resource-constrained nodes, called proxies, in order to enable a highly resource-constrained node to securely establish a session key with a remote server. Evolving from this, a new approach has been proposed to enforce the session key derivation [35]. Though performance analysis has proved that the proposed scheme can significantly reduce the consumption of resources, the set of assumptions listed in the article make it difficult to implement in generic scenarios. Considering the security aspects of the cellular M2M communication architecture, a key agreement mechanism for secure communication between entities in the cellular M2M networks has been proposed to provide a key agreement function for the reliability and efficiency of the secure cellular M2M communication networks [36].

Key management is one of the major challenges in M2M network security. Symmetric key-based key management mechanisms are more popular than asymmetric key-based schemes due to lower computation cost. With a large variety of devices deployed in the M2M system, group key management and hybrid key management, which combines symmetric and asymmetric cryptography, are possible future trends and should be addressed.

10.3.2 Solutions for Network Domain

In order to allow a large number of devices to interoperate with the Internet for extending the use of M2M applications, Internet protocol version 6 (IPv6) over low power wireless personal area networks (6LoWPAN) and constrained application protocol (CoAP) could be applied in the network domain.

10.3.2.1 Security in 6LoWPAN

Due to the large number of devices, M2M need to realize the networking of devices and the interoperability among various types of equipment. IPv6, which enables more ubiquitous computation, is a better choice for M2M sensing applications, because it has much larger address space. However, IEEE802.15.4 only prescribed the standard of PHY and MAC layers for low-rate wireless personal area networks (LR-WPANs). Other higher-level layers and interoperability sublayers are not defined in IEEE802.15.4. How to integrate IPv6 with the existing M2M network has been a hot issue. The Internet Engineering Task Force (IETF) has been developing a new standard named 6LoWPAN, which optimizes IPv6 for use with low-power, low-bandwidth communication technologies [37].

The IETF has chartered the 6LoWPAN working group to standardize protocols at various layers to connect low-power personal area networks to the open Internet. 6LoWPAN adopts the PHY and MAC layer of IEEE 802.15.4. However, the payload length supported by the 6LoWPAN bottom layer is 127 bytes and the IPv6 packet header is 40 bytes, which is relatively large. In order to connect seamlessly between the MAC layer and the network layer, the 6LoWPAN working group suggested adding an adaptation layer between the MAC layer and the network layer to achieve header compression, fragmentation, reassembly, and mesh route forwarding. Figure 10.3 shows the reference model of the 6LoWPAN protocol stack.

Sensor nodes are generally deployed in an open environment, and it is easy for messages to be attacked in the transmission process. To this end, Zhou et al. [38] propose an embedded secure gateway based on 6LoWPAN, which provides efficient, secure, and trustworthy communication between IPv6 and the wireless sensor network by combining the proxy architecture and the transmission control protocol (TCP)/IP interconnection. With the gateway, users can communicate directly with sensor nodes or query real-time data or historical data in the web server. The address mapping table transforms an IPv6 address into a short address, which improves efficiency in the 6LoWPAN network. Furthermore,

Application layer
Transport layer
IP layer
Adaptation layer
IEEE 802.15.4 media access control layer
IEEE 802.15.4 physical layer

Figure 10.3 Reference model of 6LoWPAN protocol stack.

the gateway adopts security protocols for sensor networks that include secure network encryption protocol and timed efficient stream loss-tolerant authentication protocol (μTESLA) protocol. The performance of their proposed gateway mechanism is evaluated by NS2 (Network Simulator, version 2). The result proves that the gateway design can realize communication security and good performance at the same time. Since real-world deployments of wireless sensor networks require secure communication, it is desirable to extend 6LoWPAN such that internet protocol security (IPsec) communication with IPv6 nodes is possible. Raza et al. [39] provide end-to-end secure communication between IP-enabled sensor networks and the traditional Internet. This is the first compressed lightweight design, implementation, and evaluation of 6LoWPAN extension for IPsec. IPsec is the standard method to secure Internet communication, and the authors investigate whether IPsec can be extended to sensor networks. Toward this end, they have presented the first IPsec specification and implementation for 6LoWPAN. They have extensively evaluated their implementation and demonstrated that it is possible and feasible to use compressed IPsec to secure communication between sensor nodes and hosts in the Internet. Through the application of IPsec, communication end points are able to authenticate, encrypt, and check the integrity of messages using standardized and established IPv6 mechanisms. In order to provide security for M2M communication over 6LoWPAN, secure authentication and session key exchange schemes are needed. A secure authentication and key establishment scheme (SAKES) for M2M communication in the 6LoWPAN is proposed [40]. SAKES uses pairwise key during node authentication phase and the lightweight asymmetric key cryptography during the session key establishment process. Security analysis is performed for different attack scenarios. The impact of DoS attack on the performance of the 6LoWPAN is evaluated. The evaluation is carried out by using the optimized network engineering tools (OPNET) simulation tool. Their simulation result showed the severity of DoS attack and the necessity of the proposed security scheme so as to maintain the constrained resources. As DoS attacks are considered to be an important security issue, a novel DoS detection architecture that integrates an intrusion detection system (IDS) into the network framework, developed within the Seventh Framework Programme of the European Union for Research and Technological Development (EU FP7) project, is proposed [41]. This project aims to semantically integrate the IoT into mainstream enterprise systems and support interoperable, online, end-to-end business applications. In order to evaluate the performance of the proposed architecture, a preliminary implementation was completed and tested against a real DoS attack using a penetration testing system. The result proves that their detection mechanism is successful in detecting DoS attacks on 6LoWPAN. In future, they expect to complete the implementation of this architecture and test it against different real attacks.

10.3.2.2 Security in CoAP

Due to the vast number of constrained devices in the M2M system, stack protocols such as the hypertext transfer protocol (HTTP) may not be suitable for these devices. Therefore, in March

2010, the IETF Constrained REST ful Environments (CoRE) Working Group began standardization activity on CoAP. CoAP is an application layer protocol intended to be used in very simple electronics devices that allows them to communicate interactively over the Internet [42,43]. It has been designed with a REST ful-integrated interface and used over constrained networks. It has been mainly targeted toward constrained networks such as 6LoWPAN networks.

CoAP consists of a subset of HTTP functionalities that have been redesigned taking into account the low processing power and energy consumption constraints of small embedded devices such as sensors. Various mechanisms have been modified, and some new functionalities have been added in order to make the protocol suitable for M2M applications. It is able to use the same methods as HTTP: GET, PUT, POST, and DELETE. One distinctive feature of CoAP is the use of user datagram protocol (UDP) rather than TCP as a transport layer protocol. The HTTP and CoAP protocol stacks are illustrated in Figure 10.4.

Bergmann et al. [44] present a three-phase protocol to bootstrap constrained devices in a wireless sensor network based on IPv6 and CoAP. The protocol phases include service discovery, distribution of security credentials, and application-specific node configuration, each of which is designed to lower the overall vulnerability of the system to some extent. The first phase comprises the detection of a node in the network that can assist a new node in bootstrapping. In the second phase, the new node is provided with keying material to establish a secure channel between a configuration server and the new node. The actual configuration of the new node is performed during the third phase, using the secure channel that has been set up before. Datagram transport layer security (DTLS) is the standard protocol to enable secure CoAP. A novel DTLS header compression scheme, called lightweight secure CoAP for the Internet of Things (Lithe), aiming to significantly reduce energy consumption using 6LoWPAN standard, is proposed [45]. The purpose of the scheme to achieve energy efficiency by reducing the message size and avoiding 6LoWPAN fragmentation when the size of a datagram is larger than the link layer maximum transmission unit (MTU). They evaluate their approach based on a DTLS implementation for the Contiki operating system. The evaluation demonstrates significant gains in terms of packet size, energy consumption, processing time, and network-wide response times when compressed DTLS is enabled. In addition, Ukil et al. [46] propose a novel authentication and key management scheme "Auth-Lite" over DTLS on CoAP. The proposed scheme is robust and lightweight due to its unique nonce-respecting object security along with CoAP header modification. Their solution adopts a symmetric key-based security mechanism in which key management is integrated with authentication. Along with mutual authentication and key exchange protocol, new header options in CoAP are applied to minimize resource consumption. The analysis demonstrates that Auth-Lite is lightweight, which is suitable for resource-constrained sensing nodes.

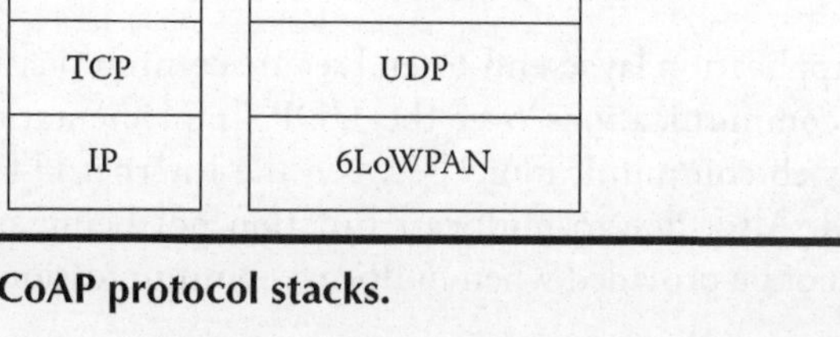

Figure 10.4 HTTP and CoAP protocol stacks.

10.4 Future Research Directions

In the previous sections, we have summarized the security issues and corresponding solutions in M2M communications, which have paved the way for the further research in this area. In this section, we explore future research directions on security issues of the M2M system comprising front-end devices, the network, and the back-end server [47].

Front-end M2M devices can obtain sensory data or gather other information and send it out to the M2M gateway or servers. Since resource-constrained M2M devices are usually deployed in unattended and accessible places, they are more easily tampered with by attackers to cause damage or take illegal action. Thus, more powerful and complex authentication mechanisms and corresponding encryption algorithms are required to prevent eavesdropping or unauthorized access to the data. Integrity protection mechanisms should be designed or enhanced. In devices equipped with universal subscriber identity module (USIM) or UICC, special functions and related security mechanisms are required for the protection of security credentials from being stolen, tampered with, or undermined.

When an attacker uses the network services to impersonate legitimate users, or takes advantage of posing as legitimate users to obtain unauthorized network services, remote validation is required to prevent this unauthorized access. For the threat of the information delivered in the communication networks being stolen or changed, security mechanisms should be designed to ensure the protection of integrity and confidentiality of data communication between M2M devices.

Back-end IT systems formed on the gateway, application, or middleware have high requirements for security. Solutions of machine and card authentication should be designed to handle the security management of code resources. To avoid security threats from replacement of operators, in order to ensure the security of the user information and reduce the risks when switching operators, appropriate security mechanisms should be applied to regulate the behavior of different operators.

As well as the future research discussed above in front-end devices, the network, and the back-end system, the number of MTC devices is rapidly increasing with the deployment of M2M technologies. When a mass of M2M devices simultaneously access the network, if each device needs to implement an independent authentication, this would cause severe signaling congestion. New, efficient group authentication mechanisms are required for future M2M communication.

Although 6LoWPAN is currently being applied to the integration of M2M applications with the Internet, the security requirements for M2M communication still cannot be met completely. Further solutions need to be developed to ensure end-to-end secure communications at the network layer between the M2M devices and the back-end hosts. Security header mapping mechanisms between the M2M 6LoWPAN domain and the Internet domain are required. Though resource-constrained M2M devices cannot currently support all IPSec functions, IPSec could be extended and used in M2M applications in future to ensure safety in the IP layer. It has become more important to promote development of key management systems for 6LoWPAN among nodes. Many other key management technologies of 6LoWPAN need to be designed and developed, including service and equipment discovery, application programming, data fusion, and so on.

At the transport and application layer, end-to-end secure communications are enabled by using DTLS to secure CoAP communications over the UDP. Implementation of end-to-end secure communications for the web communications between the Internet HTTP hosts and the M2M CoAP devices is required. Also, due to multicast function not being supported by DTLS [11], end-to-end security may not be provided when multicast communications are employed to enable a back-end or Internet host to access multiple CoAP resources. To address this issue, mechanisms to implement a proxy device need to be designed and applied.

As an emerging technology of information processing, cloud computing has proved its benefits in high scalability and functional diversity. M2M communication based on cloud computing would be a future trend. However, cloud computing architectures are vulnerable to malicious attacks, such as malicious insiders, data leakage, traffic hijacking, and so on. Certain security mechanisms are needed to defend cloud-based M2M systems against adversaries. Moreover, due to the small amount of transmitted data exchanged between M2M devices and servers, small data transmission is a feature of M2M communications, and data authenticity and integrity should be ensured, since these small data are sensitive and may be related to emergency events.

Despite the existing technologies applied in M2M communication, new communication techniques may be proposed and used in future M2M systems. Light Fidelity (Li-Fi), as a subset of visible light communications, uses light-emitting diode (LED) bulbs to transmit Li-Fi signals and photoreceptors to receive the data [48]. With a lower response time and a higher data rate, this technology could change the way in which machines communicate, and it can be used in application areas that are electromagnetically sensitive. Thus, the related security issues will be addressed.

In summary, with the development of M2M technology, the existing security mechanisms are inadequate and need to be improved to make the M2M communication environment more secure. In future, new security threats may appear, and solutions such as key management, secure routing, data encryption, and so on may also be developed to cope with security and privacy issues.

10.5 Conclusion

In this chapter, we have first introduced the background and the architecture of the M2M communication in the CPS and addressed the security issues and vulnerabilities of M2M systems. We have then reviewed the state-of-the-art security solutions for the M2M device and gateway domain and have classified them into three major categories: detection, authentication, and key management schemes. We have also introduced the 6LoWPAN and CoAP standards as the fundamental technologies of M2M communication in the future. Finally, we have explored future directions for research on security issues for the emerging M2M communications. M2M communication and CPS technologies promise to become crucial game-changing forces to make human lives much better.

Author Biographies

Yue Qiu received a BS degree in information engineering in 2011 and an MEng degree in electronics and communication engineering in 2013 from the School of Information and Electronics, Beijing Institute of Technology, China. While working toward her master's degree, her research interests were e-health systems for indoor locations and detection of falls in elderly people based on ZigBee wireless sensor network and monitoring applications based on Android. She is currently working toward a PhD degree in the Division of Communication Engineering, School of Electrical and Electronic Engineering, Nanyang Technological University, Singapore. Her research interests include machine-to-machine communication security and protocol design.

Maode Ma received his PhD in computer science from the Hong Kong University of Science and Technology in 1999. Now Dr. Ma is an associate professor in the School of Electrical and Electronic Engineering at Nanyang Technological University, Singapore. He has extensive research interests, including wireless networking and network security. He has led or participated in 18 research projects funded by government, industry, military, and universities in various countries. He has been a general chair, technical symposium chair, tutorial chair, publication chair, publicity chair, and session chair for more than 70 international conferences. He has been a member of the technical program committees for more than 180 international conferences. Dr. Ma has more than 260 international academic publications, including 120 journal papers and over 140 conference papers. He has edited 4 technical books and produced over 20 book chapters. He has delivered about 30 keynote speeches and more than 10 tutorials at various international conferences. He currently serves as the editor-in-chief of the *International Journal of Computer and Communication Engineering* and *International Journal of Electronic Transport*. He also serves as a senior editor for *IEEE Communications Surveys and Tutorials* and associate editor for the *International Journal of Network and Computer Applications*, *International Journal of Security and Communication Networks*, *International Journal of Wireless Communications and Mobile Computing*, and *International Journal of Communication Systems*. He was an associate editor for *IEEE Communications Letters* from 2003 to 2011. Dr. Ma is a fellow of the Institution of Engineering and Technology and a senior member of the Institute of Electrical and Electronics Engineers (IEEE) Communication Society and IEEE Education Society. He is the chair of the IEEE Education Society, Singapore Chapter. He is serving as an IEEE Communication Society distinguished lecturer.

References

1. Y. Zhang, W. Duan, and F. Wang. Architecture and real-time characteristics analysis of the cyber-physical system. In *Proceedings of 2011 IEEE 3rd International Conference on Communication Software and Networks* (*ICCSN*), pp. 317–320, 2011.
2. L. Sha, S. Gopalakrishnan, X. Liu, and Q. Wang. Cyber-physical systems: A new frontier. In *Proceedings of IEEE International Conference on Sensor Networks, Ubiquitous and Trustworthy Computing* (*SUTC*), pp. 1–9, 2008.
3. Q. Shafi. Cyber physical systems security: A brief survey. In *Proceedings of 2012 12th International Conference on Computational Science and Its Applications* (*ICCSA*), pp. 146–150, 2012.
4. A. A. Cardenas, S. Amin, and S. Sastry. Secure control: Towards survivable cyber-physical systems. In *Proceedings of 2008 28th International Conference on Distributed Computing Systems Workshops* (*ICDCS*), pp. 495–500, 2008.
5. I. Stojmenovic. Machine-to-machine communications with in-network data aggregation, processing, and actuation for large-scale cyber-physical systems. *IEEE Internet of Things Journal*, vol. 1, pp. 122–128, 2014.
6. J. Song, A. Kunz, M. Schmidt, and P. Szczytowski. Connecting and managing M2M devices in the future internet. *Mobile Networks and Applications*, vol. 19, pp. 4–17, 2014.
7. ETSI, TS 102 690 V2. 1.1. Machine-to-machine communications (M2M); functional architecture. 2013.
8. O. Elloumi and C. Forlivesi. ETSI M2M services architecture. In *M2M Communications*, ed: Wiley, pp. 95–140, 2012.
9. H. Chen, Z. Fu, and D. Zhang. Security and trust research in M2M system. In *Proceedings of 2011 IEEE International Conference on Vehicular Electronics and Safety (ICVES)*, pp. 286–290, 2011.
10. R. Lu, X. Li, X. Liang, X. Shen, and X. Lin. GRS: The green, reliability, and security of emerging machine to machine communications. *IEEE Communications Magazine*, vol. 49, pp. 28–35, 2011.
11. J. Granjal, E. Monteiro, and J. Silva. Security issues and approaches on wireless M2M systems. In *Wireless Networks and Security*. Springer, Berlin, pp. 133–164, 2013.

12. Z. M. Fadlullah, M. M. Fouda, N. Kato, S. Xuemin, and Y. Nozaki. An early warning system against malicious activities for smart grid communications. *IEEE Network*, vol. 25, pp. 50–55, 2011.
13. I. Broustis, G. S. Sundaram, and H. Viswanathan. Detecting and preventing machine-to-machine hijacking attacks in cellular networks. *Bell Labs Technical Journal*, vol. 17, pp. 125–140, 2012.
14. N. Gligoric, T. Dimcic, D. Drajic, S. Krco, and N. Chu. Application-layer security mechanism for M2M communication over SMS. In *Proceedings of 2012 20th Telecommunications Forum* (*TELFOR*), pp. 5–8, 2012.
15. B. S. Adiga, P. Balamuralidhar, M. A. Rajan, R. Shastry, and V. L. Shivraj. An identity based encryption using elliptic curve cryptography for secure M2M communication. In *Proceedings of the First International Conference on Security of Internet of Things*, pp. 68–74, 2012.
16. Y. Ye, Q. Yi, and R. Q. Hu. A secure and efficient scheme for machine-to-machine communications in smart grid. In *Proceedings of 2012 IEEE International Conference on Communications* (*ICC*), pp. 167–172, 2012.
17. N. Mui Van, A. Al-Saffar, and H. Eui-Nam. A dynamic ID-based authentication scheme. In *Proceedings of 2010 Sixth International Conference on Networked Computing and Advanced Information Management* (*NCM*), pp. 248–253, 2010.
18. C. Shuo, and M. Ma. A dynamic-encryption authentication scheme for M2M security in cyber-physical systems. In *Proceedings of 2013 IEEE Global Communications Conference* (*GLOBECOM*), pp. 2897–2901, 2013.
19. X. Sun, S. Men, C. Zhao, and Z. Zhou. A security authentication scheme in machine-to-machine home network service. *Security and Communication Networks*, pp. n/a-n/a, 2012.
20. Y. Lai, J. Kang, and R. Yu. Efficient and secure resource management in home M2M networks. *International Journal of Distributed Sensor Networks*, vol. 2013, p. 12, 2013.
21. H. Lee. Context-aware security system for the smart phone-based M2M service environment. *KSII Transactions on Internet and Information Systems*, vol. 6, pp. 64–83, 2012.
22. L. Hu, et al. The classic security application in M2M: The authentication scheme of mobile payment. *KSII Transactions on Internet and Information Systems*, vol. 6, pp. 131–146, 2012.
23. W. Zhang, Y. Zhang, J. Chen, H. Li, and Y. Wang. End-to-end security scheme for machine type communication based on generic authentication architecture. In *Proceedings of 2012 4th International Conference on Intelligent Networking and Collaborative Systems* (*INCoS*), pp. 353–359, 2012.
24. S. Agarwal, C. Peylo, R. Borgaonkar, and J. P. Seifert. Operator-based over-the-air M2M wireless sensor network security. In *Proceedings of 2010 14th International Conference on Intelligence in Next Generation Networks* (*ICIN*), pp. 1–5, 2010.
25. J.-M. Kim, H.-Y. Jeong, and B.-H. Hong. A study of privacy problem solving using device and user authentication for M2M environments. *Security and Communication Networks*, vol. 9, 2013.
26. B. W. J. H. Hahm. A design of advanced authentication method for protection of privacy in M2M environment. *International Journal of Smart Home*, vol. 7, p. 10, 2013.
27. J. Cao, M. Ma, and H. Li. A group-based authentication and key agreement for MTC in LTE networks. In *Proceedings of 2012 IEEE Global Communications Conference (GLOBECOM)*, pp. 1017–1022, 2012.
28. C. Lai, H. Li, R. Lu, J. Rong, and X. Shen. LGTH: A lightweight group authentication protocol for machine-type communication in LTE networks. In *Proceedings of 2013 IEEE Global Communications Conference (GLOBECOM)*, pp. 832–837, 2013.
29. C. Lai, H. Li, R. Lu, and X. Shen. SE-AKA: A secure and efficient group authentication and key agreement protocol for LTE networks. *Computer Networks*, vol. 57, pp. 3492–3510, 2013.
30. L. Chengzhe, L. Hui, L. Rongxing, J. Rong, and S. Xuemin. SEGR: A secure and efficient group roaming scheme for machine to machine communications between 3GPP and WiMAX networks. In *Proceedings of 2014 IEEE International Conference on Communications* (*ICC*), pp. 1011–1016, 2014.
31. A. Bartoli, J. Hernandez-Serrano, M. Soriano, M. Dohler, A. Kountouris, and D. Barthel. Secure lossless aggregation over fading and shadowing channels for smart grid M2M networks. *IEEE Transactions on Smart Grid*, vol. 2, pp. 844–864, 2011.
32. A. Bartoli, J. Hernandez-Serrano, M. Soriano, M. Dohler, A. Kountouris, and D. Barthel. Optimizing energy-efficiency of PHY-layer authentication in machine-to-machine networks. In *Proceedings of 2012 IEEE Globecom Workshops* (*GC Wkshps*), pp. 1663–1668, 2012.

33. A. Bartoli, J. Hernández-Serrano, O. León, A. Kountouris, and D. Barthel. Energy-efficient physical layer packet authenticator for machine-to-machine networks. *Transactions on Emerging Telecommunications Technologies*, vol. 24, pp. 401–412, 2013.
34. Y. Ben Saied, A. Olivereau, and D. Zeghlache. Energy efficiency in M2M networks: A cooperative key establishment system. In *Proceedings of 2011 3rd International Congress on Ultra Modern Telecommunications and Control Systems and Workshops* (*ICUMT*), pp. 1–8, 2011.
35. Y. Ben Saied, A. Olivereau, and M. Laurent. A distributed approach for secure M2M communications. In *Proceedings of 2012 5th International Conference on New Technologies, Mobility and Security (NTMS)*, pp. 1–7, 2012.
36. I. Doh, L. Jiyoung, L. Shi, and C. Kijoon. Key establishment and management for secure cellular machine-to-machine communication. In *Proceedings of 2013 Seventh International Conference on Innovative Mobile and Internet Services in Ubiquitous Computing* (*IMIS*), pp. 579–584, 2013.
37. X. Ma and W. Luo. The analysis of 6LoWPAN technology. In *Proceedings of Pacific-Asia Workshop on Computational Intelligence and Industrial Application (PACIIA)*, pp. 963–966, 2008.
38. Y. Zhou, Z. Jia, X. Sun, X. Li, and L. Ju. Design of embedded secure gateway based on 6LoWPAN. In *Proceedings of 2011 IEEE 13th International Conference on Communication Technology (ICCT)*, pp. 732–736, 2011.
39. S. Raza, S. Duquennoy, T. Chung, D. Yazar, T. Voigt, and U. Roedig. Securing communication in 6LoWPAN with compressed IPSec. In *Proceedings of 2011 International Conference on Distributed Computing in Sensor Systems and Workshops* (*DCOSS*), 2011, pp. 1–8.
40. H. R. Hussen, G. A. Tizazu, T. Miao, L. Taekkyeun, C. Youngjun, and K. Ki-Hyung. SAKES: Secure authentication and key establishment scheme for M2M communication in the IP-based wireless sensor network (6L0WPAN). In *Proceedings of 2013 Fifth International Conference on Ubiquitous and Future Networks (ICUFN)*, pp. 246–251, 2013.
41. P. Kasinathan, C. Pastrone, M. A. Spirito, and M. Vinkovits. Denial-of-service detection in 6LoWPAN based Internet of things. In *Proceedings of 2013 IEEE 9th International Conference on Wireless and Mobile Computing, Networking and Communications (WiMob)*, pp. 600–607, 2013.
42. T. A. Alghamdi, A. Lasebae, and M. Aiash. Security analysis of the constrained application protocol in the Internet of things. In *Proceedings of 2013 Second International Conference on Future Generation Communication Technology (FGCT)*, pp. 163–168, 2013.
43. W. Colitti, K. Steenhaut, and N. De Caro. Integrating wireless sensor networks with the web. In *Extending the Internet to Low Power and Lossy Networks* (*IP + SN 2011*), 2011.
44. O. Bergmann, S. Gerdes, S. Schafer, F. Junge, and C. Bormann. Secure bootstrapping of nodes in a CoAP network. In *Proceedings of 2012 IEEE Wireless Communications and Networking Conference Workshops* (*WCNCW*), pp. 220–225, 2012.
45. S. Raza, H. Shafagh, K. Hewage, R. Hummen, and T. Voigt. Lithe: Lightweight secure CoAP for the Internet of things. *IEEE Sensors Journal*, vol. 13, pp. 3711–3720, 2013.
46. A. Ukil, S. Bandyopadhyay, A. Bhattacharyya, A. Pal, and T. Bose. Auth-Lite: Lightweight M2M authentication reinforcing DTLS for CoAP. In *Proceedings of 2014 IEEE International Conference on Pervasive Computing and Communications Workshops (PERCOM Workshops)*, pp. 215–219, 2014.
47. J. Du and S. Chao. A study of information security for M2M of IOT. In *Proceedings of 2010 3rd International Conference on Advanced Computer Theory and Engineering (ICACTE)*, pp. V3-576–V3-579, 2010.
48. Li-Fi gets ready to compete with Wi-Fi [News]. *IEEE Spectrum*, vol. 51, pp. 13–16, 2014.

Chapter 11

Securing Embedded Systems: Cyberattacks, Countermeasures, and Challenges

Mohamed Amine Ferrag
Guelma University

Nassira Chekkai
Université Abdelhamid Mehri de Constantine

Mehdi Nafa
Badji Mokhtar University

Contents

11.1 Introduction 280
11.2 Embedded Communication System 283
11.2.1 Network Model 283
11.2.2 Threat Model 285
11.2.3 Contextual Confidentiality 286
11.3 Security Challenges in Embedded Systems 287
11.4 Attacks against Embedded Systems 288
11.5 Cryptographic Countermeasures for Embedded Systems 289
11.5.1 Symmetric Ciphers 290
11.5.2 Asymmetric Ciphers 291
11.5.3 Hash Functions 292
11.5.3.1 Message Authentication Code (MAC) 293
11.5.3.2 Digital Signatures 294

11.5.3.3 Groups of Signatures ... 294
11.5.3.4 Derivation of Symmetric Keys ... 295
11.5.4 Security Protocols ... 295
11.5.4.1 The SSL/TLS Protocol ... 295
11.5.4.2 The IPSec Protocol ... 296
11.5.4.3 The SSH Protocol ... 297
11.6 Biometrics and Embedded Systems ... 297
11.7 Future Research Directions ... 299
11.8 Conclusion ... 299
Author Biographies ... 299
References ... 300

Abstract: Embedded systems are continuously adopted in a wide range of application areas. These systems are based on the use of low-energy-consumption microprocessors or microcontrollers. The main characteristic of embedded systems is that they perform specific tasks, and they are often integrated into devices such as cellular phones, personal digital assistants (PDAs), and smart cards, which they control. According to these characteristics, security threats target embedded systems because they are physically accessible. Following a brief discussion about major challenges in embedded system development, we introduce an example of an embedded communication system, called vehicular peer-to-peer social network (VP2PSN). Based on the internal architecture and external interfaces of embedded systems, we define a taxonomy of basic cyberattacks: physical side-channel attacks and software attacks. We then focus on reviewing and discussing security requirements, cryptographic countermeasures, security protocols, and biometric systems in embedded systems. We conclude with future research directions for embedded systems security.

Keywords: Security; Embedded systems; Symmetric ciphers; Asymmetric ciphers; Hash functions; Biometrics

11.1 Introduction

A cyber-physical system (CPS) is a system of computer components that collaborate to monitor and control the physical entities. In other words, a CPS is a system in which people interact with technology ecosystem–based smart objects through complex processes. The interactions of these four components (people, smart objects, technological ecosystem, and processes) lead to the emergence of a systemic dimension within security in the CPS [1]. Furthermore, CPSs have applications in several fields including aerospace, automotive, chemical processes, civil infrastructure, energy, health care, manufacturing, and transportation.

The design of a CPS is a complex activity that requires the use of several methods and tools during the development process. However, this generation of CPSs is frequently related to embedded systems. These are bringing forward automatic control mechanisms in industrial and transportation areas. In fact, embedded systems are autonomous electronic and computer systems that contain at least one microprocessor and software designed to carry out specific tasks.

Nowadays, embedded systems are pervading our daily lives more and more, being present everywhere: in mobile phones, health, home automation, assistance to people, electronic banking, gaming, and so on (as shown in Figure 11.1).

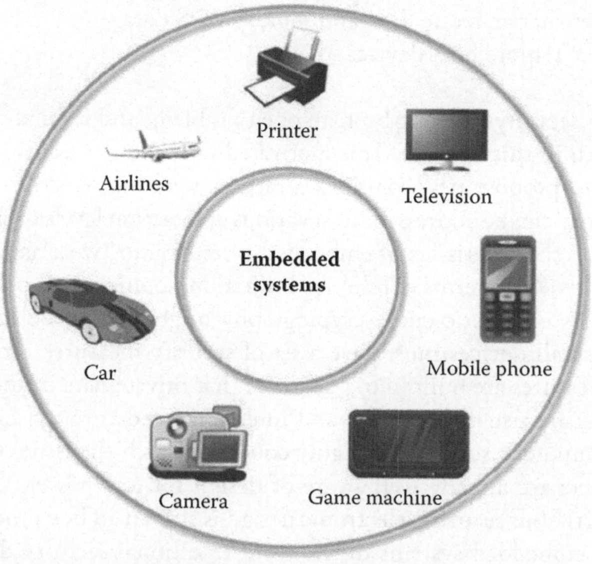

Figure 11.1 Embedded system applications.

Embedded systems may be classified according to their energy source into two categories: embedded systems connected to an external power source, such as printers, and others that depend on a dedicated power source with a finite lifetime; they are often part of the same system as mobile phones [2]. Another classification of embedded systems is in terms of the environment: autonomous systems and buried systems. An autonomous system is stand-alone equipment having an intelligence that allows it to interact directly with the environment in which it is placed, such as a global positioning system (GPS). A buried system is a coherent set of computer components that gives the ability to perform a specific set of missions.

Moreover, embedded systems are dedicated to specific tasks, unlike PCs, which have generic platforms, and they often have both energy constraints and real-time constraints [3]. These real-time events are external to the system and need to be dealt with as they occur in real time. Generally, embedded systems are supported by a wide selection of processors and architectures. The development of embedded systems has certain characteristics and needs that distinguish them from other systems: a high degree of integration of software and hardware components, parallel processing, and often distributed, and a need for hard real time [4].

Security is now a major issue in our economy, hence the need to revisit the concepts and terms related to safety in order to protect ourselves effectively against malicious adversaries. In embedded systems, security covers many issues related to the protection of circuits and the data that they handle: (i) to optimize the implementation of cryptographic algorithms in order to overcome the current limitations in terms of speed, area, power consumption, and resistance to attack; (ii) to develop bench security assessment to deepen understanding of physical attack mechanisms and the associated countermeasures; (iii) to develop new safe brick materials (TRNG, PUF) by taking into account the different execution supports (ASIC, FPGA, RFID, …); (iv) to develop design tools for the systematic realization of hardware architecture incorporating protection mechanisms; and (v) to develop solutions in hardware to protect intellectual property and prevent countevrfeiting of electronic circuits. The security threats to hierarchically managed CPSs arise from four channels [5]:

- Embedded commercial off-the-shelf information and communication technology devices
- Proprietary protocols and closed networks

- Numerous parties that generate, use, and modify CPS data
- A large number of remote field devices

Embedded systems security has long been an open problem, and it remains relevant during the development of research in this domain. This motivated us to survey security problems in embedded systems in order to propose new solutions aimed at securing sensitive information systems. Information flow security can be addressed from various abstraction levels of the system [6]. Hwang et al. have classified the characteristics of embedded systems into two classes: resource limitation and physical accessibility [7]. In terms of resource limitation, sophisticated public key cryptography techniques such as RSA or elliptic-curve cryptography might simply be infeasible. Concerning physical accessibility, small devices must have a set of security measures, since they can be easily lost or stolen. These measures are built in to guarantee that private data cannot be compromised.

Embedded systems are usually complex and interconnected through hardware systems that support embedded computers, so they are highly concerned with the issues of hardware and software security. Designers are already well aware of design for low power, small footprint, high-throughput, and so forth, but securing electronic design is still an ad hoc process [3]. However, the design of security for embedded systems differs from traditional security design [7]. To develop hardware and software security solutions for embedded systems, the security issues of these systems, whose design is often highly constrained, must be identified. These challenges can be summarized in three main areas: (i) the system must ensure authentication, confidentiality, and integrity in distributed data exchange; (ii) the system (hardware and software) must be protected against copying and reverse engineering in the context of fighting against industrial espionage; and (iii) the system must be protected against external attacks that aim to divert it from its function or to take control.

Many studies on secure processors have focused on a single microprocessor. In this area, Xu et al. and Ozdoganoglu et al. propose to guard against overflow attacks of a battery type by using a hardware stack [8,9]. Barrantes et al. present a random instruction set of a processor to make attacks more difficult [10].

Other interesting studies, related to this topic, have focused on side-channel attacks. In this perspective, we find the work of Wang and Lee, who propose to partition cache analyses in order to prevent default cache, and that of Tuck et al., who suggest using encrypted address pointers [11,12]. We also cite the studies of Suh et al. and Crandall and Chong, who propose to tag the data transmitted on a channel that is not trusted and prohibit its use as a jump target [13,14]. In parallel, Ambrose et al. inject a random code to avoid attacks by power analysis [15].

Furthermore, other proposed approaches are built around a particular firewall that is connected to the controller of the external memory bus, between communication and external memory. This firewall provides a range of security features; such as those implemented in the local firewall [16]; it also offers some cryptographic functions to protect data in terms of confidentiality and authentication [17,18].

For the prototyping of embedded systems, the use of a reconfigurable technology such as field-programmable gate array (FPGA) is an interesting solution in comparison with circuits using application-specific integrated circuit (ASIC) technology [19]. The FPGA is used to implement a board with a shorter development time while having the ability to be reconfigured to test an updated version of the embedded system, unlike ASICs, whose structure is final once they have been produced [20]. To secure communications and memories in a multiprocessor architecture embedded in a reconfigurable FPGA component, Cotret proposes the implementation of hardware mechanisms that provide monitoring functions and cryptography [21]. Indeed, these mechanisms aim to protect systems against a model of predefined threats while minimizing the impact of latency to avoid disrupting data traffic in the system.

In 2012, a European project called EURO-MILS was launched, bringing together a team of eight major industrial enterprises looking for security in embedded systems, especially in the aircraft and automotive fields [22]. The main objective of this project is to develop a virtualization technology for heterogeneous embedded systems to ensure security by isolating the system resources. During this project, Muller et al. have proposed new strategies for input-output (I/O) sharing in multiple independent levels of security (MILS) systems, mostly deployed in the special environment of avionic systems [23].

In this chapter, we provide an overview of embedded security issues and cryptographic tools, and identify the most important challenges in this emerging area. Following a brief discussion about major challenges in embedded systems development, we elaborate on embedded systems cybersecurity issues. Thus, we define a taxonomy of basic cyberattacks upon which sophisticated attack behaviors may be built. We then discuss cryptographic tools for securing embedded systems: symmetric ciphers, asymmetric ciphers, hash functions, and security protocols.

11.2 Embedded Communication System

For a decade, the automotive industry has been changing. Vehicles are no longer considered as thermomechanically controlled systems with some electronic components. Today's vehicles are complex systems whose most important functions are controlled by computer networks. There are several factors contributing to this shift in the automotive industry, such as rising fuel and vehicle pollution, potential security threats, and high-density automobile costs. For these reasons, intelligent transportation systems have been developed as a field of new information technologies and communication in the form of wireless communications, GPS tracking, and detection of obstacles and pedestrians. Internet users spend more time on social networks, communicating sensitive personal information (in some cases valuable), and hackers have the solutions to disrupting the system. In addition, the social networking service has quickly spread to mobile platforms, where people wear their multimedia content in powerful personal devices such as laptops, smartphones, and PDAs, and want to share information with their friends or find people with similar interests. Social networking on mobile equipment can be classified into two categories depending on the architecture: with and without infrastructure [24,25]. With wireless communication devices, peer-to-peer (P2P) node community, and vehicular communications, an embedded communication system called a VP2PSN can be formed, on which vehicle users exchange data-related games, rumors, and interesting information using their mobile devices with short-range wireless interfaces as well as with the P2P infrastructure. In this section, we introduce this new embedded communication system by formalizing the network model, the threat model, and contextual confidentiality.

11.2.1 Network Model

We consider a VP2PSN composed of a trust authority (TA), a P2P node community, some vehicle proxy $VP_x(x = 1, \ldots, n)$, a large number of vehicles $V = \{V_1, V_2, \ldots, V_N\}$ with the network size$|V| = N$, and some socialspots $S = \{S_1, S_2, \ldots\}$ in a city environment, as shown in Figure 11.2.

- Trust authority (TA): The TA is fully trusted by all parties in the system and in charge of the management of the whole vehicle P2P system, for example, initializing the vehicle P2P system and registering the vehicles at vehicle proxy (VP). The TA can partition its immense precinct into many domains and deploy VPs between these domains. It should

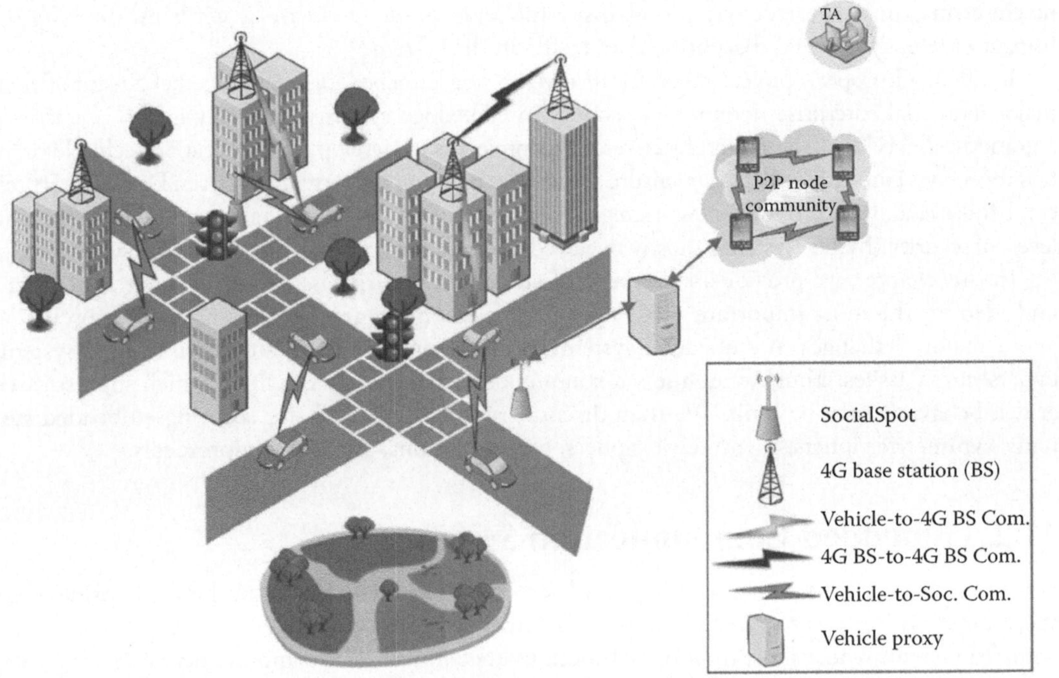

Figure 11.2 Network model under consideration.

be mentioned that the domain information is available to all entities. In addition, when the storage capability is sufficient, the TA is considered to be powered. Otherwise, it is not feasible for any adversary to compromise the TA.

- Peer-to-peer node community (P2P NC): The P2P NC is a decentralized and distributed network architecture in which individual nodes in the network (called "peers") act as both suppliers and consumers of resources.
- Socialspots $S = \{S_1, S_2, \ldots\}$: We use the notion of socialspots proposed by Lu et al., which refer to locations many vehicles will visit, for example, a shopping mall, a restaurant, or a cinema [26]. In addition, the vehicles can communicate with each other, as well as with socialspots such as the roadside units (RSUs) in a typical vehicular ad hoc network (VANET).
- Vehicles $\mathcal{V} = \{V_1, V_2, \ldots\}$: Each vehicle $V_i \in \mathcal{V}$ is equipped with the onboard unit (OBU) device; vehicles may periodically want to meet and receive the latest news stories, share experiences with other vehicles in VANET or with P2P NC, and so on. In general, the OBU device in VANET has no power-limitation issue; however, the storage is assumed to be constrained. Unlike vehicles in a typical VANET, vehicles $\mathcal{V}$ in our model have their sociality, so that a VP2PSN can be formed.
- Sociality: We use the notion of sociability used by the secure shell (SSH) scheme [27], defined as:
  - For each vehicle $V_i \in \mathcal{V}$, let sim(V_i) be the similar interests that V_i has, and soc(V_i) be V_i's sociality, and defined as

$$\mathrm{sim}(V_i) = \begin{cases} 1, & \text{if the vehicle is sociable;} \\ 0, & \text{otherwise.} \end{cases}$$

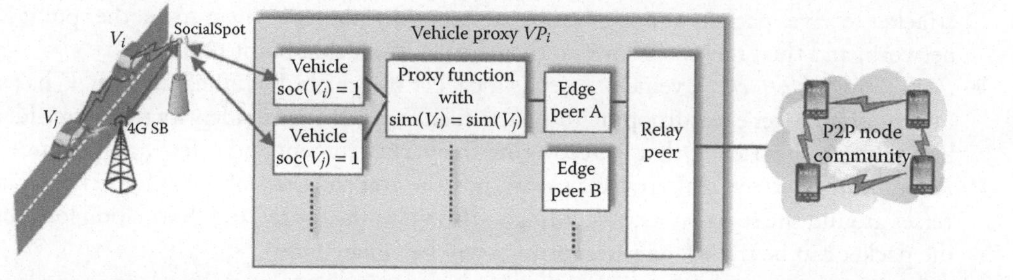

Figure 11.3 Vehicle proxy architecture.

– When two vehicles $V_i, V_i \in \mathcal{V}$ contact, the necessary conditions for establishing a social relationship based on the same similar interests are as follows:

$$\begin{cases} \text{soc}(V_i) = \text{soc}(V_j) = 1, V_i, V_j \text{ are sociable;} \\ \text{sim}(V_i) = \text{sim}(V_j), \text{ have same similar interests.} \end{cases}$$

- Vehicle proxy $\mathcal{VP} = \{VP_1, VP_2, \ldots\}$: In order to incorporate the sociable vehicles into a P2P network, we propose a vehicle proxy architecture (VPA), as shown in Figure 11.3, whereby a vehicle can virtually act as a P2P node and can perform the necessary functions in the P2P architecture based on the necessary conditions for establishing a social relationship, that is, the similar interests. In our network model, different vehicles $\mathcal{V}$ have several vehicle proxies. Each vehicle proxy $VP_i \in \mathcal{VP}$ is a virtual peer connected with the P2P network, and it can fully represent the vehicles toward the fixed and other vehicle P2P nodes, even in the situation when the vehicle is out of coverage or the PDA device lacks battery current. In addition, the VP_i is connected to the TA and the socialspots $\mathcal{S}$ by wired links in the system. They provide service for information dissemination and certificate updating. The certificates issued by a VP_i can only be used in the domain where the VP_i is located.

11.2.2 Threat Model

The vehicle P2P sharing application is subject to the following four security threats: eavesdropping attack, wormhole attack, packet analysis attack, and packet-tracing attack, which are further discussed below.

- *Eavesdropping attack*: Two vehicles V_i and V_j want to share some sensitive information with each other. Meanwhile, they do not allow other unauthorized vehicles to read the information. An eavesdropping attacker without having the appropriate secret keys may implant some malicious Trojan horse programs in the vehicle proxy, so that he can monitor the inside data flows in the vehicle proxy without being detected. This is a stronger threat model than is needed in most realistic scenarios [28].
- *Wormhole attack*: A wormhole attack is launched by a single eavesdropping attacker or by multiple eavesdropping attackers. Two vehicles V_i and V_j having similar interests want to share some sensitive information with another vehicle in VANET or with P2P NC. Based on the normal wireless transmission range of a single hop or through a direct wired link, an

attacker receives packets at one point in the network, "tunnels" them to another point in the network, and then replays them into the network from that point [29].

- *Packet analysis attack*: A vehicle V_i sends a packet to vehicle V_j, indicating that V_i has some information. After eavesdropping this packet, an attacker tries to identify the source identity by analyzing the packet, that is, recovering the packet content and inferring the source [30].
- *Packet-tracing attack*: An attacker eavesdrops the transmission of a single packet as it traverses around the socialspots. According to this view, the source and destination locations of the packet can be traced, and user privacy will be violated [30].

11.2.3 Contextual Confidentiality

In this subsection, we review some of the existing work on confidentiality [31–37]. Generally, to achieve contextual confidentiality of the embedded communication system, existing approaches can be classified into two types: the first by the confidentiality of the source location, and the second by the confidentiality of the destination location.

- *Confidentiality of the source location* consists of two techniques for location privacy (LPR): (1) the packet generation technique, wherein a recognized destination creates false sources each time a transmitter informs the destination that there are data to be sent; (2) routing on a single path, which makes the location of confidentiality by each packet generated by a source on a random path before being delivered to the destination. Another technique for protecting the LPR of the source, presented by Ozturk et al., requires a source node to send each packet through many paths to a destination, in order to make it difficult for an adversary to trace the source [31].
- *Confidentiality of the destination location*: Deng et al. describe a technique to protect destination places from a local spy chopping identification in packet header fields [34]. The authors also present four techniques to protect the location confidentiality of the destination from a local spy who is able to perform temporal correlation and tracking rate [32]. Another technique for protecting the privacy of the destination is presented in [35], where the authors propose a routing protocol for LPR toward the location confidentiality of the destination [35]. The LPR algorithm provides privacy to the destination with the help of redundant hops and fake packets when data are sent to the destination, and particularly in the case of the packet-tracing attack, in which an adversary traces the location of a receiver.

The schemes of privacy have been enhanced for different types of embedded networks. Yipin et al. propose an efficient authentication scheme with strong protection of privacy, called pseudonymous authentication scheme with strong privacy preservation (PASS), for vehicular communications [36]. Unlike traditional pseudonym authentication systems, the size of the certificate revocation list (CRL) in PASS is linear with the number of vehicles. To realize preserving the privacy of the vehicle user while increasing the efficiency of the update key-based localization in vehicular ad hoc networks, Lu et al. propose a system of key management for preserving dynamic privacy, called DynamIc privacy-preserving KEy management (DIKE) [37]. Another interesting study related to privacy is particularly interested in smart grid communications; Lu et al. provide an efficient aggregation scheme for preserving privacy, called efficient privacy-preserving aggregation scheme (EPPA) [33]. EPPA uses a super-increasing sequence structure for multidimensional data, encrypts data structured by the Paillier homomorphic encryption technology, and to reduce the cost of authentication, it adopts a batch verification technique.

There are other security objectives in order to ensure the security of embedded communication systems. We present the comparison of these security objectives in Table 11.1. It can be seen that all schemes

Table 11.1 Comparison of Security Objectives

Security Objectives	*SPRING [30]*	*SPF [26]*	*PCS [38]*	*FLIP [39]*	*Pi [40]*	*ECPDR [41]*
Privacy preserving	X	X	X	X	X	X
Optimizing vehicle DTN	X					
Resistance against attacks on privacy-related vehicles' DTN nodes	X					
Conditional preservation of confidentiality	X	X				X
Location confidentiality		X	X	X		X
Identity confidentiality			X	X		X
Interest confidentiality				X		
Stimulation of selfish DTN nodes					X	
Immutability						X
Responsibility						X
Early detection of routing attacks						X
Transparency						X
Authentication and message integrity						X
Availability of resources						X

achieve the preservation of privacy. The Social-based PRivacy-preserving packet forwardING (SPRING) scheme gives optimized vehicle delay-tolerant networking (DTN), can resist attacks on vehicles' privacy-related DTN nodes, and achieves conditional preservation of confidentiality [30]. The socialspot-based packet forwarding (SPF) scheme performs the conditional preservation of confidentiality and achieves location confidentiality [26]. The PCS scheme achieves identity confidentiality [38]. The Finding Like-minded vehIcle Protocol (FLIP) scheme reaches the same security objective as the PCS scheme and can also achieve interest confidentiality [39]. The practical incentive protocol (Pi) scheme carries only the stimulation of selfish DTN nodes [40]. The efficient conditional privacy-preservation scheme with demand response (ECPDR) scheme achieves immutability, responsibility, early detection of routing attacks, transparency, authentication, and message integrity, as well as availability of resources [41].

11.3 Security Challenges in Embedded Systems

The unique challenges of embedded systems require new approaches to security covering all aspects of embedded systems design from architecture to implementation [42]. To secure an embedded

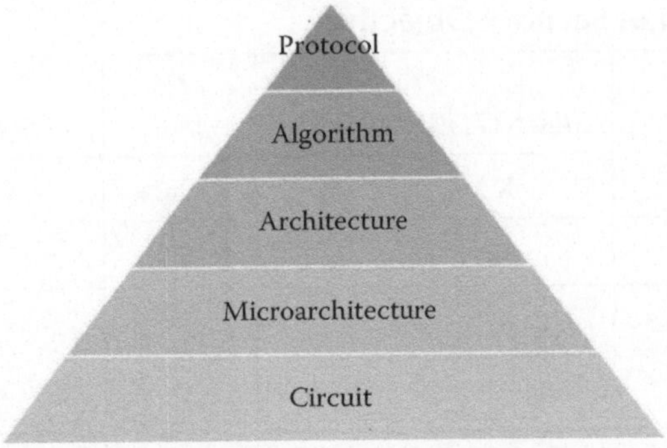

Figure 11.4 Embedded security pyramid.

system completely, Hwang et al. have designed an embedded security pyramid that presents the five primary abstraction levels in an embedded system, as shown in Figure 11.3 [7]:

- *Protocol level*: Includes the design of protocols to be performed on embedded devices to achieve such security goals as:
  - *Authentication*: Determines that something is what it purports to be. Message authentication is of vital importance in the system, because it ensures that the message received is in fact sent from legitimate and authorized parties in the system.
  - *Confidentiality*: Guarantees that the secrecy of transmitted data between communicating parties is maintained: that is, no one other than the legitimate parties should know the content of the exchanged messages.
  - *Nonrepudiation*: Prevents an authorized party from denying the existence or content of a message that is sent by itself. Additionally, it is a critical property for embedded systems, as it can prevent an attacker from denying the attacks that he/she has launched.
  - *Integrity*: Ensure that the exchanged messages between the nodes have not been subject to modifications, additions, or deletions.
- *Algorithm level*: Includes the design of cryptographic primitives (such as SHA-1, DES, RSA, etc.) used at the protocol level.
- *Architecture level:* Includes the design of secure hardware/software partitioning and embedded software techniques protect against hardware attacks such as evil maid attack, cold boot attack, firewire DMA attack, and bus attack, and software attacks such as buffer overflow attack, return-into-libc attack, and code injection attacks.
- *Microarchitecture level:* Deals with the hardware design of the modules (processors and coprocessors) required and specified at the architecture level, including watchdog checkers, memory encryption, integrity trees, and modifications to processor microarchitecture [43].
- *Circuit level:* Requires implementing the techniques on transistor level against physical attacks, namely, side-channel attacks and simple power analysis.

11.4 Attacks against Embedded Systems

Based on the internal architecture and external interfaces of embedded systems (Figure 11.5), the security attacks can be classified into two types: physical and side-channel attacks and software attacks, as shown in Figure 11.6 [44,45].

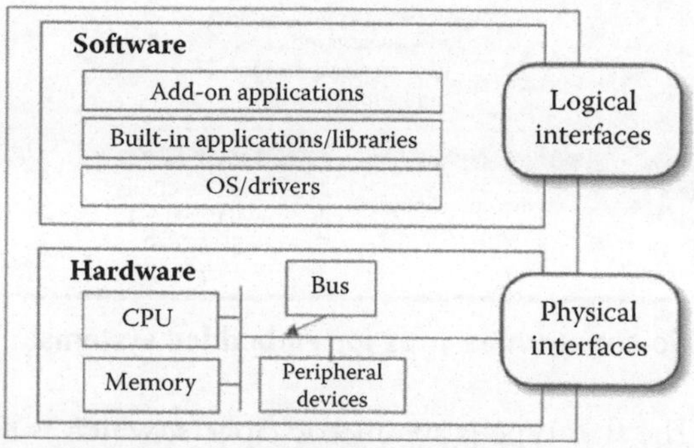

Figure 11.5 Architecture model for embedded systems.

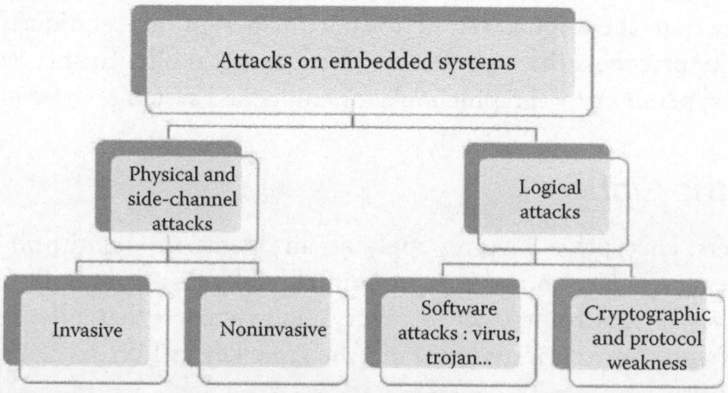

Figure 11.6 Attacks classification in embedded system.

- *Physical attacks:* They are invasive, that is, they will damage or destroy the system. Their major goal is to access elements at different levels of the component in order to reconstruct architecture (technical prepackaging or probing).
- *Side-channel attacks:* Unlike physical attacks, channel attacks are noninvasive, that is, they make an external observation of the system. This may be a power analysis (simple power analysis [SPA] and differential power analysis [DPA]) [46] or the execution time of a program on the magnetic emanations (simple electro-magnetic analysis [SEMA] and differential electro-magnetic analyses [DEMA]) [47]. These different attacks can be combined to obtain secret information as a key encryption.
- *Logical attacks:* They are based on malicious code such as viruses, worms, wabbits, Trojans, backdoors, exploits, rootkits, key loggers, dialers, and URL injectors [48].

11.5 Cryptographic Countermeasures for Embedded Systems

Cryptography has become more diverse; it provides a powerful set of tools to ensure confidentiality, integrity, and authentication. In an embedded system, with these cryptographic tools, the transmitter can send a message to a recipient so that no one can intercept it to access its contents. In addition, the sender can be confident that the message has not been altered during the transfer, and the recipient can also be sure that the message has really been sent from the appropriate sender. However, there are four types of cryptographic tools for secure embedded systems,

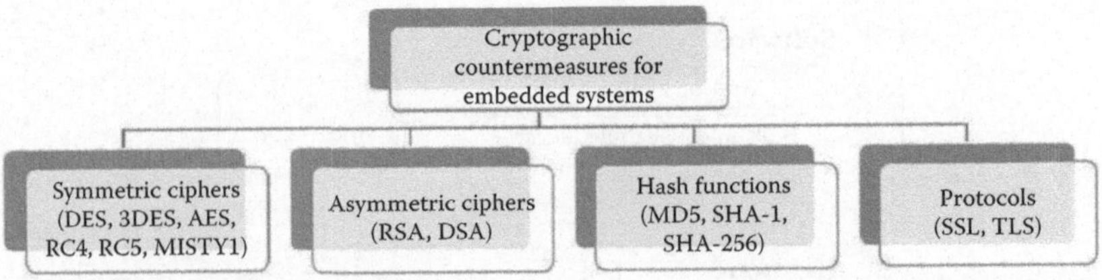

Figure 11.7 Cryptographic countermeasures for embedded systems.

as shown in Figure 11.7. The first type is symmetric ciphers, which is based on the same key to encrypt and decrypt a message, while the second type is asymmetric ciphers, which is based on the principle of two keys: a public key for encryption and a private key for decryption. The third type is the hash function, which converts a large set into a smaller one; it is impossible to decipher the latter in order to return to the original set, so it is not an encryption technique. The fourth type is the exchange security protocols that operate in a client-server mode. In this section, we examine these four different types of cryptographic tools for embedded systems.

11.5.1 Symmetric Ciphers

In symmetric ciphers, encryption involves applying an operation (algorithm) on the data to be encrypted using the private key, to make them unintelligible. Figure 11.8 illustrates the principle of symmetric ciphers. The disadvantage of this encryption system is that it does not provide nonrepudiation. In other words, my correspondent has the same key as I do, so he can create a message by spoofing my identity.

Among the symmetric encryption algorithms that are commonly used, we cite:

- Data Encryption Standard (DES) is an invention of the National Bureau of Standards (NBS), which dates from 1977 [49]. It was the first free public encryption algorithm. The data is divided into blocks of 64 bits and encoded with a secret key of 56 bits specific to a pair of users.

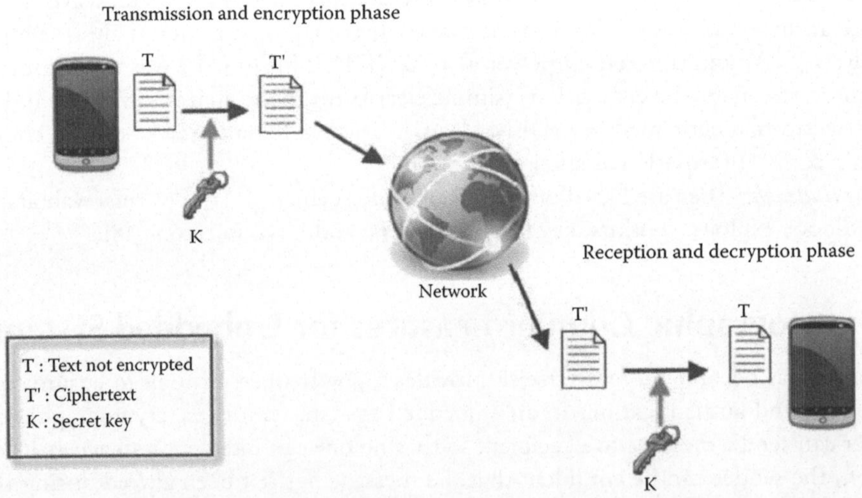

Figure 11.8 Symmetric ciphers for embedded systems.

Table 11.2 Temporal/Energy Costs of Symmetric Algorithms in a PDA (iPAQ3970 and Hx2790)

Symmetric Algorithms	*iOAQ3970*		*Hx2790*		*Ratio*	
	Temporal Costs (ms)	*Energy Costs (mJ)*	*Temporal Costs (ms)*	*Energy Costs (mJ)*	*Temporal Costs (ms)*	*Energy Costs (mJ)*
DES (64)	0.24 + 1.04*x*	0.35 + 0.64*x*	0.27*x*	0.01 + 0.32*x*	3.83	2.01
3DES (192)	0.90 + 2.66*x*	0.56 + 1.66*x*	0.02 + 0.73*x*	0.03 + 0.85*x*	3.66	1.95
AES (128)	0.02 + 0.71*x*	0.07 + 0.46*x*	0.16*x*	0.19*x*	4.44	2.38
AES (256)	0.03 + 0.97*x*	0.07 + 0.64*x*	0.21*x*	0.27*x*	4.56	2.35

- RC2, RC4, and RC5 are a set of algorithms created in 1989 by Ronald Rivest for RSA Security [50]. The acronym "RC" stands for "Ron's Code" or "Rivest's Cipher." This process allows users to select the size of the key (up to 1024 bits).
- Advanced Encryption Standard (AES) was launched in 1997 by the National Institute of Standards and Technology (NIST), and became the new encryption standard for government organizations in the United States, intended to replace DES; it is in the public domain and accepts a key size of 128, 192, or 266 bits [51].

Table 11.2 shows temporal costs and energy costs of symmetric cryptographic algorithms (encryption and decryption) for both iPAQ3970 and Hx2790 platforms, determined by Rifa-Pous and Herrera-Joancomartí [4]. It expresses the linear regression for each tested algorithm in function of the input-text size *x* in *KB*. Compaq iPAQ3970 uses an Intel XScale PXA250 processor at 400 MHz. HP Hx2790 uses an Intel XScale PXA270 processor at 624 MHz. It is clear that the results are better in the Hx2790 device, which is faster. Furthermore, the AES algorithms perform much better than DES and 3DES in both ARM processors.

The main memory of an embedded system can meet a variety of attacks that result either from the listening of an interface between a processor and memory or from a physical attack. Bus listening allows the collection of addresses, and data values can be used to reveal the behavior of the processor. To ensure confidentiality, data encryption is performed by algorithms such as AES or 3DES before external transfers. Data encrypted by these algorithms cannot be decrypted without the associated key [52,53].

11.5.2 Asymmetric Ciphers

This is a radically different approach, which appeared in 1976. Its encoding key is different from the deciphering one. The great novelty of this family of methods is that the cipher key is public. Figure 11.9 illustrates the principle of asymmetric ciphers. This concept of public key cryptography is the result of a mathematical challenge by Witfield Diffie and Martin Hellman [54]. Three American mathematicians (Ronald Rivest, Adi Shamir, and Leonard Adleman) managed to find a solution, which is now used under the name RSA [55]. In addition, this system ensures essential functions such as confidentiality and authentication. Another interesting, widely used algorithm that uses the asymmetric encryption system is the digital signature algorithm (DSA) [56].

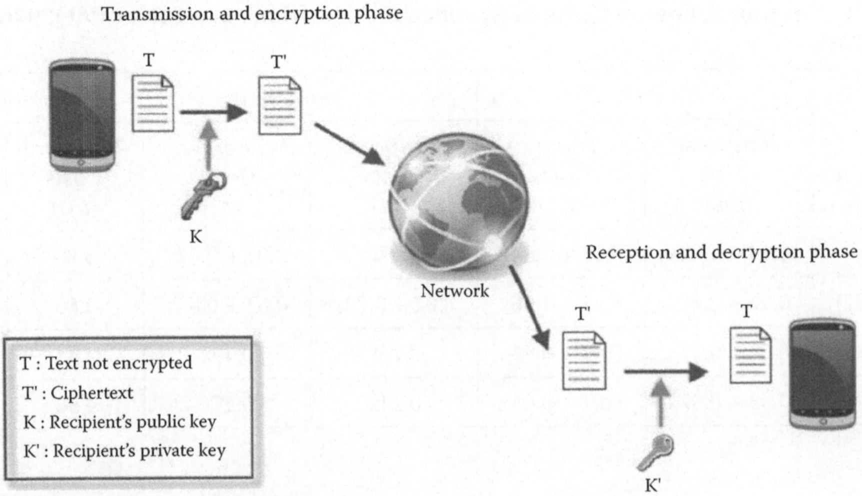

Figure 11.9 Asymmetric ciphers for embedded systems.

Table 11.3 shows temporal costs and energy costs of asymmetric cryptographic algorithms (encryption and decryption) for both iPAQ3970 and Hx2790 platforms, determined by Rifa-Pous and Herrera-Joancomartí [4]. It is clear that DSA-512 takes more time than RSA-512 because of the cost of key generation. In addition, it should be noted that the increment of time delay is influenced by the increased complexity due to the size of the key, especially when using slower microprocessors.

There are other implementations and tests similar to Rifa-Pous and Herrera-Joancomartí [4], including the work of Großschädl et al., Ramachandran et al., and Hager et al. [57–59]. Großschädl et al. launched benchmarking tests in two PDAs: iPAQ4150 with a PXA255 XScale CPU at 400 MHz, and a Dell Axim x30 with a PXA270 XScale CPU at 640 MHz [57]. Ramachandran et al. launched benchmarking tests in an iPAQ4700 with a PXA270 XScale CPU at 624 MHz [58]. Hager et al. launched benchmarking tests in a PDA with a StrongARM SA-1100 processor at 200 MHz [59].

11.5.3 Hash Functions

The hash function is an algorithm that can be used to map digital data of arbitrary size to digital data of fixed sizes. Originally, hash functions were created to facilitate the management database.

Table 11.3 Temporal/Energy Costs of Asymmetric Algorithms in a PDA (iPAQ3970 and Hx2790)

	iPAQ3970		*Hx2790*	
Asymmetric Algorithms	*Temporal Costs (ms)*	*Energy Costs (mJ)*	*Temporal Costs (ms)*	*Energy Costs (mJ)*
RSA-512	431.54	224.17	609.22	608.21
RSA-1024	2,177.21	1,186.79	2,574.12	2,839.17
DSA-512	2,616.54	1,561.21	2,050.48	1,865.25
DSA-1024	17,352.64	11,330.36	8,892.30	10,256.27

Rather than manipulating variable data, which are potentially large, we associate to these data an imprint of a fixed size, on which the comparisons can be made more quickly. The difference between this algorithm and the two types of cryptography presented above is that the latter do not constitute an encryption algorithm.

11.5.3.1 Message Authentication Code (MAC)

These algorithms are imprints dependent on a particular key K and can only be calculated by knowing K [60]. There exist some message authentication code (MAC) constructions from hash functions, the most common being keyed-hash message authentication code (HMAC) [61]. HMAC is based on the use of two constants, *ipad* and *opad*, and on a hash function H. The MAC of a message M with the key K is defined as follows:

$$\mathrm{MAC}_K(M) = H\big(K \oplus opad \,\|\, H\big(K \oplus ipad \,\|\, M\big)\big)$$

A hash function H is cryptographically secure if it satisfies the following three security properties:

1. Pre-image resistance. Given $y \in \{0,1\}\lambda$, regardless of the adversary A, the probability of finding x such that $\mathcal{H}(x) = y$ is negligible.
2. Second pre-image resistance. Given $x \in \{0,1\}^*$, regardless of the adversary A, the probability of finding $x' \neq$ x such that $\mathcal{H}(x) = \mathcal{H}(x')$ is negligible.
3. Collision resistance. Regardless of the adversary, the probability of finding a pair (x,x') such that $\mathcal{H}(x) = \mathcal{H}(x')$ and $x' \neq$ x is negligible. The experiment matching this property defines an adversary A who has access to an oracle O.$\mathcal{H}(m)$. At the end of the experiment, the adversary A returns the pair $\left(x_1^*, x_2^*\right)$. His success in this experiment is:

$$\mathbf{Succ}^{\mathcal{H}}_{\mathrm{CollRes},A}(\lambda) = \mathbf{Pr}\left[\mathcal{H}\left(x_1^*\right) = \mathcal{H}\left(x_2^*\right) \mathbf{avec} x_1^* \neq x_2^*\right]$$

A hash function $\mathcal{H}$ is called *collision resistant* if, whatever polynomial adversary A, its success $\mathbf{Succ}^{\mathcal{H}}_{\mathrm{CollRes},A}(\lambda)$ is negligible. Figure 11.10 shows the relationships between the three strength properties. A function that is resistant to collision is also resistant to the second pre-image, but the reverse is not necessarily true. A function may be collision resistant but nonresistant to the pre-image, and vice versa. A function may be collision resistant but nonresistant to the second pre-image, and vice versa [62].

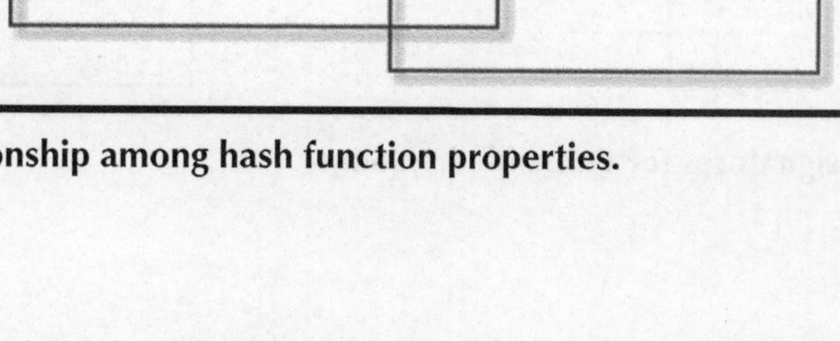

Figure 11.10 Relationship among hash function properties.

Table 11.4 Throughput/Energy Performance of Hash Algorithms in a PDA (iPAQ3970 and Hx2790)

	iPAQ3970		*Hx2790*	
Hash Algorithm	*Throughput (MB/s)*	*Energy (MB/J)*	*Throughput (MB/s)*	*Energy (MB/J)*
md5	18.12	40.19	25.57	24.06
sha-1	9.22	15.81	14.45	12.08
sha-256	1.38	2.08	8.31	6.86
sha-512	1.00	1.44	5.27	4.52

Table 11.4 shows a comparison of the quantity of data that can be hashed in a second of time and with a joule of energy, determined by Rifa-Pous and Herrera-Joancomartí [4]. It is clear that the Hx2790 device outperforms the iPAQ3970 device. In addition, MD5 and SHA-1 are more efficient in terms of energy in iPAQ3970.

11.5.3.2 Digital Signatures

Primitive signatures such as RSA, DSA, or ElGamal require a manipulation of data represented as integer's modular. Using the elliptic curve digital signature algorithm (ECDSA) requires expression as points on elliptic curves [56]. However, the size of data to be signed is constrained. To sign the data of any size, the most common solution is to apply a hash function and then apply the signature function σon the footprint obtained. The signature of a message M is then $\sigma(H(M))$. Figure 11.11 illustrates the principle of digital signature used between two embedded systems.

11.5.3.3 Groups of Signatures

The signatures of groups, introduced by Chaum and van Heyst, help to ensure the anonymity of signers [63]. Any member of the group can sign messages, but the resulting signature keeps the

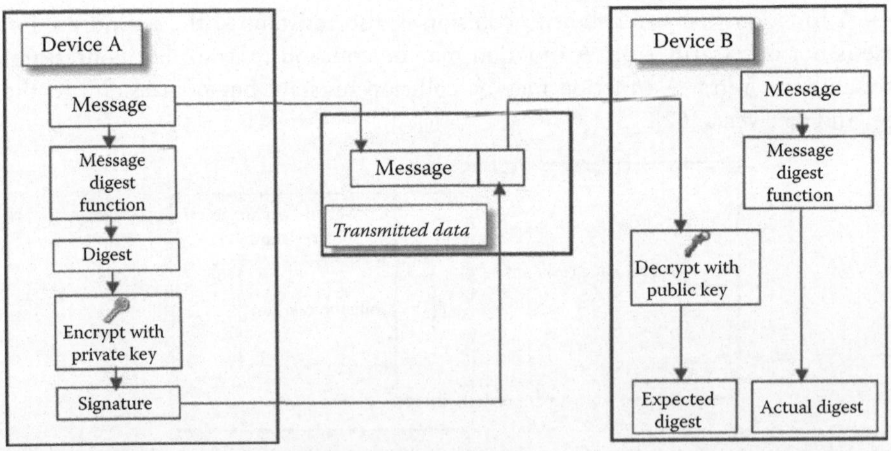

Figure 11.11 Digital signatures for embedded systems.

secret of the signer's identity. In some embedded systems, there is a third party who can trace the signature or cancel his anonymity using a special hatch. Some systems support revocation, whereby the group membership can be selectively disabled without affecting the ability to sign unrevoked members [64,65]. Currently, the most effective construction is done using bilinear groups, introduced by Jens Groth [66].

11.5.3.4 Derivation of Symmetric Keys

The cryptographic hash functions can be used to derive symmetric keys from different types of intelligence, such as the derivation from a master secret. Some communication protocols are based entirely on symmetric cryptography. Devices communicating in this case have a shared secret *S*, which is defined prior to deployment. To limit the impact of keys that are used to protect communications becoming compromised, it is necessary to renew their values regularly [67].

11.5.4 Security Protocols

Compared with the OSI layers, protocols and security services are inserted at various locations in the communication stack. In embedded networks, access points act as a point of authentication role for users. However, there are security protocols for embedded networks, such as secure socket layer (SSL) [68], transport layer security (TLS) [69], IP security protocol (IPSec) [70], and SSH protocol [71].We present these security protocols as follows.

11.5.4.1 The SSL/TLS Protocol

The SSL/TLS protocol sits between the application layer and the transport layer to ensure confidentiality, authentication, and data integrity when communicating between two embedded systems, as shown in Figure 11.12. The record layer provides basic security services to various higher-layer protocols. The handshake protocol is used to authenticate the involved parties and to ensure a secure key management mechanism. The change cipher spec protocol (CCS) allows algorithms, keys, and random numbers to be activated for the current session SSL. The alert protocol specifies the error messages sent between clients and servers. In addition, the SSL/TLS protocol can be applied to applications such as hypertext transfer protocol (HTTP), post office protocol (POP), and file transfer protocol (FTP). For example, regarding the HTTP protocol [72], it was necessary to define a new access method in the URL called HTTPS [73] to connect to the port on a server using SSL/TLS by default bringing the number 443. Figure 11.13 illustrates the principle of HTTP over SSL/TLS.

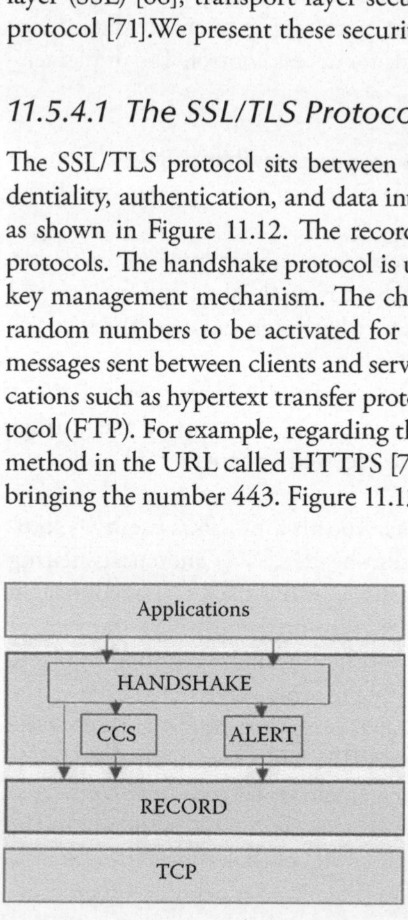

Figure 11.12 HTTP of SSL/TLS.

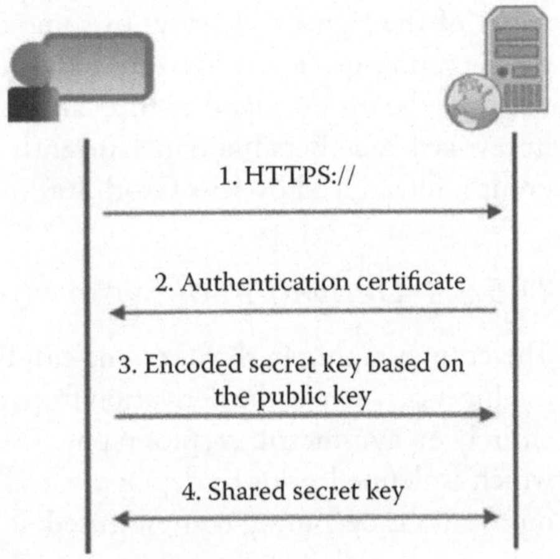

Figure 11.13 HTTP over SSL/TLS.

11.5.4.2 The IPSec Protocol

The IPsec protocol is designed to secure communications at the network layer [70]. IPv4 network is widely deployed, and full migration to IPv6 still requires a lot of time. It quickly became interesting to define security mechanisms that are common to both IPv4 and IPv6. These mechanisms are commonly referred to as IPSec. IPSec provides mechanisms of confidentiality and protection against traffic analysis; mechanisms for authentication of data; mechanisms to ensure data integrity; mechanisms of protection against replay; and mechanisms for access control. The implementations of IPSec are based on the following components:

- Security association (SA): The security association is a connection that provides security services to traffic that it carries. In addition, the SA is a data structure serving to store all the associated parameters at a communication.
- Security policy database (SPD): This ensures that the protections offered by IPSec are based on choices made in a database security policy. This database is established and maintained by an administrator. It enables deciding, for each packet, whether it will alert the security services, will be allowed to override, or will be rejected.
- Security association database (SAD): It permits management of active security associations. It uses, in fact, a database of security associations. This component contains all the settings for each SA and will be consulted on how to handle each received or transmitted packet.

The IPSec services are based on cryptographic mechanisms. To this aim, IPsec uses two security protocols in addition to conventional IP: the authentication header (AH) and encapsulating security payload (ESP) protocols [74]. AH is designed to ensure the integrity of nonconnected mode and origin authentication of IP datagram without data encryption (no privacy). The lack of confidentiality ensures that this standard will be widespread on the Internet, including in places where the export, import, or use of encryption for confidentiality purposes is restricted by law. The ESP protocol can provide data confidentiality and partial protection against traffic analysis if the tunnel mode is used, and data integrity in nonconnected mode. The SAs contain all the parameters required for IPsec, including the key used. The key management of IPsec is only connected to SA; it is not linked to other security mechanisms of IPsec. An SA can be set manually in the case of a simple situation, but the general rule is to use a specific protocol that allows the dynamic negotiation of SA and in particular the exchange of session keys [75]. The SA negotiation protocol developed for IPsec is the internet security association and key management protocol (ISAKMP). ISAKMP is actually unusable alone, and as part of the standardization of IPsec, it is associated with some secure key exchange mechanism (SKEME) and Oakley protocols [76] to give a final protocol called internet key exchange (IKE) [77].

There are two IPSec operational modes: transport mode and tunnel mode. The transport mode takes a stream of the transport level, performs the signature and encryption mechanisms, and then transmits the data to the IP layer. Specifically, in transport mode, inserting the IPsec layer is transparent between TCP and IP, so that TCP sends data to IPsec as it would to IPv4. In tunnel mode, data is sent by the application through the protocol stack until the IP layer is included, and then sent to the IPsec module. The encapsulation in IPsec tunnel mode allows address masking. Typically, the tunnel mode is used between two security gateways (router, firewall …), while the transport mode is between two hosts [78].

11.5.4.3 The SSH Protocol

SSH is a protocol that facilitates secure communications between two embedded systems connected using a client/server architecture. Furthermore, it allows users to connect to remote host server systems. However, unlike other remote communication protocols such as FTP or Telnet, SSH encrypts the login session and thus prevents any attacker from collecting unencrypted passwords [79,80].

With SSH, the client can verify that he is connecting to the same server at the previous session. The client transmits its authentication data to the server using a strong 128-bit encryption. With this encryption, decryption and reading of intercepted transmissions will be extremely difficult [81]. SSH uses a client-server architecture to provide authentication, encryption, and integrity of transmitted data over a network. Version 2 of the protocol specifies the architecture by dividing it into three protocols working together:

- The SSH transport layer (SSH-TRANS): It provides server authentication, confidentiality, and data integrity. This layer must be created for the client, who knows that he is communicating with the correct server. Then, the communication is encrypted between the client and the server by means of a symmetric encryption.
- The SSH authentication layer (SSH-AUTH): It allows the identity of the client to be certified to the server. This layer is secured by the encryption key that was described in Section 11.5. After the client has been authenticated to the server, many different services can be used safely in the connection, such as an interactive session Shell, X11 applications, and tunneled TCP/IP ports.
- The SSH connection layer (SSH-CONN): This layer is based on the authentication layer. It offers a variety of rich services to clients.

11.6 Biometrics and Embedded Systems

The advent of automatic authentication systems, particularly biometric systems, has greatly improved the security of applications that they protect. However, these systems have many flaws or drawbacks. Some are due to the nature of the biometric data used; others are more specifically related to the type of application [82]. Biometric systems dealing with live data, that is, measuring characteristics such as those of the human body, are constantly changing due to aging or trauma.

Systems must then compare these intra-individual variations to allow extended use over time [83]. Fingerprint recognition is now fairly well accepted but requires the physical presence of the person to be identified.

Modalities such as voice or face recognition cause no inconvenience to the user, and their natural appearance is very well tolerated by users [84]. Biometric authentication requires no special knowledge or possession; any individual may attempt to impersonate a client by providing a biometric recognition system. In particular, biometric authentication by voice or video data can be performed without disturbing the user, and these two methods provide a relatively high level of security [85]. Identification and verification of identity are historically the main tasks of biometric systems. A sample of biometric data *S* is supplied to the embedded system by the user with no other information on his identity. The data are compared with a characteristic of each reference *Ix* experienced by the system user, and the result of each comparison is a score [86].

There are two modes of automatic identification: in an open or in a closed environment. In a closed environment, the system automatically determines the most likely users of known identity; this must only be used in an environment in which all individuals are known. In an open environment, the automatic system has the ability to reject a user whose biometric tests do not match any of the listed identities.

To secure embedded systems using biometrics, there are several physical characteristics that seem to be unique to an individual, and there are also several ways of measuring each characteristic [86,87]:

- *Finger scan*: The basic data in the case of the fingerprint pattern is represented by the ridges and valleys of the skin. This design is unique and different for each individual.
- *Hand scan*: This type of biometric measurement is one of the most widespread. It is used to measure a number of characteristics of the hand, such as hand shape, length and width of the fingers, joint forms, inter-joint lengths, and so on.
- *Iris scan*: The individual is placed in front of a charge-coupled device/complementary metal oxide semiconductor (CCD/CMOS) camera that scans the iris [88]. This is very interesting to biometrics because it is always different (even between twins or between the left eye and the right). It is also independent of the genetic code of the individual and very difficult to falsify [89].
- *Retina scan*: This biometric measure is older than the iris technique but was less accepted by the public and users.
- *Facial scan*: This uses more or less advanced photography to extract a set of factors that specific individuals want. There are several variations of facial recognition technology. The first was developed by Kirby and Sirovich and used by Matthew Turk and Alex Pentland for classification of faces, called *Eigenface* [90,91]. Another technique, called *feature analysis*, builds on the previous information by adding the interelement distance.
- *Vein pattern scan*: This technique is usually combined with another, such as the study of the hand geometry.

There are several techniques under development at the present time; among them, we find biometrics based on the geometry of the ear [92], odors [93], and skin [94]. On the one hand, biometric data should not be used alone for strong authentication, because they are not editable, since their nature is specific to each individual. On the other hand, biometrics unfortunately has a major drawback: as it adapts to the environment, the measures change.

11.7 Future Research Directions

For several years, large companies have been working on the integration of embedded communication technologies (ECT) to provide quality services; for example, in the automotive field, researchers are trying to integrate ECT into proposed support services for navigation, traffic forecasting, or more information and audiovisual services. In the future, if we really want to use these autonomous cars based on ECT, we must be sure that they have no defects, especially in data security. However, this chapter considers leaving open a number of additional studies in the following directions:

- Protection against reverse engineering methods: It would be interesting to offer optimal solutions to protect software in embedded systems, especially against reverse engineering methods.
- Full integrity for embedded software: It would be interesting to improve data encryption for ensuring the full integrity of embedded software, namely, pairings and elliptic-curve cryptography [95].
- Detection of compromised programs: It would be interesting to propose some approaches for the detection of compromised programs by analyzing the appropriate characteristics. The validation of these approaches could be done at the time of detection of current changes such as deletion, insertion, and substitution of programs [96].
- New hardware and software platform: In an embedded sensor network, it is very interesting to look at the generation of new implications by designing additional hardware and software platforms about how an operating system manages activity, security, and privacy [97].
- Secure embedded system hardware design: It would be very interesting to improve trust protection mechanisms against physical attacks using trust zone separation, such as the approach proposed by Fournaris and Sklavos [98].

11.8 Conclusion

The embedded system helps us to stay with the rapidly evolving world of intelligent systems and industry devices [99,100]. Cybersecurity in embedded systems is an area of research that has attracted growing attention in government, industry, and academia. In this chapter, we introduced a new embedded communication system, called VP2PSN. We presented a survey of security issues in embedded systems and discussed attack prevention and defense approaches in these systems. We also presented some security protocols to achieve efficient and secure information delivery in embedded systems.

Author Biographies

Mohamed Amine Ferrag received a BSc (2008), MSc (2010), and PhD (2014) from Badji Mokhtar-Annaba University, Algeria, all in computer science. He is an assistant professor in the Department of Computer Science, Guelma University, Algeria. His research interests include wireless network security, applied cryptography, and trusted computing.

Nassira Chekkai received her Master's and PhD degrees in computer science from Constantine 2 University, Algeria, in 2010 and 2014, respectively. Currently, she is an assistant professor in the

Department of Computer Science and Its Applications, Constantine 2 University, Algeria. Her current research interests include graph theory, information filtering systems, and social networks.

Mehdi Nafa is an associate professor at the Computer Science Department of Badji Mokhtar University, Annaba, Algeria. He received his PhD in computer science in 2009 at University Evry, France, following a master's degree in computer science at Poitiers, France, in 2005 and an engineer's degree in computer science in 2003 from the University of Badji Mokhtar. His main research and teaching interests are networks, security, and cloud computing. He currently teaches computer science at the University of Badji Mokhtar and is head of the MobiMADD research team at the Network and Systems Lab (Laboratoire Réseau & Systèmes).

References

1. Riahi, A., Natalizio, E., Challal, Y., Mitton, N., and Iera, A. 2014. A systemic and cognitive approach for IoT security. In *IEEE International Conference on Computing, Networking and Communications (ICNC)*, pp. 183–188.
2. Berthier, N. 2012. Programmation synchrone de pilotes de périphériques pour un contrôle global de ressources dans les systèmes embarqués. Doctoral thesis, L'Université de Grenoble.
3. Knezevic, M., Rozic, V., and Verbauwhede, I. 2009. Design methods for embedded security. *Telfor Journal*, 1(2), pp. 69–72.
4. Rifa-Pous, H. and Herrera-Joancomartí, J. 2011. Computational and energy costs of cryptographic algorithms on handheld devices. *Future Internet*, 3(1), pp. 31–48.
5. Amin, S., Schwartz, G. A., and Hussain, A. 2013. In quest of benchmarking security risks to cyber-physical systems. *IEEE Network*, 27(1), pp. 19–24.
6. Mu, D., Hu, W., Mao, B., and Ma, B. 2014. A bottom-up approach to verifiable embedded system information flow security. *IET Information Security*, 8(1), pp. 12–17.
7. Hwang, D. A., Schaumont, P., Tiri, K., and Verbauwhede, I. 2006. Securing embedded systems. *IEEE Security & Privacy*, 4(2), 40–49.
8. Xu, J., Kalbarczyk, Z., Patel, S., and Iyer, R. K. 2002. Architecture support for defending against buffer overflow attacks. In *Workshop on Evaluating and Architecting Systems for Dependability*.
9. Ozdoganoglu, H., Vijaykumar, T. N., Brodley, C. E., Kuperman, B. A., and Jalote, A. 2006. SmashGuard: A hardware solution to prevent security attacks on the function return address. *IEEE Transactions on Computers*, 55(10), pp. 1271–1285.
10. Barrantes, G., Ackley, D. H., Palmer, T. S., Forrest, S., Stefanovic, D., and Zovi, D. D. 2003. Randomized instruction set emulation to disrupt binary code injection attacks. In *Proceedings of the 10th ACM Conference on Computer and Communications Security*, pp. 281–289, ACM, New York.
11. Wang, Z. and Lee, R. B. 2007. New cache designs for thwarting software cache-based side channel attacks. In *ACM SIGARCH Computer Architecture News*, 35(2), pp. 494–505.
12. Tuck, N., Calder, B., and Varghese, G. 2004. Hardware and binary modification support for code pointer protection from buffer overflow. In *37th International Symposium on Microarchitecture*, pp. 209–220. IEEE.
13. Suh, G. E., Lee, J. W., Zhang, D., and Devadas, S. 2004. Secure program execution via dynamic information flow tracking. In *ACM SIGPLAN Notices–ASPLOS'04*, 39(11), pp. 85–96, ACM, New York.
14. Crandall, J. R. and Chong, F. T. 2004. Minos: Control data attack prevention orthogonal to memory model. In *37th International Symposium on Microarchitecture*, pp. 221–232. IEEE.
15. Ambrose, J. A., Ragel, R. G., and Parameswaran, S. 2007. RIJID: Random code injection to mask power analysis based side channel attacks. In *Proceedings of the 44th Annual Design Automation Conference*, ACM, San Diego, CA, pp. 489–492.
16. Al-Shaer, E., Hamed, H., Boutaba, R., and Hasan, M. 2005. Conflict classification and analysis of distributed firewall policies. *IEEE Journal on Selected Areas in Communications*, 23(10), 2069–2084.

17. Gamage, C., Leiwo, J., and Zheng, Y. 1999. Encrypted message authentication by firewalls. In *Public Key Cryptography*, pp. 69–81. Springer, Berlin.
18. Oppliger, R. 1997. Internet security: Firewalls and beyond. *Communications of the ACM*, 40(5), 92–102.
19. Betz, V. and Rose, J. 1997. VPR: A new packing, placement and routing tool for FPGA research. In *Field-Programmable Logic and Applications*, pp. 213–222. Springer, Berlin.
20. Wolkerstorfer, J., Oswald, E., and Lamberger, M. 2002. An ASIC implementation of the AES SBoxes. In *Topics in Cryptology—CT-RSA 2002*, pp. 67–78. Springer, Berlin.
21. Cotret, P. 2012. Protection des architectures hétérogènes multiprocesseurs dans les systèmes embarqués: Une approche décentralisée basée sur des pare-feux matériels. PhD thesis, Université de Bretagne Sud.
22. EURO-MILS Project. Reference: 318353. [Online] https://www.euromils.eu/. Accessed December 12, 2014.
23. Muller, K., Sigl, G., Triquet, B., and Paulitsch, M. 2014. On MILS I/O sharing targeting avionic systems. In *Dependable Computing Conference (EDCC), 2014 TenthEuropean*, pp. 182–193.
24. Lu, R. 2012. Security and privacy preservation in vehicular social networks. PhD thesis, University of Waterloo, Canada.
25. Ferrag, M. A. 2014. La sécurisation des réseaux sociaux mobiles. PhD thesis, Badji Mokhtar—Annaba University, Algeria.
26. Lu, R., Lin, X., Liang, X., and Shen, X. 2010. Sacrificing the plum tree for the peach tree: A socialspot tactic for protecting receiver-location privacy in vanet. In *Global Telecommunications Conference (GLOBECOM 2010), 2010 IEEE*, pp. 1–5. IEEE.
27. Lu, R., Lin, X., Liang, X., and Shen, X. 2011. A secure handshake scheme with symptoms-matching for mhealthcare social network. *Mobile Networks and Applications*, 16(6), 683–694.
28. Lin, X., Lu, R., Shen, X., Nemoto, Y., and Kato, N. 2009. SAGE: A strong privacy-preserving scheme against global eavesdropping for ehealth systems. *IEEE Journal on Selected Areas in Communications*, 27(4), 365–378.
29. Hu, Y. C. Perrig, A., and Johnson, D. B. 2006. Wormhole attacks in wireless networks. *IEEE Journal on Selected Areas in Communications*, 24(2), pp. 370–380.
30. Lu, R., Lin, X., and Shen, X. 2010. Spring: A social-based privacy-preserving packet forwarding protocol for vehicular delay tolerant networks. In *INFOCOM, 2010 Proceedings IEEE*, pp. 1–9. IEEE.
31. Ozturk, C. and Zhang, Y. 2004. Source-location privacy in energy-constrained sensor network routing. *Proceedings of the 2nd ACM Workshop on Security of Ad Hoc and Sensor Networks*, pp. 88–93. ACM New York, Washington, DC.
32. Deng, J., Richard, H., and Shivakant, M. 2006. Decorrelating wireless sensor network traffic to inhibit traffic analysis attacks. *Elsevier Pervasive and Mobile Computing Journal*, 2(2), 159–186.
33. Lu, R., Liang, X., Li, X., Lin, X., and Shen, X. 2012. EPPA: An efficient and privacy-preserving aggregation scheme for secure smart grid communications. *IEEE Transactions on Parallel and Distributed Systems*, 23(9), 1621–1631.
34. Deng, J., Han, R., and Mishra, S. 2003. Enhancing base station security in wireless sensor networks. CU-CS-951-03: University of Colorado, Department of Computer Science Technical Report.
35. Jian, Y., Shigang, C., Zhan, Z., and Liang, Z. 2007. Protecting receiver-location privacy in wireless sensor networks. In *Proceedings of 26th IEEE International Conference on Computer Communications*, pp. 1955–1963. IEEE Computer Society, Anchorage, AL.
36. Yipin, S., Lu, R., Lin, X., Shen, X., and Su, J. 2010. An efficient pseudonymous authentication scheme with strong privacy preservation for vehicular communications. *IEEE Transactions on Vehicular Technology*, 59(7), 3589–3603.
37. Lu, R., Lin, X., Liang, X., and Shen, X. 2012. A dynamic privacy-preserving key management scheme for location based services in VANETs. *IEEE Transactions on Intelligent Transportation Systems*, 13(1), 127–139.
38. Lu, R., Lin, X., Luan, H., Liang, X., and Shen, X. 2012. Pseudonym changing at social spots: An effective strategy for location privacy in VANETs. *IEEE Transactions on Vehicular Technology*, 61(1), 86–96.

39. Lu, R., Lin, X., Liang, X., and Shen, X. 2010. Flip: An efficient privacy-preserving protocol for finding like-minded vehicles on the road. In *Global Telecommunications Conference*, Waterloo, ON, pp. 1–5.
40. Lu, R., Lin, X., Zhu, H., Shen, X., and Preiss, B. R. 2010. Pi: A practical incentive protocol for delay tolerant networks. *IEEE Transactions on Wireless Communications*, 9(4), 1483–1493.
41. Ferrag, M. A., Nafa, M., and Ghanemi, S. 2013. ECPDR: An efficient conditional privacy-preservation scheme with demand response for secure ad hoc social communications. *International Journal of Embedded and Real-Time Communication Systems (IJERTCS)*, 4(3), 43–71.
42. Ravi, S., Raghunathan, A., Kocher, P., and Hattangady, S. 2004. Security in embedded systems: Design challenges. *ACM Transactions on Embedded Computing Systems (TECS)*, 3(3), pp. 461–491.
43. Kanuparthi, A. K., Karri, R., Ormazabal, G., and Addepalli, S. K. 2012. A survey of microarchitecture support for embedded processor security. *2012 IEEE Computer Society Annual Symposium on VLSI (ISVLSI)*, New York, pp. 368–373.
44. Khelladi, L., Challal, Y., Bouabdallah, A., and Badache, N. 2008. On security issues in embedded systems: Challenges and solutions. *International Journal of Information and Computer Security*, 2(2), 140–174.
45. Ferrag, M. A., Nafa, M., and Ghanemi, S. 2014. Security and privacy for routing protocols in mobile ad hoc networks. *Security for Multihop Wireless Networks*, 19.
46. Kocher, P., Jaffe, J., and Jun, B. 1999. Differential power analysis. In *Advances in Cryptology—CRYPTO'99*, pp. 388–397. Springer, Berlin.
47. Agrawal, D., Archambeault, B., Rao, J. R., and Rohatgi, P. 2003. The EM side—Channel (s). In *Cryptographic Hardware and Embedded Systems-CHES 2002*, pp. 29–45. Springer, Berlin.
48. Dixon, J. 2006. Protected software identifiers for improving security in a computing device. U.S. Patent Application 12/063,178.
49. Coppersmith, D. 1994. The data encryption standard (DES) and its strength against attacks. *IBM Journal of Research and Development*, 38(3), 243–250.
50. Rivest, R. L. 1995. The RC5 encryption algorithm. In *Fast Software Encryption*, pp. 86–96. Springer, Berlin.
51. Daemen, J. and Rijmen, V. 2002. *The Design of Rijndael: AES—The Advanced Encryption Standard*. Springer, Berlin.
52. Jérémie, C. 2011. Sécurité haut-débit pour les systèmes embarqués à base de FPGAs. PhD thesis, Université de Bretagne Sud.
53. Elbaz, R., Torres, L., Sassatelli, G., Guillemin, P., Bardouillet, M., and Martinez, A. 2006. A parallelized way to provide data encryption and integrity checking on a processor-memory bus. In *Proceedings of the Design Automation Conference, 43rd ACM/IEEE*, pp. 506–509.
54. Diffie, W. and Hellman, M. E. 1976. New directions in cryptography. *IEEE Transactions on Information Theory*, 22(6), 644–654.
55. Rivest, R. L., Shamir, A., and Tauman, Y. 2001. How to leak a secret. In *Advances in Cryptology—ASIACRYPT 2001*, pp. 552–565. Springer, Berlin.
56. Johnson, D., Menezes, A., and Vanstone, S. 2001. The ellipticcurve digital signature algorithm (ECDSA). *International Journal of Information Security*, 1(1), 36–63.
57. Großschädl, J., Tillich, S., Rechberger, C., Hofmann, M., and Medwed, M. 2007. Energy evaluation of software implementations of block ciphers under memory constraints. In *Proceedings of the Conference on Design, Automation and Test in Europe*, pp. 1110–1115. EDA Consortium.
58. Ramachandran, A., Zhou, Z., and Huang, D. 2007. Computing cryptographic algorithms in portable and embedded devices. In *IEEE International Conference on Portable Information Devices*, pp. 1–7. IEEE.
59. Hager, C. T., Midkiff, S. F., Park, J. M., and Martin, T. L. 2005. Performance and energy efficiency of block ciphers in personal digital assistants. In *Third IEEE International Conference on Pervasive Computing and Communications*, pp. 127–136. IEEE.
60. Bellare, M., Kilian, J., and Rogaway, P. 2000. The security of the cipher block chaining message authentication code. *Journal of Computer and System Sciences*, 61(3), 362–399.
61. Krawczyk, H. Bellare, M., and Canetti, R. 1997. HMAC: Keyed-hashing for message authentication. Internet Request for Comments RFC, 2104. https://tools.ietf.org/html/rfc2104.

62. William, S. 2011. *Cryptography and Network Security Principles and Practice*, 5th edn. Prentice Hall.
63. Chaum, D. and van Heyst, E. 1991. Group signatures. In *Proceedings of Eurocrypt 1991*, pp. 257–265. Springer-Verlag.
64. Camenisch, J., and Lysyanskaya, A. 2002. Dynamic accumulators and application to efficient revocation of anonymous credentials. In *Proceedings of Crypto 2002*, pp. 61–76. Springer-Verlag.
65. Ateniese, G., Tsudik, G., and Song, D. 2003. Quasi-efficient revocation of group signatures. *Proceedings of Financial Cryptography 2002*, 2357, pp. 183–197.
66. Groth, J. 2007. Fully anonymous group signatures without random oracles. In *13th International Conference on the Theory and Application of Cryptology and Information Security*, pp. 164–180. Springer, Berlin.
67. Faust, S., Mukherjee, P., Venturi, D., and Wichs, D. 2014. Efficient non-malleable codes and key-derivation for poly-size tampering circuits. In *Advances in Cryptology–EUROCRYPT 2014*, pp. 111–128. Springer, Berlin.
68. Freier, A., Karlton, P., and Kocher, P. 2011. The secure sockets layer (SSL) protocol version 3.0. Internet Engineering Task Force (IETF), https://tools.ietf.org/html/rfc6101.
69. Dierks, T. 2008. The transport layer security (TLS) protocol version 1.2. Internet Engineering Task Force (IETF), https://tools.ietf.org/html/rfc5246.
70. Devarapalli, V. and Dupont, F. 2007. Mobile IPv6 operation with IKEv2 and the revised IPSec architecture. Internet Engineering Task Force (IETF), http://tools.ietf.org/html/rfc4877.
71. Ylonen, T. and Lonvick, C. 2006. The secure shell (SSH) protocol architecture. Internet Engineering Task Force (IETF). https://tools.ietf.org/html/rfc4251.
72. Fielding, R. T., Berners-Lee, T., and Frystyk, H. 1996. Hypertext Transfer Protocol–HTTP/1.0. Internet Engineering Task Force (IETF). http://www.hjp.at/doc/rfc/rfc1945.html.
73. Rescorla, E., and Schiffman, A. 1999. The secure hypertext transfer protocol. Internet Engineering Task Force (IETF). http://tools.ietf.org/html/rfc2660.
74. Manral, V. 2007. Cryptographic algorithm implementation requirements for encapsulating security payload (ESP) and authentication header (AH). *Internet Engineering Task Force (IETF).* http://tools.ietf.org/html/rfc4302.html.
75. Gearhart, C. M., Meyer, C., Overby Jr, L. H., and Wierbowski, D. J. 2012. Selective IPSec security association recovery. U.S. Patent No. 8,141,126. U.S. Patent and Trademark Office, Washington, DC.
76. Moravejosharieh, A., Modares, H., and Salleh, R. 2012. Overview of mobile ipv6 security. In *2012 Third International Conference on Intelligent Systems, Modelling and Simulation (ISMS)*, pp. 584–587. IEEE.
77. Das, S., Ohba, Y., Kanda, M., Famolari, D., and Das, S. K. 2012. A key management framework for AMI networks in smart grid. *IEEE Communications Magazine*, 50(8), 30–37.
78. Raza, S., Duquennoy, S., Chung, T., Voigt, T., and Roedig, U. 2011. Securing communication in 6LoWPAN with compressed IPSec. In *2011 International Conference on Distributed Computing in Sensor Systems and Workshops (DCOSS)*, pp. 1–8. IEEE.
79. Dowling, B., Bergsma, F., Kohlar, F., Schwenk, J., and Stebila, D. 2013. Multi-ciphersuite security and the SSH protocol. *IACR Cryptology ePrint Archive, 2013*, 813.
80. Ponomarev, S., Wallace, N., and Atkison, T. 2014. Detection of SSH host spoofing in control systems through network telemetry analysis. In *Proceedings of the 9th Annual Cyber and Information Security Research Conference*, pp. 21–24. ACM.
81. Ferrag, M. A., Ghanmi, S., and Nafa, M. 2012. OlsrBOOK: A privacy-preserving mobile social network leveraging on securing the OLSR routing protocol. In *Conference Proceedings of eLearning and Software for Education* (*eLSE*), pp. 133–139.
82. Chouta, T., Graba, T., Danger, J. L., Bringer, J., Berthier, M., Bocktaels, Y., and Chabanne, H. 2014. Side channel analysis on an embedded hardware fingerprint biometric comparator & low cost countermeasures. In *Proceedings of the Third Workshop on Hardware and Architectural Support for Security and Privacy*, p. 6. ACM.
83. Ghasemzadeh, H., Ostadabbas, S., Guenterberg, E., and Pantelopoulos, A. 2013. Wireless medical-embedded systems: A review of signal-processing techniques for classification. *IEEE Sensors Journal*, 13(2), 423–437.

84. Bowyer, K. W., Hollingsworth, K. P., and Flynn, P. J. 2013. A survey of iris biometrics research: 2008–2010. In *Handbook of Iris Recognition*, pp. 15–54. Springer, London.
85. Klonovs, J., Petersen, C. K., Olesen, H., and Hammershoj, A. 2013. ID proof on the go: Development of a mobile EEG-based biometric authentication system. *IEEE Vehicular Technology Magazine*, 8(1), 81–89.
86. Karaman, S. and Bagdanov, A. D. 2012. Identity inference: Generalizing person re-identification scenarios. In *Computer Vision–ECCV 2012. Workshops and Demonstrations*, pp. 443–452. Springer, Berlin.
87. Sujithra, M. and Padmavathi, G. 2012. Next generation biometric security system: An approach for mobile device security. In *Proceedings of the Second International Conference on Computational Science, Engineering and Information Technology*, pp. 377–381. ACM.
88. Holst, G. C. and Lomheim, T. S. 2007. *CMOS/CCD Sensors and Camera Systems*, Vol. 408. JCD Publishing.
89. Beenau, B. W., Bonalle, D. S., Fields, S. W., Gray, W. J., Larkin, C., Montgomery, J. L., and Saunders, P. D. 2012. Iris scan biometrics on a payment device. U.S. Patent No 8,279,042.
90. Agarwal, M., Agrawal, H., Jain, N., and Kumar, M. 2010. Face recognition using principle component analysis, eigenface and neural network. In *International Conference on Signal Acquisition and Processing, 2010. ICSAP'10*, pp. 310–314. IEEE.
91. Meytlis, M. and Sirovich, L. 2007. On the dimensionality of face space. *IEEE Transactions on Pattern Analysis and Machine Intelligence*, 29(7), 1262–1267.
92. Choraś, M. 2005. Ear biometrics based on geometrical feature extraction. *Electronic Letters on Computer Vision and Image Analysis*, 5(3), 84–95.
93. Wongchoosuk, C., Lutz, M., and Kerdcharoen, T. 2009. Detection and classification of human body odor using an electronic nose. *Sensors*, 9(9), 7234–7249.
94. Rowe, R. K. 2007. Biometrics based on multispectral skin texture. In *Advances in Biometrics*, pp. 1144–1153. Springer, Berlin.
95. Unterluggauer, T. and Wenger, E. 2014. Efficient pairings and ECC for embedded systems. In *Cryptographic Hardware and Embedded Systems–CHES 2014*, pp. 298–315. Springer, Berlin.
96. Zhai, X., Appiah, K., Ehsan, S., Cheung, W. M., Howells, G., Hu, H., and McDonald-Maier, K. 2014. Detecting compromised programs for embedded system applications. In *Architecture of Computing Systems–ARCS 2014*, pp. 221–232. Springer International Publishing.
97. Pannuto, P., Andersen, M. P., Bauer, T., Campbell, B., Levy, A., Culler, D., and Dutta, P. 2014. A networked embedded system platform for the post-mote era. In *Proceedings of the 12th ACM Conference on Embedded Network Sensor Systems*, pp. 354–355. ACM.
98. Fournaris, A. P. and Sklavos, N. 2014. Secure embedded system hardware design: A flexible security and trust enhanced approach. *Computers & Electrical Engineering*, 40(1), pp. 121–133.
99. Bhatti, S., Carlson, J., Dai, H., Deng, J., Rose, J., Sheth, A., and Han, R. 2005. MANTIS OS: An embedded multithreaded operating system for wireless micro sensor platforms. *Mobile Networks and Applications*, 10(4), pp.563–579.
100. Pillai, P. and Shin, K. G. 2001. Real-time dynamic voltage scaling for low-power embedded operating systems. In *ACM SIGOPS Operating Systems Review*, 35(5), pp. 89–102. ACM.

Chapter 12

Using Software-Defined Networking to Mitigate Cyberattacks in Industrial Control Systems

Béla Genge and Piroska Haller

Petru Maior University

Adela Beres and Hunor Sándor

Technical University of Cluj-Napoca

István Kiss

Petru Maior University and Technical University of Cluj-Napoca

Contents

12.1 Introduction 306

12.2 Industrial Control Systems and IP Networking 309

12.2.1 Overview of Industrial Control Systems 309

12.2.2 Modern IP Networking Technologies and ICSs 310

12.3 Possible SDN-Enabled Approaches to Mitigate Cyberattacks in Large ICSs 311

12.3.1 Assumptions on Network Topology and Basic Model 311

12.3.2 Approach 1: Rerouting Traffic in SDN Networks 312

12.3.3 Approach 2: Blocking Traffic in SDN Networks 312

12.4 A Novel Approach to Experiment with SDN-Enabled ICSs 314

12.4.1 Simulated versus Real ICSs 315

12.4.2 Sensei/IoT* Overview 316

12.4.3 Communication Modules Enabling Experimentation with Sensei/IoT* 316

12.4.4 Physical Process Simulators 317

12.4.5 SDN Enablers 318
12.4.6 Proposed Experimentation Approach 318
12.5 Use Case Assessment 319
12.5.1 Physical Process 320
12.5.2 Experiment 1: SDN-Based Traffic Rerouting 321
12.5.3 Experiment 2: SDN-Based Traffic Blocking 322
12.6 Conclusion 324
Acknowledgment 325
Author Biographies 325
Glossary 326
References 327

Abstract: The massive proliferation of traditional information and communication technologies (ICT) hardware and software into the heart of industrial control systems (ICSs) has given birth to a unique technological ecosystem. As a result, modern ICSs deliver advanced services and features, and facilitate the implementation of novel infrastructural paradigms such as the smart grid. Nevertheless, this technological advancement also brings new design challenges that must account for sophisticated cyber-physical attacks. To address these challenges, this work explores the applicability of state-of-the-art techniques from the field of traditional Internet protocol (IP) networks to implement advanced mitigation techniques in ICSs against complex cyberattacks. We provide an in-depth analysis of software-defined networking (SDN) and network functions virtualization (NFV) to identify intrinsic features aimed at the implementation of closed-loop intrusion detection systems. We propose a novel framework to experiment with SDN-enabled ICSs, which is subsequently applied to illustrate the impact on the outcome of cyberattacks in two scenarios: a scenario involving an SDN-enabled ICSs with the Tennessee Eastman (TE) chemical process illustrates the impact of strategic and dynamic rerouting techniques in SDN; and a large-scale SDN topology demonstrates the effectiveness of dynamic attack traffic blocking.

Keywords: Cyberattacks; Emulation; Industrial control systems; Intrusion detection systems; Network functions virtualization; OpenFlow; Security; Simulation; Software-defined networking

12.1 Introduction

Modern industrial control systems (ICSs) are complex cyber-physical environments where elements from the cyber and the physical domains are tightly glued together. The term *ICSs* refers to a wide variety of control systems that are generally used in industrial environments to control physical processes ranging from water purification systems and power grids to oil and gas pipelines. Typical ICSs subsystems and components include supervisory control and data acquisition (SCADA) systems that monitor the physical process and issue commands based on global actuation strategies; human–machine interfaces (HMI) that provide visualization and generally human–process interaction features; and programmable logical controllers (PLCs), which ensure the implementation of local actuation strategies. PLCs monitor and control the physical process based on locally implemented control loops. Nonetheless, they also send sensor measurements to

SCADA servers, from where data reaches HMI, where graphical interfaces represent the state of the process in a human-accessible fashion.

In the past, ICSs were generally perceived as isolated environments that used proprietary hardware and software. However, technological advancements in recent years have led to the adoption of traditional information and communication technologies (ICT) hardware and software across all ICSs layers. In fact, the pervasive adoption of commodity, off-the-shelf ICT in modern ICSs has led to a significant reduction in costs as well as to greater efficiency, flexibility, and interoperability between components. At the same time, it has enabled the implementation of new services and features such as remote monitoring and maintenance, energy markets, and the newly emerging smart grid.

Nevertheless, this technological shift from a completely isolated environment to a "system of systems" integration has had a dramatic impact on the security of ICSs [1]. By leveraging attack vectors that are commonly used to attack traditional computer systems, for example, phishing and USB key infections, malware aimed at the disruption of critical infrastructure systems have become effective cyberweapons [2–4].

The impact of generic malware on the normal functioning of ICSs can be devastating if we simply consider the published attack reports on ICSs. Of course, the construction of a comprehensive list of events and attacks is difficult to achieve in the industrial setting, mainly because of nondisclosure policies adopted by different stakeholders. Therefore, most of the reported events cannot be chronologically ordered, since the actual discovery date of the malware does not coincide with the actual infection time of the system.

Nevertheless, 2010 may be seen as a turning point in the perception of security in the industrial setting. This is mainly attributed to Stuxnet [2], the first malware specifically designed to attack ICSs. Its high level of sophistication and especially its ability to reprogram the logic of control hardware has served as a wakeup call for the international security community and has demonstrated how powerful such threats can be.

Subsequently, Stuxnet's "follow-ups," Duqu [5], Flame [3], and more recently Dragonfly [4] (reported in June 2014), have revealed the true dimension of cyberespionage where specially forged malware can strategically compromise significant organizations and, if needed, can cause significant damage to different industrial sectors, including defense, aviation, and energy. At the same time, the tight interconnections between ICSs and the underlying physical processes raise serious concerns regarding the ability to ensure normal functioning of *critical* services under cyberattacks. An example is the collapse of India's northern electricity grid in July 2012 [6], which affected more than 600 million people and led to the loss of critical infrastructures such as electricity grids, transportation, and health care. Similarly, the potential impact of cyberattacks on the power sector has been highlighted by the Tempe, Arizona, incident [7] in 2007. In this particular case, an improper configuration of load shedding programs caused the opening of 141 breakers and the loss of significant load, which subsequently led to a 46 min power outage affecting almost 100,000 customers. Scenarios such as these (that may also be attributed to cyberattacks) need to be recreated, analyzed, and understood in a laboratory environment to develop the necessary security measures that may be applied in real settings.

In light of the aforementioned issues, this chapter explores the applicability of state-of-the-art techniques from the field of traditional Internet protocol (IP) networks to implement advanced mitigation techniques in ICSs against cyberattacks. In traditional IP networks, we find advanced networking solutions that can significantly improve service availability and may lead to better protection mechanisms in cyberattack scenarios. In this sense, this chapter provides an in-depth analysis of software-defined networking (SDN) and network functions virtualization (NFV), and identifies intrinsic features that might be applicable in the implementation of closed-loop intrusion detection systems. SDN [8] is a recent advancement in the traditional field of IP networks. It provides the means to create virtual networking services and to implement global networking decisions. SDN relies on OpenFlow to enable communication with remote devices and it has recently been categorized as the "Next Big Technology" [9]. OpenFlow [10] is a protocol designed to ensure remote access to the forwarding plane of a network switch. On the other hand, NFV [11] uses standard information technology (IT) virtualization technologies to embody network equipment in a virtual environment. This leads to a reduction in product deployment and maintenance time, while reducing costs. In this context, we describe two techniques to mitigate cyberattacks, which are based on the features provided by SDN: the first one leverages the SDN's capability to reroute traffic, while the second technique leverages the SDN's ability to block/drop packets according to specific rules.

Subsequently, we describe a novel technique to enable experimentation with SDN-enabled ICS. The approach encompasses software simulators to recreate the physical dimension of ICS; real networks, software, and protocols to recreate the communication features of ICS; and virtualization techniques already available in modern operating system (OS) kernels to provide SDN and OpenFlow features.

In general, the study of complex systems, either physical or cyber, could be carried out by experimenting with real systems or software simulators. Experimentation with production systems suffers from the inability to control the experiment environment to reproduce results. Furthermore, if the study intends to test the resilience or security of a system, there are obvious concerns about the potential side effects (faults and disruptions) to mission-critical services. On the other hand, the development of a dedicated experimentation infrastructure with real components is often economically prohibitive and conducting disruptive experiments could be a risk to safety. Software-based simulation has always been considered an efficient approach to study physical systems, mainly because it can offer low-cost, fast, and accurate analysis. Nevertheless, it has limited applicability in the context of cybersecurity due to the diversity and complexity of computer networks. Software simulators can effectively model normal operations, but they fail to capture the way that computer systems fail. More details on choosing the most adequate cyber-physical experimentation solution can be found in [12,13].

To provide the means toward safe experimentation while ensuring high fidelity for the cyber and the physical dimensions of ICS, we propose a hybrid approach that leverages real protocols and communication networks in general for the cyber dimension of ICSs and simulation for the underlying physical process. The approach builds on an implementation [14,15] of the emerging Sensei/IoT* standard proposal [38], the Mininet network emulator [16,17], a Floodlight-based SDN controller [18], and the Assessment Platform for Multiple Interdependent Critical Infrastructures (AMICI) software simulator [19,20]. To illustrate the applicability and the advanced features of SDN-enabled networks in enhancing the security of ICSs, two different case studies are presented:

1. The first experiment leverages the simulated Tennessee Eastman (TE) chemical process model for which monitoring traffic is routed through an SDN-enabled network. The experiment shows the disruptive impact of denial-of-service (DoS) attacks, as well as the beneficial features of SDN controllers in mitigating such attacks by rerouting disruptive flows to protect industrial traffic.
2. The second experiment uses the same simulated physical process, but it places a higher emphasis on blocking the attack. We illustrate that in SDN networks, attacks can be blocked further away, closer to the source/entry point in the SDN network.

As a final note, the approaches described in this chapter uniquely combine different capabilities to enable experimentation with SDN-based networks and ICS-specific protocols, as well as a wide variety of physical processes. To the best of our knowledge, the research presented in this chapter constitutes the first documented steps that enable the integration of SDN-enabled networks into ICSs to ensure advanced experimentation capabilities combining the cyber and the physical dimensions of ICSs with SDN-controlled networks.

The remainder of this chapter is organized as follows. Section 12.2 provides an overview of ICSs as well as of state-of-the-art IP networking techniques, which might find applications in the implementation of more reliable ICSs. Then, Section 12.3 describes two possible approaches to mitigate cyberattacks in ICSs: the first approach leverages the ability of SDN controllers to monitor the network bandwidth and to take rerouting decisions, while the second one leverages external signaling software components to identify and trace back malicious flows and to finally block them. This is followed by the presentation of a novel experimentation approach in Section 12.4, which allows conducting disruptive cyber-physical security experiments on SDN-enabled ICSs. Section 12.5 presents two use cases showing the applicability of the proposed attack mitigation approaches and of the experimentation technique described in Section 12.4. Finally, the chapter concludes with Section 12.6.

12.2 Industrial Control Systems and IP Networking

This section provides an overview of ICSs architecture and an introduction to state-of-the-art IP networking solutions, which may find applications in improving the security of ICSs.

12.2.1 Overview of Industrial Control Systems

As shown in Figure 12.1, in modern ICSs architectures one can identify two different control layers [21]:

- The physical layer, which encompasses all the actuators, sensors, and hardware devices that physically perform the actions on the system, for example, open a valve or measure the voltage in a cable.

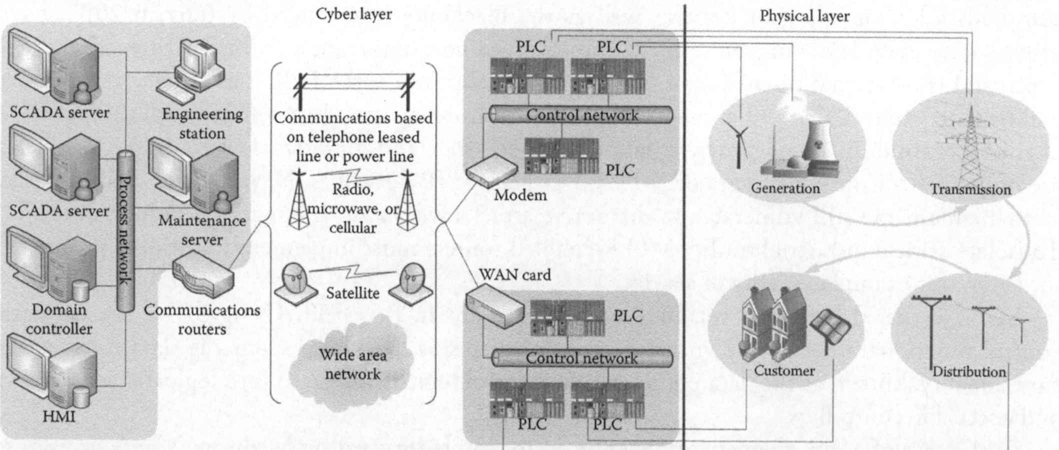

Figure 12.1 Industrial control system architecture including SCADA servers, HMI, PLCs, communication networks, and the underlying physical process.

- The cyberlayer, which is composed of all the ICT devices and software that acquire the data, elaborates low-level process strategies and delivers the commands to the physical layer. This layer typically uses SCADA protocols to manage and control the physical devices.

The "distributed control system" is typically split between two networks: the control network and the process network. The process network usually hosts all the SCADA (also known as SCADA Masters) and HMI servers. The control network hosts all the devices that on the one side control the actuators and sensors of the physical layer and on the other side provide the "control interface" to the process network. A typical control network is composed of a mesh of programmable logic controllers (PLCs). From an operational point of view, PLCs receive data from the physical layer, elaborate a "local actuation strategy," and send back commands to the actuators. PLCs also execute the commands that they receive from the SCADA servers (Masters) and additionally provide, whenever requested, detailed data regarding the physical layer. The communication between Masters and PLCs is usually implemented in two different ways: (i) through an Object Linking and Embedding (OLE) for Process Control (OPC) layer, which helps in mapping the PLC devices; and (ii) through a direct memory mapping notation making use of SCADA communication protocols such as Modbus, DNP3, Profibus, and so on [22].

12.2.2 Modern IP Networking Technologies and ICSs

Major players from the networking field on the one side and from different industrial domains on the other side are currently establishing collaborations to improve or replace or both the outdated communication infrastructure. Industrial networks have started adopting large-scale, traditional computer networking solutions, which provide increased reliability and manageability. Older communication infrastructure implementations based on frame relay, power-line carrier, and asynchronous transfer mode (ATM) are being replaced and improved with state-of-the-art networking solutions such as Internet protocol/Multiprotocol Label Switching (IP/MPLS), OpenFlow, SDN, and NFV.

An example is the partnership established between Cisco and IBM to implement a more reliable and secure networking infrastructure for the Italian electrical transmission and distribution company, Terna [23]. The damage to a high-power pylon in Switzerland, which caused loss of communication signaling in Italy, as well as the blackouts experienced by Italy in 2003, have proved that there is an urgent need to improve the communication infrastructure. Therefore, Cisco and IBM started discussions to implement a solution for the Italian electricity grid, which will be more controllable and manageable. MPLS technology was chosen for this solution. Traffic engineering, built-in support for virtual private networks, and more efficient routing capabilities are only a few of the advantages of MPLS over generic IP networks. Nevertheless, MPLS-based virtual circuits are still vulnerable to disruptive attacks with serious impact on industrial traffic. To isolate critical industrial traffic, MPLS-enabled routers must implement traditional protective measures, for example, quality of service.

SDN, as stated before, is yet another advancement in this field. Using SDN, the network control functionality, also known as the control plane, is decoupled from the data forwarding functionality, known as the data plane. All the control logic is migrated into logically centralized and accessible controllers.

In the case of SDN, the network is reduced to simple forwarding hardware, where decisions, policy enforcement algorithms, and routing protocols are integrated into carefully positioned and secured network controller(s). The forwarding hardware consists of a flow table that contains flow entries, which consist of match rules and actions performed on active flows, and a transport layer

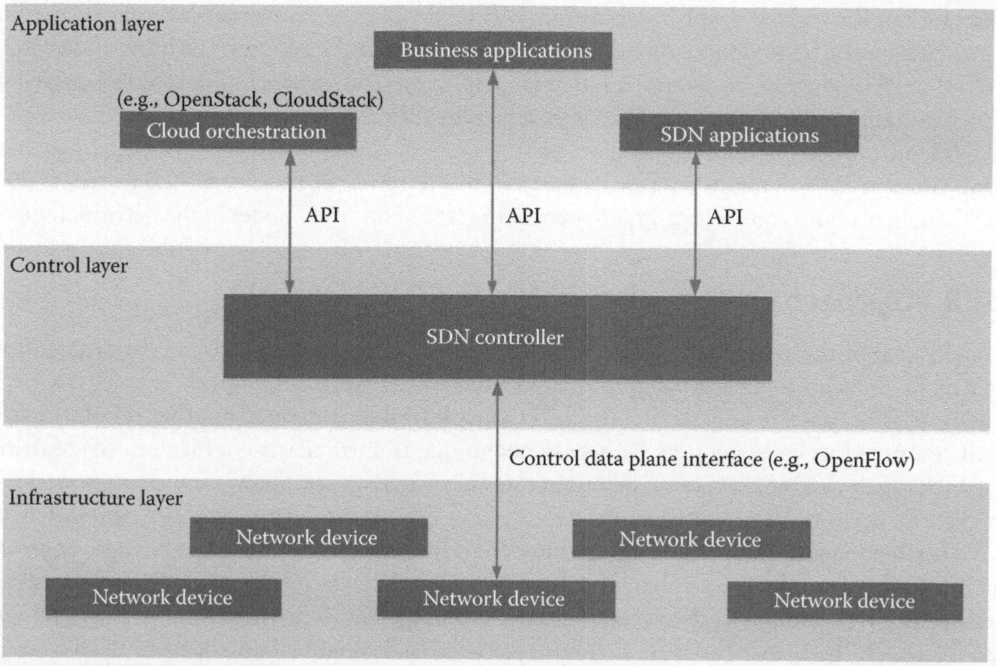

Figure 12.2 Software-defined networking building blocks.

protocol that securely communicates with a controller about new entries that are not currently in the flow table. The typical architecture of SDN is depicted in Figure 12.2.

Besides SDN, virtualization is gaining momentum and the proposal of NFV [11] represents one of the most recent trends in the field of traditional IP networks. Using NFV, one could deploy virtual routers, virtual switches, and high-volume servers in one high-power physical machine. NFV proposes to leverage standard IT virtualization technologies to embody network equipment in a virtual environment. Consequently, the adoption of NFV in real production systems, such as ICSs, would reduce the time required for a product to reach consumers, significantly reduce power consumption and costs, and enable the implementation of more flexible configurations.

12.3 Possible SDN-Enabled Approaches to Mitigate Cyberattacks in Large ICSs

This section presents two different techniques aimed at mitigating attacks in SDN-enabled ICSs environments. The first of these leverages the capabilities of SDN controllers to reroute the path of critical data flows in case of cyberattacks, while the second one blocks the attack at the farthest possible point of the network.

12.3.1 Assumptions on Network Topology and Basic Model

For a thorough understanding of the algorithms behind the two approaches, we introduce a few notations. The network infrastructure, including typical SCADA hosts, switches, and SDN-enabled networks, can be seen as a basic graph, formally denoted by $I = (V,E)$. Using this symbolic representation, for a given graph I, we define $V(I)$ to denote the set of vertices, that is, the hosts and switches, and $E(I)$ to denote the set of edges, that is, the links between the hosts and switches.

Based on this notation, we assume a rather large ICSs topology where multiple SDN-enabled networks span multiple SDN domains and are governed by different network controllers. Therefore, we need to identify special nodes providing access from one SDN domain to another, thereby interconnecting different SDN domains with each other. For this purpose, we use $S(I) \subset V(I)$ to denote the set of SDN-enabled nodes and $N(I) \subset V(I)$ to denote the set of non-SDN nodes in the network topology.

12.3.2 Approach 1: Rerouting Traffic in SDN Networks

The main goal of the rerouting technique is to find the most suitable path for the critical flows. This may be reduced to a classical graph-based problem where, given a graph topology with different weights assigned to edges, we must find the path from one node to another to minimize the overall computed weight function. This basic technique is particularly useful to mitigate disruptive attacks such as DoS, where malicious actors inject massive traffic to consume resources, for example, the network bandwidth, making the system unresponsive or even shutting it down.

We further expand the previous graph model and we assign weights to each edge. More specifically, we use D to denote a subgraph of the complete ICSs topology I, which translates to an independent SDN domain in the overall network topology. Let us further consider D as a *weighted graph* for which the helper function $\delta(e)$ returns the actual weight of an edge $e \in E(D)$. In a real system, weights, denoted by W, might correspond to different network metrics and might be associated with delays, loads, capacities, and so on. In practice, the value of W might be determined from various counters embedded in switches, which are regularly updated and are retrieved by SDN controllers from OpenFlow-enabled switches.

Next, the algorithm applies a classical *shortest path algorithm*, for example, Dijkstra, on the D graph, to minimize the overall path weight. Then, the network controller "reprograms" the switches with the newly calculated routes. It should be noted, however, that dynamic rerouting is only possible inside SDN-enabled domains. Outside these domains, specially tailored measures need to be implemented to ensure similar features.

For such cases, we assume the presence of a central administrator node that possesses all the necessary information regarding the SDN-enabled components of the infrastructure. This node needs to have detailed knowledge on boundary hosts and also needs to have access to every OpenFlow controller in the infrastructure. For this purpose, custom-built controllers can leverage communication interfaces exposed by SDN controllers, such as Floodlight's Representational State Transfer (REST) API. These provide powerful features to harmonize and orchestrate traffic across multiple SDN-enabled domains. The algorithm for traffic rerouting is summarized in Algorithm 12.1.

12.3.3 Approach 2: Blocking Traffic in SDN Networks

Contrary to the previous approach, the goal of the second technique is to localize and block the source of the attacks in the same I network topology. For this purpose, we again assume the presence of a central administration controller that is capable of communicating with different controllers from each SDN domain.

In addition to our previous assumptions, the central administrator may query each SDN controller for information such as the actual data flows in each domain identified by source and destination media access control (MAC) addresses, and the input/output ports of the switches that are involved in routing each flow.

Algorithm 12.1 Reroute Critical Flows in a Complex ICSs Network Topology

Input:	The source and destination host of the critical flow.
Output:	The list of network nodes of the calculated path.
Step 1	If the start or destination hosts are inside an SDN-enabled domain, we replace them with the nearest boundary host of the current SDN-enabled domain.
Step 2	Applies a shortest path algorithm between the start and destination host.
Step 3	Runs a shortest path (minimum weight) algorithm in each SDN-enabled domain between the nodes in the path calculated in the previous step. If the start or destination host is on the path returned by Step 2, it calculates the path between them and the representing boundary host set in Step 1.
Step 4	Submits the shortest paths calculated in the previous step by using the static flow pusher of the OpenFlow controller.
Step 5	Unifies the partial paths from Step 2 and Step 3 into the final path.

Based on this information, an attack may be traced back by following these few steps:

- The central administrator node finds the nearest switch to the attack detection point and issues a query on it about the detected flows.
- From the list of detected flows, the central administrator identifies the set of possibly malicious flows. For this purpose, we further assume that common traffic flows are well known by the central administrator nodes. This important assumption is backed by evidence from previous research [24], where it was shown that regular ICSs traffic exhibits a predictable pattern and nodes that exchange packets are well known.

The information returned by previous steps on the possibly malicious flows contains the source and the destination MAC addresses. Besides these, in each flow description received from the SDN controller, the input and output switch ports are also given. This type of information is already available in traditional switches and it is sufficient to trace back the possibly malicious flows and to identify entry points into different SDN networks, where such flows may be blocked if needed. The algorithm for traffic blocking is summarized in Algorithm 12.2.

Algorithm 12.2 Trace and Block the Source of the Attack in a Complex ICSs Network Topology

Input:	The host where the attack is detected.
Output:	The nearest SDN-enabled host to the attacker host.
Step 1	Find the source host in the current SDN-enabled domain. Set this source host as the current host.
Step 2	Look up the boundary host pairs of the current host.
Step 3	Check for each host pair on the nearest switch if there is a possibly malicious flow. If so, select this pair node as the current node and go to Step 1, otherwise the current node is the detected source.

12.4 A Novel Approach to Experiment with SDN-Enabled ICSs

The approach for conducting experiments described in this section builds on the assumption of large-scale ICSs where thousands or even millions of sensors and PLCs are spread across large geographical regions. To ensure that measurements reach their targets in such complex settings, a typical practical approach is the deployment of data concentrators. In such cases, communications are reduced to the exchange of data with data concentrators that are capable of reducing the traffic between different sites and ensuring scalable deployment of ICSs infrastructures.

In this sense, the experimentation approach described in this section embodies advanced communication capabilities based on the implementation [14,15] of the recently proposed Sensei/IoT* standard [38], multiprocess simulation capabilities based on the AMICI framework [19,20], and SDN-enabled networks using the Mininet [16,17] network simulator and a Floodlight [18] network controller. In a nutshell, the approach enables real-time cyber-physical security experimentation with SDN-enabled ICSs networks and the recently proposed Sensei/IoT* standard. It implements basic communication and architectural features defined within Sensei/IoT* and SDN, and it enables the execution of disruptive experiments against physical infrastructures through the adoption of distributed simulation software.

Fundamentally, the use of SDN in ICSs is motivated by the advanced features brought about by recent advancement in the field. Therefore, we envision the provisioning of SDN-enabled networks in the different communication layers of traditional ICSs architecture depicted in Figure 12.1. As shown in Figure 12.3, multiple SDN networks provide the communication requirements for future ICSs. At the same time, in the proposed experimentation approach, the AMICI framework ensures the re-creation of typical SCADA components, and it brings advanced simulation capabilities to ensure real-time execution of complex physical process models. Subsequently, to ensure the communication requirements for large-scale ICSs such as the future power grid, that is, smart grids, we leverage HERMIX and its support for Sensei/IoT*. These components also integrate typical security measures such as channel encryption and role-based access support, which yield a rich palette of experimentation capabilities. In this section, we provide an overview of the building

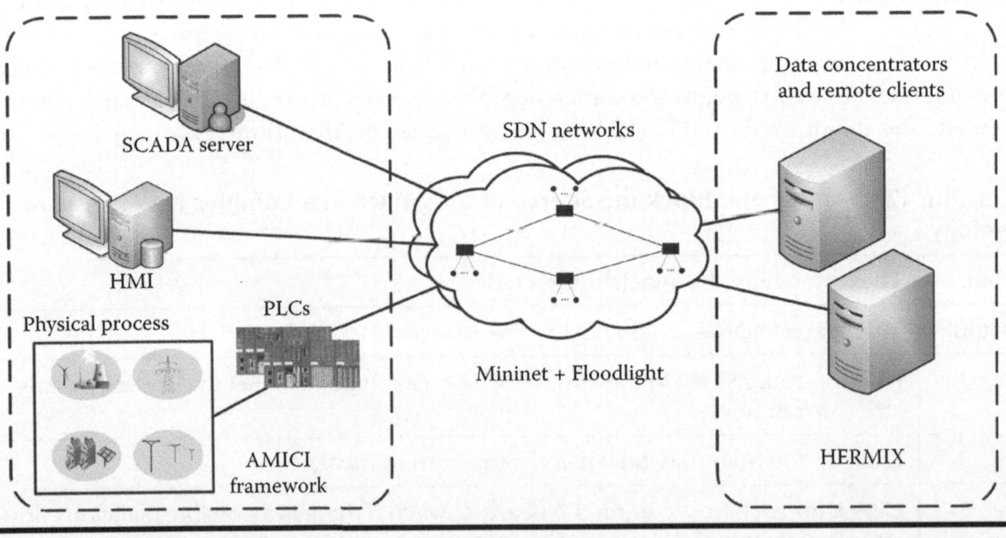

Figure 12.3 Mapping of the proposed software frameworks to the traditional ICSs architecture.

blocks of the proposed experimentation approach and we detail the intrinsic elements that fuse together different technologies in a comprehensive experimentation framework.

12.4.1 Simulated versus Real ICSs

The approaches found in the literature for conducting cyber-physical security experiments on ICSs vary considerably regarding the use of simulators and real components. In several cases, we have found approaches that use real components for the physical dimension of ICSs and partly simulated ones for the cyberparts [25–27]. Typically, in such cases, approaches leverage a real OPC server, network simulators, and possibly real PLCs and field devices to analyze ICSs.

Other researchers focused on completely simulated environments where both the cyber and the physical dimensions are recreated with the help of simulation software. An example includes Chabukswar et al.'s [28] work, the Command and Control WindTunnel (C2WindTunnel) [29] multimodel simulation environment, based on the high-level architecture (HLA) IEEE standard 1.3 [30], to enable the interaction between various simulation engines. The authors used OMNeT++ to simulate the network and Matlab Simulink to build and run the physical plant model. C2WindTunnel provides the global clock for both OMNeT++ and Matlab Simulink. With this approach, analyzing the cyber-physical effects of malware is not a trivial task, as it requires a detailed description of all ICT components and, more importantly, a detailed knowledge on the dynamics of malware, which is not always available.

More advanced experimentation techniques have recently been reported by Siaterlis and Genge [12,13]. In their work, the authors followed a hybrid approach, where an Emulab-based test bed [31] recreated the control and process networks of ICSs, including PLCs and SCADA servers, and a software simulation reproduced the physical processes.

The advantage of using such a hybrid approach is manyfold. First of all, by using real hardware and software for the cybercomponents, it is possible to test complex scenarios with real malware and to measure the impact of disturbances on real cybercomponents. At the same time, if simulation were used to carry out this task, the study of the security and resilience of computer networks would require the simulation of all the failure-related functions, behaviors, and states, most of which are unknown in principle. However, software simulation is a very reasonable approach for the physical dimension of ICSs due to its small costs, the existence of accurate models, and the ability to conduct experiments in a safe environment.

Although apparently the use of simulation seems to weaken the fidelity of the physical dimension, it is important to note that today we can find complex models of several physical systems in the open-source community. By integrating them into software simulators, the behavior of real physical systems may be accurately reproduced. A clear example is the energy sector, where simulation has become so accurate and trusted that it is commonly used to aid decision making between transmission system operators.

Based on this analysis, the approach undertaken in this chapter follows a hybrid approach as well. However, we also introduce the ability to emulate more complex switching networks by leveraging recent virtualization techniques. Consequently, compared with previous experimentation approaches, we believe that the technique presented in this chapter is more scalable and cost efficient. A possible disadvantage of this approach, however, is the limitation of software emulation for recreating disruptive experiments, which might need to be scaled, for example, reduce DoS attack bandwidth consumption, to the infrastructure's capabilities.

12.4.2 Sensei/IoT* Overview

The extensible messaging and presence protocol (XMPP), developed in 1999 by the Jabber open-source community, was intended for near real-time instant messaging, presence information, and contact list maintenance. The XMPP is an open extensible markup language (XML) protocol, which defines the method of XML content streaming. It has been used in many applications, most importantly the smart grid in the case of the Internet of Things (IoT) applications. Therefore, we believe it can also enable large-scale communications for generic ICSs installations.

Since 2002, the XMPP working group, established by the Internet Engineering Task Force (IETF), has made efforts in standardization. Initially, four specifications (RFC 3920, RFC 3921, RFC 3922, RFC 3923) were created that led to a proposed standard in 2004. In 2011, the first specifications were replaced by RFC 6120 and RFC 6121, and new ones were added, such as RFC 6122.

Besides the aforementioned core protocols, the XMPP Standards Foundation has played a part in the development of new open XMPP extensions development, also known as XEP stanzas. These efforts are not unique and other joint progress can be noticed in this direction. We mention here the ISO/IEC/IEEE P21451-1-4 XMPP standard, also known as Sensei/IoT*, which represents the first joint effort among the International Organization for Standardization (ISO), the International Electrotechnical Commission (IEC), and the Institute of Electrical and Electronic Engineers (IEEE) to design a Semantic Web 3.0 sensor standard for sensor networks, machine to machine (M2M), and the IoT.

The main features integrated into Sensei/IoT* are

- Technology agnostic and protocol independent.
- The use of the transport layer security (TLS) for data traffic encryption built into the protocol.
- Metadata isolation (MDI) and intrusion protection against cyberattacks.
- Usage of the Semantic Web 3.0 based on XML metadata for providing semantic conversation between devices.
- Usage of a service broker as a trusted intermediary to establish a trust relationship between users, applications, and devices.
- Possibility to use an identity provider (IdP) to provide single sign on (SSO).
- Support end-to-end digital signing and encryption based on RFC 3923 efficient XML interchange (EXI).

12.4.3 Communication Modules Enabling Experimentation with Sensei/IoT*

The communication infrastructure is mainly provided by the HERMIX platform, which implements most of the significant features outlined in the Sensei/IoT* standard proposal. The HERMIX platform [14,15], developed by the Vitheia consortium, is a free software, which is designed to collect, store, and analyze large amounts of data coming from a diversity of nodes, ranging from sensors to high-resolution cameras.

The platform has a layered architecture and consists of interconnected nodes representing physical resources, users, automation scripts, or services. These nodes may be either a consumer or a provider. The three layers of the platform are

- Logical management layer: Formats and extracts data, performs automated analysis and processing, manages authentication, authorization, and access control, and ensures the interconnection with other systems. This layer has a service-oriented architecture.
- Communication layer: Follows a publish–subscribe pattern for small and structured data exchange between nodes. It has an event-driven architecture.
- Data storage layer: Provides storage support and hides the underlying database system.

HERMIX uses XMPP for metadata exchange (session initiation, device managing requests, etc.) and small structured data generated by the end points. It also has an XMPP server level, which is responsible for node management, interconnection with the physical bus, authorization management, and persistent storage.

A node identified in the XMPP world by a unique Jabber ID (JID) is defined by a set of features, status information, received commands, and generated events. Taking into account the heterogeneity of existing protocols, new types can be described, but the main goal of this resource model is to provide homogeneity at the description level. A node can be dynamically created by the node manager based on an XML description or based on the image saved in the database. The node manager automatically collects and saves every modification in the registered node data in the object archive. When a saved data is required, it is loaded into the memory and transformed into its runtime C++ representation.

A discovery mechanism using the standard service discovery protocol defined in the XMPP extension XEP-0030 is used to obtain information about devices and their features or events. Events are organized hierarchically because every event has different privileges to subscribe to. State variables have the same hierarchical structure of privileges. Subsequently, a user subscribing to a node will receive events from all of the node's descendants.

The transport of the binary data from a source to multiple destinations is handled by the controller nodes. Access to the binary archives is also done indirectly, through the controllers. The controller poses two types of communication channels: one for controlling the way that data is distributed based on the XMPP and the other for actual large data transport. The controller is exposed in the middleware as a delegated node attached to a component.

The object manager also enforces permission policies managed by an authorization manager. The permission attached to an object is represented as a set of tuples (object ID, list of permission types, a set of bare JIDs, and a set of groups). When the OM needs to authorize access to an object, it will request the object's access control list (if not already cached) from the AM. The maximum caching interval is imposed by the AM and must be invalidated if it is changed. The separation between permission validation and permission management ensures third-party integration.

12.4.4 Physical Process Simulators

The AMICI [19,20] provides software simulators to recreate the physical dimension of ICSs. The AMICI was developed from the need to provide real-time multimodel experimentation capabilities supporting cybersecurity studies concerning ICSs.

Its architecture includes two main components:

- Simulation unit (Sim)
- Proxy unit (Proxy)

Each component has specific roles. The Sim runs the physical process model in real-time by coupling the model time to the system time to minimize the difference between the two. Models are created in Matlab, the corresponding "C" code is generated using the Simulink coder, and they are then integrated using an XML configuration file. This delivers a highly flexible framework in which the AMICI source code does not require changes for the encapsulation of additional physical process models.

From the Sim unit's point of view, each model is seen as a set of inputs and outputs. These are mapped to an internal memory region (I/O MEM) that is read/written by other software modules as well. The Sim unit allows open access to its I/O MEM by implementing OS-level shared memory operations. This way, AMICI enables interaction with ad hoc software that can write specific model inputs, that is, open/close a valve, and can read the status of the model, that is, the measured voltage. Interaction with other Sim units is enabled by implementing not only remote procedure call (RPC) server-side operations but also client-side calls. By using only the XML configuration file, the Sim unit can be configured to read/write inputs/outputs of models run by remote Sim units. These are mapped to the inputs/outputs of the model running locally, enabling complex interactions between models running in parallel on different machines. The Proxy unit has several roles within AMICI. First of all, it is able to run remote control code, thus enabling the integration of more complex control hardware emulators. At the same time, it can be used to handle Modbus protocol calls, transforming them to RPC calls and finally sending requests to the Sim unit.

12.4.5 SDN Enablers

Emulating an SDN-enabled network may be realized using the Mininet platform [16,17], which emulates a "network in a laptop" by using the virtualization capabilities of a modern OS. Mininet comes with Open vSwitch (OVS) preinstalled, thus providing a realistic re-creation of switching capabilities. The other features of Mininet are grouping of host-based processes together by using process name spaces, and providing communication capabilities with hosts inside the emulated network, as well as with real hosts outside the emulation domain by using virtual network interfaces.

The SDN controller is an important device in the SDN network, which may take decisions to drop packages, to run complex traffic engineering algorithms, and to reroute traffic and monitor the network. There are many open controller implementations such as NOX, POX, Beacon, Floodlight, and OpenDaylight. However, Floodlight is the most appropriate choice in the case of ICSs networks, which have a topology that requires the injection of static flows to work together with control loops. Floodlight also supports experimenting with large networks, it exposes an interface to communicate with real OpenFlow-enabled switches, and it is easy to program.

12.4.6 Proposed Experimentation Approach

The approach proposed in this chapter to experiment with large-scale ICSs may be spread across different geographically remote sites. For this purpose, the approach fuses together the communication features provided by HERMIX with the physical process simulation capabilities provided by AMICI and routes traffic through the SDN-enabled network recreated by Mininet. This way, we recreate a complex cyber-physical ICSs architecture that relies on real communication architectures and protocols, but uses simulation to enable the conducting of disruptive cyberattack scenarios in a safe environment.

The approach leverages HERMIX for the cyber dimension to provide real protocols running on real network infrastructures. On the other hand, for the physical dimension, we use simulation

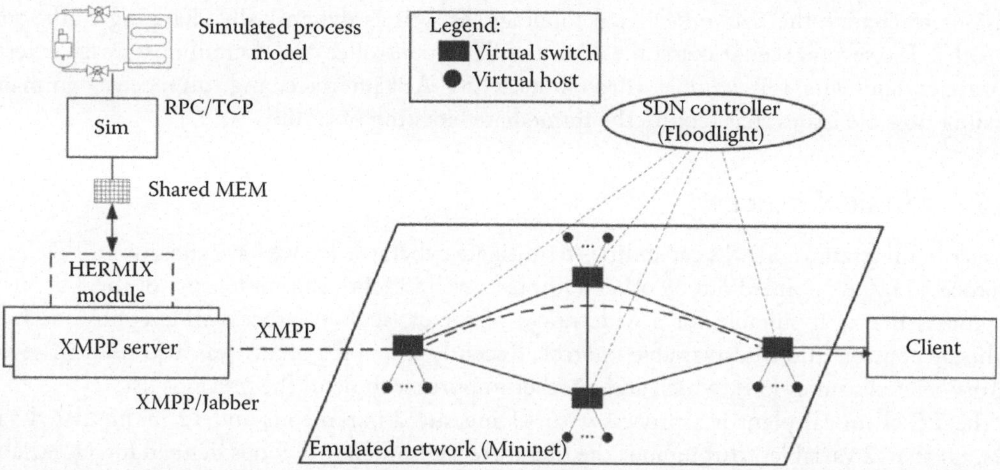

Figure 12.4 Experimentation approach architecture with main components and communication paths.

because running cybersecurity experimentation scenarios within production systems entails risks of potential side effects to mission-critical services.

The architecture (from a technological point of view) of the developed experimentation infrastructure, as a result of fusing HERMIX, AMICI, and SDN-enabled networks, is depicted in Figure 12.4. The procedure followed for this purpose exploits the features provided by each of the software platforms. As such, we implemented an additional HERMIX module to access the shared memory region created by AMICI's simulation unit. Model inputs and outputs are written and read by the implemented module, ensuring the required communication between cybercomponents and the simulated physical processes. The devices that are exposed by simulated models, for example, valves and sensors, are given different JIDs and are accessed through standard XMPP stanzas. Each device is registered in the HERMIX database (MongoDB) and users (client software) can subscribe to receive events. The proposed platform is thus compatible with any client software implementing an XMPP communication interface according to the standard description.

Additional SDN components have been naturally integrated with the developed platform since the use of real software, and the network in general facilitates the application of traditional routing features implemented in a real OS. As such, Mininet recreates the SDN network by using virtual switch technologies, while Floodlight provides SDN controller capabilities and the possibility to implement customized controller scripts to control network traffic. Components may run on the same host, thus enabling experiments on a single personal computer (PC), but they might be distributed on several hosts interconnected by real networking equipment to ensure scalable experimentation resources.

12.5 Use Case Assessment

This section provides intrinsic details on the use of the experimentation platform presented throughout this chapter. It starts with the presentation of the chosen physical process model and continues with the presentation of two experimentation scenarios. The first one assumes an extended SDN controller that is capable of monitoring network traffic throughput and of taking decisions to change the network virtual topology, as well as dynamically changing traffic routing paths. The second scenario assumes that the SDN controller can communicate with external software components, for example, through its REST API interface, and can receive commands signaling possible issues that require the immediate blocking of traffic.

12.5.1 Physical Process

In order to illustrate an SDN's capabilities to mitigate cyberattacks, we have chosen the TE chemical process [32]. As pointed out by other authors as well [33,34], the complexity of the TE chemical process makes it suitable for a wide range of topics, such as process-wide control strategy, nonlinear control, and multivariable control. Recently, the TE process was also used in several security-related studies [34], which add another important topic to the previous list.

The TE chemical plant is a process with 41 measured parameters and 12 manipulated variables. Of the 12 variables, throughout the literature we find control loops defined for 11 variables only; for the last one, the agitator speed control valve, it is not desirable to close the loop [33]. We briefly describe the process architecture and the PLCs in Figure 12.5.

The architecture of the TE process includes five main units: a two-phase *reactor*, a product *condenser*, a recycle *compressor*, a vapor/liquid *separator*, and a product *stripper*. The chemical process uses four reactants, *A*, *C*, *D*, and *E*, to generate two other products, *G* and *H*. More specifically, the combination of reactants *A*, *C*, and *D* produces *G*, while the combination of *A*, *C*, and *E* produces *H*. The three reactants *A*, *D*, and *E* are sent directly to the reactor, while reactant *C* reaches the reactor through a recycle stream. More details on the TE process can be found in the original paper by Downs and Vogel [32].

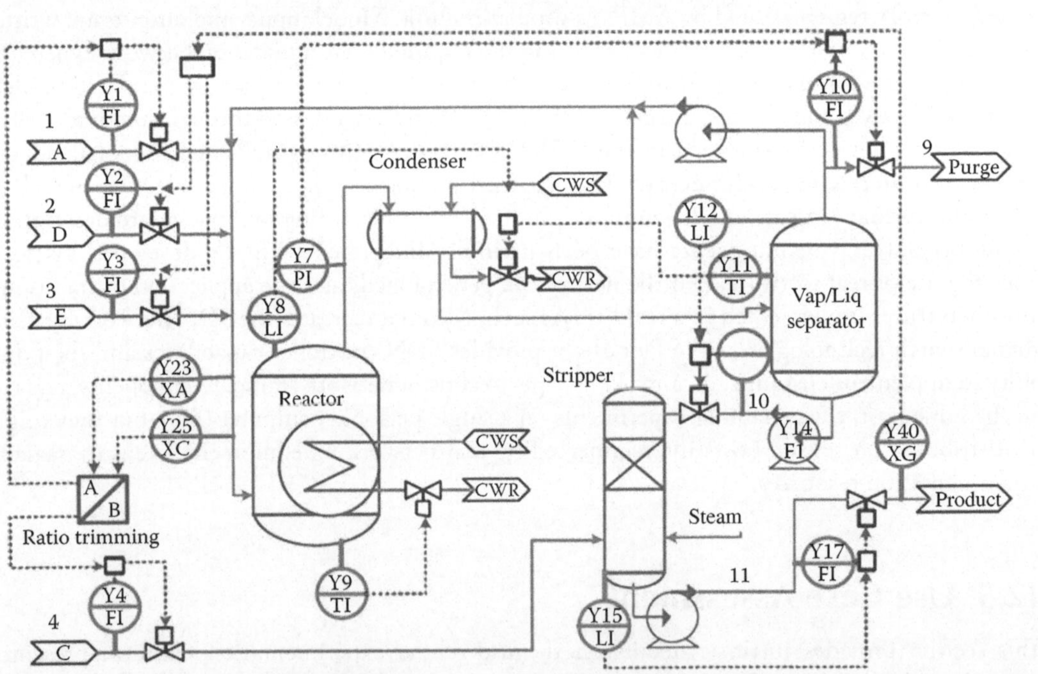

Figure 12.5 Architecture of Tennessee Eastman chemical process including process control loops.

The operation of the TE process requires a control strategy that keeps the parameters within normal operating limits. Without such a controller, the process is forced to shut down after approximately 3.6 h. The reasons for which the TE process would shut down are mentioned in [32]: high reactor pressure, high/low reactor liquid level, high reactor temperature, high/low separator liquid level, and high/low stripper liquid level. In our experiments, we employed the multiloop control system developed by Sozio [35], to keep the process parameters within normal operating limits. The primary objective of this controller is to produce the correct mixture of the *G* and *H* products at a specified rate. In his work, Sozio proposed a decentralized proportional-integral (PI) controller for the TE chemical process based on inner and outer control loops. The inner loops control the sections of the TE process with faster dynamics, while the outer loops control the slower dynamics of the system and use the inner loop set points in cascade as manipulated variables. The normal operation of the TE process is depicted in Figure 12.6.

12.5.2 Experiment 1: SDN-Based Traffic Rerouting

In the first experiment, we integrated the TE chemical process model and the control loops developed by Sozio in AMICI's software simulators and the experimentation approach described in this chapter. As a result, the TE process's 41 output variables were remotely monitored by a Python client application and communication was ensured through XMPP. A network of four

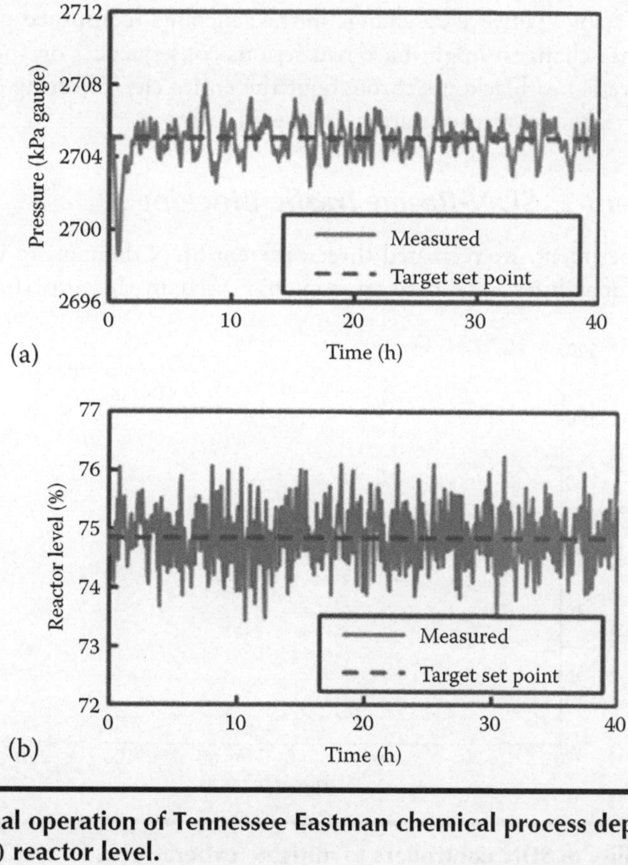

Figure 12.6 Normal operation of Tennessee Eastman chemical process depicted with (a) reactor pressure and (b) reactor level.

virtual switches was deployed with Mininet, while traffic monitoring was provided through the Floodlight network controller.

Since, in the case of this particular experiment, the emphasis is placed on highlighting the SDN's capability to mitigate attacks, we implemented a rudimentary external controller that was capable of issuing remote commands to Floodlight. The external controller relied on Floodlight's REST API interface to interrogate the state of links and to inject new static routes in case preconfigured thresholds were exceeded. Our custom controller monitored the network traffic by issuing commands to Floodlight once every second.

In the next phase of the experiment, we launched a DoS attack from one of the hosts connected to Mininet. Since the controller actively and continuously monitored the state of the network, the attack was rapidly rerouted and the traffic was not disturbed (see Figure 12.7). However, in the absence of such a controller, the network topology remains unchanged and disruptive attacks may have a serious impact on regular network traffic.

In fact, the impact of DoS attacks as defined in the first scenario is comparable to the complete loss of communications due to physical cable cuts, hardware failures, and so on. As an example, we consider the failure scenario that occurred on January 2, 2004, with Rome's remotely controlled power grid [36]. Although this was not a case of a cyberattack, the scenario may lead to a better understanding of the impact of ICT malfunctioning in ICSs. In this particular case, communications between remote sites were disabled by a broken water pipe that flooded a Telecom operator's server room and short-circuited critical hardware. The power grid operators were completely blinded and could not monitor or control the remote site. Fortunately, there were no disturbances, so the grid remained stable. However, a change in the generated–consumed power balance (possibly caused by weather changes) might have had serious consequences on the electrical grid. In Rome, this could have led to blackouts throughout the entire city, affecting other critical infrastructures as well, for example, transportation and health care.

12.5.3 Experiment 2: SDN-Based Traffic Blocking

In this particular experiment, we recreated three different SDN domains to illustrate the attack tracing algorithm's capabilities. The network topology used in this experiment is depicted in

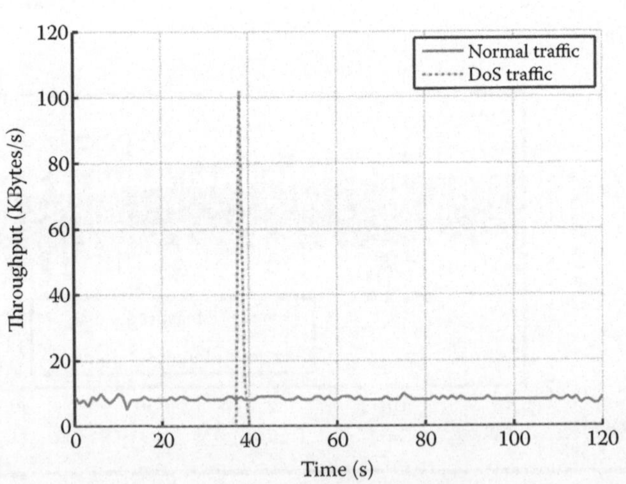

Figure 12.7 Capability of SDN controllers to mitigate cyberattacks by traffic rerouting.

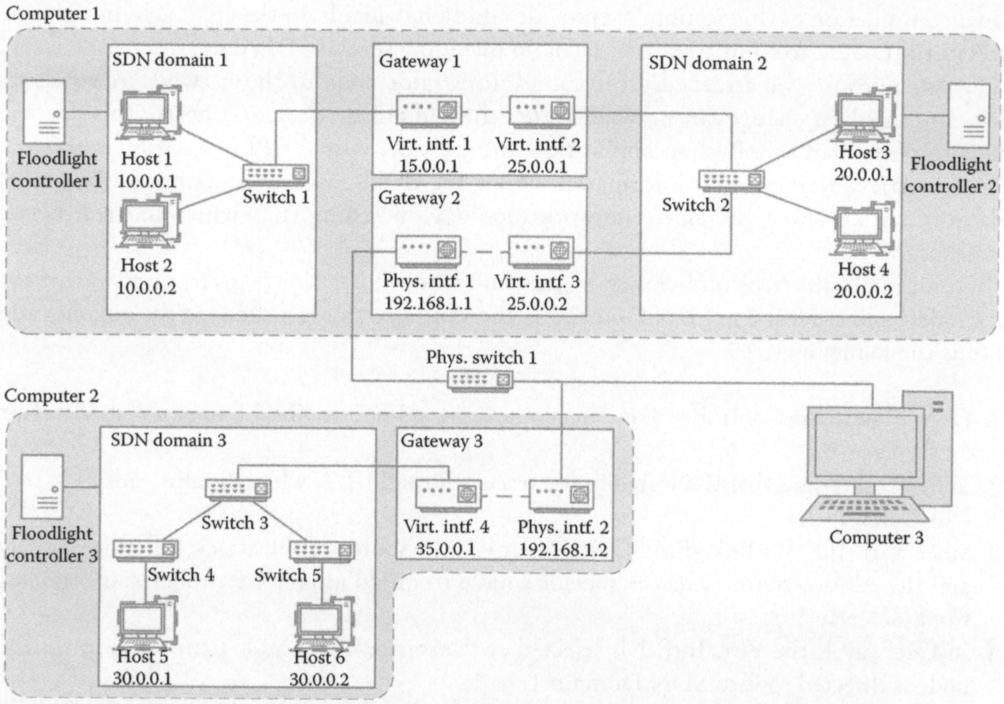

Figure 12.8 Multiple SDN domain network topology used in the second experiment.

Figure 12.8. Given the high complexity of the procedure for recreating such a complex topology, in the description that follows special emphasis is placed on the presentation of intrinsic technical details, which will also guide the reader in recreating similar experiments.

To perform the experiment, the network infrastructure shown in Figure 12.8 was recreated. The network topology was built using real computers interconnected with an Ethernet switch, as well as using virtual networks structured in different SDN domains with the help of Mininet.

As depicted in Figure 12.8, Computer 1 runs two instances of Mininet in parallel, namely, SDN Domain 1 and SDN Domain 2, while Computer 2 runs a third Mininet instance, namely, SDN Domain 3. Computer 3 connects to the network infrastructure through the Ethernet switch as a physical host. The interconnection of the different parts of the network is realized with Gateways 1, 2, and 3.

The attack implemented in this particular scenario uses real packets generated with the Scapy tool [37], a powerful packet manipulator program based on the Python interpreter. This tool provides the ability to generate and send out different network packets at different network layers. As a result, we were able to test the behavior and the effect of different attack types on the constructed network topologies.

To simulate a DoS attack launched from Host 1, a series of user datagram protocol (UDP) packets were generated with the help of Scapy and were sent out through the network infrastructure. All the sent packets had the same destination IP address (30.0.0.2), which is the address of Host 6. However, to simulate a realistic DoS attack where source IP addresses are hidden and chosen randomly to reduce the chances of successful source host detection, we randomly allocated IP addresses from 10.0.1.0/24 IP block and we varied the range of destination UDP ports.

In a continuation of this section, we provide additional details on the approach undertaken to map Algorithm 12.2 to a fairly realistic scenario including several SDN domains.

For this purpose, we attached a central administrator node to the network infrastructure, which is notified on changes in network traffic throughput by detection hosts. This particular node is implemented as a Python application and uses the REST API of each Floodlight controller to retrieve the required information about the SDN-enabled domains. Additionally, it holds information about the entire network topology, including the virtual and real network infrastructure.

To understand the steps undertaken by the central administration host, let us assume that the attack is detected at Host 6 in SDN Domain 3. The administrator is notified of the ongoing attack and runs the following steps:

1. From Floodlight Controller 3, it detects the entry point into SDN Domain 3 as Virt. Intf. 4 on Gateway 3.
2. The next interface that is selected in the trace is Phys. Intf. 2, which finally leads to Virt. Inf. 3 in Gateway 2.
3. Since Virt. Inf. 3 is linked to SDN Domain 2, the source of the attack is further inspected and the administrator finds the specific source from Floodlight Controller 2 as originating from Gateway 1.
4. In Gateway 1, the Virt. Intf. 1 is selected as the source of the attack and the administrator node is directed toward SDN Domain 1.
5. In SDN Domain 1, it requests from Floodlight Controller 1 the known traffic flows and correctly identifies the malicious flow.
6. Finally, the administrator host issues a blocking command to Floodlight Controller 1 to drop all packets originating from Host 1.

In this particular scenario, we assumed that the attacker host is part of an SDN-enabled network. Nevertheless, in other settings when the attack is traced outside the supervised SDN domains, the administrator node will not be able to effectively isolate and block the attack, since for the same MAC address, there might be multiple flows detected. However, this scenario highlights the beneficial effects of supervised and SDN-enabled networks, where attacks are traced back and blocked far away from the target host.

12.6 Conclusion

Modern malware exploiting the cyber and the physical dimensions of ICSs have led to a new type of cyberwar, where disturbances caused by malicious software may have significant repercussions in the physical world. We are actually witnessing the rise of multidimensional malware, which may efficiently exploit zero-day software vulnerabilities as well as knowledge of the underlying physical infrastructures to cause significant service disruptions.

In light of the aforementioned issues, it is therefore imperative that novel technologies and novel methods are developed and deployed to provide better protection and more secure and resilient ICSs. Nevertheless, the ICSs sector has a different, slower dynamics when it comes to the adoption of new technologies, compared with the traditional ICT sector. Therefore, approaches need to be tested and designed in such a way as to be integrated and to function alongside a mixture of outdated and new software and hardware.

In this sense, in this chapter, we explored the applicability of novel emerging techniques from the field of traditional IP networks to ICSs. In fact, experience from the past [23] has shown that a joint effort across different sectors can lead to significant improvements in services and can deliver better and more reliable infrastructures. Based on these observations, this chapter has highlighted the applicability of emerging technologies such as SDN and NFV in the implementation of effective security strategies in ICSs. Using SDN controllers, the traffic is rerouted or even blocked in the case of an attack, making the system more reliable. In this sense, the chapter presented intrinsic details on two techniques to mitigate cyberattacks by leveraging the advanced features of SDN-enabled networks. The first technique showed the capabilities to mitigate cyberattacks by rerouting malicious traffic. The second technique went further and showed the ability of SDN controllers in multiple SDN-enabled networks to trace back attacks and to block them as far as possible from the target host.

It is important, however, to note that the adoption of techniques for ICSs is usually followed only after thorough testing in environments that are able to recreate real systems and components while supporting experiments with real malware in a safe way. Therefore, this chapter proposed a novel experimentation architecture that recreates the cyber and the physical dimensions of ICSs while encompassing state-of-the-art techniques from traditional IP networks. More specifically, the approach embodies software simulators combined with specific components to recreate typical ICSs elements and communication infrastructures. It was shown that communication across a large-scale system may be effectively performed with the implementation of standard proposals such as Sensei/IoT*, while preserving the particular properties and protocols of ICSs.

Finally, the chapter presented two use cases. The first use case leveraged a single SDN domain and used the TE chemical process as the underlying industrial process. The second use case recreated a more complex scenario with three different SDN domains. In both cases, the effectiveness of supervised SDN networks was shown.

As future work, we envision an in-depth assessment of the security measures integrated into Sensei/IoT* and their applicability and suitability to ICS. At the same time, we foresee the development of more complex decision algorithms where additional parameters will be taken into account in the SDN-based decision-making process, for example, network delays and traffic prioritization.

Acknowledgment

This research was supported by a Marie Curie FP7 Integration Grant within the 7th European Union Framework Programme.

Author Biographies

Béla Genge is a Marie Curie Fellow and senior lecturer at Petru Maior University, Târgu Mureş, Romania. He obtained his PhD from the Technical University of Cluj-Napoca, Romania, in the field of network security. His research interests include critical infrastructure protection, anomaly detection systems, and network security in general. In 2014, he was awarded the prestigious Marie Curie Career Integration Grant. He has authored and coauthored papers in prestigious journals (*IEEE Communication Surveys and Tutorials*, *Communications of the ACM*, *IEEE Transactions on Emerging Topics in Computing*) and conferences/workshops (*Networking*, *Critical Infrastructure Protection*, *EUROSEC*). He is a reviewer for journals including *IEEE Transactions on Smart Grid* and *Computers and Electrical Engineering*. Before his employment at Petru Maior University, Dr. Genge was a postdoctoral researcher at the Institute for the Protection and Security of the Citizen, Joint Research Centre, Ispra, Italy, where he conducted experimental network security research on cyber-physical systems.

Hunor Sándor is a PhD student at the Technical University of Cluj-Napoca, Romania. He obtained his MSc in information technology and his BSc in systems engineering from the Petru Maior University, Târgu Mureş, Romania. He also graduated in informatics from the Sapientia Hungarian University of Transylvania, Romania. His research interests are network-based control, Internet of Things, and network security in distributed systems. He has scientific and industrial experiences in the field of the Internet of Things. In 2014, he received a research grant from the National Excellence Program of the European Union and the State of Hungary for the topic bilateral teleoperation over wireless networks.

Piroska Haller obtained her PhD from the Technical University of Cluj-Napoca, Romania, in the field of distributed multimedia systems. She is currently associate professor at Petru Maior University, Târgu Mureş, Romania. She is a reviewer for *Control Engineering Practice*, *IEEE Infocom*, and *Information Sciences*. Her research interests include networked control systems, the design, optimization, and development off large-scale distributed systems, and system security in general.

Adela Bereş is a PhD student at the Technical University of Cluj-Napoca, Romania, in the field of cloud computing and network security. Her research interests include cloud infrastructure, cloud security, critical infrastructure integration with cloud, and network security. She has authored and coauthored papers in journals and conferences (*International Symposium on Digital Forensics and Security*, *International Universities' Power Engineering Conference*). Before starting her PhD, she completed her master's studies at Petru Maior University, Târgu Mureş, in information technology.

István Kiss received a BS degree in systems engineering and an MS degree in information technology from Petru Maior University, Târgu Mureş, Romania, in 2011 and 2013, respectively. He is currently a PhD student at the Technical University of Cluj-Napoca, Romania, in the field of computer science, and is employed as a researcher at Petru Maior University, Târgu Mureş, Romania. His research interests include industrial control systems security, critical infrastructure protection, sensor and actuator networks, industrial protocols, anomaly detection, and data mining. Until 2014, he worked as an automation engineer in the natural gas production industry in Romania, where he was involved in the development of several novel monitoring and control applications.

Glossary

AMICI: Assessment Platform for Multiple Interdependent Critical Infrastructures
ATM: asynchronous transfer mode
DoS: denial of service
EXI: efficient XML interchange
HMI: human–machine interfaces
ICSs: industrial control systems

ICT: information and communication technologies
IdP: identify provider
IETF: Internet Engineering Task Force
IP: Internet protocol
JID: Jabber ID
MDI: metadata isolation
MPLS: Multiprotocol Label Switching
NFV: network functions virtualization
OLE: object linking and embedding
OS: operating system
OVS: Open vSwitch
PLC: programmable logical controller
RPC: remote procedure call
SCADA: supervisory control and data acquisition
SDN: software-defined networking
SSO: single sign on
TE: Tennessee Eastman
TLS: transport layer security
XML: extensible markup language
XMPP: extensible messaging and presence protocol

References

1. R. Anderson, R. Hundley. *The Implications of COTS Vulnerabilities for the DoD and Critical U.S. Infrastructures.* RAND National Security Research Division Report, RAND, Santa Monica, CA, 1998.
2. M. Hagerot. Stuxnet and the vital role of critical infrastructure operators and engineers. *International Journal of Critical Infrastructure Protection*, vol. 7, no. 4, pp. 244–246, 2014.
3. CrySiS Lab. sKyWIper (a.k.a. Flame a.k.a. Flamer): A complex malware for targeted attacks. Laboratory of Cryptography and Systems Security, Budapest University of Technology and Economics, 2012.
4. M. Presser, P. M. Barnaghi, M. Eurich, and C. Villalonga. The SENSEI project: Integrating the physical world with the digital world of the network of the future. *IEEE Communications Magazine*, vol. 47, no. 4, pp. 1–4, 2009.
5. Symantec. W32.Duqu. The precursor to the next Stuxnet, 2011.
6. *The Economic Times.* Northern & eastern grids collapse: Biggest power failure in India, July, 2012.
7. J. Weiss. *Protecting Industrial Control Systems from Electronic Threats.* New York, Momentum Press, 2010.
8. Open Networking Foundation. Software-defined networking (SDN) definition. https://www.opennetworking.org/sdn-resources/sdn-definition, accessed July 2014.
9. R. K. Ackerman. Software-defined networking looms as next big technology. *Signal Online Magazine*, May 12, 2014.
10. OpenFlow, OpenFlow News. http://archive.openflow.org/, accessed July 2014.
11. ETSI. Network functions virtualisation. An introduction, benefits, enablers, challenges & call for action, White paper, Sophia-Antipolis Cedex, France, pp. 1–16, 2012.
12. C. Siaterlis, B. Genge. Cyber-physical testbeds. *Communications of the ACM*, vol. 57, no. 6, pp. 64–73, 2014.
13. C. Siaterlis, B. Genge, and M. Hohenadel. EPIC: A testbed for scientifically rigorous cyber-physical security experimentation. *IEEE Transactions on Emerging Topics in Computing*, vol. 1, no. 2, pp. 319–330, 2013.

14. P. Haller, A. Bica, and I. C. Szanto. Middleware for heterogeneous subsystems integration in health care services. In *Interdisciplinarity in Engineering International Conference*, Tirgu Mures, pp. 349–354, 2012.
15. Vitheia, Hermix software, http://vitheia.com/, accessed July 2014.
16. N. Handigol, B. Heller, V. Jeyakumar, B. Lantz, and N. McKeown. Reproducible network experiments using container-based emulation. In *Proceedings of the 8th International Conference Emerging Networking Experiments and Technologies*, New York, pp. 253–264, 2012.
17. B. Lantz, B. Heller and N. McKeown. A network in a laptop: Rapid prototyping for software-defined networks. In *Proceedings of the 9th ACM SIGCOMM Workshop on Hot Topics in Networks*, Article No. 19, 2010.
18. Project Floodlight. http://www.projectfloodlight.org/floodlight/, accessed July 2014.
19. B. Genge, C. Siaterlis, and M. Hohenadel. AMICI: An assessment platform for multi-domain security experimentation on critical infrastructures. In *7th International Conference on Critical Information Infrastructures Security*, Lillehammer, Norway, Lecture Notes in Computer Science 7722, pp. 228–239, 2012.
20. AMICI project, http://sourceforge.net/projects/amici/, accessed July 2014.
21. B. Galloway, G. P. Hancke. Introduction to industrial control networks. *IEEE Communications Surveys Tutorials*, vol. 15, no. 2, pp. 860–880, 2013.
22. S. East, J. Butts, M. Papa, and S. Shenoi. A taxonomy of attacks on the DNP3 protocol. In *IFIP Advances in Information and Communication Technology*, Springer, Boston, vol. 311/2009, pp. 67–81, 2009.
23. IBM and Cisco. Cisco and IBM provide high-voltage grid operator with increased reliability and manageability of its telecommunication infrastructure. IBM Case Studies, 2007.
24. B. Genge, D. A. Rusu, and P. Haller. A connection pattern-based approach to detect network traffic anomalies in critical infrastructures. In *2014 ACM European Workshop on System Security (EuroSec2014)*, Amsterdam, The Netherlands, pp. 1–6, 2014.
25. W. Chunlei, F. Lan, and D. Yiqi. A simulation environment for SCADA security analysis and assessment. In *Proceedings of 2010 International Conference on Measuring Technology and Mechatronics Automation*, Changsha City, China, pp. 342–347, 2010.
26. I. NaiFovino, A. Carcano, M. Masera, and A. Trombetta. An experimental investigation of malware attacks on SCADA systems. *International Journal of Critical Infrastructure Protection*, vol. 2, no. 4, pp. 139–145, 2009.
27. C. Queiroz, A. Mahmood, J. Hu, Z. Tari, and X. Yu. Building a SCADA security testbed. In *Proceedings of the 2009 Third International Conference on Network and System Security*, Gold Coast, Australia, pp. 357–364, 2009.
28. R. Chabukswar, B. Sinopoli, G. Karsai, A. Giani, H. Neema, and A. Davis. Simulation of network attacks on SCADA systems. In *First Workshop on Secure Control Systems, Cyber Physical Systems Week*, April, 2010.
29. S. Neema, T. Bapty, X. Koutsoukos, H. Neema, J. Sztipanovits, and G. Karsai. Model based integration and experimentation of information fusion and C2 systems. In *Proceedings of 12th International Conference on Information Fusion*, Seattle, WA, pp. 1958–1965, 2009.
30. J. O. Calvin, R. Weatherly. An introduction to the high level architecture (HLA) runtime infrastructure (RTI). In *Proceedings of the 14th Workshop on Standards for the Interoperability of Defence Simulations*, Orlando, FL, pp. 705–715, 1996.
31. T. Benzel, R. Braden, D. Kim, C. Neuman, A. Joseph, K. Sklower, R. Ostrenga, and S. Schwab. Experience with DETER: A testbed for security research. In *Proceedings of the International Conference on Testbeds and Research Infrastructures for the Development of Networks and Communities* (Barcelona, March 1–3). IEEE, New York, pp. 379–388, 2006.
32. J. J. Downs, E. F. Vogel. A plant-wide industrial process control problem. *Computer Chemical Engineering*, vol. 17, no. 3, pp. 245–255, 1993.
33. T. J. McAvoy, N. Ye. Base control for the Tennessee Eastman problem. *Computer Chemical Engineering*, vol. 18, no. 5, pp. 383–413, 1994.
34. B. Genge, C. Siaterlis. Physical process resilience-aware network design for SCADA systems. *Computers & Electrical Engineering*, vol. 40, no. 1, pp. 142–157, 2014.

35. J. C. Sozio. Intelligent parameter adaptation for chemical processes. Master's thesis, Virginia Polytechnic Institute and State University, Blacksburg, VA, 1999.
36. A. Bobbio, G. Bonanni, E. Ciancamerla, R. Clemente, A. Iacomini, M. Minichino, A. Scarlatti, R. Terruggia, and E. Zendri. Unavailability of critical SCADA communication links interconnecting a power grid and a telco network. *Reliability Engineering and System Safety*, vol. 95, no. 12, pp. 1345–1357, 2010.
37. Scapy, http://www.secdev.org/projects/scapy/, accessed July 2014.
38. Symantec. Dragonfly: Cyber espionage attacks against energy suppliers. Symantec Security Response, 2014.

Chapter 13

Tackling Cross-Site Scripting (XSS) Attacks in Cyberspace

Al-Sakib Khan Pathan and Imran Yusof

International Islamic University Malaysia

Contents

13.1 Introduction....332
13.2 Operational Method of Cross-Site Scripting....333
13.3 Major Types of Cross-Site Scripting....334
13.3.1 Persistent XSS....334
13.3.2 Nonpersistent XSS....334
13.3.3 Document Object Model–Based XSS....335
13.4 XSS Prevention and Detection Initiatives: Literature Review....335
13.5 Our Approach....338
13.5.1 Filtering Event Handlers....338
13.5.2 Filtering Data URI....340
13.5.3 Filtering Insecure Keywords....342
13.5.4 Filtering Character Escaping....342
13.5.5 Filtering Common Words in XSS Payload....342
13.5.6 Filtering XSS Buddies....343
13.5.7 Effectiveness of Our Approach....344
13.6 Future of XSS Attacks in Cyber-Physical Systems....344
13.7 Conclusions and Future Work....345
Author Biographies....345
References....346

Abstract: One of the most prominent attacks against web applications is the cross-site scripting (XSS) attack. Whenever a *server* gives a client access to any website or web application via cyberspace, irrespective of the environment in which the service is offered, a security threat such as XSS remains. This is because of the way that the XSS attacks operate by taking advantage of the *client–server* model and their communications through cyberspace. While a cyber-physical system (CPS) is considered a multidimensional environment combining various concepts, it would also have some cybercomponents and a cyberspace-like virtual world within it. Our concern is thus to analyze the current experiences of and proposals for tackling XSS attacks in cyberspace and to offer an effective solution to mitigate such attacks. In this chapter, alongside showing the effectiveness of our approach, we review some prominent past efforts of defending against XSS attacks.

Keywords: Attack; Cross-site scripting; Cyberspace; Exploitation; JavaScript; Malicious; Sanitization

13.1 Introduction

The concept of a cyber-physical system (CPS) links the notion of cyberspace with the physical world through a network of interrelated elements, such as sensors and actuators, robotics, and computational engines. A CPS is an environment in which different kinds of systems would use cybertechnologies for different tasks with high automation, intelligence, and collaboration. Some of the envisioned examples include energy-neutral buildings, zero-fatality highways, personalized medical devices, and so on. Our take from this idea is that whenever these systems are in place for actual use, any kind of cyberactivity would have the same vulnerabilities as in the usual cyberspace. In fact, in a sense, there is a real possibility of an increase in loopholes in the systems as a CPS could be very dynamic in nature with different kinds of devices with varying resources and security mechanisms, which would interact among themselves. Hence, in such a scenario, whenever any web application/website is provided as a service to the user, the chance of cross-site scripting (XSS) would remain. With this understanding, in this chapter, we discuss ways of defending against the common types of XSS attacks.

XSS is basically a very well-known computer security vulnerability that is typically associated with web applications, which enables malicious attackers to inject client-side script into web pages viewed by other users [1,2]. An XSS attack was first discussed in a Computer Emergency Response Team (CERT) advisory in 2003 [3].

A huge number of vulnerabilities plague today's web applications. While there are many security flaws that are exploited by attackers to achieve various kinds of objectives, XSS is often ignored. Proper attention should be given to XSS attacks as they are very prevalent nowadays. XSS is basically a type of injection problem in which malicious scripts are injected into a trusted website. Attackers use XSS to execute script in a victim's browser and the malicious script can access any cookie, session token, or other sensitive information stored by the browser. According to WhiteHat Security, 43% of web applications have XSS vulnerabilities [4]. Hence, some kind of efficient mechanism is needed to deal with such a security flaw, which could be a great threat to web users. This is the main motivation behind this work.

The rest of the chapter is organized as follows: Section 13.2 discusses how XSS attacks work; Section 13.3 notes the types of XSS; Section 13.4 reviews the XSS prevention and detection initiatives that are available in the literature; Section 13.5 presents our proposed mechanism with examples, explanations, and the outcomes of various experiments; Section 13.6 explores the rationale behind this work and future expectations; and finally, Section 13.7 concludes the chapter with future scopes of research.

13.2 Operational Method of Cross-Site Scripting

Whenever some *untrusted* data (in the plural sense here—singular is *datum*) are taken by an application and then sent to a web browser without proper validation and escaping, XSS flaws could occur. *Escaping* technically means to take the data that someone may already have and help secure it prior to rendering it for the end user. Using XSS, attackers can execute malicious scripts in the victim's browser, which can hijack user sessions, deface websites, or redirect the user to malicious sites. Hence, an XSS attack allows an attacker to acquire the personal credentials of a legitimate user and possibly impersonate the same user during the time of interaction with a specific website.

Often, a website may contain a script that returns a user's input (some parameter values) in a hypertext markup language (HTML) page. In such cases, if proper sanitizing is not carried out, it is possible to launch an XSS attack. To clarify, *sanitization* is the process of removing sensitive information from a document or other medium, so that it can be distributed to a broader audience. Another technical meaning is the removal of malicious data from a user input, such as form submissions.

If there is any such flawed mechanism (as noted in the previous paragraph) of getting user input—for instance, an input consisting of JavaScript code to be executed by the browser when the script returns this input in the response page (without proper *sanitization*)—in this case, it is possible to make links to the site where one of the parameters consists of malicious JavaScript code. This code will then be executed by a user's browser in the site context, granting it access to cookies that the user has for the site, and other windows in the site through the user's browser.

Given the severity of the threat, XSS was ranked second in the Open Web Application Security Project (OWASP) Top 10 Most Critical Web Application Security Risks report 2010 and third in the OWASP Top 10 Most Critical Web Application Security Risks report 2013 [5]. According to Google's vulnerability reward program's statistics [6], XSS is the most reported issue (see Figure 13.1). With this current trend, we expect that in the future, XSS will be extensively used by attackers in any kind of cyberspace—especially when 69% of all attacks are XSS, it would be difficult to reduce this percentage quickly due to the complexity of the attack methods and the

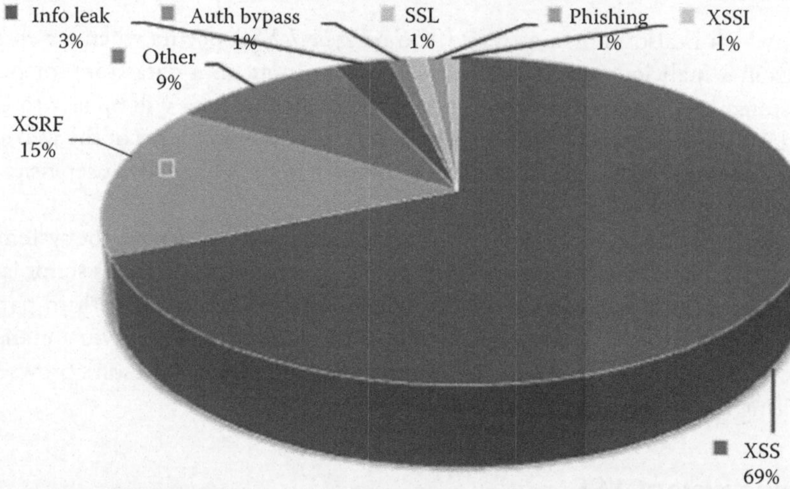

Figure 13.1 Google vulnerability reward program's statistics (generated from the data available at http://www.nilsjuenemann.de/2012/12/news-about-googles-vulnerability-reward.html).

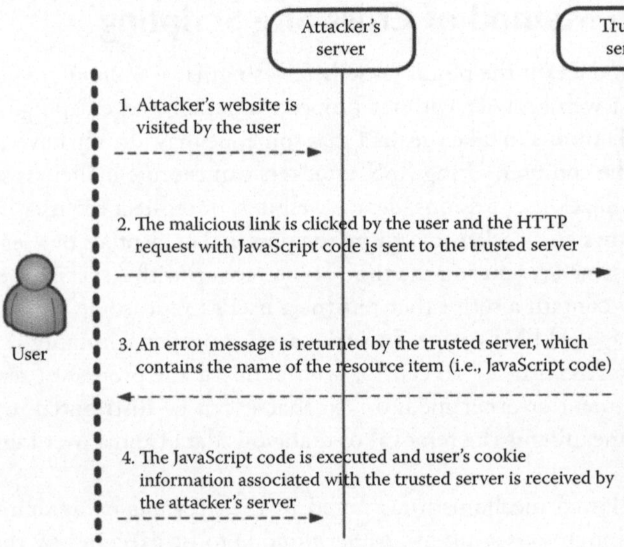

Figure 13.2 An example scenario of cross-site scripting.

inherent vulnerabilities in web applications (that could be exploited for XSS attacks). A typical XSS scenario is depicted in Figure 13.2 (adopted from [7]).

13.3 Major Types of Cross-Site Scripting

There are three major types of XSSs: (i) *persistent*, (ii) *nonpersistent*, and (iii) *document object model (DOM)-based*.

13.3.1 Persistent XSS

Persistent XSS, which is also known as *stored XSS* or *Type-I XSS*, occurs when a web application gathers input from a malicious user, and then stores that input in a data store for possible later use [8]. If the stored input is not properly filtered, the malicious data will appear to be a part of the website and it will be run within the user's browser under the privileges of the web application. This kind of XSS does not need a malicious link to be exploited. Whenever a user visits a web page with a stored XSS, a successful exploitation occurs.

Persistent XSS is often difficult to detect and could cause serious harm to the system. This type of XSS is considered more harmful than other types as an attacker's malicious script is used automatically, without any need to individually target victims or lure them to a third-party website. For instance, an attacker could be a seemingly innocuous blog user who leaves a malicious script in the comment field of a vulnerable blogging web application. Thus, a person's browser would be affected by visiting the blog with the malicious script.

13.3.2 Nonpersistent XSS

Nonpersistent attacks are also called *reflected XSS* attacks. When a web application is vulnerable to this type of attack, it will pass invalidated input, which is sent through requests to the client.

A typical example is when the attacker engineers the social behavior of the user or attracts a user to load an offending uniform resource identifier (URI) on his or her browser, which then executes the offending code using the credentials of the user.

13.3.3 Document Object Model–Based XSS

The DOM-based XSS is also sometimes called *Type-0 XSS*. There are some similarities between this type of XSS and the *nonpersistent* type; however, in this case, the JavaScript payload does not have to be echoed back from the web server. Often, it is simply the value from a uniform resource locator (URL) parameter that is echoed back onto the page on-the-fly when loading an already resident JavaScript. It occurs when the XSS vector executes as a result of a DOM modification on a website in a user's browser. Here, the hypertext transfer protocol (HTTP) response does not change on the client side; however, the script executes in a malicious manner. This exploit only works if the browser does not modify the URL characters [9]. This is recognized as the most sophisticated and least-known type of XSS. As many application developers simply do not understand how it works, it can occur frequently. Following this brief review of the basic mechanism behind XSS and its types, in the next section, we look at the various efforts that researchers and experts have exerted in the past.

13.4 XSS Prevention and Detection Initiatives: Literature Review

Garcia-Alfaro and Navarro-Arribas [10] present a survey on detection techniques for the prevention of XSS attacks on various web applications. As prevention techniques, the authors mainly talk about the analysis and filtering of the exchanged information and runtime enforcement of web browsers. Given the work's publication year (2007–2008), though many of the issues discussed are still relevant today, not all the information presented in the paper would relate to current web applications. This is obvious because even over a short period of time, the types of web applications as well as innovative attack techniques using XSS and other methods constantly change. The same authors of [10] conclude in [11] that an efficient solution to prevent XSS attacks would be the enforcement of security policies defined at the server side and deployed over the end point. In their work, they suggest that a set of actions over those browser's resources belonging to the web application must be clearly defined by their developers or administrators or both, and enforced by the web browser.

Madou et al. [12] state in their work that appropriate coding is the best way to prevent XSS attacks. However, an additional layer of defense could be created by simply introducing some XSS vulnerabilities. This could be used to record and distinguish normal and abnormal behavior, based on which further protection in coding could be applied. Their approach defends web applications mainly from two types of attacks: *reflected* and *persistent* XSS attacks. There are two phases to how it works:

Phase 1: The target application is monitored during an attack-free training period with a finite duration, which generates likely invariants on normal program behavior. In the field of mathematics, the term *invariant* means a property of a class of mathematical objects that remains unchanged when transformations of a certain type are applied to the objects. Here, with a similar meaning, the invariants are those conditions that always hold during the training period. They are all related to the types of output that the program writes to the HTTP response.

Phase 2: Once a set of likely invariants are developed, the application is monitored for an indefinite period of time in a potentially hostile environment. The objective is to make sure that the application does not deviate from normal behavior. A problem is reported when a program behavior violates one or more likely invariants.

This kind of mechanism is also the basic working principle of different kinds of intrusion detection systems (IDSs).

An argument is presented in [13] that input validation or filtering is not always sufficient to prevent XSS attacks on the server side. The authors state that it is ineffective in preventing several instances of attacks, especially when user input includes content-rich HTML. With this understanding, they propose a new framework called *XSS-GUARD*, which is a prevention mechanism against XSS attacks on the server side. The essence of the framework is that it dynamically learns the set of scripts that a web application intends to create for any HTML request. A mechanism is used to detect and remove any suspicious script in the output that is not intended by the web application. Although the framework seems to be a good approach to deal with the issue and to introduce another line of defense, in reality, the finding that input validation (i.e., filtering) is not enough is obvious. Careful filtering is a must for such XSS attack prevention mechanisms.

In [14], the authors present a dynamic cookie rewriting mechanism to thwart impersonation attacks that could be launched by attackers using XSS. When a user is browsing a website, the small piece of data that is sent from the website and stored in the user's web browser is known as a *cookie*, also known as a HTTP cookie, a web cookie, or a browser cookie. Cookies are used for identifying and authenticating users. Each time a user loads the website, the web browser sends the cookie back to the server to notify the website of the user's previous activity. Cookies are designed as a reliable mechanism for websites to remember stateful information (such as items in a shopping cart) or to record a user's browsing activity (including clicking particular buttons, logging in, or recording which pages were visited by the user as far back as months or years ago). Hence, once a user is authenticated or the user's information is sent to the server, every subsequent request that contains the valid cookies will be automatically allowed by the web applications without any further authentication. This is one of the mechanisms that could be targeted by XSS attackers. Realizing this threat, the authors of this work outline a set of rules and implement their mechanism of dynamic cookie rewriting. The authors note that it is possible to implement the mechanism in the web proxy without any change required to either the web browser or the web server. The core idea is that the web proxy will automatically rewrite the value of the name attribute in the cookie with a randomized value before sending the cookie to the browser. This would ensure that the browser keeps the randomized value in its database instead of the original value sent by the web server. Consequently, the returned cookie from the browser would also be rewritten back to its original value in the web proxy before forwarding to the web server. The trick here is that as the database in the browser side does not have the original values of the cookies, even if XSS attacks are used to steal the cookies from the browser's database, the attackers would be unable to use the information for launching impersonation attacks later.

Shar and Tan [15] mention that XSS vulnerabilities are mainly caused by the failure of web applications to *sanitize* user inputs embedded in web pages. They argue that even though several advanced mechanisms have been developed, often it is difficult to tackle XSS vulnerabilities because of the difficulty of adopting the advanced techniques, the often partial implementation of the solutions, and the lack of proper understanding of various types of XSSs. To address these issues, the authors propose a code-auditing approach, which would recover the defense model that is implemented in a program source code and they then suggest guidelines for checking the adequacy of the recovered model against XSS attacks. They show that their approach is effective in recovering all the XSS defense features implemented in the test subjects. However, one of the main weaknesses of this approach is manual auditing, which would be cumbersome to employ for large, complex applications. In fact, the test subjects that are used in this work are simple and do not include enough complexity to claim real effectiveness against sophisticated XSS attack scenarios.

A machine learning (ML)-based method is presented in [16] to detect XSS attacks in web pages. ML is basically a subfield of computer science (CS) and artificial intelligence (AI), which deals with the construction and study of systems that can learn from data, rather than only following explicit programming instructions. In this work, the authors carry out their experiments with two ML methods: (i) naive Bayes and (ii) support vector machines (SVM). Here, naive Bayes and SVM deal with a set of labeled sample data, which include positive and negative samples whether web pages are infected with XSS code or not. The performance analysis based on these methods shows satisfactory results for the automatic classification of XSS attacks on web pages. The weakness of the work is that the experiments are not thorough or subject to parameter manipulation. Only two ML methods are used and other methods have not been experimented. Also, it does not provide a guarantee of detecting all types of XSS attacks, though large databases were used for the experiments.

An XSS attack detection algorithm is proposed in [17], which extracts an attack feature of an XSS attack considering the appearance, position, and frequency of symbols. In their scheme, the authors present their classification rule and their calculation of the degree of importance of symbols. The basic idea behind this scheme is to set a particular threshold and detect the attack feature value. In the process of learning the attack feature value threshold, the rank of symbols is determined. From the rank of symbols, it is possible to compute the attack feature value against an input. If the input has a higher rank/frequency of symbols (high attack feature value) than the threshold, it is detected as an attack. Experiments show that this scheme successfully detects 99.5% of attack test samples and 97.5% of normal test samples. However, the major drawback of this scheme is the processing costs of each input and the complexity of choosing an appropriate threshold as the calculation and learning process may not always be correct. A valid input may be incorrectly detected as an attack script if the threshold is wrongly set for a particular scenario.

Sun and He [18] propose an automatic modeling method for defending against XSS attacks. The idea behind this work is to judge an operational behavior if it conforms to the requirements of the legal behavior of a website. Bugs were detected for various website implementations based on the automatic modeling algorithm for HTML code. However, the scope of the paper's work was narrow and not all types of website implementations were checked—which is a limitation of this work. Another automatic detection algorithm of XSS with the nonstationary Bernoulli distribution is presented in [19]. The authors of this work mathematically formulated the XSS detection problem in terms of the statistical decision theory. The proposed algorithm was obtained by calculating the Bayes optimal prediction under the nonstationary Bernoulli process. To illustrate, in probability and statistics, a Bernoulli process is a finite or infinite sequence of binary random variables, so it is a discrete-time stochastic process that takes only two values, canonically 0 and 1. Despite showing good results with the proposed algorithm, one critical drawback that the authors also noted is the instability of the algorithm. Of course, the overall complexity of implementing this scheme would be relatively high with uncertainty about its actual effectiveness in practical scenarios.

A hybrid solution, named *XSS-Dec*, for mitigating XSS attacks is presented in [20]. This solution combines the benefits of a control flow analysis and anomaly detection to protect client systems against XSS attacks. The authors call it a *security-by-proxy solution*, which relies on a proxy component for vulnerability analysis and detection. As is common knowledge, a proxy acts as a middleman between the server and the client's devices. The browsing activities of the users are thoroughly monitored to analyze whether an attack is occurring. The scheme basically uses feature extraction to determine an attack. The authors developed a prototype, which was tested; however, the scalability of the approach in a distributed setting was not tested.

Lan et al. [21] analyze XSS attacks that are based on encoding. The authors identify the limitations of a traditional web proxy, and then describe a binary-encoded XSS attack and N-ray alphabets encoding XSS attacks. Then, they propose their dynamic access control mechanism to mitigate encoding-based XSS attacks. The basic idea is that the attacks can be mitigated by using a k-threshold approach, which would only allow a maximum of k static links with the same domain in the page, and if the number of the same domain static links is greater than k, the proxy would warn the user. They note that, in practice, many normal web pages contain multiple static links with the same domain, which makes the threshold k difficult to set. In fact, if the value of k is too large, the proxy would not be useful against XSS attacks, and if the value of k is too small, it would generate a high rate of false positive. Hence, to strike a balance between these, the dynamic access control scheme would enhance the prevention policy of the web proxy based on the observation that: "Even if a page contains more than k links to some external domain, it might still be safe for the user to click a small number of these links without leaking too much information." The experimental setup showed good performance of the approach; however, the technique was not tested against other types of attacks, and the details of the full experiment, which are available in the paper, raise some queries about the credibility of the approach.

After analyzing all of these works, our understanding is that input validation and careful choice of easily implementable steps could be the best remedy to defend against XSS attacks. In the next section, we describe our approach together with all the necessary details of various facets of such attacks.

13.5 Our Approach

To defend against persistent XSS attacks, a simple task must be performed for input filtering: Any data from the input must be transformed or filtered in such a way that it is not executed by a browser if it is sent to it. To avoid XSS, developers must sanitize the user's input before storing it in the database. The conceptual model of filtering persistent XSS vulnerabilities is designed based on the analysis of the results of various experimentations.

Figure 13.3 shows the conceptual model to prevent persistent XSS attacks and Figure 13.4 illustrates the process of filtering persistent XSS attacks. Figure 13.4 depicts user inputs that are taken from a web browser as untrusted data, which go through a filtering process to get a *clean* status. These clean data are stored in the database to generate clean output after output sanitization.

13.5.1 Filtering Event Handlers

Event handlers are JavaScript codes that are not added inside the <script> tags, but rather are added inside the HTML tags, which execute JavaScript when something happens, such as pressing a button, moving the mouse over a web link, or submitting a form [22]. When any event occurs, the function that is assigned to an event handler runs. Some examples of well-known event handlers are onError (when the loading of a document or an image causes an error), onClick (if someone clicks on a form), onLoad (an attacker executes the attack string after the window loads),

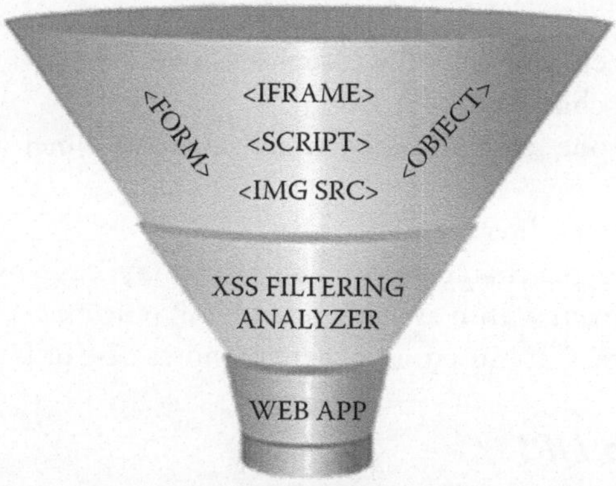

Figure 13.3 Conceptual model of the persistent XSS filter.

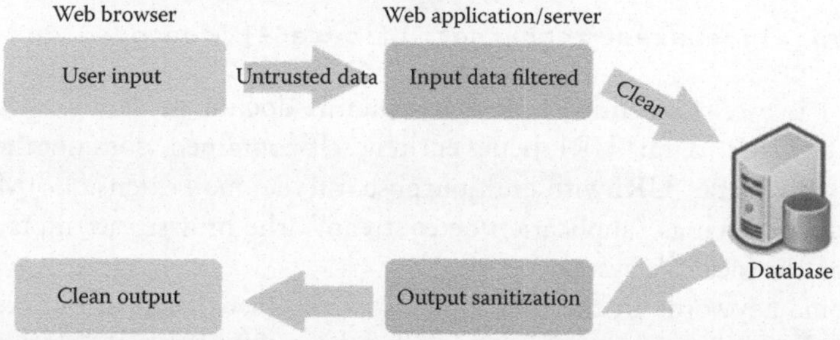

Figure 13.4 Persistent XSS filtering process.

and onMouseOver (the cursor moves over an object or area). Examples of XSS vectors using this method are [23]:

```
<img/src=`%00` onerror=this.onerror=confirm('XSS') ?>
<///style///><span %2F onmousemove=alert&lpar;1&rpar;>SPAN
<input/onmouseover="javaSCRIPT&colon;confirm&lpar;1&rpar;"
<img/&#09;&#10;&#11; src=`~` onerror=prompt(1)>
<iframesrcdoc='&lt;bodyonload=prompt&lpar;1&rpar;&gt;'>
```

These kinds of XSS vectors do not require the use of any variants of “javascript:” or “<SCRIPT...” for the attacker to accomplish the XSS attack. By applying pattern of regular expression as noted next, we can filter these kinds of XSS vectors.

```
/on\w+=|fscommand/i
```

When an attacker submits or injects an XSS vector into a web application that implements or uses this pattern filtering, that web application will filter out the event handler in the input submitted by the attacker by replacing it with null. Thus, the XSS payload would become invalid. Figure 13.5 shows how this filter can be used in a hypertext preprocessor (PHP) class.

```
public function filter_event_handlers($str)
{
    $pattern = '/on\w+=|fscommand/i';
    return preg_replace($pattern, '', $str);
}
```

Figure 13.5 PHP method for filtering event handlers.

Explanation:

1. `on` matches the characters on literally; case insensitive.
2. **`\w+`** match any word character [a-zA-Z0-9].
3. Quantifier: Between one and unlimited times, as many times as possible, giving back as needed.
4. = matches the character = literally.
5. **`fscommand`** matches the characters *fscommand* literally; case insensitive. (Attacker can use this when executing from within an embedded Flash object.)
   `i` modifier: insensitive. Case-insensitive match ignores case of [a-zA-Z].

13.5.2 Filtering Data URI

The data URI format is pretty simple and was presented in RFC 2397 [24]. The basic format of the data URI is as follows [25]:

```
data:[<mimetype>][;charset=<charset>][;base64],<encoded data>
```

The data URI is a self-contained link that contains document data and metadata entirely encapsulated in the URI; "data:" URI, being entirely self-contained, does not include a filename. When presented with "data:" URI with multipurpose Internet mail extensions (MIME) types that trigger the save dialog such as "application/octet-stream", the browser attempts to save the URI content as a file on the local file system.

The use of some keywords in the user input has been blacklisted in our web application—keywords such as JavaScript, alert, script, round brackets, double quotes, and colon. Generally, a <script> tag must be used to execute a JavaScript. Here, the attacker cannot use the <script> tag because the application validates the user input against specific keywords. Hence, to execute a JavaScript, the attacker tries using a data URI. In this attempt, the attacker can now inject the following payload:

```
<object data="data:text/html;base64,PHNjcmlwdD5hbGVydCgiWFNTIik7PC9zY3Jp
cHQ+"></object>
<object data="data:image/gif;base64,R0lGODlhEAAJANUrAB4aGyAcHfHx8fb19fb2
9vX19fLy8lZTVCklJkNAQOXk5fX09C0qKkVCQ/T09J2bm////5mXmOnp6SUhIqSioz05OuDf4
IeFhVRRUj87PFVSUyomJ/39/a6sre/u7lBNTWhlZjk1NrCur9nY2cPCw/f393p4eB4bG7++v
l9dXSMfIP///wAAAAAAAAAAAAAAAAAAAAAAAAAAAAAAAAAAAAAAAAAAAAAAAAAAAAAA
AAAAAAAAAAAAAAAAAACH/C1hNUCBEYXRhWE1QPD94cGFja2V0IGJlZ2luPSLvu78iIGlkPS
JXNU0wTXBDZWhpSHpyZVN6TlRjemtjOWQiPz4gPHg6eG1wbWV0YSB4bWxuczp4PSJhZG9iZTp
uczptZXRhLyIgeDp4bXB0az0iQWRvYmUgWE1QIENvcmUgNS4zLWMwMTEgNjYuMTQ1NjYxLCAy
MDEyLzAyLzA2LTE0OjU2Oj13ICAgICAgICAiPiA8cmRmOlJERiB4bWxuczpyZGY9Imh0dHA6L
y93d3cudzMub3JnLzE5OTkvMDIvMjItcmRmLXN5bnRheC1ucyMiPiA8cmRmOkRlc2NyaXB0aW
9uIHJkZjphYm91dD0iIiB4bWxuczp4bXA9Imh0dHA6Ly9ucy5hZG9iZS5jb20veGFwLzEuMC8
iIHhtbG5zOnhtcE1NPSJodHRwOi8vbnMuYWRvYmUuY29tL3hhcC8xLjAvbW0vIiB4bWxuczpz
dFJlZj0iaHR0cDovL25zLmFkb2JlLmNvbS94YXAvMS4wL3NUeXBlL1Jlc291cmNlUmVmIyIge
G1wOkNyZWF0b3JUb29sPSJBZG9iZSBQaG90b3Nob3AgQ1M2IChNYWNpbnRvc2gpIiB4bXBNTT
pJbnN0YW5jZUlEPSJ4bXAuaWlkOkUxQjk5RTZERkQ2RjExRTNBRkM5OUE5QUFGMTY0NDlGIi
B4bXBNTTpEb2N1bWVudElEPSJ4bXAuZGlkOkUxQjk5RTZFRkQ2RjExRTNBRkM5OUE5QUFGMT
Y0NDlGIj4gPHhtcE1NOkRlcml2ZWRGcm9tIHN0UmVmOmluc3RhbmNlSUQ9InhtcC5paWQ6RTF
COTlFNkJGRDZGMTFFM0FGQzk5QTlBQUYxNjQ0OUYiIHN0UmVmOmRvY3VtZW50SUQ9InhtcC5
kaWQ6RTFCOTlFNkNGRDZGMTFFM0FGQzk5QTlBQUYxNjQ0OUYiLz4gPC9yZGY6RGVzY3JpcHRp
b24+IDwvcmRmOlJERj4gPC94OnhtcG1ldGE+IDw/eHBhY2tldCBlbmQ9InIiPz4B//79/Pv6
+fj39vX0 8/Lx8O/u7ezr6uno5+bl5OPi4eDf3t3c29rZ2NfW1dTT0tHQz87NzMvKycjHxsXE
```

```
w8LBwL++vby7urm4t7a1tLOysbCvrq2sq6qpqKempaSjoqGgn56dnJuamZiXlpWUk5KRkI+O
jYyLiomIh4aFhIOCgYB/fn18e3p5eHd2dXRzcnFwb25tbGtqaWhnZmVkY2JhYF9eXVxbWllY
V1ZVVFNSUVBPTk1MS0pJSEdGRURDQkFAPz49PDs6OTg3NjU0MzIxMC8uLSwrKikoJyYlJCMi
ISAfHh0cGxoZGBcWFRQTEhEQDw4NDAsKCQgHBgUEAwIBAAAh+QQBAAArACwAAAAAEAAJAAAG
Q8CVcEgsGo/FhYFQIBAhhcFAUFqhGoDThKSgCCKAQCA1EnoyKtWmokqkVaDi5fBhvEMYTQdp
MSEeEkIcSCsOIoSIREEAOw==" /></object>
```


The executions of the injected payloads are shown in Figures 13.6 and 13.7.

A data URI attack can be prevented by applying the following regular expression pattern filtering in our web application (see Figure 13.8):

```
/data\s*:[^\\1]*?base64[^\\1]*?,/i
```

Explanation:

1. **`data`** matches the characters data: literally case insensitive
2. **`\s*`** match any white space character [\r\n\t\f]
   Quantifier: Between zero and unlimited times, as many times as possible, giving back as needed.
3. : matches the character: literally
4. **`[^\\1]*?`** match a single character not present in the list below:
   Quantifier: Between zero and unlimited times, as few times as possible, expanding as needed.
   \\ matches the character \ literally
   `1` the literal character 1
   `base64` matches the characters base64 literally (case insensitive)
5. **`[^\\1]*?`** match a single character not present in the list below:
   Quantifier: Between zero and unlimited times, as few times as possible, expanding as needed.
   \\ matches the character \ literally
   `1` the literal character 1, matches the character, literally.
6. **`i`** modifier: insensitive. Case insensitive match ignores case of [a-zA-Z].

By implementing pattern filtering as mentioned earlier, our web application would be free from this kind of attack.

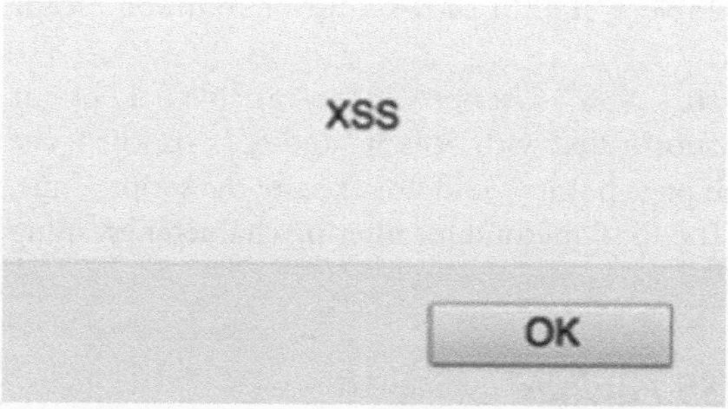

Figure 13.6 Data URI HTML JavaScript.

Figure 13.7 Data URI HTML image.

```
public function filter_data_uri($str)
{
    $pattern = '/data\s*:[^\\1]*?base64[^\\1]*?,/i';
    return preg_replace($pattern, '', $str);
}
```

Figure 13.8 PHP method for filtering data URI.

```
public function filter_blacklisted($str)
{
    strtolower($str);
    $blacklisted = array(
        'document.cookie'    => '',
        'document.write'     => '',
        '<!--'               => '&lt;!--',
        '-->'                => '--&gt;',
        '<![CDATA['          => '&lt;![CDATA[',
        '<comment>'          => '&lt;comment&gt;',
        '.parentNode'        => '',
        '.innerHTML'         => '',
        'window.location'    => '',
        '-moz-binding'       => '',
        '<embed'             => '',
        '<applet'            => '',
        '<object'            => '',
        '<script'            => ''
    );

    $str = str_ireplace(array_keys($blacklisted), $blacklisted, $str);
    return $str;
}
```

Figure 13.9 PHP method for filtering unsecure keywords.

13.5.3 Filtering Insecure Keywords

An insecure keyword belongs to a list of known bad data that block illegal content from being executed. We have to filter the pattern that should not appear in the user input. If a string matches this pattern, it is marked as invalid and removed or replaced with equivalent words. Examples of insecure keywords are shown in Figure 13.9.

Basically, we would compile a list of all blacklisted words, and then verify that the input received from the user is not one of these blacklisted words.

13.5.4 Filtering Character Escaping

To help prevent XSS attacks, a web application needs to ensure that all variable outputs in a page are encoded before being returned to the end user. Preventing XSS attacks means substituting every special character that is used in these attacks. We can escape dangerous characters by using the &#sequence followed by its character code. Table 13.1 [26] shows a list of common escape codes.

For instance, if an attacker injects <script>alert ("XSS")</script> into a variable field of our web application, a character such as <, > will be substituted with &#x3C and > then, the browser would display the script as part of the web page but it would not execute the script. Thus, we could prevent our web application from XSS. The PHP method for filtering character escaping is shown in Figure 13.10.

13.5.5 Filtering Common Words in XSS Payload

XSS attacks are constantly evolving. Every day, new vectors are created. By implementing common words in the XSS payload, we can defend our web application from a malicious code injection. As an example, the following payload will be filtered by our web application.

```
<iframe %00 src="&Tab;javascript:prompt(1)&Tab;"%00>
```

Table 13.1 List of Common Escape Codes

Display	*Numerical Code*	*Hex Code*
"	"	"
#	#	#
&	&	&
'	'	'
(	(	(
)	)	)
/	/	/
;	;	;
<	<	<
>	>	>

Source: ASCII to Hex [Online]. Available: http://www.asciitohex.com. With permission.

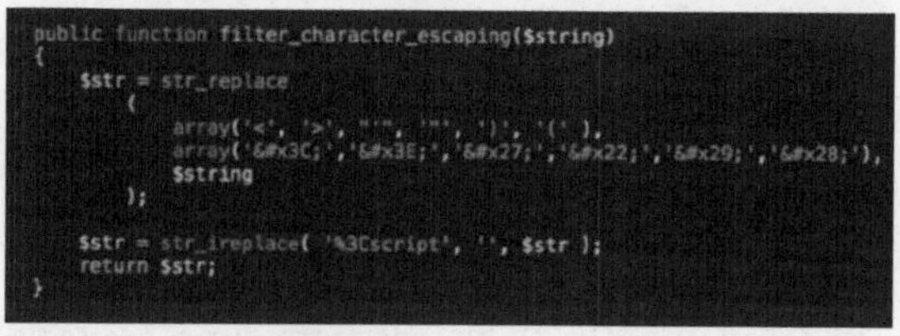

Figure 13.10 PHP method for filtering character escaping.

Explanation:

1. **`javascript`** matches the characters JavaScript literally case insensitive.
2. **`s*`** match any white space character [\r\n\t\f].
3. Quantifier: Between zero and unlimited times, as many times as possible, giving back as needed.
4. **`:`** matches the character: literally.
   `i` modifier: insensitive. Case-insensitive match ignores case of [a-zA-Z].

The PHP method for filtering common XSS words is shown in Figure 13.11.

13.5.6 Filtering XSS Buddies

The friend of my enemy is my enemy. HTML elements such as `<isindex>`, `<meta>`, `<form>`, `<object>`, `<style>`, `<script>`, and so on, should be filtered out from user input to protect our web application from XSS code injection. The following is an example of an XSS payload filtered by this method:

```
<iframe src=j&Tab;a&Tab;v&Tab;a&Tab;s&Tab;c&Tab;r&Tab;i&Tab;p&Tab;t&Tab;:
a&Tab;l&Tab;e&Tab;r&Tab;t&Tab;%28&Tab;1&Tab;%29></iframe>
<form><button formaction=javascript&colon;alert(1)>CLICKME
```

```
public function filter_common_xss($str)
{
    $common_xss = array(
        'javascript\s*:',
        'expression\s*(\(|&\#40;)',
        'vbscript\s*:',
        'iframe\s*',
        'redirect\s+302',
    );

    foreach ($common_xss as $xss) {
        $str = preg_replace("#$xss#is", '', $str);
    }
    return $str;
}
```

Figure 13.11 PHP method for filtering common XSS words.

```
public function filter_xss_buddies($str)
{
    $pattern = array
        (
            '/<isindex[^>]*>[\s\S]*?/i',
            '/<script[^>]*>[\s\S]*?/i',
            '/<meta[^>]*>[\s\S]*?/i',
            '/<object[^>]*>[\s\S]*?/i',
            '/<style[^>]*>[\s\S]*?/i',
            '/<form[^>]*>[\s\S]*?/i',
            '/<applet[^>]*>[\s\S]*?/i',
            '/<iframe[^>]*>[\s\S]*?/i',
            '/[\s\S]xlink:href[\s\S]/i',
            '/[\s\S]formaction[\s\S]]/i',
            '/[\s\S]@import[\s\S]/i'
        );

    $replace_with = array('', '', '', '', '', '', '', '', '', '', '');
    return preg_replace($pattern, $replace_with, $str);
}
```

Figure 13.12 PHP method for filtering XSS buddies.

As presented in Figure 13.12:

1. **`<isindex`** match the characters <isindex literally; case insensitive.
2. **`[^>]*`** match a single character not present in the following list:
   Quantifier: Between zero and unlimited times, as many times as possible, giving back as needed.
   > a single character in the list > literally case insensitive
   > matches the characters > literally
3. **`[\s\S]*?`** match a single character present in the following list:
   Quantifier: Between zero and unlimited times, as few times as possible, expanding as needed
   `\s` match any white space character [\r\n\t\f]
   `\S` match any nonwhite space character [^\r\n\t\f]

13.5.7 Effectiveness of Our Approach

We have tested and evaluated a series of XSS attack scenarios. A collection of XSS cheat sheets [27–29] were used, which were filtered and sanitized effectively. It has been proved that the proposed mechanism is sufficiently effective in filtering out various malicious XSS vectors.

13.6 Future of XSS Attacks in Cyber-Physical Systems

People see a CPS from different perspectives. Sometimes, it is considered a ubiquitous system that is meant for power systems or transportation networks or industrial control processes or critical infrastructures of any kind that use the cyberconcept, and so on [30]. Irrespective of the environment in which the cyberspace exists, whenever a client and a server are involved and the client needs to access web applications located at the trusted server, there would be vulnerabilities exploiting which XSS attacks could be launched. For instance, the smart grid infrastructure would heavily depend on the CPS structure. In fact, the way that the CPS portrays its envisioned services, the smart grid can rely on it for those users who interact via cyberspace with servers that keep track of electricity usage. The CPS for the smart grid will be able to monitor, share, and manage information and perform actions for various types of tasks including business activities [31]. All these systems need to operate reliably when faced with unforeseen errors, vulnerabilities, and external malicious attacks. Hence, our work will still be relevant for any such emerging technology that uses the web for facilitating interactions between users and the servers.

13.7 Conclusions and Future Work

Using an XSS attack, it is possible to steal or manipulate a victim's sessions and cookies, which may be used to impersonate a legitimate user of a system. Hence, it is very important to filter user input to secure any web application. Our main concern in this chapter is that the applications should perform input and output filtering to achieve an appropriate level of protection for their users. With our various experiments and investigation, the proposed XSS attack prevention model has been found to be very effective. However, various kinds of tricks and techniques are being devised all the time [32]—hackers are not sitting idle, in fact their attacks are getting more and more sophisticated as time moves on. Therefore, there is no 100% guarantee that the solution that we have presented in this chapter would work in the coming years in the same way. It is highly likely that XSS attacks could spread to emerging technologies such as the CPS, the Internet of Things (IoT), and so on.

Given these facts, the best way to prevent or defend against an XSS attack is to code the web applications with *security* in mind and to use proper escaping mechanisms in the right places. In this case, it is better never to trust the data coming from the user(s). Every piece of data must be validated, filtered, and escaped on output. For our future work, we plan to thoroughly investigate how our prevention model can be extended and applied to nonpersistent and other types of XSS.

Author Biographies

Al-Sakib Khan Pathan received a PhD degree (a master's leading to a PhD) in computer engineering in 2009 from Kyung Hee University, South Korea. He received a BSc degree in computer science and information technology from the Islamic University of Technology, Bangladesh, in 2003. He is currently an assistant professor in the computer science department of the International Islamic University Malaysia, Malaysia. Up to June 2010, he served as an assistant professor in the Computer Science and Engineering Department in BRAC University, Bangladesh. Prior to holding this position, he worked as a researcher at Networking Lab, Kyung Hee University, South Korea till August 2009. His research interest includes wireless sensor networks, network security, and e-services technologies. Currently, he is also working on some multidisciplinary issues. He is a recipient of several awards/best paper awards and has several publications in these areas. He has served as a chair, organizing committee member, and technical program committee member in numerous international conferences/workshops such as GLOBECOM, International Conference on Communications, GreenCom, Advanced Information Networking and Applications, Wireless

Communications and Networking Conference, High Performance Computing & Simulation, Algorithms and Architectures for Parallel Processing, International Wireless Communications & Mobile Computing Conference, Vehicular Technology, High Performance Computing and Communications, and so on. He was awarded the Institute of Electrical and Electronics Engineers Outstanding Leadership Award and a Certificate of Appreciation for his role in the IEEE GreenCom 2013 Conference. He is currently serving as an area editor of the *International Journal of Communication Networks and Information Security*; associate editor of the *International Journal of Computer Science Engineering* and the *International Journal of Computer Application* (IASTED/ACTA Press); and he is guest editor of many special issues of top-ranked journals and editor/author of 12 published books. One of his books has been included twice in Intel Corporation's Recommended Reading List for Developers, in the second half of 2013 and the first half of 2014; three other books were included in the IEEE Communications Society's Best Readings in Communications and Information Systems Security 2013, and a fifth book is in the process of being translated to simplified Chinese language from its English version. Also, two of his journal papers and one conference paper were included under different categories in the IEEE Communications Society's Best Readings Topics on Communications and Information Systems Security 2013. He also serves as a referee of numerous renowned journals. He has received some awards for his reviewing activities such as being one of the most active reviewers of the *International Arab Journal of Information Technology* (2012) and received recognized reviewer status of *Computers and Electrical Engineering* (March 2014) and *Ad Hoc Networks* (April 2014). He is a senior member of the IEEE, United States.

Imran Yusof is currently pursuing his master's degree in the Department of Computer Science, KICT, International Islamic University Malaysia, Malaysia. He received his BSc degree in computer science in 2013 from the same university. He is a security consultant and an experienced web developer. He has been involved in several projects under various organizations including the Ministry of Defense (Malaysia) for penetration testing, the Ministry of Labor (Saudi Arabia) for front-end web development and web security measures, and the Ministry of Finance (Malaysia) as a consultant for MyResults web application. His research interests include cybersecurity, web application vulnerabilities, and countermeasures.

References

1. M. Dabbour, I. Alsmadi, and E. Alsukhni, Efficient assessment and evaluation for websites vulnerabilities using SNORT, *International Journal of Security and Its Applications*, Vol. 7, No. 1, pp. 7–16, 2013.
2. I. Yusof and A.-S. K. Pathan, Preventing persistent cross-site scripting (XSS) attack by applying pattern filtering approach, in *5th International Conference on Information and Communication Technology for the Muslim World (ICT4M 2014)*, November 17–19, 2014, Kuching, Sarawak, Malaysia.
3. CERT, Malicious HTML tags embedded in client web requests, CERT advisory ca-2000-02, February 2000.
4. WhiteHat Security. Website security statistics report. WhiteHat Security [Online]. Available: https://www.whitehatsec.com/assets/WPstatsReport_052013.pdf, May 2013.
5. OWASP. OWASP Top 10–2013: The ten most critical web application security risks. OWASP [Online]. Available: https://www.owasp.org/index.php/Category:OWASP_Top_Ten_Project, 2013.
6. Juenemann, J. Google's vulnerability reward program [Online]. Available: http://www.nilsjuenemann.de/2012/12/news-about-googles-vulnerability-reward.html, December 16, 2012.

7. E. Kirda, C. Kruegel, G., Vigna, and N. Jovanovic, Noxes: A client-side solution for mitigating cross-site scripting attacks, in *Proceedings of the 2006 ACM Symposium on Applied Computing (SAC'06)*, New York, pp. 330–337, 2006.
8. OWASP. Cross site scripting [Online]. Available: https://www.owasp.org/index.php/Cross-site_Scripting_(XSS), April 4, 2014.
9. A. Klein. DOM based cross site scripting or XSS of the third kind. Web Application Security Consortium [Online]. Available: http://www.webappsec.org/projects/articles/071105.shtml [accessed July 10, 2014], 2005.
10. J. Garcia-Alfaro and G. Navarro-Arribas, A survey on detection techniques to prevent cross-site scripting attacks on current web applications, in CRITIS 2007, LNCS 5141, Springer, Berlin/Heidelberg, pp. 287–298, 2008.
11. J. Garcia-Alfaro and G. Navarro-Arribas, Prevention of cross-site scripting attacks on current web applications, in OTM 2007, Part II, LNCS 4804, Springer, Berlin/Heidelberg, pp. 1770–1784, 2007.
12. M. Madou, E. Lee, J. West, and B. Chess, Watch what you write: Preventing cross-site scripting by observing program output, in *Application Security Conference*, May 19–22, 2008, Ghent, Belgium. Available: https://www.owasp.org/images/9/9d/OWASP-AppSecEU08-Madou.pdf, 2008.
13. P. Bisht and V. N. Venkatakrishnan, XSS-GUARD: Precise dynamic prevention of cross-site scripting attacks, in D. Zamboni (Ed.): DIMVA 2008, LNCS 5137, pp. 23–43, Springer, Berlin/Heidelberg, 2008.
14. R. Putthacharoen and P. Bunyatnoparat, Protecting cookies from cross site script attacks using dynamic cookies rewriting technique, in *2011 13th International Conference on Advanced Communication Technology (ICACT 2011)*, pp. 1090–1094, February 13–16, 2011.
15. L. K. Shar and H. B. K. Tan, Auditing the XSS defence features implemented in web application programs, *IET Software*, Vol. 6, No. 4, pp. 377–390, 2012.
16. A. E. Nunan, E. Souto, E. M. dos Santos, and E. Feitosa, Automatic classification of cross-site scripting in web pages using document-based and URL-based features, *2012 IEEE Symposium on Computers and Communications (ISCC)*, pp. 702–707, 2012.
17. T. Matsuda, D. Koizumi, and M. Sonoda, Cross site scripting attacks detection algorithm based on the appearance position of characters, in *2012 Mosharaka International Conference on Communications, Computers and Applications (MIC-CCA)*, pp. 65–70, October 12–14, 2012.
18. Y. Sun and D. He, Model checking for the defense against cross-site scripting attacks, in *2012 International Conference on Computer Science & Service System (CSSS'12)*, pp. 2161–2164, August 11–13, 2012.
19. D. Koizumi, T. Matsuda, and M. Sonoda, On the automatic detection algorithm of cross site scripting (XSS) with the non-stationary Bernoulli distribution, in *2012 Mosharaka International Conference on Communications, Computers and Applications (MIC-CCA)*, pp. 131–135, October 12–14, 2012.
20. S. Sundareswaran and A.C. Squicciarini, XSS-Dec: A hybrid solution to mitigate cross-site scripting attacks, in N. Cuppens-Boulahia et al. (eds): DBSec 2012, LNCS 7371, 2012, pp. 223–238.
21. D. Lan, W. ShuTing, Y. Xing, and Z. Wei, Analysis and prevention for cross-site scripting attack based on encoding, in *2013 IEEE 4th International Conference on Electronics Information and Emergency Communication (ICEIEC)*, pp. 102–105, November 15–17, 2013.
22. JavaScript Kit. Understanding "event handlers" in JavaScript [Online]. Available: http://www.javascriptkit.com/javatutors/event1.shtml.
23. A. Javed. XSS vectors [Online]. Available: http://www.bugsheet.com/cheat-sheets/100-xss-vectors-by-ashar-javed, https://twitter.com/soaj1664ashar [Last accessed: 6 June 2015].
24. L. Masinter. The "data" URL scheme, RFC 2397, Internet Engineering Task Force, August 1998.
25. I. Devlin. HTML5 media and data URIs [Online]. Available: http://www.iandevlin.com/blog/2012/09/html5/html5-media-and-data-uri, September 16, 2012.
26. ASCII to hex [Online]. Available: http://www.asciitohex.com.
27. Universitat Oberta de Catalunya. XSS cheat sheet [Online]. Available: http://seguretat.wiki.uoc.edu/index.php/XSS_Cheat_Sheet.
28. Break the Security. Complete cross site scripting (XSS) cheat sheets [Online]. Available: http://www.breakthesecurity.com/2012/02/complete-cross-site-scriptingxss-cheat.html.

29. OWASP. XSS filter evasion cheat sheet [Online]. Available: https://www.owasp.org/index.php/XSS_Filter_Evasion_Cheat_Sheet, September 9, 2014.
30. F. Pasqualetti, F. Dorfler, and F. Bullo, Attack detection and identification in cyber-physical systems, *IEEE Transactions on Automatic Control*, Vol. 58, No. 11, pp. 2715–2729, 2013.
31. S. Karnouskos, Cyber-physical systems in the smartgrid, in *2011 9th IEEE International Conference on Industrial Informatics (INDIN)*, Caparica, Lisbon, Portugal, pp. 20–23, July 26–29, 2011.
32. D. A. Kindy and A.-S. K. Pathan, A detailed survey on various aspects of SQL injection in web applications: Vulnerabilities, innovative attacks and remedies, *International Journal of Communication Networks and Information Security*, Vol. 5, No. 2, pp. 80–92, 2013.

Chapter 14

Trojan-Resilient Circuits

Jean-Pierre Seifert and Christoph Bayer

TU Berlin and Deutsche Telekom Laboratories

Contents

14.1 Introduction 350
14.2 Definitions and Preliminaries 352
14.2.1 Boolean Circuits 352
14.2.2 Integrated Circuits 352
14.2.3 Probabilistically Checkable Proofs 352
14.2.4 Gál and Szegedy's Model of Fault-Tolerant Boolean Circuits 353
14.2.4.1 Loose Computation 353
14.2.4.2 Faulty Gates and Circuits 354
14.2.4.3 ε-Halvers 354
14.2.4.4 Construction for Symmetric Functions 355
14.2.4.5 Arbitrary Boolean Functions 355
14.3 Hardware Trojans 355
14.3.1 Formal Attack Scenario 357
14.4 Trojan-Resilient Circuit Construction 358
14.4.1 Faulty Wires and Circuits 358
14.4.2 ε-Halvers 358
14.4.2.1 Construction for Symmetric Functions 359
14.4.2.2 Arbitrary Boolean Functions 361
14.5 Future Research 363
14.6 Conclusions 363
Appendix 363
Appendix A: ε-Halvers with Faulty Gates and Faulty Wires 363
Appendix B: Valiant–Vazirani Uniqueness Reduction 364
Appendix C: Example: A Resilient Half Adder 365
Author Biographies 366
References 367

Abstract: Integrated circuits (ICs) can contain malicious logic or backdoors, known as hardware trojans, which may impede them from functioning properly. These hardware trojans include the bug attacks presented by Biham et al. [1]. To protect ICs against such hardware trojans and bug attacks, we present an effective method to efficiently construct "trojan-resilient" circuits. We revisit the fundamental work on fault-tolerant circuits by Gál and Szegedy. We extend their attack model, and from this extended adversary scenario, we derive a mathematical definition of "IC resilience" against well-defined hardware trojans. In our model, we allow an all-powerful adversary to modify a constant fraction of the gates and wires at each level of the resilient circuit in an arbitrary way. We prove that every Boolean circuit can be transformed into another Boolean circuit with the same functionality as the original circuit even in the presence of an adversary tampering with the "resilient" circuit. The transformation is polynomial time computable and yields a circuit, which has a logarithmic depth in the size of the original circuit. To the best of our knowledge, this is the first work to counteract hardware trojans with a rigorous mathematical security proof—backed up by a practical and meaningful model.

Keywords: Bug attacks; Error-correcting codes; Hardware backdoors and trojans; Probabilistically checkable proofs; Reliable and secure circuits; Resilient circuit design; Security and trust

14.1 Introduction

Bug attacks of Biham et al. [1] make use of deterministic errors in the hardware implementation of cryptosystems (such as Pohlig and Hellman [2] and Rivest–Shamir–Adleman [RSA] [3]). Using a single chosen ciphertext or a larger number of ciphertexts (in the case of RSA, optimal asymmetric encryption padding [OAEP] [4]), the full secret key can be computed. Even if there is only one error in the multiplication of a single pair of numbers, this can be exploited by an adversary. The errors, which are utilized by attackers, can occur due to accidental bugs such as the Intel division bug. More alarming is the problem of maliciously tampered hardware. Until recently, integrated circuits (ICs) were assumed to be secure against malicious activities. However, it is questionable if this assumption is still valid. ICs are becoming increasingly vulnerable to malicious alterations, known as hardware trojans, as many in-house steps of an IC fabrication process are being outsourced to third parties. This risk is presented in [5–7]. In particular, hardware trojans have drawn attention to the potential threats to governmental and military systems as well as financial infrastructure and transportation security. For all mission-critical areas and to prevent bug attacks, it is essential to use computer systems that ensure their correct functionality in all circumstances. Thus, a reasonable and challenging question is whether ICs can be designed in such a way that the functionality intended by the designers is guaranteed—even if a malicious adversary is allowed to tamper with the ICs during certain production steps. That means that we consider the scenario in which the design process is trusted, but the subsequent production steps are not trustworthy. Due to the so-called fabless trend, this scenario is the most relevant one as outsourcing to silicon foundries is by virtue untrusted. This challenge was explicitly presented in [8] as the first of three key topics and it was also mentioned in [5]: "Given an IC corresponding to a known design, does the IC that is delivered do what it is supposed to do and nothing more? This is the case when the fabrication facility is not trusted, but the design process is."

Our chapter answers the central question affirmatively by presenting a resilient IC design that ensures equivalent IC functionality even if a malicious adversary physically alters the IC in the fabrication phase. In a real-world scenario, an attacker will only slightly alter a chip since large-scale alterations would later be detected during the testing phase. This scenario goes along with the model of bug attacks, in which only a single multiplication needs to be incorrect for the attack to work. Thus, our concept for a resilient IC design fulfills the requirement that small changes to the IC do not affect its correct functionality, whereas more serious changes should be detected otherwise. Such a design could, for example, prevent the danger of so-called kill switches [6] and bug attacks [1].

Since the topic of hardware trojans is rather new, recent research has followed other approaches. In [9–11], hardware trojans have been constructed and practically investigated. There are various approaches to a hardware trojan taxonomy [12–14]. This is necessary as adversaries have many different objectives, and hence the developed hardware trojans are vastly different as well. Several contributions to the topic of hardware trojans focus exclusively on trojan detection [12,14–19]. However, little research has gone into design techniques that detect hardware trojans at runtime or counteract them at runtime [16,17,20]. The proposed directions are rather heuristic and do not cover all hardware backdoors. Ishai et al. [21,22] examine the problem of privacy in circuits, which is motivated by side-channel attacks. They define a formal threat model, and suggest provably secure methods to counteract probing attacks on circuits.

Compared with all other existing research concerning proper IC functionality, this chapter develops a trojan-resilient IC model, which is provably secure. To achieve this, we first revisit the model of fault-tolerant Boolean circuits by Gál and Szegedy [23]. Their work deals with deliberate nonrandom faults in Boolean circuits. We extend their work and introduce a formal attack scenario that targets the malicious altering of ICs. This hardware trojan model is mapped into a real-world taxonomy [13] as well. By leveraging Gál and Szegedy's techniques of fault-tolerant computations, we prove that it is indeed possible to design ICs that maintain their correct functionality even if they are infected by hardware trojans. To the best of our knowledge, there is no prior work relating the area of fault-tolerant circuit computation with hardware trojans.

Research in the area of fault-tolerant circuits has mainly been based on the model of random faults by von Neumann [24]. In this model it is assumed that all gates of a Boolean circuit fail, that is, they produce a faulty value, independently and with probability bounded by some small constant. From this early research it is known that any function can be reliably computed by another circuit of size $L \log L$, where L is the size of the error-free circuit that computes the given function [24–26]. However, hardware trojans cannot be described by this classical fault model since maliciously altered hardware closely resembles deliberately inserted faults. Gál and Szegedy deal with this more difficult case when the faults are not random [23]. In their model, an adversary may arbitrarily choose a small constant fraction of the gates at each level of a Boolean circuit to be faulty. They introduce a constructive way to efficiently build fault-tolerant Boolean circuits with small redundancy even in the presence of nonrandom faulty gates. Their construction makes use of very elaborated techniques from the field of probabilistically checkable proofs (PCPs) among many others, cf. [27]. The PCP theorem guarantees an efficient proof system with "robust" proofs for every problem of the class Nondeterministic Polynomial time (NP). In the notion of PCPs, proofs can be efficiently encoded and provide enough redundancy such that a proof of a false statement will result in many errors. Additionally, a verifier only has to read a constant number of proof bits, but will still catch faulty proofs with high probability. These PCP encodings are used to construct fault-tolerant circuits for arbitrary Boolean functions.

The chapter is structured as follows. The next section introduces background knowledge on Boolean circuits, ICs, and PCPs. Furthermore, it revisits the adversary model of fault-tolerant circuits that was presented in [23]. Our attack model is explained in Section 14.3, and consequently the trojan is defined. In Section 14.4, the model of [23] is extended and the presented techniques are applied to counteract the trojan. Finally, in Section 14.5, our work is concluded; open questions and future research directions are also presented.

14.2 Definitions and Preliminaries

This section briefly introduces Boolean circuits, PCPs, and basic fault-tolerant circuit constructions due to Gál and Szegedy [23,28]. We consider combinational, synchronous circuits with a single output bit; for a thorough treatment, we refer to [23,28–30].

14.2.1 Boolean Circuits

A *Boolean circuit* C with N_I input bits and one output bit is defined as an acyclic directed graph, in which every vertex (called *gate*) corresponds to either a Boolean function from the set $B = \{AND, OR, NOT\}$ or an input gate (of in-degree 0) labeled by one of the N_I input bits. Every edge represents a *wire*. One gate is labeled as the output gate. A Boolean circuit C computes a *Boolean function* $f : \{0,1\}^{N_I} \rightarrow \{0,1\}$. We can assume that AND and OR gates have in-degree 2, NOT gates have in-degree 1, and all gates have a maximum out-degree of 2. A *combinational* (or *combinatorial*) *circuit* with N_I inputs and one output is a Boolean circuit C with N_I input bits $x_1, \ldots, x_{N_I}$ and one output bit z. A circuit is called *synchronous* (or *synchronized*) if for any gate g all paths from the inputs to g have the same length. Let C be a circuit and let g be any gate in C. The *depth* of g is the length of the longest path from any input to g and the *circuit depth* $D(C)$ is defined as the maximal depth of an output gate. The *size* $S(C)$ of a circuit C is defined as the total number of gates it consists of. The *i-th level* of a circuit consists of all gates with a depth equal to i. A circuit C is synchronous if and only if every wire in C is between adjacent levels.

14.2.2 Integrated Circuits

An *IC* is composed of combinational logic having some inputs, which are output derived, cf. [31]. There may also be independent inputs. All or some of the outputs are fed back into the input. We denote by C the combinational logic, by $x_1, \ldots, x_I$ the independent inputs to C, and by Y the output of C that is also fed back to C as input y. The output value Y, called the *state vector*, may be *clocked* (*delayed*) and becomes an input y to C. Because of these possible delays, the output Y and the corresponding input y may differ, therefore we denote them differently. Without loss of generality, we can assume that C is a synchronous circuit [29]. For simplicity, only ICs with one output bit are considered. This single output bit is fed back into the input.

14.2.3 Probabilistically Checkable Proofs

Conventional proofs have to be checked by a verifier step by step since a false theorem could be "proven" by a proof that contains only one incorrect clause. PCPs are more robust and a verifier can decide much more efficiently whether a proof is valid or not.

Let $L \in$ NP be a set. A PCP verifier V receives an input x and gets access to a proof π. It is allowed to read some $O(r)$ random bits, but at most $O(q)$ bits from the proof. Using $V^{\pi}(x, \rho)$ denote the output of V on proof π, input x, and randomness ρ. Then the class PCP[r, q] is the set of all languages L, for which there exists such a verifier V with the following properties:

- (*completeness*) If $x \in L$, then there exists a proof π such that $\text{Prob}_{\rho}[V^{\pi}(x, \rho) \text{ accepts}] = 1$.
- (*soundness*) If $x \notin L$, then it holds true for all proofs π that $\text{Prob}_{\rho}[V^{\pi}(x, \rho) \text{ accepts}] \leq 1/2$.

The PCP theorem states that NP = PCP[log n, 1] and is proved in [32,33]. Improvements concerning proof length, query complexity, and fault tolerance were achieved in [32–36]. In [36], PCPs of length n exp(poly(loglog n))^2 and query complexity poly(loglog n) are presented. Compared with this, in [35] the PCPs have length n poly(log n) and can be verified by poly(log n) queries. PCPs are closely related to so-called locally testable codes, on which we will not elaborate in this chapter. However, they may be of interest to practically implement PCPs. In each case [35,36], constructions for more efficient, locally testable codes are presented.

14.2.4 Gál and Szegedy's Model of Fault-Tolerant Boolean Circuits

The conventional scenario of fault-tolerant Boolean circuits deals with natural random errors. To address the more difficult scenario of nonrandom faults, Gál and Szegedy define a model, in which an adversary is allowed to maliciously choose at most a constant fraction of the gates at each level of the circuit to be faulty [23]. This means that gates may be destroyed or gate types may even change. The wires of the circuit are assumed to work correctly. This model is equivalent to the idea that a constant number of absolutely reliable gates is used for the last few levels of a circuit. Such an assumption is reasonable because more expensive and reliable hardware may be used for certain parts of a circuit. As tiny alterations to the IC should not affect its functionality, the circuit is required to compute a given function only "loosely." However, if the IC is substantially altered, the loose version of the function is undefined and thus the malicious modification should be detected. Gál and Szegedy define and prove the following fundamental insights toward their model.

14.2.4.1 Loose Computation

Let f: $\{0, 1\}^n \rightarrow \{0, 1\}$ be a Boolean function and M be any computational device. We say that M δ-*loosely computes* f if the following holds:

1. If $f(x) = 1$, then $M(x) = 1$
2. If $f(y) = 0$ for every y with $d(x, y) \leq \delta n$, then $M(x) = 0$

where $d(x, y)$ denotes the Hamming distance between x and y. If an input x does not belong to one of the two categories, M can output an arbitrary value or no value at all. Combined with an appropriate error-correcting code, the loose computation behaves like the usual evaluation of a given function. For an error-correcting code, E_n, with code words of length q_n and a function f: $\{0, 1\}^n \rightarrow \{0, 1\}$, we define the function $f \circ E_n : \{0,1\}^{q_n} \rightarrow \{0,1\}$ as follows:

1. $(f \circ E_n)(z) = 0$ for all z where z is not a code word of E_n.
2. If $z = E_n(x)$, then $(f \circ E_n)(z) = f(x)$.

Lemma 14.1

If the Hamming distance of any two code words in an error-correcting code E_n with code words of length q_n is at least δq_n and M is a computational device that computes $f \circ E_n$ δ-loosely, then $M(E_n(x)) = f(x)$ on any input x.

It is known from coding theory, cf. [37], that there exist linear binary codes E_n with the required properties. The matrix of E_n can be polynomially computed in n. (This also means that the length of the code word q_n is polynomial in n.) The Hamming distance of any two code words in E_n is at least δq_n for some small constant δ.

14.2.4.2 Faulty Gates and Circuits

Formal definitions for the intuitive notions of errors, faulty gates, and faulty circuits are now given. Denote by $g(x_1, x_2)$ the function that gate g is supposed to compute on inputs x_1 and x_2. A gate g is called *faulty* if its output is different from $g(x_1, x_2)$. Let C be a circuit with no faulty gates and let $\tilde{C}$ be a copy of the same circuit with possibly faulty gates. The output of a gate of $\tilde{C}$ is *incorrect* if it is different from the value computed by the same gate in C. Note that the output of a gate may be incorrect because the gate is faulty or because the inputs of the gates are incorrect. Let $\tilde{C}$ be a circuit with possibly faulty gates, but correctly working wires. If a gate g receives an incorrect input, at least one of the previous adjacent gates that provide the inputs to g computed an incorrect output. We say that a circuit C is *γ-faulty* if at most a γ fraction of the gates on each level is faulty. A circuit C for a function f is called *fault tolerant* if it computes f δ-loosely even if it is γ-faulty.

14.2.4.3 ε-Halvers

Using the techniques presented by Gál and Szegedy, it is possible to construct a synchronous fault-tolerant circuit for every symmetric function [23]. The construction for symmetric functions makes use of ε-halvers from Ajtai et al. [38]. An ε-halver is a bounded depth comparator network with the following property: For any set of the l smallest (largest) inputs, where $l \leq n/2$, at most εl elements will be among the last (first) $n/2$ outputs. Equivalently, an ε-halver can be defined as a halver (a network that separates the $n/2$ largest and the $n/2$ smallest inputs into two disjoint sets) that may misplace at most an ε fraction of the elements. For 0–1 inputs, ε-halvers can be implemented by monotone Boolean circuits. Each comparator can be realized by an *AND–OR* gate pair, where the *AND* gate computes the minimum and the *OR* gate computes the maximum of the two common input bits. We will consider ε-halvers with faulty gates and examine the number of faults and their propagation. At level d of an ε-halver with faulty gates, the number of incorrect outputs is at most the number of incorrect outputs at level $d - 1$ plus the number of faulty gates at level d. For an ε-halver, we denote by L_1 (L_0) the number of 1's (0's) in the lower part of the output, and by U_1 (U_0) the number of 1's (0's) in the upper part of the output. The following two lemmas from [23] deal with the propagation of faults in ε-halvers.

Lemma 14.2

Consider a γ-faulty ε-halver of depth c with m inputs and let the number of 0's in the input be a. If $a \geq m/2$, then $L_1 \leq \varepsilon(m - a) + c\gamma m$ and $(a - m/2) - c\gamma m \leq U_0 \leq (a - m/2) + \varepsilon m/2 + c\gamma m$. If $a \leq m/2$, then $U_0 \leq \varepsilon a + c\gamma m$ and $(m/2 - a) - c\gamma m \leq L_1 \leq (m/2 - a) + \varepsilon m/2 + c\gamma m$.

Lemma 14.3

Consider a 0–1 string of length m, such that there are z 0's followed by m – z 1's. Denote by z_L *(*z_U*) the number of 0's in the lower (upper) part of this ordered string. Consider a γ-faulty ε-halver of depth c with m inputs and let the number of 0's in the input be a, such that* $|a - z| \leq r$*. Then* $|U_0 - z_U| \leq r + (\varepsilon + 2c\gamma)m/2$ *and* $|L_0 - z_L| \leq r + (\varepsilon + 2c\gamma)m/2$*. A similar statement holds for the number of 1's in the output.*

14.2.4.4 Construction for Symmetric Functions

ε-Halvers are building blocks of so-called overwhelming majority functions and threshold functions. These can be computed correctly on all defined inputs by γ-faulty circuits, and they are used to construct fault-tolerant circuits for symmetric functions [23].

The overwhelming majority function Maj_k^m has value 1 (respectively 0) if the number of 1's (0's) in the input is at least k, and it is undefined otherwise. Let $k > 3/4m$. Then, for some $\gamma > 0$ there is a γ-faulty circuit of size $O(m)$ and depth $O(\log m)$ computing Maj_k^m correctly on every input belonging to its domain, cf. [23]. The threshold function Th_k^n has value 1 if and only if at least k of the n input bits have a value of 1. For any $\delta > 0$, there is a $\gamma > 0$ such that for any threshold function Th_k^n there is a synchronous circuit such that, cf. [23], if an adversary destroys a γ fraction of the gates on every level (including the input level), the circuits still compute Th_k^n in a δ-loose manner. The size of the circuit is $O(n)$. The depth of the circuit is $O(\log n)$.

The abovementioned results constitute a central result of [23], showing that it is indeed possible to construct a synchronous fault-tolerant circuit for every symmetric function.

Theorem 14.1.

For any $\delta > 0$ *there is a* $\gamma > 0$ *such that for any symmetric function f with n inputs there is a synchronous circuit with the following properties. If an adversary destroys a γ fraction of the gates on every level (including the input level), the circuit still computes f in a δ-loose manner. The size of the circuit is* $O(n)$ *and the depth of the circuit is* $O(\log n)$*.*

14.2.4.5 Arbitrary Boolean Functions

Synchronous fault-tolerant circuits can be obtained for any Boolean function in this model if certain error-correcting codes are applied. In addition to ε-halvers, the fault-tolerant circuits for arbitrary Boolean functions are also based on techniques from the area of PCPs as defined by Arora et al. [32]. As we extend this construction from [23] for arbitrary Boolean functions to our new hardware trojan model, we will thoroughly present the adapted and extended proof later as our main result.

14.3 Hardware Trojans

The risk of using maliciously altered hardware has increased over the years and poses a real threat to critical computer systems. Since hardware is the lowest layer of a computer system, it controls everything running on it. Not surprisingly, it is also very difficult to detect and prevent such

Hardware trojans

Insertion phase	Abstraction level	Activation mechanism	Effects	Location
Specification	System level	Always on	Change the functionality	Processor
Design	Development environment	Triggered	Downgrade performance	Memory
Fabrication	Register-transfer level	▷ Internally	Leak information	I/O
Testing	Gate level	• Time-based	Denial of service	Power supply
Assembly and package	Transistor level	• Physical-condition-based		Clock grid
	Physical level	▷ Externally		
		• User input		
		• Component output		

Figure 14.1 Hardware trojan taxonomy according to [13]. The properties of our hardware trojan are shaded.

attacks on this lowest level of control, cf. [9–11]. Additionally, there is no convenient hardware solution to repair altered hardware afterward. This means that there is no equivalent to the usual software updates. Due to the plethora of different hardware trojans, there is also a huge taxonomy [12–14] of different hardware trojans. Figure 14.1 shows the taxonomy presented by Karri et al. [13] based on five attributes.

In order to focus on feasible problem solutions and to counteract bug attacks, this chapter considers hardware trojans that might alter the proper functionality of an IC. The central idea is that small changes to the IC should not affect the functionality of a “resilient” IC, while more serious changes could be detected otherwise. It is obvious that massive design changes are clearly visible by a simple mask comparison with the IC die under investigation. So, even if an adversary knows about this resilient design method and the thresholds defining small and massive changes, he or she cannot arbitrarily destroy the IC too much. Hence, although the proposed solution seems to be static, it is virtually impossible for an adversary to circumvent it.

Let us consider the development cycle of an IC [8,39] and the trustworthiness of its stages. In the specification phase, the characteristics of the system, for example, its expected function, are defined. Next, the specification is transformed into a chip design taking account of logical and physical requirements. These two steps take place in trusted research laboratories. During the fabrication phase, the physical design layout is transformed into a set of mask layouts. A set of masks is then produced from these layouts and wafers can be processed by the masks. We will consider the case when the specification and design processes are trustworthy, but the mask and fabrication phase is not. Since the mask and fabrication process is often outsourced to untrusted factories, our approach is well-founded [5,8] in practice. At these or some later stages, an adversary may have the opportunity to change the mask or even change the IC during production. It is likely that an adversary subtly tampers with the mask or the complex IC production process itself. This is because major changes could be detected during the trusted testing phase, and will thus force the adversary to make only tiny deliberate alterations.

In this chapter, we consider adversaries that change the existing gates and wires of the combinational logic of an IC. Since an adversary who can tamper with a mask will not only change the gates but also the wires, this is a very natural assumption and a logical extension of Gál and Szegedy’s model [23]. Gates may be destroyed or gate types may be changed, and wires may be cut or swapped. This work does not address the adversarial additions of logic to an IC directly, as presented, for example, in [10]. We hereby follow one of the presented scenarios from [8], in which only “destructive” alterations are taken into account. However, in current ICs there is usually a large surplus of logic elements anyway that could be exploited by an attacker [40]. These logic elements are not essential for the proper functionality of the IC. Instead, they are used to implement built-in self-tests for debugging facilities such as the Joint Test Action Group (JTAG) [40,41] and they provide the last possibility to patch nonfunctional electronic devices after an erroneous fabrication. Suppose there was a secure IC design against added malicious logic such as the hardware trojan in [10]. When it comes to practice, even in such a design model an attacker could take advantage of the abovementioned additional test components, which are integral features of the device by design. Our model is not limited to special components of a system. However, it might be reasonable to examine components with certain attributes, for example, a trusted input, separately.

14.3.1 Formal Attack Scenario

Consider an IC with synchronous and combinational logic *C*. An adversary is allowed to choose at most a small constant fraction $\alpha < 1$ of the gates at each level of *C* to be faulty. Additionally, he or she is allowed to choose at most a fraction $\beta < 1$ of the wires between all levels of *C* to be faulty. That means that the adversary may choose at most a $\gamma := \alpha + \beta$ fraction of the gates at each level to produce *incorrect outputs*. Observe that the last gate and the outgoing wire that reconnects the single output of *C* with the input of *C* via the clock must work correctly since the adversary is only allowed to destroy a $0 \leq \beta < 1$ fraction of this connection. The gates and wires of the last few levels are very likely to remain unchanged since alterations would be too obvious and would be detected during the testing phase.

Definition 1

We call an IC infected by a hardware trojan if an adversary has tampered with it for some $\gamma > 0$ *according to our model. After the adversary has tampered with an IC the way that is described for our hardware trojan, its combinational circuit C is called* γ*-faulty* (Figure 14.2).

Definition 2

A circuit C′ for a function f is said to be γ*-resilient if C′ computes the function f even if C′ has been tampered with by a hardware trojan for some* $\gamma > 0$*. Additionally, an IC that contains C′ is also called* γ*-resilient.*

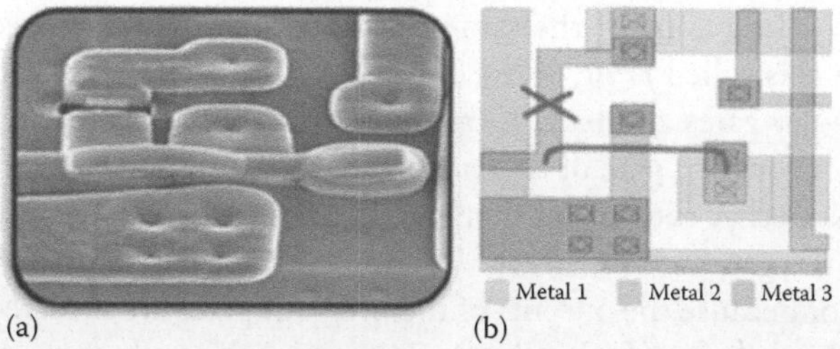

Figure 14.2 An infected IC. (a) The intended layout with three metal layers for the correct design where malicious design alterations are highlighted by black lines in the correct layout. (b) An x-ray of the modified silicon is shown where the line in Metal 1 was cut (cross in layout image) and was instead connected to another via (bridge in layout). In terms of Table 14.1, this trojan was realized via focused ion beam (FIB) postfabrication on the physical level, which is always on, changes the functionality, and might affect all elements of the IC (processor, memory, I/O, power supply, and the clock grid).

The previously defined hardware trojan covers a large and important variety of hardware trojans. It can be classified according to the taxonomy of [13] in the following way (see Figure 14.1):

- Insertion phase during the development cycle: after the design phase.
- Hardware abstraction level: gate level or below.
- Activation mechanism: always on. However, depending on the gates and wires, which are destroyed, the trojan might only make an impact if it is triggered by some event.
- Effects on the target device: change of functionality, denial of service.
- Location in a system: not limited to a special component.

Since this attack scenario is similar in its consequences to the one described in Section 14.3.2, namely, a γ-faulty circuit, we can apply similar techniques to the combinational logic of an IC. In the next section, we will extend the adversary model from [23] to faulty wires to cover our model of hardware trojans. Thus, the combinational circuit is provided with more robustness and redundancy and is able to reliably compute the intended function. Having transformed a circuit C according to these techniques into a fault-tolerant circuit C', C' is clearly γ-resilient. If C' is the combinational component of an IC, this IC is γ-resilient as well. These γ-resilient ICs of course counteract the predefined hardware trojan, and hence prevent computer systems from adversarial misuse.

14.4 Trojan-Resilient Circuit Construction

The model of Gál and Szegedy is limited to the alteration of gates [23]. As seen in the previous sections, an adversary is interested in tampering with the wires as well. Hence, in our extended model, an adversary is allowed to maliciously choose at most a constant fraction of the gates at each level and wires between adjacent levels to be faulty. All in all, we assume that at most a constant fraction of the gates on each level newly produces incorrect outputs because of faulty gates or wires. The corresponding definitions of Section 14.2 are extended and stronger results are proved.

14.4.1 Faulty Wires and Circuits

Let g_1 and g_2 be two adjacent gates connected by a wire w in a circuit without faults where g_1 provides an input to g_2. In a copy of the same circuit, which may have been tampered with by an adversary, the wire w is called *faulty* if the output of g_1 is different from the input to g_2. Let C be a circuit with no faulty gates and let $\tilde{C}$ be a copy of the same circuit with possibly faulty gates and faulty wires. The output of a gate of $\tilde{C}$ is *incorrect* if it is different from the value computed by the same gate in C. Note that the output of a gate may be incorrect because the gate is faulty or because the inputs of the gates are incorrect. The inputs of the gate may be incorrect because the input wires are faulty or because the outputs of the previous gates are incorrect. At most, a γd fraction of the outputs at level d of a γ-faulty circuit is incorrect. Note that this modified definition of a γ-*faulty* circuit does not contradict the definition from Section 14.2, since in that model all wires work correctly. Hence, $\beta = 0$ and $\gamma = \alpha$ is the maximum fraction of faulty gates on each level.

14.4.2 ε-Halvers

As in Section 14.2, we will use ε-halvers. However, the ε-halvers may now contain faulty gates and faulty wires. Gál and Szegedy's lemmas, Lemmas 1 and 2 in Section 2.4.3, easily translate to ε-halvers with faulty gates and wires. This is implied by the proposition stated and proved in Appendix A.

14.4.2.1 Construction for Symmetric Functions

We will construct γ-faulty circuits, which can correctly compute overwhelming majority functions and threshold functions for all defined inputs, and base our techniques on [23].

Lemma 14.4

Let $k > 3/4m$. Then for some α, β > 0 and γ := α + β, there is a γ-faulty circuit of size O(m) and depth O(log m) computing Maj_k^m correctly on every input belonging to its domain. At most, an α fraction of the gates on each level and a β fraction of the wires between all levels are faulty.

Proof. The construction is based on *majority preservers*. In [42], this component is defined as a comparator network with m inputs and $m/2$ outputs that guarantees that if at least a given constant fraction greater than 1/2 of the m inputs has the same value, this value appears in at least the same given constant fraction of the $m/2$ outputs. A majority preserver, which tolerates a small constant fraction of errors at each of its levels, can be constructed by triplets of ε-halvers. An m-input ε-halver, denoted by *M-halver*, is applied to the m inputs. Next, one $m/2$-input ε-halver is applied to the upper part and another one is applied to the lower part of the output of the M-halver. They are called the *U-halver* and the *L-halver*. The output of this majority preserver consists of the upper part of the output of the L-halver and the lower part of the output of the U-halver. A family of ε-halvers of depth c with the same parameters ε and c for all input lengths exists for an appropriate choice of the constants ε and c.

Now, let a be the number of 0's in the input of the majority preserver. Suppose $a \geq (3/4 + c\gamma)$ m. By $L_0(M)$ (respectively $U_0(M)$), the number of 0's in the lower (upper) part of the output of the M-halver is denoted. A similar notation is used for the U-halver and the L-halver. From Lemma 14.2 it follows that $L_0(M) \geq m/2 - (\varepsilon + 2c\gamma)m/2$ and $U_0(M) \geq m/4$. Denote by $I_0(L)$ (respectively $I_0(U)$) the number of 0's in the input of the L-halver (U-halver). As the M-halver is connected to the L-halver (U-halver) by $m/2$ wires, at most $\beta m/2$ wires may be faulty. Hence, $I_0(L) \geq m/2 - (\varepsilon + 2c\gamma)m/2 - \beta m/2$ and $I_0(U) \geq m/4 - \beta m/2$. Applying Lemma 14.3 to the L-halver and the U-halver yields $U_0(L) + L_0(U) \geq (1 - 2(\varepsilon + 2c\gamma + \beta))m/2$. If the number of 0's in the input of a majority preserver is at least a $(3/4 + c\gamma)$ fraction of the input, then at least a $(1 - 2(\varepsilon + 2c\gamma + \beta))$ fraction of its output is 0 as well.

Since several majority preservers will be combined by feeding the outputs of one as inputs to the next, we have to consider the faulty wires of these connections. Connecting an $m/2$-output majority preserver with an $m/2$-input majority preserver, it holds for the number of 0's $I_0(MP)$ in the input of the second majority preserver that $I_0(MP) \geq (1 - 2(\varepsilon + 2c\gamma + \beta))m/2 - \beta m/2$. A similar statement can be shown for the number of 1's. Choose α, β, and γ α + β small enough so that $k > 3/4 + c\gamma$ and $-3\beta + 1 - 2(\varepsilon + 2c\gamma) \geq 3/4 + c\gamma$. By feeding the outputs of one majority preserver as inputs to the next, we combine j majority preservers. This construction with $n/2^j$ outputs has the property that its overwhelming majority is the same as the overwhelming majority of the input. Once $n/2^j < \min\{1/\alpha, 1/\beta\}$, the computation can be finished by a small circuit that has fewer than $1/\alpha$ gates at each of its levels and fewer than $1/\beta$ wires between all levels, and that computes the usual majority of its inputs. In this small circuit, the adversary can destroy neither gates nor wires—according to our model.

q.e.d.

Theorem 14.2.

For any $\delta > 0$ there are α, $\beta > 0$ and $\gamma := \alpha + \beta$ such that for any threshold function Th_k^n *there is a synchronous circuit such that the following holds. If an adversary destroys an α fraction of the gates on each level (including the input level) and a β fraction of the wires between all levels, the circuit still computes* Th_k^n *in a δ-loose manner. The size of the circuit is* $O(n)$ *and the depth of the circuit is* $O(\log n)$.

Proof. As the circuit is supposed to compute the threshold function in a δ-loose way, the circuit has to output 1 if the number of 0's is $\leq n - k$, 0 if the number of 0's is $\geq n - k + \delta n$, and an arbitrary value otherwise. Assume that the input is correctly ordered and consider the set of bits at positions $n - k + 1, \ldots, n - k + \delta n$. Whenever the circuit has to output 1 (respectively 0) all these bits are 1 (respectively 0). The parameters t and l are chosen such that $ln/2^t \geq n - k$ and $(l + 1)n/2^t \leq n - k + \delta n$; t depends on n and δ, but not on k. Let T be the set of elements at positions $ln/2^t + 1, \ldots, (l + 1)n/2^t$ of the correctly ordered input, and let z_T be the number of 0's in T.

The construction consists of two components. First, a circuit, denoted by C_1, is constructed, which has n inputs and $n/2^t$ outputs. The number v of 0's in its output should satisfy $|v - z_T| \leq (\varepsilon + \alpha + 2\beta + 2c\gamma)n$, where ε and c are the parameters of the ε-halvers that are used. The second component is the construction from Lemma 14.4, which computes the overwhelming majority function Maj_s^m of the outputs of C_1, where $m = n/2^t$ and $s = (1 - 2^t(\varepsilon + \alpha + 2\beta + 2c\gamma))m$. In order to apply this lemma, it is necessary that $1 - 2^t(\varepsilon + \alpha + 2\beta + 2c\gamma) \geq 3/4 + c\gamma$. Parameters ε, α, β, and $\gamma = \alpha + \beta$ are determined by this inequality. Depending on the kind of ε-halvers that are used and depending on ε, c can be computed.

Circuit C_1 is a comparator network consisting of t γ-faulty ε-halvers each of depth c. The i-th ε-halver has $n/2t^{-1}$ inputs and $n/2t$ outputs. Using $l_1, \ldots, l_t$, denote the binary representation of l.

- If $l_t = 0$, the input to the $i + 1$-st ε-halver is the lower part of the output of the i-th ε-halver.
- If $l_t = 1$, the upper part is fed to the next ε-halver.

The number of 0's in the correct input is denoted by a_0. However, the adversary may destroy an α-fraction of the input gates of C_1. So, let a be the number of 0-valued input gates. Then $a_{0\,-}\,\alpha n \leq a \leq a_0 + \alpha n$. Lemma 14.3 can be applied repeatedly with $r = \alpha n$. Since at most a β fraction of the wires between the i-th and i + 1-st ε-halver may be faulty, these errors have to be considered by introducing the summand depending on β. It follows that $|v - z_T| \leq \alpha n + \Sigma_{i=1}^{t}(\varepsilon + 2\beta + 2c\gamma)n / 2^i \leq (\varepsilon + \alpha + 2\beta + 2c\gamma)n$.

q.e.d.

Theorem 14.3

For any $\delta > 0$ there is a $\gamma > 0$ such that for any symmetric function f there is a synchronous circuit with the following properties. If an adversary destroys an α fraction of the gates on each level (including the input level) and a β fraction of the wires between all levels and $\gamma := \alpha + \beta$, the circuit still computes f in a δ-loose manner. The size of the circuit is $O(n)$ *and the depth of the circuit is* $O(\log n)$.

Proof. Every symmetric function f can be described by a binary string of length $n + 1$. The i-th element of the string is 1 if and only if the value of f is 1 on inputs containing exactly i 1's. Suppose every set of consecutive 0's in this string has length $<\delta n$. In this case, the δ-loose computation of *f* becomes trivial since the value 1 can be output for every input. Now consider the case that the string contains $h \geq 1$ sets of consecutive 0's of length $\geq \delta n$. Using (l_i, u_i), denote the *i*-th set. In order to compute *f* in a δ-loose way, it is sufficient to compute each $\neg \mathrm{Th}^n_{l_i}$ and each $\mathrm{Th}^n_{u_i}$. These $2h$ functions can be computed in parallel. They can all be computed in a δ-loose way using the constructions in Theorem 14.2 because the negated threshold functions may be computed analogously to the presented techniques.

Set $\alpha := \tilde{\alpha} / 2h$, $\beta := \tilde{\beta} / 2h$, and $\gamma := \tilde{\gamma} / 2h$, and choose $\tilde{\alpha}$, $\tilde{\beta}$, and $\tilde{\gamma}$ according to Theorem 14.2. The parameters $\tilde{\alpha}$, $\tilde{\beta}$, $\tilde{\gamma}$, δ, ε, and *c* can be chosen in such a way that they have the same value for all $2h$ circuits, cf. [23]. By this choice, the number of gates and wires at the corresponding levels of all circuits is the same. If an attacker destroys at most an α fraction of the gates at each level, at most an $\tilde{\alpha}$ fraction of the gates at each level of any one of the $2h$ circuits will be destroyed. There is a similar correlation between β and $\tilde{\beta}$ concerning the wires of the circuits. As for the parameters, it is true that $h < 1/\delta < 1/2\gamma$ (from [23]) and $1/2\gamma \leq \min\{1/2\alpha, 1/2\beta\}$, the $2h$ values can be combined without having to consider any faulty gates or faulty wires.

q.e.d.

14.4.2.2 Arbitrary Boolean Functions

As in the original model, it is possible to design fault-tolerant circuits if the input is specifically encoded. The circuit constructions for symmetric Boolean functions are used as well as the aforementioned PCP techniques [32]. First, the Boolean circuit computing a given function is transformed into a PCP verifier consisting of several circuits. Then, the resulting circuits are structured, and finally the techniques of fault-tolerant circuits for symmetric functions are used to recombine them. We now state the main theorem of our chapter, which shows how to efficiently construct provable, secure, trojan-resilient circuits.

Theorem 14.4.

Let C be a Boolean circuit and let $f: \{0, 1\}^n \rightarrow \{0,1\}$ *be the corresponding Boolean function computed by C. A code* $E = \mathrm{E}_C$ *and a circuit C′ exist such that C′ computes* $f \circ E$ *in a δ-loose manner for every* $\delta > 0$, *even if an adversary destroys an α fraction of the gates at each level of C′ as well as a β fraction of the wires between all levels of C′. Moreover, E and C′ have the following properties:*

1. $|E(x)| \leq q(|x|)$ *for some polynomial q independent of C.*
2. *The Hamming distance* $d(x, y)$ *between any two code words x and y of E is at least* $\delta_0|E|$ *for some* $0 < \delta_0 < 1$ *independent of C* (δ_0 *is a function of* δ).
3. $D(C') \leq O(\log S(C))$. *This implies that* $S(C')$ *is polynomial in* $S(C)$.
4. *C′ can be computed from C in probabilistic polynomial time and E(x) can be computed from C and x in polynomial time.*

Before we present the proof of the main theorem, we will simplify the PCP properties 1 (completeness) and 2 (soundness) into a single property. Consider the subset C^1 of tuples from $\{0, 1\}^n$, for which *C* evaluates to 1 and the analogously defined subset C^0. Arora et al. presented a procedure to transform a circuit *C* into a family $\{C_i\}_{i\in I}$ of constant size circuits with input $(G(x), Y)$ [32].

Here, $G(x)$ is an adequate error-correcting encoding of the input x to C, and Y is an advise string (both have length polynomial in $S(C)$). For this family $\{C_i\}_i$, we have

1. For every $x \in C^1$ there is a Y such that for all $i \in I$: $C_i(G(x), Y) = 1$.
2. For every $x \in C^0$ and for every Y, it is true that $\text{Prob}_{i \in I}[C_i(G(x), Y) = 0] \geq \varepsilon$, for some ε.

Now, by applying the techniques due to Valiant and Vazirani, see Lemma 7 in Appendix B, we can modify the circuit family C_i such that Y of Property 1 is unique for every x and Property 2 holds for every Y. Thus, Properties 1 and 2 can be combined into a single property, where $|\cdot|$ denotes the binary length of the argument and $d(\cdot,\cdot)$ is the Hamming distance between its arguments.

Lemma 14.5

For every $x \in C^1$ there is, with high probability, a unique Y_x such that for all $i \in I$: $C_i(G(x), Y_x) = 1$. Also, for every $\delta > 0$ there exists $\varepsilon > 0$ such that $\text{Prob}_{i \in I}[C_i(H, Y) = 0] < \varepsilon$ implies that $d((H, Y), (G(x), Y_x)) \leq \delta\, |(H, Y)|$ for some $x \in C^1$.

Originally, Gál and Szegedy [23] cited an unknown construction due to Lund and Spielman to guarantee a unique witness Y_x for the PCP completeness. However, their construction was neither clear nor described in [23]. Due to this lack of detail, we developed our own Y_x uniqueness construction. Details can be found in the appendices.

Proof of Theorem 14.4. The circuit C' will consist of several parts. Circuit C' should contain all members of the modified family $\{C_i\}_{i \in I}$ with the property that:

For every $x \in C$ there is a unique Y_x such that for all $i \in I$: $C_i(G(x), Y_x) = 1$. Also, for every $\delta > 0$ there exists $\varepsilon > 0$ such that $\text{Prob}_{i \in I}[C_i(H, Y) = 0] \leq \varepsilon$ implies that $d((H, Y), (G(x), Y_x)) \leq \delta |(H, Y)|$ for some $x \in C^1$.

The members of the family should have disjoint inputs, which can be achieved by transforming $G(x)$ into $G'(x)$ and Y_x into Y_x'. $G'(x)$ is formed by repeating the bits of $G(x)$ and Y_x' is formed by repeating Y_x as many times as the number of times for which they appear as input to some $\{C_i\}$, $i \in I$. By this construction, each bit of $G(x)$ (respectively Y_x) will be repeated for the same number of times [23]. Next, the error-correcting code E is defined. If $x \in C^1$, $E(x) := (G'(x), Y_x')$, and if $x \in C^0$, $E(x) := (G'(x), 0, \ldots, 0)$. Finally, C' is constructed in the following way. The family $\{C_i\}_{i \in I}$ is transformed into a family of synchronous circuits such that all of its members have disjoint inputs and all outputs are at the same level. To ensure that the groups of repeated bits consist of identical bits, extra tests are added. Therefore, a bounded degree expander is introduced over each group of input bits that have to be identical, cf. [30, 43]. For every edge of these expanders, equality is checked. This family is referred to as $\{D_j\}_{j \in J}$ and the circuits have to be synchronized with the members of $\{C_i\}_{i \in I}$ so that all the outputs are at the same level. Furthermore, the sizes of I and J have to be the same within a constant factor. Clearly, $\wedge_{i \in I} C_i(H, Y) \wedge \wedge_{j \in J} D_j(H, Y) = f \circ E(H, Y)$. Since the construction for threshold functions can be used to compute the Boolean *AND* function, this technique is applied to combine the output bits of the circuits C_i, $i \in I$, and D_j, $j \in J$. Theorem 14.2 and Lemma 14.1 conclude the proof that C' computes $f \circ E$ in a δ-loose way even if an α fraction of the gates at each level of C' and a β fraction of the wires between all levels are destroyed for adequate α and β.

q.e.d.

14.5 Future Research

The presented design for trojan-resilient ICs is worthwhile developing further; especially from a practical point of view when it comes to the very elaborate PCP construction. First, the theoretical techniques of PCP constructions may be improved, as there have been many advancements in the fields of PCPs and related codes, cf. [33–36]. Second, it is important to examine the practical PCP implementation, its complexity and costs. Just recently, another approach was presented, which uses PCPs to solve a very practical problem [44] Indeed, this recent work puts forward the thesis that PCP usage can be put into practice. Thus, we are optimistic that further achievements in Moore's law will enable us to spend many transistors on their sole usage of Boolean circuit resilience.

14.6 Conclusions

This chapter connects the fundamental work on fault tolerance for Boolean circuits by Gál and Szegedy [23] with the very vibrant research area of hardware trojans. Their work was enhanced in a natural way and extended to fully cover faulty wires as well. Developing their approach further, it was shown how to efficiently design fault-tolerant Boolean circuits in this extended model of deliberate faults on gates *and* wires. A corresponding and natural trojan model affecting the functionality of an IC, practically backed up by the Defense Advanced Research Projects Agency's (DARPA) problem challenge [8], was also defined. This hardware trojan fits very well into the model of deliberate faults. Thus, in theory, we can design ICs that reliably compute their intended functions even if they are infected by a hardware trojan from our model. Our finding is highly relevant to industries, in which trust in computer systems is crucial, cf. [5]. As bug attacks require only very small errors, adversaries launching such attacks will only slightly alter the affected hardware as well. The overhead of additional circuits arising from our constructions might therefore be kept within reasonable limits. In Appendix C, a very simple example of a resilient circuit construction is shown.

Appendix

Appendix A: ε-Halvers with Faulty Gates and Faulty Wires

In Section 14.4, we consider ε-halvers with faulty gates and faulty wires. We therefore examine the possible malicious alteration of wires between comparators of level $d-1$ and level d. Assume that there are no faulty gates. An adversary may cut a wire near the output of a gate so that two input bits are affected. Formally, two wires are faulty. He or she may also cut a wire so that only one wire is faulty, and hence, one input bit is affected. In both cases, at most one of the two output bits is incorrect. Finally, an adversary could swap two wires, which means that two wires are faulty. This leads to lemmas similar to the ones from Gál and Szegedy presented in Section 14.2 concerning faulty ε-halvers. Their Lemmas 14.2 and 14.3 easily translate to (extended) ε-halvers with faulty gates and wires. This is implied by the following proposition.

Proposition 1

1. *In a comparator with correctly working gates but faulty wires, the number of incorrect output bits is at most the number of faulty wires.*

2. *At level d of an* ε-halver with faulty gates and faulty wires, the number of incorrect outputs is at most the number of incorrect inputs at level d plus the number of faulty gates at level d. The number of incorrect inputs at level d is at most the number of incorrect outputs at level d – 1 *plus the number of faulty wires between levels d – 1 and d.*

Proof. We prove the second statement. Level d of an ε-halver consist of disjoint comparators. A comparator in such that an ε-halver is an *AND–OR* gate pair with common inputs. It is sufficient to show that the number of incorrect output bits of a comparator at level d is at most the number of its faulty gates plus the number of faulty wires feeding the comparator plus the number of incorrect output bits of the adjacent gates at level $d - 1$. Hence, it is enough to deal with a single comparator with two inputs and two outputs at a time. From the previous observations and the first statement, the proposition follows.

q.e.d.

Appendix B: Valiant–Vazirani Uniqueness Reduction

We briefly describe the fundamental Valiant–Vazirani uniqueness reduction, cf. [45]. This is a probabilistic method that can be applied to reduce the number of satisfying assignments of a satisfiable formula to a single one. We will follow the notation of [46].

Lemma 14.6

There is a probabilistic polynomial time algorithm that on input, ϕ (a CNF formula) and an integer k outputs a formula ψ such that

- *If ϕ is unsatisfiable then ψ is unsatisfiable.*
- *If ϕ has at least 2^k and less than 2^{k+1} satisfying assignments, then there is a probability of at least 1/8 that the formula ψ has exactly one satisfying assignment.*

The proof of Lemma 14.6 will easily follow from certain other definitions and results, which will be presented first.

Let H be a family of functions of the form h:,$\{0, 1\}^n \rightarrow \{0, 1\}^m$. We say that H is a *family of pairwise independent hash functions* if, for every two different inputs $x, y \in \{0, 1\}^n$ and for every two possible outputs $a, b \in \{0, 1\}^m$, we have

$Prob_{h \in H}[h(x) = a \wedge h(y) = b] = 2^{-2m}$.

For m vectors $a_1, \ldots, a_m \in \{0, 1\}^m$ and m bits $b_1, \ldots, b_m$, define $h_{a_1,\ldots,a_m,b_1,\ldots,b_m} : \{0,1\}^n \rightarrow \{0,1\}^m$ as $h_{\mathbf{a},\mathbf{b}}(x) = (a_1 \cdot x + b_1, \ldots, a_m \cdot x + b_m)$, and let H′ be the family of functions defined this way. Then H′ is a family of pairwise independent hash functions. This construction implies the following simple result.

Lemma 14.7

Let $T \subseteq \{0, 1\}^n$ be a set such that $2^k \leq |T| < 2^{k+1}$ and let H *be a family of pairwise independent hash functions of the form h: $\{0,1\}^n \rightarrow \{0,1\}^{k+2}$. Then, if we pick h at random from* H, *there is a constant probability that there is a unique element $x \in T$ such that $h(x) = 0$. Precisely,*

$\text{Prob}_{h \in H}\left[\left|\{x \in T : h(x) = 0\}\right| = 1\right] \geq 1/8$.

Now we can prove the famous uniqueness reduction due to Valiant and Vazirani.

Proof. In order to prove Lemma 14.7, the following algorithm is presented. The algorithm randomly chooses vectors $a_1,\ldots, a_{k+2} \in \{0, 1\}^n$ and bits $b_1,\ldots, b_{k+2}$ and produces a formula ψ that is equivalent to the expression $\phi(x) \wedge (a_1 \cdot x + b_1 = 0) \wedge\ldots\wedge (a_{k+2} \cdot x + b_{k+2} = 0)$. By construction, the number of satisfying assignments of ψ is equal to the number of satisfying assignments x of ϕ such that $h_{a_1,\ldots,a_{k+2},b_1,\ldots,b_{k+2}}(x) = 0$. If ϕ is unsatisfiable, then, for every possible choice of a_i, ψ is also unsatisfiable. If ϕ has between 2^k and 2^{k+1} assignments, then Lemma 14.6 implies that with a probability of at least 1/8, there is exactly one satisfying assignment for ψ.

q.e.d.

Consider the subset C^1 of tuples from $\{0, 1\}^n$, for which a Boolean circuit C evaluates to 1 and the analogously defined subset C^0. Arora et al. presented a procedure to transform C into a family $\{C_i\}_{i\in I}$ of constant size circuits with input $(G(x), Y)$ [32], where $G(x)$ is an adequate error-correcting encoding of the input x to C, and Y is an advise string (both have length polynomial in $S(C)$). For this family $\{C_i\}_i$ we have

1. For every $x \in C^1$ there is a Y such that for all $i \in I$: $C_i(G(x), Y) = 1$.
2. For every $x \in C^0$ and for every Y, it is true that $\text{Prob}_{i\in I}[C_i(G(x), Y) = 0] \geq \varepsilon$, for some ε.

The previously described techniques of Valiant and Vazirani guarantee the uniqueness of Y in Property 1. Properties 1 and 2 can now be combined; $|\cdot|$ denotes the binary length of the argument and $d(\cdot,\cdot)$ denotes the Hamming distance between its arguments.

Lemma 14.8

For every $x \in C^1$ there is, with high probability, a unique Y_x such that for all $I \in I$: $C_i(G(x), Y_x) = 1$. Also, for every $\delta > 0$, there exists $\varepsilon > 0$ such that $\text{Prob}_{i\in I}$ $[C_i(H, Y) = 0] < \varepsilon$ implies that $d((H, Y), (G(x), Y_x)) \leq \delta|(H, Y)|$ for some $x \in C^1$.

Proof. The equivalence of Property 1 and the first part of the lemma is obvious. Hence, we focus on Property 2 and the second part. Assume for the contrary that the second part is not true. Then there does not exist an $x \in C^1$: $G^{-1}(H) = x$. Hence, there is an $x_0 \in C^0$: $G^{-1}(H) = x_0$ and $\text{Prob}_{i\in I}[C_i(H, Y) = 0] = \text{Prob}_{i\in I}[C_i(G(x_0), Y) = 0] < \varepsilon$. For the other direction, assume that Property 2 does not hold true. Then there exist $x \in C^0$ and Y such that $\text{Prob}_{i\in I}[C_i(H, Y) = 0] < \varepsilon$. Since $x \in C^0$ and $H = G(x)$, it holds for all $x_1 \in C^1$ that $d((G(x),Y),G(x_1,Y_{x_1})) \geq \delta_0 \,|\, E \,|\geq \delta \,|\, (G(x),Y) \,|$.

q.e.d.

Appendix C: Example: A Resilient Half Adder

In this appendix, parts of the construction are illustrated by the simple example of a half adder. A half adder adds two bits x and y, and it has two outputs, s ("sum") and c ("carry"). Table 14.1 displays the truth table of a half adder. A simple construction, which contains only elementary gates, is presented in Figure 14.3.

Table 14.1 Truth Table of a Half Adder

x	y	s	c
0	0	0	0
0	1	1	0
1	0	1	0
1	1	0	1

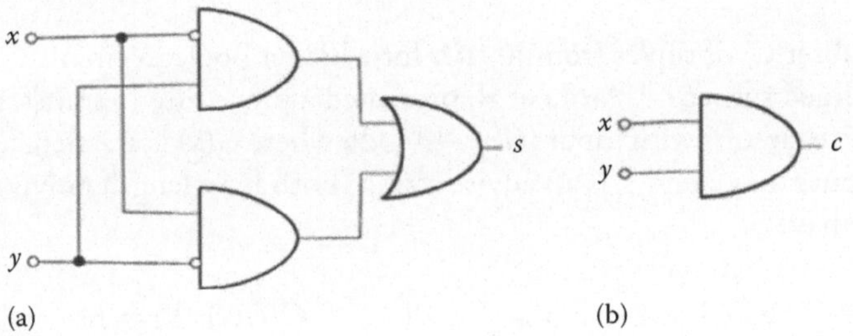

Figure 14.3 Simple design of a half adder, which computes (a) the sum and (b) the carry.

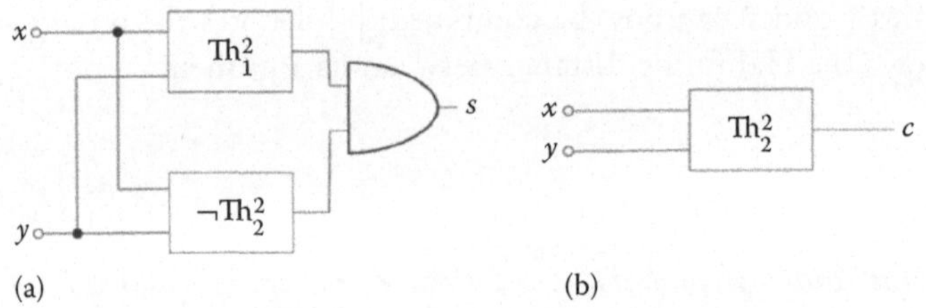

Figure 14.4 Resilient design of a half adder, which computes (a) the sum and (b) the carry.

The two outputs s and c can be computed by circuits consisting of resilient components. These components implement resilient circuits of threshold functions from Theorem 2 and analogously constructed resilient circuits of negated threshold functions. Output c can be computed by the function Th^2_2, and output s can be computed by functions $\neg\mathrm{Th}^2_2$ and Th^2_1. Figure 14.4 shows the new, resilient circuits. The precise constructions of the circuits, which compute the threshold functions, depend on the kind of ε-halvers that are used and on the parameter δ for the δ-loose computation of the threshold functions.

Author Biographies

Jean-Pierre Seifert, is head of Security in Telecommunications at the Technical University of Berlin and at Telekom Innovation Laboratories (as of January 2015). Jean-Pierre Seifert studied computer science and mathematics at Johann-Wolfgang-Goethe-University at Frankfurt/Main. Here, he received his PhD in 2000 with Professor Dr. Claus Schnorr, one of the most important theoretician in the field of secure information systems. Afterward, Seifert gained intensive practical experience working in the research and development departments for hardware security at Infineon, Munich and Intel, United States. At Intel, United States (2004–2006), Professor Seifert was responsible for the design and integration of new central processing unit (CPU) security instructions for microprocessors, which are going to be integrated in all Intel microprocessors. From 2007 to 2008, he developed for Samsung Electronics the first worldwide commercial secure cell phone based on the Linux operating system. Since the end of 2008, Jean-Pierre Seifert has been professor heading the group "Security in Telecommunications" at the Technical University of Berlin. This professorship is at the same time related to the management of the identically named research field at Telekom Innovation Laboratories, the research and development institute of Deutsche Telekom at the Technical University of Berlin. In 2002, Professor Seifert was honored by Infineon with the award "Inventor of the Year" and he also received two Intel Achievement Awards in 2005 for his new CPU security instructions for the Intel microprocessors. Approximately 40 patents have been granted to Professor Seifert in the field of computer security.

Christoph Bayer received his diploma in mathematics in 2011 from the Technical University of Berlin, Germany, and he is an information technology security consultant. During his studies at the technical universities in Kaiserslautern and Berlin, he focused on algebra, number theory, and cryptography. After his graduation, he was a research assistant at the chair "Security in Telecommunications" at the Technical University of Berlin. His research interests include asymmetric cryptography and hardware security. The first topic comprises the theory and implementation as well as the analysis of cryptographic algorithms. The second topic comprises the theoretical foundation of secure and reliable hardware and its application in practice to thwart hardware trojans.

References

1. E. Biham, Y. Carmeli, and A. Shamir. Bug attacks. In *Advances in CRYPTO'08*, Springer, Berlin, pp. 221–240, 2008.
2. S. C. Pohlig and M. E. Hellman. An improved algorithm for computing logarithms over GF(p) and its cryptographic significance. *IEEE Transactions on Information Theory*, 24(1): 106–111, 1978.
3. R. L. Rivest, A. Shamir, and L. Adleman. A method for obtaining digital signatures and public-key cryptosystems. *Communications of the ACM*, 21(2): 120–126, 1978.
4. M. Bellare and P. Rogaway. Optimal asymmetric encryption—How to encrypt with RSA (Extended Abstract). *EUROCRYPT 1994*, Springer, Berlin, pp. 92–111, 1995.
5. Defense Science Board Task Force. On high performance microchip supply, Washington, DC, 2005.
6. S. Adee. The hunt for the kill switch. *IEEE Spectrum*, 45(5): 34–39, 2008.
7. J. I. Lieberman. National security aspects of the global migration of the U.S. semiconductor industry, White paper, 2003.
8. D. Collins. DARPA "TRUST in IC's" effort. In *DARPA Microsystems Technology Symposium*, San Jose, CA, 2007.
9. C. Sturton, M. Hicks, D. Wagner, and S. King. Defeating UCI: Building stealthy and malicious hardware. In *Proceedings of the 2011 IEEE Symposium on Security and Privacy*, Oakland, CA, pp. 64–77, 2011.
10. S. King, J. Tucek, A. Cozzie, C. Grier, W. Jiang, and Y. Zhou. Designing and implementing malicious hardware. In *Proceedings of the 1st USENIX Workshop on Large-Scale Exploits and Emergent Threats*, Washington, D.C., pp. 1–8, 2008.
11. L. Lin, M. Kasper, T. Güneysu, C. Paar, and W. Burleson. Trojan side-channels: Lightweight hardware trojans through side-channel engineering. *Cryptographic Hardware and Embedded Systems-CHES 2009*, Springer, Berlin, pp. 382–395, 2009.

12. M. Tehranipoor and F. Koushanfar. A survey of hardware trojan taxonomy and detection. *IEEE Design & Test of Computers*, 27(1): 10–25, 2010.
13. R. Karri, J. Rajendran, K. Rosenfeld, and M. Tehranipoor. Trustworthy hardware: Identifying and classifying hardware trojans. *IEEE Computer Magazine*, 43(10): 39–46, 2010.
14. X. Wang, M. Tehranipoor, and J. Plusquellic. Detecting malicious inclusions in secure hardware: Challenges and solutions. In *Proceedings of IEEE Int'l Workshop Hardware-Oriented Security and Trust (Host 08)*, IEEE CS Press, pp. 15–19, 2008.
15. F. Koushanfar and A. Mirhoseini. A unified framework for multimodal submodular integrated circuits trojan detection. *IEEE Transactions on Information Forensics and Security*, 6(1): 162–174, 2011.
16. A. Waksman and S. Sethumadhavan. Tamper evident microprocessors. In *Proceedings of the 2010 IEEE Symposium on Security and Privacy*, Washington, DC, pp. 173–188, 2010.
17. M. Hicks, M. Finnicum, S. King, M. Martin, and J. Smith. Overcoming an untrusted computing base: Detecting and removing malicious hardware automatically. In *Proceedings of the 2010 IEEE Symposium on Security and Privacy*, pp. 159–172, 2010.
18. D. Agrawal, S. Baktir, D. Karakoyunlu, P. Rohatgi, and B. Sunar. Trojan detection using IC fingerprinting. In *Proceedings of the 2007 IEEE Symposium on Security and Privacy*, Oakland, CA, pp. 296–310, 2007.
19. F. Wolff, C. Papachristou, S. Bhunia, and R. S. Chakraborty. Towards trojan-free trusted ICs: Problem analysis and detection scheme. In *Design, Automation and Test in Europe (DATE) 2008*, Munich, Germany, pp. 1362–1365, 2008.
20. A. Waksman and S. Sethumadhavan. Silencing hardware backdoors. In *Proceedings of the 2011 IEEE Symposium on Security and Privacy*, Washington, DC, pp. 49–63, 2011.
21. Y. Ishai, A. Sahai, and D. Wagner. Private circuits: Protecting hardware against probing attacks. In *Proceedings of CRYPTO'03*, Berlin, pp. 462–479, 2003.
22. Y. Ishai, M. Prabhakaran, A. Sahai, and D. Wagner. Private Circuits II: Keeping secrets in tamperable circuits. In *Advances in Cryptology—EUROCRYPT 2006*, Springer, Berlin, pp. 308–327, 2006.
23. A. Gál and M. Szegedy. Fault tolerant circuits and probabilistically checkable proofs. In *Proceedings of Structure in Complexity Theory. 10th Annual IEEE Conference*, Atlanta, pp. 65–73, 1995.
24. J. Von Neumann. Probabilistic logics and the synthesis of reliable organisms from unreliable components. In C. E. Shannon and J. McCarthy (eds), *Automata Studies*, vol. 34, pp. 329–378, Princeton University Press, 1956.
25. N. Pippenger. On networks of noisy gates. In *Proceedings of 26th IEEE Symposium on the Foundations of Computer Science*, Portland, OR, pp. 30–36, 1985.
26. R. Dobrushin and S. Ortyukov. Upper bound on the redundancy of self-correcting arrangements of unreliable functional elements. *Problems of Information Transmission*, 13(3): 203–218, 1977.
27. S. Arora and S. Safra. Probabilistic checking of proofs. In *Proceedings of the 33rd IEEE Symposium on Foundations of Computer Science*, New York, pp. 2–13, 1992.
28. A. Gál. Combinatorial methods in Boolean function complexity. PhD thesis, University of Chicago, 1995.
29. I. Wegener. *The Complexity of Boolean Functions*. Wiley-Teubner, Chichester, 1987.
30. S. Arora and B. Barak. *Computational Complexity: A Modern Approach*. Cambridge University Press, 2009.
31. D. A. Pucknell. *Fundamentals of Digital Logic Design: With VLSI Circuit Applications*. Prentice Hall, New York, 1990.
32. S. Arora, C. Lund, R. Motwani, and M. Sudan. Proof verification and hardness of approximation problems. In *Proceedings of the 33rd Annual Symposium on Foundations of Computer Science*, pp. 14–23. IEEE, 1992.
33. I. Dinur. The PCP theorem by gap amplification. *Journal of the ACM*, 54(3): 12, 2007.
34. A. Polishchuk and D. Spielman. Nearly-linear size holographic proofs. In *Proceedings of the Twenty-Sixth Annual ACM Symposium on Theory of Computing*, Montreal, pp. 194–203, 1994.
35. E. Ben-Sasson and M. Sudan. Short PCPs with polylog query complexity. *SIAM Journal on Computing*, 38(2): 551–607, 2008.
36. E. Ben-Sasson, O. Goldreich, P. Harsha, M. Sudan, and S. Vadhan. Robust PCPs of proximity, shorter PCPs, and applications to coding. *SIAM Journal on Computing*, 36(4): 889–974, 2006.

37. F. J. MacWilliams and N. J. A. Sloane. *The Theory of Error-Correcting Codes*. North-Holland, Amsterdam, 1977.
38. M. Ajtai, J. Komlós, and E. Szemerédi. An O(n log n) sorting network. In *Proceedings of the Fifteenth Annual ACM Symposium on Theory of Computing*, volume 129, pp. 1–9. ACM, 1983.
39. N. H. E. Weste and K. Eshraghian. *Principles of CMOS VLSI Design: A Systems Perspective*. Addison-Wesley, Boston, MA, Second edition, 1994.
40. K. Rosenfeld and R. Karri. Attacks and defenses for JTAG. *IEEE Design & Test of Computers*, 27(1): 2–13, 2010.
41. C. Stroud, M. Ding, S. Seshadri, I. Kim, S. Roy, S. Wu, and R. Karri. A parameterized VHDL library for on-line testing. In *Proceedings of the 1997 IEEE International Test Conference*, Washington, D.C., pp. 479–488, 1997.
42. S. Assaf and E. Upfal. Fault tolerant sorting network. In *Proceedings of 31st IEEE Symposium on Foundations of Computer Science*, pp. 275–284. *IEEE Comput. Soc. Press*, 1990.
43. S. Hoory, N. Linial, and A. Wigderson. Expander graphs and their applications. *Bulletin of the American Mathematical Society*, 43(04): 439–562, 2006.
44. S. Setty, R. McPherson, A. Blumberg, and M. Walfish. Olive: Making argument systems for outsourced computation practical (sometimes). To appear in *Proceedings of the Network & Distributed System Security Symposium (NDSS)* San Diego, 2012.
45. L. Valiant and V. Vazirani. NP is as easy as detecting unique solutions. *Theoretical Computer Science*, 47(3): 85–93, 1986.
46. L. Trevisan. Lecture notes on computational complexity. Computer Science Division, UC Berkeley, 2004.

Chapter 15

Intrusion Detection, Prevention, and Response System (IDPRS) for Cyber-Physical Systems (CPSs)

Jianguo Ding
University of Skövde

Contents

15.1 Introduction 373
15.2 CPSs 373
15.2.1 Definition of CPSs 373
15.2.2 Characteristics of CPSs 374
15.2.3 Performance Requirements of CPSs 375
15.3 Security in CPSs 376
15.3.1 Security Requirements in CPSs 376
15.3.1.1 Sensing Security 376
15.3.1.2 Storage Security 376
15.3.1.3 Communication Security 376
15.3.1.4 Actuation Control Security 377
15.3.1.5 Feedback Security 377
15.3.1.6 Application Security 377
15.3.2 Security Challenges in CPSs 377
15.3.2.1 Suffering New Attacks 377
15.3.2.2 Security in Integrated SoS 377
15.3.2.3 Security on Dynamic Evolving Systems 378
15.3.2.4 Physical Environment Protection 379
15.3.2.5 Human-Involved Security 379
15.3.2.6 Resilience of CPSs 379

15.3.2.7 Control Security 380
15.4 IDPRS for CPSs 380
15.4.1 Intrusion Detection System 380
15.4.2 Intrusion Prevention System 380
15.4.3 Intrusion Response System 381
15.4.4 Intrusion Detection Analysis/Models 381
15.4.4.1 Anomaly-Based IDS 381
15.4.4.2 Signature-Based IDS 382
15.4.4.3 Stateful Protocol Analysis 382
15.4.5 Types of IDPRS 382
15.4.5.1 Network-Based IDPRS 382
15.4.5.2 Host-Based IDPRS 383
15.4.5.3 Network Behavior Analysis 383
15.4.5.4 The Hybrid Model 383
15.4.6 Challenges for IDPRS 383
15.4.6.1 Wider Detection 383
15.4.6.2 Monitor the Interaction Procedure 384
15.4.6.3 Human Intrusion 384
15.4.6.4 False Positives and Negatives 384
15.4.6.5 Proactive Defense 384
15.4.6.6 Micro-Scope Solution 385
15.5 Solutions 385
15.5.1 Emerging Computer Models and CPS Security 385
15.5.1.1 Nomadic Computing, Mobile Services 385
15.5.1.2 Autonomic Computing 385
15.5.1.3 Pervasive Computing 387
15.5.1.4 Opportunistic Computing 387
15.5.1.5 Scalable Computing 388
15.5.1.6 Physical Computing 388
15.5.1.7 Probabilistic Computing 388
15.5.2 Technical Strategies 389
15.6 Conclusions 390
Author Biography 390
References 390

Abstract: Cyber-physical systems (CPSs) are integrated physical, engineered, and social systems whose operations are monitored, coordinated, controlled, and integrated by a computing and communication core. Due to the dynamic structure of CPSs, the security measurements are often complex. Given this fact, the objective of this chapter is to present the intrusion detection, prevention, and response system (IDPRS) for such a dynamic environment.

Keywords: Intrusion detection; Intrusion prevention; Intrusion response; Cyber-physical systems

15.1 Introduction

Cyber-physical systems (CPSs) are integrated physical, engineered, and social systems whose operations are monitored, coordinated, controlled, and integrated by a computing and communication core. This intimate coupling between the cyberworld, physical world, and social world will be manifested from the nano-world to large-scale wide-area systems of systems (SoS), from the physical environment to social society. The Internet transformed how humans interact and communicate with one another, revolutionized how and where information is accessed, and even changed how people buy and sell products. CPSs will transform how humans interact with and control the physical, cyber, and social world around us [1].

CPSs have cybertechnologies, both hardware and software, deeply embedded in and interacting with physical components, and sensing and changing the state of the real world, and managed by humans, and must have high levels of reliability, safety, security, dependability, resilience, and usability.

In general, CPS security has three main security properties: confidentiality, integrity, and availability. Confidentiality prevents an unauthorized user from obtaining secret or private information. Integrity prevents an unauthorized user from modifying the information. Availability ensures that the resource can be used when requested.

With the proliferation of CPS extension, remote management, and control of CPSs, security plays a critically important role. Compared with current cyberinfrastructures, the physical component of CPS infrastructure adds significant complexity that greatly complicates security.

From the perspective of the defender, more complex systems require dramatically more effort to analyze and defend, because of the state–space explosion when considering combinations of events [2].

An intrusion detection, prevention and response system (IDPRS) is one important technical solution to protect complex CPSs. However, IDPRS still has some challenges and is not sufficient for dealing with potential security threats, which come from the complexity, dynamics, probabilistic environment, and uncertain human involvement. Thus, systematic, intelligent, autonomic, and comprehensive technical and management solutions should be embraced in IDPRS for the detection and defense of challenging attacks in CPSs.

This chapter surveys the present challenges in CPS security and investigates the possible solutions to improve existing IDPRS and to depict the road map for future IDPRS design and security protection for evolving CPSs.

15.2 CPSs

15.2.1 Definition of CPSs

CPSs are physical, biological, social, and engineered systems whose operations/computations are integrated, monitored, or controlled by a computational core. Components include all the networked elements at various scales. Computing is deeply embedded into every physical component, possibly even into materials. CPSs not only indicate the physical connection between all networked components but also indicate the deep integration of various computations.

CPSs can be found in areas such as aerospace, automotive, chemical processes, civil infrastructure, military, medical system, energy, health care, manufacturing, factory automation, building and environmental control, robotic systems, transportation, entertainment, and consumer appliances. As a complex SoS, a CPS should be dependable, safe, secure, resilient, efficient, and real-time.

The concept of CPSs can be extended to a macrosystem in which cyber-physical systems are involved. In this chapter, CPSs are used in both macro- and microdomains.

15.2.2 Characteristics of CPSs

An extension of current network and distributed systems, CPSs help to integrate the physical world, the cyberworld, and the social world into a sociotechnical system (Figure 15.1).

The characteristics of CPSs are as follows [3,4]:

1. Integration
   a. Integration of complex, heterogeneous large-scale systems, creating universal definitions for representing ultra-large heterogeneous systems, building an interconnected and interoperable shared development infrastructure, and developing an abstraction infrastructure to bridge digital and physical system components
   b. Macrointegration of C (the cyberworld) with P (the physical world) with S (the social world), extending the informatization of the physical world, network scale, and network applications
   c. Microintegration of heterogeneous networked system, platform, protocol, interaction of devices, and so on
   d. Interaction between humans, physical systems, and cybersystems, enabling natural, more seamless human–CPS interactions, with computational and physical processes tightly interconnected and coordinated to work together effectively, often with humans in the loop.
2. Dynamics
   a. Inherent mobility of physical system
   b. Changes to individual CPS components (hardware, software, protocol, etc.)
   c. Changes to applications/services
   d. Changes of CPS users/operators and their behavior
   e. Mobile and wireless communications involved

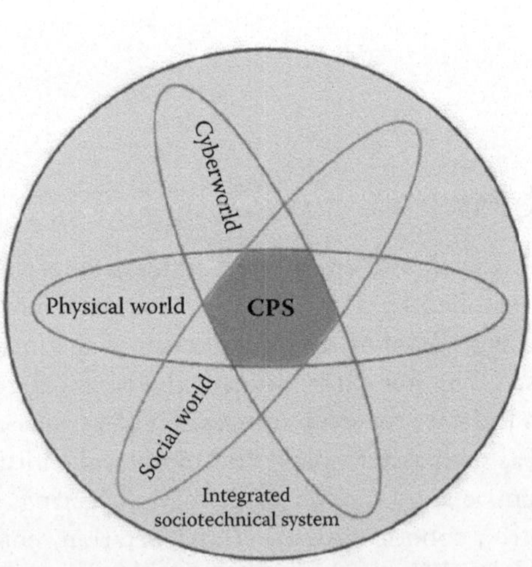

Figure 15.1 Integrated sociotechnical systems with CPS.

   f. Changes to CPS structure (deployment/topology) and functions
   g. Parallel local and global changes in CPSs
   h. Changes to social system/environment
3. Unbalance
   a. Unbalanced deployment/structure
   b. Unbalanced computing resources
4. Multilayered
   a. Networked at multiple layers and extreme scale
   b. CPS built with layered stack structure, such as layered protocols
   c. Application models layered
5. Real-time performance
   a. Real-time communication
   b. Real-time data processing
   c. Real-time information fusion
   d. Real-time system protection
6. Large scale
   a. Large geographical distribution
   b. Large-scale control of SoS
7. Federation-based distributed management and control
8. Uncertainty of the complex system
9. Autonomic and automation
10. Emerging computing models
    a. As CPSs become more dependent on computational processes, it becomes increasingly important to adapt and embrace the new computing models in a unified way: nomadic computing, autonomic computing, pervasive computing, cognitive computing, opportunistic computing, scalable computing, physical computing, and situation computing.
11. CPSs engineered to be reliable, secure, safe, sustainable, and resilient

15.2.3 Performance Requirements of CPSs

To maintain the high performance of CPSs, the system should have the following properties [5]:

- Extendable in system deployment and functional extension
- Adaptable to the context/situation change and new applications/services
- Autonomic in system management and system protection
- Efficient
- Functional
- Robust and resilient in unhealthy environments
- Reliable, safe, and secure
- Controllable
- Manageable
- Supporting dynamic computing
- Dealing with uncertainty
- Predictable in system behavior and performance
- Available and usable in various scenarios
- Involving humans in a sociotechnical system

15.3 Security in CPSs

15.3.1 Security Requirements in CPSs

As an emerging distributed SoS, CPS security architecture should be designed to meet the requirements outlined by Venkatasubramanian [6]. Figure 15.2 shows the security framework in CPSs.

15.3.1.1 Sensing Security

As CPSs are closely related to the physical process, the validity and accuracy of the sensing process have to be ensured. Sensing security needs techniques for authentication of physical stimuli, so that any data measured from the physical process can be trusted.

15.3.1.2 Storage Security

Once the data has been collected and processed, it may need to be stored over time for future access. Any tampering with this stored data can lead to errors in future data processing requirements. Storage security involves developing solutions for securing stored data in CPS platforms from physical or cybertampering.

15.3.1.3 Communication Security

An important aspect of CPSs is that they are networked in nature. This allows them not only to form a network for data fusion and delivery to back-end entities but also to take coordinated response actions (in both passively active and active operational modes). Communication security needs the development of protocols for securing both inter- and intra-CPS communication from active (interferers) and passive (eavesdroppers) adversaries.

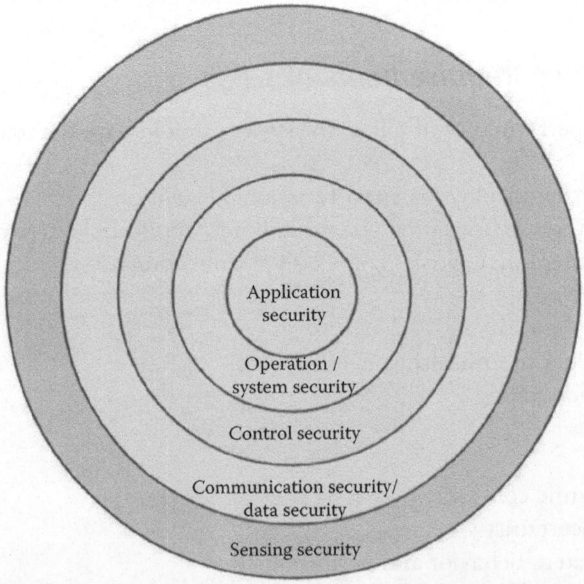

Figure 15.2 CPS security framework.

15.3.1.4 Actuation Control Security

This refers to ensuring that, during the passive or active mode of operation, no actuation can take place without the appropriate authorization. The specification of the authorizations has to be dynamic, as CPS requirements change over time.

15.3.1.5 Feedback Security

This refers to ensuring that the control systems in a CPS, which provide the necessary feedback for effecting actuation, are protected. The current security solutions focus on data security only, but their effects on estimation and control algorithms have to be studied in order to provide an in-depth defense against attacks.

15.3.1.6 Application Security

Applications/services should be protected and secured. Application security is mostly overlapped with the traditional network application security, such as encryption, authentication, authorization, auditing, data privacy and protection, and so on. Application security is the final, ultimate service protection in CPSs.

15.3.2 Security Challenges in CPSs

Security is a critical aspect of CPSs on many levels, including the protection of national infrastructure, privacy of individuals, system integrity, and intellectual property. Attacks on CPSs are becoming increasingly sophisticated, targeted, and coordinated. The ideal security protection will cover the whole CPS (sociotechnical system) (see Figure 15.3).

The emerging challenges are [6,7]:

15.3.2.1 Suffering New Attacks

The combination of cyber and physical vulnerabilities may lead to attack models that are fundamentally new and hard to analyze and carry a substantial risk to maintaining the physical integrity of critical systems. The deep interaction with a distributed physical environment increases the risks (e.g., the potential physical damage due to a security breach) and offers new opportunities (e.g., the use of physical data to authenticate nodes or detect intruders).

New threats, particularly on the main components of CPSs and the interfaces between CPSs and other subsystems and SoS, are serious. Stuxnet attack is a typical example involving supervisory control and data acquisition (SCADA) systems [8].

15.3.2.2 Security in Integrated SoS

CPS security needs to be integrated with system theory to guarantee resilience of the SoS, which use widespread sensing, communication, and control to operate safely and reliably.

- Dependence on widespread computing and networking naturally increases security concerns, as the availability, integrity, and secrecy of the data carried may be compromised.
- The presence of the physical system widens the range of possible attacks and constrains the set of feasible countermeasures.

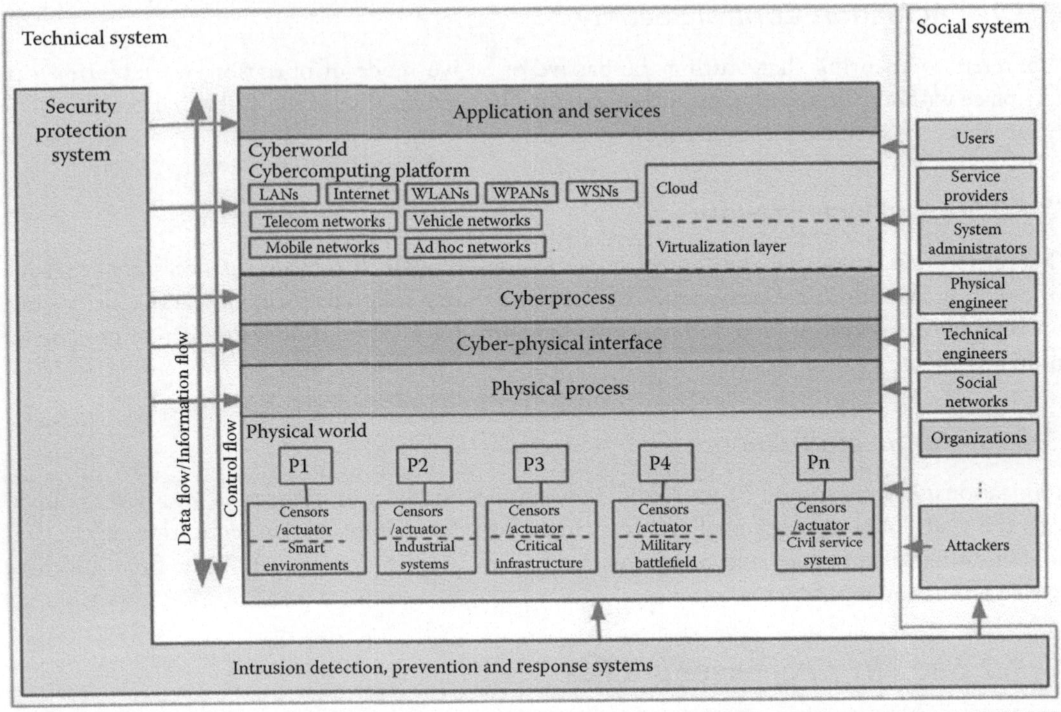

Figure 15.3 Architecture of CPS.

- The interaction between the cyber and the physical dimensions offers many opportunities for detection and response when the physical system is equipped with computational and communications capabilities.
- Each function of a CPS (sensing, communication, storage, actuation and feedback, etc.) has its own set of security requirements, which are function dependent.
- CPSs have to deal with cross-organizational security information sharing, which is necessary but hard to manage in current scenarios.
- As CPSs are federated systems, CPS security needs to be considered architecturally, not as a separate security architecture but as a secure architecture for the deployment of such applications.
- The structure of data placement, system control, and monitoring of the system as a whole must consider the security implications.

15.3.2.3 Security on Dynamic Evolving Systems

The environment, structure, sensing process, data analysis, function modification, real-time feedback control, and varying security requirements put CPSs into a dynamic, evolving situation. The evolution in CPSs is paralleled with individual cyber-physical systems and integrated cyber-physical systems, particularly as systems become interconnected with legacy systems and across industry boundaries. Any change within the CPS, whatever the physical changes or system behavior changes, can result in unpredictable vulnerabilities. Static and fixed protection strategies mostly are not valid. Moreover, the running dynamic data flow, information flow, and control flow should be under protection. Thus, the security task includes the need to dynamically reassign monitoring, correlation, and intrusion detection management responsibilities to nodes as the topology evolves; to maintain availability and provide continuous coverage; and to address various risks that compromised nodes will be assigned responsibilities that enable them to subvert the architecture from within.

15.3.2.4 Physical Environment Protection

CPS security solutions depend upon the physical environment to enable security. Attacks on the physical environment can be potentially used to prevent the security solutions from functioning correctly. Attackers can artificially change the environment around the cyberelements of a CPS, causing unexpected results with security threats, including denial of service (DoS). The physical environment can be tampered with in CPSs such as power grids and unmanned aerial vehicles (UAVs), since they are unmanned. Attackers can potentially control the sensors in a data center (DC) to cause overload of the air conditioner.

Security for sensors and actuators in the field needs to be considered as well. A technique for detecting tampering and validating the inputs provided by these sensors is important to prevent these control inputs to the CPS from being recruited by adversaries (e.g., botnets).

Some tiny smart devices, because of their limited computing capability and resources and because they are deployed unprotected in the physical environment, are very weak under technical attacks or may even suffer physical damage. Therefore, the physical environment itself should be safe and secure, and protection strategies and mechanisms for authenticating the sensed value are required [9].

15.3.2.5 Human-Involved Security

The deployment of CPSs is not limited to specialized systems managed by tech-savvy people. Many of the applications of CPSs are systems in everyday use operated by nontechnical people—medical monitoring systems, smart infrastructures, and so on. Therefore, security solutions for CPSs should have a high degree of usability—plug-n-play nature and security transparency—a characteristic that today's cyber-only security solutions do not consider [9].

15.3.2.6 Resilience of CPSs

Resilience is defined as the ability to prepare for and adapt to changing conditions and to withstand and recover rapidly from disruptions. Resilience includes the ability to withstand and recover from deliberate attacks, accidents, or naturally occurring threats or incidents. The terms *security* and *resilience* are often used together. Both share common roots and requirements: the need to assess threats and vulnerabilities; the need to develop plans and procedures; and the need to have access to accurate and timely information. CPS, such as energy systems, are often safety critical, as the lives of many depend on their correct operation. Consequently, resilience becomes a key property; the system needs to continue operating under attacks, perhaps at a reduced performance, while still guaranteeing the basic safety properties through graceful degradation. Physical and analytical redundancies should be combined with security principles (e.g., diversity of and separation of duty) to adapt or reschedule its operation during attacks [10].

15.3.2.7 Control Security

The property of control systems in CPSs with security is that software patching and frequent updates are not well suited for control systems. For example, upgrading a system may require months of advance planning to take the system off-line; it is, therefore, economically difficult to justify suspending the operation of an industrial computer on a regular basis to install new security patches. Some security patches may even violate the certification of control systems [10].

Another property of control systems in CPSs is the real-time requirements of control systems. Control systems are autonomous decision-making agents that need to take decisions in real time. Real-time availability provides a stricter operational environment than most traditional IT systems. CPSs with large industrial control systems may have a large number of legacy systems. Most of the efforts made with legacy systems should be considered short-term solutions. To secure critical control systems properly, the underlying technology must satisfy some minimum performance requirements to allow the implementation of well-tested security mechanisms and standards.

15.4 IDPRS for CPSs

IDPRS for CPSs are composed of an intrusion detection system (IDS), an intrusion prevention system (IPS), and an intrusion response system (IRS).

15.4.1 Intrusion Detection System

An IDS is a device or software application that monitors network or system activities, gathers and analyzes information from various areas within information systems for malicious activities or policy violations, coming from both intrusions (attacks from outside the organizations) and misuse (attacks from within the organizations), and produces reports to a management station.

Attackers are using a number of evasion techniques, such as fragmentation, avoiding defaults, coordinated low-bandwidth attacks, address spoofing/proxying, pattern change evasion, and so on.

The typical intrusions include [11]

- Attempted break-ins, which are detected by atypical behavior profiles or violations of security constraints. An IDS for this type is called anomaly-based IDS.
- Masquerade attacks, which are detected by atypical behavior profiles or violations of security constraints. These intrusions are also detected using anomaly-based IDS.
- Penetrations of the security control system, which are detected by monitoring for specific patterns of activity.
- Leakage, which is detected by atypical use of system resources.
- DoS, which is detected by atypical use of system resources.
- Malicious use, which is detected by atypical behavior profiles, violations of security constraints, or use of special privileges.

15.4.2 Intrusion Prevention System

IPS are network security appliances to identify malicious activity, log information for this activity, attempt to block/stop it, and report it. IPS are considered extensions of IDS because they monitor network traffic and system activities for malicious activity. Unlike IDS, IPS are placed in-line and are able to actively prevent/block intrusions that are detected. More specifically, IPS can take such actions as sending an alarm, dropping the malicious packets, resetting the connection, or blocking the traffic from the offending destinations. An IPS can also correct cyclic redundancy check (CRC) errors, unfragment packet streams, prevent transmission control protocol (TCP) sequencing issues, and clean up unwanted transport and network layer options [12].

15.4.3 Intrusion Response System

IRS are systems to produce a corresponding response for system intrusion. A good response must consist of preplanned defensive measures that include an incident response team and ways to collect IDS logs for future use and for evidence when needed. The IRS have responsibility for: keeping up to date with the latest threats and incidents; generating notifications whenever an incident occurs; assessing the damage and impact of every incident, to avoid exploitation of the same vulnerability; and making decisions to recover from the incident [13].

IDS, IPS, and IRS do not work independently. They share a common knowledge base and update the knowledge in the common base. Most of the time, they work together, or integrated into one security protection system, to maximize the protection functions of the whole IDRPS (see Figure 15.4).

15.4.4 Intrusion Detection Analysis/Models

IDS detection models comprise anomaly-based detection, signature-based detection, stateful protocol analysis, and hybrid detection [14].

15.4.4.1 Anomaly-Based IDS

An IDS that is anomaly based will monitor network behavior and compare it against an established baseline. The baseline will identify what is "normal" for that network, such as what sort of bandwidth is usually used, what protocols are used, and what ports and devices mostly connect to each other, and alert the administrator or user when traffic is detected that is anomalous or

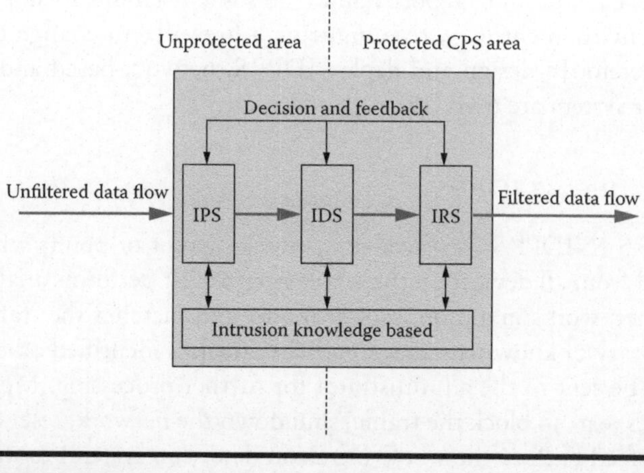

Figure 15.4 IDPRS architecture.

significantly different from the baseline. Anomaly-based IDS can be used in dynamic network environments to adapt the behavior dynamics. The issue is that it may raise a false-positive alarm for a legitimate use of bandwidth if the baselines are not intelligently configured or updated in time with the system dynamics.

15.4.4.2 Signature-Based IDS

A signature-based IDS (termed a *misuse detection* system) will monitor network behavior and compare it with a database of signatures or attributes from known malicious threats. Identification engines perform well by monitoring these patterns of known misuse of system resources. This is similar to the way most antivirus software detects malware. Signature-based IDS can only be efficient within stable systems. There will be a lag following a new threat being discovered in the wild, because the signature is not yet recorded in the detection system for the new threats.

15.4.4.3 Stateful Protocol Analysis

Stateful protocol analysis identifies deviations of protocol states. Once the protocols are fully decoded, the intrusion detection system analysis engine can evaluate different parts of the protocol for anomalous behavior or exploits against predetermined profiles of generally accepted definitions of benign protocol activity for each protocol state.

It is often difficult or impossible to develop completely accurate models of protocols, because (1) it is very resource intensive and (2) it cannot detect attacks that do not violate the characteristics of generally acceptable protocol behavior. An example would be monitoring requests with their corresponding response; every request should have a predictable response, and those responses that fall outside of expected results will be flagged and analyzed further.

In applications, a hybrid model, combining anomaly-based and signature-based models and stateful protocol analysis is often used to adapt to dynamic new threats to CPSs.

15.4.5 Types of IDPRS

IDPRS typically record information related to observed events, notify security administrators of important observed events, produce reports, and take some reactions to stop the attack itself, to change the security environment (e.g., reconfiguring a firewall), to change the attack's content, and to recover the system. In design and deploy IDPRS, network-based and host-based systems and network behavior system are used [15].

15.4.5.1 Network-Based IDPRS

Network-based IDPRS (NIDPRS) is placed at a strategic point or points within the network to monitor traffic to and from all devices on the whole network. It performs analysis for passing traffic on the entire subnet, works in a promiscuous mode, and matches the traffic that is passed on the subnets to the library of known attacks. Once the attack is identified or abnormal behavior is sensed, the alert can be sent to the administrator for further processing. Meanwhile, the system can start the responses (e.g., to block the traffic, shut down the network, reset the communication, trace the attack, and feed back to the whole intrusion detection system) to mitigate the potential damages in time.

In practice, IDPRS can cooperate with firewalls to implement multilayer detection and protection with high performance. When necessary, both inbound and outbound traffic is monitored.

15.4.5.2 Host-Based IDPRS

Host-based IDPRS (HIDPRS) run on individual hosts or devices on the CPS. A HIDPRS monitors the inbound and outbound packets from the device only and will alert the user or administrator if abnormal/misuse activity is detected, and the response to the alert will be executed, such as to deactivate the device, reset the device, and so on.

In CPSs, some smart devices have limited computing resources and computing capability. It is hard or not feasible to install HIDPRS directly in all the smart devices. In this case, the HIDPRS will be installed in a host computer, which manages the smart devices. The control mechanism in the CPS will support the IDPRS as well.

15.4.5.3 Network Behavior Analysis

Network behavior analysis (NBA) examines network traffic to identify threats that generate unusual traffic flows, such as DoS and distributed denial of service (DDoS) attacks, certain forms of malware (e.g., worms, backdoors), and policy violations (e.g., a client system providing network services to other systems).

NBA systems are most often deployed to monitor flows on an organization's internal networks, and are also sometimes deployed where they can monitor flows between an organization's networks and external networks (e.g., the Internet, business partners' networks). NBA technologies can also be deployed if organizations desire additional detection capabilities for DoS and DDoS attacks, worms, and other threats that NBAs are particularly good at detecting.

NBA can be an embedded component in both NIDPRS and HIDPRS.

15.4.5.4 The Hybrid Model

For most CPS environments, a combination of NIDPRS and HIDPRS is needed for an effective intrusion detection solution.

- NIDPRS and HIDPRS each patrol their own area on the network for unwanted and illegal network traffic. They complement each other, however. Both bring to the security of the CPS their own strengths and weaknesses, which nicely complement and augment the security of the CPS.
- The hybrid model will depend to a great extent on how well the interface receives and distributes the incidents and integrates the reporting structure between the different types of sensors in the NIDPRS and HIDPRS spheres. Furthermore, the interface should be able to smartly and intelligently gather and report data from the CPS being monitored.

15.4.6 Challenges for IDPRS

15.4.6.1 Wider Detection

CPSs provide technical support for the integration of various related IT systems into one large-scale system. However, most of the current IDPRS target the monitoring, detection, and control of data flow. In SoS-based CPSs, wider elements/factors will be detected, such as control flow, information flow, information content, physical environment, operation, network behavior, and human behavior. With the evolution of CPSs, the detection will be extended to any potential domain.

15.4.6.2 Monitor the Interaction Procedure

IDPRS mainly monitor the various traffics in CPSs, but the CPS interaction procedure (physical interactions, cyber-physical interactions, human-physical interactions, and human-cyber interactions) is not yet fully monitored and detected. CPS interactions with components within a system must be modeled as control and data channels and human-involved channels. Such modeling of CPS interactions is likely to be application domain specific, for example, modeling the effect of phase imbalance on critical infrastructure, such as the power grid, or flow constraints within an oil or gas pipeline. The monitoring, detection, and protection of the interactions in CPSs are rather important to maintain a robust, safe security system.

15.4.6.3 Human Intrusion

In the sociotechnical system, human behavior plays a significant role throughout the CPS operation, from physical environment to cybersystem, control procedure, information process, and final application and management. IDPRS can take the role of regulating and controlling human behavior toward CPSs, particularly identifying potential innocent and malicious operation in the system. As a nonoptional role, human behavior should be modeled and integrated in systems in various levels and procedures.

15.4.6.4 False Positives and Negatives

IDPRS technologies cannot provide completely accurate detection. When an IDPRS incorrectly identifies benign activity as being malicious, a false positive has occurred. When an IDPRS fails to identify malicious activity, a false negative has occurred.

It is not possible to eliminate all false positives and negatives; in most cases, reducing the occurrence of one increases the occurrence of the other. The reasons behind this are incomplete system understanding, unexpected system dynamic and incidents, existing bugs from hardware and software, uncertain physical environment, and human behavior. System noise can severely limit IDPRS effectiveness.

Many organizations choose to decrease false negatives at the cost of increasing false positives, which means that more malicious events are detected but more analytical resources are needed to differentiate false positives from true malicious events. Altering the configuration of an IDPRS to improve its detection accuracy is known as tuning. But, finally, it is hard to get a balance between false positives and false negatives.

15.4.6.5 Proactive Defense

Because of the constantly changing CPS running environment, new attacks, the evolution of CPSs, and emergence of organized cybercrime groups capable of conducting intrusions into CPSs, the risks of new or rare failure events cannot be ignored. Potential attacks cannot be identified and defended against in time. Moreover, cyberwarfare is projected to become the future of armed conflict. CPSs should have the capability for proactive detection and defense [16].

15.4.6.6 Micro-Scope Solution

Most of the current IDPRS technology puts more effort into micro-scope technical solutions, such as:

- Attack target-based solution
- Patch and fix strategies
- Not including the changes from global/neighbor factors
- Not including global structure change
- Not including hidden security causes, which can propagate along the multilayered networks

Thus, IDPRS should embrace a macro-scope/systematic solution to bring the whole CPS under holistic protection.

15.5 Solutions

15.5.1 Emerging Computer Models and CPS Security

The foundational challenges of CPS security require top-to-bottom rethinking of the emerging computing models [17]. New security models and paradigms are needed to adapt to and to be supported by the computing models for CPS security.

15.5.1.1 Nomadic Computing, Mobile Services

Nomadic computing (mobile computing) is the use of portable CPS devices, or mobile CPS services in conjunction with mobile communications technologies, to enable users to access the CPS from anywhere in the world. Nomadic computing provides a rich set of computing and communication capabilities and services to nomads as they move from place to place in a transparent, integrated, and convenient form. Subsequently, more users and devices are connected and have direct dynamic communication links and dynamic data transactions in CPSs. Mobile CPSs pose unique challenges to identity due to mobility, resource constraints, scale, and heterogeneity.

Nomadic security protection models should consider all the dynamic factors and the vulnerabilities from nomadic behavior, and finally support a secure dynamic CPSs and applications.

15.5.1.2 Autonomic Computing

Autonomic computing is the development of computer systems capable of self-management to overcome the rapidly growing complexity of computing systems management and to reduce the barrier that complexity poses to further growth. In other words, autonomic computing refers to the self-managing characteristics of distributed computing resources, adapting to unpredictable changes while hiding their intrinsic complexity from operators and users. An autonomic system makes decisions on its own, using high-level policies; it will constantly check and optimize its status and automatically adapt itself to changing conditions.

Besides enhanced user experience for human-to-human (H2H) or human-to-machine (H2M) interactions, autonomous machine-to-machine (M2M) interaction has gained significant importance. This mechanism improves and extends CPS application and performance. Autonomic security will be of great benefit to protection of complex dynamic CPSs.

Context-aware computing, situation-aware computing, and self-management mechanisms will support autonomic computing in various aspects.

15.5.1.2.1 Context-Aware Computing

Context-aware computing refers to a general class of mobile systems that can sense their physical environment and adapt their behavior accordingly [18]. Three important aspects of context are: location; identity; and resource/behavior. CPS transactions and processes will be automated and will take place based on autonomous decisions without any human intervention. These will often be based on or influenced by context information obtained from the physical world, without the requirement of human input to describe the situation. Context awareness is a good property for IDPRS in dealing with challenging threats and attacks in dynamic scenarios.

15.5.1.2.2 Situation-Aware Computing

Situation awareness is the perception of environmental elements with respect to time or space, the comprehension of their meaning, and the projection of their status after some variable has changed, such as time, or some other variable, such as a predetermined event. It is meaningful to have cybersituation awareness to safeguard sensitive data, sustain fundamental operations, and protect critical infrastructure in CPSs. Comprehensive cybersituation awareness involves computing and network components, threat information, and mission dependencies [19,20].

- Network awareness
  - Disciplined asset and configuration management
  - Routing vulnerability auditing
  - Patch management and compliance reporting
  - Recognizing and sharing incident awareness across the organization
- Threat awareness
  - Identify and track internal incidents and suspicious behavior
  - Incorporate knowledge of external threats
  - Participate in cross-industry or cross-government threat-sharing communities on possible indicators and warnings
- Mission awareness
  - Develop a comprehensive picture of the critical dependencies (and specific components) to operate in CPSs
  - Understand these critical dependencies to support mission impact in forensic analysis, triage, and real-time crisis-action response risk/readiness assessments prior to task execution and informed defense planning

15.5.1.2.3 Self-Management

Self-management is the process by which CPSs can manage their own operation without human intervention.

- Self-configuration: automatic configuration of components
- Self-healing: automatic discovery and correction of faults; automatically applying all necessary actions to bring the system back to normal operation
- Self-optimization; automatic monitoring and control of resources to ensure optimal functioning with respect to the defined requirements
- Self-protection: proactive identification and protection from arbitrary attacks

15.5.1.2.4 Cognitive Computing

Cognitive computing is about engineering the mind by reverse engineering the brain. A cognitive network (CPS) is a network composed of elements that, through learning and reasoning, dynamically adapt to varying network conditions in order to optimize end-to-end performance. In a cognitive CPS, decisions are made to meet the requirements of the system as a whole, rather than the individual networked components. Cognitive systems can be characterized by their ability to perform their tasks in an autonomous fashion by using their self-attributes, such as self-managing, self-optimizing, self-monitoring, self-repair, self-protection, self-adaptation, and self-healing, to adapt dynamically to changing requirements or component failures while taking into account the end-to-end goals.

Cognitive networks use the self-configuration capability to respond and dynamically adapt to operational and context changes. The main function components of self-configuration are self-awareness and auto-learning, which are implemented by network-aware middleware and normally distributed across network components. Applications and devices adapt to exploiting enhanced network performance and are agnostic of the underlying reconfigurations, in accordance with the seamless service provision paradigm. A cognitive infrastructure consists of reconfigurable elements and intelligent management functionality that will progressively evolve policies based on past actions [21].

Context awareness, situation awareness, and cognitive mechanisms not only help to build an intelligent and robust CPS, but also help to realize the safe, secure, and resilient CPS.

15.5.1.3 Pervasive Computing

Pervasive computing is the trend toward increasingly ubiquitous, connected computing devices in the environment, a trend being brought about by a convergence of advanced electronic, wireless technologies and CPSs. Pervasive computing devices vary from large computing to tiny smart devices, either mobile or embedded in almost any type of object imaginable, including cars, tools, appliances, clothing, and various consumer goods, all communicating through increasingly interconnected networks. Pervasive computing supports the creation of a CPS that is pervasively and unobtrusively embedded in the environment, completely connected, intuitive, effortlessly portable, and constantly available [22].

The final goal of pervasive security is to design advanced devices, networks, systems, and software to support the secure operation and services.

15.5.1.4 Opportunistic Computing

Opportunistic computing exploits humans' mobility and their gregarious nature to enable a transmission only if two users are sufficiently close. Opportunistic computing can benefit from the research outcomes in pervasive and sensor systems, distributed and fault-tolerant computing, and mobile ad hoc networking. Technological advances in CPSs are leading to a world replete with mobile and static sensors, user mobile devices, and vehicles equipped with a variety of sensing and computing devices, thus paving the way for a multitude of opportunities for pairwise device contacts. Opportunistic computing exploits the opportunistic communication between pairs of devices (and applications executing on them) to share each other's content, resources, and services.

Opportunistic networks (oppnets) are formed by small devices that communicate with each other. These devices are either mobile, personal devices carried by a user or fixed devices mounted at a dedicated location. Oppnets have an outstanding potential for a truly beneficially "disruptive" effect on existing technologies. They can make applications more effective and efficient, in particular, by providing these applications with a wealth of communication modes, sensing devices, and other tools. By their very nature of relying on growth and expansion, Oppnets are highly adaptive and can be exploited for achieving highly reliable and dependable operation in highly dynamic and unforeseeable situations [23].

Technologies in opportunistic computing and opportunistic networks should be extended and enhanced to support the security protection in opportunistic applications of CPSs.

15.5.1.5 Scalable Computing

Scalable computing involves using a computer system that can adapt to the need for more powerful computing capabilities. Scalability is a desirable quality for CPSs. The evolution of CPSs brings new challenges to scalability. Examples include the extension of physical systems, cyberapplication, and flexible evolution.

CPS security should be flexible and extendable to support the scalable computing in evolving CPSs.

15.5.1.6 Physical Computing

Physical (or embedded) computing, in the broadest sense, means building interactive physical systems by the use of software and hardware that can sense and respond to the analog world. In practice, it means using sensors and microcontrollers to translate analog input to a software system, and/or control electromechanical devices such as motors, servos, lighting, or other hardware. CPSs or Internet of Things (IoT) are typical systems to implement physical computing.

The goals of physical computing are to instrument and interconnect all physical things and to ensure that all those physical things are intelligent.

Physical computing brings the idea that all physical components (things) can be networked and can be sufficiently intelligent to interact with each other and, further, to undertake some transactions. However, all the physical components (things) should reside in a safe, secure, and resilient environment where they can provide reliable services without being tampered with by malicious attacks.

15.5.1.7 Probabilistic Computing

Probabilistic computing means to exploit uncertain knowledge to learn from data, infer its probable causes, make calibrated predictions, and choose effective action. For evolving complex CPSs, uncertainty is an unavoidable characteristic, which comes from unexpected hardware defects, unavoidable software errors, incomplete system information, dependency relationships between the considered entities, and dynamic behavior in the system. It is not always possible to build precise models for CPS computing. The imprecision of the information supplied by specialists very often causes great difficulties. The expressions "very high", "normal," and "sometimes" are inherently imprecise and may not be directly incorporated into the knowledge basis of a conventional rule-based system. Moreover, due to the fact that the configuration frequently changes in CPSs, the more detailed a model is, the faster it will become outdated.

An effective security protection for CPSs should deal with the uncertainty and suggest probabilistic reasoning for various protection tasks.

15.5.2 Technical Strategies

To mitigate current weaknesses in IDPRS and CPS protection, the following technical strategies should be taken into consideration:

1. System design in CPSs should be design by security. Most of the current IT system vulnerabilities come from insufficient security design. A later fix cannot create a perfectly secure system. In CPSs, all the security control and security management functions should be embedded during the system design. This includes embedding the security functions into all the parts in the CPS security architecture, such as hardware, smart devices, software, protocols, data communication and data processing, and the interaction procedure between CPS components.
2. Intelligent technologies should be integrated into the IDPRS solutions to support autonomic properties (such as context awareness, situation awareness, self-management and cognitive properties) and resilience in CPS protection. Intelligent data analysis and process technology are useful in mining potential security (attack) patterns in large-scale security raw data (big data). The emerging organic computing [24] can support the implementation of optimized technical systems such as CPSs, which act more independently, flexibly, and autonomously; that is, they will need to exhibit lifelike properties. This technical progress can finally set up promising security protection solutions in CPSs.
3. Formal security models are good candidates to model complex security systems. CPSs are characteristic of these, integrating many new IT technologies and heterogeneous IT systems. Security threats to this complex SoS mainly cannot be controlled with the current patch and repair solution. Particularly, it is not easy to verify whether the defense approach fully covers the attack pattern. Thus, formal and security theories are necessary to model and analyze secure systems and the machine-assisted verification of their security properties. Such models and verification methods and tools should be effective in real applications and should be demonstrated for many different kinds of systems: for example, to ensure secure information flow in programs, operating systems, and hardware; to verify the security of cryptographic protocols; to verify properties of cryptographic functions; and to defend web-based systems from various security attacks.
4. Holistic social-technical security solutions are a macrocomprehensive approach to CPS security protection. Pure technical solutions can only solve the technical problems on the micro scale. Obviously, CPSs are not only pure technical systems, but integrated sociotechnical systems. Thus, not only the physical system and the cybersystem, but also the business models, social regulations, government policies, economic status, education training, lifestyle, culture fostering, law system, human social behaviors and regulation, psychology, and public-private partnerships (PPP) should be included in the systems security strategies. Without the holistic solution, we cannot obtain a secure CPS and secure applications.

15.6 Conclusions

CPSs have additional security requirements due to the addition of physical control and communication channels, real-time requirements, and their common application to critical infrastructure. IDPRS have to meet the new challenges to security. To implement a reliable security protection system, we need to take security into account at the very start of the design process in CPSs by enumerating the specific information flow, control, and availability requirements and ensuring that those requirements are met through all parts of the design of the system, rather than attempting to meet them only with add-on security mechanisms. Intelligent technologies are good tools to deal with the challenging situations in CPS security using the intelligent information process, intelligent decision, and autonomic models. Formal and theoretic models for CPS security will help to simplify the complexity in numerous security threats and emerging attacks. As a socio-technical system, a holistic solution should be included in the whole CPS security infrastructure. Physical world protection, cyber-physical world protection, social world protection, and all the interactions between the different components throughout CPS transactions should be embraced in one security framework and be coordinated with each other. Finally, complete, efficient, robust, and resilient CPSs with full security are expected in realistic applications. Technical engineers, users, academic researchers, government sectors, and all CPS players should work together to build a usable and secure CPS.

Author Biography

Jianguo Ding is a senior lecturer at the University of Skövde, Sweden. Jianguo Ding holds the degree of a doctor engineer (Dr.-Ing.) in electronic engineering from the University of Hagen, Germany. He was a senior researcher at the University of Luxembourg from 2010 to 2013. He was awarded the European Research Consortium for Informatics and Mathematics "Alain Bensoussan" postdoctoral fellowship, which supported his research work at University of Luxembourg and the Norwegian University of Science and Technology from 2008 to 2010. Jianguo Ding is a senior member of the Institute of Electrical and Electronics Engineers and a member of the Association for Computing Machinery. His current research interests include network management and control, network security, wireless and mobile networks, network performance evaluation, intelligent technology, probabilistic reasoning, and complex networks. Dr. Ding has published several books, book chapters, journal papers and peer-reviewed conference papers in these areas. He serves on the editorial board for several international journals and serves as chair for several international workshops and conferences.

References

1. Rajkumar, R., Lee, I., Sha, L., and Stankovic, J. Cyber-physical systems: The next computing revolution. In *Proceedings of the 47th Design Automation Conference (DAC'10)*. ACM, New York, pp. 731–736, 2010.
2. Mo, Y., Kim, T. H.-H., Brancik, K., Dickinson, D., Lee, H., Perrig, A., and Sinopoli, B. Cyber–physical security of a smart grid infrastructure, *Proceedings of the IEEE*, vol. 100, no. 1, pp. 195–209, January 2012.
3. Lee, E. A. Cyber physical systems: Design challenges. In *11th IEEE International Symposium on Object Oriented Real-Time Distributed Computing (ISORC)*, Orlando, FL, pp. 363–369, May 5–7, 2008.

4. Sha, L., Gopalakrishnan, S., Liu, X., and Wang, Q. Cyber-physical systems: A new frontier. In *Machine Learning in Cyber Trust*, pp. 3–13. Springer, Berlin, 2009.
5. Gunes, V., Peter, S., Givargis, T., and Vahid, F. A survey on concepts, applications, and challenges in cyber-physical systems. *KSII Transactions on Internet and Information Systems*, pp. 4242–4268, 2014.
6. Venkatasubramanian, K. Security solutions for cyber-physical systems. PhD Dissertation. Arizona State University, Tempe, AZ, 2009.
7. Sinopoli, B. Cyber-physical security: A whole new ballgame. *IEEE Smart Grid*, November 2012.
8. Karnouskos, S., Stuxnet worm impact on industrial cyber-physical system security. In *IECON 2011—37th Annual Conference on IEEE Industrial Electronics Society*, pp. 4490–4494, November 7–10, 2011.
9. Banerjee, A., Venkatasubramanian, K. K., Mukherjee, T., and Gupta, S. K. S. Ensuring safety, security, and sustainability of mission-critical cyber–physical systems. *Proceedings of the IEEE*, vol. 100, no. 1, pp. 283–299, 2012.
10. Cardenas, A., Amin, S., Sinopoli, B., Giani, A., Perrig, A., and Sastry, S. Challenges for securing cyber physical systems. In *Workshop on Future Directions in Cyber-physical Systems Security*, DHS, Newark, NJ, July 23, 2009.
11. Sundaram, A. An introduction to intrusion detection. *Crossroads*, vol. 2, no. 4, pp. 3–7, 1996.
12. Scarfone, K., and Mell, P. *Guide to Intrusion Detection and Prevention Systems (IDPS)*. Computer Security Resource Center (National Institute of Standards and Technology), Gaithersburg, MD, pp. 800–894, 2007.
13. Stakhanova, N., Basu, S., and Wong, J. A taxonomy of intrusion response systems. *International Journal of Information and Computer Security*, vol. 1, no. 1/2, pp. 169–184, 2007.
14. Whitman, M. E., and Mattord, H. J. Principles of information security. *Cengage Learning EMEA*. Thomson Course Technology, Boston, MA, pp. 289–, 2009.
15. Liao, H., Lin, C. R., Lin, Y., and Tung, K. Review: Intrusion detection system: A comprehensive review. *Journal of. Network and Computer Application*, vol. 36, no. 1, pp. 16–24, 2013.
16. Amin, S., Schwartz, G. A., and Hussain, A. In quest of benchmarking security risks to cyber-physical systems. *IEEE Network*, vol. 27, no. 1, pp. 19, 24, 2013.
17. Ding, J., Bouvry, P., and Balasingham, I. Management challenges for emerging wireless networks. In: Makaya, C., and Pierre, S. (Eds.), *Emerging Wireless Networks: Concepts, Techniques and Applications.* CRC Press, Boca Raton, FL, pp. 3–34, 2012.
18. Bellavista, P., Corradi, A., Fanelli, M., and Foschini, L. A survey of context data distribution for mobile ubiquitous systems. *ACM Computer Surveys*, vol. 44, no. 24, 45, pp. 1–24, 2012.
19. Franke, U., and Brynielsson, J. Cyber situational awareness—A systematic review of the literature. *Computers & Security*, vol. 46, pp. 18–31, 2014.
20. MITRE. http://www.mitre.org/capabilities/cybersecurity/situation-awareness. Accessed on January 22, 2014.
21. Thomas, R. W., DaSilva, L. A., and MacKenzie, A. B. Cognitive networks. In *Proceedings of 1st IEEE International Symposium on New Frontiers in Dynamic Spectrum Access Networks (DySPAN)*, pp. 352–360, 2005.
22. Conti, M., Das, S. K., Bisdikian, C., Kumar, M., Ni, L. M., Passarella, A., Roussos, G., Tröster, G., Tsudik, G., and Zambonelli, F. Looking ahead in pervasive computing: Challenges and opportunities in the era of cyber–physical convergence. *Pervasive and Mobile Computing*, vol. 8, no. 1, pp. 2–21, 2012.
23. Leszek, L., Gupta, A., Kamal, Z., and Yang, Z. Opportunistic resource utilization networks: A new paradigm for specialized ad hoc networks. *Computers & Electrical Engineering*, vol. 36, no. 2, pp. 328–340, 2010.
24. Würtz, R. P. (Ed.) *Organic Computing (Understanding Complex Systems)*. Springer, Berlin, 2008.

Chapter 16

Security-Integrated Quality-of-Service Paradigm for Cyber-Physical Systems

Zubair Md. Fadlullah
Tohoku University

Contents

16.1 Introduction ... 394
16.2 Overview of CPS Characteristics and QoS–Security Requirements ... 396
16.3 QoS–Security Integration Initiatives: Literature Review ... 397
16.4 Interaction between QoS and Security Metrics ... 399
16.5 A QoS–Security Integration Technique ... 402
16.6 Future Directions ... 404
16.7 Conclusion ... 405
Author Biography ... 406
References ... 407

Abstract: In many organizations, separate groups are responsible for dealing with security and quality of service (QoS). Hence, services requiring assured delivery could end up reserving excessive resources and potentially denying service to other applications that are security (but not QoS) critical. This could be a big problem in cyber-physical systems (CPSs), which are becoming more dominant and have recently gained much attention. Therefore, QoS and security requirements must be considered together rather than in isolation. In this vein, a simple yet effective network policy framework has been designed that is able to identify the conflicting goals of security and QoS requirements that are perceived by the users. Our framework offers security-integrated QoS for resolving QoS–security (QoSec) conflicts in a balanced fashion.

Keywords: Cyber-physical systems (CPSs); Quality of service (QoS); Joint QoS security (QoSec)

16.1 Introduction

At the beginning, the Internet was egalitarian in terms of providing service guarantees. The general meaning of best-effort delivery in the Internet implied a likelihood that a given user's packets might be dropped due to congestion or overloading. Because all users were supposedly "friendly," deliberate overloading (which later became infamously known as the denial-of-service [DoS] attack) was not perceived as a viable threat. Also, it was mutually agreed among users that the protocols requiring strict service guarantees were not suitable for Internet applications. These simple assumptions were practical for that era when the bandwidth was indeed limited (readers may refer back to the original Internet [i.e., the Advanced Research Projects Agency Network—ARPANET], which operated up to 56 Kbps!). As a consequence, the original Internet excluded most real-time communications applications such as voice calls, video streaming, and so forth. As the communication bandwidth continued to increase and communication delays were dramatically reduced due to the invention and wide adoption of faster and reliable transmission media, the Internet could accommodate real-time services (e.g., half- and full-duplex audio and video services) with strict delay and jitter requirements. However, accommodation of such real-time services was done through resource reservation to satisfy the delivery goals.

The Internet has come a long way since its origin. The once-simple Internet is evolving toward the Internet of Things (IoT), which maintains a hierarchy of communication networks that collect information by sensing, exploring, processing, aggregating, and distributing it in a demand-driven and controlled way. The IoT aims at functional connectivity and relationships in the physical space (between analog and digital entities) that arises in various cyber-physical systems (CPSs), a current research hotspot. These CPSs integrate analog and computational hardware, middleware, and cyberware, thereby creating synergy between the entities of the physical space and cyberspace. A CPS essentially merges the physical equipment with computation elements for specific purposes. The cyber and physical elements of a CPS are tightly combined to allow effective coordination between them. The CPSs that have frequently appeared in the recent literature are typically physical and engineered systems whose operations are monitored. For instance, CPSs can nowadays be found in a plethora of areas including the smart energy grid, health care, chemical processes, the automotive and aerospace industry, the transportation sector, civil and military infrastructure, and so forth. CPSs have clearly defined quality-of-service (QoS) requirements that are specifically driven by the dynamics of the physical environment in which they operate. The QoS of a CPS is directly related to its performance. The research, implementation, and deployment of a CPS-centric QoS primarily focus on challenges including bandwidth guarantees, packet loss rate, end-to-end delay, delay variance or jitter, and other performance-related quality guarantees when transmitting information over the CPS. In the literature, QoS provisioning models such as Integrated Services (IntServ) [1] and Differentiated Services (DiffServ) [2] architectures are the most well-known ones to provide QoS for real-time traffic. However, recent developments in CPSs have unlocked new directions for researchers in the field of QoS. In other words, communication networks have evolved and have become quite complex, particularly when combined with physical systems. Consider a simple example of a smart energy grid, which is deemed by many to be an excellent example of a CPS where the power generation and supply grid consist of both physical equipment (e.g., transformers and sensors) and communication infrastructure (control center, smart energy meters, etc.). The smart energy meters provide great convenience for customers to communicate with their electricity company so that in addition to checking their energy use, they can express their energy demand in advance. The communication delay between the electricity company's control center and its customers should be minimal and reliable to estimate the demand and the actual supply of electricity according to hourly need. Thus, these are certain QoS requirements from the point of view of customers. Customers can access their energy usage report, energy bills, energy demand requests, and so forth via wireless devices, for example, laptop computers, portable data assistants (PDAs), or smartphones. In such a CPS, the use of wireless technology is anticipated to increase by leaps and bounds for transmitting QoS-sensitive applications, which often comprise sensitive and crucial information. Thus, in addition to the stringent QoS requirements, security is also a critical issue in the CPS. As a consequence, it is also essential to provide security along with QoS in a CPS. In addition, depending on the particular nature of each application that is used (e.g., non-real-time applications or real-time applications with non-adaptive or adaptive requirements), its security levels may be perceived differently by the end users of a CPS. The conventional QoS provisioning approaches may allow such applications to receive assurance on particular QoS parameters such as bandwidth and delay. However, these approaches do not have the adequate support of integrated and differentiated levels of security. Therefore, in order to introduce the research of QoS in these new frontiers of CPS, the concept of QoS must be integrated with multilevel security in an effective way.

Security leaks can be considered to increase with the scalability of the CPS. In the existing literature, even cryptographic protocols, which are used to provide secure communications, were often found to be under threat from diverse attacks. In a large-scale CPS, security concerns cannot be combatted by merely deploying conventional intrusion detection and prevention systems. The conventional intrusion detection systems (IDSs) rely heavily on inspecting the payload contents, and therefore may increase the communication delay while performing such an inspection. As a consequence, it becomes more difficult to provide the best possible QoS for the services provided during ongoing security attacks and intrusion detection–based countermeasures. In fact, the few conventional approaches that exist in the literature for including security parameters with QoS parameters could lead to further security risks because they consider only one or two QoS parameters in isolated cases rather than taking into account all of the QoS and security parameters in a tightly coupled fashion. Therefore, in addition to detecting security attacks, it is also essential to design a framework that tightly combines both QoS and security aspects.

Although theoretically simple, in practice it has been difficult to offer end users multiple levels of security with multiple levels of performance choices [3]. In order to address this important issue, the concept of quality of security services (QoSS) has evolved and gained acceptance among researchers aiming to protect sensitive information while maintaining QoS in an effective manner. QoSS approaches take into consideration security attributes such as the choice of authentication scheme, the selection of the cryptographic algorithm, and the lengths of the encryption/decryption keys. In fact, the protection of information exchanges over a CPS is usually achieved by exploiting well-known security mechanisms and cryptographic protocols. One limitation of such security enforcements is that they might lead to QoS degradation because of their impacts on the QoS attributes, for example, resources, bandwidth, and delay requirements. The development of a CPS with both QoS and security is, however, a challenging task because of their conflicting objectives, a set of joint QoS–security (QoSec) design decisions. In this chapter, to address these issues, we develop a game theoretic real-time system for a CPS that provides an appropriate QoSec level.

The remainder of the chapter is structured as follows. In Section 16.2, we provide an overview of the characteristics of a CPS and its QoS as well as its security requirement. Section 16.3 briefly describes a literature review covering the existing QoSec integration initiatives. In Section 16.4, the interaction between the QoS and security metrics is explained. A QoSec integration technique is presented for CPSs in Section 16.5. In Section 16.6, open issues along with future directions of QoSec integration in CPSs are discussed. Finally, Section 16.7 summarizes the content of the chapter.

16.2 Overview of CPS Characteristics and QoS–Security Requirements

Figure 16.1 shows a number of diverse autonomous CPSs. What is common among these CPSs is that each CPS comprises a large number of physical devices (i.e., for measuring and instrumenting data, and computation), which are embedded and interconnected through a cybernetwork (facilitated by fixed and mobile communication nodes), as shown in the figure. The various autonomous subsystems of these CPSs provide certain services for the end users. For example, in the medical system, medical information sharing is achieved by connecting different medical sensors, emergency health-care units (e.g., ambulances), and so forth, over an appropriate communication network. Since the vital sign measurement data should be processed with high priority, the computational time should be minimal and reliable, and the time to report to the appropriate medical personnel over the communication network needs to be as early as possible to take prompt medical action. In other words, these are the specific QoS requirements of the medical CPS. On the other hand, in a cyber-physical traffic control system aiming to provide intelligent transportation, traffic lights, radars, and motion detecting sensors, surveillance cameras are interlinked so that the traffic information can be collected and processed in real-time to apprise users (car drivers, police patrols, and so forth) of the prevailing traffic conditions, navigational instructions, and so forth. The QoS requirement of the traffic control CPS can be described in terms of the requirement that the provided instructions should not be laggy and must be reliable so as to minimize travel time and avert potential accidents. The smart grid system has also often been considered as a large-scale CPS whereby users can communicate bidirectionally with their power supplier. Various power generation units in addition to the power retailer form localized microgrids that focus on renewable energy production, exploiting solar panels, wind turbines, hybrid car batteries, and so forth. It is worth noting that in the smart grid, different equipment is used such as power generation

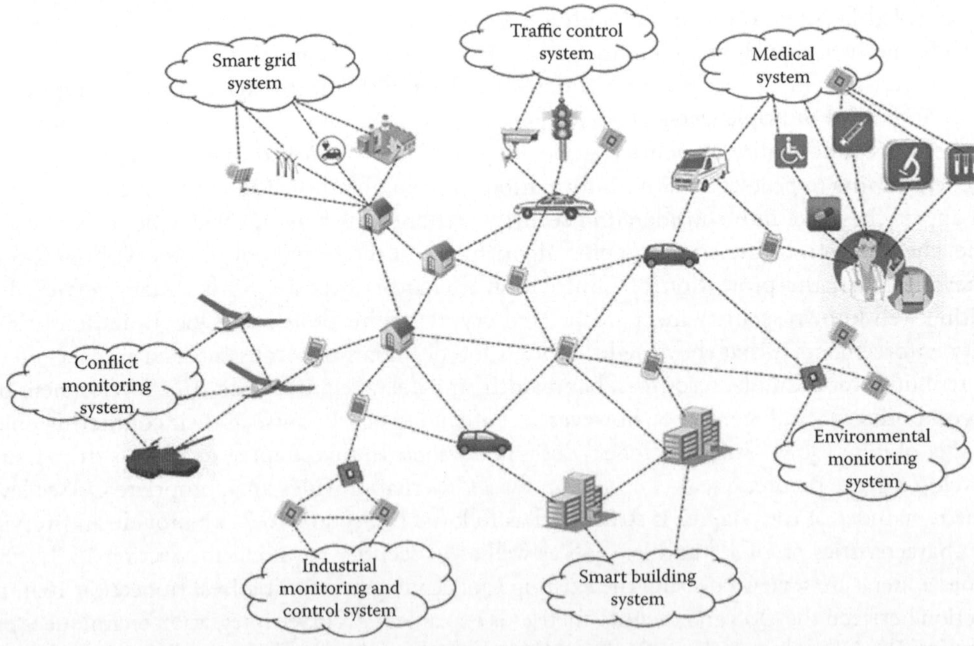

Figure 16.1 Different CPSs require specific QoS requirements.

elements, transformers, measurement devices, monitoring sensors, and smart meters, which are all essential components of the cyber-physical power grid. To realize the smart grid vision, it is indeed important to have guaranteed QoS for the communication and networking technology that is used in its various stages including power generation, transmission, and distribution to the customer applications. For example, low-cost wireless protocols (e.g., IEEE 802.15.4 Zigbee and IEEE 802.15.1 Bluetooth) are particularly useful for power distribution system monitoring and customer applications. However, they inherently lack the support of QoS, and typically have a short propagation distance. In a similar vein, examples of other CPSs shown in Figure 16.1 include a conflict monitoring system, an industrial monitoring and control system, a smart building system, and an environmental monitoring system, each of which has its specific QoS needs. Thus, it can be said that in the near future, we can anticipate that CPSs will become widespread in virtually all areas of science and engineering, for example, industry, health care, traffic planning, defense, environmental science, and the energy grid, as well as our everyday life. From an abstract viewpoint, the communication technology serves the CPS as an interface between the cybersystem and the physical system. The communication elements gather information about the physical world by exploiting the communication technology, and based on the obtained information, the actuators respond appropriately by taking relevant actions on the physical world. In this way, the communication systems enable the cybersystems to monitor and exploit the behavior of the physical world. As a result, the performance level and eventual usability of a CPS are subject to the fulfillment of the QoS requirements of the underlying communication technology. In other words, if the QoS requirements of the cyberside of the CPS can be satisfied, we will be able to improve our quality of life by better interacting with our physical world.

In addition to the QoS requirement of the CPS, what is often overlooked yet is always cherished by any human user is the ability to maintain security in terms of safeguarding his or her relevant data from prying eyes. Security is a sensitive issue, whether you consider the physical world or the cyberworld. Again refer to Figure 16.1, for instance. Consider the health-care cyber-physical system, which we refer to as the medical CPS. Thousands of patients visit a city hospital; their information is supposed to be protected by a "doctor–patient" confidentiality agreement. While the medical CPS offers convenience to users (i.e., doctors, patients, and emergency caregivers) to access information, there is a chance that confidential information could be leaked if the information is not accessed in a "secure" manner. From capturing the vital signs of patients to transmitting them to a computational element for information processing and then sending the processed information to the users, security measures should be adopted so as to avert leakage of confidential information to any third party. Similar examples can be provided for all the CPSs shown in Figure 16.1, readily showing the readers the importance of securing information collection and transmission in a CPS. Therefore, the CPS can be characterized as a cyber-physical system that has stringent QoS and security issues. None can be overlooked. However, is it possible to consider both of them at the same time? More technically speaking, is it possible to priortize one without jeopardizing the other? This is the core question that we will address in the remainder of this chapter.

16.3 QoS–Security Integration Initiatives: Literature Review

To the best of our knowledge, existing CPS architectures address QoS requirements and security requirements in an isolated manner. The closest research work that we can derive in the literature involving QoSec integration is usually in the small-sized wireless communication networks. In this section, we will review recently introduced ideas to facilitate security-integrated QoS in different wireless networks. This will help the readers to understand how challenging it is to combine the security requirements with QoS demands in a CPS.

The work conducted in [4] clarified that QoS and security have conventionally been considered as two independent entities. However, it was also pointed out that they always impact on each other in different scenarios; therefore, it is important to study the optimization between them. The work in [4] proposed algorithms to evaluate security levels with three main characteristics, namely authentication, data integrity, and confidentiality. Furthermore, a model was proposed to measure the interaction between QoS delay and security in various scenarios, heterogeneous users, and disparate services. The model was shown to be useful to get better performance for network service, especially in rigorous network circumstance.

Encouraging research on the QoS combined with security was conducted in [5], which illustrated how security could be added to the conventional QoS framework as an extra dimension. A middleware was designed through which IEEE 802.11-based wireless ad hoc network users can express their security needs along with one specific QoS requirement, namely end-to-end delay. Based on a user's selected level of security and delay requirements, the middleware tries to obtain the minimum end-to-end delay while offering the highest possible security level to the user that is somewhat proportional to the encryption key length. In this way, the middleware could achieve a balance or a trade-off between delay and security levels under changing traffic loads. Even though this tunable bandwidth security framework for QoS delay and security requirements was one of the first substantial works found in the literature, it has its shortcoming. In particular, a bandwidth consuming attack might exploit the way in which the encryption key lengths are dynamically downgraded to maintain a reasonable end-to-end delay requirement for the user, enabling the attacker to execute cryptographic attacks more effectively and quickly because of the weakened encryption level. In one of our earlier works [6], the significance of the problem of dynamically adjusting the lengths of the encryption keys with varying end-to-end delays was illustrated.

The research work conducted in [7] shows two different ways of combining QoS and security in multimedia communication. The first way is to enforce security at the gateway level by performing security authentication when end-to-end QoS is violated. The second way is a QoS parameter protection security approach that is accomplished on the router level during the set-up phase. This is aimed at protecting the end-to-end QoS setup for multimedia transmission. These examples demonstrate that the interconnection between security and QoS is possible. It was also noted that this is the prerequisite for providing a careful selection of QoS and security mechanisms and policies at the right places at the right time. Security services such as encryption/decryption may introduce additional latencies, which may violate the delay requirements. Furthermore, the cryptographic algorithms, the processing time of which is data dependent, may lead to additional end-to-end delay and jitter. The infrequent cryptographic operations (e.g., rekeying and rehasing) may also cause similar issues. Security services may benefit from QoS measures, which somewhat limit delay and jitter. On the other hand, industry QoS usually operates under a commercial model that needs the assurance of network management services for provisioning, auditing, and billing. As a consequence, these QoS mechanisms may well exploit the existing network security services. For further information, readers are encouraged to review the reports published by the Center for Information Systems Security Studies and Research [8,9].

Some researchers consider the conflicting goal of simultaneously achieving QoS and security requirements as a problem, which may be solved by selecting an adequate adaptive theory. For instance, game theory, which has been applied to various disciplines such as economics, political science, and computer science, may be applied for choosing the adequate QoSec level. Game theory consists of a multiplayer decision problem whereby multiple players with different objectives may compete and interact/cooperate with one another to maximize their respective benefits. For instance, the two works in [10,11] exploit the cooperative game theory–based strategies to model the interaction between intruders and the IDS in a wired and a mobile ad hoc network, respectively. The applicability of game theory was demonstrated to be useful in various decision, analysis, and control algorithms in intrusion detection [12]. This work addressed the trade-offs among fundamental network security issues and attempted to find an appropriate decision from contrasting goals. On the other hand, the Bayesian Nash algorithm was employed in the work conducted by Liu et al. [13] to analyze the interaction between an intruder and a defender in both static and dynamic network settings with the aid of monitoring systems. Nash equilibrium–based game theoretic studies have also been conducted toward solving QoS problems (i.e., without any security incorporation) involving power and rate control problems where network users compete with each other to obtain maximum throughput with minimum energy consumption [14,15].

While the aforementioned research works focused on a few QoS or security aspects or both, they did not provide a broad picture of the QoSS model. In this chapter, we aim to present a complete QoSS solution based on game theory. In the next section, we describe our considered system model whereby the network users can negotiate with the system regarding their service and security level requirements.

16.4 Interaction between QoS and Security Metrics

In this section, the interaction between the QoS and security metrics is investigated. The QoS and security parameters that are usually taken into consideration in the existing literature are shown in Figure 16.2. It is worth noting that we consider these same QoS and security metrics from the existing literature for CPS communication. The QoS metrics include throughput (bandwidth use), delay, jitter, packet drop, fairness index, and reliability. On the other hand, the security parameters include authentication, authorization, message integrity, confidentiality, nonrepudiation, and so forth. In the following, we show some examples of the opposing or contrasting requirements of the QoS metrics and the security parameters.

Through the Tequila project, it has been found that the integrated security protocol impacts on resources during the initialization phase in which the security context is established (i.e., during key generation, negotiation of the used algorithms, and so forth). This consumes the processing power of the end host's memory, and also contributes to end-to-end delay. The specific protocol data (Internet protocol security [IPSec]/transport layer security [TLS] header) also consumes a

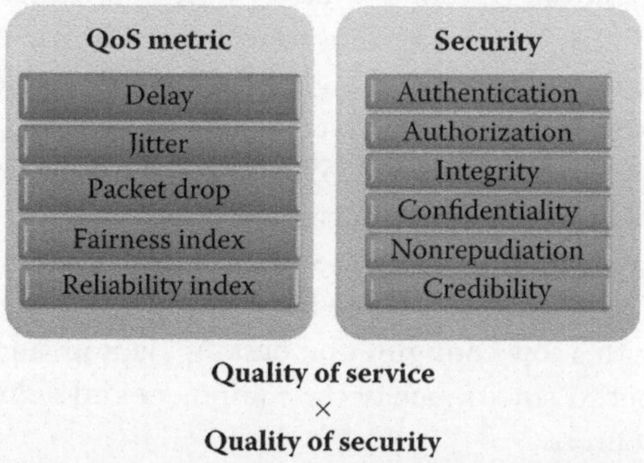

Figure 16.2 QoS and security parameters that need to be considered for a CPS.

Table 16.1 Cost of Bandwidth for Security-Enforced Protocols over User Datagram Protocol (UDP) and IPSec

Protocol		*Initialization Bandwidth (BW)*	*Streaming Bandwidth (BW/packet)*
UDP		Not applicable	1358
IPSec and AH	Authentication and integrity	1688	1382
IPSec and ESP	Authentication and integrity	1712	1382
IPSec and ESP	Confidentiality	1712	1378
IPSec and ESP	Confidentiality, authentication, and integrity	1712	1390

Source: S. Duflos, V. C. Gay, B. Kervella, and E. Horlait. Improving the SLA-based management of QoS for secure multimedia services. In Proceedings of 8th International Conference on Management of Multimedia Networks and Services (MMNS'05), Barcelona, Spain, October 2005.

higher bandwidth. To determine the precise impact of the security protocol on the network bandwidth, different security levels applied on IPSec revealed the bandwidth costs for a Moving Picture Experts Group (MPEG) video and a DVD sequence.

It was found that while the multimedia sequence quality, the confidentiality level, and the authentication and integrity level do not impact bandwidth costs, the choice of security services and the protocol have an impact on them. Table 16.1 [16] lists the increased bandwidth costs before and after the inclusion of security parameters. Bandwidth costs during the initialization phase and during streaming are expressed in bytes and bytes per second, respectively. Table 16.1 demonstrates that the bandwidth initialization cost only depends on the security protocol (i.e., encapsulating security payload [ESP] consumes more resources than the authentication header [AH]). During the streaming phase, the bandwidth consumption changes as per the chosen security services. On the other hand, confidentiality consumes less bandwidth in contrast to authentication and integrity.

Ong et al. [17] found how authentication delays might impact a desktop, laptop, and a portable tablet. Four authentication methods were taken into consideration, namely, password, message digest, 512-bit signature, and 1024-bit signature. For the password-based authentication, the delays experienced by the desktop, laptop, and tablet were approximately 30, 190, and 285 ms, respectively. The message digest–based authentication led to similar delays on the desktop and the laptop; however, it contributed to a much higher delay on the tablet (approximately 314 ms). The signature-based authentication using 512 bits, on the other hand, increased the delay on all three types of machines (approximately 464, 1559, and 3970 ms on the desktop, laptop, and the tablet, respectively). The delays dramatically increased when 1024-bit signatures were employed for authentication. The delays experienced by the users on the desktop, laptop, and tablet leaped to approximately 6,378, 15,656, and 59,078 ms, respectively. It is worth noting that the findings from [17] were associated with a low configuration desktop, laptop, and tablet; however, they can still be useful in the CPS context since much of the equipment and many of the sensors are usually equipped with low-spec resources.

Next, we briefly describe and explain the multilevel security model [5] for dynamically adjusting the security levels for the varied QoS delay requirements of the users, as shown in Table 16.2.

Table 16.2 Average Delays for Performing Cryptographic Operations at End Users for Different Cryptographic Key Sizes

Cryptographic Key Size (bits)	*Contributed Delay (ms)*
512	24
256	16
192	14
128	10

In this case, the results obtained are from a wireless network scenario whereby different key sizes (128, 192, 256, and 512 bits) for encryption are used. The larger key size implies stronger security, which is more difficult for malicious users to crack. This means that a user is likely to select and use the highest key size to ensure that the packets that he or she is sending and receiving are well secure. However, the encryption key size does have an impact on the QoS end-to-end delay, as shown in Table 16.2. In fact, the relationship between the encryption key size and the end-to-end delay was found to be almost linear in this particular scenario. This means a CPS with many users, where each user wants to use the largest encryption key, may lead to significant communication delay, which may substantially degrade the quality of experience of the users. Therefore, if the users have the chance to flexibly lower their security choice by selecting a weaker encryption key in a dynamic fashion, it might be possible to communicate with acceptable delay (which again depends on the application used in the CPS). For the readers to easily grasp this idea, Figure 16.3 demonstrates how an increased security level in terms of the encryption key impacts QoS end-to-end delay. Indeed, this gives rise to the idea of multilevel security levels, which can be integrated with the different QoS levels. For a multiuser scenario in a CPS, the main challenge is how to dynamically determine both the QoS and security levels for a number of users so that they can experience acceptable communication with sufficient security.

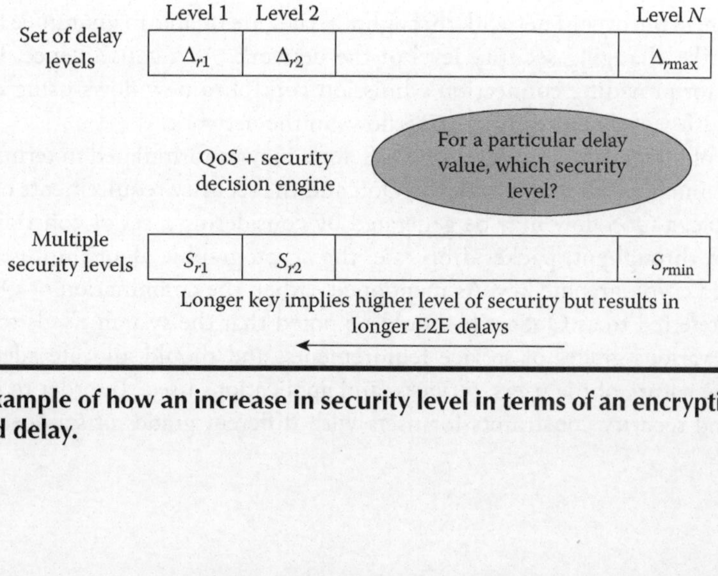

Figure 16.3 Example of how an increase in security level in terms of an encryption key impacts QoS end-to-end delay.

16.5 A QoS–Security Integration Technique

As a continuation of [6], where the problem of the impact of security on the QoS is stated, the objective of QoSec integration is to design a flexible framework that ensures a high level of protection for the network from malicious attacks. However, in the absence of a potential threat, the framework, in an autonomic way, should be able to relax the system's overall security requirements in case the required QoS levels are not being met under the current security settings. The basic concept of the framework is depicted in Figure 16.4, which shows a network security advisory system. The advisory system is used for network monitoring and diagnosis. The security advisory system defines the threat level of the network based on the events reported by IDSs or other entities or both, such as firewalls and the IDSs of other collaborating networks. In other words, an IDS can be part of this advisory system that monitors network intrusions or malicious attacks to enable it to determine a number of threat levels ranging from low to severe. The advisory system analyzes the events in specific time slots and constantly updates the threat level. For each threat level and each associated security level, a particular defensive measure can be applied. Threat Level 1 (i.e., low) corresponds to a normal network state when no malicious activities are reported. In contrast, threat level "severe" implies that the system is either under potential attack or is in grave danger of encountering a particular attack. The threat level of a given time slot may be decided by the increasing/decreasing number of anomalous or suspicious events that exceed a detection threshold that is decided a priori.

Based on the alert level indicated by the security advisory system, we are interested in designing a security/QoS policy control that indicates the security level that should correspond to a desired QoS level. When under the indicated threat level, the security advisory system recommends a range of security levels (e.g., range of encryption/decryption key lengths, anomaly detection score, and worm signature lengths). We are interested in finding out the highest security level that should be selected so that the QoS requirements of users are not compromised. If, for a particular security level from within the recommended range, the QoS requirements of users cannot be satisfied (i.e., this can be inferred from a learning phase), the security/QoS policy control unit asks for security relaxation. It should be noted here that if the network is under potential attack and the security advisory system recommends the highest security level, the system has to stick to the recommended level although this decision may compromise the required QoS. QoS relaxation thus becomes mandatory in such a case.

Traditional opportunistic scheduling approaches (e.g., the work in [5]) can exploit the multiuser diversity gain and the dynamic nature of wireless channels. However, while such approaches attempt to maximize the overall network throughput, they are unable to guarantee flexible resource reservation with the changing security level of the network. As a consequence, it is essential to devise a scheme for providing connection admission control to new flows using their impact on the QoS and security level of already existing flows in the network.

The problem of integrating security with QoS flows may be formulated in terms of a set of constraints that take into consideration both the QoS and the security requirements of the concerned users. For example, a QoS flow may be generated by considering a set of constraints comprising end-to-end delay, throughput, packet drop rate, the cryptographic algorithm used, and also the length of the used cryptographic key. As mentioned earlier, the combination of QoS and security requirements is referred to as QoSec. It should be noted that the system needs to explicitly consider users with various grades of service requirements, and should allocate adequate resources depending on the nature of the users, services, and applications used. In order to guarantee these multiple QoS and security constraints for users with different grades of service, the underlying

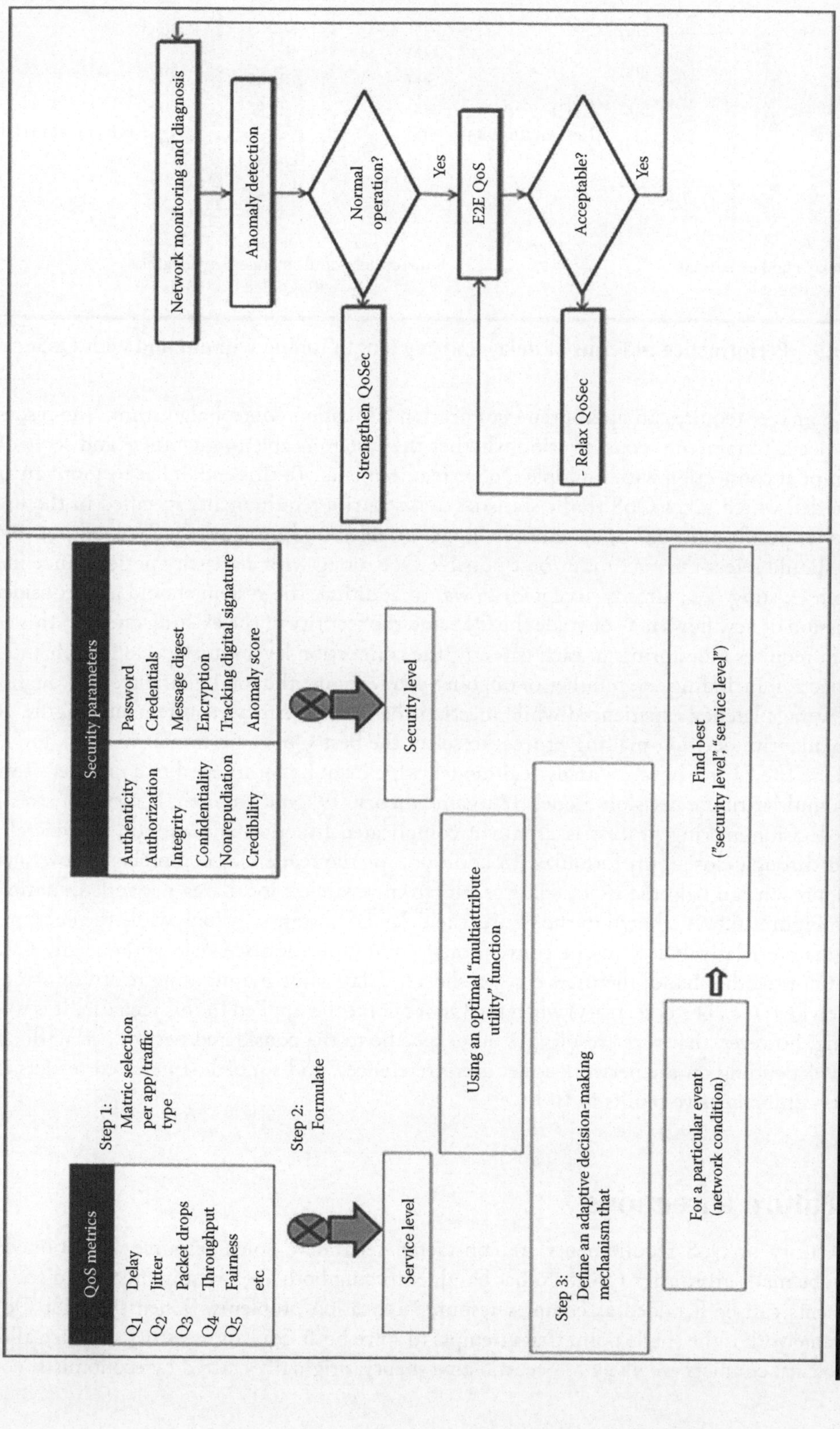

Figure 16.4 Concept of QoS and security integration (QoSec).

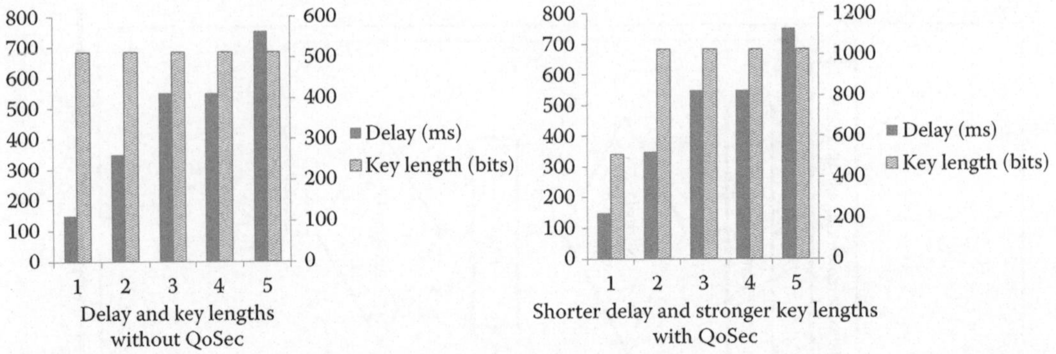

Figure 16.5 Performance in terms of delay and key length tuning without and with QoSec.

resource manager requires an appropriate connection admission control algorithm. The resource manager needs to take into consideration whether the system is able to guarantee and serve each new attempt at connection with multiple QoSec requirements. To this end, it has to adopt an analytical model, which takes QoS traffic statistics and security requirements specified in the users' service level specifications (SLS) as multiple input variables, and provides QoSS as output. By so doing, it should select the maximum/best possible QoS along with a security performance index made from existing (i.e., already accepted) flows. In addition, the system should also consider if the admission of new flows may degrade the QoS and the security of the existing ones. To this end, the system requires monitoring, at each gateway, the connection level statistics along each end-to-end connection including the number of ongoing connections, the total guaranteed throughput, and the average latency experienced while meeting the users' security requirements. Figure 16.4 shows an adaptive decision-making process to select the best QoSec performance index for each connection. The figure shows an analytical model, which can be formulated in a number of ways such as a multiattribute decision model [18], game theory [19], and so forth. It is worth stressing that the decision-making process is usually a complicated function and cannot, in general, be expressed through close-form formulas. In addition, for the readers to comprehend how such a QoSec approach can help the users, some results from a wireless local area network scenario are shown in Figure 16.5. As shown in the figure, the delay is substantially long while the encryption key lengths are relatively low in the conventional communication scenario without any QoSec control. On the other hand, the users enjoy a shorter delay while maintaining relatively stronger encryption keys (i.e., better security) when the QoSec control is applied in this scenario. It is worth reminding, however, that these results are quite specific to the considered network scenario, and may vary depending on the network scale, user preferences, and so forth. Interested readers may find more comprehensive results in [19].

16.6 Future Directions

When security or QoS requirements are considered separately, some resource allocation decisions can be made arbitrarily. On the other hand, enforcing both QoS requirements and security requirements can be heralded as complex resource allocation problems. When the joint QoSec policy framework is the single point that attempts to solve both QoS and security resource allocation problems, conflicts are likely to occur. Game theory, originally crafted by economists, could be a potential avenue in resolving such conflicts as it has been extensively utilized in solving many conflict problems arising in computer networks. One problem with the game theory is, however, that it considers the involved players as humans whereas the CPSs mainly deal with machines. To take into account the subjectivity of humans and the objectivity of machines, prospect theory in conjunction with game theory could also be considered in solving such complex resource allocation problems. However, it should be noted that the balanced QoS and security levels offered to all users by adopting such approaches might not necessarily indicate that each and every user receives the "best" QoS or security level or both. In other words, such approaches may or may not be able to achieve optimized (from a traditional optimization point of view) QoSec levels. How to guarantee the optimal allocation of joint QoS and security levels remains an open research issue. Furthermore, current policy framework systems can adequately deal with the static resolution of requirements for security or QoS. However, it is going to be a big leap to deal with security and QoS together as the requirements tend to become more dynamic in nature. As a consequence, the policy framework systems will have to continue to evolve to deal with interactions between administrative domains, more dynamic network requirements, and new network services.

16.7 Conclusion

In many organizations, separate groups are responsible for dealing with security and QoS. As a result, services that require assured delivery could reserve excessive resources and potentially deny service to other applications that are security (but not QoS) critical. Furthermore, the protocols that are used for negotiating QoS agreements may be subject to attack or interference by nonparticipating users. Additionally, security services such as encryption/decryption can result in a delay requirements violation since they introduce additional delays. Cryptographic algorithms, the timing of which is data dependent, could contribute to additional jitter (i.e., irregularities in the transmission delay). Irregular operations such as rekeying may also lead to additional jitter. Therefore, there is a need to incorporate QoS measures into security, and vice versa, to such an extent that the QoS measures limit delay and jitter in an appreciable way while meeting the security needs of users. The motivation behind this chapter was, therefore, to reveal the fact that security services can ensure the safety of both the users and the service providers of a CPS, and complement the QoS. Indeed, both QoS and security services affect the entire network infrastructure. However, security and QoS attributes impact one another. For instance, without adequate information pertaining to the correct QoS requirements of the end users, a poor choice of encryption algorithms and cryptographic key size, or a strict level of security enforcement by the IDS may reduce the effectiveness of the QoS performance. On the other hand, in the absence of information regarding the security requirements, a poor allocation of QoS levels may lead to a DoS.

As a consequence, QoS and security requirements must be taken into consideration together. To this end, we showed how a simple yet effective network policy framework can identify the conflicting goals of security and QoS requirements that are perceived by users. The security and QoS requirements can be entered into the framework using the feedback obtained from an alert/advisory system, which is typically an IDS. The security policy (including a library and taxonomy of different threats and the best possible countermeasure against each threat), along with the QoS policy, should be carefully implemented in the advisory system so that it can tune the QoSec parameters in an appropriate manner, and the QoSec framework can obtain sufficient information about the network system, security requirements, and QoS requirements, thereby identifying and resolving their conflicting requirements.

To summarize, enforcing both security and QoS requirements can be considered a complex resource allocation problem. The existing literature with similar problems reveals that treating the conflicts between QoS and security metrics as a risk management problem could be a useful way to design and build a QoSec-integrated system for resolving their conflicts in a balanced manner. Using this approach, risk factors such as the resource conflict among QoS and security services can be readily identified by obtaining feedback from users. On identifying the risk factors, appropriate risk mitigation techniques can be adopted to address the resource allocation trade-offs pertaining to the QoS and security services in the CPS.

Author Biography

Zubair Md. Fadlullah is an assistant professor at the Graduate School of Information Sciences, Tohoku University, Japan. He also serves as a computer science faculty member at the prestigious international Islamic University of Technology in Bangladesh. He is a senior member of the Institute of Electrical and Electronics Engineers and the Institute of Electrical and Electronics Engineers Communications Society. Dr. Fadlullah holds a PhD in applied information sciences, which he obtained from Tohoku University in March 2011. He has made a noteworthy contribution to the research community through his technical papers in scholarly journals, magazines, and international conferences in various areas of networking and communications. In recognition of his outstanding research contributions, he was awarded the prestigious Dean's and President's Awards from Tohoku University in March 2011. He was also acclaimed with the best paper award at Globecom 2014 and the International Wireless Communications & Mobile Computing Conference 2009. He was a member of the Japanese team involved with the prestigious A3 Foresight Project supported by the Japan Society for the Promotion of Science, the National Natural Science Foundation of China, and the National Research Foundation of Korea, which comprised prominent researchers in the field of networking and communications from the mentioned countries.

Dr. Fadlullah was a cochair in the Ad Hoc and Sensor Networking Symposium of the Institute of Electrical and Electronics Engineers International Conference on Communications 2014 and a chair in the invited session on smart grid in the 2011 International Conference on Wireless Communications and Signal Processing. He has been serving as a technical committee member for several Institute of Electrical and Electronics Engineers Globecoms, International Conference on Communications, Symposium on Personal, Indoor and Mobile Radio Communications, Wireless Communications and Networking Conference, and Wireless Communications and Signal Processing conferences for a number of years. He is an associate editor of the Institute of Electrical and Electronics Engineers Internet of Things (IoT). He also served as an editor of the *Ad Hoc & Sensor Wireless Networks* journal. He has also been actively engaged in helping editorial members of prestigious Institute of Electrical and Electronics Engineers transactions (including Transactions on Vehicular Technology, Transactions on Parallel and Distributed Systems, and Transactions on Smart Grid) to manage and delegate reviews in an efficient manner. He was a recipient of the Meritorious Service Certificate as "Top Quality Reviewer" awarded by the Institute of Electrical and Electronics Engineers Transactions on Parallel and Distributed Systems. His research covers a wide range of areas including the smart grid, energy efficiency in wireless networks, sensor and ad hoc networking, network security, and the application of game theory in computer networking problems.

References

1. R. Braden, D. Clark, and S. Shenker. Integrated services in the Internet architecture: An overview. Internet Engineering Task Force, RFC 1633, June 1994.
2. S. Blake, D. Black, M. Carlson, E. Davies, Z. Wang, and W. Weiss. An architecture for differentiated services. Internet Engineering Task Force, RFC 2475, December 1998.
3. S. N. Foley, S. Bistarelli, B. O'Sullivan, J. Herbert, and G. Swart. Multilevel security and quality of protection. In *First Workshop on Quality of Protection*, Como, Italy, September 2005.
4. J. Chen, H. Zeng, C. Hu, and Z. Ji. Optimization between security and delay of quality-of-service. *Journal of Network and Computer Applications*, vol. 34, no. 2, pp. 603–608, 2011.
5. W. He and K. Nahrstedt, An integrated solution to delay and security support in wireless networks. In *Proceedings IEEE Wireless Communications and Networking Conference (WCNC)*, Las Vegas, NV, April 2006.
6. Z. Fadlullah, T. Taleb, N. Nasser, and N. Kato. Exploring the security requirements for quality of service in combined wired and wireless networks. In *Proceedings of IWCMC'09*, Leipzig, Germany, June 2009.
7. L. S. Cordoso. Quality and security usability. *ITU-T Workshop on End-to-End QoE/QoS*, Geneva, Switzerland, June 2006.
8. C. Irvine, T. Levin, E. Spyropoulou, and B. Allen. Security as a dimension of quality of service in active service environments. In *Proceedings on Active Middleware Services Workshop*, San Francisco, CA, August 2001.
9. E. Spyropoulou, C. Irvine, T. Levin, and B. Allen. Managing costs and variability of security services. In *IEEE Symposium on Security and Privacy*, Oakland, CA, May 2001.
10. H. Otrok, M. Mehrandish, C. Assi, M. Debbabi, and P. Bhattacharya. Game theoretic models for detecting network intrusions. *Computer Communications*, vol. 31, no. 10, pp. 1934–1944, June 2008.
11. H. Otrok, N. Mohammed, L. Wang, M. Debbabi, and P. Bhattacharya. A game-theoretic intrusion detection model for mobile ad hoc networks. *Computer Communications*, vol. 31, no. 4, pp. 708–721, March 2008.
12. T. Alpcan and T. Basar. A game theoretic analysis of intrusion detection in access control systems. In *Proceedings of 43rd IEEE Conference on Decision and Control (CDC)*, Paradise Island, Bahamas, December 2004.
13. Y. Liu, C. Comaniciu, and H. Man. A Bayesian game approach for intrusion detection in wireless ad hoc networks. In *Proceedings on ACM GameNets'06*, Pisa, Italy, October 2006.
14. L. Chen and J. Leneutre. A game theoretic framework of distributed power and rate control in IEEE 802.11 WLANS. *IEEE Journal on Selected Areas in Communications*, vol. 26, no. 7, pp. 1128–1137, September 2008.
15. L. Chen and J. Leneutre. Selfishness, not always a nightmare: Modeling selfish mac behaviors in wireless mobile ad hoc networks. In *Proceedings of ICDCS'07*, Pisa, Italy, October 2007.
16. S. Duflos, V. C. Gay, B. Kervella, and E. Horlait. Improving the SLA-based management of QoS for secure multimedia services. In *Proceedings of 8th International Conference on Management of Multimedia Networks and Services (MMNS'05)*, Barcelona, Spain, October 2005.
17. C. S. Ong, K. Nahrtedt, and Y. Wanghong. Quality of protection for mobile multimedia applications. In *Proceedings of International Conference on Multimedia and Expo (ICME'03)*, July 2003.
18. T. Taleb and Y. Hadjadj-Aoul. QoS2: A framework for integrating quality of security with quality of service. *Security and Communications Network*, vol. 5, no. 12, pp. 1462–1470, December 2012.
19. Z. M. Fadlullah, A. V. Vasilakos, and N. Kato. A game theoretic approach to integrate security with quality of service. In *Proc. IEEE ICC'12*, Ottawa, Canada, June 2012.

References

[illegible]

Index

A

ABC, *see* Attribute-based credentials (ABC)
ABE, *see* Attribute-based encryption (ABE)
ABP, *see* Attribute-based privacy (ABP)
Abstract Syntax Notation One (ASN1), 20, 21
ACE, *see* Authentication and Authorization for Constrained Environments (ACE)
Active attacker, 123, 131, 133, 134
Active attacks, 121, 130–131
Address space layout permutation (ASLP), 65, 80–81
Address space randomization, 64, 65, 68, 80, 82
Advanced encryption standard (AES), 65, 135, 267, 291
AH, *see* Authentication header (AH)
AIR, *see* Anonymous information retrieval (AIR)
AMControl, 136
AMReceive, 136
AMSend, 136
Anomaly, 210–211, 337, 402
Anomaly-based detection, 177, 210
Anomaly-based intrusion detection system, 381–382
Anonymous information retrieval (AIR), 179
Application programming interface (API), 37–38, 84, 322, 324
Application simulator/federate, 181, 185
Application-specific integrated circuit (ASIC), 282
AS, *see* Authentication system (AS)
Ashton, K., 223
ASIC, *see* Application-specific integrated circuit (ASIC)
ASLP, *see* Address space layout permutation (ASLP)
ASN1, *see* Abstract Syntax Notation One (ASN1)
Assessment Platform for Multiple Interdependent Critical Infrastructures (AMICI), 314, 317–319, 321
Asymmetric ciphers, 290, 291–292
Attack classifications, in VANET environment, 171
Attacker profiles, in VANET environment, 171
Attribute-based credentials (ABC), 179
Attribute-based cryptography, 268
Attribute-based encryption (ABE), 212
Attribute-based privacy (ABP), 179
Authentication algorithms
  cryptography, 265–266
  general schemes, 266–269
  group authentication and, 269–270
  physical layer authentication and, 270
Authentication and Authorization for Constrained Environments (ACE), 251
Authentication and identification attacks, 172–173
Authentication header (AH), 248, 296, 400
Authentication server, 268
Authentication system (AS), 176, 179, 297
Auth-Lite scheme, 273
Authorization, 176, 226, 251, 377, 399
Automatic detection algorithm, of cross-site scripting, 337
Autonomic computing, 385–386
  cognitive computing, 387
  context-aware computing, 386
  self-management, 386–387
  situation-aware computing, 386
Autonomous vehicles, 198
  research areas in vehicular security, 213–214
  security challenges
    availability risks, 205–206
    confidentiality risks, 204–205
    integrity risks, 205
    mixed risks, 206–207
  security mechanisms for vehicular networks and, 207–213
  vehicular computing
    architectures, 199–200
    elements, 202–204
    scenarios, 201–202

B

Baseload generation, 4
Base station (BS), 122, 125, 127, 133–135, 140, 153–154
Basic Encoding Rules (BER), 20
Bayesian Nash algorithm, 399
BER, *see* Basic Encoding Rules (BER)
Bernoulli process, 337
BGP, *see* Border gateway protocol (BGP)
Big6™, 98

Biometrics and embedded systems, 297–298
BioSENSE (Biologically Inspired Secure Elastic Networked Sensor Environment), 79
Bitwise rotation, 85
Black-hole attack, 172, 173, 231
BLE, *see* Bluetooth low energy (BLE)
BLS, *see* Boneh, Lynn, Shacham (BLS) scheme
Bluetooth low energy (BLE), 251
Boneh, Lynn, Shacham (BLS) scheme, 15, 16
Boolean circuits, 351, 352; *see also* Gál and Szegedy model of fault-tolerant Boolean circuits
Border gateway protocol (BGP), 229
Border router (BR), 245, 249, 250
Botnets, 69, 206, 207, 213, 244, 379
BR, *see* Border router (BR)
British Standards Institute (BSI), 3
brk(), 81
Broadcast tampering attack, 172
Brute-force attacks, 67, 174, 226, 264
BS, *see* Base station (BS)
BSI, *see* British Standards Institute (BSI)
Buffer overflow attack, 56, 65, 80–84
Bug attacks, 350–351, 356, 363
Build diversity, 78

C

C2WindTunnel, *see* Command and Control WindTunnel (C2WindTunnel)
CA, *see* Certificate authority (CA)
CAMs, *see* Cooperative awareness messages (CAMs)
CAN, *see* Controller area network (CAN)
CARAVAN system, 208
CC, *see* Cyber-cyber (CC) threats
CCA, *see* Clear channel assessment (CCA)
CCS, *see* Change cipher spec (CCS) protocol
CCs, *see* Control centers (CCs)
Cell-oriented architecture (COA), 78–79
Central point, 122, 125, 127
Certificate authority (CA), 170, 171, 175, 176, 179
Certificate revocation list (CRL), 176, 179, 286
ChameleonSoft, 66, 78
Change cipher spec (CCS) protocol, 295
Character escaping filtering, 342
China, 102
Cikhaj 2012 and social interactions, 151–152
Cikhaj 2013 and attacker detection, 152–154
CIP, *see* Critical Infrastructure Protection (CIP)
Circuit breakers, 5, 11–13, 17, 22, 33, 46
Clear channel assessment (CCA), 146
Client-server protocols, 12
Cloud robotics and assisted in-pipe inspection, 95–96
COA, *see* Cell-oriented architecture (COA)
CoAP, *see* Constrained application protocol (CoAP)
Cognitive computing, 387
Collection Tree Protocol (CTP), 133, 135–136
  routing tree discovery, 143, 146, 147–148
Collision resistance, 293
CombinedData configuration structure, 137
Command and Control WindTunnel (C2WindTunnel), 315
Common words filtering in cross-site scripting payload, 342–343
Communication networks, 29, 46, 262, 268, 308, 394; *see also individual entries*
  tools
    Network Simulation Version 2 (NS-2), 40–41
    Network Simulation Version 3 (NS-3), 41
    OMNeT++, 41–42
    OPNET Modeler, 41
Confidentiality, 69, 168, 175, 233, 245, 263
  attacks, 173, 231
  contextual, 286–287
  lack of, 296
  risks, 204–205
Configuration attack, 264
Configuration protocols, 12
Congestion avoidance and vehicular computing, 201
Congestion issues, in electrical grids, 5
Constrained application protocol (CoAP), 243, 245
  security in, 272–273
Constrained environments security, 245–246
  data security, 250
  IoT security standardization, 250–251
  message security, 246–249
  network security, 249–250
Constrained Restful Environments (CoRE), 229, 273
Context-aware computing, 386
Context verification, 177
Control centers (CCs), 42, 46, 52
  ICT model, 53–54
Controller area network (CAN), 203, 210–211
Controller security, MTD techniques for, 75–76
  buffer overflow attack, 80–81
  deception attack, 76–77
  worms and virus, 77–80
Cookies, 253, 333, 336
Cooperative awareness messages (CAMs), 184
CoRE, *see* Constrained Restful Environments (CoRE)
Core network attack, 264
CPPS, *see* Cyber-physical power system (CPPS)
CPS, *see* Cyber-physical system (CPS)
Critical Infrastructure Protection (CIP), 3
CRL, *see* Certificate revocation list (CRL)
Cross-site scripting (XSS), 332
  buddies filtering, 343–344
  character escaping filtering, 342
  common words filtering in XSS payload, 342–343
  data URI filtering, 340–342
  event handlers filtering, 338–340
  future, in cyber-physical system, 344–345
  insecure keywords filtering, 342
  operational method of, 333–334
  prevention and detection initiatives, 335–338

types of
document object model-based XSS, 335
nonpersistent XSS, 334–335
persistent XSS, 334
Cryptanalysis attack, 85–86, 232
Cryptography, 135, 190, 214, 229, 265–266, 289; *see also individual entries*
asymmetric/public key, 175, 207–208, 291
protections, 175
symmetric/private key, 175
CTP, *see* Collection Tree Protocol (CTP)
Cyber-cyber (CC) threats, 8
Cyber-physical coupling, 8
Cyber-physical power system (CPPS), 92–93
design challenges, 98
design knowledge dynamics, 99
design knowledge incompleteness, 98–99
hypothesized solution, and cloud robotics and assisted in-pipe inspection, 95–96
literature review
cyber-physical system, 93–94
embedded system design for in-pipe inspection, 94–95
PFWSB framework
behavior, 101
constraint, 102–103
design description, 103, 104
discussion, 111, 113–114
environment, 102
function, 101
knowledge flow representation and understanding via, 107–111
purpose, 100–101
reasons to employ, 103, 105
structure, 102
use, to understand and represent knowledge, 105–107
working space, 103
security challenges, relevant to hypothetical solution, 96
hardware, 96
network, 97–98
software, 96–97
Cyber-physical security, for IEC 61850, 14–15
Cyber-physical system (CPS), 29, 93–94, 260, 280, 332; *see also* Autonomous vehicles; Moving target defense (MTD); Transportation cyber-physical systems
applications of, 30
architecture of, 378
characteristics of, 374–375
communication performances, 57
computer models and security
autonomic computing, 385–387
nomadic computing and mobile services, 385
opportunistic computing, 387–388
pervasive computing, 387
physical computing, 388
probabilistic computing, 388–389
scalable computing, 388
definition of, 373
general architecture of, 261
intrusion detection system for, 380
anomaly-based, 381–382
signature-based, 382
stateful protocol analysis, 382
intrusion prevention system (IPS) for, 380–381
intrusion response system (IRS) for, 381
performance, 55–56
indices for communication, 57
requirements, 375
quality of service (QOS), 394–395
quality of service and security metrics, interaction between, 399–401
quality of service–security
integration initiatives, 397–399
integration technique, 402–404
requirements, 396–397
real-time simulator example, 42–44
security challenges in, 377
control security, 380
physical environment protection, 379
resilience, 379
security in integrated SOS, 377–378
security on dynamic evolving systems, 378–379
suffering of new attacks, 377
security requirements in, 376
actuation control security, 377
application security, 377
communication security, 376
feedback security, 377
sensing security, 376
storage security, 376
simulator, 31
time-stepped synchronization examples in, 35
XSS attacks future in, 344–345

D

Data center, 84–85, 379
Data correlation, 178
Data Encryption Standard (DES), 290–291
Datagram transport layer security (DTLS), 248, 249, 251, 273, 274
in Constrained Environments (DICE), 251
Data intrusion, 74
Data packets, 44, 49–56, 172, 246
D/D/m/K queuing system, 48–49
DDoS, *see* Distributed denial-of-service (DDoS) attack
Decentralized environment notification messages (DENM), 184
Deception attack, 76–77, 82
Decision node (DN), 105, 107–108, 110–111

Dedicated short-range communications (DSRC), 165, 167, 199, 203
Default-allow policy, 98
Default-deny policy, 98
Delay
  authentication, 400
  average, for performing cryptographic operations, 401
  communication, 394–395, 401
  end-to-end, 398, 399, 401, 402
  performance in terms of, 404
  quality of service (QOS), 398, 400
Delay-tolerant networking (DTN), 287
Delete action, 84
Denial-of-service (DoS) attacks, 69–71, 171–172, 322
  jamming attack and, 186, 189–190, 228
  on L1-L3 communication protocol, 229
  on SCADA, 29
  severity and impact of, 272
  simulation of, 323
DENM, *see* Decentralized environment notification messages (DENM)
Department of Homeland Security, United States, 3
DES, *see* Data Encryption Standard (DES)
Destination location confidentiality, 286
Destination-oriented directed acyclic graph (DODAG), 245
Differentiated Services (DiffServ), 394
DiffServ, *see* Differentiated Services (DiffServ)
Digital signature, 15, 16, 177, 294
Digital signature algorithm (DSA), 15, 16, 291
DIgSILENT PowerFactory, 33, 36–37, 42
Dijkstra algorithm, 312
DIKE, *see* DynamIc privacy-preserving KEy management (DIKE)
Discretionary access control policy, 97
Dispatcher training environment, 30
Distributed coloring algorithm, 79
Distributed denial-of-service (DDoS) attack, 205, 228
DN, *see* Decision node (DN)
DNS, *see* Domain Name System (DNS) server
Document object model-based cross-site scripting, 335
DODAG, *see* Destination-oriented directed acyclic graph (DODAG)
Domain Name System (DNS) server, 74
DoS, *see* Denial-of-service (DoS) attacks
DOT, *see* U.S. Department of Transportation (DOT)
Driving safety and vehicular computing, 201
DSA, *see* Digital signature algorithm (DSA)
DSRC, *see* Dedicated short-range communications (DSRC)
DTN, *see* Delay-tolerant networking (DTN)
Duarouter.exe, 184
DynaBone, 70–71, 74, 75, 77
Dynamic data, 67
Dynamic networks, 66, 382, 405
Dynamic platforms, 66–67
DynamIc privacy-preserving KEy management (DIKE), 286
Dynamic rating, 5
Dynamic runtime environment, 65
Dynamic software, 65–66
DYNAT, 66

E

EAP, *see* Extensible authentication protocol (EAP)
Eavesdropping attack, 73–75, 173, 208, 227, 230, 285–286
ECC, *see* Elliptic-curve cryptography (ECC)
ECDSA, *see* Elliptic curve digital signature algorithm (ECDSA)
ECPDR, *see* Efficient conditional privacy-preservation scheme with demand response (ECPDR)
EEPROM memory, 134–139, 151, 153
Efficient conditional privacy-preservation scheme with demand response (ECPDR), 287
Efficient privacy-preserving aggregation scheme (EPPA), 286
ε-halvers, 354–355, 358–359
  with faulty gates and wires, 363–364
Electric vehicles (EVs), 6, 190
Electronic license plates (ELPs), 177
ELF, *see* Executable and linking format (ELF) file
Elliptic-curve cryptography (ECC), 208, 266, 282
Elliptic curve Diffie-Hellman (ECDH), 269
Elliptic curve digital signature algorithm (ECDSA), 15, 16, 167, 269, 294
ELPs, *see* Electronic license plates (ELPs)
Embedded systems, 70, 280–283
  applications, 281
  architectural model for, 289
  attacks against, 288–289
  biometrics and, 297–298
  for communication, 283
    contextual confidentiality, 286–287
    network model, 283–285
    threat model, 285–286
  cryptographic countermeasures for, 289–290
    asymmetric ciphers, 291–292
    hash functions, 292–295
    security protocols, 295–297
    symmetric ciphers, 290–291
  design, for in-pipe inspection, 94–95; *see also* Cyber-physical power system (CPPS)
  future directions, 299
  security challenges, 287–288
EMS, *see* Energy management system (EMS)
Encapsulated security payload (ESP), 248, 296, 400
Encrypt action, 84
Encryption key, 130, 175, 267, 398, 401, 404
Encryption problem, 15–16
End-to-end (E2E) security, 244–247, 250
  at network layer, 248
  at transport layer, 248–249

Energy management system (EMS), 30, 54
Environment attack, 232
EPPA, *see* Efficient privacy-preserving aggregation scheme (EPPA)
Error-correcting codes, 353–355, 362, 365
ESP, *see* Encapsulated security payload (ESP)
Ethernet, 14, 17–19, 28, 32, 50, 53–54
  switch, 323
ETSI, *see* European Telecommunications Standards Institute (ETSI)
E2E, *see* End-to-end (E2E) security
EURO-MILS, 283
European Telecommunications Standards Institute (ETSI), 261
EUROSTAG®, 38
Event data recording, 178
Event handlers filtering, 338–340
EVs, *see* Electric vehicles (EVs)
eWorld event simulator, 185
Exchange security protocols, 290
Executable and linking format (ELF) file, 80–81
Extensible authentication protocol (EAP), 227
Extensible messaging and presence protocol (XMPP), 316, 317, 319, 321
  Standards Foundation, 316
External attacker, 123

F

Fabless trend, 350
Facial scan, 298
Fault diversity, 79
Fault-tolerant circuits, 351–352, 354, 355, 358, 361
FBS, *see* Function-behavior-structure (FBS)
Federal Communications Commission (FCC), 165
FES, *see* Function-effect-structure (FES) model
Field-programmable gate array (FPGA), 282
Finding Likeminded vehIcle Protocol (FLIP), 287
Finger scan, 298
Firewall, 97, 246, 250, 282, 383, 402
  limitations of, 98
  and router, 52–55
FLIP, *see* Finding Likeminded vehIcle Protocol (FLIP)
Floodlight, 318, 322
  Representational State Transfer (REST) API, 322, 324
FPGA, *see* Field-programmable gate array (FPGA)
Free branch, 67, 81
Function-behavior-structure (FBS), 100, 103
Function-effect-structure (FES) model, 103

G

GAA, *see* Generic authentication architecture (GAA)
Gadgets, 81, 236
Gál and Szegedy model of fault-tolerant Boolean circuits, 353
  arbitrary Boolean functions, 355
  ε-halvers, 354–355
  faulty gates and circuits, 354
  loose computation, 353–354
  symmetric functions construction, 355
γ-faulty combinatorial circuit, 357, 358
γ-resilient C circuit, 357, 358
Gates, 351–353, 359–361
  α fraction of, 359–362
  faulty, 351, 354, 357, 358–359, 361, 363–364
  γ fraction of, 355
  and wires, 352, 354, 356–359, 363–364
GBA, *see* Generic bootstrapping architecture (GBA)
Generic attacks, 229
Generic authentication architecture (GAA), 268
Generic bootstrapping architecture (GBA), 268
Generic header compression (GHC), 244
Generic Object Oriented Substation Events (GOOSE), 11–18
  IEC 61850 exploitation, 18–19
    attack results, 21–22
    normal function, 19–20
    practical cyberattack building technical details, 20–21
    script building, 21
Generic Substation Event (GSE), 11
Generic Substation State Events (GSSE), 11
Georgia, 65
G-Free, 67, 81
GHC, *see* Generic header compression (GHC)
Global attacker, 123
Global event-driven approach, 35
  examples, 36
Global positioning systems (GPS), 209
  spoofing/position faking attack, 172–173
Global security architecture, 178
GOOSE, *see* Generic Object Oriented Substation Events (GOOSE)
GPS, *see* Global positioning systems (GPS)
Grayhole attack, 172
Greedy behavior attack, 172
Group signatures, 176, 208
GSE, *see* Generic Substation Event (GSE)
GSSE, *see* Generic Substation State Events (GSSE)

H

Half adder, 365–366
Hamming distance, 353, 354, 362, 365
Handbook Emission Factors for Road Transport (HBEFA) version 3.1 database, 187
Hand scan, 298
Hardware backdoors, *see* Trojan-resilient circuits
Hardware-in-the-loop (HIL), 32, 42
  off-line simulation and, 33
  real-time simulation and, 32–33
Hardware tampering, 174

Hardware Trojans, 350, 351, 355–357, 363
formal attack scenario, 357–358
Hash computation, 135
Hash functions, 290, 292–293
digital signatures, 294
group of signatures, 294–295
message authentication code, 293–294
symmetric keys derivation, 295
HBEFA, *see* Handbook Emission Factors for Road Transport (HBEFA) version 3.1 database
Heap overflow, *see* Buffer overflow attack
Heap randomization, 81
HERMIX, 314, 316–319
HIDPRS, *see* Host-based intrusion detection, prevention, and response system (HIDPRS)
Hijacking attack, 265
HIL, *see* Hardware-in-the-loop (HIL)
HITL, *see* Human-in-the-loop (HITL)
HKS, *see* Horizontal knowledge stream (HKS)
HMAC, *see* Keyed-hash message authentication code (HMAC)
HMI, *see* Human–machine interface (HMI)
Home network, 267
Horizontal knowledge stream (HKS), 105
Host-based intrusion detection, prevention, and response system (HIDPRS), 383
Human-in-the-loop (HITL), 190
Human–machine interface (HMI), 186, 306
Hypertext preprocessor (PHP)
to filter
character escaping, 343
common XSS words, 344
data URI, 342
event handlers, 339
unsecure keywords, 342
XSS buddies, 344
Hypervisor, 129

I

IBE, *see* Identity-based encryption (IBE)
ICs, *see* Integrated circuits (ICs)
ICSs, *see* Industrial control systems (ICSs)
ICT modeling, 28–30
cyber-physical system (CPS) performance, 55–56
cyberpower systems cosimulation and, 30–31
real-time CPS simulator example, 42–44
simulation tools coupling, 31–36
simulation tools, 36–42
of integrated cyberpower systems, 44–46
cybersystem and transmission operator layers, 47–55
power system layer, 46–47
transmission operator console, 55
simulation results, 56–58
Identity-based encryption (IBE), 266
IDSs, *see* Intrusion detection systems (IDSs)
IEDs, *see* Intelligent electronic devices (IEDs)
IEEE, *see* Institute of Electrical and Electronics Engineers (IEEE)
IETF, *see* Internet Engineering Task Force (IETF)
IKE, *see* Internet key exchange (IKE) protocol
Illusion attack, 173–174
Implementation diversity, 78
Incident warning application (IWA), 185–189
Industrial control systems (ICSs), 6–9, 75, 77, 306–309
case assessment, 319–320
physical process, 320–321
SDN-based traffic blocking, 322–324
SDN-based traffic rerouting, 321–322
and IP networking
modern IP networking technologies and ICSs, 310–311
overview, 309–310
novel approach to experiment with SDN-enabled, 314–315
physical process simulators, 317–318
proposed experimentation approach, 318–319
SDN enablers, 318
Sensei/ IoT, 316–317
simulated *vs.* real ICSs, 315
SDN-enabled approaches to mitigate cyberattacks in
network topology assumption and basic model, 311–312
rerouting traffic in SDN networks, 312, 313
traffic blocking in SDN networks, 312–313
Industrial robots, 94
Information from a server, 12
Innerlays, 70–71, 74, 75
In-pipe inspection robot systems, 94
cloud robotics and, 95–96
and design, 113
embedded system design, 94–95
Insecure keywords filtering, 342
Inside authentication, 267
Insider attacker, 125, 126
Insider supervisor attacker, 129
Institute of Electrical and Electronics Engineers (IEEE), 9
39-bus system model at power system layer, 47, 48
802.1Q, 12, 17, 19
802.11, 167, 203, 398
802.11p, 167, 184, 203
802.15.4, 146, 225, 229, 244, 247, 271
802.3, 11, 19
1609, 167
Instruction set randomization, 65, 81
Integrated circuits (ICs), 350, 352
development cycle and trustworthiness of, 356
infected by hardware Trojan, 357
Integrated Services (IntServ), 394
Integrity, 173–178, 234, 263, 288, 295, 373
data, 245–246, 296, 297

and data trust attacks, 173–174
full, 299
message, 168
protection, 247, 274
risks, 205
source, 246
Intelligent electronic devices (IEDs), 11, 14–16, 18, 44, 50, 52
ICT simulation model for, 51
output status, 22
sensing and actuating capabilities, 51
Intelligent transportation systems (ITS), 165, 190, 283
Internal attacker, 123
International Electrotechnical Commission (IEC) 61850 Standard
attack consequences, 17–18
attacks mitigation, 18
attack vectors and techniques, 17
background, 9–11
challenges and vulnerabilities, 13–17
exploitation via GOOSE, 18–22
functionality example, 12–13
overview, 11–12
International Society of Automation (ISA), 3–4, 9
International Telecommunication Union (ITU), 223, 224
Internet Engineering Task Force (IETF), 229, 251, 271, 316
Internet key exchange (IKE) protocol, 248
Internet of Things (IoT), 223, 242–244
constrained environments security, 245–246
data security, 250
IoT security standardization, 250–251
message security, 246–249
network security, 249–250
devices, security threats in, 230–231, 232
ICT technologies vulnerabilities and, 227
denial-of-service (DoS) attacks, 228
distributed denial-of-service (DDoS) attacks, 228
eavesdropping attacks, 227
spoofing attacks, 227
issues, approaches to mitigate
architecture protection schemes, 234–235
IoT protocols protection against security threats, 235
NFC protection, 236
preventive measures against privacy issues, 236–237
RFID protection, 235–236
open research issues, 237
privacy challenges, 251–252
cookies, 253
education, 255–256
k-anonymity, 255
legal frameworks, 255
media access control protection, 254
network address translation (NAT), 254
privacy aware design, 254–255
privacy preserving with homomorphic encryption, 255
radio signals, 253
resource constraints, 253
scale and ubiquity, 252
semantics and annotations, 254
sensing capabilities, 252
third-party services, 253
privacy issues in, 231–232
protocols
constrained application protocol (CoAP), 245
IPv6 over low-power personal area network (6LoWPAN), 244–245
routing protocol for low-power and lossy network, 245
protocols, vulnerabilities in, 229
DoS attack on L1-L3 communication protocol, 229
generic attacks, 229
redirection attacks, 230
security requirements, 232
auditing, 233
confidentiality, 233
identity management, 233
integrity, 234
secure data communication, 233
secure execution, 233
tamper resistance, 233
user authentication, 232–233
technologies, 223–224
near field communication (NFC), 224–225
radio-frequency identification, 224
security issues in, 225–227
security threats in core, 230, 231
supporting, 225
wireless sensor networks (WSNs), 224
Internet of Vehicles (IoV), 165
Internet protocol version 4 (IPv4), 68, 72, 225, 296
Internet protocol version 6 (IPv6), 68, 72, 225, 296, 394; *see also* Internet of Things (IoT)
constrained application protocol (CoAP), 245
over low-power personal area network (6LoWPAN), 225, 229, 243–250
security in, 271–272
routing protocol for low-power and lossy networks (RPL), 243, 245, 250
Internet security association and key management protocol (ISAKMP), 297
IntrusionDetect, 139
Intrusion detection, prevention, and response system (IDPRS), 373–380; *see also* Cyber-physical system (CPS)
architecture, 381
challenges for
false positives and negatives, 384
human intrusion, 384

interaction procedure monitoring, 384
micro-scope solution, 385
proactive defense, 384
wider detection, 383–384
for cyber-physical system (CPS)
intrusion detection analysis, 381–382
intrusion detection system, 380
intrusion prevention system, 380–381
intrusion response system, 381
solutions
emerging computer models and CPS security, 385–389
technical strategies, 389
types of, 382
host-based IDPRS (HIDPRS), 383
hybrid model, 383
network behavior analysis (NBA), 383
network-based (NIDPRS), 382–383
Intrusion detection systems (IDSs), 121, 133–134, 209, 228, 246, 250
anomaly-based, 381–382
and jamming experiment, 146, 149
signature-based, 382
Intrusion prevention system (IPS), 380–381
Intrusion response system (IRS), 381
IntServ, *see* Integrated Services (IntServ)
IoT, *see* Internet of Things (IoT)
IoV, *see* Internet of Vehicles (IoV)
IP for Smart Object Alliance (IPSO), 225
IPHC, *see* IP header compression (IPHC)
IP header compression (IPHC), 244
IP hopping technique, 68, 72, 74, 75, 77
IPS, *see* Intrusion prevention system (IPS)
IPsec, *see* IP security (IPsec)
IP security (IPsec), 248, 272, 400
IPSO, *see* IP for Smart Object Alliance (IPSO)
IPv4, *see* Internet protocol version 4 (IPv4)
IPv6, *see* Internet protocol version 6 (IPv6)
Iris scan, 298
IRS, *see* Intrusion response system (IRS)
ISA, *see* International Society of Automation (ISA)
ISAKMP, *see* Internet security association and key management protocol (ISAKMP)
iTETRIS, 181, 182
ITS, *see* Intelligent transportation systems (ITS)
ITU, *see* International Telecommunication Union (ITU)
IWA, *see* Incident warning application (IWA)

J

Jamming attack, 69, 146, 171–172, 186–189, 228, 263
Japanese Industrial Robot Association, 94
Java in simulation time/scalable wireless ad hoc network simulator (JiST/SWANS), 181, 183, 184–185
JavaScript, 333–335, 338–341, 343
JiST/SWANS, *see* Java in simulation time/scalable wireless ad hoc network simulator (JiST/SWANS)
Joint Test Action Group (JTAG), 356
JTAG, *see* Joint Test Action Group (JTAG)

K

k-Anonymity, 255
Key and/or certificate replication attack, 173
Key derivation, 135, 271
Keyed-hash message authentication code (HMAC), 293
Key generate center (KGC), 269
KGC, *see* Key generate center (KGC)
Knowledge input, 108, 113
k-threshold approach, 338

L

LAN, *see* Local area network (LAN)
Latency, 15, 20, 30, 55–56, 72, 129
LEA, *see* Low-entropy authentication (LEA)
Legitimate person, 127
LGTH, *see* Lightweight group authentication (LGTH)
L-halver, 359
Lightweight group authentication (LGTH), 269
Lightweight secure CoAP for the Internet of Things (Lithe), 273
LNS, *see* Log-normal shadowing (LNS)
Load-following units, 4
Local area network (LAN), 10, 11, 16, 46, 50, 54
Local attacker, 123
Local operating network (LON), 50
Location privacy (LPR), 286
Logical attacks, 289
Logical device, 11, 12
Logical nodes, 12
Log-normal shadowing (LNS), 150
LON, *see* Local operating network (LON)
Long-term evolution (LTE), 10, 265, 269
Lookup table (LUT), 85
Low-entropy authentication (LEA), 133
Low-rate wireless personal area networks (LR-WPANs), 271
LPR, *see* Location privacy (LPR)
LR-WPANs, *see* Low-rate wireless personal area networks (LR-WPANs)
LTE, *see* Long-term evolution (LTE)
LUT, *see* Lookup table (LUT)

M

MAC, *see* Media access control (MAC)
Machine communication identity module (MCIM), 264
Machine learning (ML)-based method, 337
Machine-to-machine (M2M) communications, 11, 261
device and gateway domain solutions, 265

authentication algorithms, 265–270
detection schemes, 265
key management, 270–271
future directions, 274
high-level architecture for, 262
network domain solutions
CoAP security, 272–273
6LoWPAN security, 271–272
security, 262–263
requirements, 263
threats, 263–264
Machine type communication (MTC), 264, 268, 269, 274
McLuhan, M., 223
Majority preserver, 359
Malware attack, 172
Mandatory access control policy, 97
MANETs, *see* Mobile ad hoc networks (MANETs)
Man-in-the-middle attack, 174
Manufacturing message specification (MMS), 12, 15
Masquerading attack, 173
Master-slave approach, 34
examples, 34
MATLAB®, 33, 34, 39, 46, 48, 266
Simulink, 37, 40, 42, 181, 315, 318
MatrikonOPC Simulation Server, 42–43
Maximum transmission unit (MTU), 244
MCIM, *see* Machine communication identity module (MCIM)
MD, *see* Movement detected (MD) message
Media access control (MAC), 12, 72–73, 229, 270
protection, 254
Medium access control, 178
Message authentication codes, 269, 293–294
Message authentication *vs.* latency, 15–16
Message digest–based authentication, 400
Message integrity codes (MIC), 246
M-halver, 359
MIC, *see* Message integrity codes (MIC)
MIME, *see* Multipurpose Internet mail extensions (MIME)
Mininet, 318, 322, 323
Mirov 2014, 155–156
mmap(), 81
MME, *see* Mobile management entity (MME)
MMS, *see* Manufacturing message specification (MMS)
MNO, *see* Mobile network operator (MNO)
Mobile ad hoc networks (MANETs), 167
Mobile management entity (MME), 269
Mobile network operator (MNO), 264
Mobile sensor nodes, 122, 125, 127, 146, 150, 152
Model-based numerical simulation, 31
Motion detection sensors, 123
Move action, 84
Movement detected (MD) message, 153
Moving target defense (MTD), 64
attack on techniques
brute force/bypass MTD techniques, 67
movement choice limiting, 68
movement disabling, 68
techniques prediction, 68
for controller security, 75–76
buffer overflow attack, 80–81
deception attack, 76–77
worms and virus, 77–80
cyber-physical system (CPS) and, 68–69
at different system layers, 65
dynamic data, 67
dynamic networks, 66
dynamic platforms, 66–67
dynamic runtime environment, 65
dynamic software, 65–66
for network security, 69
denial of service (DoS), 69–71
eavesdropping attack, 73–75
packet-scheduling attacks, 71–73
for physical system security, 81–82
buffer overflow, 82–84
deception attacks, 82
physical attack, 84–86
MPLS, *see* Multiprotocol label switching (MPLS)
MSIECV, *see* Multiple Simulator Interlinking Environment for C2CC in VANETs (MSIECV)
MTD, *see* Moving target defense (MTD)
MT6D IP hopping technique, 72–73
MTU, *see* Maximum transmission unit (MTU)
M2M, *see* Machine-to-machine (M2M) communications
Multicast filtering, 14
Multilevel security levels, 400–401
Multiple Simulator Interlinking Environment for C2CC in VANETs (MSIECV), 181
Multiprotocol label switching (MPLS), 310
Multipurpose Internet mail extensions (MIME), 340

N

Naive Bayes, 337
NAT, *see* Network address translation (NAT)
National Bureau of Standards (NBS), 290
National Cyber Leap Year (NCLY) Summit (2009), 65
NBA, *see* Network behavior analysis (NBA)
NBS, *see* National Bureau of Standards (NBS)
NCLY, *see* National Cyber Leap Year (NCLY) Summit (2009)
Near field communication (NFC), 224–225, 230, 231
protection, 236
NEPLAN, 37, 38
NERC, *see* North American Electric Reliability Corporation (NERC)
Netconvert.exe, 184
Network address translation (NAT), 254

Network-based intrusion detection, prevention, and response system (NIDPRS), 382–383
Network behavior analysis (NBA), 383
Network functions virtualization (NFV), 308, 311, 325
Network layer security, 248
Network model, 283–285
Network security, MTD techniques for, 69
- denial of service (DoS), 69–71
- eavesdropping attack, 73–75
- packet-scheduling attacks, 71–73

Network Simulation Version 2 (NS-2), 40–41
Network Simulation Version 3 (NS-3), 41
Neumann computer architecture, 108
Next header compression (NHC), 244
NFC, *see* Near field communication (NFC)
NFV, *see* Network functions virtualization (NFV)
NHC, *see* Next header compression (NHC)
NIDPRS, *see* Network-based intrusion detection, prevention, and response system (NIDPRS)
NIST, *see* U.S. National Institute of Standards and Technology (NIST)
Node impersonation attack, 173
Nonce value, 73
Nonpersistent cross-site scripting, 334–335
Nonrepudiation, 168, 173–177, 204, 226, 263, 288
- violation of, 173, 174

North American Electric Reliability Corporation (NERC), 3
Ns-2 network simulator, 181
N-variant system, 74–75

O

OBD, *see* Onboard diagnostic (OBD) system
Object linking and embedding for process control (OPC), 29, 33, 37, 42–44, 47, 51
OBUs, *see* Onboard units (OBUs)
OCSP, *see* Online certificate status protocol (OCSP)
OMG, *see* Open Management Group (OMG)
OMNEST, 41
OMNeT++, 41–42, 141–142, 181, 315
Onboard diagnostic (OBD) system, 187, 211
Onboard short-range radar system, 209
Onboard units (OBUs), 165, 168, 171
OnClick, 338
OnError, 338
Online certificate status protocol (OCSP), 179
OnLoad, 338
OnMouseOver, 339
OnStar satellite, 203, 211
OPC, *see* Object linking and embedding for process control (OPC)
Open Distribution System Simulator (OpenDSS), 38–39
OpenDSS, *see* Open Distribution System Simulator (OpenDSS)
OpenFlow, 308, 312, 318
Open Management Group (OMG), 251
Open shortest path first (OSPF), 229
OpenStreetMap files, 185
Open Systems Interconnection (OSI), 12, 17
Open Web Application Security Project (OWASP), 333
Operating system (OS), 96–97
OPNET, *see* Optimized network engineering tools (OPNET) simulation tool
OPNET Modeler, 41
Opportunistic computing, 387–388
Optimized network engineering tools (OPNET) simulation tool, 272
OS, *see* Operating system (OS)
OSI, *see* Open Systems Interconnection (OSI)
OSPF, *see* Open shortest path first (OSPF)
Outerlay, 70
Outsider attacker, 125, 126
Overwhelming majority function, 355
OWASP, *see* Open Web Application Security Project (OWASP)

P

Packet analysis attack, 286
Packet generation technique, 286
Packet-scheduling attacks, 71–73
Packet-tracing attack, 286
Palo Verde Nuclear Generating Station (PVNGS), 17
Paramics traffic simulator, 181
PASS, *see* Pseudonymous authentication scheme with strong privacy preservation (PASS)
Passive attacker, 123, 133
Passive attacks, 130
Password-based authentication, 400
PC, *see* Physical-cyber (PC) threats
PCPs, *see* Probabilistically checkable proofs (PCPs)
Peaking plants, 4
Peer-to-peer node community (P2P NC), 284
PEM, *see* Privacy-enhancing model (PEM)
Per-hop security, 247–248
Persistent cross-site scripting, 334
- filter, 339

Pervasive computing, 387
PEV, *see* Plug-in electric vehicle (PEV)
PFWSB, *see* Purpose-function-working space-structure-behavior (PFWSB)
Phantom routing, 133
Phasor measurement units (PMUs), 28
PHEM, *see* Passenger car and Heavy duty vehicle Emission Model (PHEM)
Phishing attack, 231, 307
PHP, *see* Hypertext preprocessor (PHP)
Physical attack, 84–86, 131, 232, 263–264, 289
Physical computing, 388
Physical-cyber (PC) threats, 8
Physical-physical (PP) threats, 8

Physical system security, MTD techniques for, 81–82
  buffer overflow, 82–84
  deception attacks, 82
  physical attack, 84–86
Pi, *see* Practical incentive (Pi) protocol scheme
PIOC, *see* Predefined in IEC 61850 (PIOC)
PKI, *see* Public key infrastructure (PKI)
Platooning and vehicular computing, 202
PLCs, *see* Programmable logic controllers (PLCs)
Plug-in electric vehicle (PEV), 6
PMUs, *see* Phasor measurement units (PMUs)
Poland, 65
Policy tree (PT), 212–213
Port security, 14
PowerServer, 32
Power systems, 2–3
  communication protocols, 42
  as critical infrastructure, 3–4
  distribution, 5–6
  generation, 4
  industrial control systems (ICSs), 6–9
    culture, 8
    cyber-physical coupling, 8
    design lifetime, 8–9
    distributed systems, 8
    objectives, 7
    performance, 8
    regulation and standards, 9
    risk management, 9
  International Electrotechnical Commission (IEC) 61850 Standard
    attack consequences, 17–18
    attack vectors and techniques, 17
    attacks mitigation, 18
    background, 9–11
    challenges and vulnerabilities, 13–17
    exploitation via GOOSE, 18–22
    functionality example, 12–13
    overview, 11–12
  load, 6
  transmission, 4–5
Power systems computer-aided design (PSCAD)/ electromagnetic transient (EMTDC), 39–40
Power system tools, 36
  DIgSILENT PowerFactory, 36–37
  EUROSTAG®, 38
  NEPLAN, 37, 38
  Open Distribution System Simulator (OpenDSS), 38–39
  power systems computer-aided design (PSCAD)/ electromagnetic transient (EMTDC), 39–40
  PowerWorld, 38, 39
  SIEMENS PSS®E, 37
PowerWorld, 38, 39
PP, *see* Physical-physical (PP) threats
Practical incentive (Pi) protocol scheme, 287
Predefined in IEC 61850 (PIOC), 12
Pre-image resistance, 293
Privacy attacks, 174
Privacy component, 139
Privacy-enhancing model (PEM), 179
Privacy-preserving detection of abuses of pseudonyms (P2DAP), 177
Privacy risks, in VANET, 178–179
Private key, 15, 207, 269, 290cryptography, 175
Proactive/reactive multiplexer (PRM), 70–71
Probabilistically checkable proofs (PCPs), 351–353, 355, 363
Probabilistic computing, 388–389
Problem solution using a device and user authentication (PSDUA), 268
Programmable logic controllers (PLCs), 77, 306–307, 310, 314
Proprietary system design, 177
Protection relay logical device, 12
Protection trip condition (PTRC), 12, 13
ProtectLayerC, 137
ProtectLayerConfigurator, 138–139
PSDUA, *see* Problem solution using a device and user authentication (PSDUA)
Pseudonym, use of, 208
Pseudonymous authentication scheme with strong privacy preservation (PASS), 286
PSS®SINCAL, 37
PT, *see* Policy tree (PT)
PTRC, *see* Protection trip condition (PTRC)
P2DAP, *see* Privacy-preserving detection of abuses of pseudonyms (P2DAP)
P2P NC, *see* Peer-to-peer node community (P2P NC)
Public key, 15, 170, 179, 268cryptography, 175, 207–208, 229, 291
Public key infrastructure (PKI), 176, 177
Purpose-function-working space-structure-behavior (PFWSB), 100
  behavior, 101
  constraint, 102–103
  design description, 103, 104
  discussion, 111
    contributions, 111, 113
    future work, 113–114
  environment, 102
  function, 101
  knowledge flow representation and understanding via, 107–111
  purpose, 100–101
  reasons to employ, 103, 105
  structure, 102
  use, to understand and represent knowledge, 105–107
  working space, 103
PVNGS, *see* Palo Verde Nuclear Generating Station (PVNGS)
Python, 20, 323

Q

QOS, *see* Quality of service (QOS)
QoSec, *see* QoS–security (QoSec)
Quality of security services (QoSS), 395, 399, 404; *see also* Quality of service-security (QoSec)
Quality of service (QOS), 394–395; *see also* Quality of service-security (QoSec)
  and security metrics, interaction between, 399–401
Quality of service-security (QoSec), 395
  integration initiatives, 397–399
  integration technique, 402–404
  requirements, 396–397
Queuing theory and system, 47, 56

R

Radio-frequency identification (RFID), 122, 156, 230, 231
  active, 224
  passive, 224
  protection, 235–236
Radio signals, 253
RAS, *see* Remedial action scheme (RAS)
REA, *see* Reconfigurable symmetric encryption architecture (REA)
Reactive power, 6, 46
Real power, 6
Reauthentication, 267
Received signal strength indicator (RSSI) radio signal strength experiment, 143, 144–146, 150
Recloser, 13
Reconfigurable symmetric encryption architecture (REA), 85–86
Redirection attacks, 230
Reflected XSS, *see* Nonpersistent cross-site scripting
Regular visitor, 129
Relay attack, 230, 231
Remedial action scheme (RAS), 17
Remote procedure call (RPC), 318
Remote terminal units (RTU), 12, 30, 44, 50
  ICT model for, 52
Replay attack, 77, 172, 173
Replay protection, 246
Representational state transfer (REST), 245, 273, 312, 320, 322, 324
Requirement-function-behavior-structure, 100
Rerouting technique, 184, 186, 312, 313, 321–322
REST, *see* Representational state transfer (REST)
Retina scan, 298
Return-oriented programming (ROP), 67, 81
Return-to-libc attack, 67
RFID, *see* Radio-frequency identification (RFID)
RINSE, 32
RIP, *see* Routing information protocol (RIP)
Rivest, Shamir and Adleman (RSA) algorithm, 15, 16, 208, 350
Roadside units (RSUs), 165, 168, 171, 183, 184, 200
Roaming authentication, 267
ROP, *see* Return-oriented programming (ROP)
Routing, on single path, 286
Routing information protocol (RIP), 229
RPC, *see* Remote procedure call (RPC)
RSA, *see* Rivest, Shamir and Adleman (RSA) algorithm
RSSI, *see* Received signal strength indicator (RSSI) radio signal strength experiment
RSUs, *see* Roadside units (RSUs)
RTU, *see* Remote terminal units (RTU)

S

SA, *see* Still alive (SA) message
SAD, *see* Security association database (SAD)
SAKES, *see* Secure authentication and key establishment scheme (SAKES)
Sampled measured values (SMV), 12
Sanitization, 333
S-box, 86
SCADA, *see* Supervisory control and data acquisition (SCADA)
Scalable computing, 388
Scapy, 20, 323
SCL, *see* Substation configuration language (SCL)
SDN, *see* Software-defined networking (SDN)
SE, *see* State estimation (SE)
SE-AKA, *see* Secure and efficient authentication and key agreement (SE-AKA)
Second pre-image resistance, 293
Secure and efficient authentication and key agreement (SE-AKA), 269
Secure and efficient group roaming (SEGR), 269
Secure authentication and key establishment scheme (SAKES), 272
Secure Boot, 209
Secure routing protocols (SRPs), 178
Security association, 296
Security association database (SAD), 296
Security-by-proxy solution, 337–338
Security-integrated quality-of-service paradigm, 394
  future directions, 404–405
  quality of service (QOS), 394–395
  quality of service and security metrics, interaction between, 399–401
  quality of service–security
    integration initiatives, 397–399
    integration technique, 402–404
    requirements, 396–397
Security issues, in Internet of Things (IOT), 225–226
  insecure architecture
    application layer issues, 227, 228
    network layer issues, 226–227, 228
    perception layer issues, 226, 228
Security policy database (SPD), 296
Security protocols, 295; *see also individual entries*

IPSec protocol, 296–297
secure shell (SSH) protocol, 297
secure socket layer/transport layer security (SSL/TLS) protocol, 295–296
SEGR, *see* Secure and efficient group roaming (SEGR)
Self-management, 386–387
Semantics and annotations, 254
Sensei/ IoT*, 314
communication modules enabling experimentation with, 316–317
overview, 316
Sensor nodes, 120–121, 131, 140, 143, 153, 271
hardware-enhanced, 156
mobile, 122, 125, 127, 146, 150, 152
static, 122, 123, 125, 127–129, 151
Sequence event recorder (SER), 22
Service level specification (SLS), 404
SG-CAT, *see* Smart grid communication assessment tool (SG-CAT)
SharedData component, 137
Short message service (SMS), 266
Side-channel attack, 231, 289
SIEMENS PSS®E, 37
SIEMENS SICAM PAS, 42
Signature-based authentication, 400
Signature-based detection, 177
Signature-based intrusion detection system, 382
SimAuto, *see* Simulator Automation server (SimAuto)
SimEvents, 42, 48, 49
Simulation for urban mobility (SUMO) traffic simulator, 181, 183, 185, 187
Simulation tools
communication network tools
Network Simulation Version 2 (NS-2), 40–41
Network Simulation Version 3 (NS-3), 41
OMNeT++, 41–42
OPNET Modeler, 41
power system communication protocols, 42
power system tools, 36
DIgSILENT PowerFactory, 36–37
EUROSTAG®, 38
NEPLAN, 37, 38
Open Distribution System Simulator (OpenDSS), 38–39
power systems computer-aided design (PSCAD)/electromagnetic transient (EMTDC), 39–40
PowerWorld, 38, 39
SIEMENS PSS®E, 37
Simulator Automation server (SimAuto), 38
Simulink, 37, 40, 42, 181, 315, 318
Sinkhole attack, 126, 127, 131, 172
Situational trust, 210
Situation-aware computing, 386
SLS, *see* Service level specification (SLS)
Smart grid, 64, 71–73, 265, 345
Smart grid communication assessment tool (SG-CAT), 41
Smart meter, 69–71, 77, 81–82, 84, 261, 265
SMS, *see* Short message service (SMS)
SMV, *see* Sampled measured values (SMV)
Social-based PRivacy-preserving packet forwardING (SPRING), 287
Social engineering, 174
Sociality, 284–285
Socialspot-based packet forwarding (SPF), 287
Socialspots, 284
Software attack, 232; *see also* embedded system
Software-defined networking (SDN), 18, 307–308, 310–311; *see also* Industrial control systems (ICSs)
building blocks, 311
Software diversity, 65–68, 79
Software fault tolerance, 74
SolidWorks®, 98
Source location confidentiality, 286
Spamming attack, 172
SPD, *see* Security policy database (SPD)
Spectrum Power TG, 42
SPF, *see* Socialspot-based packet forwarding (SPF)
SPHeader, 139
Spoofing attacks, 20, 170, 172–173, 227, 290, 231
SPRING, *see* Social-based PRivacy-preserving packet forwardING (SPRING)
SRPs, *see* Secure routing protocols (SRPs)
Stability limit, 5
Stack overflow, *see* Buffer overflow attack
State estimation (SE), 77
Static sensor nodes, 122, 123, 125, 127–129, 129, 151
Still alive (SA) message, 153
Stored XSS, *see* Persistent cross-site scripting
Stuxnet worm, 17, 77–78, 307, 377
Substation configuration language (SCL), 11, 12
Substation ICT model, 50–53
Substitution-permutation network, 85
SUMO, *see* Simulation for urban mobility (SUMO) traffic simulator
Supervisor, 129
Supervisory control and data acquisition (SCADA), 28–29, 42, 44, 46, 55, 309–310
cosimulation platform for test bed, 33
cybersecurity enhancement for, 30
development planning and performance assessment, 30
mimics, 55
overall performance index, 56
Support vector machines (SVM), 337
Suppressing/fabricating/modifying/tampering messages, 173
SVELTE, 250
Sybil attack, 130, 168, 170, 172, 177, 207
Symmetric ciphers, 290–291
Symmetric key, 73, 175, 237, 269, 273
derivation, 295
System diversity, 78

T

TA, *see* Trust authority (TA)
Tags, 122, 123, 125, 129, 224, 236
TALENT, *see* Trusted Dynamic Logical Heterogeneity System (TALENT)
Tamperproof device/hardware, use of, 177, 178
Tamper-resistant hardware for vehicles, 208–209
TCP/IP, *see* Transmission control protocol/Internet protocol (TCP/IP)
TDS, *see* Time domain simulations (TDS)
TD-SCDMA, *see* Time division synchronous code division multiple access (TD-SCDMA) network
TE, *see* Tennessee Eastman (TE) chemical process model
TelosB and MICAz performance platform comparison, 139–140
Tennessee Eastman (TE) chemical process model, 308
- architecture, 320–321
- normal operation, with reactor pressure and level, 321

TESLA approach, 207–208
Thermal limits, 5
Third Generation Partnership Project (3GPP) Security Workgroup, 263, 268, 269
Third-party services, 253
Threat model, 285–286
3GPP, *see* Third Generation Partnership Project (3GPP) Security Workgroup
Threshold function, 355, 360
Time division synchronous code division multiple access (TD-SCDMA) network, 267
Time domain simulations (TDS), 30, 39, 44, 47
Time-stepped approach, 34–35
- examples, 35

Time synchronization
- in cosimulation, 33–34
  - global event-driven approach, 35–36
  - master-slave approach, 34
  - time-stepped approach, 34–35
- cosimulation without, 33

Timing attack, 174, 189
TinyOS operating system, 136, 137, 146
TLS, *see* Transport layer security (TLS)
TO, *see* Transmission operator (TO)
TPMs, *see* Trusted platform modules (TPMs)
Transformers, 4–5, 11, 12, 46
Transmission control protocol/Internet protocol (TCP/IP), 12, 28, 37–38, 97
Transmission operator (TO), 46
- console, 29, 42, 44, 55
- ICT model, 54–55
- layers, and cybersystem, 47–55

Transportation cyber-physical systems, 164–166
- case study
  - evaluation results, 187–190
  - evaluation scenarios, 186–187
  - real-world data set, 183
  - simulation inputs and parameters, 183–185
  - V2X simulation framework, 180–183
- countermeasures for security and privacy in, 174–180
  - cryptography mechanisms, 175
  - cryptography protections, 175
  - public key infrastructure (PKI), 176, 177
- future research, 190
- VANET
  - applications, 166
  - architecture, 166, 190
  - characteristics, 167–168
  - public key infrastructure (VPKI), 176
  - security and privacy challenges, 169–174
  - security and privacy requirements, 168–169
  - security architectures, 178–180
  - security countermeasures for securing, 176–177
  - specific security solutions for, 177–178
  - standards, 167

Transport layer security (TLS), 248–249
Trojan-resilient circuits, 350–352
- Boolean circuits, 351, 352
- construction, 358
  - arbitrary Boolean functions, 361–362
  - ε-halvers, 358–359
  - faulty wires and circuits, 358
  - symmetric functions construction, 359–361
- Gál and Szegedy model of fault-tolerant Boolean circuits, 353
  - arbitrary Boolean functions, 355
  - ε-halvers, 354–355
  - faulty gates and circuits, 354
  - loose computation, 353–354
  - symmetric functions construction, 355
- hardware Trojans, 355–357
  - formal attack scenario, 357–358
- integrated circuits, 352
- probabilistically checkable proofs (PCPs), 352–353

Tru-Alarm system, 77
Trust authority (TA), 283–284
Trusted Dynamic Logical Heterogeneity System (TALENT), 67
Trusted platform modules (TPMs), 165, 174, 209
Trust Validation Model (TVM), 179
Tuning, 384
Tunneling attack, 173, 264, 286
TVM, *see* Trust Validation Model (TVM)
Two-way authentication, 267
Type-0 XSS, *see* Document object model-based cross-site scripting
TYPE-I XSS, *see* Persistent cross-site scripting

U

UART, 137, 139
UCD, *see* University College Dublin (UCD)
UDP, *see* User datagram protocol (UDP)

U-halver, 359
UICC, *see* Universal integrated circuit card (UICC)
UMTS, *see* Universal mobile telecommunications system (UMTS)
Uniform resource identifier (URI), 335
  data, filtering, 340–342
Uniform resource name (URN), 225
Universal integrated circuit card (UICC), 264
Universal mobile telecommunications system (UMTS), 265
University College Dublin (UCD), 56
Uploader, 138
URI, *see* Uniform resource identifier (URI)
URN, *see* Uniform resource name (URN)
U.S. Department of Transportation (DOT), 200, 203
User data and identity privacy attack, 264
User datagram protocol (UDP), 244, 249, 273, 323, 400
U.S. National Institute of Standards and Technology (NIST), 3, 9, 15, 291

V

V2I, *see* Vehicle-to-infrastructure (V2I) communications
V2V, *see* Vehicle-to-vehicle (V2V) communications
V2X simulation runtime infrastructure (VSimRTI), 180–183
  high-level architecture with coupled federates, 182
  necessary basic federates using, 182
Valiant–Vazirani uniqueness reduction, 364–365
VANETs, *see* Vehicular ad hoc networks (VANETs)
Vehicle Infrastructure Integration (VII) program, 200
Vehicle proxy (VP), 283
  architecture, 285
Vehicle-to-infrastructure (V2I) communications, 165
Vehicle-to-vehicle (V2V) communications, 165, 203, 206
Vehicular ad hoc networks (VANETs), 165, 199–200, 206, 284; *see also* Transportation cyber-physical systems
  applications, 166
  architecture, 166, 190
  characteristics, 167–168
  public key infrastructure (VPKI), 176
  security and privacy
    challenges, 169–174
    requirements, 168–169
  security architectures, 178–180
  security countermeasures for securing, 176–177
  security mechanisms, 207
    access control to vehicle-generated data, 211–213
    hardening vehicles against compromise, 210–211
    tamper-resistant hardware for vehicles, 208–209
    vehicle messages authentication, 207–208
    vehicle trustworthiness determination and messages, 209–210
  specific security solutions for, 177–178
  standards, 167
Vehicular cloud approach, 200, 206, 211–212, 213
Vehicular peer-to-peer social network (VP2PSN), 283
Vein pattern scan, 298
Verification on demand (VoD), 167
Vertical knowledge stream (VKS), 105
VII, *see* Vehicle Infrastructure Integration (VII) program
VIP visitor, 129
Virtualization support, 212
Virtual LAN (VLAN), 12, 14, 17–19
Virtual private network (VPN), 32
VISSIM traffic simulator, 181
Vitheia consortium, 316
VKS, *see* Vertical knowledge stream (VKS)
VLAN, *see* Virtual LAN (VLAN)
VoD, *see* Verification on demand (VoD)
Voltage limits, 5
VP, *see* Vehicle proxy (VP)
VP2PSN, *see* Vehicular peer-to-peer social network (VP2PSN)
VPN, *see* Virtual private network (VPN)
VSimRTI, *see* V2X simulation runtime infrastructure (VSimRTI)

W

WAN, *see* Wide area network (WAN)
WAVE, *see* Wireless access in vehicular environments (WAVE)
WECC, *see* Western Electricity Coordinating Council (WECC)
Western Electricity Coordinating Council (WECC), 18
WhiteHat Security, 332
Wide area network (WAN), 44, 46, 49, 226
WiMAX, *see* Worldwide Interoperability for Microwave Access (WiMAX)
Wireless access in vehicular environments (WAVE), 167
Wireless sensor networks (WSNs), 224, 230, 231, 243, 247, 250; *see also* WSNProtectLayer
Wires, 353
  β fraction of, 359–361
  and gates, 352, 354, 356–359, 363–364
Wireshark, 21–22, 114
Worldwide Interoperability for Microwave Access (WiMAX), 10, 166, 269
Wormhole attack, 131, 172, 207, 231, 285–286
Worms and virus, 77–80
WSNProtectLayer, 120–122, 131–132
  cryptography component, 135
  experiments, 140
    Cikhaj 2012 and social interactions, 151–152
    Cikhaj 2013 and attacker detection, 152–154
    CTP routing tree discovery, 143, 146, 147–148
    development test bed building, 140–143
    IDS and jamming experiment, 146, 149
    localization experiment, 146, 150
    Mirov 2014, 155–156

RSSI radio signal strength experiment, 143, 144–145
test bed 2013 and movement and item detection, 154–155
test bed 2014, 156–157
future work, 157–158
implementation details, 136–137
configuration component, 137
logging, 137–138
packet acknowledgements, 139
ProtectLayerC component, 137
TelosB and MICAz performance platform comparison, 139–140
uploader and ProtectLayerConfigurator, 138–139
intrusion detection component, 133–134
key establishment component, 134
middleware lifecycle, 135–136
privacy component, 133
scenario analysis
attacks summary, 131
building monitoring, 128–131
mobile emergency unit, 127–128
warehouse monitoring, 124–127
scenario description
assumptions, 122
attacker model, 123–124
device types, 122
WSNs, *see* Wireless sensor networks (WSNs)

X

XMPP, *see* Extensible messaging and presence protocol (XMPP)
XOR, 67, 83, 85
XSS-Dec, 337
XSS-GUARD, 336

Z

ZCZ, *see* Zero correlation zone (ZCZ)
Zero correlation zone (ZCZ), 266